ROUTLEDGE HANDBOOK OF AFRICAN POLITICS

Providing a comprehensive and cutting-edge examination of this important continent, the *Routledge Handbook of African Politics* surveys the key debates and controversies, dealing with each of the major issues to be found in Africa's politics today.

Structured into six broad areas, the *Handbook* features over 30 contributions focused around:

- The state
- Identity
- Conflict
- Democracy and electoral politics
- Political economy and development
- International relations

Each chapter deals with a specific topic, providing an overview of the main arguments and theories and explaining the empirical evidence on which they are based, drawing on high-profile cases such as the Democratic Republic of Congo, Kenya, Nigeria, Somalia, South Africa, Rwanda, and Zimbabwe. The *Handbook* also contains new contributions on a wide range of topical issues, including terrorism, the growing influence of China, civil war, and transitional justice, making it required reading for non-specialists and experts alike.

Featuring both established scholars and emerging researchers, this is a vital resource for all students of African Studies, democratization, conflict resolution, and Third World politics.

Nic Cheeseman is University Lecturer in African Politics at the University of Oxford, joint editor of *African Affairs*, and founder of www.democracyinafrica.co.uk.

David M. Anderson is Professor of African Politics at the University of Oxford, and a Fellow of St Cross College.

Andrea Scheibler is a DPhil candidate in African History at the University of Oxford, and a member of St Hugh's College.

ROUTLEDGE HANDBOOK OF AFRICAN POLITICS

Edited by
Nic Cheeseman, David M. Anderson, and Andrea Scheibler

Routledge
Taylor & Francis Group

LONDON AND NEW YORK

First published 2013
by Routledge
2 Park Square, Milton Park, Abingdon, Oxon OX14 4RN

Simultaneously published in the USA and Canada
by Routledge
711 Third Avenue, New York, NY 10017

Routledge is an imprint of the Taylor & Francis Group, an informa business

British Library Cataloguing in Publication Data
A catalogue record for this book is available from the British Library

Library of Congress Cataloging in Publication Data
Routledge handbook of African politics / edited by Nic Cheeseman, David M. Anderson and Andrea Scheibler.
    p. cm.
  Includes bibliographical references and index.
  1. Africa–Politics and government–1960- 2. Africa–Economic policy. I. Cheeseman, Nicholas, 1979- II. Anderson, David, 1957- III. Scheibler, Andrea, 1981-
  JQ1875.A1R68 2013
  320.96–dc23
                        2012029309

ISBN: 978-0-415-57378-8 (hbk)
ISBN: 978-0-203-07068-0 (ebk)

Typeset in Bembo
by Taylor & Francis Books

Printed and bound in Great Britain by MPG Printgroup

This *Handbook* would not have been possible without our exceptional editorial team. Many thanks to Benjamin Armstrong and Martin Williams for their assistance, and special thanks must go to our senior editorial assistant, Zoe Marks.

CONTENTS

Contents

ILLUSTRATIONS

Figures

CONTRIBUTORS

Rita Abrahamsen, University of Ottawa, Canada

Chris Alden, London School of Economics, UK

David M. Anderson, University of Oxford, UK

Joel D. Barkan, University of Iowa & Center for Strategic and International Studies, USA

Matthijs Bogaards, Jacobs University Bremen, Germany

Michael Bratton, Michigan State University, USA

Stephen Brown, University of Ottawa, Canada

Nic Cheeseman, University of Oxford, UK

Phil Clark, School of Oriental and African Studies, UK

Devon Curtis, University of Cambridge, UK

Stephen Ellis, Vrije University & The African Studies Centre Leiden, Holland

Gero Erdmann, German Institute of Global and Area Studies, Germany

Bill Freund, University of KwaZulu-Natal, South Africa

Peter Geschiere, University of Amsterdam, Holland

Gerrie ter Haar, Erasmus University Rotterdam, Holland

Göran Hydén, University of Florida, USA

Michael Jennings, School of Oriental and African Studies, UK

Tim Kelsall, Africa Power and Politics Program, UK

Gilbert M. Khadiagala, University of the Witwatersrand, South Africa

Staffan I. Lindberg, University of Florida, USA, and University of Gothenburg, Sweden

Gabrielle Lynch, University of Warwick, UK

Amina Mama, University of California, USA

Andreas Mehler, German Institute of Global and Area Studies, Germany

Ken Menkhaus, Davidson College, USA

Richard E. Mshomba, Le Salle University, USA

Jean-Pierre Olivier de Sardan, LASDEL, Niger

Philip Roessler, The College of William and Mary, USA

Andrea Scheibler, University of Oxford, UK

Jeremy Seekings, University of Cape Town, South Africa

Ricardo Soares de Oliveira, University of Oxford, UK

Rotimi T. Suberu, Bennington College, USA

Leonardo A. Villalón, University of Florida, USA

Peter VonDoepp, University of Vermont, USA

Nicolas van de Walle, Cornell University, USA

Martin Williams, London School of Economics, UK

ACKNOWLEDGEMENTS

The editors would like to thank the contributors for their remarkable patience and hard work – it has been a real privilege to work with such a committed and talented group of authors. We are also grateful for the consistent support of the team at Routledge, despite the considerable time and effort that it has taken to complete this ambitious project. Our appreciation must also go to the African Studies Centre and the Department of Politics and International Relations, University of Oxford, which have financially supported our endeavours. Finally, we would like to thank our colleagues and families, who have offered much-needed warmth and support throughout the process.

AN INTRODUCTION TO AFRICAN POLITICS

David M. Anderson and Nic Cheeseman

It has now been more than half a century since the newly independent states of sub-Saharan Africa first emerged onto the world stage as independent nations, beginning a process of political liberation that spanned nearly 40 years. The bulk of the continent threw off the shackles of colonial rule between the mid-1950s and late 1960s, with the fall of the Portuguese empire in 1974 sparking the later decolonizations in southern Africa, culminating in the ending of apartheid rule in South Africa in 1994. The prospects for the political development and economic growth of Africa's 'new' nations has remained a key element in scholarship on the region ever since, highlighted most recently in the creation of Africa's two youngest nations – the secession of Eritrea from Ethiopia in the 1990s, and South Sudan's separation from its northern neighbour in 2011.

Africa's politics has been in flux over all these years, as the transitions from colonial rule and liberation first saw the emergence of fragile and short-lived democratic structures, which in turn were typically swept aside by military rulers and one-party states in the 1970s. By the 1980s, Africa had become synonymous with an image of bad government, poverty, and economic stagnation, problems that structural adjustment only partially addressed. Then, in the early 1990s, Africa entered its second major political transition of the twentieth century – a return to electoral democracy, driven by both internal pressures for change and external global forces brought to bear at the end of the Cold War. Two decades on, Africa is still in the midst of this latest political transition, with most of its countries now identified as democracies, but ones that are still struggling to consolidate and strengthen their democratic practices and institutions.

The turmoil of transition marks African politics in the current century, and the study of these processes – the successes and the failures, the triumphs and the setbacks – has given enormous impetus to the growth of political studies on the continent. To understand politics in Africa one must grapple with the limitations of the African state; the strength of ethnic identities and their influence on political behaviour; the prevalence of conflict and civil wars; the delicate politics of peacebuilding; the struggles for economic development and political democracy; and the reasons for and the implications of the continent's continued international marginalization. All of these themes are covered in this collection of essays, which focuses on the most important contemporary debates and current controversies.

1

Dealing with the data

Africa's politics are now widely studied and extensively written about, but scholars are inevitably still constrained by their sources. One of the most significant barriers to political research in Africa has been the difficulty of collecting accurate and comprehensive data, and it is a problem that has both limited our knowledge of specific processes and restricted our ability to draw meaningful comparative insights. Authoritarian governments are not known for their willingness to open their archives or talk to researchers, and Africa has had more than its fair share of such regimes. In countries such as Angola, Ethiopia, and Eritrea, state control has made it extremely difficult – and at times impossible – for scholars to function. Within Africa itself there is a dearth of university departments of politics, in part because the study of politics has not always been welcomed by military dictators and one-party rulers. In other conflict-prone countries, such as the Democratic Republic of Congo (DRC) and Somalia, it has often been too dangerous for researchers to spend the necessary time on the ground. Even where the research environment has been more hospitable, reliable census data and economic indicators have been conspicuous by their absence. Moreover, in Africa the rise of the Internet did not initially generate 'off-the-shelf' data sets upon which researchers in other parts of the world thrived, adding to an information gap that widened the gulf between the study of politics in Africa and in North America and Europe.

Instead, researchers in Africa have been energetic and imaginative in identifying and collecting their own data, piecing together material from diverse sources, and often making extensive use of interviews, local newspaper sources and archives, and drawing upon research reported in the grey literature of non-governmental organizations (NGOs), human rights organizations, donors, and international agencies. This has had a profound impact on the way that the analysis of African politics has evolved. The tools used in the study of African politics have often been closer to those utilized by historians and anthropologists than they have to the methods adopted by political scientists working on modern Western democracies, and so the literature produced on Africa has also been different. The absence of easily available data encouraged researchers to focus their efforts on the construction of careful case studies through months of painstaking fieldwork in previously understudied countries, often investigating themes that would not be accessible through more conventional data sources. This has had its strengths, but it has also contributed to a fragmenting of Africa's political studies, making it harder to compare across a large number of countries with any confidence. Without obviously comparable data, Africanists have been dissuaded from conducting 'large-*n*' projects. Thus, whereas the general trend in comparative politics over the last 50 years has been toward more comparative and quantitative methods, research on African politics has tended to be smaller in scale and more attentive to local context. Perhaps for these reasons, those who work on politics have often been uncomfortable with research that seeks to make broader generalizations about the continent. It is of more than semantic significance that many people who study African politics would never refer to themselves as 'political scientists', but see themselves as inhabiting a field best described as 'political studies'.

However, since the turn of the present century this picture has been undergoing rapid change. The World Bank (www.data.worldbank.org) and a number of other international organizations have steadily improved the scope and accuracy of the data they make available on Africa. Google, for example, has teamed up with some governments to increase access to information, most notably through open data web portals, such as the one launched with the Kenyan government in 2011 (www.opendata.go.ke). More significantly, in 1999 a team of researchers from the Centre for Democratic Development (CDD-Ghana), Michigan State University, and the Institute for Democracy in South Africa (IDASA) launched the

Afrobarometer – a survey of public opinion in Africa. Afrobarometer surveys were run in 12 countries in the first round (1999–2000), 16 in the second (2002–03), 18 in the third (2005–06), and 20 countries in the fourth (2008–09). The creation of a vast and easily accessible dataset on ordinary people's attitudes on everything from economic policy to the quality of democracy has resulted in an explosion of research: by 2012, some 138 articles had already been posted in the Afrobarometer's Working Papers series (www.afrobarometer.org). Some of the main findings of this body of work are summarized in Michael Bratton's contribution to this volume. Especially in the United States, the availability of the Afrobarometer and other 'off-the-shelf' data sets, such as the democracy ratings provided by Freedom House (www.freedomhouse.org) and the Polity Project (www.systemicpeace.org/polity), has encouraged more Africanists to engage in quantitative and 'large-*n*' comparative research. Put another way, there are far more Africanist political scientists than there used to be. As a result, the methods used to study Africa and the type of research produced continues to evolve and diversify – the innovation that marks the field continues but is now consolidated and endorsed by a stronger and growing comparative and quantitative body of work.

The African state and identity politics

The essays brought together in this *Handbook* display all of the richness that is evident in the field of African politics, including the diversity of sources and methods. The chapters are organized around six key themes that allow us to survey the breadth of the field. The opening set of essays looks at different aspects of the state in Africa. Wrestling with the problem of how to understand and categorize the modern state in Africa has generated a large and vibrant literature over the past two decades. To date, much of this literature has essentially sought to tackle one of two questions. The first relates to the strength of the state – its coercive capacity, physical reach, and ability to protect and provide for its citizens. From the very first years of independence, the weakness of African states has been apparent. Aristide Zolberg (1969) was first to document a centre-periphery divide, noting that the power of African governments appeared to dissipate the further away from the capital city one went. Numerous other studies followed, including Jackson and Rosberg's (1982) influential article suggesting that African states did not have an 'empirical' reality, but only continued to survive because they were recognized by the international state system that worked to protect them. Later authors, perhaps most notably Jeffrey Herbst (2000), expanded on these early insights, demonstrating that the centre-periphery divide was related to the lack of infrastructural development during the colonial period and the absence of inter-state conflict. According to Herbst, the key factor was that African governments had failed to invest in the creation of strong borders – in sharp contrast to their European counterparts who built their states through conflicts at their borders.

The second main strand of literature on understanding the state in Africa has sought to explain its weakness by demonstrating its incompatibility with the forms of political organization present within pre-colonial African societies. Following Médard's classic 1982 formulation, the African state was understood to be 'neopatrimonial' – the product of the clash between the 'modern' colonial state and 'traditional' forms of patrimonial authority (in short, the tendency of leaders to treat the resources of the community as if they were their personal possessions). The most valuable insight of this literature was that neither the state nor traditional forms of authority emerged unchanged from this collision. As patrimonial leaders found themselves in charge of centralized state bureaucracies upon independence, the scope and power of the continent's 'big men' increased dramatically. At the same time, the ability of patrimonial leaders to use their personal networks to undermine official constitutional and legislative rules meant that key institutions of accountability and security failed to function according to the official rules. Indeed, one of the reasons that the concept of neopatrimonialism has proved to be so durable is precisely because it is so well suited to explaining the descent of a number of high-profile African states into authoritarian rule and corruption.

Explanations of the weakness of the state that reference neopatrimonialism, or other theories that similarly focus on the clash between culture and institutions, such as those most famously offered by Bayart (1993) and Chabal and Daloz (1999), are intimately connected to the literature on ethnic, linguistic, and religious politics. After all, it is through their position as the leaders of ethnic groups – or other forms of community – that 'big men' draw their authority. For this reason, the second section of the *Handbook* addresses the politics of identity. Commentators have long noted the tendency for people of the same community to line up behind their community leaders, whether chiefs during the colonial era, 'big men' under authoritarian rule, or political leaders under multi-partyism (Horowitz 1985; Posner 2005). There is considerable evidence that in many countries the situation worsened since the 1990s, over a period when democratization has been in vogue. Research conducted by scholars from a variety of disciplines, including anthropologists and historians, as well as political scientists, has documented the worrying development of 'ethnic politics' in many parts of the continent, in which communities that claim to be the original 'sons of the soil' – 'autochthons' – reject the rights of other 'immigrant' communities to vote, stand as candidates, or access resources, outside of their home area. The rise of this 'politics of belonging' has intensified local disputes over land and power and has made identity politics a key theme. It is therefore understandable that ethnicity is often posited as being at the root of Africa's ills, from poor economic performance, to civil war (see, for example, Easterly and Levine 1997).

Investigations into the identity politics of ethnicity in Africa have allowed us to appreciate much about mobilization and electoral politics in particular, but other strands of this research into ethnicity have demonstrated that, in reality, the African state and the politics of identity are more complex than predominant narratives allow. For one thing, African states have not been equally weak and the rule of law has not been equally abused. Ruling parties in one-party states, such as those in Kenya, Senegal, Tanzania, and Zambia, were able to effectively hold on to power for two to three decades precisely because they maintained a mixture of coercive control and political legitimacy. So it is that, while neopatrimonialism remains an over-arching theme, other chapters included here on the importance of state bureaucracies, the struggles to restore and maintain the rule of law, the resilience of forms of one-party rule and the influence of the military, the privatization of violence, and the options offered by federalist approaches to government, all provide further evidence of the workings of the state in Africa.

Similarly, the dominant narrative of ethnic politics, which remains essential to any understanding of African politics, also needs to be put into context. In practice, ethnic identities have been shown to be remarkably malleable in many parts of Africa: more open and inclusive during times of peace and common need, and more closed and hostile during times of conflict. One of the main findings of the literature on communal identities is that the development of pronounced ethnic identities and distrust is not a natural process, but rather is often the product of the deliberate efforts of local cultural entrepreneurs and political leaders to shape communal identities for their own agendas (Ranger 1983; Vail 1989).

The emphasis on ethnicity has also served to obscure the significance of other markers of political identities, such as class, religion, and gender. Although often more subtle, these forms of identification affect politics in powerful ways – a point that has received far greater acceptance following the rise of radical Islamic movements in Somalia and, more recently, Nigeria. Given this, it is important to always keep ethnicity in context and not to give it too great an explanatory power: rather, we should follow the example of the best research on ethnic politics in Africa and ask how ethnicity, religion, and other forms of communal identity interact, and through what processes they become more overtly politicized. Our chapters on political ethnicity and the politics of belonging therefore need to be read in tandem with those dealing with class, Muslim politics, religion and witchcraft, and gender.

The conflict continent?

The weakness of the African state and the strength of communal identities represent important foundations for the understanding of contemporary domestic politics on the continent. Our third section gathers together chapters on the theme of conflict – work that has often traced incidents of political disorder and violence back to the combination of weak states, predatory leaders, and intense competition over scarce resources (Bates 2008). The logic here has been intuitive. Neopatrimonial leaders in countries with highly politicized ethnic identities face few barriers to corruption and strong pressure to reward their supporters, and so are more likely to steal state resources and divert them to consolidate their position within their communities. When this happens, rival communities learn that losing power means losing economic opportunities. As a result, the stakes of political competition increase (Cooper 2002) to the point where no group is willing to accept defeat: the winner must take all, and so competition too easily spills over into conflict.

While African states have rarely fought against each other since the 1950s, civil conflicts have been all too common. Botswana is perhaps the only resource-rich state that has escaped this particular curse, managing its bounties in a way that has actually contributed to long-term economic growth and national unity. Too often, Botswana has simply been presented as the exception – a place of tranquillity in a continent of conflict. However, the notion that Africa's history since the 1960s has been a story only of conflict is both inaccurate and misleading. Military coups and insurrections have been multiple, to be sure, but a study of patterns and trends in African conflicts reveals peaks in intensity at the end of the Cold War and a more recent decline (Strauss 2012).

It is therefore important to consider not only what causes these conflicts – how states enter conflict – but also how they have avoided it and how they can emerge out of it. It is true that the strongest predictor that a country will have a civil war in the future is that it has had a civil war in the past (Collier and Hoeffler 2004), but it is also true that countries experiencing civil wars have a very bad impact upon their neighbours. It is therefore not surprising that African states have been playing an increasing role in seeking settlements to conflicts on the continent. Countries do not passively accept their 'destiny'; instead, we have seen concerted efforts by brave coalitions of domestic and international actors – peacemakers and peacekeepers – to break the cycles of violence in places such as Liberia and Sierra Leone. These efforts have empowered people in these states to imagine new futures, even if their countries still have a long way to go before the spectre of violence will begin to recede and the infrastructure of the state is restored. While considering the importance of the 'resource curse' in Africa's oil politics and the prevalence of civil war, it is thus also essential to understand the mechanisms of power-sharing, peacebuilding, and the imposition of transitional justice.

Democratic transitions and the politics of development

Much of the analysis of African politics since the end of the Cold War has focused on the question of whether or not democracy can be built in countries that lack the rule of law, have recently emerged from conflict, and in which political behaviour is so strongly shaped by ethnic identity (Ake 2000). This is the theme of our fourth set of essays.

One of the most fundamental reasons why democracy is so valued in much of Africa is that it provides the opportunity to 'vote the rascals out'. Democratic electoral politics promises more accountable and effective governance, and rule-bound leadership. However, if unscrupulous leaders can legitimate themselves by diverting resources to their communities through neopatrimonial structures, then they may be able to mobilize support even when they have performed poorly in terms of the economy or national security. Under these conditions, the relationship between political competition and accountability, as it has been commonly understood in Western democracies, breaks down.

It is therefore unsurprising that research and media coverage of democracy in Africa has reported a mixed picture. South Africa is often identified as a leading democratic light, but has often been kept out of the headlines by the continuing failure of democratic institutions in neighbouring Zimbabwe. Ghana has managed to escape from a history of coups and counter-coups to establish a stable democracy in which both main parties have been willing to accept defeat, but elections in nearby Nigeria have been denounced as a farce. Some of those countries that were once thought to be among Africa's more stable states, such as Côte d'Ivoire and Kenya, have suffered significant episodes of unrest following the reintroduction of multi-partyism. All of this has raised inevitable – and very important – questions regarding the suitability of introducing divisive electoral competition into Africa's divided societies (Chua 2002). Michael Mann (2005) perhaps put this point most starkly when he argued that the Rwandan genocide – in which over 800,000 Tutsi and moderate Hutu were killed in a genocide led by a faction of the government desperate to retain power at all costs – should be interpreted as a manifestation of the 'dark side of democracy'.

Yet the news about democratization has not been all bad. Progress might be slow, but there have been genuine advances. Posner and Young (2007) have argued that African politics is becoming more 'institutionalized'. Their research shows that more African leaders than ever before are leaving power through constitutional means, in part because term limits on pre-sidential office are increasingly being respected, forcing a change of president even where countries have not witnessed a transfer of power between parties. In a similar optimistic vein, Cheeseman (2010) suggests that ruling parties are much more vulnerable to electoral defeat when they are forced to change their presidential candidate: it is under these conditions that African elections can act as vehicles of change. Moreover, there is some evidence that formal checks-and-balances institutions, such as legislatures, are starting to become more effective in protecting term-limits but also in exposing corruption and debating policy, at least in those countries that have established a basic level of political rights and civil liberties. The 'mixed bag' of democratization in sub-Saharan Africa is examined here over chapters that range through the resilience of electoral authoritarianism, the power of elections to effect change, the rise of African legislatures, the evolution of political parties, and the growing place of public opinion in democratic consolidation.

Given that development is a constant demand from African voters, at both the national and local level, it might have been expected that the reintroduction of multi-partyism would have led to a dramatic improvement in the quality of healthcare, education, and other public services on the continent. However, this would be to ignore both the patchy progress towards political liberalization and the economic constraints on African governments. The loans that African countries accepted from the World Bank and the International Monetary Fund, combined with poor economic performance during the 1970s and particularly the 1980s, left many African governments saddled with debts they could not pay, and dependent on aid from international donors. Our essays dealing with this theme, in section five, document the restrictions that current patterns of aid and trade place on the choices available to African leaders, and of the historical reliance on NGOs – what some would call civil society – to provide public services. A further essay here revisits the significance of ingrained sets of informal rules and behaviours that govern inter-personal relationships and patterns of exchange, this time with a focus on the impact of the 'economy of affection' on development and economic management.

The picture is not all gloomy, however. By the second decade of the twenty-first century many African countries were growing again, while debt relief had allowed many more African governments to spend an increasing share of government revenue on public services. While the provision of clean water and electricity remains highly uneven across the continent, an impressive number of countries have invested in free primary school education, and while states such as South Africa were terribly slow to respond to the HIV/AIDS pandemic, many are now providing antiretroviral medication and expanding still-limited coverage. These more positive developments are highlighted by chapters that address recent developments in social policy, and the possibility that by better understanding the local politics of development, it will be possible to promote effective economic growth and public services provision in certain types of neopatrimonial regimes.

Regional and international dimensions

Our final section turns attention to Africa's international relations. A concerted literature on Africa's international relations has not yet really emerged, in part, one suspects, because international relations theorists have typically assumed that African countries are simply too weak to be able to shape outcomes at the international level in a meaningful way (see Clapham 1996). African states have thus often been treated as a residual category without effective agency: the plaything of global actors, rather than a genuine player on the world stage. This is unfortunate, because sovereignty has been a key concern of those studying African politics since the ending of colonial rule. In the 1950s and 1960s, during the rise of African nationalism, research naturally focused on these new political organizations, the prospects for independence, and the capacity of African states for self-rule (Scott 1971). In the years that followed, the debate shifted to ask whether political independence was meaningful if African countries were effectively confined to the periphery of the international system, locked in a system of never-ending economic dependency (Rodney 1972; see also Leys 1996).

This view, known as dependency theory, eventually became unfashionable, in part because the success of countries such as Botswana and Mauritius demonstrated that there was nothing inevitable about African poverty. The capacity of leaders such as Uganda's Yoweri Museveni to manipulate the strategic importance of their countries to secure support and resources from international actors with far more wealth and military might has also demonstrated that, sometimes, the tail can wag the dog. Despite this, though, it is clear from the chapters collected here that concerns about the sovereignty of African states being undermined by the agendas of foreign powers remain as prominent as ever, whether the focus is the unfair treatment of African producers at the World Trade Organization, the attempts by Western donors to promote democracy in Africa, the potential militarization of the continent as a result of the 'war on terror', or the impact of the rise of China on prospects for African democracy. It should therefore come as no surprise that the need for, and limitations of, the unity of African states continues to be one of the most debated issues within the continent's regional organizations.

Bibliography

Ake, C. (2000) *The Feasibility of Democracy in Africa*, Dakar: CODESRIA.

Bates, R.H. (2008) *When Things Fell Apart: State Failure in Late Century Africa*, New York, NY: Cambridge University Press.

Bayart, J.-F. (1993) *The State in Africa: The Politics of the Belly*, London: Longman.

Bratton, M. and van de Walle, N. (1997) *Democratic Experiments in Africa: Regime Transitions in Comparative Perspective*, Cambridge: Cambridge University Press.

Chabal, P. and Daloz, J.-P. (1999) *Africa Works: Disorder as Political Instrument*, Oxford: James Currey.

Cheeseman, N. (2010) 'African Elections as Vehicles for Change', *Journal of Democracy* 21(4): 139–53.

Chua, A. (2002) *World on Fire: How Exporting Free Market Democracy Breeds Ethnic Hatred and Global Instability*, New York, NY: Anchor Books.

Clapham, C. (1996) *Africa and the International System: The Politics of State Survival*, Cambridge: Cambridge University Press.

Collier, P. and Hoeffler, A. (2004) 'Greed and Grievance in Civil War', *Oxford Economic Papers* 56(4): 563–95.

Cooper, F. (2002) *Africa Since 1940: The Past of the Present*, Cambridge: Cambridge University Press.

Easterly, W. and Levine, R. (1997) 'Africa's Growth Tragedy: Policies and Ethnic Divisions', *Quarterly Journal of Economics* 112(4): 1203–50.

Herbst, J. (2000) *States and Power in Africa: Comparative Lessons in Authority and Control*, Princeton, NJ: Princeton University Press.

Horowitz, D.L. (1985) *Ethnic Groups in Conflict*, Berkeley, CA: University of California Press.

Jackson, R.H. and Rosberg, C.G. (1982) 'Why Africa's Weak States Persist: The Empirical and Juridical in Statehood', *World Politics* 35(1): 1–24.

Mann, M. (2005) *The Dark Side of Democracy: Explaining Ethnic Cleansing*, Cambridge: Cambridge University Press.

Médard, J.F. (1982) 'The Underdeveloped State in Africa: Political Clientelism or Neo-patrimonialism?', in C. Clapham (ed.) *Private Patronage and Public Power: Political Clientelism in the Modern State*, New York, NY: St Martin's Press.

Leys, C. (1996) *The Rise and Fall of Dependency Theory*, London: James Currey.

Posner, D.N. (2005) *Institutions and Ethnic Politics in Africa*, Cambridge: Cambridge University Press.

Posner, D.N. and Young, D.J. (2007) 'The Institutionalization of Political Power in Africa', *Journal of Democracy* 18(3): 126–40.

Ranger, T. (1983) 'The Invention of Tradition in Colonial Africa', in E. Hobsbawm and T. Ranger (eds) *The Invention of Tradition*, Cambridge: Cambridge University Press.

Rodney, W. (1972) *How Europe Underdeveloped Africa*, London: Bogle-L'Ouverture Publications.

Scott, R. (1971) *The Politics of New States*, London: Allen and Unwin.

Strauss, S. (2012) 'Wars Do End! Changing Patterns of Political Violence in sub-Saharan Africa', *African Affairs* 433(111): 179–201.

Vail, R. (1989) *The Creation of Tribalism in Southern Africa*, Oxford: James Currey.

van de Walle, N. (2001) *African Economies and the Politics of Permanent Crisis, 1979–1999*, Cambridge: Cambridge University Press.

Zolberg, A. (1969) *Creating Political Order: The Party States of West Africa*, Chicago, IL: Rand McNally.

PART I

The politics of the state

1

NATIONALISM, ONE-PARTY STATES, AND MILITARY RULE

Nic Cheeseman

Following the reintroduction of multi-party politics in Africa in the early 1990s it is easy to assume that topics such as the one-party state and military rule are no longer relevant. After all, these were the subjects that Africanists studied in the 1980s when authoritarian rule was ubiquitous and there was little to celebrate. What relevance could such issues have for the era of democratization? In fact, the legacy of authoritarian rule continues to loom large on the continent. The prospects for long-term economic development and democratic consolidation are shaped by whether or not a country was a one-party state or a military regime, was governed by a benign 'philosopher King' or a unscrupulous dictator, or experienced relative stability or endemic conflict. Nationalism, one-party states, and military rule thus remain important topics because they help us better to understand both the past and the present.

This chapter has three main aims. The first is to demonstrate the lasting significance of nationalism to African politics. Nationalism has consistently exerted a powerful hold on the continent's trajectory, from the fragmentation of nationalist movements in the 1960s, which contributed to the emergence of one-party states and military rule, through to the continued use of nationalist discourse by political leaders, most notably Robert Mugabe, in the contemporary period. The second is to show that not all authoritarian regimes were the same. In fact, Africa has witnessed a broad range of undemocratic governments that have varied dramatically in terms of their commitment to human rights and political participation. Some, such as Mobutu Sese Seko's brutal military dictatorship in Zaire (now the Democratic Republic of Congo – DRC) denied citizens any meaningful political rights. Others, though, such as Julius Nyerere's one-party state in Tanzania, prohibited opposition parties but allowed citizens to enjoy a degree of free speech and to participate in elections in which they could choose their local representative, if not their government.

The third and final aim of the chapter is to trace the legacies of one-party and military rule, in order to show how they continue to influence political developments today. It is not possible to understand fully the international and domestic resonance of the power-sharing model of government – a form of inclusive government with no opposition, which has often been introduced as a way to end periods of conflict – without first recognizing that the one-party state was the most stable form of government in the years that followed independence. It is also not possible to fully understand the scepticism of many Africanists towards American plans to channel increasing resources to the continent's armies through the recently formed US Africa

Command (AFRICOM) without first appreciating the record of African militaries in power since independence.

Nationalism and after

The fight against colonial rule is often remembered across the continent as a moment of great national unity; of course, in many ways it was. Consider the proud history of the African National Congress (ANC) in South Africa. Formed in 1912 as the South African Native National Congress (SANNC), the ANC fought a struggle that was impressively inclusive of different black African ethnic groups, coloureds, Asians, and whites. This was remarkable because the apartheid government elected by white voters in 1948 employed a range of divide-and-rule strategies that were deliberately designed to prevent the emergence of a united opposition. By creating separate 'homelands' for black ethnic groups, the National Party sought to strengthen individual group identities and thus make it harder for a united black nationalist movement to emerge (Lodge 1983). By transferring modest amounts of patronage and power to black African leaders willing to engage with the state, the apartheid regime also hoped to create a tier of conservative black figures who would find it in their interests to defend the status quo.

This strategy was not without success. For example, having established the Inkatha Freedom Party (IFP) in 1975, Inkosi Mangosuthu Buthelezi, son of the Zulu Chief Mathole Buthelezi, became the chief minister of the 'semi-autonomous' KwaZulu homeland. Although the ANC initially accepted the new party, radical nationalists soon accused Buthelezi of being an apartheid collaborator (Mare and Hamilton 1987). For his part, Buthelezi recognized that his privileged status depended on the ongoing support of the apartheid government; his power was therefore threatened by the prospects of majority rule. As a result, following the negotiations to bring an end to apartheid rule in the early 1990s, Buthelezi initially refused to participate in democratic elections and only agreed to stand after ANC leader Nelson Mandela and National Party leader F.W. de Klerk had promised that they would recognize the special status of the Zulu monarchy after the polls.

However, although such fissures existed, the ANC proved able to win and retain the loyalty of the vast majority of the black population over some 100 years. Despite being banned and forced into exile by one of the most effective authoritarian states in sub-Saharan Africa, the message of the movement's Freedom Charter – that South Africa belongs to all those who live in it, black and white – continued to resonate. The hold of the party over the South African political imagination shows no signs of abating: after 20 years of multi-party elections, the ANC's share of the vote has yet to drop below 62 per cent.

Yet the notion of the late colonial period as a time of African unity was also a necessary myth, valuable to leaders in both colonial times and the post-colonial era because it allowed those in power to gloss over internal schisms and to obscure competing visions of how power should be distributed. As the case of the ANC and IFP suggests, even the most effective nationalist movements contained deep divisions (Hodgkin 1956). The boundaries of African states had been drawn not with respect to the location and history of different ethnic groups, but according to a geo-strategic logic. Even if European cartographers had been more sensitive to local context, they would have struggled to design states that made economic and cultural sense: the average African polity is at least twice as ethnically diverse as New York or London, and the high number of small ethnic groups in countries such as the DRC, Ethiopia, Nigeria, and Uganda would have made it impossible to design polities that would have been both ethnically homogenous and large enough to be viable. It is therefore unsurprising that African states group together a range of different communities with little sense of a common identity, and that subsequent inter-communal relations have often been characterized more by competition than by a sense of solidarity.

Prior to independence, ethnic identities were reified and entrenched by colonial practices of codifying groups and mapping the location of ethnic groups, appointing and solidifying the role of chiefs over distinct ethnic communities, and playing divide-and-rule politics. Taken together, these policies served to institutionalize identities while simultaneously providing Africans with incentives to organize as ethnic communities to be better able to press their demands on the colonial regime. Following Ranger, one might say that colonial governments believed in tribes, and Africans gave them tribes to believe in (see Ranger 1983, 1993). In turn, more politically salient ethnic identities made it less likely that political movements would remain united – a major problem for nationalist movements but a boon for authoritarian incumbents seeking to defend their positions after independence (see Lynch, this volume).

Inter-ethnic tensions were also fostered by the impact of the colonial era on local political economies, which varied within countries as well as between them. The communities that lived near sites of colonial settlement usually suffered the greatest disruption as a result of occupation, but were also the groups that benefitted the most from the opportunities colonial rule had to offer. Mission education may have provided the basis for self-advancement, but it was proximity to wage labour and positions in the colonial administration that facilitated the emergence of a new elite. Because the communities that suffered the most painful consequences of colonial rule, such as land alienation, often also enjoyed higher levels of education, know-how, and capital, their leaders typically had both the motivation and the confidence required to campaign for a rapid transition to independence. The Kikuyu of Kenya illustrate this pattern well. The reservation of land in the Rift Valley for white settlers helped to radicalize the Kikuyu community, ultimately leading to the violent Mau Mau rebellion of the 1950s (Anderson 2005b).

Simultaneously, high levels of missionary education and the greater employment options available in Nairobi ensured that the Kikuyu community assumed an economically privileged position. Many Kikuyu did not join Mau Mau, but rather became 'loyalists' and worked for the colonial regime (Branch 2009). As a result, the Kikuyu were both strongly represented within the colonial administration and were at the forefront of the nationalist movement: it was predominantly leaders from the Kikuyu and Luo communities that in 1960 established the Kenyan African National Union (KANU) to push for the speedy end of colonial rule, confident that they had the necessary skills and opportunity to reap the benefits of independence.

By contrast, economically and politically marginal communities faced a more uncertain future. For such groups, independence promised not a new set of freedoms, but rather the prospect of being dominated by their rivals. In Kenya, the Nandi, Maasai, and coastal communities were numerically smaller and less economically advanced than the Luo and Kikuyu. They thus established their own 'nationalist' organization, the Kenya African Democratic Union (KADU), which pushed a far more conservative agenda. Encouraged by European settlers – who also had good reason to fear majority rule – KADU campaigned for a more gradual transition to independence and for the introduction of a *majimbo* (regionalist) constitution that would allow Kenya's communities a degree of local self-government (Anderson 2005a). Subsequent competition between KANU and KADU split the nationalist movement in two and resulted in considerable inter-party violence.

While a number of more homogenous countries, such as Botswana, did not have to face these challenges, Kenya was far from alone in struggling to manage the tension between the need for unity within the nationalist movement and the desire of sub-national communities for a degree of self-government and protection against the threat of the tyranny of the majority. These internal contradictions meant that the struggle against colonial oppression was often more messy – and divisive – than official narratives of nationalism allow. Such fissures proved to be particularly significant in the post-colonial period because, when mishandled by post-colonial political leaders, they formed the foundations of civil conflict and unrest.

In addition to the internal contradictions within many nationalist coalitions, there was a deep tension in the ideas that motivated nationalism. On the one hand, the cry of freedom resonated everywhere. In East Africa, the nationalist struggle was known as the battle for *uhuru* (freedom). In South Africa, the ANC's Freedom Charter guided successive anti-apartheid campaigns, including that of the United Democratic Front (UDF) in the mid- to late 1980s. Freedom was a particularly effective rallying call because it could mean all things to all people: freedom from colonial oppression, freedom from poverty and unemployment, freedom to fulfil one's aspirations.

However, the demand for freedom went hand-in-hand with a call to unity. In the eyes of philosopher-kings such as Leopold Senghor of Senegal, unity had instrumental value because internal divisions would weaken the effectiveness of African nationalism. It also had intrinsic value, though, because it reflected a common African heritage and culture that needed to be preserved against the challenges that would come from within and without. The call to unity took a variety of forms. In the hands of Kwame Nkrumah, Ghana's influential independence leader, it became a message of pan-Africanism – a call to move beyond colonial borders and to celebrate the continent's common history and needs. Other founding fathers, such as Jomo Kenyatta in Kenya, were rhetorically supportive of pan-Africanism but in practice were more concerned to ensure domestic unity, which they saw as being necessary first to secure independence and later to meet the challenge of nation-building (for a full discussion see Khadiagala, this volume).

These two key goals of freedom and unity continue to exert a great hold over the political imagination, yet they have existed in perpetual tension. Post-colonial regimes typically viewed disunity as the forerunner of civil conflict and responded by promoting unity at any costs, even when this meant imposing significant constraints on the freedoms of ordinary people to speak and act freely. As a result, the quest for unity frequently gave rise to the emergence of an authoritarian form of politics that often has been viewed as more acceptable by domestic and international actors because of its rhetorical roots in the nationalist struggle.

Especially where the liberation struggle was longer and more violent, as in Angola, Mozambique, and Zimbabwe, governments have been particularly concerned to maintain the unity that was essential to the success of their former guerrilla/military operations in order to establish political hegemony. Some former liberation movements have managed to maintain a balance between the quest for control with a respect for civil liberties, as in Namibia and South Africa, but in cases in which former liberation parties have suffered a decline in popularity but were unwilling to contemplate losing power, they have often proved adept at manipulating the memory of the liberation struggle in order to depict opposition groups or dissenting individuals as 'sell-outs' and 'traitors', and thus as legitimate targets of state violence. The response of Robert Mugabe's Zimbabwe African National Union (ZANU) to the threat posed by the Movement of Democratic Change (MDC) opposition is a classic example of the use of 'patriotic history' to cow dissent (Tendi 2010). Although the quest to maintain political order did not always lead to such repressive consequences, in the struggle between freedom and unity it was typically the latter that won out.

Authoritarian rule

Chris Allen (1995) has described how, following the victory over colonial rule, many of the nationalist coalitions began to fragment under the weight of their own contradictions. Across the continent, leaders struggled to hold their alliances together as competition over power and patronage intensified both between and within ethnic groups. As leaders scrambled to maintain order, they drew on the nationalist rhetoric of unity to justify the extension of political control, paving the way for the marginalization of rival parties and the steady erosion of political space. The consequence was a decade of democratic backsliding and political unrest.

However, as Allen points out, there was no single 'African' experience. Instead, two main trajectories emerged. In those states where ruling parties had a national reach, and the executive was able to retain control of the party machinery, the nationalist crisis was resolved by the construction of one-party states, in which power was centralized under the president and democratic institutions were downgraded. It was not always feasible to establish a one-party state. In countries where no party was able to establish a dominant position, ethno-regional divisions were pronounced, trust among the political elite was low, and leaders found it far harder to consolidate their rule and maintain political order. In turn, mounting instability and the descent into what Allen calls 'spoils politics' de-legitimated democratically elected governments, generating a power vacuum that facilitated the entrance of the military onto the political stage.

These trajectories were important to later developments, because while in many military regimes political participation was all but eradicated, in some one-party states elements of representative government lived on, albeit to varying degrees. Different experiences of authoritarian rule therefore shaped the political landscape within which the transition to multi-partyism in the 1990s took place.

One-party states

The one-party state proved to be one of the most durable and common forms of government in Africa after independence. At various times, Angola, Benin, Burkina Faso, Burundi, Cameroon, Cape Verde, the Central African Republic (CAR), Chad, Comoros, Congo-Brazzaville, Côte d'Ivoire, the DRC (then Congo-Kinshasa), Djibouti, Equatorial Guinea, Ethiopia, Gabon, Ghana, Guinea-Bissau, Kenya, Liberia, Malawi, Mali, Mauritania, Mozambique, Niger, Rwanda, São Tomé and Príncipe, Senegal, Seychelles, Sierra Leone, Somalia, Sudan, and Togo all claimed single-party status. In many of these countries 'one-party rule' meant little more than the creation of a façade of a political organization to legitimize what was in effect a brutal military regime. However, a small but important sub-set of one-party states evolved out of civilian regimes that initially won power at the ballot box and retained their legitimacy over the first decade or so of independence. For example, in Côte d'Ivoire (1960), Kenya (1969), and Senegal (1966) *de facto* one-party systems emerged after opposition to the ruling party collapsed, disbanded, or was banned.

Ruling parties in Tanzania (1965), Zambia (1972), and Kenya (under second President Daniel arap Moi in 1982), went a step further, establishing *de jure* single-party systems through constitutional amendments that rendered opposition parties illegal, but only after their parties had won large majorities in open elections. As a result, the single-party systems established by the likes of the Democratic Party of Côte d'Ivoire (PDCI), the Tanzanian African National Union (TANU), the Kenya African National Union (KANU), and Zambia's United National Independence Party (UNIP), initially had a strong claim to be the legitimate representation of the national will. Of course, not all civilian one-party states remained politically open. In Ghana, the single-party system of Kwame Nkrumah became increasingly intolerant of opposition until he was deposed in a coup in February 1966. However, it was those one-party states that were able to combine participation and control that proved to be the most stable and durable.

Control was maintained through the centralization of power under a dominant executive, the downgrading of representative institutions, such as the legislature, and the effective (if not official) prohibition of criticism of the executive. Where opposition to the system emerged, it was typically repressed through the targeted use of intimidation, exile, and in extreme cases, assassination. In Kenya, Pio Gama Pinto (1965), Tom Mboya (1969), J.M. Kariuki (1975), and Robert Ouko (1990) were allegedly killed because they posed too great a threat to the incumbent cabal.

At the same time, ruling parties typically expanded their reach to regulate an increasing proportion of political and social activity. As part of the broader centralization of power, the TANU constitution emulated the image of mass socialist parties by making provision for a party youth league, women's section, and elders' section. By co-opting trade union and youth leaders into the party hierarchy, Nyerere and Kenyatta brought potentially destabilizing groups to heel. However, for other regimes where unions were larger and better organized, as in Zambia, this strategy proved to be difficult to implement.

The extension of control was legitimated by the maintenance of avenues of political participation, most notably through one-party elections in which voters could choose between candidates from the ruling party. Although it is impossible to be certain, these elections appear to have been mostly free and fair, at least in the first decade of independence, and they allowed voters occasionally to give the government a bloody nose. In Zambia, Kenneth Kaunda replaced presidential elections with a referendum that allowed the electorate to accept or reject his candidacy. In the 1978 election, a strong 'no' vote in many areas, including the Southern and Northern Provinces, forced UNIP leaders to think up ever more imaginative ways to secure a healthy majority for the president, such as using widely despised animals like the hyena as the symbol for the 'no' option on the ballot paper.

In most other one-party states, presidential polls were abandoned and elections were restricted to first-past-the-post constituency polls in which constituencies were able to vote for their member of parliament (MP) from a list of candidates approved by the ruling party. These contests served many purposes for the government. Significantly, they legitimated the regime and facilitated elite rotation, enabling younger political leaders with new ideas to enter parliament. One-party polls also created mechanisms of local accountability that kept MPs on their toes: elections typically resulted in around half of all sitting MPs losing their seats. The willingness of voters to reject candidates who paid them insufficient attention encouraged legislators to focus on constituency service and to raise locally sensitive issues on the floor of the House (Barkan, this volume). However, the rapid turnover of MPs also had a downside as it undermined the level of expertise within the legislature and so further empowered the executive to control the parliamentary agenda.

Unsurprisingly, single-party elections developed their own distinctive dynamics. Because all of the candidates belonged to the same party, and elections focused on the constituency level, they became obsessively local. This reduced the potential for divisive open competition between larger ethnic and regional communities, and so made it easier to maintain national unity. It also reduced the importance of a candidate's ethno-regional background because most rural constituencies were fairly homogenous and the vast majority of constituencies were rural: as a result, most contests occurred between candidates of the same ethnicity. Consequently, voters were unable to differentiate between candidates on the basis of communal identity (unless constituencies were split into rival clans or kinship networks), and so had to find other ways of distinguishing between aspiring political leaders. Under these conditions, a candidate's record and personal qualities became of central importance.

Ironically, the main challenge for most civilian one-party rulers was not so much maintaining national unity as sustaining the ruling party itself. The absence of a common enemy against which to mobilize support, and a chronic lack of resources, typically resulted in an atrophy of members and office holders after independence. For example, although Kaunda claimed that it 'Pays to Belong to UNIP' and that the party was supposed to be the vehicle through which the government and the Zambian people communicated, by 1984 UNIP had a remarkable 172,930 unfilled posts. Presidents typically responded to this process of institutional decline in one of two ways. In Kenya, Kenyatta was not a party man and was suspicious of the more radical leaders who had created the party during his incarceration by the British. He was therefore happy to allow KANU to decay and instead to rule through his powerful patron-client networks and the prefectural structure of the Provincial Administration that he inherited from colonial rule. Consequently, Kenya soon evolved into a 'no-party' state centred on Kenyatta's personalized rule.

More typically, leaders attempted to extend the life of their parties by fusing them with state structures. For Nyerere and Kaunda this served two purposes: allowing them to use state resources to fund the ruling party; and to radicalize the bureaucracy to nationalist ends (Nyerere 1961). In Zambia, this development resulted in a bureaucratic/party hybrid that was given the unfortunate name of the Party and Its Government (popularly – or perhaps more accurately, unpopularly – known as PIG). The conflation of party and state structures kept UNIP from complete collapse but only at the cost of creating bloated committees, unclear authority structures, and institutional blockages, as technocrats and party officials competed for supremacy. Although in principle this system generated more avenues through which people could engage with their rulers, in reality the labyrinthine world of committee systems was often so unresponsive that ordinary citizens began to lose faith in the value of political participation.

Military rule and politics without politicians

In the DRC (1960), Benin (1963), Congo-Brazzaville (1963), Togo (1963), CAR (1966), and Ghana (1966), independence was quickly followed by a military coup. These were not isolated examples: by 1980, more than two-thirds of sub-Saharan African states had experienced some form of military rule. Coup leaders typically justified their actions by invoking the national interest and promising to rectify the economic and political failings of the civilian regimes that they replaced (First 1970). However, such rhetoric often masked a more self-interested reality. As Samuel Decalo has argued, military intervention in the 1970s and 1980s was typically triggered by threats to the status of the military itself, such as government proposals to reduce the terms of service of the security forces, to sideline particular factions within the officer class, or to promote a dominant ethnic group via privileged access to state resources (Decalo 1990). Despite this, the rhetoric of coup leaders was often taken at face value. Indeed, some early commentators talked up the potential of the military to act as a transformative force capable of delivering unity and modernization, and domestic and international actors frequently welcomed coups as a positive development (see Mazrui 1976 for an interesting discussion).

In the wake of the harrowing and violent legacy of Idi Amin's rule in Uganda, it is easy to forget that the coup that brought Amin to power in 1971 inspired celebrations in the streets and was initially welcomed in the metropole. Following the uncertainty and authoritarianism that had characterized the government of Milton Obote, Amin's coup encouraged Ugandans to dream of an efficient, orderly, and responsive government. Indeed, Amin went out of his way to cultivate these expectations, publishing a list of 18 failings of the Obote regime that his government would put right, including the use of forced labour and thuggery, the denial of freedom of speech, and the failure to hold free and fair elections.

Although Amin's criticism of Obote was well founded, the failure of multi-partyism in Uganda served to facilitate, rather than inspire, his seizure of power. Amin's real motivation seems to have been self-protection: he knew that Obote planned to replace him as Commander of the Army, which would have left him vulnerable to prosecution over his alleged involvement in the murder of Brigadier P.Y. Okoya, who had been Amin's main rival within the military. As in Benin, the CAR, and Ghana, military leaders in Uganda were above neither the self-interest nor the petty squabbles that frequently undermined their civilian predecessors. Given this, it is perhaps unsurprising that there was little that was distinctive about the achievements of military governments, which often proved to be more venal and authoritarian than the regimes they replaced.

In Uganda, Amin's increasingly paranoid and violent rule wholly undermined the basic institutions of the government and resulted in over 100,000 deaths, with some estimations as high as half a million. This pattern was repeated elsewhere, as indicated by several African countries' poor ratings on political rights and civil liberties. Evaluated on the basis of a 1–7 scale in which lower scores denote 'more free' countries, Nigeria, Mauritania, and the CAR all averaged over 5.5 from 1975 to 1990 (Freedom House 2012). The performance of military regimes on issues such as corruption and the economy was not much better. In Nigeria, General Ibrahim Babangida, who took power from General Muhammadu Buhari in a palace coup in 1985, appears to have misappropriated over US$6 billion of state funds despite his pretensions to order and discipline (Diamond *et al.* 1997). Meanwhile, authoritarian rule in the CAR was as ineffective as it was corrupt, resulting in an average rate of gross domestic product (GDP) growth of just 1.16 between 1975 and 1990.

While there was nothing unique about the record of military regimes, they did face a distinctive dilemma in government. Like their civilian counterparts who established one-party states, military leaders associated inter-communal tension with multi-party competition. However, unlike single-party states where the ruling party lived on (at least in principle) as a vehicle of popular participation, military leaders were often distrustful of the political class and so limited their presence in the government. Military leaders were also reluctant to maintain elections because competition, even at the local level, was unpredictable and had the potential to exacerbate pre-existing tensions, endangering the unity of the military itself.

Nigeria provides an apt example. The period of coup and counter-coup that marked the demise of civilian rule was in part the product of a struggle for power within the military between Hausa-Fulani and Igbo officers: to re-engage with political leaders even at the regional level threatened to intensify existing divisions. Practising politics without politicians brought its own problems, however. Most notably, it made it harder for governments to legitimate themselves and to anticipate shifts in public opinion. Military leaders thus faced a difficult choice between engaging in representative government and endangering the unity of the armed forces on the one hand, and banning politicians and elections at the risk of not being able to anticipate the public mood on the other.

Henry Bienen's research in Western State in Nigeria in the early 1970s illustrates the difficulty of conducting the day-to-day business of ruling a territory in the absence of politicians. Having come to power via the second coup of 1966, General Yakubu Gowon initially set out to establish a technocratic administration in order to complete the job of nation-building before handing power back to civilian leaders. However, the need to maintain the legitimacy of his regime, especially in the context of the Nigerian civil war, encouraged Gowon to compromise and incorporate more civilian figures within the government. To this end, in June 1967 he announced that a civilian Federal Executive Council (FEC) would be established to share executive authority with the Supreme Military Council (SMC). The civilians appointed were called commissioners because Gowon believed that his countrymen 'were not anxious to see those who in recent years participated in politics back in ministerial seats'

(Bienen 1978: 211). Similar reforms were introduced with some variations in each of Nigeria's 12 states.

However, this technocratic/hybrid failed to resolve the challenges facing the Gowon government. The attempt to generate a more responsive political system without engaging with politicians was largely unsuccessful because many of the 'civilians' appointed to the FEC (and its regional equivalents) had previously been political leaders. They therefore saw themselves as representing specific parties, whether these organizations officially existed or not. Consequently, civilian commissioners began to engage in a disorganized form of party politics, which undermined the ability of the military to claim political neutrality and thus threatened to bring broader social tensions into the very heart of the military. At the same time, although they operated as very much political animals, the military's civilian representatives failed effectively to connect the government to local communities. The small number of commissioners and their lack of an effective party machine rendered it nigh on impossible to reach out to the grassroots.

This failure had significant consequences in Western State, where Bienen (ibid.) finds that the lack of information on public opinion resulted in the failure of the government to anticipate a widespread wave of riots in 1968 and 1969 in which farmers refused to pay taxes. Once the riots had started, the absence of effective political structures further hampered attempts to identify the source of the dispute and broker a resolution. Consequently, the military was forced to utilize increasingly coercive strategies in lieu of effective systems of representation and participation. Subsequent Nigerian military regimes struggled with the same conundrum and typically also resorted to repression to compensate for inadequate mechanisms of representation.

Authoritarian legacies

Variations in the institutional structure of authoritarian rule in the 1970s and 1980s shaped the pathways different countries took to multi-partyism. In the mid-1990s Bratton and van de Walle (1994) argued that the more participation and competition there had been in the *ancien régime*, the better the prospects for democratic consolidation. Their logic was that more participatory forms of authoritarian rule were more likely to have fostered strong civil society groups, inculcated norms of electoral representation, and produced active and democratically conscious societies. By contrast, more competitive forms of authoritarian rule were more likely to have developed norms in favour of representative government and institutions capable of maintaining their independence from the executive. Given this, they predicted that former one-party states and dominant-party systems would enjoy the smoothest transition to multi-partyism. The fate of the continent's one-party and military regimes provides some support for this intuition. The existence of norms of accountability, electoral systems, and judiciaries that occasionally demonstrated the capacity for independent action in countries such as Senegal, Tanzania, and Zambia, paved the way for slow but steady processes of political liberalization.

The legacy bequeathed by less participatory and more coercive military regimes was often far less positive. Take the example of the CAR, where the military government of Colonel Jean-Bédel Bokassa gradually undermined both the capability and independence of the state and the space for dissenting voices to be heard. After seizing power in 1965, Bokassa effectively dismantled the state and castrated the bureaucracy. Fearful of losing power following a series of coup attempts between 1974 and 1976, Bokassa systematically purged his administration of individuals of talent and factions that he feared could pose a potential threat to his own position. By the time he was overthrown in 1980, Bokassa had effectively destroyed the country's representative institutions and replaced them with the foundations of a political landscape in which power was understood not to derive from the popular will, but from control over coercive forces. Ever since, the CAR has failed to overcome the twin challenge of establishing representative government and sending the military back to barracks. Attempted transitions to multi-partyism in 1981 and 1993 were both ultimately curtailed by coups. Although the CAR is an extreme example, it reflects a wider trend in which military regimes across the continent have struggled to re-civilianize politics.

Yet although institutional legacies are often critical to understanding the state of democracy in a particular country, it is important to keep in mind that many countries have moved between categories over time, blurring the distinction between different types of regime. In Benin, President Mathieu Kérékou, for example, effectively transformed a military government into a civilian one-party state. By contrast, in Malawi, President Banda's regime was officially a one-party state under the Malawian Congress Party (MCP), but in reality the weakness of party structures meant that it was closer to a personal dictatorship wholly reliant on a vast array of security forces to maintain control. The implications of the institutional legacy of Benin and Malawi therefore take some time to unpack.

At the same time, the long and contingent nature of processes of democratization, in which political trajectories may be radically altered by unanticipated crises and the idiosyncratic decisions of individual leaders, means that the hold of institutional legacies is likely to fade over time. It is therefore not surprising that while former one-party states such as Senegal, Tanzania, and Zambia have remained stable under multi-party rule, others have witnessed the emergence of civil strife and political disorder, as in Côte d'Ivoire and Kenya. Similarly, while many former military regimes have struggled to establish a genuinely civilian form of government that respects the independence of civil society, as in the CAR and Nigeria, some, such as Ghana, have emerged as among Africa's leading democratic lights.

Conclusion

The political systems and ideas developed in the immediate post-independence period continue to reverberate in Africa today. Although Posner and Young (2007) find that the number of leaders leaving power through a coup, overthrow, or violent assassination has dropped precipitously, it is also true that the military remains a central political actor in many African states. Most obviously, coups have yet to be eliminated. Over the past two decades civilian regimes have been unseated in countries such as the CAR, Gambia, Guinea-Bissau, Madagascar, Mali, Mauritania, and São Tomé and Príncipe. Second, in many countries civilian governments are staffed by military figures who have taken off their uniforms but rarely sever their ties with the army. Of the 91 presidents and prime ministers that have held office on the continent in civilian regimes since 1989, fully 45 per cent could boast some form of military experience (see Table 1.1).

The dividing line between military and civilian rule is therefore less clear in practice than it is in theory. This is important, because while governments of all stripes have engaged in democratic backsliding, there are good reasons to think that regimes infused with military figures are more likely to respond to criticism by seeking to close down political space. Militaries are based on strong hierarchical structures and are imbued with cultures that prioritize obedience. The rebel movements that came to power through post-conflict elections in countries such as Angola, Burundi, and Mozambique were not set up to facilitate discussion or formulate economic policy, and had little time to re-establish themselves as civilian organizations prior to elections (Curtis, this volume).

Moreover, leaders schooled in a military environment may find it harder to accept the principles of open participation and free speech that are central to democratic government. In

Table 1.1 'Civilian' African executives with military/rebel experience, 2010

Country	Name	State military (S)/ Rebel & non-state (RNS)
Angola	Jose Dos Santos	S
Botswana	Ian Khama	S
Burkina Faso	Blaise Compaore	S
Burundi	Pierre Nkurunziza	S
CAR	François Bozizé	S
DRC	Joseph Kabila	RNS
Equatorial Guinea	Teodoro Obiang	S
Ethiopia	Girma Wolde-Giorgis	S
Guinea-Bissau	João Bernardo Vieira	S
Mali	Amadou Toumani Touré	S
Mozambique	Armando Emílio Guebuza	RNS
Namibia	Sam Nujoma	S
Nigeria	Olusegun Obasanjo	S
Rep. of Congo	Denis Sassou-Nguesso	RNS
Rwanda	Paul Kagame	RNS
South Africa	Jacob Zuma	RNS
Tanzania	Jakaya Kikwete	S
Sudan	Omar al-Bashir	S
Uganda	Yoweri Museveni	RNS
Zimbabwe	Robert Mugabe	RNS

Note: Only civilian regimes holding elections are included in this table.

Botswana, one of the most long-standing African democracies, critics of President Ian Khama – who was trained at the Royal Military Academy at Sandhurst (UK) and was a Commander in the Botswana Defence Force – claim that he has 'militarized' the government, reducing the scope for debate and proposing legislation that would restrict the civil liberties of the Batswana (Good 2010).

It is against this background that the increased funding currently being channelled to African militaries is a cause for concern (e.g. Abegunrin 2007; Keenan 2008). The aim of AFRICOM is to boost the capacity and professionalism of African security forces so that they can promote development and better protect their own citizens and, perhaps more importantly, so that they can better protect Western allies against terrorist networks (Menkhaus, this volume). In line with AFRICOM's raison d'être, American expenditure on military training in Africa has increased dramatically over the past decade. Under the George W. Bush Administration, the value of US arms deliveries and training programmes increased from about $100 million in 2001 to around $700 million in 2008. At the same time, the State Department's expenditure on International Military Education and Training (IMET) and Foreign Military Financing (FMF) increased from $20.6 million in 2008, to $23.6 million in 2009, and $33.1 million in 2010.

There can be no doubt that many African militaries are in dire need of greater training. Organizations such Amnesty International and the International Crisis Group continue to expose criminality and human rights violations – including drug smuggling, rape, and murder – by armies across the continent (e.g. Amnesty International 2012). The question is whether or not these reforms can be done in a way that professionalizes African militaries in the long term, and so ensure that the greater firepower being transferred to the armed forces is used responsibly.

In this regard there are three main dangers. First, and most obviously, strengthening the capacity of militaries effectively increases the coercive capacity of African governments. Given that many of the continent's multi-party systems are already guilty of using the armed and security forces for political purposes (van de Walle, this volume), there is a real danger that sooner or later the military's greater strength will be used against ordinary African people rather than active terrorists. Second, the more generous funding accruing to military leaders from external sources may render them less accountable locally, because such international transfers often bypass legislatures and domestic political processes. Moreover, the more revenue militaries receive, the more likely they are to emerge as strong political players *vis-à-vis* civilian factions within a government.

Finally, there is a danger that the scope of military activities will expand, transforming the balance between civilian and military power. One of the ways in which AFRICOM initially sought to legitimize itself was by pledging that it would do more development work, and would empower African militaries to do the same. Yet militaries are not skilled at development projects, and critics fear that allowing the functions performed by the military to expand will only serve to further blur the line between military and civilian actors (Abegunrin 2007). Although initial criticism of these plans to further link security and development resulted in AFRICOM pulling back on some of its initial pronouncements, 'mission creep' remains a possibility.

The shadow of the one-party state also continues to fall across the continent. Most notably, the perception that multi-party competition represents a grave danger to social harmony, and that inter-communal conflict is best managed by reducing competition and promoting inclusive forms of participation is still popular among political elites and donors. Indeed, contemporary strategies of ending political crises through the creation of power-sharing 'unity' governments in which there is no formal political opposition have all but reintroduced one-party states in a number of African countries, if only temporarily. It is therefore important to learn the right lessons from Africa's authoritarian experience. One-party states were comparatively stable and often did a good job of maintaining, but they also blunted accountability, facilitated corruption, and became chronically inefficient. Power-sharing may therefore be necessary in some cases, but it is rarely desirable (Mehler, this volume). The past thus remains an important, if incomplete, guide to the future.

Bibliography

Abegunrin, O. (2007) 'AFRICOM: The U.S. Militarization of Africa', *ACAS Bulletin* 78, http://concernedafri cascholars.org/bulletin/78/abegunrin/ (accessed 2 June 2012).

Allen, C. (1995) 'Understanding African Politics', *Review of African Political Economy* 65(22): 301–20.

Amnesty International (2012) '"If You Resist, We'll Shoot You": The Democratic Republic of the Congo and the Case for an Effective Arms Trade Treaty', www.amnestyusa.org/research/reports/if-you-resist-we-ll-shoot-you-the-democratic-republic-of-the-congo-and-the-case-for-an-effective-arm (accessed 13 June 2012).

Anderson, D. (2005a) '"Yours in the Struggle for Majimbo": Nationalism and the Party Politics of Decolonization in Kenya, 1955–64', *Journal of Contemporary History* 40(3): 547–64.

——(2005b) *Histories of the Hanged: The Dirty War in Kenya and the End of Empire*, London: Weidenfeld & Nicholson.

Bienen, H. (1977) *Kenya: The Politics of Participation and Control*, Princeton, NJ: Princeton University Press.

——(1978) 'Military Rule and Political Process: Nigerian Examples', *Comparative Politics* 10(2): 205–25.

Branch, D. (2009) *Defeating Mau Mau, Creating Kenya: Counterinsurgency, Civil War and Decolonization*, Cambridge: Cambridge University Press.

Bratton, M. and van de Walle, N. (1994) 'Neopatrimonial Regimes and Political Transitions in Africa', *World Politics* 26(4): 453–89.

——(1997) 'Neopatrimonial Regimes and Political Transitions in Africa' *World Politics* 46(4): 453–89.

Cooper, F. (2002) *Africa Since 1940: The Past of the Present*, Cambridge: Cambridge University Press.

Decalo, S. (1990) *Coups and Army Rule in Africa: Motivations and Constraints*, New Haven, CT: Yale University Press.

Diamond, L., Kirk-Green, A. and Oyediran, O. (eds) (1997) *Transition Without End: Nigerian Politics and Civil Society Under Babangida*, Boulder, CO: Lynne Rienner Publishers.

First, R. (1970) *Barrel of a Gun: Political Power in Africa and the Coup d'État*, London: Allen Lane, The Penguin Press.

Freedom House (2012) 'Freedom in the World', www.freedomhouse.org/report-types/freedom-world (accessed 11 July 2012).

Good, K. (2010) 'The Presidency of General Ian Khama: The Militarization of the Botswana "Miracle"', *African Affairs* 109(435): 315–24.

Hodgkin, T. (1956) *Nationalism in Colonial Africa*, London: Frederick Muller.

Keenan, J. (2008) 'US Militarization in Africa: What Anthropologists Should Know About AFRICOM', *Anthropology Today* 24(5): 16–20.

Lodge, T. (1983) *Black Politics in South Africa Since 1945*, London: Longman.

Mare, G. and Hamilton, G. (1987) *An Appetite for Power: Buthelezi's Inkatha and South Africa*, Bloomington, ID: Indiana University Press.

Mazrui, A. (1976) 'Soldiers as Traditionalizers: Military Rule and the Re-Africanization of Africa', *World Politics* 28(2): 246–72.

Nyerere, J. (1961) 'One Party Government', *Transition* (2): 9–11.

Posner, D.N. and Young, D.J. (2007) 'The Institutionalization of Political Power in Africa', *Journal of Democracy* 18(3): 126–40.

Ranger, T. (1983) 'The Invention of Tradition in Colonial Africa', in E. Hobsbawm and T. Ranger (eds) *The Invention of Tradition*, Cambridge: Cambridge University Press.

——(1993) 'The Invention of Tradition Revisited: The Case of Colonial Africa', in T. Ranger and O. Vaughan (eds) *Legitimacy and the State in Twentieth Century Africa: Essays in Honour of A.H.M. Kirk-Greene*, London: MacMillan.

Tendi, M. (2010) *Making History in Mugabe's Zimbabwe: Politics, Intellectuals and the Media*, Oxford: Peter Lang.

2

FEDERALISM AND DECENTRALIZATION

Rotimi T. Suberu

Although Africa boasts only three relatively established federations – Nigeria, Ethiopia, and South Africa – federalist ideas and institutions for combining self-rule with shared rule in multi-level governance systems have tremendous appeal, resonance, and relevance across most of the continent's 54 states. Federal principles for the intergovernmental division of powers have been used explicitly or implicitly in Africa not only to construct multi-ethnic or multi-racial federations, but also to foster political decentralization in unitary states, and to promote inter-African or supranational relations and institutions among different states.

At the same time, federalist experiments in Africa, not unlike other formal political institutions in the continent, have an unimpressive and uninspiring track record. The federal systems in Nigeria, Ethiopia, and South Africa, for instance, face enormous political and economic strains that challenge the federal character of these polities. In those three federations, and in the less established federal system of Comoros, as well as in decentralizing unitary states like Senegal and Uganda, the relations between national and sub-national orders of government remain fundamentally lopsided, precarious, or conflicted. Similarly, the intergovernmental institutions designed to promote international (continental/regional and sub-regional) integration in Africa are mostly weak, rudimentary, and problematic. Indeed, a hiatus exists between the obvious attractions and imperatives of federalism in Africa and the absence and paucity of the structural and political conditions that are conducive to the development of federal institutions (Kymlicka 2006).

This chapter explores Africa's chequered experiences with federalism. It begins by discussing the federal idea and the principles and properties that have made it paradoxically both appealing and unviable in the African context. A consideration of the implementation and performance of federalist principles and arrangements in Africa's federations and decentralized unitary states is then offered, and the final section draws together the main implications of my argument: that the limited success of federal structures thus far is unlikely to dampen their allure in the future.

The architecture and attractions of federalism

Like many other important social science concepts, federalism is, analytically, a highly contested, elusive, and ambiguous term. The concept has been persuasively used to describe radically different political systems, including confederations, federations, devolutionary arrangements in unitary states, international unions, and hybrids combining characteristics of different governmental designs (Watts 2008: 10–11). This conceptual nightmare may be mitigated by distinguishing between federalism as a generic paradigm and philosophy of political design, on the one hand, and the practical applications of this design in specific governmental systems and institutions – notably federations, decentralized unitary states, confederations, and international unions – on the other.

As a broad genus, federalism is a philosophy of governance that advocates and promotes the combination of shared rule and self-rule in voluntary, multi-tiered political systems that can advance such normative principles as subsidiarity (the idea that a higher authority should only undertake those functions that cannot be accomplished by lower levels of authority), unity in diversity, power-sharing, liberty, competitive innovation and experimentation, prosperity, democracy, conflict management, peace, and security. The classic governmental expression of federalism is federation, which is a political system involving the constitutionally entrenched division of powers between regional governments and a central government as well as the representation of the regional governments in the machinery of the central government.

Aside from a written and rigid constitution specifying the governmental division of powers, the key institutional properties associated with federations include: a bicameral legislature, one of which represents the people of the federation as a whole and the other the constituent units; an umpire, usually a supreme or constitutional court, that rules on intergovernmental constitutional disputes; allocation of revenue resources between regional and central governments in order to ensure genuine autonomy for each order of government; and 'processes and institutions to facilitate intergovernmental collaboration for those areas where governmental responsibilities are shared or inevitably overlap' (Watts 2008: 9). According to two leading experts on federalism, 28 countries – accounting for over 40 per cent of the world's population – currently either call themselves federations or are generally considered to be so (Anderson 2008; Watts 2008). These include six African countries, namely, Comoros, Democratic Republic of Congo (DRC), Ethiopia, Nigeria, South Africa, and the former Sudan (before the July 2011 independence of South Sudan). However, in the Comoros, as in the so-called Transitional Federal Government (TFG) of the collapsed state of Somalia, the federal characteristics of the polity have been rendered inchoate by chronic political instability and chaos. Similarly, the federal credentials of the DRC are dubious not only because of the incomplete reconstitution of the failed Congolese state and the non-implementation of some of the more decentralist features of its 2006 Constitution, but also because the country has officially avoided an explicit federal identity. Another African country with a contested or ambiguous federalist identity is the federacy of Tanzania, where an otherwise unitary (albeit decentralized) state has developed a (con)federal relationship with approximately 3 per cent of its population living in Zanzibar, which has its own distinctive constitution, presidency, legislature, judicature, bureaucracy, local government system, and electoral political dynamics. Described as the only variation between federal and unitary states, a federacy involves the asymmetrical grant of political autonomy to a distinct, usually peripheral, community in a state, while the core population of the state remains under unitary rule (Stepan 1999).

Indeed, in an overwhelming majority of African countries, devolution or decentralization within a unitary framework, rather than federation, has been the preferred mode for institutionalizing self-rule and shared rule since the third wave of democratization inspired a corresponding wave of territorial political reforms across the continent in the 1990s. This is partly because federation entails a degree of territorial autonomy that is considered by central authorities in Africa and most of the developing world to be potentially subversive of state continuity, stability, and unity. In most decentralized unitary arrangements, unlike in federations, the powers of lower levels of government are not constitutionally entrenched. Rather, sub-national powers are devolved by a central government, the authority of which to decentralize also includes the ability to re-centralize power. Furthermore, unitary arrangements do not typically provide for the representation of sub-national authorities in the machinery of the central government.

Yet, the distinction between federations and decentralized unitary arrangements can be very imprecise and ambiguous for several reasons. For one, because a country's self-identity as federal or unitary may have 'deep historical and symbolic meanings', identical labels 'may resonate differently in different contexts' (USAID 2009: 18). South Africa, for instance, has adopted all the basic features of federations while formally rejecting a federal identity because of the label's association with the country's history of racial apartheid. Second, several polities in Africa, as elsewhere, include features from different constitutional systems, thereby defying any rigid or rigorous classification into unitary and federal types. Third, and related to the above, decentralization or the shift of powers and resources to sub-national orders of government can theoretically take place in both unitary polities and federations. Consequently, although federations are usually 'more decentralized than unitary countries, federations can be quite centralized and unitary countries can in fact be highly decentralized' (ibid.: 19).

The formally decentralized polities highlighted in this chapter include Kenya, Uganda, Cameroon, and the DRC, where decentralization was preceded by failed attempts to experiment with federation or quasi-federation. Also noteworthy are Mozambique, Mali, and Senegal, where decentralization processes have included significant elements of *devolution* (the transfer of autonomous competencies and resources from higher orders of government to elected sub-national provincial and/or local governments), as distinct from mere *deconcentration* (the execution of central government functions by the centre's own field staff) or *delegation* (the implementation of central directives and functions by sub-national authorities).

Federalism's appeal in Africa derives from its presumed capacity to facilitate the three overarching aspirations of the developing world – unity, democratic development, and socio-economic progress. Federalism can be especially apt for managing the multi-ethnicity of most African states, enabling these countries to diffuse and defuse ethnic conflict. Specifically, the grant of autonomy to territorial sub-units in multi-ethnic states can empower or appease ethnic minorities, transforming them from national minorities to sub-national majorities. Such territorial autonomy can also: compartmentalize conflict so that the conflicts of one sub-unit do not polarize or destabilize the rest of the state; generate potentially cross-cutting, intra-ethnic competition in ethnically homogeneous sub-units; promote inter-ethnic cooperation and political socialization in more ethnically heterogeneous sub-units; stimulate alignment on non-ethnic issues as regions controlled by different ethnic groups forge functional lines of cooperation or coalesce to defend their collective interests; and reduce ethnic or horizontal inequalities through schemes for inter-regional redistribution or equalization (Horowitz 1985).

Federalism can deepen and broaden democracy in a number of ways: by facilitating citizen engagement at sub-national or local levels; by enhancing the accountability and responsiveness of government to citizen needs; by making government more representative of the diversity of the population; by furnishing checks and balances on the powers of the central state; and by providing opportunities for the political opposition at the national level to exercise power at the sub-national level and thus, to acquire a direct stake in the development of the democratic political system (Diamond 1999). Federalism can also engender economic efficiency and prosperity through inter-jurisdictional or inter-governmental competition. Indeed, the most economically dynamic and prosperous countries in the world today are either fully-fledged federations or, like China, highly decentralized unitary states. This is because, as claimed by the theory of market-preserving federalism, competition between sub-units for capital and labour can reduce corruption and mismanagement, stimulate innovation and experimentation, and generate a credible political commitment to 'limited government' and the preservation of productive private economic activity (ibid.: 153).

Yet, especially in the developing world, federalism and decentralized governance has often failed to fulfil its advertised advantages. Rather, a substantial countervailing literature exists linking federal institutions to the exacerbation of inter-ethnic discrimination and ethno-secessionist conflict, the creation of authoritarian enclaves, and the complication of macro-economic management. More pertinently, however, recent scholarly writings on federalism have moved beyond simplistic generalizations regarding the benign or malign consequences of federalism, and focus instead on the institutional and structural conditions that may produce federalism's beneficial or baneful effects.

Constraints on federalism in Africa

Six interrelated factors have undermined the successful implementation of federalism and decentralization in Africa. First, the arbitrariness, artificiality, and perceived illegitimacy of Africa's colonially imposed boundaries are at odds with federalism, which ultimately 'requires a voluntary will to federate' (Adamolekun and Kincaid 1991: 180). Africa's multi-ethnic states continue to struggle fundamentally with this issue of their territorial legitimacy, as underscored by the constant demands for a 'sovereign national conference' to discuss the desirability and modalities of federal union in Nigeria, or by the formal insertion of a voluntary exit or secession clause in the Ethiopian Constitution, and in the Comprehensive Peace Agreement (CPA) for Sudan. Yet, this issue has generally been avoided in Africa, where the prevailing norm is to maintain existing state boundaries at all costs, rather than to accept their negotiability or reversibility through democratic processes.

Second, African states are inherently weak economically and politically, and therefore are largely bereft of the critical capacities required for sustaining federalism (see also Abrahamsen, this volume). These capacities not only enable central authorities to promote a 'common roof' of rights and liberties, and 'minimum floor' of socioeconomic opportunities throughout the state, but also give sub-national administrations the resources to establish their own autonomy; exercise legislative, administrative, and fiscal powers; and engage constructively in intergovernmental relationships (Diamond 1999; Simeon and Murray 2004). Without these capacities, federalism can compromise rather than aid democracy, stability, and development. Thus, although decentralization is often promoted as a pragmatic response to the inability of African states effectively to control their hinterlands or peripheries, 'only governments that [are] strong at the [centre], both politically and administratively, could take the risk and find the resources to decentralize important programs or functions' (Stren and Eyoh 2007: 6). Not surprisingly, Africa's insecure central elites have rarely promoted genuine local autonomy. Rather, they have often manipulated the rhetoric and institutions of decentralization to subvert, 'coopt, demobilize, usurp, bypass, or modify' sub-national institutions (Boone 2003: 369).

Third, although Africa's diverse territorially based ethnic constituencies are considered to make federalism a 'natural option' for the continent's states (Kymlicka 2006: 46), the often fragmentary, fluid, and multi-layered – yet parochial and discriminatory – nature of those identities can pose difficult challenges for federal design. Where groups lack internal homogeneity and stable external boundaries, the establishment of viable units of sub-national governance may be problematic. Rather, an inclusive multi-ethnic coalition in the central state apparatus, as distinct from territorial self-rule at the sub-state level, may be a more sustainable strategy of ethnic conflict management. The case against territorial autonomy is strengthened by the pervasiveness of discourses and practices of discriminatory autochthony or indigenousness in most African communities. These practices promote inter-group conflict at the sub-national level, militate against the development of a common civic state citizenship, and undermine the inter-jurisdictional mobility that is required to engender 'market-preserving' intergovernmental competition, experimentation, and innovation (Ndegwa 1997).

Fourth, basic flaws in the design and implementation of federalist schemes have discredited and undermined federalism in Africa. Some of the more common design flaws include sub-optimal numbers of constituent units, dramatic inequalities in the sizes of sub-units, unsustainable asymmetries in the powers of sub-units, the over-concentration of functions and/or revenues in the central government, the failure to incorporate strong incentives for sub-national units to generate their own resources, and the belated implementation of federalist schemes after ethnic feelings of injustice and exclusion have hardened, leading to the development of federal arrangements that are more divisive than integrative. As underscored by the Sudanese and Ethiopian federal experiments, the price for such belated separatist federalism may include the suicidal enshrinement of secession as an explicit principle of constitutional design rather than as something that may implicitly evolve 'out of piecemeal democratic negotiations' (Kymlicka 2006: 55).

Fifth, while federalism is democracy's territorial correlate, most African countries have simply lacked the basic democratic architecture required for federalism to take root and flourish. In particular, federalism in Africa has been severely degraded and truncated by electoral processes lacking in transparency, credibility, and fair, inter-party competition for control of central and sub-central government. Thus, the credibility and vitality of federalism and decentralization in Africa has been undermined by 'the prevalence of dominant-party states' in countries as diverse as Botswana, Burkina Faso, Ethiopia, Mozambique, Nigeria, South Africa, Tanzania, and Uganda (Dickovick and Riedl 2010: 10). Finally, the African regional context or system of inter-state relations has been particularly inauspicious for the development of federalism. Essentially, the combination of artificial colonial boundaries, weak states, and insecure state elites have militated against the development of a pan-African consensus on values – like democracy and the rights of ethnic and political minorities – that are necessary for federalism to flourish both nationally and internationally.

Federations

Nigeria is Africa's most established federation, having instituted a three-region federation under British colonial auspices in 1954 to hold together its three major ethnic groups, hundreds of smaller ethno-linguistic communities, and roughly equal numbers of Muslims and Christians. This tri-regional federal system, however, exacerbated Nigeria's ethnic divisions, leading to the destabilization and collapse of the country's first post-independence republic (1960–66), bloody ethno-military infighting, and three years of civil war (1967–70). Since the country's first military coup in 1966, Nigeria's most important achievement as a federation consists of the progressive transformation of this centrifugal three-region structure into a much more centripetal, multi-unit federal system, which currently consists of a federal government, 36 states, and 776 constitutionally designated local governments.

Despite its remarkable success in preventing a recurrence of ethno-secessionist warfare and state collapse, Nigeria's current federal system suffers from several pathologies and contradictions that graphically illustrate the limitations of federalism in African contexts. Since the inception of the country's fourth civilian republic in 1999, for instance, the Nigerian federation has witnessed thousands of deaths in ethnic clashes arising from discrimination against so-called non-indigenes (Nigerians resident in sub-units outside their presumed ancestral communal roots) by ethnic indigenes in control of state and local governments. The communal bloodletting has been aggravated by the terrorist insurgency of the Islamic sect Boko Haram, which has killed and campaigned for the expulsion of southern Nigerian Christians living in the predominantly Muslim north, partly in retaliation for violent attacks against Muslims by indigenous non-Muslim groups in Jos and other cities in Nigeria's ethnically and religiously mixed Middle Belt. Nigeria's federal constitution abets the conflict by mandating the equitable representation of indigenes of each constituent state in the central government and then defining such indigenes in terms of ethnic autochthony and genealogy rather than geographical residence (Geschiere, this volume).

Nigerian federalism has also been degraded by violent insurgency in the Niger Delta, the ecologically and economically neglected and ethnic minority-populated region that produces all the oil revenues on which Nigeria's federal, state, and local governments are completely dependent. In addition to engendering a sense of economic grievance and deprivation in the Delta, the centralized collection and redistribution of oil revenues in Nigeria has undermined economic decentralization and diversification, promoted fiscal irresponsibility and political corruption (including massive electoral fraud perpetrated to gain control of central, state, and local governments), and spawned significant agitations for a 'true federalism' that would dismantle some of the military's centrist reforms and establish more financially viable and democratically accountable sub-national authorities.

The formal design of the current Ethiopian federal system, following failed experiments in the Ethiopia-Eritrea Federation (1952–62) and in unitary nationalization (1962–91), contains several features that many Nigerian advocates of 'true federalism' will endorse. This includes the organization of its nine constituent regional states on an explicitly ethnic basis, the endowment of constituent units with their own constitutions and police agencies, the promotion of ethnic political parties, the formal granting of a right to self-determination (up to and including secession) to ethnic communities, and the demarcation of the federation into a small number of relatively large states (rather than a large number of mostly small or weak states).

Yet, Ethiopian federalism is vexed by contradictions that are not unlike the failings of the Nigerian system. While contributing significantly to the regulation of national-level ethno-political conflict in Ethiopia, for instance, the policy of ethnic federalism has aggravated such conflict at the regional and local level. This is especially evident in states like Beninshangul-Gumuz, Gambela, Oromia, and the Southern Nations, Nationalities, and People's Region (SNNPR), where ethno-linguistic communities considered non-autochthonous to these states suffer discriminatory practices that effectively reduce them to second-class citizens (Fiseha and Habib 2010: 154–55).

The Ethiopian federal system is also heavily centralized financially, with the federal government controlling more than 80 per cent of aggregate revenue in the country, leading to high and sustained regional dependency on central financial subsidy. This vertical fiscal imbalance contributes to a centrist political and policy process that 'enhances central political leaders' domination, kills regional incentives to innovate and be flexible, discourages challenge to the status quo, and makes lower level politicians and office holders insecure' (Chanie 2007: 367). Such economic and policy centralization is nurtured and reinforced by the political hegemony of the Ethiopian Peoples' Revolutionary Democratic Front (EPRDF) coalition, the member and affiliated parties of which control all governments at the federal and regional levels. Indeed, the EPRDF has demonstrated extreme intolerance to the development of any vibrant political opposition spaces at national and sub-national levels, and has instead established a Soviet-style authoritarian party state. In essence, while ethnic federalism has contributed significantly to the reconstruction and stabilization of the Ethiopian state, the federation still has a long way to go 'in terms of enhancing the autonomy of the states, strengthening the institutions of democracy, and protecting minorities in the regional states' (Fiseha and Habib 2010: 140).

Unlike Nigeria and Ethiopia, post-apartheid South Africa does not explicitly define itself as a federation. Indeed, federation is supported primarily by narrowly based minority parties – the white-dominant National Party and Democratic Alliance (DA), and the Zulu nationalist Inkatha Freedom Party – and remains unpopular with most black supporters of the dominant African National Congress (ANC), who favour a strong, centrist, and consolidated developmental state. Reflecting the inclusive, consociation-oriented nature of South Africa's political transition to multi-racial democracy, however, the country's Constitution recognized national, provincial, and local authorities as 'distinctive, interdependent, and interrelated' spheres of governance (Simeon and Murray 2004: 277).

Inspired by the German national cooperative model of federalism, the South African federal system is strongly centrist, 'with the predominance of legislative power assigned to the center, with a centralized system of public finance, and with considerable central powers to oversee provincial performance' (Simeon and Murray 2004: 297). Although they are constitutionally empowered to develop their own constitutions, all of South Africa's current nine provinces lack real political and decision-making autonomy. Rather, their authority is subject to the overriding prerogatives of the centre to maintain the country's security and unity, and their major role has been effectively limited to implementing and delivering the services mandated by the national government. Like their counterparts in Nigeria and Ethiopia, the South African provinces are very weak financially, depending on central revenue transfers for over 90 per cent of their resources. Unlike the more financially autonomous localities, which collect property taxes, the South African provinces do not have any significant base of own-source taxation or revenue.

A major centralizing force in South Africa remains the overwhelming electoral dominance of the centrist ANC. Unlike Ethiopia and Nigeria, however, South Africa is a credible electoral democracy, with genuine freedom for opposition parties to organize and mobilize politically at national and sub-national levels. The potential for this relative electoral integrity to eventually develop into a more viable political pluralism and federalism is reflected in the significant electoral and governance successes of the DA, first in Cape Town, and then in the Western Cape Province.

Despite their political and economic over-centralization, the federal systems in Nigeria, Ethiopia, and South Africa have emerged as largely durable and stabilizing features of government and politics in these countries. The Comoros, on the other hand, remains a very fragile and conflicted federation. The Comoros is a union of three small islands, one of which (Grande Comoros) is more populous than the other two (Anjouan and Moheli) combined. Reflecting this blatant structural imbalance, the federation has witnessed intense inter-island rivalries, separatist movements, numerous coups and attempted coups, and repeated constitutional overhauls and political reforms designed to create a less precarious federation.

A profoundly multi-racial, multi-ethnic, multi-religious, and multi-lingual state, Sudan is a prime example of the limited viability of federation when the system is introduced after inter-group conflicts have escalated and hardened to a disintegrative stage. The first Sudanese federalist autonomy arrangement (1973–83) was introduced under the 1972 Addis Ababa Peace Agreement after 17 years of violent rebellion mounted by the country's southern, non-Muslim, black African minority, against political and cultural subjugation by the Arab-Islamic unitary government in Khartoum. When Khartoum unilaterally abrogated the Addis agreement in 1983, the South resumed its rebellion, which killed more than 2 million people, and displaced an additional 4 million, over a 20-year period (1983–2005).

Following protracted international mediation, federalism was reintroduced in Sudan as a cornerstone of the historic 2005 Comprehensive Peace Agreement (CPA). Reflecting the legacy of two bitter civil wars, however, the CPA was a classic partitionist blueprint, elaborately providing not only for power-sharing, oil revenue-sharing, and security arrangements between Northern and Southern Sudan, but also for a referendum on secession in the South. Predictably, in January 2011 Southern Sudan voted overwhelmingly to become an independent country in its own right. Yet, in addition and despite their internal heterogeneity and ethnic conflict, the two Sudanese successor states have clashed violently over boundary demarcations, oil revenues, and new citizenship arrangements. Consequently, federalism and decentralization will remain indispensable to any constitutional proposals for their stabilization.

Decentralized unitary states

To reiterate, some of the more ambitious experiments in political decentralization in Africa since the 1990s have taken place in countries with a previous, often contentious, history of experimentation with federation. Uganda's 1962 Independence Constitution, for instance, provided for the devolution of powers to local councils and four historic kingdoms, including the Buganda kingdom, which enjoyed a special, asymmetric federal status, and where enthusiasm for *federo* (federalism) remains strong to this day. The dismantling of this quasi-federal structure in 1966 under the authoritarian rule of Milton Obote marked the beginning of an extended process of state failure and implosion in Uganda. Under the charismatic leadership of Yoweri Museveni, the National Resistance Movement (NRM) progressively seized control of Uganda in the mid-1980s, establishing 'resistance councils in the areas under their control in order to mobilize and politicize the masses' (Steiner 2008: 42). Since its official legalization in 1987, the resistance council system has developed into an elaborate five-tier devolutionary structure, with elected councils and committees at the village, parish, sub-county, county, and district levels. The system involves the extensive transfer of planning, legislative, and executive powers to elected subnational authorities on the basis of the subsidiarity principle. Coexisting with this comprehensive devolution scheme is a deconcentration element, including the office of the district commissioner, a presidential appointee who supervises the local implementation of functions (defence, security, and so on) that are not devolved.

Decentralization in Kenya also has been implemented against a background of initial experimentation with, and continuing debates about, federalism. The country came into independence in 1963 on the basis of a constitution that largely enshrined the demands of many of Kenya's non-Kikuyu smaller ethnic communities for 'majimboism, or regionalism' (Ndegwa 1997: 605). The key federalist features of this constitution included a bicameral national parliament, the decentralization of powers and resources to relatively strong regional governments with their own legislatures and executives, and a requirement for the approval of any changes to regional powers by super-majorities in each house of the bicameral national parliament or in a national referendum. Within a year of Kenya's independence, however, the ruling Kenya African National Union (KANU) dismantled the constitutional architecture of regional autonomy and transformed the country into a unitary, one-party state. Kenya's transition to multi-party politics in the 1990s, however, revived the *majimbo* debate.

Following prolonged struggles and debates over political reform, a new Constitution for Kenya was approved in a referendum and promulgated in August 2010. Aside from enshrining a separation of powers between the executive and the legislature, the 2010 Kenya Constitution provided for the devolution of power to county (district) levels of government and reintroduced a bicameral federal parliament, with each county being represented by a Senator in the upper house of the parliament. Each of the country's 47 counties will also have a county executive headed by a county governor and a county assembly made up of representatives of wards within the county. The counties will have powers over matters of local concern as well as enjoy guaranteed revenues based on proposals of a newly established Commission on Revenue Allocation. Although its decentralist provisions were less far-reaching than those of the 1963 Majimbo Constitution, which had devolved powers to the much larger regions/provinces, the 2010 Kenyan Constitution represents a remarkably ambitious and rigorous experiment in democratic decentralization within an otherwise unitary polity in Africa.

In the DRC, a formally decentralized system has emerged as a compromise solution to the political struggles between proponents of federalism and unitarism. The basic law that ushered the DRC into independence in 1960 had significant federal features, including the grant of autonomous legislative and executive powers to the country's original six provinces. Changes to this basic law in the immediate post-independence period – including the expansion of the number of provinces to 21, in order to enhance the ethnic homogeneity of these units – consolidated the federal character of the Congolese state. Yet, this period was defined by catastrophic ethnic instability and political chaos, including the mutiny of the national army, the assassination of the country's first prime minister, and the emergence of a violent ethno-secessionist movement in Katanga Province. This political disarray led to the takeover of power by army commander Joseph Mobutu, who imposed a centralized one-party dictatorship. The implosion of Mobutu's predatory government in the wake of the introduction of multi-party competition in the early 1990s plunged the DRC into an extended period of violent disintegrative conflict, which officially ended with an internationally mediated peace and political transition process during 2002–06.

A highlight of the Congolese transition was the making of the 2006 Constitution, the decentralizing features of which represent a 'radical break with Congo's long history of pseudo-centralized rule' (Tull 2010: 653). The new Constitution, for instance, mandates the expansion of the number of provinces from the existing 11 to 26, provides for the division of powers and revenues between the provinces and central government, establishes a Senate and a Conference of Governors to 'give voice to the provinces', and creates a constitutional court to arbitrate centre-provincial conflicts. The revenue-sharing provisions of the Constitution are especially remarkable, providing for the retention by the provinces of 40 per cent of fiscal revenues generated from their territory, while establishing an equalization fund that would allocate up to 10 per cent of national finances to developmental projects in poorer provinces. Yet, reflecting the troubled state of democratization and post-conflict reconstruction in the DRC, the fiscal provisions of the 2006 Constitution and the envisaged territorial reconfiguration of the country into 26 provinces have not been implemented.

Procrastination and ambivalence toward political decentralization has been a characteristic political strategy in several other African states, including the previously federal country of Cameroon. Established in 1961 following the reunification of former British and French trusteeship territories in the old German colony of Kamerun, the Cameroon federation was riddled with multiple imperfections and contradictions from birth. These included: the existence of only two federal sub-units, one of which (Francophone East Cameroon) was vastly superior in population and influence to the other (Anglophone West Cameroon); failure to specify a clear division of powers and resources between the central and sub-national orders of government; the non-establishment of a federal legislative chamber, thereby denuding the federal arrangement of a key mechanism for representing regional interests in the national government; extensive federal intervention in the territorial administration of the federal sub-units through presidential appointees, like the federal inspector and the district officers; and the imposition of unitary, single-party rule in 1968. In essence, the formal abrogation of the federation following a referendum in 1972 merely put an end to an experiment that was more 'shadow than reality' (Stark 1976).

Cameroonian politics continues to be vexed by the Anglophone agitation for the territorial reform of the francophone-dominated centralized unitary state. While denouncing federation as a recipe for separatism, the Cameroonian central authorities have formally and explicitly embraced the transformation of the country into a decentralized unitary state. Constitutional reforms introduced in 1996, for instance, not only instituted the principle of political autonomy for two decentralized tiers of sub-national government (the commune councils and the regional council), but also introduced a 100-member Senate as a quasi-federalist second chamber of the national parliament, with 10 senators representing local governments in each of the country's 10 regions. However, the Senate and the regional councils were not established.

Despite its discouraging record in countries such as the DRC and Cameroon, decentralization has been embraced in several African countries that have emerged from a centralist Francophone or Lusophone administrative colonial tradition, including Mali, Senegal, and Mozambique. Malian decentralization has, for instance, been described as the 'heart' of the country's democracy. Originally initiated in 1992 to placate separatist Tuareg groups in the north of the country, decentralization in Mali has sought ambitiously to develop a 'local-level democratic vitality' through the establishment of elected and representative councils (with administrative and financial authority over basic health, education, and infrastructure) at the levels of commune, the circle, and the region, as well as the creation of a High Council of Local Government as a form of second national legislative house that represents commune governments at the national level (Pringle 2006). However, the resurgence of Tuareg separatism in 2012 (following an influx of arms from the 2011 Libyan conflict) and a subsequent military coup highlights the unstable regional context of multi-level governance in Africa, as well as the deficits of decentralization in Mali, where sub-national autonomy is seriously constrained by 'a limited fiscal base and the practice of central state tutelage' (Dickovick and Riedl 2010: 67).

In Senegal, decentralization has produced a complex, multi-level political structure. This includes regional governments with elected councils, and a centrally appointed administrative governor; elected urban and rural localities (communes and *communautes rurales*); and centrally appointed departments and *arrondissements* with oversight powers over local governments. Decentralization laws in 1996 introduced elections for the regions, established new revenue transfers for regional and local authorities, and expanded sub-national responsibility for the delivery of nine basic social services, including health and education (Dickovick 2005: 188). In Mozambique, the creation in the 1990s of politically autonomous municipalities (*autarquias*), with elected mayors and municipal assemblies, has significantly opened up an otherwise centralized dominant party state. The creation of the *autarquias* has produced substantial improvements in service delivery, encouraged the development of sub-national revenue autonomy and fiscal capacity, and enabled opposition control of power and challenges to the hegemony of the ruling *Frente de Libertação de Moçambique* (FRELIMO, Liberation Front of Mozambique) party that are not feasible at the national level (Linder 2009).

While acknowledging the 'bourgeoning trend of decentralization in Africa', however, the scholarly literature has documented several interrelated shortcomings of this process that echo many of the flaws that also afflict the continent's fully fledged federations (Dickovick 2005: 184). These shortcomings include:

- The ambiguous, ambivalent, and often rhetorical approach of Africa's mostly centrist, presidentialist, and authoritarian regimes to political decentralization as a policy.

- Central government political interference in, and administrative control of, elected sub-national governments.
- Weak, incomplete, or poorly designed legal frameworks for devolution.
- Severe shortfalls in the administrative, fiscal, and managerial resources or capacities of sub-national authorities.
- Over-dependence of sub-national authorities on central governments or even the international donor community for financial, institutional, and related resources.
- Conflicts or poor coordination between different levels or tiers of sub-national government.
- Tensions between autochthonous and immigrant groups over citizenship rights in devolved jurisdictions.
- The arbitrary, contested, unstable, or unviable boundaries of sub-national units.
- Weak engagement of sub-national authorities with local civil society, including community development associations and other forms of informal and self-organized institutions of community governance.
- The pervasiveness of corruption, clientelism, and political patronage in sub-national governments.

Overall, recent achievements in the establishment of new legal frameworks for devolution in Africa have not been matched by *de facto* advances in decentralization. Rather, sub-national fiscal autonomy, developmental capacity, public service provision, and democratic political accountability have lagged behind the formal institutionalization of decentralized legal authority (Dickovick and Riedl 2010: 1–6). As multifaceted and complicated as these shortcomings of decentralization may appear, they pale in comparison to the enormity of the impediments that afflict experiments at promoting inter-governmental relations at the international level in Africa (see Khadiagala, this volume).

Conclusion

Federalist governance principles have been extensively, if often grudgingly and unsuccessfully, invoked and implemented in Africa. These principles are a fundamental feature of the architecture of governance in some of the continent's larger and more ethnically complex states, including Nigeria, South Africa, and Ethiopia. While they have abandoned or resisted fully fledged federal constitutions, most of the continent's multi-ethnic states have used federal principles of self-rule and shared rule for the decentralization of their unitary governmental systems. These same principles have provided the basis for organizing the continent's evolving supranational institutions that are designed to meet collective governance challenges at the international (regional and sub-regional) levels.

Yet, there can be little doubt that the record of federalism in Africa has been uninspiring. Indeed, a prime contradiction of African politics involves the obvious imperatives and relevance of federalism as a governance strategy on the continent on the one hand, and the absence of propitious conditions for the effective working of federal institutions and processes on the other. Most African states lack the fiscal resources, administrative capacities, and political cultures necessary to make federalism and decentralization flourish as instruments of democratic consolidation, political stability and unity, and economic development. Thus, Africa's federations and decentralized unitary states have been too centralized to be authentic and successful experiments in self-rule and shared rule. The continent's supranational or international integration schemes, on the other hand, have been too decentralized, fissiparous, or incoherent to make for the effective and constructive development and deployment of collective solutions to continental and sub-regional governance challenges.

All of this is not to understate the positive contributions of federalism to African governance and politics. The adoption or reconfiguration of federalist institutions has contributed to the relative stabilization of post-civil war Nigeria and Ethiopia, the consolidation of multi-racial democracy in South Africa, and the durability of the union of Zanzibar and mainland Tanzania. Decentralization has aided post-conflict reconstruction in Uganda, restrained political authoritarianism in Mozambique, and spurred governance reform in Kenya, among other countries. Furthermore, it is difficult to envisage any viable political alternative to democratic federalism and/or decentralization in conflicted states like the two Sudans and the DRC. Federal strategies and theories for designing intergovernmental relations will remain important for developing and improving Africa's nascent institutions for supranational governance. For these reasons, federal ideas, principles, and options will continue to have tremendous appeal, relevance, and resonance in Africa.

Bibliography

Adamolekun, L. and Kincaid, J. (1991) 'The Federal Solution: An Assessment and Prognosis for Nigeria and Africa', *Publius: The Journal of Federalism* 21(4): 173–88.

Anderson, G. (2008) *Federalism: An Introduction*, Oxford: Oxford University Press.

Boone, C. (2003) 'Decentralization as Political Strategy in West Africa', *Comparative Political Studies* 36(4): 355–80.

Chanie, P. (2007) 'Clientelism and Ethiopia's post-1991 Decentralization', *Journal of Modern African Studies* 45(3): 355–84.

Diamond, L. (1999) *Developing Democracy: Toward Consolidation*, Baltimore, CO, and London: Johns Hopkins University Press.

Dickovick, T. (2005) 'The Measure and Mismeasure of Decentralization: Subnational Autonomy in Senegal and South Africa', *Journal of Modern African Studies* 43(2): 183–210.

Dickovick, T. and Riedl, R. (2010) *Comparative Assessment of Decentralization in Africa: Final Report and Summary of Findings*, Washington, DC: USAID.

Fiseha, A. and Habib, M. (2010) 'Ethiopia', in Luis Moreno and Cesar Colino (eds) *Diversity and Unity in Federal Countries*, Montreal and Kingston: McGill-Queen's University Press.

Horowitz, D. (1985) *Ethnic Groups in Conflict*, Berkeley, CA: University of California Press.

Kymlicka, W. (2006) 'Emerging Western Models of Multination Federalism: Are They Relevant for Africa?' in D. Turton (ed.) *Ethnic Federalism: The Ethiopian Experience in Comparative Perspective*, Oxford: James Currey.

Linder, W. (2009) 'On the Merits of Decentralization in New Democracies', *Publius: The Journal of Federalism* 40(1): 1–30.

Ndegwa, S. (1997) 'Citizenship and Ethnicity: An Examination of Two Transition Moments in Kenyan Politics', *American Political Science Review* 91(3): 599–616.

Pringle, R. (2006) *Democratization in Mali: Putting History to Work*, Washington, DC: United States Institute of Peace.

Simeon, R. and Murray, C. (2004) 'Multi-Level Governance in South Africa', in B. Berman, D. Eyoh and W. Kymlicka (eds) *Ethnicity and Democracy in Africa*, Oxford: James Currey.

Stark, F. (1976) 'Federalism in Cameroon: The Shadow and the Reality', *Canadian Journal of African Studies* 10(3): 423–42.

Steiner, S. (2008) 'Constraints on the Implementation of Decentralization and Implications for Poverty Reduction: The Case of Uganda', in G. Crawford and C. Hartmann (eds) *Decentralization in Africa: A Pathway out of Poverty and Conflict?* Amsterdam: Amsterdam University Press.

Stepan, A. (1999) 'Federalism and Democracy: Beyond the US Model', *Journal of Democracy* 10(4): 19–34.

Stren, R. and Eyoh, D. (2007) 'Decentralization and Urban Development in West Africa', in D. Eyoh and R. Stren (eds) *Decentralization and the Politics of Urban Development in West Africa*, Washington, DC: Woodrow Wilson International Center for Scholars.

Suberu, R. (2009) 'Federalism in Africa: The Nigerian Experience in Comparative Perspective', *Ethnopolitics* 8(1): 67–86.

Tull, D. (2010) 'Troubled State-Building in the DR Congo: The Challenge from the Margins', *Journal of Modern African Studies* 48(4): 643–61.

USAID (United States Agency for International Development) (2009) *Democratic Decentralization Programming Handbook*, Washington, DC: USAID.

Watts, R. (2008) *Comparing Federal Systems*, Montreal and Kingston: McGill-Queen's University Press.

3

THE RULE OF LAW AND THE COURTS

Peter VonDoepp

The rule of law is today a major theme in the discourse on governance in African countries. Donors, intellectuals, and activists on the ground in African societies now highlight it as one of the key ingredients needed to promote social stability and economic development on the continent. Whereas the first three decades of Africa's independence were characterized by the weakness, if not absence, of the rule of law in most countries, circumstances today are more favourable. African political systems are more 'rule-governed' than in the past, civil liberties have improved, and judicial and legal actors occupy more important positions in many societies. Yet the picture is not entirely positive. Executives are still the dominant players in African politics, and many of them operate with little regard for the legal boundaries on their authority. Judiciaries remain weak in terms of their capabilities and independence, and corruption continues to undermine the institutions charged with promoting the rule of law (Olivier de Sardan, this volume). All this serves as an important reminder that the rule of law still faces many challenges in sub-Saharan Africa.

In this chapter, I offer an overview of the rule of law and the courts in Africa. I begin with a brief discussion that reviews the concept of the rule of law and the importance assigned to it in contemporary conversations about governance and development. Thereafter, I review the historical experience with the rule of law in African countries since independence, dividing my discussion between the first three decades of independence and the period since the early 1990s, when many countries witnessed a substantial liberalization of their political systems. I conclude by considering the courts and the challenges that judiciaries face as the primary institutions tasked with promoting the rule of law.

Understanding the rule of law

What precisely is meant by the rule of law? In conventional usage, the term is associated with themes such as judicial independence, constitutionalism, rights protection, and social predictability and stability. All of these surely speak to the notion of the rule of law, but the concept deserves some elaboration beyond this, even if we must accept that there is no clear agreement on the precise meaning of the concept among scholars.

One way to begin thinking about the rule of law is that the concept refers to a situation where those in power exercise their authority in a manner that complies with the formal/legal rules of the political system (Maravall and Przeworski 2003: 1). Where the rule of law operates, governments act in accordance with the law and comply with the law (Diamond 1999: 90). Understood in this way, the rule of law is a property of political systems, varying across contexts, which can be observed in the extent to which power holders respect and are constrained by the extant legal regime (Sanchez-Cuenca 2003: 67). The notion of 'constitutionalism' obtains special relevance in this regard, as it attempts to capture the degree to which political life reflects and operates within established constitutional principles. The rule of law necessarily implies high levels of constitutionalism.

Beyond the notion of compliance with a legal order, some emphasize that the rule of law implies a legal system characterized by certain specific features: principles of natural justice, referring to basic fairness in legal processes, should operate; laws should be general, consistent, and prospective in nature; and the courts should be independent and accessible (World Bank n.d.; Sanchez-Cuenca 2003: 68; Raz 1977: 198–202). Others highlight that in practice, especially in Anglophone contexts, the rule of law has been associated with the protection of basic civil liberties (Donnelly 2006: 42). In this regard, the character of the legal system and even the substance of the law deserve attention when considering the extent to which the rule of law obtains in a given context.

As indicated above, independent judicial institutions represent a primary institutional foundation of the rule of law. Indeed, one can scarcely imagine the operation of the rule of law without an independent court system. Courts, for instance, provide a venue for the resolution of private disputes, which in the absence of formal systems of arbitration might degenerate into violence and disorder – signal features of the breakdown of law. Courts also help to identify and, potentially, sanction government behaviour that violates established rules of the political system. One key component of this is their role in protecting individuals, whether by ensuring that principles of natural justice are adhered to when governments attempt to deprive them of liberty or property, or simply by confirming the basic rights of individuals as laid out in legal documents (Donnelly 2006: 42–43).

Notably, the rule of law does not necessarily imply the existence of democracy, nor does it even demand a regime with high regard for human rights. The basic feature of the rule of law is a government that adheres to the formal rules of the political system, accepting that it cannot change those rules by fiat. While certain individual rights might be implied by the rule of law – access to the courts, due process, and so on – the actual substantive outcomes of legal proceedings may themselves appear at odds with human rights. Deprivations of property, limits on speech, and even state-sanctioned violence against individuals are all quite conceivable where the rule of law obtains.

When seeking to capture empirically the extent to which the rule of law operates in a given society, different bodies have developed indices that speak to many of the themes raised above. For example, Freedom House uses a 'Rule of Law' category as part of its assessment of civil liberties in different countries. The organization bases its evaluation of the rule of law on four questions (Freedom House 2008: 875):

- Is there an independent judiciary?
- Does the rule of law prevail in civil and criminal matters? Are police under direct civilian control?
- Is there protection from political terror, unjustified imprisonment, exile, or torture, whether by groups that support or oppose the system? Is there freedom from war or insurgencies?
- Do laws, policies and practices guarantee equal treatment of various segments of the population?

Although these do not directly address the issue of government behaviour and compliance with the law, they do reference features of the legal system, such as equality before the law, and directly focus on the autonomy of judicial institutions.

The Bertelsmann Institute, a German organization that also undertakes regular assessments of governance conditions, also relies on four questions in its assessments of the rule of law (Bertelsmann Stiftung 2010):

- To what extent is there a working separation of powers (checks and balances)?
- To what extent does an independent judiciary exist?
- To what extent are there legal or political penalties for officeholders who abuse their positions?
- To what extent are civil rights guaranteed and protected, and to what extent can citizens seek redress for violations of these liberties?

As is clear, the Bertelsmann assessment focuses more on the workings of government and behaviour of its officials – a likely advance over Freedom House – but also considers the independence of the courts and substantive workings of the legal system in terms of civil liberties.

Yet this discussion of the concept necessarily begs a second question: why be concerned with the rule of law at all? The simple answer is that it matters. The extent to which societies are characterized by the rule of law has major consequences for their political and developmental fortunes. This point is fairly intuitive. Many scholars recognize that democracy requires the rule of law. As democracy hinges on the operation of specific rules, the system presupposes a rule-governed polity. The rule of law is also considered critical for economic development. The protection of property rights is especially important in this regard as this enables investment, which is critical for economic growth. Further, by protecting individuals through contract laws, the rule of law facilitates economic interchange. The predictability and order associated with the rule of law is more conducive to development than lawlessness and conflict (Haggard *et al.* 2008: 207–9).

Since 2000, research has substantially confirmed many of the assumptions about the positive effects of the rule of law. Kaufmann and Kraay (2002) found that higher scores on the World Bank rule of law measure contributed to higher levels of per capita income, but that the reverse relationship did not obtain. Other work by Feld and Voigt (2003) has indicated that higher levels of *de facto* judicial independence lead to increased gross domestic product (GDP) growth. Given these types of findings, it is little wonder that many bodies seeking to promote economic development, such as the World Bank and International Monetary Fund (IMF), are increasingly supporting programmes to enhance the rule of law in Africa and elsewhere (Carothers 1998).

The rule of law in post-colonial Africa

As those with even a perfunctory knowledge of post-colonial political life in Africa are surely aware, the rule of law did not flourish in the first three decades of independence. While there have been tangible advances in parts of Africa with respect to the rule of law since the end of the Cold War, major challenges remain.

The first three decades

Although constitutions, independent courts, and provisions for civil liberties were often established during the 1950s and 1960s when many African countries were achieving independence, in the aftermath, these institutions, and the rule of law itself, ceased to be primary elements of the governance situation in most countries. Their erosion occurred in the context of a general turn to authoritarianism and personal rule. The situation that emerged in most African countries was starkly at odds with the type of political system envisioned by the rule of law framework. Instead, the actual conduct of politics came to reflect the individual pro-clivities and personalities of those holding presidential power (Jackson and Rosberg 1982). Legal strictures rarely interfered with the exercise of power, and when they did, the law was changed to suit the needs of the power-holder. Constitutions, in this respect, had little relevance for politics.

Other institutions associated with the rule of law suffered similarly. The courts, for example, were emasculated and undermined in most contexts, leaving them to play a largely peripheral role in a political world dominated by the executive. In the early 1970s, for instance, the Hastings Banda regime in Malawi removed the authority of the common law courts over criminal matters and, in their place, revived a system of 'traditional courts'. The latter came to be the primary venue where Banda tried political opponents and those suspected of disloyalty to his government. Notably, within the traditional courts defendants were denied rights to legal representation, the right to call witnesses, or the ability to appeal to the common law courts. In this context, the formal court system ceased to play any real function in protecting civil liberties or due process, much less checking the arbitrary rule of the executive.

Ghana affords other examples. The courts lost substantial authority shortly after independence when the government of Kwame Nkrumah established special courts to hear cases of treason and sedition. A roughly similar development took place under the Jerry Rawlings regime in the early 1980s, when the government created a system of 'Public Tribunals' (or 'People's Courts') with the authority to hear cases regarding economic sabotage, smuggling, corruption, embezzlement, abuse of power, and subversion, and to render death sentences in those cases. The right to have decisions appealed or reviewed simply did not exist (Howard 1985: 341). In Uganda in the early 1970s, legal changes gave military tribunals the power to try civilians accused of offenses against the government (Widner 2001: 116).

In addition to actions that institutionally undermined (or replaced) the courts, judges themselves were the frequent targets of actions to subvert their independence. In the late 1960s, for instance, ruling party members stormed court offices in Lusaka, Zambia, which led ultimately to the resignation of the chief justice and several other judges. At later points, the government of Kenneth Kaunda enacted legislation that increased presidential control over court appointments. Legislation passed during Daniel arap Moi's reign in Kenya stripped judges of security of tenure in 1988 and many judges were subjected to extra-legal transfers that undermined their autonomy (Mutua 2001). In Uganda, judges became one of the many targets of Idi Amin's repressive rule. The chief justice himself was dragged from his chambers and never seen again, while the pre-sident of the Industrial Court was murdered. In the aftermath of his rule, conditions improved only marginally, as judges were unconstitutionally removed from office, arrested, and forced into exile (Widner 2001: 116).

Civil liberties also suffered markedly. Although sedition and preventative detention laws had been used by colonial authorities to suppress nationalist movements, these same laws were often kept on the books and in other cases, reintroduced and strengthened by post-independence governments. In Ghana, Kwame Nkrumah expanded the provisions for preventative detention in 1958, allowing the government to hold individuals without trial for five years. Uganda's Milton Obote implemented similar legal changes, while Julius Nyerere's regime in Tanzania and Jomo Kenyatta's government in Kenya did the same in 1962 and 1966, respectively. In Malawi and Zambia similar detention laws were put to use against political opponents within the first few years on independence (see Harding and Hatchard 1993).

How can we understand this general decay in the rule of law in the post independence era? Part of the explanation lay in the general condition of governance in many African countries, and the dilemmas confronting post-independence leaders. On the one hand, leaders of nationalist movements frequently came to power on a wave of anti-colonial sentiment, but actually lacked solid legitimacy once in office. Combined with the weakness of Africa's new states, this served to limit the authority of many executives, which in turn undermined their ability to accomplish their objectives and even left them vulnerable to challenges from rivals. Moreover, post-independence leaders typically had very lofty ambitions of fostering nation-building, development, and modernity. Unity came to be prized as a means to these ends, while competitive politics was seen as a distraction.

In this context, the dominant mode of political adaptation was the closing of political systems and the creation of new formulas of governance designed to consolidate and increase the power of the incumbent. Liberal politics and the rule of law were luxuries that a leader could ill afford lest his security and ambitions be undermined. The demands of security and unity were used to justify the suspension of *habeas corpus* laws, and the idea that a court system might protect those suspected of plotting the demise of the executive quickly became anathema.

Coupled with this, the courts and the legal system frequently encountered legitimacy problems in their own right. As Howard (1985: 324) wrote, 'constitutionalism and the rule of law in Commonwealth Africa were originally imposed from above; hence, they may still be seen as both foreign and colonial institutions'. These legitimacy problems became more acute when the courts rendered judgments that were seen to conflict with local sentiments. The Zambian courts, and the white judges who sat on the bench, for instance, garnered considerable popular resentment in 1969 when they rendered a judgment against the state in favour of two Portuguese soldiers. Subsequent government badgering of the courts was seen less as an intrusion on judicial independence than an articulation of popular grievances. The Malawian courts also faced problems of popular support. Distrust of the courts heightened in the context of decisions in criminal cases in favour of accused individuals held to be guilty in the court of public opinion. In the early 1970s, President Banda decried acquittals of accused murderers based on 'mere technicalities' and moved forward with plans to reform the judicial system in a manner that allowed the 'Malawian sense of justice' to prevail, facilitating the introduction of 'traditional courts' (Williams 1978: 252–54).

Finally, it is worth noting that liberalism, the idea that the state should be limited and that individual rights should be protected, was hardly cultivated under colonial rule. In the imagery of *bula matari*, the colonial state was driven by a vocation of domination (Young 1994). Colonial subjects had few rights and were usually victimized by systems of indirect rule that utilized 'traditional' rulers as agents of control and extraction. Frequently such traditional rulers fused both executive and judicial functions, leaving individuals no effective legal redress against the state (Mamdani 1996: 53). On top of this, preventative detention laws were used by colonial authorities against those who challenged the colonial system and sedition laws were routinely used to control political protest and expression. Finally, colonial authorities themselves were quite unconstrained, encountering few limitations in the form of checks and balances and the separation of powers (Howard 1985: 325–27). Given this, constitutional orders creating a framework for the rule of law had very shallow roots in new African countries. To the contrary, especially in the case of preventative detention laws, the colonial system often left the legal tools to undermine the rule of law.

Under these circumstances, actors within legal and judicial systems who might have worked to promote and defend the rule of law came to play a relatively subservient role. Judges, for example, operating from positions of institutional weakness and personal insecurity, tended to defer to the interests of executives in their rulings (Howard 1985; VonDoepp 2009). Yet it is notable that in most contexts, the idea of the rule of law never died entirely. Judges and lawyers worked to preserve the narrow spheres of authority and competence granted to them. At times, these actors actually did take steps to challenge over-reaching executives in defence of constitutionalism and individual rights.

Widner's account of the activities of Francis Nyalali, former chief justice of Tanzania, serves as testament to this. In 1977 Nyalali began serving as chief justice within Nyerere's relatively 'soft' single-party system. During the 1980s, a number of incidents raised fears about the direction of the country. Judges became especially alarmed with the passage of an Economic Sabotage Act in 1983 that created a special economic crimes tribunal outside of the supervision of the judiciary. Beyond this, those accused under the act lacked rights of bail, legal representation and appeal. With the support of other judges, Nyalali appealed first to the president and then to the party central committee, voicing concerns about the law and the implications for the rule of law in the country. The law was later revised, removing its more draconian elements and reinstating the authority of the common law courts (Widner 2001: 145). At later points, Nyalali played an important role in pushing for the effective implementation of a bill of rights that had been passed in 1984 (ibid.: 192).

Judges in other parts of Africa also worked in limited ways to support the rule of law. While Zambian judges tended to support the executive (even endorsing the government's exercising detention powers under state of emergency provisions) they also sometimes took an independent line. The Supreme Court in the 1980s acquitted individuals who had been found guilty of treason at the High Court. In two important cases, the courts ruled that the government had to have reasonable grounds to detain individuals, and that the court was competent to adjudicate such matters (VonDoepp 2009).

Lawyers were also active in these respects. In 1982, for example, the Ghana Bar Association decided to boycott the People's Courts because of their violations of the basic principles of the rule of law. In Kenya, although lawyers were generally supportive of Moi's authoritarian system, some were active in representing political opponents and civil society activists. As such activism increased in the mid- to late 1980s, lawyers themselves became the target of government. In 1986, two lawyers were detained for their alleged connection to a dissident group, while in 1987 the government detained a prominent Nairobi lawyer for filing a *habeas corpus* application on behalf of a dissident (Mutua 2001: 102).

These actors also played important roles in the liberalization processes that took place in much of Africa in the early 1990s. Lawyers were especially important players in the movement to reform Kenya's political system, even taking leadership roles. In Malawi and Zambia, bar associations were part of broader civic organizations that worked for political liberalization. Individual lawyers also made use of court systems to support political reform, working for the release of multi-party advocates who had been imprisoned and challenging incumbents' efforts to stall reform. Finally, lawyers in all three countries played important roles in drafting the constitutional revisions undertaken to liberalize political systems.

The same was true of judges. Francis Nyalali, while serving as Tanzania's chief justice, served as the head of a presidential commission on political change and in that capacity was a primary advocate for the introduction of a multi-party system in the country (Widner 2001: 306). At a less visible level, judges in countries such as Malawi and Zambia rendered a number of decisions that were supportive of processes of political change. This included releasing detained multi-party advocates and challenging government actions that undermined the integrity of polling processes – developments that were critical to the democratization process (VonDoepp 2009).

The rule of law in the multi-party era

With the transition to multi-party politics in many countries since the early 1990s, the prospects for the rule of law have improved considerably. Not only is the context more supportive of constitutionalism and rights protection, but there is also tangible evidence that clear advances have been registered. At the same time, very real challenges remain.

One development that has improved the environment for the rule of law is the elevated normative importance that is now assigned to 'constitutionalism' in many countries. Many of the political transitions of the early 1990s entailed not only the reintroduction of elections, but also efforts to re-establish constitutional governance. This often took the form of pressing for and sometimes negotiating constitutional changes, leading to the adoption of new constitutions in a number of countries. Since that time, questions of constitutional reform have remained on the forefront of national issues in countries such as Zambia and Kenya. As a partial reflection of this, discourse in African countries has increasingly focused on the concept of constitutionalism, both in terms of its abstract meaning and practical application. This is true at an intellectual level, as witnessed in the increased number of conferences taking place and publications emerging on the issue. It is also true at a popular level, where the question of constitutionalism is discussed in newspaper editorials and radio programmes. Indeed, a simple LexisNexis search by the author of the Internet source 'Africa News' provided nearly 2,000 references to 'constitutionalism' in African newspapers since 2001.

The international climate for the rule of law has improved as well. On the one hand, this is evident in the increased discourse devoted to rights and the rule of law at a global level. On the other hand, international institutions have prioritized civil liberties and the rule of law in their interactions with African governments. The US government Millennium Challenge Corporation, for example, considers the status of the rule of law and civil liberties when evaluating whether countries should receive funding from the Millennium Challenge Account. The World Bank also issues regular evaluations of countries' progress with the rule of law as part of its assessments of governance. Given this prioritization of the rule of law, governments seeking to remain in good standing with international donors have had clear incentives to at least maintain the institutional edifice of the rule of law.

On top of this, political and economic conditions have elevated the importance of the legal system and the infrastructure for the rule of law. On the economic side, over the last 15 years, most African states have undertaken efforts to reduce the role of the state in the economy, opening up more room for private-sector activity. As a partial reflection of this, foreign investment in Africa has increased dramatically in the past decade (Lewis 2010: 198). This return of market economics and greater economic pluralism has significant implications for the rule of law. As scholars have argued, increasing socioeconomic complexity and diversity generate a greater need for mechanisms to ensure economic predictability, contract enforcement, and dispute resolution (Bill Chavez 2003: 420). This serves to boost the development of key elements of the rule of law – a court system, delimited rights to property, and codified law.

The development of more open political environments has also contributed to the rule of law. Open discussions of issues such as constitutionalism and judicial independence help to enhance normative support for the rule of law. Moreover, the density and number of civil society organizations have increased dramatically in many African countries over the past two decades. These organizations have proven especially important in countries such as Malawi and Zambia, where broad-based social movements challenged and thwarted executives who sought to amend constitutions to increase or enhance their power. Finally, competitive politics in the form of electoral contestation has increased the importance of the legal and judicial institutions, which are often called upon to resolve disputes about electoral processes and outcomes. To be sure, robust electoral competition, coupled with substantial judicial involvement in politics, can sometimes put judicial institutions in the firing line of incumbents seeking to maintain power (VonDoepp 2009). Nonetheless, open and competitive politics has increased the relevance of judicial institutions in national political life.

The improved status of the rule of law in Africa can be witnessed in a number of different respects. Consider the change over the last three decades in terms of sub-Saharan Africa's civil liberties scores from Freedom House, as displayed in Figure 3.1 (lower scores indicate better conditions with respect to civil liberties). These scores include a specific measure for the rule of law as described above, as well as a number of other measures focusing on the status of civil liberties in countries. As is evident, substantial improvements were realized in the early 1990s, while gradual improvements have continued throughout the last decade.

Moreover, as Posner and Young (2007) have ably argued and demonstrated, the formal rules of the game matter today much more than they did 20 or 30 years ago. While African leaders used to leave office through coup, violent overthrow, or assassination, over 1990–2005 incumbents have most often left office through constitutional means, either through electoral defeat or as a result of the imposition of term limits. In other words, leaders have increasingly demonstrated respect for constitutions and constitutional processes when making decisions about whether – and how – to leave office (Lindberg, this volume). Notably, virtually all of those who attempted to change the rules of the game – for example by removing or extending term limits – did so through constitutional processes, and all three who failed acquiesced to the final outcome and left power (Posner and Young 2007).

Finally, lawyers and judges are playing increasingly visible roles in African countries, which is in itself a reflection of the increasing significance of formal rules in political life. It also demonstrates the increasingly plural and competitive nature of politics, which engenders the need for mechanisms of dispute resolution. Courts especially have been charged with rendering decisions with major consequences for national life. In Malawi and Zambia, for instance, courts have been centrally involved in electoral politics, determining issues such as whether certain candidates can legally stand for office, whether electoral processes were conducted fairly, and whether national election results should be upheld. In both countries courts have also rendered judgments regarding freedom of expression and the right of citizens to demonstrate, and have adjudicated disputes about the proper exercise of executive authority.

Moreover, in dramatic contrast with previous periods, court decisions in these kinds of cases have frequently, if inconsistently, indicated that judges are willing to uphold the rule of law

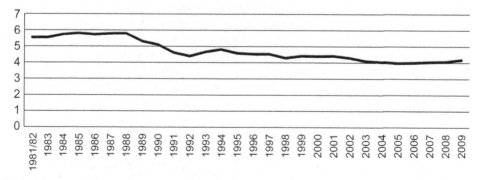

Figure 3.1 Civil liberties in Africa, 1981–2009
Source: Based on author calculations in 48 African countries.

even when it conflicts with the executive's interests. For instance, court decisions in Malawi and Zambia that halted executive measures designed to undermine protests and demonstrations played an important role in preventing the amendment of the constitution to allow the sitting president to stand for a third term (VonDoepp 2005). At times, Zambian and Malawian courts have also extended protection to journalists charged by the government with infractions related to their reporting of political events. So while courts have also rendered a number of decisions that have supported executives, sometimes in ways that would appear deleterious for checks and balances and a liberal political dispensation, the key point is that they can no longer be considered mere lapdogs of government (VonDoepp 2009).

All of this said, there remain substantial challenges for the rule of law in Africa. Although the formal rules matter in ways that they did not in previous years, personalist and neopatrimonial tendencies still operate in political life. One extension of this is that executives continue to place a very high premium on holding and maintaining power. This can place pressure on the legal and constitutional frameworks designed to structure political life, as rulers bend, circumvent, and change rules in the exercise and pursuit of power. As indicated above, many presidents have attempted to alter rules of the game to allow them to stand for third presidential terms. In so doing, they have sometimes stretched the limits or openly violated the rule of law. In Niger, the effort by former president Mamadou Tandja to extend his time in office led to the actual suspension of the constitution, which itself precipitated his extra-constitutional removal from office by the military in the months that followed.

The volatile and tense character of political life can also lead presidents to take steps that place strains on the rule of law. During his first term in office, Malawian president Bingu Mutharika was forced to govern in a situation where the legislature was controlled by his opponents. While Mutharika faced persistent gridlock and paralysis with respect to policy initiatives and appointments, he was also forced for two years to deal with a persistent impeachment threat brought by his opponents in the legislature. This led to measures such as the closing of parliament in 2008 in a manner that had dubious legal backing. Moreover, fearing that his opponents had supporters in the state apparatus, and facing a legislature that was unwilling to approve new appointments to government posts, the president attempted to make a number of personnel changes that violated the legal procedures for doing so. In another instance, the government defied a court order requiring it to restore the security and other entitlements of the vice-president (the president's opponent) after these had been withdrawn (Kanyongolo 2006).

It also needs to be remembered that in their routine dealings with the state, citizens in many African countries continue to experience predation, arbitrary decisions, and abuse, with little recourse to legal instruments for redress. As Englebert (2009) has so effectively described it, those in state positions, such as local police officers, agricultural extension workers, market supervisors, etc.; have the power of 'legal command'. This allows them to exercise power over citizens and prey on them for resources, and so state authorities routinely violate the legal mandates of their office during face-to-face interactions with citizens – a key sign of weakness in the rule of law. A survey conducted by Transparency International in Kenya in 2004 indicated that 78 per cent of citizens were asked to pay bribes when engaging with law enforcement and regulatory officials. On average, urban Kenyans reported paying 16 bribes per month. A similar study undertaken in Zambia indicated that nearly 60 per cent of Zambians were asked for a bribe in 2009. In almost all cases, refusal to pay a bribe leads to the denial of the service.

One additional challenge is that very few citizens have means of legal redress when they suffer inappropriate treatment at the hands of state authorities. As a number of studies have documented, for most poor citizens, legal systems are inaccessible owing to the skills and resources needed to make use of them. On top of this, lower-level courts are often perceived to be corrupt and woefully inefficient, creating further disincentives for average citizens to attempt to work through the legal system. This problem takes on special relevance with respect to women, who face unique barriers to the realization of their constitutional rights (see Mama, this volume). These barriers include the need to negotiate customary law in matters of inheritance and divorce and social norms that work against women's empowerment.

Ongoing challenges for courts

A final challenge for the rule of law concerns the need to preserve and enhance judicial independence, especially in those countries experimenting with democratic rule. Judiciaries have the potential to serve as a key mechanism to promote governmental accountability to the law. This is most apparent when they render decisions that define the scope and boundaries of executive authority. They can also play an important role in solidifying individual rights *vis-à-vis* the state. This includes upholding citizens' rights to association, free expression, and due process, as well as rights against unlawful detention or loss of property at the hands of the state.

As indicated earlier, judiciaries in several countries in Africa have distinguished themselves by demonstrating that they will not simply bow to executive interests and priorities when rendering decisions in important political cases. The Ugandan and Malawian judiciaries have stood out especially in this regard over the past 15 years, but judicial independence nonetheless faces a number of different challenges in Africa today.

By virtue of their lack of control over key resources, such as enforcement powers, money, or public platforms, courts are inherently the weakest branch of government. While this is true in nearly all cases, it is especially the case in African countries given the traditional dominance of executives in political life. The behaviour of executives *vis-à-vis* the courts remains one of the key challenges that judiciaries face. For one, as indicated above, the executive may not comply with the decision of the courts. A report by the African Peer Review Mechanism on Kenya indicates that prominent government officials have either disobeyed or threatened to disobey court orders, a tendency, it maintains, that 'strikes at the heart' of the rule of law (Lansner 2010: 331).

Beyond this, courts in many countries remain institutionally subservient to other branches. Executives in most countries have substantial influence over appointments to the highest echelons of the judiciary and the funding of the judicial system. When the courts have asserted their authority they have sometimes become the target of aggressive acts by government. President Yoweri Museveni of Uganda twice sent soldiers to the courts to prevent the implementation of bail decisions. In other countries, judges have been targeted with impeachment efforts, criminal investigations, and personal harassment in the wake of rendering decisions against governments (VonDoepp and Ellett 2011).

Finally, judiciaries in many countries suffer from a perception that judges themselves are corrupt. Some executives have provided material benefits to judges or members of their families in ways that have surely compromised the independence of the courts (VonDoepp and Ellett 2011). Public opinion surveys from Ghana indicate that nearly 80 per cent of the public consider the judiciary to be corrupt (Gyimah Boadi 2010: 202). Similarly, perceptions of judicial corruption in Kenya were so severe that the judiciary became the target of a major effort to clear the courts of corrupt individuals. By some accounts, the effort has only achieved modest successes (Transparency International 2007: 224).

Conclusion

As Widner (2001) has pointed out, courts can themselves be active agents in remedying these challenges to their independence and integrity. By improving their efficiency and engaging in more effective public education, for example, they can help to build the popular legitimacy that can dissuade governments from openly interfering with them. Moreover, international agencies remain very keen to support judicial institutions, with efforts to improve efficiency and accountability at the forefront of many programmes.

Whether the glass is half full or half empty with respect to the rule of law is of course a matter of perception. What is most important to recognize is that the advances that have been registered are not irrevocable. In most African countries, constitutions, civil liberties, and courts operate in environments in which personalist tendencies remain and in which state authority is often abused by those holding office. Given this, and given the importance of the rule of law for both the overall trajectories of African polities and the everyday lives of citizens, it is quite right that the issue receives the attention that it does.

Bibliography

Bertelsmann Stiftung (2010) 'Transformation Index of the Bertelsmann Stiftung 2010: Manual for Country Assessments', Gütersloh: Bertelsmann Stiftung, www.bti-project.de (accessed 10 January 2011).

Bill Chavez, R. (2003) 'The Construction of the Rule of Law: A Tale of Two Provinces', *Comparative Politics* 35(4): 417–37.

Carothers, T. (1998) 'The Rule of Law Revival', *Foreign Affairs* 77(2): 95–106.

Diamond, L. (1999) *Developing Democracy*, Baltimore, MD: Johns Hopkins University Press.

Donnelly, S. (2006) 'Reflecting on the Rule of Law: Its Reciprocal Relation with Rights, Legitimacy and Other Concepts and Institutions', *Annals of the American Academy of Political and Social Science* 603(1): 37–53.

Englebert, P. (2009) *Africa: Unity, Sovereignty, and Sorrow*, Boulder, CO: Lynne Rienner Publishers.

Feld, L. and Voigt, S. (2003) 'Economic Growth and Judicial Independence: Cross-Country Evidence Using a New Set of Indicators', *European Journal of Political Economy* 19(3): 497–527.

Freedom House (2008) 'Freedom in the World: 2008', New York, NY: Rowman and Littlefield.

——(2010) *Freedom of the Press 2010: Broad Setbacks to Global Media Freedom*, New York, NY: Freedom House.

Gyimah-Boadi, E. (2010) 'Ghana', in Freedom House, *Countries at the Crossroads 2010*, New York, NY: Rowman and Littlefield.

Haggard, S., MacIntyre, A. and Tiede, L. (2008) 'The Rule of Law and Economic Development', *Annual Review of Political Science* 11: 205–34.

Harding, A. and Hatchard, J. (1993) *Preventative Detention and Security Law: A Comparative Survey*, Boston, MA: Martinus Nijhoff Publishers.

Howard, R. (1985) 'Legitimacy and Class Rule in Commonwealth Africa: Constitutionalism and the Rule of Law', *Third World Quarterly* 17(2): 323–47.

Jackson, R. and Rosberg, C. (1982) *Personal Rule in Black Africa*, Berkeley, CA: University of California Press.

Kanyongolo, F.E. (2006) 'Malawi–Justice Sector and the Rule of Law', London: Open Society Initiative for Southern Africa, www.soros.org/reports/malawi-justice-sector-and-rule-law (accessed 10 January 2011).

Kasfir, N. (2010) 'Uganda', in Freedom House, *Countries at the Crossroads 2010*, New York, NY: Rowman and Littlefield.

Kaufmann, D. and Kraay, A. (2002) 'Growth Without Governance', World Bank Policy Research Working Paper No. 2928, Washington, DC: World Bank Institute.

Lansner, T. (2010) 'Kenya', in Freedom House, *Countries at the Crossroads 2010*, New York, NY: Rowman and Littlefield.

Lewis, P. (2010) 'African Economies' New Resilience', *Current History* 109(727): 193–98.

Mamdani, M. (1996) *Citizen and Subject: Contemporary Africa and the Legacy of Late Colonialism*, Princeton, NJ: Princeton University Press.

Maravall, J.M. and Przeworski, A. (2003) 'Introduction', in J.M. Maravall and A. Przeworski (eds) *Democracy and the Rule of Law*, New York, NY: Cambridge University Press.

Mutua, M. (2001) 'Justice Under Siege: The Rule of Law and Judicial Subservience in Kenya', *Human Rights Quarterly* 23(1): 96–118.

Posner, D. and Young, D. (2007) 'The Institutionalization of Political Power in Africa', *Journal of Democracy* 18(3): 126–40.

Raz, J. (1977) 'The Rule of Law and its Virtue', *The Law Quarterly Review* 93: 197–211.

Sanchez-Cuenca, I. (2003) 'Power, Rules and Compliance', in J.M. Maravall and A. Przeworski (eds) *Democracy and the Rule of Law*, New York, NY: Cambridge University Press.

Transparency International (2007) 'Global Corruption Report 2007: Corruption in Judicial Systems', New York, NY: Cambridge University Press.

VonDoepp, P. (2005) 'The Problem of Judicial Control in Africa's Neopatrimonial Democracies: Malawi and Zambia', *Political Science Quarterly* 120(2): 275–301.

——(2009) *Judicial Politics in New Democracies: Cases from Southern Africa*, Boulder, CO: Lynne Rienner Publishers.

VonDoepp, P. and Ellett, R. (2011) 'Reworking Strategic Models of Executive-Judicial Relations: Insights from New African Democracies', *Comparative Politics* 43(2): 147–65.

Widner, J. (2001) *Building the Rule of Law: Francis Nyalali and the Road to Judicial Independence in Africa*, New York, NY: W.W. Norton and Co.

Williams, D.T. (1978) *Malawi: The Politics of Despair*, Ithaca, NY: Cornell University Press.

World Bank. (n.d.) 'Rule of Law as a Goal of Development Policy', http://web.worldbank.org/WBSITE/EXTERNAL/TOPICS/EXTLAWJUSTINST/0,contentMDK:20763583~menuPK:1989584~pagePK:210058~piPK:210062~theSitePK:1974062~isCURL:Y~DIR_PATH:WBSITE/EXTERNAL/TOPICS/EXTLAWJUSTINST/,00.html (accessed 10 January 2011).

Young, C. (1994) *The African Colonial State in Comparative Perspective*, New Haven, CT: Yale University Press.

4

SECURITY AND THE PRIVATIZATION OF FORCE AND VIOLENCE

Rita Abrahamsen

Private security in Africa has a long, complex, and controversial history. Early European expansion on the continent was facilitated by private force, with chartered companies like Cecil Rhodes's British South African Company recruiting their own armies, and later colonial commercial enterprises like De Beers employing private police to secure their concessions. After independence, and particularly during the height of the Cold War, Africa became the favourite playground for the world's soldiers of fortune, with mercenaries involved in numerous civil wars, conflicts, and military coups d'état. In the 1990s, the South African mercenary company Executive Outcomes was hired by beleaguered state rulers to intervene in the civil wars of Angola and Sierra Leone, inflicting significant loss of life while banking high profits and lucrative diamond concessions. Today, private security is arguably more pervasive than ever before. A plethora of different private actors, ranging from global private security companies to local vigilantes, now inhabit the security field, raising important questions about the African state, its sovereignty, and its relationship to the security of citizens.

In Max Weber's classic definition the state is a set of enduring institutions with a monopoly of the legitimate means of violence within its territory (Weber 1958). The ideal-typical Weberian state in perfect control of the legitimate means of violence is always and everywhere just that – an ideal type rather than an empirical description of actually existing states, whether in Africa, Europe, or elsewhere. Nevertheless, this notion of the state continues to exercise a powerful hold on our political imaginations and practices. So much so that the history of European state formation is told as the story of the centralization of force in the hands of the uniformed agents of the state. African states came to independence with a state security apparatus fashioned from the same Weberian cloth: a police force focused on maintaining domestic law and order and a military dedicated to defence against external enemies. Some 50 years after independence, it is the increased role of private actors that many fear is eroding this public monopoly on violence – and with it, the state itself.

Ever since Executive Outcomes (EO) intervened in Angola and Sierra Leone, private security on the African continent has been associated with state weakness and potential state failure. Even as direct military actions by mercenary armies appear to have subsided, anxiety and unease continue to follow in the footsteps of private security actors. As commercial security companies and local vigilantes proliferate across the continent, the power and authority of the state is perceived to decrease in almost equal measure, as if the rise of the private sector is necessarily at the expense of the public. In the most despairing visions, social and political fragmentation is the inevitable endpoint of a downward spiral in which the wealthy retreat to their privately fortified enclaves, the poor rely on vigilante justice, and the state abandons any notion of security as a public good equally available to all.

This chapter unravels the relationship between the African state and the privatization of force and violence, and uses private security as a lens through which to explore broader transformations of the contemporary state. While there are many reasons to be concerned about the growth of private security on the continent, the chapter argues that what is at stake in security privatization is much more than a simple transfer of previously public tasks to private actors. Instead, it involves a complex reconfiguration of the public and the private, with important implications for how we understand the state and its sources of legitimacy and authority. By approaching the public/private distinction as both historically constructed and as foundational to our conception of politics and political community, the chapter shows that the rise of private security actors cannot be understood simply with reference to state weakness or state failure, wherein the rise of the private is necessarily at the expense of the public in a zero-sum power struggle. Instead, it shows how the public/private distinction has always been highly contested in debates about the African state, and how the contemporary rise of private security actors is as much about transformations of the state and forms of governance as it is about privatization or state failure in any narrow understanding of those terms. Security privatization, in all its various forms, is thus best understood and analysed as part of Africa's 'real governance' (Olivier de Sardan 2008), and rather than treating the state and its monopoly of security as fixed and unchanging, the chapter argues that contemporary security provision and governance take place within global security assemblages that include a multiplicity of public and private, and global and local actors (Abrahamsen and Williams 2011).

The public/private distinction

It is no exaggeration to say that the public/private distinction is at the heart of most debates in the study of African politics, especially as they relate to the state. Again, these debates take their inspiration from Weber's classic notion of the legal-rational state. For Weber, legitimate authority in the modern legal-rational state arises in part from the clear distinction and separation between public office and private interest, thus distinguishing legal-rational legitimacy from his other ideal-types of legitimation – charismatic and patrimonial. As the colonial era came to an end on the African continent, the newly independent states inherited bureaucracies that were formally (and hastily) organized along legal-rational lines. However, it soon became apparent that the distinction between the public and the private did not readily map onto African realities, as public office was frequently awarded and executed on the basis of personal favour and interest. This gave rise to the concept of the neopatrimonial state, in which all the formal trappings of the legal-rational state exist but have been superimposed on societies and structures governed at least in part by private or personal loyalties (Erdmann, this volume). The African state is thus frequently described as a 'hybrid' state, wherein formal legal-rational principles and informal personal loyalties and obligations co-exist – and sometimes compete – within the same institutions and practices. While this dualism is often expressed in terms of a modern/traditional divide, it is important to note that the practices associated with personal loyalties are as rooted in the contemporary as they are in some distant past.

It is not necessary to endorse the neopatrimonial description of the African state to see how it effectively illustrates aspects of the problematic nature of the public/private distinction, and the manner in which the two are more delineated in theory than in practice. The public and private realms co-exist and interact in multiple, complex ways, with the private at times firmly lodged within the public and vice-versa. In the security field, this finds its articulation in the widespread use of the public security apparatus for private gains or for regime security. As Hills argues, policing in Africa has generally been preoccupied with 'the enforcement of order on behalf of a regime', rather than with crime prevention and public protection (Hills 2000: 162). This preoccupation with regime survival has its historical roots in the colonial origins of the state and its police forces, and has been further reinforced by the lack of popular legitimacy of many governments. The period of neo-liberal restructuring in the 1980s and 1990s is crucial in this context; by eroding the state's economic ability to provide for its citizens, it alienated ever-larger sections of the population, thus intensifying the need for regime security yet further. At the same time, political elites often showed little inclination toward tightening their own belts, and instead privatised elements of the state in the interest of their own survival and reproduction. The security apparatus thus came to be utilized more and more often for explicitly political purposes. In many countries an ostensibly public police force has been increasingly acting in defence of the narrow private interests of political elites, significantly problematizing any simplistic public/private distinction.

At the individual level, the use of public authority for private purposes is also evident. With declining public resources, the wages and status of public security officers deteriorated, sometimes to the point of significant hardship and deprivation. Inevitably, the temptation to turn the public authority arising from being the uniformed agent of the state into private coping strategies increased; as living standards dropped across the continent, elements of the police turned to corruption, bribery and collusion with criminals. The notion that the police are tasked with the protection of the public is thus increasingly at odds with the public's actual experience, and in many countries the population encounters the police primarily as a source of intimidation, extortion, and insecurity. The net result is a progressive erosion of public trust in the police.

Approached from this perspective, the proliferation of private security actors appears primarily as a reaction to the failure or neglect of the state to provide the public good of security: as the state has been unable or unwilling to provide adequate protection, people have turned to (or become subject to) other responses and actors, be they neighbourhood watches, traditional policing structures, militias, vigilantes, or commercial security companies. On the one hand, such initiatives respond to the perceived security needs of specific groups and populations, filling a gap or void left by the retreating state. On the other, their multiplication creates the conditions for predatory violence, protection rackets and generalized fear, as all security actors, whether public or private, are also potentially actors of insecurity.

Against the canvas of the Weberian state, these developments appear as an unquestionable indication of state decline or state failure. Discussions of security privatization rarely miss the opportunity to highlight the links between state failure and private security, be it as cause or effect. It is undoubtedly the case that many African states deviate substantially from the Weberian model of providing a full range of public services, including security. Approaching security privatization primarily as a reflection of and contribution to state decline and failure, however, is problematic. Although it clearly captures some aspects of an explanation, it also comes with severe risks. The discourse of failure encourages a focus on absences, on what Africa lacks, rather than on what is actually taking place within these areas. Like the neopatrimonial perspective, the danger lies in overly negative and culturalist interpretations, wherein Africa and its politics is not only judged according to Western standards, but also somehow perceived as trapped within a static and all-encompassing culture of primordialism and failure. By focusing on the absence of a fully functioning state, the state itself becomes reified, a fixed and ahistorical entity, thus blinding us not only to its evolving and historically constituted character but also to the manner in which governance and security are actually produced and assembled in interactions between public and private institutions.

Analytically this points towards the merits of a less state-centric perspective, wherein the question of how authority and order emerge and are maintained is open to investigation. Several recent studies, for example, have drawn attention to the continuation of service delivery in states frequently perceived as failed, demonstrating that even where the state has retreated from public provisions, alternative services emerge, and order and authority prevail in some form that does not necessarily threaten or further undermine the state (Trefon 2004; Lund 2006). Applied to the security sector – whether in so-called failed or successful states – this raises the possibility that private actors do not necessarily act at the expense of state authority and legitimacy, and that private security is not always and everywhere an indication of state weakness or impending collapse. The relationship of the private to the public becomes instead an empirical question to be investigated through careful analysis of how public and private actors interact, negotiate, and compete to produce and govern security. As the discussion below reveals, most private security actors stand in some relationship to the state or the public, and some are actively encouraged and promoted by states and global trends in security policy. Others legitimate themselves by reference to the state, and even those that emerge in explicit opposition to the state's failure to protect do not necessarily threaten its authority. Approached in this manner, security privatization emerges as a more complex process and as an expression of broader transformations of governance, where the private is increasingly lodged within the state and has various degrees of authority and autonomy.

The remainder of this chapter provides a bird's-eye view of private security actors in Africa. The category of private force and violence is to some extent too vast to be meaningful, and the differences between a private soldier fighting a foreign civil war, an unarmed guard half-asleep outside an up-scale shopping centre, and a local vigilante patrolling his village or neighbourhood are obvious. By the same token, there is no one common causal logic underlying the rise of these disparate actors, nor one unified analytical frame for understanding their implications. The ensuing discussion hence makes no attempt at comprehensiveness, but rather focuses on how the public and private interact and are negotiated to produce different forms of security and governance, and how, in the process, the very categories of the public and the private are being transformed.

Private security in war and conflict

Among Africa's multiple private security actors, the mercenary and, above all, the South African company Executive Outcomes (EO) is the undoubted cause célèbre. EO's spectacular and violent involvement in Sierra Leone and Angola have had an enduring impact on the interpretation of the relationship between private security and the state in Africa, and despite the fact that the company no longer exists, no discussion of private security is considered complete without revisiting EO's operations (Avant 2005; Singer 2003). EO was founded at the end of the Cold War by senior figures from the apartheid military apparatus and primarily enlisted former soldiers from the various battalions and divisions that had spearheaded South Africa's destabilization strategy in the frontline states. Approximately 70 per cent of EO's soldiers were black Africans, including many Angolans who had fought with the South African Defence Forces during the apartheid era and who subsequently found themselves without employment. One of EO's more long-standing operations was in Angola, where it trained and fought alongside government troops against the rebel movement National Union for the Total Independence of Angola (UNITA) after its refusal to accept the 1992 election results. Its other main operation in Africa was in Sierra Leone in 1995, when the beleaguered government of Captain Valentine Strasser contracted EO to fight against the Revolutionary United Front (RUF). In military terms, the EO intervention was highly successful. Within a month of its arrival, EO and government forces had cleared major towns of RUF forces and pushed the rebels to the Liberian border. Hundreds of RUF fighters were reportedly killed, while even more allegedly deserted. Later the same year, EO-led forces re-captured the all-important diamond mining areas, again inflicting significant losses on the RUF.

EO's involvement in Sierra Leone and Angola exemplifies the extreme privatization and extraversion of the state, where rulers hire foreign private forces to maintain their power and strengthen the 'shadow state' (Reno 1998). Importantly in this regard, EO was paid in Sierra Leone in part through future diamond concessions, through which the country's rulers mortgaged future income for their own immediate survival. Complex transnational networks of power and interaction, linking elements of the state, private security actors, and transnational capital enabled these rulers to lever foreign resources in their struggle against opponents and thus strengthen their personalized control over the state's economic resources. At the same time, it is often claimed that the EO presence enabled sufficient stability for multi-party elections to be held, and thus potentially contributed to the possibility of a more democratic, legal-rational state. The newly elected President Ahmed Tejan Kabbah continued to rely on the services of EO until January 1997, but when the contract was terminated, the RUF advanced again. In the long term, the state's ability to control the use of force seems to have been further eroded through the contract with EO and later with Sandline International, a British-based mercenary firm. The privatization of military power in states such as Sierra Leone and Angola thus appears to diffuse power and control toward the private military corporations (PMCs), as they gained influence over key political decisions. Military outsourcing in Sierra Leone also strengthened local social forces such as the Kamajor militias, which were trained and deployed by EO. As the Kamajors' primary loyalty was not necessarily to the government, but to their ethnic chiefs, the contract with EO can be seen to have created future challenges for state reconstruction and consolidation. Importantly, political control and influence also passed to the outside mining companies which financed the military operations and subsequently received lucrative concessions. These operations thus draw attention to the unstable relationship of public authority to private force.

EO ceased operations in 1999, and the activities of most contemporary private security firms that operate at the military end of the spectrum bear relatively little resemblance to the combat roles so widely associated with events in Sierra Leone and Angola. To be sure, private armies and soldiers are still to be found in African conflicts, as witnessed by reports that Liberian mercenaries were fighting in Côte d'Ivoire's post-election crisis and speculations that Saracen International, a company with connections to Uganda, South Africa, and the founder of Blackwater (known for its Iraq involvement) might be entering Somalia. At the same time, the face of the private military in Africa is today decidedly more 'corporate', and the rogue, active combat soldier finds his contemporary avatar in the employ of legally sanctioned private military companies. As Northern countries have become increasingly preoccupied with security and the so-called 'war on terror', the merging of development and security has opened up new opportunities for the private military sector. The vast expansion of reforms and training initiatives to strengthen and improve African security forces now routinely incorporate a plethora of private military companies and consultants working alongside public security officials. Companies like the American Military Professional Resource Incorporated (MPRI), DynCorp International, and Pacific Architects Engineers (PAE), as well as the British ArmorGroup (now part of Group4Securicor) have come to play key roles in efforts to strengthen the capacities of African militaries, reform police services, train anti-terrorist squads, and so on – often as part of broader security sector reform programmes funded by donor governments. Key examples are Liberia, where the United States contracted DynCorp International to restructure and rebuild the country's military sector, and Nigeria, where MPRI has been involved in an extensive US-funded project to professionalize the military forces.

Arguably then, while the spectacular interventions of mercenaries have waned, the presence of international private military actors in Africa has increased since the time of EO, and their relationship to the state – both in Africa and overseas – differs in important respects from that of previous mercenary companies. While the latter operated on the fringes of legality, the former are often funded by overseas development and security programmes with the intention of strengthening the legal-rational state and its monopoly of force. The results and implications of such security arrangements are as yet poorly researched and understood, but they are indicative of a significant transformation in the manner in which military force is assembled in the contemporary security arena. Through such extensive programmes, private global security actors might be attaining important positions of power and authority within local public security institutions in terms of shaping security norms, practices, knowledge, and action. In the process, the distinctions between the public and the private, the global and the local are further eroded, problematizing not only our conception of the public but also raising important questions for democracy and accountability within state borders.

Militias and rebel groups constitute another diverse category of private security actors that have proliferated in recent years, particularly in Africa's war-torn areas such as the Democratic Republic of Congo (DRC), Somalia, Côte d'Ivoire, and Liberia. Perceived simply as an expression of state collapse and disorder, militias are associated first and foremost with predation, greed, and ruthless self-preservation. While there is no denying the senseless violence perpetrated by many militias, recent studies have drawn attention to the manner in which they may also become incorporated and engaged in the production of governance and forms of regulation. In the midst of war and political crisis, and in the absence of public services, militias sometimes perform state-like functions such as the provision of security and the collection of taxes. On the Congo–Ugandan border, for example, Raeymaekers (2010) has shown how rebels did not just engage in economic predation, but sold protection to transnational traders. Both rebels and traders benefitted from sharing the spoils of cross-border trade, and the protection offered by rebels in turn enabled local entrepreneurs to provide services such as financing schools and healthcare, constructing and maintaining roads, hospitals, and even a local airport. The state was not entirely absent from these arrangements, and a range of state authorities participated in regular meetings to discuss security in the area. Put differently, security can emerge in a complex negotiation between public and private actors, wherein the power and authority of the private is not necessarily at the expense of the public but emerges through interaction and negotiation with it.

Similar observations have been made in the context of Somalia (Menkhaus 2006). Despite having been without a central government since January 1991 (the official but ineffective administration of the Transitional Federal Government notwithstanding), multiple informal systems of governance have emerged where key state functions such as security and law and order are performed and negotiated by a range of private actors. What these examples show is that even in war and conflict zones, in which the state is by definition struggling to maintain its hegemony and legitimacy, the implications of private security cannot be captured through simply equating them with state failure or weakness. Instead, they draw attention to the possibility of different modes of governance, where the state is one of many actors in the security field.

The privatization of everyday security

Outside the military arena, the day-to-day delivery of security in Africa has also become increasingly privatized. While far from a new phenomenon, commercial private security companies (PSCs) have expanded at an astonishing rate in the last two decades. Their services, ranging from basic manned guarding, risk management, and CCTV monitoring, to armed response services, close protection, and cash-in-transit, have become an integral part of Africa's security landscape. A few statistics illustrate the point: Group4Securicor, the world's largest PSC, is present in 29 African countries, employs over 106,500 people on the continent and is, according to some estimates, Africa's largest private employer. Measured as a percentage of gross domestic product (GDP), South Africa has the largest private security sector in the world: 6,392 PSCs employ 375,315 security officers with access to 80,000 vehicles. By comparison, the South African Police Service has 114,241 sworn police officers and only 37,000 vehicles. In Nigeria, the continent's most populous country, estimates indicate there are 1,500 to 2,000 private security companies. In Kenya, some 2,000 companies employ approximately 48,000 people. In Angola, there are at least 300 PSCs with about 35,000 personnel; in Uganda, the number of private guards equals that of police officers; and in many other African countries private security is one of few sectors of employment growth and expansion. In Sierra Leone, for example, there were only two private security companies before the civil war; there are now at least 20. There are no signs that the expansion of commercial security is slowing. By contrast, the market for private security in Africa – as well as in other so-called emerging markets – is expanding more rapidly than in the rich Northern countries. As a result, these areas are now targeted by the aggressive global expansion strategies of the world's leading PSCs, who estimate that by 2015 emerging markets will account for 35 per cent of a global private security market that is forecast to be worth some US$230 billion (all numbers from Abrahamsen and Williams 2011).

The phenomenal expansion of PSCs on the continent demonstrates the extent to which daily security in Africa is in the hands of private actors rather than the uniformed agents of the state. For individuals and families, small businesses, large corporations, non-governmental organizations (NGOs), and international organizations, the first line of defence against theft, intrusion, and violation is not the police, but privately hired guards, often employed by global security companies. The United Nations' (UN) instructions to its foreign staff in Kenya's capital Nairobi are instructive in this regard: 'in the event of a security breach at your home, you should call your own security company first, which will provide the fastest response' (UN 2005). The statement is, on the one hand, a clear indictment of the Kenyan police and their inability to provide adequate security, whilst on the other, it shows the extent to which the growth of private security is linked to Africa's globalization: with increased risk awareness, international personnel stationed abroad in the service of 'development' (or commerce) require 'first world' security.

While PSCs clearly thrive in the absence of a fully functioning or trustworthy public police force, it would be a mistake to regard these private security actors as existing in opposition to the state. Instead, security privatization frequently occurs at the instigation of the state, as part of policies of outsourcing, cost recovery, and efficiency. Security privatization is also a key aspect of international discourses of police reform and governance, whereby the public police is actively encouraged to enter into partnerships with private policing actors such as commercial companies, neighbourhood watches, and other so-called 'stakeholders'. A striking example can be found in Cape Town, where security of the city centre has effectively been outsourced to the world's largest security company, Group4Securicor, through the public-private partnership 'Cape Town Central City Improvement District'. Group4Securicor provides 24-hour patrols of the city, on foot, horseback, and wheels, with a street presence that far exceeds that of the public police. However, the state police are not absent from this security arrangement and often work in close cooperation with the private company in terms of patrols, surveillance, and security planning. The Cape Town Central City Improvement District is representative of the global security assemblages and the new forms of security governance emerging on the African continent. Within such assemblages, power and authority cannot be fitted into the neat grip of the territorial nation-state or clear public/private distinctions. Instead, significant power and authority over domestic territory and security decisions reside with international actors (in this case Group4Securicor, but also international policymakers and discourses more broadly). As a result, security governance emerges out of a combination of the private and the public, the global and the local, highlighting the limitations of regarding private security as an automatic threat to the authority of the state.

While PSCs have become part of daily life for international personnel, the wealthy, and Africa's expanding middle classes, the majority of poor people are unable to afford even the most basic of commercial security services. Faced with an unresponsive and/or overstretched police force, many communities and neighbourhoods have organized their own solutions in the form of informal, non-commercial security initiatives, often referred to as vigilantes. Again such initiatives appear to have proliferated in the last two decades, even if some groups clearly have a much longer history that stretches back to the pre-colonial period. The term vigilante conceals a wide variety of different non-state security initiatives, defined by Pratten as groups that focus on the 'protection and care of the community encompassed within these boundaries', and which 'involves maintaining surveillance and taking action against threats to this community' (Pratten 2006: 711). That said, vigilante groups that begin as popular schemes for imposing order in the absence of adequate state provision and control may subsequently degenerate into violent gangs, protection rackets, or militias that increase social and political disorder. They can thus be sources of security and insecurity at the same time.

The relationship of vigilantes to the state is far from straightforward. Vigilantes usefully illustrate the multiple ways in which the public and the private sectors are interlinked in Africa's security landscape. Police officers might be vigilantes by night, just as soldiers might shed their uniforms in favour of rebel outfits at the end of a shift; and retired police commanders may own successful private security companies. Powerful political actors have also mobilized vigilante groups for political thuggery during election campaigns. In Kenya, for example, Anderson (2002: 542) has highlighted how vigilantes 'all too easily become a political instrument in the hands of those with money to pay', playing key roles in electoral and post-election violence so as to ensure a particular electoral outcome. Conversely, while the very term 'vigilante' seems to indicate opposition to the state and formal law – a defence of a particular community against the neglect or hostility of the state – this is not necessarily the case. Much recent research has shown that even those groups that have emerged as a reaction to the perceived failure of the state to provide adequate security have connections to the state and do not necessarily threaten its authority and legitimacy. In the case of the Sungusungu in Tanzania and Kenya, for example, local responses to the growing problem of cattle theft have been hailed as highly successful, drawing on traditional practices, but also the formal law of the state (Heald 2007). As such, vigilante groups can be seen to be involved in state-like performances, and their existence and activities are better perceived as a constant negotiation of the boundaries between the public and the private rather than an automatic threat to the authority of the state (Buur and Jensen 2004).

Conclusion

Private security, in all its various forms, has become ubiquitous in contemporary Africa. From capital cities to isolated resource enclaves, from shopping centres to rural villages, people often rely on private actors rather than the state for their everyday provision of security. While these developments are frequently perceived to lead to an automatic weakening of state power and authority, a less state-centric approach shows that this is not always and everywhere the case, nor is it necessarily the most productive approach in terms of understanding security governance on the continent. Rather than defining the state in an absolutist Weberian sense, where the public and private are fixed categories, there is much to be gained from abandoning the state-centrism that permeates contemporary political analysis in favour of a focus on how social and political order or governance is actually produced.

Approached from this perspective, security privatization becomes a lens on contemporary transformations in statehood on the African continent. Rather than approaching the state as an ideal-type with strict public/private boundaries, the state can be perceived as the effect of a wider range of dispersed forms of power, where various non-state actors can be seen to help produce and enact the state in the eyes of many of its inhabitants, making the state more real and tangible in everyday practices (Mitchell 1999). Although private security can work to undermine state power and authority, many private security initiatives operate with the active endorsement and encouragement of state authorities and within contemporary neoliberal strategies of governance. The private delivery and governance of security is thus, more often than not, part of state policy. Rather than existing in opposition to the state, today's PMCs, PSCs, vigilantes, and other private agencies are often part of complex security networks that knit together public and private, global and local, actors. Private actors, such as vigilantes and militias, who have emerged in opposition to the (neoliberal) state or in reaction to its failure, often interact with public actors and give rise to new forms of governance and regulation. These complex security networks, stretched across national territories and continents, have given rise to the emergence of global security assemblages. These are settings where security is shaped and influenced by actors, values, and normative orders beyond the nation-state, and by the growing power of private actors who interact with the state to such a degree that it is often difficult to determine where the public ends and the private begins. Indeed, in global security assemblages the very categories of public/private and global/local are being reconstituted and reconfigured. What is at stake in security privatization is thus not merely a transfer of previously public functions to private actors, but instead a broader transformation of the relationship between security and sovereignty, as well as the traditional relationship between the public and the private, the global and the local.

Bibliography

Abrahamsen, R. and Williams, M.C. (2011) *Security Beyond the State: Private Security in International Politics*, Cambridge: Cambridge University Press.

Anderson, D. (2002) 'Vigilantes, Violence and the Politics of Public Order in Kenya', *African Affairs* 101(405): 531–55.

Avant, D. (2005) *The Market for Force*, Cambridge: Cambridge University Press.

Buur, L. and Jensen, S. (2004) 'Introduction: Vigilantism and the Policing of Everyday Life in South Africa', *African Studies* 63(2): 139–52.

Heald, S. (2007) 'Controlling Crime and Corruption from Below: Sungusungu in Kenya', *International Relations* 21(2): 183–99.

Hills, A. (2000) *Policing Africa: Internal Security and the Limitations of Liberalization*, Boulder, CO: Lynne Rienner Publishers.

Lund, C. (ed.) (2006) *Twilight Institutions: Public Authority and Local Politics in Africa*, Oxford: Blackwell.

Menkhaus, K. (2006) 'Governance without Government in Somalia', *International Security* 31(3): 74–106.

Mitchell, T. (1999) 'Economy and the State Effect', in G. Steinmetz (ed.) *State/Culture: State Formation after the Cultural Turn*, Ithaca, NY: Cornell University Press.

Olivier de Sardan, J.-P. (2008) 'Researching the Practical Norms of Real Governance in Africa', Discussion Paper No. 5, London: Africa Power and Politics Programme.

Pratten, D. (2006) 'The Politics of Vigilance in Southeastern Nigeria', *Development and Change* 37(4): 707–34.

Raeymaekers, T. (2010) 'Protection for Sale? War and the Transformation of Regulation on the Congo-Ugandan Border', *Development and Change* 41(4): 563–87.

Reno, W. (1998) *Warlord Politics and African States*, Boulder, CO: Lynne Rienner Publishers.

Singer, P.W. (2003) *Corporate Warriors: The Rise of the Privatized Military*, Ithaca, NY: Cornell University Press.

Trefon, T. (2004) *Reinventing Order in the Congo: How People Respond to State Failure in Kinshasa*, London: Zed Book.

UN (United Nations) (2005) 'Karibu Kenya: An Orientation Guide for United Staff Working in Kenya', www.unon.org/karibukenya (accessed 14 December 2011).

Weber, M. (1958) *Max Weber: Essays in Sociology*, H.H. Gerth and C. Wright Mills (eds), Oxford: Oxford University Press.

5

NEOPATRIMONIALISM AND POLITICAL REGIMES

Gero Erdmann

'Neopatrimonialism' refers to the coexistence and interaction of formal and informal institutions or a widespread informal behaviour within a formal polity such as a modern state. In other words, it is a concept that systematically includes both formal and informal institutions. Scholars often struggle with the interaction of the formal and informal dimension of governance, particularly outside the Western world. However, although the concept is often associated with African studies, from the beginning it was intended to be a universal model. In fact, it can be applied to understand politics in areas such as Southeast and Central Asia, the Middle East, and even Southeast and post-communist Europe; the phenomenon is not confined to these areas, nor does it reduce politics to 'big man syndrome'.

In African studies, there has been a tendency for scholars to reject the idea that formal institutions, which were equated with the (formal) 'Western' modern state, are of any relevance at all. Many scholars perceived African politics to be dominated by informal institutions or at least by informal behaviour (Chabal and Daloz 1999; Hydén 2006: 98), despite the fact that in most African states formal institutions matter to some degree. However, recent research on African politics indicates that crucial formal institutions become increasingly institutionalized (Solt 2001; Posner and Young 2007; Lindberg 2006). Hence, the coexistence of formal institutions with informal institutions and informal behaviour is becoming an increasingly pertinent area of research (see Olivier de Sardan, this volume).

History

The origin of the concept of neopatrimonialism dates back to the developmental studies of the early 1970s when Eisenstadt (1973) is thought to have coined the term. During the 1970s it was part of the general debate about 'modernization'. He challenged the dichotomous paradigm of modernization theory by arguing that there is not only a traditional society and modernity; rather, within the modern world there are also systems that do not comply to the 'nation-state model' and are best captured by terms such as 'patrimonialism' and 'neopatrimonialism'. From the beginning, the concept had a universalistic claim applicable to developing countries in general (e.g. Theobald 1982; Roth 1987). On this basis, Médard (1982) and Clapham (1985) developed and applied the concept to Africa. Only Le Vine (1980) explicitly adapted neopatrimonialism to a particular African variant of patrimonialism. During the 1980s the concept suffered a decline in usage in developmental studies, but experienced a revival in African studies during the 1990s. Above all, it became a frequent explanation for failures in transition processes from authoritarian to democratic rule (Bratton and van de Walle 1997). Neopatrimonialism was also used to explain the continued economic crisis in Africa (Englebert 2000; van de Walle 2001).

It is important to note that all those scholars who discussed the formation of the concept linked it to Max Weber's ideal types of domination that were themselves conceived as universal concepts. In this tradition, scholars conceptualized neopatrimonialism as a 'mixed type', comprising elements of patrimonial and legal-rational bureaucratic domination (see below). However, there were frequent complaints about conceptual shortcomings (Le Vine 1980: 663; Theobald 1982: 555; Clapham 1982: 32; Erdmann and Engel 2007: 97–104; de Grassi 2008; Pitcher *et al.* 2009), some of which will be reiterated here.

Against this background of a Weberian scholarship, it is evident that the concept is not linked to the 'neo-liberal project' of the 1990s as some authors claim (Olukoshi 1998: 14), nor should it be completely misrepresented as a 'personalist approach' that seeks to describe African behaviour as in effect 'genetic' and 'preordained' (Bauer and Taylor 2005: 9–10).

Definition

As indicated above, until the mid-1990s, the concept of neopatrimonialism was ill defined. Most often the distinction between patrimonialism and neopatrimonialism was blurred, the meaning of both conflated. Sometimes neopatrimonialism was just used as a synonym for personal rule, clientelism, and patronage. Others scholars provide a sort of 'dense' description of the phenomenon. Often the prefix 'neo' was used to describe a somehow modern or area-specific variant of patrimonialism without much specification (Erdmann and Engel 2007; Pitcher *et al.* 2009). The varied meanings and application of the concept have contributed to frequent claims that it has become a 'catch-all concept' with diminished analytical power (ibid.; de Grassi 2008).

Indeed a recent survey of how neopatrimonialism is used in African studies has identified four different applications, which can be interrelated. Scholars have depicted the concept as:

- A set of social relations at either the community or nation-state level, mediated by personal loyalty and governed by bonds of dependence and subordination.
- The rent-seeking behaviour and personalist patterns of authority practised by leaders in selected country settings.
- An economic logic distinguished by the continual blurring of public service and private gain, with serious implications for economic development.
- A characteristic regime type associated with countries not only during periods of authoritarian rule, but also in the period of democratization.

(Adapted from Pitcher et al. 2009: 131)

Scholars have only recently sought to be more specific in their use of the term. Michael Bratton and Nicolas van de Walle (1997), in their seminal work *Democratic Experiments in Africa*, opened up the space for a more precise understanding of neopatrimonialism. They were the first to define neopatrimonialism as being clearly distinct from patrimonialism.

Max Weber distinguished 'three pure types of legitimate domination' ('authority' = *Herrschaft*):[1] legal-rational bureaucratic domination, traditional domination, and charismatic domination. Patrimonialism is one type of traditional domination. Under traditional domination, 'obedience is owed to the person … who occupies the traditionally sanctioned position of authority', but not to the enacted rules: 'Personal loyalty, not the official's impersonal duty, determines the relations of the administrative staff to the master' (Weber 1978: 227). By contrast, legal rational domination is based on obedience to the 'legally established impersonal order'. The three most fundamental categories of rational legal authority are a 'continuous rule-bound conduct of official business', a 'specific specified sphere of competence (jurisdiction)', and the 'organization of offices follows the principle of hierarchy' (ibid.: 215–18). Its formal incarnation is the bureaucratic administration of the modern Western state.

According to Bratton and van de Walle (1997: 62), neopatrimonialism is characterized by customs and patterns of patrimonialism that coexist with, and suffuse, rational-legal institutions. Based on a critical discussion of their concept, the following definition was proposed:

> Neopatrimonialism is a mixture of two types of domination: namely, patrimonial and legal-rational bureaucratic domination. Under patrimonialism, all power relations between ruler and ruled, political as well as administrative relations, are personal relations; there is no differentiation between the private and the public realm. However, under neopatrimonialism the distinction between the private and the public, at least formally, exists and is accepted ... Neopatrimonial rule takes place within the framework of, and with the claim to, legal-rational bureaucracy or 'modern' stateness. Formal structures and rules do exist, although in practice the separation of the private and public sphere is not always observed. In other words, two role systems or logics exist next to each other, the patrimonial of the personal relations, and the legal-rational of the bureaucracy.
>
> *(Erdmann and Engel 2007: 105)*

This means that the two spheres are not isolated from each other; the patrimonial penetrates the legal-rational system, twists its logic, functions, and output, but does not take exclusive control over the legal-rational logic. Formal and informal institutions and behaviour are intimately linked to each other in various ways and by varying degrees and this mixture becomes institutionalized. Within this system, people have a certain degree of choice as to which logic they want to employ to achieve their goals and best realize their interests. Thus, the crucial feature of neopatrimonialism is the insecurity about the role of state institutions and the behaviour of their agents. The systematic uncertainty about which rules or which relationship are best utilized in any particular situation in order to achieve a particular goal – either the legal-rational (formal) or the patrimonial (informal) – shapes the behaviour of individuals and organizations. All actors strive to overcome their insecurity, but they do so by employing different combinations of the two underlying logics that operate within neopatrimonial systems. Ultimately, this inherent insecurity is reproduced in a systematic way. One additional remark must be made. Within such a pattern of social and political relations, formal state institutions cannot fulfil their (supposed) universalistic purpose; but they might fulfil other purposes and perform other functions for a different 'system' in which particularistic interests determine politics and policies.

Conceptual shortcomings

To begin, it is worth noting a general observation about the way in which the term neopatrimonialism is used, which illuminates a major problem with the concept. Neopatrimonialism is usually applied as an independent variable in research projects. This means the concept is taken as 'given' and used to explain something else – for example, an ill-functioning democracy, a poor policy outcome, or an economic crisis. I know of only one study that takes neopatrimonialism as a dependent variable or as something that needs to be explained. Moreover, I know of no study that investigates thoroughly whether a form of domination (regime or system) is actually neo-patrimonial or is better described another way. This observation indicates a number of conceptual problems that will be discussed below.

The problem of delineation

Regardless of how we make use of the concept, even using it as a meaningful independent variable, we must be able to answer the following questions: How can we recognize a neopatrimonial type of domination? How can we distinguish such a type from others? To answer these questions, we need to be able to identify clearly defined attributes or components (properties or indicators) that would allow us to determine the specific character of a given type of domination and to distinguish it from others. Unfortunately, such clear and explicit criteria are missing in all definitions and descriptions of the concept.

This unresolved issue reveals what I refer to as the 'delineation' or 'benchmark' problem of the concept. Without specifying such attributes it will be impossible to identify a neopatrimonial form of domination. For this purpose, we must be in a position to distinguish between a patrimonialism, neopatrimonialism, and legal-rational type of domination. Exactly where should we draw the borders?

At a first glance, neopatrimonialism is defined quite clearly as a mixture of two other types; hence, it is not patrimonial or legal-rational bureaucratic domination, but a fusion of the two. However, if we go a step further we then need to answer the question of how much of a system needs to be patrimonial or rational-legal for it to qualify as neopatrimonial? Is it about 50–50? Or is a minimum of 25 per cent on one side sufficient? We can also ask this question the other way round. In systems recognized as being legal-rational bureaucratic, there are usually informal elements or non-rule-bound behaviours and informal institutions, some of which are even required to make the formal institutions work. So how many 'patrimonial defects' in a legal-rational bureaucratic system are necessary for it to be called neopatrimonial? Or the other way round, how much legal-rational bureaucracy is required to turn a patrimonial regime into a neopatrimonial one?

It is surprising that there is no discussion about the delineation or threshold issue and how to solve this problem among scholars who use the concept. Instead, there is hardly any explication as to why a given system is termed 'neopatrimonial', apart from general references to non-formal politics, clientelism, and patronage. This leads directly to the next problem: how to apply the concept in empirical research.

The problem of operationalization

As implied above, only a few authors have explicitly addressed the challenge of operationalizing neopatrimonialism. Snyder (1992: 379) identified 'an extensive network of personal patronage', which determined the character of neopatrimonial regimes, and stated that the penetration of state institutions by these networks 'tend[s] to be uneven'. However, he did not explain how we can establish the existence of an extensive network of personal relations and the degree of penetration into state institutions. Based on the assumption that there is a vital link between patrimonialism and broader socioeconomic factors, Theobald (1982: 559) related specific instances of patrimonialism to 'these contextual variables'. However, he confined himself vaguely to 'three sets of variables' that, apart from casually naming some (the size and composition of gross domestic product (GDP) and the subsistence sector; the general nature of the relationship between the political executive and the administration), he did not elaborate further with regard to their relationship to each other. Possibly as a result of the very general nature of these variables (for example the rate of social mobilization), the literature on neopatrimonialism has made no systematic use of Theobald's suggestion.

More recently, Bratton and van de Walle (1997) suggested another substantive approach to the problem. They identified three informal political institutions that are said to be typical of neopatrimonial regimes. First, 'presidentialism', which here means the 'systematic concentration of political power in the hands of one individual, who resists delegating all but the most trivial decision-making tasks' (ibid.: 63). Second, 'systematic clientelism', which implies that the president or 'strongman' relies on awarding of personal favours, for example the distribution of public-sector jobs and public resources through licenses, contracts, and projects (ibid.: 65–66). Third, the 'use of state resources for political legitimation', which is closely linked to clientelism (ibid.: 66–67). The first problem with this proposition is that the first variable is not indicative of neopatrimonialism, but of a kind of patrimonialism, for everything is left to the discretion of the unrestrained ruler. The crucial question of whether or not presidential powers are applied according to formal constitutional rules (if presidential powers were rule-based then this could be rule-bound behaviour) is not addressed. Another problem is that the second variable is underspecified – 'use of state resources for political legitimation' is not very precise. This phenomenon can be identified in all sorts of political regimes; even in the best of all democracies, politicians will try to find policies that use state resources in order to please the majority of the electorate in order to build support for the next elections. What Bratton and van de Walle probably meant was simply that political office is used for appropriating public wealth for private enrichment as well as selective patronage, but this would require a different phrasing of the indicator.

It is worth further exploring the possibility of employing patronage or clientelism as *one* indicator of neopatrimonialism because both turn up in most descriptions and definitions of the concept. The systematic analysis of the distribution of public resources, including development projects, to particular regions, districts, or ethnic (sub-)groups, along with the distribution of ministerial and other major political and administrative posts, might generate an indicative pattern of patronage or clientelistic politics. However, adopting this strategy simply swaps one conceptual problem for another; instead of neopatrimonialism, we would have to know how to operationalize patronage or clientelism.

As Landé (1983: 440) has observed, there are three problems related to comparative research on clientelism: conceptualization, observation, and explanation. Taking them in order: (1) there is no basic agreement as to what is to be included in the study of clientelism; (2) the 'amorphousness', the 'latency', and the 'elusiveness' of clientelism make measurement extremely difficult; and finally, (3) due to methodological questions we have failed to satisfactorily explain the existence of clientelism. Because confusion about terminology and methodology remain, and because we still lack clear criteria to distinguish 'clients' from 'non-clients', it is still very difficult to deal with 'clientelism' in empirical and comparative research. This lack of conceptual clarity applies to 'patronage' as well: indeed, patronage and clientelism are often conflated or not sufficiently distinguished (Erdmann and Engel 2007: 106–8).

Building on Bratton and van de Walle, Christian von Soest has further refined the concentration-of-power indicator by suggesting an 'and-connection' between the concentration of power in the hands of the president and a high turnover of five key cabinet members (von Soest 2009: 56). In addition, he operationalizes the clientelism indicator by looking at the 'size and the composition of the ministerial cabinet', and measures the third informal institution, the 'misuse of state resources', by using the corruption ratings of Transparency International's Corruption Perception Index (CPI) and the World Bank Governance Index in respect to 'control of corruption' (ibid.: 57–58).

All this is an improvement over Bratton and van de Walle's original operationalization. However, it does not really solve the aforementioned because all of the new indicators are vague: they do not tell us the exact number of turnovers of key cabinet ministers, or which cabinet size, or which ranking in one of the corruption indexes, turns a legal-rational bureaucratic type of domination into a neopatrimonial one. Once again, the problem is that we lack clearly defined benchmarks.

Moreover, it is unclear whether these indicators really measure what they are supposed to. Beyond the claim that these indicators are highly correlated with neopatrimonialism, there is very little conceptual discussion about their usefulness, not to mention any test of their validity. The size of a cabinet could be dictated by various political reasons that might have nothing to do with neopatrimonial practices. For example, having a bigger cabinet might be an attempt to include as many different political groups as possible in order to keep peace, to unite all political forces behind one particular goal, or to integrate a heterogeneous polity – all of which may occur whether or not there is clientelist politics, the misuse of state resources for private gains, and a largely corrupt political system. These issues need to be thoroughly discussed before we can be sure of the suitability of the indicator. For example, there is a problem with using corruption indices to measure the misuse of state funds by the political elite in government because both of the indexes mentioned above appraise both grand and petty corruption; hence, they are 'second-best indicators' (ibid.: 58) when it comes to the specific purpose of indicating corruption among the political elite.

Finally, there are two other unresolved problems. One is that the indicators discussed in detail here are related to the political sphere, which is much less formally rule-based than the bureaucracy proper and so may underestimate the degree of rule following in a given country – a crucial issue which I shall discuss in the next sub-section. The other problem is related to what Bratton and van de Walle refer to as the informal institutions of neopatrimonialism. Scholars relying on an institutionalist approach often view behaviour that does not follow formal rules as being attributable to the presence of informal institutions. However, there is a general tendency in neopatrimonialist or patrimonialist studies to view informal or non-rule-bound behaviour not as an institution but as something 'ingrained' or culturally or traditionally embedded. Helmke and Levitzky (2006: 6–8) have emphasized the distinction between informal behaviour and informal institutions. In other words, not all non-rule-bound behaviour constitutes an informal institution. A formal rule might not be observed, but that does not mean that deviant behaviour is guided by a different institution or set of rules. Therefore, the challenge is to distinguish between non-rule-bound behaviour according to a formal institution and behaviour according to an informal institution. How to distinguish between informal behaviour and institutions, and the problems this raises for institutionalist approaches, has not been discussed at all.

It is therefore impossible to avoid the conclusion that neopatrimonialism remains poorly operationalized for empirical research. The indicators or properties that have been put forward for this purpose are very 'soft' and ill defined and it is therefore difficult to establish whether or not the concept is able to 'catch' the phenomenon it claims to describe.

The significance of the political and administrative sphere

The most recent operationalizations of neopatrimonialism focus on the political dimension of the concept, which means that they focus on only one dimension and tend to ignore the second: the administrative dimension. Claiming that a political system is neopatrimonial based on observing only its political side may be highly misleading. One has to take into account that there might be strong patrimonial behaviour in the political sphere, while the public administration operates largely according to legal-rational bureaucratic principles. Put another way, focusing only on political issues conflates the two dimensions of government and governance, which, at least for analytical purposes, should be kept separate. The reason that maintaining this distinction is valuable is that the political sphere of government (and governance) is much less regulated by formal rule than the administrative sphere. The government proper, which is the arena of politicians who might be elected, nominated, or self-nominated by force, is not entirely sub-mitted to legal-rational bureaucratic rule, not even in a democracy. Most of the political decisions are at the discretion of the politicians, although they have to observe certain procedural rules and some basic values and norms that are embedded in the constitution. The sphere of the admin-istration – the state bureaucracy and its administrative staff – is much more closely regulated by legal-rational bureaucratic rules.

This distinction between governmental spheres is perfectly at one with Weber's concept of rational domination: 'There are very important types of rational domination which, with respect to the [head of administrative staff], belong to other types ... ; this is true of the hereditary charismatic type ... and of a pure charismatic type of a president chosen by plebiscite' (Weber 1978: 219, 222, own translation). The implication is: 'at the top of a bureaucratic organisation, there is necessarily an element which is at least not purely bureaucratic' (Weber 1980: 126, own translation). Presidents, prime ministers, and cabinet ministers are not proper 'officials' (*Beamte*) within the legal-rational bureaucracy, which requires staff to have technical qualifications. Membership in a ministerial cabinet requires 'political' qualifications only; the nomination of cabinet members is usually left to the discretion of the head of government, and the number of cabinet members is usually not regulated by the constitution (only the nomination procedure is prescribed). This means there is always a personal or patrimonial dimension in even the most advanced or pure type of legal-rational bureaucratic domination. There is, however, a differ-ence between authoritarian and democratic regimes as regards to the scope of the personal or patrimonial sphere: a democratically elected leader or head of government is subjected to legal-rational rules himself (the rule of law) much more than an authoritarian ruler (for a discussion of these issues, see the next section).

We therefore need a separate analysis of each of the two dimensions of government: first, the conduct of political office and, second, the conduct of bureaucratic office. For the first, the well-known criteria that allow the distinction between authoritarian and democratic governance can be applied. For the second, one might use specific indicators that allow administrative behaviour to be assessed – for example, a list provided by Max Weber – although these are clearly not exhaustive. To do this an analysis of how the bureaucracy operates is required. Hence, we have to establish how far the stipulated rules are observed, how the offi-cials concur with their formal obligations of the legal-rational roles, and to what extent and frequency they deviate from the conception of their role. This should provide an answer to the question of the degree to which formal bureaucratic behaviour is routinized *vis-à-vis* informal behaviour. Yet so far hardly any studies of neopatrimonialism have included an analysis of the functioning of the state administration proper, with the exception of von Soest (2009, 2007), who tried to assess the legal-rational and neopatrimonial behaviour of the tax administration in Zambia and Botswana.

The problem of subtypes

Since neopatrimonialism can have different empirical manifestations – closer to patrimonialism or closer to legal-rational domination – and these may have different effects, authors have suggested the formation of subtypes in order to increase the analytical power of the concept (Snyder and

Mahoney 1999: 112, 118; Erdmann and Engel 2007: 114). Although no elaborated subtypes have been suggested or developed yet within African Studies, a number of scholars of Central Asian studies have made an attempt to differentiate the concept for classificatory purposes based on Bratton and van de Walle's discussion, and have developed the following subtypes (Fisun 2003; Gawrich and Franke 2009):

- *Sultanistic neopatrimonialism* has a very strong concentration of power in an impermeable narrow circle of power elites. There is low or no elite competition.
- *Oligarchic neopatrimonialism* may be characterized by rent-seeking cycles, which may be linked with government institutions. There may be strong competition between these groups.
- *Bureaucratic neopatrimonialism* shows a monopolization of power, which is based on informality in bureaucracy. State mechanisms are dominated by bureaucracy (parallel to weak parliaments), especially due to the lack of party power.
- *Soft neopatrimonialism* is defined as governance systems, which are already based on less informal mechanisms. Accordingly strong competition is expected.

(Adapted from Gawrich and Franke 2009: 5)

A major advantage of this typology is that it uses Weberian terminology, which fits with the conceptual roots of neopatrimonialism. However, the two major challenges for each typology – first, exclusiveness (are the types sufficiently distinctive or specific?), and second, exhaustiveness (are they sufficiently inclusive?) – are not so neatly addressed. The 'exhaustiveness' criterion is not such a problem in this case, as the four types cover a wide empirical range that spans from the first type, which is close to patrimonialism, to the fourth type, which is close to legal-rational bureaucratic rule (although the authors need to do more to explain exactly where the dividing lines between these categories lie in practice).

The 'exclusiveness' of the typology is more of a problem. The explication of the different types comes in the form of very short descriptions and the phrasing is not very precise ('competition may be strong'). Another problem is that one particular subtype is defined through an economic behaviour: 'rent-seeking'. Is this a behaviour that is relevant for neopatrimonialism only? Why is it a feature of only one subtype? More fundamentally, while 'informality in the bureaucracy' is a defining attribute of neopatrimonialism, how can this be used as a defining attribute of one subtype? There is no in-depth discussion of these issues. As a result, the subtypes proposed by Gawrich and Franke are not sufficiently specific in their definitions or consistent in the criteria they specify to be effectively applied to empirical research.

The most recent suggestion of 'regulated and predatory forms of neopatrimonialism' based on African cases (Bach 2011: 277–79; see also Bach 2012) is not very helpful either, as it suffers from all the same familiar problems mentioned above; in particular, it once again conflates patrimonialism with neopatrimonialism and remains vague about how to distinguish between these two 'forms'.

Neopatrimonialism and regime types

Another contentious issue is the debate about how neopatrimonialism relates to the classical regime types. There are several questions related to the issue. First, is neopatrimonialism a regime type of its own? Second, how does neopatrimonialism relate to democratic and/or authoritarian regimes? Often the application of the concept suggests that neopatrimonialism is a type of its own, a hybrid type of regime somewhere between democracy and dictatorship. At the same time, there seems to be an agreement that neopatrimonial domination belongs to the realm of non-democratic regimes. However, only a few authors explicitly address this question. Critical discussions of the concept claim that it is not a regime type of its own (Erdmann and Engel 2007: 111; Pitcher *et al.* 2009: 126). However, this raises further contentious questions: Is it possible to have a neopatrimonial democracy? Would such a regime be a hybrid regime or a defective democracy? Is it possible to observe a non-neopatrimonial autocracy – or is this a contradiction in terms?

Democracy is closely linked to the rule of law and thus dependent on a functioning legal-rational bureaucracy and its rules (VonDoepp, this volume). Consequently, legal-rational domination finds its logical incarnation in a democratic framework. However, as mentioned above, even the purest type of legal-rational bureaucratic domination accommodates some patrimonial elements as well. Along with many other political scientists, I would argue that liberal democracy and neopatrimonialism are not compatible with each other – by definition they exclude each other – but that neopatrimonialism may be compatible with defective democracies (see van de Walle, this volume).

Ann Pitcher and her colleagues have challenged this view. They argue with the example of Botswana that liberal democracy and neopatrimonialism are compatible: the political regime is 'neopatrimonial, yet democratic' (Pitcher *et al.* 2009: 144). They acknowledge that elections are widely regarded as fair and substantially free of fraud, and although elections have not resulted in a handover of power to an opposition party, the latter were able to secure lower-level election victories. Quoting the Botswana expert Kenneth Good (1992), they describe the regime as an 'open elite democracy' in which patrimonialism has not been abandoned by the elite. The elite has built a 'democratic state on the foundation of traditional and highly personalised reciprocities and loyalties' (Pitcher *et al.* 2009: 145).

The point of disagreement here is foremost not an empirical but rather a conceptual one (from which empirical problems arise). The conceptual problem is twofold. Like many others, Pitcher and her colleagues do not clearly explicate how they distinguish between a neopatrimonial and a legal-rational bureaucratic form of domination or define the concept of liberal democracy. In other words, the real question is whether or not Botswana should be called a 'democracy'. Without going into details, one way out of this disagreement would be to agree that if an increasing 'share' of patrimonialism impacts, for example, the practice of the rule of law, *even if the electoral regime as the core regime of a democracy is unaffected*, one would want to call the country in question not a liberal democracy but a defective or more precisely an 'illiberal', 'delegative', or 'electoral' democracy (Merkel 2004; O'Donnell 1994; Freedom House 2011). If we follow this line of reasoning, a defective democracy might be compatible with a weak ('low-intensity') kind of neopatrimonialism, but this would not be true of liberal democracies. Of course, here again the crucial question is how most accurately to distinguish between a liberal and an illiberal democracy.

Although neopatrimonialism may not be compatible with liberal democracy, authoritarian rule should not be equated with neopatrimonialism. There is considerable evidence that a legal-rational bureaucracy can exist within an authoritarian regime, which, for example, might have a corporatist character, as in many cases in Latin America. Another classic example of non-neopatrimonial authoritarianism is Germany during the second half of the nineteenth century, during which the country was largely governed by a legal-rational bureaucracy and the rule of law, although this version of the rule of law was not based on basic political or human rights. Hence, various possible combinations of the type of regime and the type of bureaucracy are possible, which demonstrates how important it is to differentiate and devote attention to the two spheres of government: the political and the bureaucratic.

Significantly, clarifying how different authoritarian regimes function is crucial if we are accurately to assess their chances of successfully democratizing. Bratton and van de Walle (1994) make this point well with regards to the different outcomes of transitions in Africa. They argue that transitions in Latin America and in Southern and Eastern Europe took place in authoritarian regimes that were corporatist in nature, while authoritarian regimes in Africa were distinctly neopatrimonial, which provided a major institutional impediment to democratic consolidation. In fact, while the majority of Latin American countries succeeded in establishing at least defective democracies, in Africa democratic transitions were much less successful. Based on a few cases in Africa, Asia, and Latin America, Snyder (1992; see also Brownlee 2002) made a similar argument when he observed that transitions from neopatrimonial authoritarian regimes tend to result in non-democratic rule.

Conclusion

Neopatrimonialism is still characterized by several conceptual weaknesses: it lacks a clear and useful definition; there is no delineation to other related concepts; and it is poorly operationalized. Discussions of the concept are often one-sided and unbalanced, and no convincing subtypes have yet been developed. One consequence of these flaws is that it is difficult, if not impossible, to identify and clearly explain why or why not a regime should be described as neopatrimonial. All this makes it problematic to use the concept in empirical research. However, the term maintains its heuristic value by directing our attention to the unresolved problem of how to investigate the widespread phenomenon of the interaction between formal institutions and informal behaviour and/or institutions in politics. To overcome these limitations, further conceptual elaboration is required.

Note

1 For the translation of the German *Herrschaft*, both 'domination' and 'authority' are used alternatively by Weber's translators and editors.

Bibliography

Bach, D.C. (2011) 'Patrimonialism and Neopatrimonialism: Comparative Trajectories and Readings', *Commonwealth and Comparative Politics* 49(3): 275–94.
——(2012) 'Patrimonialism and Neopatrimonialism. Comparative Receptions and Transcriptions', in D.C. Bach and M. Gazibo (eds) *Neopatrimonialism in Africa and Beyond*, London: Routledge.
Bauer, G. and Taylor, S.D. (2005) *Politics in Southern Africa: State and Society in Transition*, Boulder, CO: Lynne Rienner Publishers.
Bayart, J.-F. (1993) *The State in Africa: The Politics of the Belly*, London: Longman.
Bratton, M. and van de Walle, N. (1994) 'Neopatrimonial Regimes and Political Transitions in Africa', *World Politics* 26(4): 453–89.
——(1997) *Democratic Experiments in Africa*, Cambridge: Cambridge University Press.
Brownlee, J. (2002) 'And Yet They Persist: Explaining Survival and Transition in Neopatrimonial Regimes', *Studies in Comparative International Development* 37(3): 35–63.
Chabal, P. and Daloz, J.-P. (1999) *Africa Works: Disorder as Political Instrument*, Oxford: James Currey.
Clapham, C. (1982) 'Clientelism and the State', in C. Clapham (ed.) *Private Patronage and Public Power: Political Clientelism in the Modern State*, London: Frances Pinter.
——(1985) *Third World Politics*, London: Helm.
de Grassi, A. (2008) '"Neopatrimonialism" and Agricultural Development in Africa: Contributions and Limitations of a Contested Concept', *African Studies Review* 51(3): 107–33.
Eisenstadt, S.N. (1973) *Traditional Patrimonialism and Modern Neopatrimonialism*, London: Sage Publications.
Englebert, P. (2000) 'Pre-Colonial Institutions, Post-Colonial States, and Economic Development in Tropical Africa', *Political Research Quarterly* 53: 7–36.
Erdmann, G. and Engel, U. (2007) 'Neopatrimonialism Reconsidered: Critical Review and Elaboration of an Elusive Concept', *Commonwealth and Comparative Politics* 45(1): 95–119.

Fisun, O. (2003) 'Developing Democracy or Competitive Neopatrimonialism? The Political Regime of Ukraine in Comparative Perspective', paper presented at the Centre for Russian and Eastern European Studies, University of Toronto, Toronto, 24 October 2003, www.utoronto.ca/jacyk/Fisun-CREES-workshop.pdf (accessed 28 January 2011).

Freedom House (2011) 'Analysis: Freedom in the World. Draft FIW Front Page 2010 Edition', www.freedom house.org/template.cfm?page=351&ana_page=363&year=2010 (accessed 30 January 2011).

Gawrich, A. and Franke, A. (2009) 'Informal Institutions and Negative Stability in Post-Soviet Rentier States – The Cases of Kazakhstan and Azerbaijan', paper presented at the 5th ECPR General Conference, Panel 215, Section 24, on 'Informal institutions in the age of globalization – different world regions compared', Potsdam, 10–12 September.

Good, K. (1992) 'Interpreting the Exceptionality of Botswana', *Journal of Modern African Studies* 30(1): 69–95.

Helmke, G. and Levitzky, S. (2006) 'Introduction', in G. Helmke and S. Levitzky (eds) *Informal Institutions and Democracy: Lessons from Latin America*, Baltimore, MD: Johns Hopkins University Press.

Hydén, G. (2006) *African Politics in Comparative Perspective*, Cambridge: Cambridge University Press.

Landé, C.H. (1983) 'Political Clientelism in Political Studies. Retrospect and Prospects', *International Political Science Review* 4(4): 435–54.

Le Vine, V.T. (1980) 'African Patrimonial Regimes in Comparative Perspective', *Journal of Modern African Studies* 18: 657–73.

Lindberg, S.I. (2006) *Democracy and Elections in Africa*, Baltimore, MD: Johns Hopkins University Press.

Médard, J.F. (1982) 'The Underdeveloped State in Africa: Political Clientelism or Neo-patrimonialism?' in C. Clapham (ed.) *Private Patronage and Public Power*, London: Frances Pinter.

Merkel, W. (2004) 'Embedded and Defective Democracies', *Democratization* 11(5): 33–58.

O'Donnell, G. (1994) 'Delegative Democracy', *Journal of Democracy* 5(1): 55–69.

Olukoshi, A.O. (1998) '*The Elusive Prince of Denmark: Structural Adjustment and the Crisis of Governance in Africa*', Research Report No. 104, Uppsala: Nordiska Afrikainstitutet.

——(1999) 'State Conflict and Democracy in Africa: The Complex Process of Renewal', in R. Joseph (ed.) *Conflict and Democracy in Africa*, Boulder, CO, and London: Lynne Rienner Publishers.

Pitcher, A., Moran, M.H. and Johnston, M. (2009) 'Rethinking Patrimonialism and Neopatrimonialism in Africa', *African Studies Review* 52(1): 125–56.

Posner, D.N. and Young, D.J. (2007) 'The Institutionalisation of Political Power in Africa', *Journal of Democracy* 18(3): 126–40.

Roth, G. (1987) *Politische Herrschaft und persönliche Freiheit*, Frankfurt am Main: Suhrkamp.

Snyder, R. (1992) 'Explaining Transitions form Neopatrimonial Dictatorships', *Comparative Politics* 24(4): 379–400.

Snyder, R. and Mahoney, J. (1999) 'The Missing Variable: Institutions and the Study of Regime Change', *Comparative Politics* 32(1): 103–22.

Solt, F. (2001) 'Institutional Effects on Democratic Transitions: Neo-Patrimonial Regimes in Africa, 1989–94', *Studies in Comparative International Development* 36(2): 82–91.

Theobald, R. (1982) 'Patrimonialism: Research Note', *World Politics* 34(4): 548–59.

van de Walle, N. (2001) *African Economies and the Politics of Permanent Crisis, 1979–1999*, New York, NY: Cambridge University Press.

von Soest, C. (2007) 'How does Neopatrimonialism Affect the African State? The Case of Tax Collection in Zambia', *Journal of Modern African Studies* 45(4): 621–45.

——(2009) *The African State and Its Revenues*, Baden-Baden: Nomos Verlag.

Weber, M. (1978) *Economy and Society: An Outline of Interpretive Sociology*, with G. Roth and C. Wittich (eds) Berkeley, CA, and London: University of California Press.

——(1980) *Wirtschaft und Gesellschaft*, fifth edition ed. by J. Winckelmann, Tübingen: Mohr.

6

THE INFORMAL PRACTICES
OF CIVIL SERVANTS

Jean-Pierre Olivier de Sardan

One area of consensus in the sea of literature on African states, governments, and public services is the significant divergence between the *official norms* that govern these institutions and the *actual behaviour* of their employees, regardless of whether the literature emanates from the field of political science, anthropology, sociology, or administrative science, and regardless of the theoretical currents present and scientific positions taken in this literature. Across the board there is acknowledgement that legislation, regulations, procedures, specifications, and organizational structures, all of which have largely been patterned on Western models, are rarely adhered to by government officials and users alike (see Erdmann; VonDoepp, both this volume).

There is no doubt that in any social institution, in any country, and at any time, divergences exist between norms and practices. However, the scope and form of these divergences vary considerably depending on the context. In the case of public sector jobs in Africa, this divergence is particularly sharp and becomes manifest in a variety of forms. Most assessments of these processes are normative and evaluative. The divergence between official norms and actual behaviour is usually critiqued on the basis of value judgements. 'Poor governance' is condemned, as is corruption, ethnic allegiance, or clientelism, with implicit reference being made to the democratic and technocratic model of Northern countries, which is often idealized.

However, beyond this somewhat accusatory and Western-centric subtext, divergences between norms and practices among African government officials are also the object of various scholarly works, although empirical studies have unfortunately been scarce until recently. It is true that there is a huge contrast between the literature on the sociology of organizations, which has developed grounded analysis of the actual behaviour of civil servants in Europe, and the lack of such studies in Africa, but this contrast is becoming less and less pronounced.[1] For many reasons, corruption has been undoubtedly the most frequent entry point for empirically studying informal practices of civil servants: corruption is obviously 'breaking' the rules of bureaucracies, ignoring the law of the state, and departing from the official norms with which civil servants are supposed to comply.

Corruption

In most African countries, corruption is now systemic and omnipresent, in the form of 'petty corruption', which takes place between civil servants and citizens, and in the form of 'big corruption', which involves senior civil servants, members of parliament (MPs), members of the government, international companies, and so on. While 'big corruption' is opaque and quite impenetrable, to be investigated by policemen, judges, or newsmen, petty corruption is a typical job for anthropologists: it is a visible daily practice involving rank and file actors which is open to everyone, situated as it is at the interface between 'street level bureaucrats' (Lipsky 1980) and users of public services. For the social sciences, the word 'corruption' is little more than an entry point to the study informal practices, which are against the law from a legal point of view.

> In order to take into account this overlap between corrupt practices and all of the 'real' everyday practices of state services, we adopted the broadest possible acceptation of the 'complex of corruption' and one which is far removed from strictly legal definitions, i.e. all practices involving the use of public of office that is improper, i.e. illegal and/or illegitimate from the perspective of the regulations in force or from that of users, and gives rise to undue personal gain.
>
> *(Blundo and Olivier de Sardan 2006: 6)*

Daily corruption is at the core of many of the informal behaviours of civil servants. This systemic corruption has multiple forms: commissions for illicit services (the payment of money to officials for unjustified favours that are granted to the user, most commonly at the expense of the public purse); unwarranted fees for public services (undue remuneration that is given in exchange for rendering public services to which one is anyway entitled and which are supposed to be carried out 'free of charge'); more or less 'required' gratuities (gratitude has to be shown to a public official who has 'done his work well' by offering 'something'); string-pulling (favouritism, cronyism, and 'recommendations', which result in a general exchange of favours); tributes and tolls (levies are extorted, the service supplied being legal or illegal); sidelines (the use of company materials and resources by workers for the completion of private paid work); and misappropriations (illegal appropriation – or theft – of public commodities). The list goes on. The first four forms (commission, unwarranted fee, gratuity, and string-pulling) involve *transactions* of either a monetary or material nature, or transactions that are based on personal or identity-based ties. This does not apply to the last three forms, which instead involve forms of extortion (toll) or privative appropriation of public goods (sideline and misappropriation). These multiple forms are often interlinked. In other words they are hybrid and ambiguous patterns frequently entangled in daily reality: the *ex post* gratuity may be 'expected' or 'solicited' in a way that is more akin to a form of unwarranted fee or commission; the over-billing of a medical service may involve not only a levy, but also an unwarranted fee and, similarly, the 'toll' may conceal a commission.

Corruption unites people in continuous business relationships and leads to a kind of 'informal privatization' of the state, insofar as a government official does not do his work, or any work, unless he gets a direct remuneration from the user or the colleague. Corruption structures itself according to organized and even reciprocal networks (the police officer must give 'his share' to the sergeant, who gives his to the police chief; the trader importing goods has 'his' custom officer, as well as the truck driver); it can be punctual, dyadic, and regular.

Links may also exist between monetary and non-monetary transactions. For example, a commission or toll may also be paid in kind: if a 'development project' finances the renovation of a minister's house, it may be interpreted not only as a form of 'misappropriation', but also as either a 'commission' that is paid so that the minister will play the role of intermediary, enabling the project to benefit from favours granted by the administration, or a toll that is paid to secure the simple freedom to operate.

Certain aspects of such transactions are more or less spontaneous, at least from the perspective of the actors involved. This is most clearly the case when corruption takes the form of gratuities and string-pulling. Others are the outcome of negotiation and bargaining, which is the case with commissions and, sometimes, unwarranted fees; and others again are an expression of an outright power relationship, for example the toll. In previous work, we also noted that all of these forms of corruption are viewed ambiguously, depending on whether the informant has a direct or indirect relationship with the practice in question. Everyone disapproves of it in some contexts, but everyone lends legitimacy to it in other contexts.[2] Nonetheless, this does not prevent each individual form of corruption from occupying a specific place on the scale of legitimacy/illegitimacy.

Popular semiology conveys very well the multiple dimensions of corruption and its daily omnipresence: *'The goat grazes where it is tied.'* *'The one who pounds always keeps a mouthful for himself.'* One has to give *'the money for the ingredients of the sauce'*, *'to put a stone on a file, so that it does not fly away'*, *'to lubricate the mouth'*.

Corruption is also omnipresent in the perceptions of people about administrations. This leads to a vicious circle: if people assume (or are convinced) that the civil servants they have to deal with are corrupt and respond only in venal terms, civil servants are likely to react and behave accordingly, often by taking advantage of corrupt offers and therefore further reinforcing existing popular attitudes. However, this does not mean that there is a complete absence of rules and regulations, or that corrupt practices are merely a matter of the 'law of the market' or simple power relations. On the contrary, everyday corruption is a social activity that is regulated *de facto* and in accordance with complex rules and is tightly controlled by a series of tacit codes that differ significantly from public codes and official or legal norms. This is also true of other non-corrupt, informal practices of civil servants.

The embeddedness of corruption in daily practices of civil servants

Corruption does not take place in a world of its own and corrupt transactions can often not easily be differentiated from non-corrupt practices. For example, it may be hard to know where to draw the line between legitimate commission and tips on one hand, and illegal *pots-de-vin* such as bribes on the other hand. Corruption is embedded in the day-to-day routine of civil servants to such an extent that it often becomes difficult to distinguish between corrupted practices and the everyday informal practices through which the civil service operates. To see this, let us consider some key characteristics of African bureaucracies.

Clientelism

Although no administration is monolithic, and civil servants are not all alike, some informal practices are very common in most African administrations. For instance, the numerous phenomena of factional solidarity, patronage, bonds of affiliation, and partisan preference that one meets daily at all levels of African administrative services could be grouped into the category of clientelism. Thus, appointments, assignments, promotions, or pushing 'somebody on one's side' often follows the rather systematic logics of network building and of individualized protection and redistribution, which has little to do with duly established profiles of positions or competence criteria.

The formal and the real

Organization charts, official texts, regulations, schedules, and plans are far from lacking in African administrations and suggest the contours of an integrated and functional bureaucratic world. Yet reality is different and is very far from this smooth image. For instance, the tasks carried out are not the ones that were planned; the agents do things other than those for which they are officially recruited and paid; voluntary and other informal back-up agents, not of the formal payroll, assume and perform a considerable part of the regular tasks; budgets are purely fictional; or posted instructions are never respected. The real daily functioning of any administrative service in most African countries cannot be inferred from the written guidelines governing it.

The 'each one for oneself-ism'

In spite of slogans and stereotypes praising community solidarity, African administrations are the kingdom of the 'each one for oneself-ism'. In the administrative services, teamwork is more or less unknown: no one interferes in his/her colleague's work. Meetings involving collective discussions aimed at improving quality or work effectiveness are extremely rare. Each acts in a kind of 'bubble' (two or three people can, of course, professionally live together in the same bubble) wherein no outsiders penetrate. Everyone applies the proverb '*If you go through a village of one-eyed people, close an eye and walk!*'

'Areas of suspicion'

Any form of collective action immediately gives rise to considerable suspicion, rumours, and accusations, from inside as well as from outside. There is hardly a head of department who is not potentially corrupted, partial, or partisan in the eyes of his collaborators and subordinates. Similarly, any decision of a judge is automatically suspected of having been taken to please *X*, or because *Y* offered a bribe-containing 'envelope'. We cannot say anything about the truthfulness of all these accusations: some are probably unfounded or slanderous. What remains confirmed, however, is the extent of these 'areas of suspicion' in the administrative service; significantly, they militate against the construction of the minimal relations of trust or safety that are necessary to the satisfactory delivery of public services.

'Privilegism'

Any position in the public services is first and foremost valued in terms of the access to privileges that it permits. Since the wages are derisory and never increasing almost anywhere, and as the commitment to the work itself is weak, the privileges – formal or informal, licit or illicit – make the difference. The goal is, to some extent, to extend these privileges to the utmost, as far as possible, sometimes immoderately, either because of the material interest, or because of the prestige they provide. The advantages of one's position are thus genuine markers of status and operate as signs of 'distinction' (in the sense of Bourdieu 1979) *vis-à-vis* colleagues, subordinates, and users.

Contempt for anonymous users

Whether in a public service, a post office, a registry office, a police station, or a medical centre, the anonymous user will make a bad start, likely finding himself in a hostile field. He believes he has to go round an assault course and nobody will help him, whereas in reality it is often quite the contrary. The civil servants regard him as an intruder and troublemaker, even as prey, and intend to be as little disturbed by him as possible. His ignorance of procedures does not invite help, but rather reprimand. Whereas the external social world privileges the values of propriety, hospitality,

73

and respect, the bureaucratic universe, on the contrary, seems to be based on the contempt of the user and, in particular, of his time.

The generalized exchange of favours

However, this contempt stops where the recommendations (for example, from a superior, a neighbour, or a family member) start. Any person directly or indirectly recommended is, on the contrary, rather well served, often at the expense of waiting anonymous users. For a relative or an acquaintance, the civil servant improves politeness and will ease the access to the required service, readily leaving his place to guide his host. The 'recommendation networks' are multiple: members of the extended family, neighbours, people originating in the same region, colleagues, former schoolmates, leisure mates, party comrades, and so on. The favour rendered won't necessarily be returned by the debtor, but by other acquaintances that will render services: this is why we can talk of a 'generalized exchange of favours'. You have to know somebody, or know somebody who knows somebody, in order to survive in an administrated territory. Faced with an administrative problem that needs to be solved, one does not try to find out about the procedure to be followed, but whom to see – who could pull the strings for you.

The 'culture of impunity'

The absence of real penalties for serious professional misconducts (such as embezzlement or corruption) is confirmed by empirical studies. The worst that can generally happen is re-assignment, a change of working place. Many heads of department told us they were unable to sanction an incompetent, negligent, or venal subordinate because any sanction immediately raises a flood of protestations and interventions in favour of the sanctioned agent. Such defences are mounted either in the name of solidarity or are a form of power struggle for patronage or clienteles, whether or not bound to political parties. We should add the fact that the indelicacies of each offender are well known to the other offenders and thus, vertically or horizontally, 'everybody has a hold over everybody else'. This helps us to understand why such a culture of impunity prevails nowadays.

Other logics

Of course, the above informal practices are not the only ones that can be identified. Individuals may also intervene on the basis of other logics (charity or pity, for instance) and of course African civil servants sometimes follow official norms and behave partly in conformity with bureaucratic rules. The acknowledgement of competence, merit-based promotions, legal-rational logics, deference to professional ethics, and respect for procedures are not uncommon – even if they are exceptions – or are mixed with opportunistic strategies. Also, 'islands of effectiveness' (Crook 2010) may be noticed here and there. We must keep in mind that as far as logics of action among civil servants are concerned, pluralism, code switching, and straddling are the rule. So we need new theoretical tools in order to understand more acutely how civil servants 'play' between formal practices and informal ones. Here the concept of 'practical norms' may help.

Practical norms

Let us begin with this starting point: the informal professional practices of public actors are neither anarchic nor random. Africa is not the continent of anomia; it is not 'Ubu's kingdom'. We should distrust the expression of 'failed states', too hastily used about Africa, which implies a world without structures and regulations. African states are true states, and informal practices of civil servants are structured and regulated. When informal practices lead individuals away from following official norms, they are following other norms. We term them *practical norms*. Practical norms are informal regulations, tacit or latent, underlying actors' practices when they do not follow official norms. They help to understand why and how informal practices converge and are not anarchic.

Practical norms always coexist with official norms. So, *the informal practices of civil servants in Africa are not the product of a lack of norms, but of an excess.* Of course, practical norms are not formalized, they are not even necessarily conscious and are scarcely expressed as such by social actors: they are more often than not automatic and routine, existing in a vein more implicit than explicit. One could even say – to use Bourdieu's (1992) expression – that these practical norms are incorporated into a *habitus*,[3] in that they are not directly seen. They are at times similar to linguistic norms. It is therefore the responsibility of the researcher to isolate, identify, and analyse them, based on the practices and views of the actors.

Such an approach, involving a multiplicity of practical norms coexisting with official norms, runs counter to the unifying interpretation of norms that has pervaded all social sciences since Durkheim's time, according to which members of the same society necessarily share common norms, either official or social. This conception is even more common where Africa is concerned: there are plenty of clichés and stereotypes about the absence of individuality and the pressure of community in Africa, and the weight of a so-called traditional African culture. This is the 'culturalist-traditionalist' argument. For many people, the informal practices of civil servants ignore official norms and actually follow social norms inherited from the African past, but practical norms are much more diverse, innovative, and syncretic than social (traditional) norms; they are more often than not modern outcomes, produced inside the African administrative world through interactions between civil servants and users and between civil servants themselves as the product of a contemporary history in which colonization looms large.

There is no shortage of examples in which it is not possible to attribute the current practices of public officials (which are not in line with professional norms) to surrounding social norms and 'African cultures'. Take, for example, a very topical case. Virtually everywhere in Africa nurses are well known for the disdain they show toward patients from poor backgrounds. This attitude has been highlighted in numerous studies (Jaffré and Olivier de Sardan 2003; Jewkes *et al.* 1998). The odds are very high that in a hospital in Bamako, Niamey, or Conakry, a young nurse who receives an elderly female patient in a threadbare *pagne* (loincloth) from the rural area will show no consideration for her, will not greet her, or even ask her to take a seat. Such an attitude is completely at variance with the respect accorded to the elderly in 'African cultures', in other words with traditional norms of decorum. It also represents a departure from what is taught in medical faculties and from the respect that should be accorded to the sick.

In the same vein, what we have termed 'each one for oneself-ism' is a practical norm. This widespread lack of teamwork in public services norm is not a social (traditional) norm. Indeed, it seems quite difficult to incorporate 'each-for-oneself-ism' into traditional African culture. Thus when the practices of public officials in Africa do not follow official norms, they do not necessarily follow social (traditional) norms either. Practical norms in the public sphere should not be confused with social norms in the private sphere, even if some links of course do exist. Social norms (as moral norms, kinship norms, and propriety norms) are visible and openly prescriptive. They are present in social relations just as official norms are in the public space. They are publicly told and taught in the framework of institutions and organizations (for instance churches or brotherhoods for religious norms, or family for courtesy norms), so they are not informal at all. They are formalized in teachings, dogmas, codes, moral standards, precepts, and so on. By contrast, practical norms are truly informal because they are absent from the public discourse and absent from official moral rhetoric and teaching. They informally regulate practices that diverge from both official and social norms.

In Africa, the school of legal pluralism (Moore 1978; Benda-Beckmann 1981) has rightly underlined the multiplicity of norms, but it has been only concerned by the coexistence of official laws with various social norms, used in daily life as quasi laws, and highly formalized. Legal pluralism has been most widely illustrated in the context of land tenure: thus, in the Sahelian countries, one observes the coexistence of 'Western' land law, Islamic law, and various customary rights (*cf.* VonDoepp, this volume). This is an example of pluralism of norms, where official bureaucratic norms coexist with social norms, the latter being sometimes recognized by the state. However, the school of legal pluralism ignored both the gap between official norms and informal practices in the public domain and the gap between social norms and real practices in the private one.

This is why the concept of practical norms is useful and important. Practical norms can never be separated from official norms: we should always remember that civil servants 'play' between official norms and practical norms, according to contexts, personal options, and the type of interactions. To navigate this terrain, civil servants may develop opportunistic strategies as well as follow ethical precepts, or may react to 'taken-for-granted expectations', and adopt what March and Olsen (1984) have called *rules of appropriateness* (to behave in a way that seems appropriate to the context). Practical norms are resources for actors as well as constraints.

Many combinations of practical norms and official ones are to be found in Africa, from complementarity or substitution to antagonism. In the bureaucratic world in which we are interested, three types can be distinguished:

- Sometimes practical norms are not so far away from official norms and derive from the room for interpretation that surrounds official norms. These are *adaptive practical norms*. Giorgio Blundo has given examples of many informal 'arrangements' imagined by environmental agents in Senegal and Niger *(Eaux et Forêts)* to make the service functional despite operating in a context of deprivation (Blundo 2011).
- Sometimes practical norms contravene and disobey official norms. These are *breaking practical norms*. Many types of corruption are cases in point.
- Sometimes practical norms oppose official norms and present themselves as counter-norms. These are *rebel practical norms*. The 'everyday peasant resistances', to use James Scott's (1986) expression and for which we have many examples since colonization, are rebel practical norms.

So what are official norms and practical norms about? To answer this question we must consider the core administrative tasks and duties in order to link civil servants' practices with their institutional settings.

Bureaucratic mode of governance and professional cultures of civil servants

Civil servants are supposed to provide public goods and services, directly or indirectly. Most official norms are professional norms revolving around this service delivery. Most informal practices concern service delivery, and so do practical norms, but in Africa there are in fact many configurations of service delivery, many configurations of official norms (many institutional settings), and, of course, many types of games that can be played between official norms and practical norms in the course of service delivery. In other words, official norms and practical norms are embedded in different modes of governance. The complex articulation of a multiplicity of modes of governance is with no doubt a specificity of the African context.

Taking the concept of governance in a purely descriptive and analytical sense, we can define a mode of governance as *any organized method of delivering public or collective services and goods according to specific set of norms (official and practical), and to specific forms of authority and legitimacy.* This definition of governance enables us to complete the traditional social anthropological approach to the state in Africa, which, most of the time, has ignored the role of the state as the deliverer of goods and services and as the manager of this delivery (or more specifically as co-deliverer and co-manager alongside other institutions) in favour of a focus on other functions of the state that are already well known, most notably the despotic or repressive functions (typically Foucault or Scott are abundantly quoted). However, even in undemocratic Africa the 'repressive state' does not exhaust all the functions of the state. We must also consider the African state as a provider of services (the 'delivery state'). This approach is much more productive when considering the actual practices of civil servants. Of course, this is not a statement on the quality of service delivery. In fact, according to most users, the services delivered are of bad quality. This definition of governance has another advantage: it takes into account the diversity of modes of governance in Africa. Today, thanks to structural adjustment, neo-liberal policies, or commitment to 'civil society', more and more public or collective goods or services are delivered in Africa by other institutions than the state and its bureaucracy: development agencies, non-governmental organizations (NGOs), community-based organizations, chiefdoms, the private sector, and so on.

> There is no longer any public service in Africa whose deliverance does not include the greater or lesser involvement of the four following instances: the state administrative services, the development administration (NGOs and international agencies), the 'community-type' organizations (from associations to the municipal council), and private operators.
>
> *(Blundo and Le Meur 2009: 15)*

The coexistence of many modes of governance, on the local level as well the national, is a central characteristic of African countries. The process of 'stacking up' modes of governance in local arenas has become generalized: when a new form of political authority or type of management is set up (either by the state or by development agencies) it does not substitute for the layers of institutionality already in place but adds to them. None of them has truly disappeared, but all have been recycled and reconstituted, interlinked and interwoven.

The consequence is that the bureaucratic mode of governance coexists and interacts today with many other modes. Civil servants have lost the monopoly of delivering public goods and services and should collaborate with other actors (development agents, activists, local 'big men', NGOs' leaders, chiefs, entrepreneurs, and so on), whose behaviour is regulated by other patterns, formal or informal.

Empirical studies show that at least eight modes of governance may be distinguished in African contexts today (Olivier de Sardan 2011): the bureaucratic mode (services provided by the state apparatus); the municipal mode (services provided by local governments and city councils); the associational mode (services provided by management boards, cooperatives, community-based organizations, local associations); the chiefly mode (services provided by traditional or neo-traditional chiefs); the project-based mode (services provided by development projects); the sponsorship-based mode (services provided by 'big men'); the religious mode (services provided by churches or brotherhoods); and the merchant mode (services provided by private operators).

This diversity of modes of governance can be apprehended not only externally (several 'modes of governance' coexist), but also internally (a single mode of governance involves different players, institutions and rules of the games). Inside the bureaucratic mode of governance we have a multiplicity of professions, each one with specific competencies, knowledge, and duties, delivering very different services. In rural Africa, for instance, there is a strong distinction between, on the one side, very diverse technical professions (nurses and doctors, teachers, hydraulics specialists, and agricultural extension agents), and, on the other, the official actors representing the state sovereignty (from governors and district administrators to policemen).

Each profession within the bureaucratic mode of governance has its own *professional culture*, which includes official norms specific to this profession as well as local practical norms, but also reflects the training process, division of labour, management patterns, international connections, and tricks of the trade. It follows that informal practices in African administrations are shared to some degree by more or less all civil servants, whatever their domain of activity (they are common to the bureaucratic mode of governance), but are also specific to particular professions and vary according to professional cultures and local settings.[4] For example, the contempt toward anonymous users is widespread among bureaucrats, but features of the 'negotiation process' with traders are distinctive of custom officers.

Conclusion

This normative pluralism as manifested in Africa is not fundamentally different from what various currents in modern sociology and anthropology have described: from the diffuse and interactive mechanisms by which norms and practices are continually produced and recomposed in the countries of the North. The sociology of organizations, work, and professions all share an epistemological position that accords an active role to social actors and are concerned by the gap between public norms and regulated practices. In Africa, however, the extent of the gap, the style of the informal practices, and the registers of practical norms are of course distinctive.

One of the modalities of the famous and unacceptable 'great divide' between North and South would be falsely to assume that in the North norms and practices are ceaselessly produced, questioned, and recomposed through interactive processes, while maintaining that in Africa they take the form of a cultural traditional determinism that continues to impose itself on behaviour. Our firm position is that the advances of the social sciences in Europe must be taken into account in Africa, and that normative pluralism and the local production of practical norms in different modes of governance must be recognized. Indeed in several respects this normative pluralism and the local production of norms are actually – on the basis of empirical evidence and for historical reasons – more important in Africa than in Europe.

However, public administrations are not comfortable with normative pluralism. On the contrary, for political leaders and experts in management, an ideal administration is one that functions in complete conformity with coherent professional norms, without any significant divergences, following a perfectly designed logical frame. In such a world, the problem of informal practices would be non-existent. In an ideal administration divergences would be minimized as much as possible. This is exactly the dream of the international institutions and development agencies that engage with Africa. 'Good governance' approaches are based on the increase in and strengthening of official norms, and on the constant refinement of procedures to monitor their application. In order to improve the normative framework in Africa and boost its efficiency, this implies introducing New Public Management techniques (McCourt and Minogue 2001): more and more sophisticated technologies to manage and streamline public action, in ways that are increasingly quantified and computerized, in order to promote greater compliance of formal rules by public actors.

Nothing is less likely to take place. The weight of informal practices and practical norms in the bureaucratic mode of governance and the professional cultures of civil servants in Africa should not be underestimated, and they have the capacity to by-pass and undermine New Public Management techniques. One has good reason to doubt the success of such measures that are designed and implemented by 'reformers from the outside'. However, this does not mean that the situation will not change. Practical norms and professional culture are not homogeneous and may evolve along their own dynamics, which are more often than not different from donors' injunctions and the International Monetary Fund's conditionalities, but which may nevertheless improve step-by-step the quality of services delivered by public agents in Africa, even in an informal way.

Notes

1 Among the recent empirical studies in English on bureaucracies and civil servants in Africa, one may mention: Anders (2010); Bierschenk (2007, 2008); Blundo and Le Meur (2009); Blundo and Olivier de Sardan (2006); Chalfin (2010); Crook (2010); Therkildsen (2005). Publications in French are also growing.
2 For a detailed description of the everyday forms of corruption in Africa, as well as for a popular semiology of corruption, see Blundo and Olivier de Sardan (2006); this chapter relies heavily on chapter 3, which is written jointly with Giorgio Blundo. Regarding the 'moral economy of corruption', see Olivier de Sardan (1999).
3 'Habitus' refers to the set of socially learnt dispositions, skills, and ways of acting that are often taken for granted by 'insiders' and invisible to 'outsiders', and which are acquired through practice.
4 There are good illustrations of this at two levels: Anders (2010) has studied the core features of the common informal practices of civil servants in Malawi, while Chalfin (2010) has conducted a detailed study of custom officers in Ghana.

Bibliography

Anders, G. (2010) *In the Shadow of Good Governance: An Ethnography of Civil Reform in Africa*, Leiden: Brill.
Benda-Beckmann, K.V. (1981) 'Forum Shopping and Shopping Forums: Dispute Processing in a Minangkabau Village in West Sumatra', *Journal of Legal Pluralism and Unofficial Law* 19: 117–59.
Bierschenk, T. (2007) 'L'éducation de base en Afrique de l'Ouest francophone: Bien privé, bien public, bien global', in T. Bierschenk, G. Blundo, Y. Jaffré and M. Tidjani Alou (eds) *Une anthropologie entre rigueur et engagement: Essais autour de l'œuvre de Jean-Pierre Olivier de Sardan*, Paris: Karthala.
——(2008) 'The Everyday Functioning of an African Public Service: Informalization, Privatization and Corruption in Benin's Legal System', *Journal of Legal Pluralism and Unofficial Law* 57: 101–39.
Blundo, G. (2011) 'Une administration à deux vitesses: Projets de développement et construction de l'État au Sahel', *Cahiers d'Études Africaines* 202(203): 427–52.
Blundo, G. and Le Meur, P.Y. (eds) (2009) *The Governance of Daily Life in Africa: Ethnographic Explorations of Public and Collective Service*, Leiden: Brill.
Blundo, G. and Olivier de Sardan, J.P. (eds) (2006) *Everyday Corruption and the State: Citizens and Public Officials in Africa*, London: Zed Books.
Bourdieu, P. (1979) *La distinction: Critique sociale du jugement*, Paris: Éditions de Minuit.
——(with Wacquant, L.) (1992) *Réponses: Pour une anthropologie réflexive*, Paris: Seuil.
Chalfin, B. (2010) *Neo-liberal Frontiers: An Ethnography of Sovereignty in West Africa*, Chicago, IL: The University of Chicago Press.
Crook, R. (2010) 'Rethinking Civil Service Reform in Africa: "Islands of Effectiveness" and Organisational Commitment', *Commonwealth and Comparative Politics* 48(4): 479–504.

Jaffré, Y. and Olivier de Sardan, J.P. (eds) (2003) *Une médecine inhospitalière: Les difficiles relations entre soignants et soignés dans cinq capitales d'Afrique de l'Ouest*, Paris: Karthala.

Jewkes, R., Naeemah, A. and Zodumo, M. (1998) 'Why Do Nurses Abuse Patients? Reflections from South African Obstetric Services', *Social Science and Medicine* 47(11): 1781–95.

Jordan Smith, D. (2006) *A Culture of Corruption: Everyday Deception and Popular Discontent in Nigeria*, Princeton, NJ, and Oxford: Princeton University Press.

Lipsky, M. (1980) *Street-level Bureaucracy: Dilemma of the Individual in Public Services*, New York, NY: Russell-Sage Foundation.

McCourt, W. and Minogue, M. (eds) (2001) *The Internationalization of Public Management: Reinventing the Third World State*, Northampton, MA: Edward Elgar.

March, J. and Olsen, J.P. (1984) 'The New Institutionalism: Organisational Factors in Political Life', *American Political Science Review* 78(3): 734–49.

Moore, S.F. (1978) *Law as Process: An Anthropological Approach*, London: Routledge and Kegan Paul.

Olivier de Sardan, J.P. (1999) 'A Moral Economy of Corruption in Africa?' *The Journal of Modern African Studies* 37(1): 25–52.

——(2011) 'The Eight Modes of Local Governance in West Africa', *IDS Bulletin* 42(2): 22–31.

Reno, W. (1995) *Corruption and State Politics in Sierra Leone*, Cambridge: Cambridge University Press.

Scott, J. (1986) 'Everyday Forms of Peasant Resistance', *The Journal of Peasant Studies* 13(2): 5–35.

——(1990) *Domination and the Arts of Resistance: Hidden Transcripts*, London: Yale University Press.

Therkildsen, O. (2005) 'Understanding Public Management Through Neo-patrimonialism: A Paradigm for all African Seasons?' in U. Engel and G.R. Olsen (eds) *The African Exception*, Aldershot: Ashgate.

PART II

The politics of identity

7

CLASS POLITICS

Bill Freund

To use the concept of social class effectively in the African context requires some work not just defining, but in effect taking a position on, class and its validity. Just as culture dominates anthropological theory, sociological theory has no greater vessel than class with which to discuss human forms of integration. Yet, and of course precisely for this reason, using class today is deeply controversial. One representative view in a much used 'key ideas' series insisted that: '[t]he sociological significance of classes is that class relationships ... are the key to the social structure in general, and economic and political life in particular. It is in this sense that industrial capitalist nations, such as Britain and America, are still class societies' (Edgell 1993: 116).

By contrast, a contemporary pair of Australian sociologists considers that 'the intellectual armoury of class theory is about as useful for the contemporary social scene as a cavalry brigade in a tank battle' (Pakulski and Waters 1996: 152). Although we should also note their view that 'during the nineteenth and early twentieth century the social question of class was at the centre of the political agenda, class imagery was strong and clear and class identification was firm' (ibid.).

How can such opposing views both be seriously held? One obvious reason is that so many intellectuals are captivated by the breathtaking vision of Karl Marx that the proletarianized industrial workers would be the revolutionary force that would overcome alienation in the modern world. They would become more numerous and more homogeneous, and so the logic of their coming together culturally, socially, and politically to transcend the oppressive aspects of capital accumulation under capitalism would become ever stronger. Here, the Pakulski and Waters view has its merits; this is hardly how the world's historical trajectory looks today.

Marxist views of class under capitalism fitted the politics of the century after the writing of the *Communist Manifesto* far better than it does our own. The industrial proletariat is stagnant or declining in size globally, the situation of workers is increasingly heterogeneous, inequality is not such an important feature of some capitalist societies – especially where left-of-centre parties have legislated for equality – and classic worker political instruments and forms of organization have declined to the point that they struggle to have a purchase on the contemporary world. Nor is there a bourgeoisie hovering around a class of buccaneering capitalist owner-operators of firms. However, a meticulous study like Wright's *Class Counts* (1997) shows that it is still possible to comprehend industrial society in terms of class agendas as we consider mobility, skill levels, social identity, and even politics. Wright marries an abiding belief in the importance of class politically with an American tradition of empirical stratification studies. The value of this process in grasping social change over time, of not simply considering social categories independent of their place in the economy (or perhaps abandoning social categories entirely), seems patent even if class antagonisms are abandoned as the moving force in history.

In Africa, to make use of class with any conviction one has to abandon both the proletariat and the bourgeoisie as master-classes; both classes exist today in Africa, but neither is strong or numerically dominant, at least in the form Marx or Weber would have considered critical. Moreover, they have if anything regressed. It is interesting, however, that even Pakulski and Waters admit to the historic importance of class, and what else but history should be the proper study of the historian? It is argued here that looking at other class categories and considering them *vis-à-vis* the question of exploitation or surplus extraction can be a valuable, if not sufficient, way of exploring the African past and the African present.

Class in African history

To a specialist in African history, Pakulski and Waters's disinterest in the past and in the delineation of class outside of capitalist societies seems peculiar. In fact, the latter issue has been very important for some Africanists. How do we characterize pre-colonial societies and with what implications for modern history? To what extent did modernization in enclave form coexist with older values and social forms in the colonial period and since? In one classic study, for instance, the question of class in colonial Kenya led Gavin Kitching (1980) to suggest that class formation existed within a society that could not really be assessed in terms of a single mode of production.

So class in this sense is closely aligned to a question raised in the 1970s and early 1980s around the concept of mode of production – a concept that is more implicit and descriptive in the writings of Karl Marx than explicit (Crummey and Stewart 1981; Freund 1985). Marx felt that the roots of social formation lay in the mode of production, the means by which a surplus is systematically, socially, and economically formed through the power of one class over another. Considering this issue forces historians to confront not only the issue of inequality in society but also the relationship of ruler to ruled, of how an economic surplus is systematically pumped out, no doubt in conjunction with a system of sacred beliefs. Those interested in this debate were generally concerned with the issue of state formation and the impact of long-distance commerce rather than with establishing a schema of progressive change over the course of history, as was Marx. My own view was and is that this concept was a very useful and stimulating touchstone, but that if applied too rigidly or simply as part of a formula it is unlikely to teach us much. The concept of class, closely allied to the attempt to identify how production and power intersected, is rather similar. It has raised very interesting questions and suggested further lines of research, but quickly turns sterile when used merely as a classificatory device.

There are parts of sub-Saharan Africa where class relationships belonged to everyday consciousness and where the link between power, wealth, and status can certainly be investigated quite directly. One of these areas is lowland northern Nigeria, in particular the core emirate territories that accepted the authority of the Sultan of Sokoto in the nineteenth century. Here there certainly was a peasantry that paid taxes and tributes and a horse-riding aristocracy that could wield power. Up to a point, wealthy people could own estates as well as landed property in towns. There was a radical edge to the religious wars that created the Sokoto polity and denounced this form of earthly inequality. The emirate system attempted a revolutionary political reform, as did equivalent *jihad*s in other parts of Sudanic Africa, but the reformed polities, however austere and severed from any association with ancient sacred kingships, came to exhibit their own forms of exploitation felt by the masses. The republican (and in some respects egalitarian) Islamists of the Futa Djallon promoted the hunting and selling of pagan Africans in

Guinea and Sierra Leone. Within the Sokoto caliphate there were rebellions of slaves and others in the name of Islam, the 'sword of truth'. However, the success of the rebels only led to the foundation of political units that mimicked the very emirates that had failed to stamp out the pre-*jihad* injustice of the Hausa rulers called Habe. In its heyday, the emirates presided over enough peace so as to promote internal and external commerce and, with it, wealth. The greatest of the towns, Kano, was a massive trading emporium as well as a centre for handicraft production that attracted hundreds of traders from Egypt and North Africa alone during the trading season. This was a society where rich merchants ran businesses but their status *vis-à-vis* the religious state and the sword-bearing class was not entirely certain. It was only after the coming of the British that they were permitted to build their houses as tall as those considered the legitimate rulers of society.

A major feature of the society was the massive presence of slavery. Slaves were sometimes soldiers, worked in the fields on private estates, became skilled craftsmen and craftswomen, or became the wives of powerful individuals in a juridical regime where descent was recognized through the male line. A few were eunuchs; probably the majority in fact were women. It is most uncertain whether slaves were exploited 'more' than free peasants and poor clients. Often no doubt they worked side by side. If (or once) slaves were Muslim, they also enjoyed being part of a theological discourse of human equality. However, there was exploitation and there was certainly a surplus to be extracted (Lovejoy 1978; Usman 1974).

Class is therefore an important factor for understanding the social forces that motivated and justified these *jihad*s, as well as for understanding revolts against the new regime and the reactions to the coming of colonial rule. Indeed, this latter tended to prop up that regime through the system of indirect rule, even if it was shorn of most elements of state power.

There are parallels across the whole immense belt of Africa north of the equatorial forests and the dry lands of upper East Africa. The surviving chronicles that tell us a little about life in the kingdom of Songhay, occupying much of what is today Mali, mention substantial agricultural estates worked by slaves at least as far back as the sixteenth and seventeenth centuries. In his magnum opus, Donald Crummey tells us that:

> the main, ongoing way in which, through the centuries, the Ethiopian state and rulers affected the lives of ordinary people and limited their productive autonomy was through its system of taxation and tribute, known by the term of *gult*, an institution of land tenure which brought together producers and privileged, farms and rulers, and provided the means whereby the former supported the latter. This would suggest it is of central importance for understanding the workings of historic Ethiopia.
>
> *(Crummey 2000: 5)*

In Ethiopia, the church, too, was a factor in land ownership and surplus extraction from the bulk of the peasantry. Closer to the Sahara, nomadic clans also exhibited social stratification, despite what one might think was the unlikelihood of pastoralists creating unequal societies. Reluctant as they were to acknowledge adherence to a state, they nonetheless held agricultural populations in oases to the status of slaves or semi-slaves. Of course, it is worth noting that some scholars would be more comfortable understanding such a society as one of caste, which they would choose to delineate sharply from class.

Slavery, trade, and inequality

One should not discount the importance of commerce in bringing about change in Africa in the nineteenth century and, with reference to the slave trade, even earlier in coastal West Africa. It is difficult to forget the argument of Walter Rodney, considering the upper Guinea coast, who argued that slaving over time created inequality, stoking massive violence and what he called social oppression even where large state formations were not in question (Rodney 1966). Certainly social strata emerged, occasionally of mixed racial origins, which depended for their existence on maritime commerce, if not in slaves then in other commodities.

Slaving polities such as Dahomey or the Kongo kingdom raided their peripheries ceaselessly and demanded tribute in people, but they kept dense communities of individuals focused on the core controlled by the ruler. Catherine Coquery-Vidrovitch has suggested that slaves, once no longer used for overseas trade, were put to work once the palm oil trade began to flourish on the coast of what is today the republic of Bénin (Coquery-Vidrovitch 1971). Similarly, Boubacar Barry indicates that the *ceddo* warrior caste of the Senegal River valley became more oppressive as these societies became more money- and trade-orientated, and also more violent – an oppression that rendered the arrival of the French not entirely unwelcome (Barry 1972). The rise of slave-based economies in other regions has also been attested (Cooper 1977; Sheriff 1987; Campbell 2005).

Returning briefly to West Africa, Emmanuel Terray proposed that Akan-speaking people formed strong states (the greatest of which was Asante) in what is today Ghana and Côte d'Ivoire due to the ability to control the production of gold, probably through the use of slave labour. Here was an area that for a long period sold gold rather than slaves, and actually imported slaves commercially. However, research has suggested that producers in gold mines were not slaves, that the state did secure revenue but largely through taxing trade, and that merchants, rather than producers, were able to do very well out of lucrative gold-producing areas. It is difficult here to say whether gold production intensified the existing earlier forms of inequality that were reproduced through the economy or helped to create them (Dumett 1998).

In contrast to arguments that link slavery to the intensification of class through an antagonistic process of social stratification, Harms (1981) and Horton (1969) have shown how massive slaving went together with the rapid absorption of slaves into trading societies formed along transport routes in the Congo River valley as well as in the Niger Delta. By contrast with, say, Asante, slave origins could be rapidly forgotten where individual initiative was highly valued. Southeastern Nigeria was a massive source of slaves for the Americas, but it was and remains a very densely populated region famous for its relatively egalitarian villages with authority vested in title societies, masquerade societies, and other social forms, some of them consisting only of women. The Igbo-speaking peoples honoured individual achievement and did not turn slaving into a particularly hierarchical set of social values.

Further to the west, Yoruba speakers, also massively involved in the slave trade, formed societies based on concentrated urban communities where massive households included master and slave, creditor and debtor, rich and poor, and were to some degree gathered together in common fortune. When the British made their first incursion into this world by occupying Lagos, the question of what happened to the slaves become especially salient. The answer, Kristin Mann found, was that for reasons of safety and identity they needed to stay associated if at all possible with powerful households even if their status was no longer so clear cut and they could be legally emancipated if they wished (Mann 2007). Throughout most of Africa, large and diverse social units emerged along similar lines and typically overrode or masked the existence of potentially antagonistic class relations. As Marcia Wright showed for East and East-central Africa in the late nineteenth century, women unable to attach themselves to such units were women 'in peril', and proved to be particularly interested in finding succour in mission settlements when they appeared (Wright 1975). So trade and violence did not necessarily lead to societies where class distinctions hardened into the main building blocks of social relations.

In other parts of this diverse continent, inequality was less significant, the economy far less commodified, and class relations seem largely irrelevant before the nineteenth century. Certainly this holds for most of the southern third of Africa. Much of this land was characterized by the practice of extensive forms of agriculture, largely carried out by women (often using wooden hoes), and with men concentrating on the keeping and herding of cattle wherever suitable. Here the common wisdom of Africanists, which I shall not challenge, is that it was labour – not land – that was scarce. This may have encouraged human movements to have a violent element, involving the seizure of captives and systematic apparent enslavement. Over time, however, there was also a strong inducement to incorporate the captives into mainstream society and to establish a new form of loyalty to the village, the chief, or the household head that represented potential prosperity and safety. The extended reproduction of these societies was more effective due to the absorption of new members on a relatively egalitarian basis – except for the general issue of exploitation of women – rather than the formation of a permanent exploitable underclass. So here it is the very absence of class that leads us into sociological insights.

As commercial life intensified in Africa, it is notable that by the seventeenth century in coastal Ghana and by the nineteenth in the central West African savannah travellers and merchants found that a pool of men (and perhaps women?) were prepared to work in return for a fixed sum of money or a wage. One might assume that the massive caravans bearing ivory tusks from what is today the eastern Democratic Republic of the Congo all the way to ports on the Indian Ocean, a region where pack animals could not be kept in good health, were full of slaves. However, in fact they were dominated by relations of free labour and organized according to hierarchies with the particular interest of specific ethnic groups (Rockel 2006). Eventually railways and roads ended the careers of porters as they did those of transport riders in southern Africa, but colonialism brought with it demands for labour on the plantations, mines, and transport infrastructures inherent to the new economies, and so labour-induced migration continued.

Continuity and change in the colonial era

How to define these issues in class terms presents a variety of problems. Slavery, for one thing, did not die out immediately but tended to dissipate gradually, as was also true of debtor–creditor relations mediated through clientelist labour relations. Nor can slaves be defined strictly as a class. Early colonialism made wide use of forced labour, even if some pay changed hands. The wild rubber trade of the central African equatorial forests was tied to the notorious forced labour regime where massive violence caused a scandal that forced the end of the private regime of the Congo Free State of Belgium's King Leopold II. However, equivalent abuses continued in the French colonies on the other side of the Congo and the Ubangi for long after (Coquery-Vidrovitch 1972) – a region that also witnessed a huge death toll in the construction of the all-French Congo-Océan railway, completed in the 1930s. The *indigénat* which authorized forced labour in French colonial Africa survived until after the Second World War and abusive forced labour typified the Portuguese colonies even later. Increasingly characteristic of African labour systems was the presence of very large numbers of men who worked as migrants on mines and plantations (but also on African-owned farms, for example in the coffee fields of Uganda or the cocoa farms of south-central Ghana) but who also retained membership in home communities where they sought to maintain and build up households based on agriculture and craft activities. Being able to play two economic systems against one another could be advantageous. The reluctance of colonial rulers to introduce or spread private land tenure outside towns intensified this tendency.

As a result, the colonial workforce can be looked at in two ways. For some writers, particularly anthropologists, it has been important to de-emphasize the issue of class and examine the way that entry into new labour situations impacted on other aspects of the social firmament. The average unskilled mine worker in northern Nigeria, for instance, not only remained deeply involved in a different economy back home (and many came from distant areas) but participated in a recruitment process that took place along patrimonial lines that the white mine managers knew very little about (Freund 1981). The more such workers fended for themselves, the lower wages could be and the less involved in problems outside the mining situation they had to be.

To see wage workers as the equivalent of the proletariat in Europe, even when one could find pockets of complete landlessness, is therefore deceptive and leads social scientists to unrealistic expectations in terms of social identity and political practice. In 1946, after considerable inflationary pressures, a massive strike of South African gold miners took place. There clearly were a group of militant communist activists who supported and wished to be seen as the very heart of the strike. However, Dunbar Moodie has argued that it was the violation of a kind of 'moral economy' that more or less had determined what would be a reasonable wage for miners that angered them enough to take on the mighty mining companies (Moodie 1986). Yet of course strike they did. Cooper has shown how relatively well-intentioned French post-war administrators struggled to find a regime that would work in pay and welfare terms for railway workers and the like that also accorded with European ideas at the time, but their efforts did not mean the railway workers were unable to mount and sustain an epic strike that had powerful historic reverberations (Cooper 1996).

Moreover, the picture is more complex especially if we look at categories such as railway workers. Ralph Grillo wrote an excellent monograph on East African railway workers and found that they came largely from one ethnic group, moved from city to city across territorial lines, and had a strong sense of community, of being 'railway men'. They also had specific skills, even if not always recognized as such (Grillo 1973). In the late colonial period, several eminent figures focused on the large population of copper miners in the territory of Northern Rhodesia, today Zambia. Their interest was spurred by several major strikes, notably in 1935 and 1940, which suggested the ability to act in common across ethnic borders and on a very large scale. It is interesting that several scholars of this 'Rhodes-Livingstone' school actually shifted disciplines, from anthropology to sociology. Whatever else the workers might be, according to Max Gluckman and others, on the mines they were miners and acted accordingly in response to a classic situation. The extent to which the miners melded into the urban population of the Copperbelt, however, was somewhat limited by their continued presence on rented mines premises, albeit eventually with families of their own. James Ferguson has recently characterized the outlook of miners as 'modern'; they possessed a definite, Western-influenced sense of their place in a modern, independent country, and their union was a powerful social force in early independent Zambia (Ferguson 1990, 1999). In my view, therefore, understanding wage workers in colonial Africa can be understood as an important new class, but this point needs qualification and pursuit of particular configurations rather than limiting analysis to a classificatory exercise (Freund 1988).

As workers, in struggles with bosses and the state or effectively buttressing anti-colonial agitation, they played an important historic role. However, they did not necessarily abandon their affiliation to a world of autonomous cultivators and their situation as workers could shift dramatically in the ups and downs of a colonial economy. Some writers on colonial and post-colonial Africa have also given class overtones to the relationship of the rural population, once it paid taxes and was subject to regimes that seemed to adopt threatening policies. When elements of this population could accumulate, creating exploitation within the village community as well, the question of the peasantry as a distinct class is laid open (Freund 1988; Hydén 1980; Lamb 1974; Feierman 1990).

The social historians of colonial Africa have also been extremely interested in what was usually identified as a Westernized elite, which today we might be more apt to call an emergent middle class. African beneficiaries of the colonial system might potentially include cash crop farmers (or, more likely, the leaders of milling cooperatives, licensed buyers of crops, merchants, or town women investing in property) but these more elusive categories have been much less attended to than the mission boys who acquired leading-edge education. These were, of course, the potential future politicians who would shape nationalist movements and were thus of critical importance to colonial systems as devolution began to loom. In *A Modern History of Tanganyika*, Iliffe (1979), one of the most influential historians of modern African society, gives such figures attention. Terence Ranger, probably as influential or more so, has equally focused on them in much of his work (e.g. Ranger 1995).

However, were such men (and their families) a nascent bourgeoisie? Perhaps Paul Bomani, the power behind the Tanganyika cotton cooperatives, eager to displace millers of Indian descent, was a figure of this type. So were Bamako or Kano merchants (such as the Dantata family), who widened their range of business and knowledge with time. On the whole, though, the tendency before independence was rather to invest in education – which often became a platform for entering politics – rather than in industry organized on capitalist lines.

In some parts of Africa, however, settler power was considerable and they were able, through the diffusion of private property, to establish a conventional European-style capitalist society. As it developed, settler society contained industrialists, capitalists who focused on resources and agrarian cultivation, sometimes mimicking elements of pre-capitalist landlord culture, small independent businessmen, skilled workers, and, in a few cases (such as Algeria but especially South Africa) even semi-skilled and unskilled workers as well as farm employees without land. Local politics and the rise of interest groups and trade unions paralleled this process. In the southern half of Africa, there was (very contested) space for a large Indian merchant class that, especially after the Second World War, engaged in industry as well as other economic activities even while it lacked political rights.

South Africa was, of course, the site of the most sweeping transition to capitalism, the territory where fortunes (made in mining especially) remained in the country as settlers sought to create a local equivalent of Canada or Australia. However, even here a major theme, theorized as the key element to understanding capitalism in South Africa by its most interesting sociologist, Harold Wolpe, was the continual effort to prop up pre-capitalist social and property relations in a small but significant part of the country where much of the conquered African population resided. The survival of apparently tribal society in these Reserves was coupled with the long shadow of semi-feudal, non-cash economic relationships in many parts of white-owned rural South Africa. This system was fundamental to the period of state-building that followed the formation of the Union of South Africa as an effectively independent country in 1910. However, the intensified economic growth and industrialization from the late 1930s, which brought a very large number of African men and some women to the cities, increasingly threatened to bring it into crisis (Wolpe 1972). The black proletariat (for that it surely became), while unlike its Western counterpart in both cultural and political terms, became a force with which to reckon at every level. However, the racial divide between black and white (as well as black and Indian/coloured) remained an important feature of working-class life. Of course, this kind of boundary-setting in the working class is hardly unique to South Africa (Greenberg 1980). Well before the end of apartheid, however, observers considered the growth of class stratification and the formation of a middle class within the theoretically bounded black population to be of real significance (Kuper 1965; Brandel-Syrier 1971). At the same time, in the political language of black South Africans, whites and capitalists were synonymous and remained so after the end of the apartheid system.

Literature from the late colonial period, and even after, took seriously the idea that independence for Africa would mean a major expansion of the working class and the continued growth of trade union power. In part this was due to the salience of unions in being able to call out labour strikes on the part of strategic workers, especially workers in mining and infrastructural sectors (railways, ports, post offices, and so on), which was a key feature of the nationalist struggle in many territories. Many scholars also worked with the assumption that independence would lead to the growing capacity and influence of African capitalists who would play a major role in the economy, at least as partners to Western firms.

Independence and after

Neither of these expectations were realized. The new one-party and military regimes that emerged were suspicious and uneasy with any autonomous voices from civil society and worked hard to assimilate the unions into the state apparatus, even if the progressive-minded regimes tried, where and when possible, to improve the workers' situation (Berg and Butler 1964). There were exceptions. In Zambia, trade unions remained a thorn in the flesh of Kenneth Kaunda and held on to some of the collective gains of the past while probably pushing the ruling party into a more left-wing stance. In time, a union candidate would defeat Kaunda when one-party rule was abandoned, in part under foreign pressure. From the 1970s, a new trade union movement came about in South Africa that achieved a growing ability to challenge business and then the state itself. It also attracted intellectuals who envisioned a working class-centred state and displayed impressive vigour and variety as well as discipline (Friedman 1987). Other than this, however, unions tended to lose much of their ability to cow governments but were able to survive and provide coherence to their members. Jon Kraus (2007) has made the case that in several important instances unions were crucial to the emergence of democratic practices. In Zimbabwe, the unions have been the core of the Movement for Democratic Change challenging the Mugabe government, to date without success. Sadly, given its history, union strength has also faltered in Zambia, where working class strength on the mines has been shattered (Ferguson 1990; Larmer 2007).

To some extent this held as well for the business world. A few Africans began to accede to unheard-of wealth but this now emanated directly from the governments, which used their hold on society to enrich a small class of people on clientelist lines. One could point, say, to merchants as important in the opposition to the left-wing regime of Modibo Keita in Mali, but overall it would be hard to say that the new states reflected the rise of a significant new class with its feet placed in civil society. Indeed in Julius Nyerere's Tanzania, where relatively objective and honest practices characterized the growing bureaucracy, these educated civil servants, if not rich, manifested themselves as a new class. However, the typical African governments of the later twentieth century were predatory rather than developmentalist.

The explanation for the stagnation of class formation lay in Africa's poor economic performance; critical structures in African economies were unable to adjust to the growing shifts in international trade, where primary products fell in value. Foreign aid in the form of Cold War gifts gave way to loans, which created dependency in new forms and led to attempts to force African states to behave in accordance with 'good governance' criteria as conceived by the World Bank (see Williams, this volume). The dominant pattern during this period was of

Western disinvestment, apart from select – and lucrative – mineral projects. Perhaps Botswana and Mauritius constitute the only exceptions to this pattern of decline and international marginality, along with a few oil-rich states in the final quarter of the twentieth century.

At the same time, African cities were starting to grow apace and absorb an ever larger percentage of the population. The older ways of living on the land were no longer acceptable to many Africans and political crises with the threat of social breakdown intensified the movement off the land in many places. The peasantry, as Iliffe understood the term, began to lose coherence. The result was the rapid growth of what was clearly a proletariat in the original Roman sense of the word – the landless urban crowd – but only a few of these could find work in industry. Thus, the formal, state-recognized wage earning system became a marginal part of how individuals survived in large cities such as Lagos and Kinshasa.

From the 1970s, starting with Keith Hart's (1973) work in Ghana and the International Labour Organization's (ILO) report on Kenya, the so-called informal sector became a major standing feature in any discussion of African economies. This frankly incoherent sector included a great variety of activities: commercial, service-orientated, repair and maintenance work, and some productive labour, especially in countries with strong craft and apprentice traditions and a long history of urban life. How to comprehend this increasingly important population, and whether it contains elements that would permit substantial accumulation and upward mobility, is certainly a matter of debate. For some, Africa is simply developing classic third world cities of slums in which non-governmental organizations (NGOs) and charity just about keep the population surviving. In fact, the human development indices are higher for the slum cities than for rural populations. For others, these are slums of hope in which Africans are inventing new cultural forms and transforming older ways of living, with increasing scope for women to operate outside male- and elder-centred households and increased access for everyone to international trends (Rakodi 1997). In the first generation of independence, many African governments responded to the emergence of this 'excess' population by trying to pack lorry loads of the poor back to the countryside, just as they continue to try to expel foreigners during episodes of apparent social tension. These expulsions did not resolve the problem, however, and so the best way forward with regards to the urban masses remains a crucial question. It may be useful to consider them a working class but clearly not one for whom homogeneous conditions and the discipline of factory work will naturally lead to class-based effective organization. Although some intellectuals continue to see this pool of people as a constant potential threat to the state, in reality they are almost impossible to organize coherently. Either way, they are a critical social reality.

Conclusion

After a generation of crisis, decline, and violent upheavals in quite a few countries, the African situation has shifted again. Primary products are again bringing in good prices, even in agriculture where we may be seeing a turn to industrially orientated and more productive forms of cultivation, but also in forms that are further disrupting peasant life in at least some countries (Oya 2010). New entrants such as Chad, Sudan, Ghana, and Uganda are beginning to exploit substantial oil reserves. Copper, bauxite, and other minerals are once again valuable. The result is a certain stabilization and a return to some of the values of the early nationalist era, as loans from the International Monetary Fund and the threat of aid withdrawal become less crucial for many countries. Secondary industry is not growing rapidly but is reviving to a limited extent, and wage labour is certainly expanding in infrastructural and commercial sectors while hundreds of thousands of Africans find employment through emigration on uncertain time frames outside the continent.

African cities are showing signs of investment and restructuring by a more stable class of employees (whom we might call middle class), which is growing in size, competence, and buying power, furthermore fortified by foreign remittances. The breakdown of often-irrelevant colonial urban planning and control legislation has been to the advantage of a new class that has structured transport routes, shopping opportunities, and the presence of privatized services in health and education to its own advantage. Upon re-examination, studies that look at this as post-colonialism (i.e. culturally), or as a mark of changes in gender relations or the rise of so-called civil society, actually reveal the rising significance of the middle class (Tati 2001; Tripp 1997). This is something that has also been noted in Maputo by Jenkins (2009), while Hanlon and Mosse (2010) suggest that we can find in Mozambique today the germs of a class project that uses the state to promote development and its own interests simultaneously. Business journals highlight the emergence of a small number of African billionaires, including some white South African moguls but also black men with diverse interests in cell phones, oil, and even secondary industry. Here we might recall the judgement by Colin Leys on the dependency debate of the 1960s and 1970s that, for all the extent to which Kenyan development was tied to Western-dominated patterns of growth, there were real possibilities for a capitalist society to take root in Kenya. As Leys recognized, structural conditions did not render this impossible; rather, it was the failings of Kenyan institutions and the Kenyan state which slowed down the process (Leys 1996).

South Africa has often been condemned for its post-1994 development strategy, which saw the rapid emergence of a wealthy elite (Bond 2004). In a country where there is the possibility of real wealth accumulation for well-connected and ambitious entrepreneurs, a massive class formation process is underway. I would suggest that this is emblematic and typical – not exceptional – of today's Africa. It is much easier for the accumulators, the educated professionals, to make their weight felt as a class than it is for the difficult-to-organize informal sector. In some ways, though, South Africa is also atypical, most notably in that it continues to have an often tense but very potent alliance between the ruling party and the trade union movement, which, at least in principle, allowed workers to influence government policy. However, this must be understood as the product of a specific set of historical process such as high levels of industrialization and protective labour structures that were not replicated in many other countries and are unlikely to be in the future (Buhlungu 2004). Of course the terms of this alliance benefit far more the small emergent class of wealthy Africans and the much larger black middle class.

Although class remains uneven and sometimes ephemeral in contemporary Africa, it remains of considerable importance as an analytical tool to explain collective feeling and collective action. If we wish to look below the surface, surely Seekings and Nattrass (2005) are right when they emphasize the growing analytical importance of class trumping race as a way of grasping social reality in South Africa, even if it is just what politicians are reluctant to promote and remains muted in their discourse. Class therefore retains importance for all those trying to develop a full understanding of Africa in the new century.

Bibliography

Barry, B. (1972) *Le Royaume du Waalo: Le Sénégal avant la Conquête*, Paris: Maspero.

Berg, E. and Butler, J. (1964) 'Trade Unions', in J. Coleman and C. Rosberg (eds) *Political Parties and National Integration in Tropical Africa*, Berkeley, CA: University of California Press.

Bond, P. (2004) *Talk Left, Walk Right: South Africa's Frustrated Global Reforms*, Pietermaritzburg: University of KwaZulu-Natal Press.

Brandel-Syrier, M. (1971) *Reeftown Elite: A Study of Social Mobility in a Modern African Community on the Reef*, London: Routledge & Kegan Paul.

Buhlungu, S. (2004) 'A Question of Power: Co-determination and Trade Union Capacity', *African Sociological Review* 3(1): 111–29.

Campbell, G. (2005) *The Economic History of Imperial Madagascar 1750–1895: The Rise and Fall of an Island Empire*, Cambridge: Cambridge University Press.

Cooper, F. (1977) *Plantation Slavery in Kenya and Zanzibar*, New Haven, CT: Yale University Press.

——(1996) *Decolonization and African Society: The Labor Question in French and British Africa*, Cambridge: Cambridge University Press.

Coquery-Vidrovitch, C. (1971) 'De la traite des esclaves à l'exportation de l'huile de palme et des palmistes au Dahomey: XIXe siècle', in C. Meillassoux (ed.) *The Development of Indigenous Trades and Markets in West Africa*, Oxford: Oxford University Press.

——(1972) *Le Congo au temps des grandes compagnes concessionaires 1898–1930*, Paris: Mouton.

Crummey, D. (2000) *Land and Society in the Christian Kingdom of Ethiopia from the Thirteenth to the Twentieth Century*, Oxford: James Currey.

Crummey, D. and Stewart, C.C. (eds) (1981) *Modes of Production in Africa: The Precolonial Era*, London: Sage.

Dumett, R. (1998) *El Dorado in West Africa: The Gold-Mining Frontier, African Labour, and Colonial Capitalism in the Gold Coast, 1875–1900*, Athens, OH: Ohio University Press; Oxford: James Currey.

Edgell, S. (1993) *Class*, London: Routledge.

Feierman, S. (1990) *Peasant Intellectuals: Anthropology and History in Tanzania*, Madison, WI: University of Wisconsin Press.

Ferguson, J. (1990) 'Mobile Workers, Modernist Narratives: A Critique of the Historiography of Transition on the Zambian Copperbelt', Parts One and Two, *Journal of Southern African Studies* 16(3–4): 385–412, 603–21.

——(1999) *Expectations of Modernity: Myth and Meanings of Urban Life on the Zambian Copperbelt*, Berkeley, CA: University of California Press.

Freund, B. (1981) *Capital and Labour on the Nigerian Tin Mines*, Harlow: Longman.

——(1985) 'The Modes of Production: A Debate in African Studies', *Canadian Journal of African Studies* 19(1): 23–29.

——(1988) *The African Worker*, Cambridge: Cambridge University Press.

Friedman, S. (1987) *Building Tomorrow Today: African Workers in Trade Unions 1970–84*, Johannesburg: Ravan.

Greenberg, S. (1980) *Race and State in Capitalist Development: South Africa in Comparative Perspective*, Johannesburg: Ravan.

Grillo, R. (1973) *African Railwaymen*, Cambridge: Cambridge University Press.

Hanlon, J. and Mosse, M. (2010) 'Mozambique's Elite – Finding its Way in a Globalized World and Returning to Old Development Models', United Nations University WIDER Working Papers 2010/105.

Harms, R. (1981) *River of Wealth, River of Sorrow: The Central Zaire Basin in the Era of the Slave and Ivory Trade 1500–1891*, New Haven, CT: Yale University Press.

Hart, K. (1973) 'Informal Income Opportunities and Urban Employment in Ghana', *Journal of Modern African Studies* 11(1): 61–89.

Horton, R. (1969) 'From Fishing Village to City-State: A Social History of New Calabar', in M. Douglas and P. Kabery (eds) *Man in Africa*, London: Tavistock.

Hydén, G. (1980) *Beyond Ujamaa in Tanzania: Underdevelopment and an Uncaptured Peasantry*, Berkeley, CA: University of California Press.

Iliffe, J. (1979) *A Modern History of Tanganyika*, Cambridge: Cambridge University Press.

Jenkins, P. (2009) 'African Cities: Competing Claims on Urban Land', in F. Locatelli and P. Nugent (eds) *African Cities: Competing Claims on Urban Spaces*, Amsterdam: Brill, 81–108.

Kitching, G. (1980) *Class and Economic Change in Kenya: The Making of an African Petty Bourgeoisie 1905–70*, New Haven, CT: Yale University Press.

Kraus, J. (2007) *Trade Unions and the Coming of Democracy in Africa*, New York, NY: Palgrave Macmillan.

Kuper, L. (1965) *An African Bourgeoisie: Race, Class and Power in South Africa*, New Haven, CT: Yale University Press.

Lamb, G. (1974) *Peasant Politics: Conflict and Development in Murang'a*, London: Julian Friedman.

Larmer, M. (2007) *Mineworkers in Zambia: Labour and Post-Colonial Africa*, London: I.B. Tauris.

Leys, C. (1996) *The Rise and Fall of Development Theory*, Nairobi: East African Educational Publishers; Bloomington, IN: Indiana University Press; Oxford: James Currey.

Lovejoy, P. (1978) 'Plantations in the Economy of the Sokoto Caliphate', *Journal of African History* 19(3): 341–68.

Mann, K. (2007) *Slavery and the Birth of an African City, Lagos 1760–1900*, Bloomington, IN: Indiana University Press.

Moodie, D. (1986) 'The Moral Economy of the Black Miners' Strike', *Journal of Southern African Studies* 13: 1–35.

Oya, C. (2010) 'Agro-pessimism, Capitalism and Agrarian Change: Trajectories and Contradictions in Sub-Saharan Africa', in V. Padayachee (ed.) *The Political Economy of Africa*, London: Routledge, 85–109.

Pakulski, J. and Waters, M. (1996) *The Death of Class*, London: Sage.

Rakodi, C. (ed.) (1997) *Urban Management in Africa: Growth and Management of its Large Cities*, London: United Nations University Press.

Ranger, T. (1995) *Are We Not Also Men? The Samkange Family and African Politics in Zimbabwe 1920–1964*, Harare: Baobab; London: James Currey.

Rockel, S. (2006) *Carriers of Culture: Labor on the Road in Nineteenth-Century East Africa*, Portsmouth, NH: Heinemann.

Rodney, W. (1966) 'African Slavery and Other Forms of Social Oppression on the Upper Guinea Coast', *Journal of African History* 7(3): 431–43.

Seekings, J. and Nattrass, N. (2005) *Class, Race and Inequality in South Africa*, New Haven, CT: Yale University Press.

Sheriff, A. (1987) *Slaves, Spices and Ivory in Zanzibar*, London: James Currey.

Tati, G. (2001) 'Responses to the Urban Crisis in Cameroun and Congo: Patterns of Local Participation in Urban Management', in A. Tostensen, I. Tvedten and M. Vaa (eds) *Associational Life in African Cities: Popular Responses to the Urban Crisis*, Uppsala: Scandinavian Institute of African Studies.

Tripp, A. (1997) *Changing the Rules: The Politics of Liberalization and the Urban Informal Economy in Tanzania*, Berkeley, CA: University of California Press.

Usman, Y. (1974) 'The Transformation of Katsina c.1796–1903', unpublished PhD thesis, Ahmadu Bello University.

Wolpe, H. (1972) 'Capitalism and Cheap Labour in South Africa: From Segregation to Apartheid', *Economy and Society* 1(4): 425–56.

Wright, E.O. (1997) *Class Counts: Comparative Studies in Class Analysis*, Cambridge: Cambridge University Press.

Wright, M. (1975) 'Women in Peril: A Commentary on the Life Stories of Captives in Nineteenth Century East-Central Africa', *African Social Research* 20: 800–18.

8

THE POLITICS OF ETHNICITY

Gabrielle Lynch

Ethnic identity is an essentially contested concept and there is no formulation for the delimitation of group membership that holds for every recognized group. Nevertheless, ethnic groups can be distinguished from other kinds of groups – nations, races, classes, and interest groups – due to 'the symbolism which they employ' (Bates 1986: 154). This symbolism relates to a sense of in-group connectedness and distinctiveness that is rooted primarily in a notion of cultural peoplehood, whereby individuals of different age, status, and wealth are linked (and simultaneously differentiated from ethnic others) through a conjoining of cultural similarity and perception of common descent.

In the mid-twentieth century, there was debate as to whether ethnic identities were the result of primordial attachments that stemmed from the 'assumed "givens" of social existence' (Geertz 1963: 109), or whether they were the product of a false consciousness that was cultivated and used by self-interested political elites as a way to mobilize support and suppress class-based dissent (e.g. Mafeje 1971). These primordialist and instrumentalist schools provided opposing accounts of the origins and political salience of ethnic or tribal identities, but both associated such cultural affiliation with traditional or uneducated people, and predicted the decline of ethnic identification and rise of national and/or class consciousness in the face of modernization.

These expectations were not realized. Instead, in a number of countries – for example, Burundi, the Democratic Republic of the Congo (DRC), Kenya, Nigeria, Rwanda, Sierra Leone, and Zimbabwe – questions of ethnic identity became more relevant in the post-colonial period as ethnic consciousness was shaped and fostered (rather than negated) by globalization, urbanization, capital accumulation, class formation, political competition, democratization, decentralization, and population growth. Moreover, the recent origins of many ethnic groups in Africa – for example, the Mijikenda, Luhya, and Kalenjin communities in Kenya (which date back to the 1920s, 1930s, and 1950s, respectively) – together with the initial articulation of some ethnic traditions and cultural practices in urban contexts (Mitchell 1956), poses further challenges to a primordialist understanding. In turn, instrumentalist explanations are brought into question by subaltern studies, analyses that incorporate local politics and bottom-up dynamics as well as often more visible, top-down processes (e.g. Lynch 2011a), and high levels of political consciousness and political rationality at local levels (Barkan 1976).

Today, a constructivist approach dominates. Most Africanist scholars view ethnic groups as socially constructed imagined communities (*cf.* Anderson 1983) and as moral and historic communities that struggle, not because they exist, but because they have come into existence out of a process of struggle (*cf.* Thompson 1978: 147–49). This conceptualization has led most scholars to reject the term 'tribe' in favour of 'ethnic group'. Both terms refer to cultural and linguistic units, however, tribe carries additional connotations of primitive or static traditions and an assumption of long-standing mechanisms for the discipline and control of group members across a recognized territory, which is a characterization that has never accurately captured more complex and dynamic local realities, as discussed below.

Among today's Africanist scholars the common understanding is that: pre-colonial African identities were relatively fluid, permeable, overlapping, and complex; and that the more bounded and politically pertinent ethnic identities of today are (at least to a certain extent) the product of a colonial order of delineated control and of dual processes of invention and imagination. This is not to say that there is no disagreement. On the contrary, areas of debate include:

- The scope for ethnic invention;
- The role of Europeans and Africans in processes of invention and imagination;
- Key motivations for becoming and being a member of a particular ethnic group over time;
- The extent of (and motivation for) people's negotiation and renegotiation of ethnic identities in contemporary contexts;
- The role and importance of ethnic identities in political competition.

This chapter provides an introduction to some of these issues from the processes of invention and imagination in the colonial period to the negotiation and renegotiation of ethnic identities and political salience of ethnic identities in contemporary contexts. The analysis is biased towards Anglophone Africa and to countries – such as Kenya and Nigeria – where ethnic identities have been central to colonial orders and post-colonial politics.[1]

Ethnic invention, imagination, and motivations in colonial Africa

The idea that 'every African belonged to a tribe, just as every European belonged to a nation' (Iliffe 1979: 323) was central to how colonial rulers understood sub-Saharan Africa and to how they justified colonial projects. The concept of 'tribe' comprised a central element of the discursive repertoires through which the continent was conceptualized as a dark continent in need of civilization and development. In particular, the British model of indirect rule, and specifically its reliance on a hierarchy of provincial administrators, had as its basic premise a notion of ethnic territoriality in which tribal chiefs were presumed to enjoy authoritative powers to legitimately define local duties and responsibilities, proscribe punishment, and measure justice over a certain area and local people. However, many pre-colonial African societies – from highly centralized kingdoms to stateless societies – did not fit this categorization, highlighting the extent to which this portrait of 'tribal Africa' was an invention of the colonial mind.

Nevertheless, this image was central to the justification of foreign rule and to how colonial authorities sought to control new territories with limited resources and questionable authority. For colonial officials, the control or disciplinary powers of chiefs and elders – on whom they were largely dependent for law and order, tax collection, and labour supply – were inherently intertwined with their understandings of local cultural practices and hierarchal relations. As Bruce Berman (1990) highlights, African colonial states were simultaneously weak and strong. Largely reliant on local collaborators, they were coercive, intrusive, overly repressive, disproportionately reactionary, and obsessed with the control of subjects rather than the development of territories. As a result, colonial authorities feared 'detribalized' natives who, freed from the yoke of traditional power, would stretch policing powers thin. Together with the limitations of the colonial state and perceived experiences of industrialization and urbanization in Europe, this prompted colonial officials to find and delineate tribes and tribal leaders with whom they could work, a process that often involved the creation of entirely new ethnic communities (Iliffe 1979).

European missionaries also helped to define the shape and relevant content of emergent ethnic communities through the standardization of local languages to facilitate the dissemination of 'God's Word', whilst anthropologists provided 'authoritative' studies on 'traditional' culture and society (Berman 1998: 322). However, many analysts have emphasized the role of African agency in imagining ethnic content rather than in inventing groups and boundaries. Thus, Terence Ranger argued that 'European classifications and inventions of race, or tribe or language in effect created a series of empty boxes, with bounded walls but without contents. It was all very well to write of "the Ndebele" or "the Kikuyu", but to give meaning to that identity was a much more complex and contested business', which was bound to be a matter of internal struggle within African societies (Ranger 1993: 27). According to Ranger, modern African ethnicities were constructed during the colonial period, when – as a result of colonial administrative and economic practice, the influence of European missionaries and anthropologists, and African responses – a colonial view of tribal Africa was invented by Europeans and imagined by Africans.

Clearly, the notion of 'tribal Africa' was an invention of the colonial mind. In turn, the process of demarcating and administering Africans as members of supposedly bounded tribes helped foster a sense of local ethnic consciousness, while various facets of the new administrative reality provided Africans with powerful incentives to imagine ethnic content and to think and act ethnically. Africans (both collectively and individually) were catalogued and labelled, their movements often monitored and regulated outside of 'home' areas, and 'aliens' were sometimes forced to incorporate into the 'local' majority. Moreover, collaborators tended to benefit from the clarification and ossification of customary laws and local decision-making processes, which often justified and bolstered their own privileged position.

The fact that chiefs, headmen, and local leaders became the key interface linking state and society – especially in British colonies where they constituted the major channel for distributing state largesse and principal instrument of state control – also provided many Africans with reasons to invest in their relationships with ethnic leaders. Such relations provided a way to access centralized resources and avoid state violence (Berman 1998), and for men in particular to try to assert control over local contexts at a moment of rapid social change (Vail 1989). In turn, reference to common kinship became a way to approach, petition, and plead with administrators and ethnic kin, just as reference to ethnic difference could help one question the legitimacy of administrative powers or the presence of ethnic 'outsiders'. Colonial officials also encouraged such strategies by supporting ethnic claims and providing them with periodic public forums, while simultaneously suppressing efforts to articulate interests and organize resistance at the national level.

The growth of social and spatial inequalities across the sub-continent also helped foster a sense of ethnic difference – especially in contexts where colonial authorities believed, and acted as if certain communities were relatively 'advanced' and others 'backward' – due to an overlap (both real and perceived) between livelihoods, class schisms, and ethnic groupings (see Cohen 1969 on Nigeria; Prunier 1995 on Rwanda). Parallel developments occurred in urban centres, where migrants tended (and were often encouraged) to reside near kin and residents from home areas. Several factors encouraged these residents to identify themselves and others as 'tribesmen', including the uncertainties of urban life, similarities in language, culture, and culinary tastes; the overriding logic of 'tribal Africa' and related ethnic stereotypes (which included assumed skills and common proclivities); the establishment of ethnic welfare associations and social groups; and persistent attachment to land in rural areas.

Yet, it is an oversimplification to argue that Africans simply imagined the content of invented ethnic units. First, much of the information used to delineate Africans into tribes and catalogue ethnic content was offered by African collaborators. Such 'knowledge' allowed collaborators to influence and manipulate the process of invention according to their own understandings and vested interests (Willis 1992). Second, processes of invention and imagining did not take place in a vacuum but also drew heavily from, and were built upon, existing realities and real linguistic, cultural, and socioeconomic similarities and differences (Lentz and Nugent 2000).

Moreover, many modern ethnic groups – such as the Twa of Central Africa, Kalenjin in Kenya, Maasai in Kenya and Tanzania, Somalis in the Horn of Africa, and Tswana in Botswana and South Africa – do not neatly fit colonial boundaries. Case study analyses of such groups point to the importance of European administrators, missionaries, anthropologists, as well as African culture brokers, in the creation of ethnic groups and imagining of ethnic content, whilst also highlighting a range of motivating factors for ethnic association (e.g. Lynch 2011a).

For many Africans, the appeal of constructing and internalizing ethnic identities in this way was linked to a close association of people and place. This association is not unique to Africa, as reflected in a pervasive politics of belonging that differentiates 'locals' from 'outsiders' around the world (Geschiere 2009). However, it was an approach that was endorsed and institutionalized with particular effect in colonial Africa. Colonial subjects in British Africa were encouraged to associate with a particular area, as geographic space became intertwined with a sense of legitimate control and rightful occupancy by particular ethnic communities. This association was promoted and ossified in different ways in different contexts, but measures included: the establishment of reserves in settler colonies; the removal of 'aliens' who refused to become initiated into local tribes; the passage of laws, sometimes including the requirement to carry a pass; colonial opposition to national organizations; and community-orientated agricultural and development schemes. This approach encouraged a two-tier conception of citizenship that distinguished between national and local citizenship, wherein understandings of who is really 'local' tied the relevant *demos* with a spatially fixed *ethnos* (Mamdani 1996).

At the same time, economic imperatives often encouraged the controlled migration of ethnic 'outsiders' into certain territorial spaces. In parts of west, central, and southern Africa, this process of 'mobilizing and fixing labor and populations' (Marshall-Fratani 2006: 15) involved the migration of Africans from neighbouring territories and has been associated with fierce debate and violent confrontations between self-professed autochthons, or 'sons of the soil', and those cast as 'foreigners' in postcolonial contexts. In contrast, pastoralist communities in colonial Kenya were pushed off fertile lands in the Rift Valley, which were set aside for European settlement, with European labour needs largely met by the recruitment and migration of other communities. The contradiction of economic imperative and administrative practice fuelled competing territorial claims to rich agricultural land in the Rift Valley between those who enjoyed rights as previous owners and those with user and purchase rights – differences that were articulated around independence in 1963 and periodically revived at times of political uncertainty (Lynch 2011a).

The colonial experience thus encouraged Africans to think and act ethnically in three principal ways:

- The categorization and administration of Africans as tribesmen helped inform and promote processes of ethnic invention and imagining;
- The growth of real and perceived economic and social inequalities, and the notion of 'advanced' and 'backward' communities, helped encourage a sense of difference and competition; and

- The association of discrete ethnic groups with the ownership and control of particular geographic areas fuelled a sense of difference and tension between 'locals' and 'outsiders', especially in cosmopolitan areas where 'locals' felt (or feel) that 'outsiders' have benefited from unfair advantages (either as a result of group action, market economics, state bias, or external interventions).

These processes occurred to different extents between and within individual countries. As a consequence, these historical differences – together with varied post-colonial trajectories – can help account for why ethnic identities have proved much more salient and divisive in some contexts than others.

The benefit of a constructivist approach – as compared to primordial or instrumental explanations of ethnic identification – is that it can incorporate all three of these processes. More important still, it can allow for the instrumental use of ethnic identity for political and socioeconomic gain as well as the 'non-instrumental, deeply affective and emotional character of ethnicity', through a recognition of how '[e]thnic identity cannot be conjured out of thin air, [but] must be built on real cultural experience' (Berman 1998: 309, 312). This limitation of invention is important and stems from the fact that ethnic bonds require a level of intra-intelligibility – most commonly, a sense of linguistic and cultural similarity, an assumed history of union, and some sense (or rehearsed debate) about what is right and just in terms of intra- and inter-communal relations and group rights. The possibilities of invention are also limited by the fact that the boundaries of 'we-groups' have mutated from pre-colonial times onward (Lentz and Nugent 2000) and have always drawn (however selectively or creatively) from existing notions of 'us' and 'them'.

While common language, cultural practices, and home area can be used to assert ethnic commonality, the constructivist approach also recognizes that small distinctions of dialect and custom, local debate on relevant borders and geographic units, and divergent histories of migration and interaction can be used to assert ethnic difference. For a sense of common ethnic identity to emerge and persist, similarities in cultural materials must be regarded as relevant or salient and be attended by a sense of a shared past or myth of collective ancestry and an associated conception of rights and social justice. The result is a dynamic reality in which ethnic groups are moral and historic communities, 'the outcome of an endless process in which they are always simultaneously old and new, grounded in the past and perpetually in the process of creation' (Berman 1998: 312). As a consequence, the existence and perpetuation of ethnic identities can never be assumed, but must always be explained.

Negotiation and renegotiation

Colonial experiences encouraged Africans to think and act ethnically, but they did not leave a legacy of fixed and unchanging ethnic signifiers. Instead, a number of recent accounts of ethnic identification in sub-Saharan Africa highlight how people make use of confused terrains of cultural politics to debate and reinterpret ethnic brands, content, allies, and cousins through four distinct but potentially interrelated avenues of ethnic negotiation and renegotiation: ethnic migration; assertions of difference; ethnic amalgamation; and ethnic branding or positioning (e.g. Comaroff and Comaroff 2009; Hodgson 2011; Lynch 2011a). This section will take a brief look at each of these avenues.

First, an ability to migrate from one ethnic community to another stems from an ability to redefine one's individual or collective ethnic identity on the basis of a re-reading of complex histories (both recent and past). Complexities include past administrative boundary changes, developments in anthropological categorization, the existence of cross-cutting clans, and local histories of inter-marriage, migration, forced removals, incorporation, and cultural borrowing, all of which can allow people (individually or collectively) to look back and redefine themselves according to the assumed ethnic identity of parents, forebears, or 'original' ancestors. One example is provided by a small number of Kalenjin in western Kenya who – in the context of opportunities in a local settlement scheme and burgeoning global indigenous people's movement in the early 1990s – chose to look back at family histories of migration, forced removals, and intermarriage, and conclude that they were not Pokot or Kipsigis as they had previously thought, but Sengwer, another Kalenjin sub-group (Lynch 2006).

In contrast, members of an ethnic sub-group can also assert their difference from a larger ethnic group, or call for the amalgamation of their sub-group with linguistically or culturally similar 'others'. This stems in large part from the multiplicity of ethnic sets. Individual ethnic groups usually consist of various clans and sub-groups, but also often form part of larger linguistic or regional blocs, nations, or ethnic 'families' (such as Cushitic, Bantu, and Nilotic). As a result, ethnic identities can 'expand and contract in inverse relation to the scale of inclusion and exclusion of the membership' (Cohen 1978: 387). An assertion of difference occurs when members of a sub-group draw upon cultural or linguistic differences or contested histories of origins and migration to declare that they are distinct and separate from the larger ethnic group with which they are usually associated. In contrast, ethnic amalgamation occurs when people decide – on the basis of cultural, linguistic and/or socioeconomic similarity, interpretations of ethnic pasts, and an assessment of current politics – that two or more groups, which are usually regarded as distinct, actually comprise part of a larger and more inclusive ethnic grouping (e.g. Lynch 2011a).

Instances of migration, assertions of difference, and amalgamation involve debates about relevant ethnic content, boundaries, friends, and foes. However, people can also debate ethnic typology – of whether, for example, a group constitutes a race, a nation, an ethnic minority, a marginalized community, an autochthonous society, or an indigenous people. Such debates are best thought of as a form of ethnic branding or positioning in response to economic, socio-legal, and political 'markets' or audiences. Thus, the Comaroffs show how ethnic groups can be commodified for 'consumers of the exotic, of spiritual reclamation, [or] jungle adventure', or be converted into 'corporations' (Comaroff and Comaroff 2009: 2–4). Similarly, Hodgson reveals how Maasai activists in Tanzania positioned themselves as indigenous and later as pastoralists in their efforts to pursue local political and economic struggles (Hodgson 2011: xi). Alternatively, the Endorois in Kenya provide an example of local culture brokers who chose to assert their ethnic difference from Kalenjin neighbours as a strategy of legal argument to strengthen claims to land and resources on the basis of special economic and cultural attachment (Lynch 2012).

In contemporary Africa, the two most common examples of ethnic branding or positioning are assertions of autochthony and indigeneity, which are similar and sometimes overlap, but are subtly different (see Geschiere, this volume). The minimum requirement of autochthony is a sense that your community belongs to an area more than 'others', while indigeneity rests on the idea that one's culture and sense of self is tied to a specific geographic space. In some accounts, assertions of autochthony are said to rely 'on nothing but the claim to have been in a certain space first' (Dunn 2009: 121). However, on closer inspection such a language of belonging lacks even that requirement. Thus, there are numerous communities that proudly recall histories of migration and recognize local indigenous communities, but still employ the notion of being 'sons of the soil' as a way to differentiate themselves from more recent migrants (Leonhardt 2006).

Africanist academics have highlighted how, according to such logic, those who have 'come from elsewhere' – so-called foreigners, migrants, outsiders, aliens, or allogenes – do not enjoy the same kind of naturalized claims as 'locals'. History provides many examples of where this sense of differential rights has been used to paint 'others' as second-class citizens who should not enjoy equal access to local resources or elected office, determine political outcomes, or even be residents (Lynch 2011a). In addition, complex migration patterns together with the cross-cutting layers of ethnic appellations (which result from changes to administrative boundaries and ethnic terminology over time) leads to a disjuncture between autochthony's promise of 'basic security' and the term's 'haunting uncertainty' (Geschiere 2009: 31). Such uncertainty can foster apprehension about autochthons' 'own authenticity [and a] need to prove itself by unmasking "fake" autochthons' (Ceuppens and Geschiere 2005: 403). Especially in contexts where 'being local' is an important means of laying claims to resources and political power, where 'dead certainty' is sometimes only 'achieved through death and dismemberment' (Marshall-Fratani 2006: 38).

In contrast, the language of indigeneity in Africa goes beyond a general sense of belonging, to place ownership and control of land at the very centre of communal identity, as critical to livelihood, culture, and religious practice. The African indigenous peoples' movement began in the late 1980s and early 1990s, when communities such as the Maasai of Tanzania became involved in international networks and forums. This engagement, together with a common argument that all Africans are indigenous to Africa, led to a redefinition of what it is to be indigenous at the supra-national level, as attention shifted away from an emphasis on original residence to 'certain forms of inequalities and suppression' (ACHPR 2005: 87). Thus, according to the African Commission on Human and People's Rights, the term 'indigenous' does not simply refer to 'first people' but to:

> a global movement fighting for rights and justice for those particular groups who have been left on the margins of development and who are perceived negatively by dominating mainstream development paradigms, whose cultures and ways of life are subject to discrimination and contempt and whose very existence is under threat of extinction.
>
> *(ACHPR 2005: 87)*

This understanding, together with the legacies, memories, and interpretations of colonial and post-colonial histories, as well as a close association between many African ethnic groups and 'the land' (which can include burial and spiritual sites, flora and fauna, and livelihoods), means that it is surprisingly easy for Africans to position themselves as indigenous in contemporary contexts (Lynch 2012). The main motivation for doing so stems from benefits (both real and perceived) at the global level. These include involvement in the indigenous people's movement, new inter-national agreements and laws, and possibility of assistance from international non-governmental organizations (NGOs) who want to work with small and politically marginalized communities. Becoming and being indigenous is thus usually a 'strategy of extraversion', a means to mobilize resources and moral, political, and legal advantage at the global level (Igoe 2006). In contrast, indigenous peoples often gain little recognition from African states, a reality that has led local Maasai activists in Tanzania to shift from basing 'political claims on discourses of indigeneity to discourses of livelihoods' at the turn of the twenty-first century in a 'conscious effort to find less confrontational and more effective ways to engage state policy (and policymakers) in Tanzania' (Hodgson 2011: xi, 175).

Processes of ethnic migration, differentiation, amalgamation, and branding are – like processes of ethnic invention and imagining – constrained by recognizable similarities and available memory due to the need for popularly accepted ethnic narratives to find resonance at the local level. However, the complexity and confusion that surround ethnic pasts, the ambiguous nature of ethnic identities, and multiplicity of ethnic sets provides ample room for debate.

Finally, processes of negotiation and renegotiation are inherently instrumental as culture brokers and leaders use the language of ethnicity to secure access to political and economic resources and to bolster arguments for social justice. This negotiability of ethnic identities complicates academic study, but it also heightens the concept's utility, since it provides space for debate, contestation, and reformulation. Indeed, it is this dynamism that enables ethnic narratives to adapt and respond to an ever-changing world and thus remain relevant to ordinary people and useful to political elites.

Political salience

Political action across sub-Saharan Africa is informed by many factors, including divisions other than ethnicity (such as class, religion, generation, and gender), pertinent issues (such as opposition to graft and the logic of trickle-down Reaganomics), personal characteristics (such as political record and clever use of idiom), and perceptions of likely outcomes. However, in contexts like contemporary Kenya and Nigeria, ethnic identities are clearly central to political debates and alliances. Given the constructed, situational, and negotiable nature of ethnic identities, such examples of politicized ethnicity raise at least two important questions: How and why are ethnic identities formed and sustained? How and why does a particular line of ethnic cleavage acquire and retain political significance?

Generally, the blame for politicized ethnicity and associated divisions and conflicts is placed squarely at the door of African elites who choose to mobilize support along ethnic lines, either for practical political reasons of easy mobilization and tactical advantage in the relative absence of other major social cleavages, or to protect and promote vested economic and class interests (Molteno 1974). At one extreme, such strategies of political mobilization are portrayed as a 'ploy or distortion' on the part of African elites who use ethnic identities to 'conceal their exploitative role' and as a 'mark of false consciousness on the part of the supposed tribesmen, who subscribe to an ideology that is inconsistent with their material base and therefore unwittingly respond to the call for their own exploitation' (Mafeje 1971: 259).

However, most analyses reject explanations that are wholly dependent upon popular self-deception and irrationality and look for alternatives that lend greater agency and reasoning to non-elites.

The standard approach is of economic rationalism with emphasis placed on the immediate material advantages gained from support for ethnic patrons. Molteno (1974: 84–85) hints at such relations in his argument that a conflict of interests between urban and rural populations was mitigated by networks of communication and assistance. Many have expanded on this notion of mitigation through networks to argue that patron-client ties (or clientelism) link politicians and supporters through:

> a largely instrumental friendship in which an individual of higher socio economic status (patron) uses his own influence and resources to provide protection or benefits, or both, for a person of lower status (client) who, for his part, reciprocates by offering general support and assistance, including personal services, to the patron.
>
> *(Scott 1972: 92)*

In post-colonial Africa, this is often believed to have resulted in neopatrimonial regimes 'where the chief executive maintains power through personal patronage, rather than through ideology or law' (Bratton and van de Walle 1994: 458), and in which the 'customs and patterns of patrimonialism co-exist with, and suffuse, rational-legal institutions' of the modern bureaucratic state (ibid.: 62; see also Erdmann, this volume).

In turn, much of the literature on ethnic politics in sub-Saharan Africa lays principal or even sole emphasis on logics of short-term material gain. In so doing, scholars often look (at least in part) to popular political metaphors for evidence, and in particular to the common reference to the African state as a 'cake', to politics as eating, and to popular demands for 'our turn to eat' (e.g. Bayart 1993). However, in addition to motivations of immediate consumption, individuals also invest in patron-client networks as a way to defend personal and communal interests against a dangerous and unpredictable state. Everyday experiences of nepotism, ethnic bias, and corruption produce a vicious circle that reinforces 'reliance on the ethnic solidarity and patron-client networks that dominate bureaucratic processes in post-colonial African states' (Berman 2004: 39). The perception that others are gaining from their ethnic identity and connections leads people to invest in and support their own ethnic leaders, both in the hope of future assistance and the fear of losing out if ethnic 'others' gain power. In such contexts, ethnically biased leadership becomes a reinforcing cycle of expectation and action, as voting for 'one of your own' becomes a rational response to the system as perceived. Moreover, it is a cycle that becomes particularly vicious in multi-party contexts where the electoral process is viewed as 'a zero-sum game with definite winners and losers among a country's ethno-regional communities' (Lemarchand 1992: 104), since, while victory in such instances appears to open the door to various opportunities, defeat carries the threat of marginalization, dispossession, and even persecution.

Over time, such rational calculations of short-term material loss and gain can become intertwined and reinforced by more economically irrational feelings of affection, resentment, anger, and hatred. In short, feelings of belonging instil ethnic identities with strong emotive force (and thus political utility) when they are linked with strong remembered or interpreted collective histories of victimhood, marginalization, and entitlement. These histories provide a discursive lens through which the notion of 'others' and the morality and justice of different political and economic dispensations can be viewed. In such contexts, ethnically delineated political support can be economically rational in the short to medium term; reactive to the actual and assumed behaviour of others; and highly emotive due to the link between collective pasts, group status, self-worth, and assumed prospects. However, while such behaviour may be reactive and emotive, it can still be regarded as rational for two closely related reasons. This is because of logics of 'exclusionary ethnicity', or a focus on who should 'not get power and control the state's resources' (Mueller 2008: 201), as well as 'speculative ethnic loyalty', or calculation regarding the advantages of electing community spokesmen who promise assistance but who also successfully portray themselves as strong defenders of local interests (Lynch 2011a). The latter often includes a commitment to tackle past injustices, such as historical land injustices, state neglect, or repression. Unfortunately, this dual logic further fuels a reinforcing cycle of ethnically biased leadership and political support, and can help justify participation in inter-communal violence in instances where the opportunities or threats appear to be particularly strong.

In contexts where such political dynamics are visible, support for ethnic leaders becomes embedded in assistance broadly understood as immediate material reward and longer-term security as well as a promotion of 'rights', 'social justice', and 'status'. In this regard, a politician's perceived ability and commitment to defend and lobby for local 'interests' is usually more important than campaign expenditure and financial promises per se. Interpretations of this ability are formed through an ongoing interaction between perceptions of a politician's past performance and future potential, perceptions of stasis or flux, communal narratives of suffering and desert, and institutional frameworks.

Finally, this understanding of ethnic groups as moral *and* historic communities complicates a common distinction between good and bad ethnicity as 'ethnicity from below' versus 'ethnicity from above' (Eyoh 1999: 273). In such analyses, the positive aspect of ethnic association refers to largely depoliticized in-group relations of interdependence and assistance and bottom-up pressures for redistribution, while the negative aspect refers to highly politicized external relations of inter-communal competition and conflict, associated with top-down processes of political mobilization. In African studies, this distinction is often articulated through reference to moral ethnicity – 'the contested internal standard of civic virtue against which we measure our personal esteem' – and 'unprincipled "political tribalism" through which groups compete for public resources' (Lonsdale 1994: 131). Lonsdale presents moral ethnicity as having the potential to provide a 'culture of personal accountability' and common political morality (Lonsdale 2004: 95). However, while Lonsdale is cautious as to the practical impact of moral ethnicity, others insist on the democratic and anti-democratic nature of moral ethnicity and political tribalism, respectively (e.g. Klopp 2002). This is an oversimplification that distorts the more nefarious logic that can imbue both elite and non-elite thinking, which ensure that internal moral debates and a sense of competition can become conflated and confused.

First, and as Cheeseman has argued with respect to the Kenyan context, moral ethnicity is largely grounded in 'the idea that MPs are personally responsible for funding local development and all manner of other local needs' (Cheeseman 2009: 13). This places a heavy financial burden on political elites, provides an incentive to abuse state funds, and explains why ordinary citizens do not unite against their leaders. Second, since ethnic groups are also historic communities, communal memories of past injustice, marginalization, suffering, and achievement can be used to lay claims to protection and entitlement in the present. In this way, evidence of a eader's assistance of his kin can appear highly immoral for communities that believe they have been neglected or marginalized. In turn, such remembered pasts can form the basis of claims that it is 'our turn to eat', while the relative advancement of 'others' can become a strong source of resentment, especially when they are deemed to be ethnic 'outsiders' (Chua 2003).

Thus, while top-down processes of mobilization and incitement are critical for explaining instances of politicized ethnicity in sub-Saharan Africa, the availability and success of such strategies should be assessed through a comprehensive analysis that recognizes the potentially dubious morality of bottom-up pressures. Consequently, more attention should be given to the highly personalized and localized nature of much African politics, which ensures that public political forums provide opportunities for the expression of intimacy and conviviality, as well as subjection and domination (Mbembe 2001). The realm of public political 'theatre' provides local citizens with an opportunity to express perceptions, expectations, and fears, if only through their silence, body language, or sliding scale of applause. In turn, while politicians play a critical role in constructing ethnic identities and in mobilizing ethnic support, they also need to respond to and can be constrained by messages from below. These are not only performed at political rallies but are also discussed and developed in other contexts, from vernacular radio stations to church pulpits and local markets. Politicians can soon find themselves politically isolated if they ignore (at least too blatantly) local fears, grievances, interests, and divisions, while easy political mileage can often be gained from playing upon local communal narratives of angst and moral outcomes. The discursive repertoires of ethnicity thus produce a complex, confused, and often contradictory moral terrain of politics that can be manipulated by elites but which, in highly divided societies, is often foolhardy for them to ignore.

Conclusion

The construction, negotiation, and politicization of ethnicity are thus instrumental in motivation and opportunistic in character, but simultaneously rooted in linguistic, cultural, and ethnographic similarities, and communal experiences of marginalization, neglect, injustice, and achievement. These communal pasts can acquire strong emotive force as historical layers of interaction influence everyday conceptions of bodily, socioeconomic, and political fortunes and future prospects. The corollary is that ethnic identities can lose emotive force if such factors are absent or if they are countered by strong, ethnically neutral leadership and institutions.

Consequently, the realities of ethnically delineated political support reflect pragmatism and expectations of patronage, as well as the significance of remembered pasts and associated narratives of justice and strategies of acquisition. Such discursive repertoires provide a list of grievances that elites can use to foster a sense of difference and mobilize local support bases, but also provide non-elites with a means to question and counter intra- and inter-communal differences and thus social and spatial inequalities. Ethnic identification and political support are thus rational but not for the simple reasons that classic neopatrimonial accounts suggest. Consequently, a comprehensive understanding of the nature and political salience of ethnic identities can help us better to understand those contexts where ethnic identities are central to political dynamics as well as those where such consciousness has limited political importance.

Note

1 This chapter draws extensively from previously published material, most notably Lynch 2011a, but also Lynch 2006, 2011b, 2011c, 2012.

Bibliography

ACHPR (African Commission on Human and People's Rights) (2005) *Report of the African Commission's Working Group of Experts on Indigenous Populations/Communities*, New Jersey: Transaction Publishers/ ACHPR and IWGIA.

Anderson, B. (1983) *Imagined Communities: Reflections on the Origin and Spread of Nationalism*, London: Verso.

Barkan, J. (1976) 'Comment: Further Reassessment of "Conventional Wisdom": Political Knowledge and Voting Behaviour in Rural Kenya', *American Political Science Review* 70(2): 452–55.

Bates, R. (1986) 'Modernization, Ethnic Competition, and the Rationality of Politics in Contemporary Africa', in M. Doro and N. Stultz (eds) *Governing in Black Africa: Perspectives on New States*, New York, NY: Africana.

Bayart, J.-F. (1993) *The State in Africa: The Politics of the Belly*, New York, NY: Longman Publishing.

Berman, B. (1990) *Control and Crisis in Colonial Kenya: The Dialectic of Domination*, London: James Currey.

——(1998) 'Ethnicity, Patronage and the African State: The Politics of Uncivil Nationalism', *African Affairs* 97: 305–41.

——(2004) 'Ethnicity, Bureaucracy and Democracy: The Politics of Trust', in B. Berman, D. Eyoh and W. Kymlicka (eds) *Ethnicity and Democracy in Africa*, Oxford: James Currey.

Bratton, M. and van de Walle, N. (1994) 'Neopatrimonial Regimes and Political Transitions in Africa', *World Politics* 46(4): 453–89.

Ceuppens, B. and Geschiere, P. (2005) 'Autochthony: Local or Global? New Modes in the Struggle over Citizenship and Belonging in Africa and Europe', *Annual Review of Anthropology* 34: 385–407.

Cheeseman, N. (2009) 'Kenya Since 2002: The More Things Change the More They Stay the Same', in A.R. Mustapha and L. Whitfield (eds) *Turning Points? The Politics of African States in the Era of Democracy*, Oxford: James Currey.

Chua, A. (2003) *World on Fire: How Exporting Free Market Democracy Breeds Ethnic Hatred and Global Instability*, London: Arrow Books.

Cohen, A. (1969) *Custom and Politics in Urban Africa: A Study of Hausa Migrants in Yoruba Towns*, London: Routledge and Kegan Paul.

Cohen, R. (1978) 'Ethnicity: Problem and Focus in Anthropology', *Annual Review of Anthropology* 7: 379–403.

Comaroff, J.L. and Comaroff, J. (2009) *Ethnicity, Inc.* Chicago, IL: Chicago University Press.

Dunn, K. (2009) '"Sons of the Soil" and Contemporary State Making: Autochthony, Uncertainty and Political Violence in Africa', *Third World Quarterly* 30(1): 113–27.

Eyoh, D. (1999) 'Community, Citizenship, and the Politics of Ethnicity in Post-Colonial Africa', in E. Kalipeni and P. Zeleza (eds) *Sacred Spaces and Public Quarrels: African Cultural and Economic Landscapes*, Trenton, NJ: Africa World Press, Inc.

Geertz, C. (1963) 'The Integrative Revolution: Primordial Sentiments and Civil Politics in the New States', in C. Geertz (ed.) *Old Societies and New States: The Quest for Modernity in Asia and Africa*, New York, NY: Free Press of Glencoe.

Geschiere, P. (2009) *The Perils of Belonging: Autochthony, Citizenship and Exclusion in Africa and Europe*, Chicago, IL: University of Chicago Press.

Hodgson, D. (2011) *Being Maasai, Becoming Indigenous: Postcolonial Politics in a Neoliberal World*, Bloomington, IN: Indiana University Press.

Igoe, J. (2006) 'Becoming Indigenous Peoples: Difference, Inequality, and the Globalization of East African Identity Politics', *African Affairs* 105(420): 399–420.

Iliffe, J. (1979) *A Modern History of Tanganyika*, Cambridge: Cambridge University Press.

Klopp, J. (2002) 'Can Moral Ethnicity Trump Political Tribalism? The Struggle for Land and Nation in Kenya', *African Studies* 61(2): 269–94.

Lemarchand, R. (1992) 'Africa's Troubled Transitions', *Journal of Democracy* 3(4): 98–109.

Lentz, C. and Nugent, P. (eds) (2000) *Ethnicity in Ghana: The Limits of Invention*, Basingstoke: St Martin's Press.

Leonhardt, A. (2006) 'Baka and the Magic of the State: Between Autochthony and Citizenship', *African Studies Review* 49(2): 69–94.

Lonsdale, J. (1994) 'Moral Ethnicity and Political Tribalism', in P. Kaarsholm and J. Huttin (eds) *Inventions and Boundaries: Historical and Anthropological Approaches to the Study of Ethnicity and Nationalism*, Roskilde: Institute for Development Studies, Roskilde University.

——(2004) 'Moral and Political Argument in Kenya', in B. Berman, D. Eyoh and W. Kymlicka (eds) *Ethnicity and Democracy in Africa*, Oxford: James Currey.

Lynch, G. (2006) 'Negotiating Ethnicity: Identity Politics in Contemporary Kenya', *Review of African Political Economy* 33(107): 385–410.

——(2011a) *I Say to You: Ethnic Politics and the Kalenjin in Kenya*, Chicago, IL: University of Chicago Press.

——(2011b) 'Kenya's New Indigenes: Negotiating Local Identities in a Global Context', *Nations and Nationalism* 17(1): 148–67.

——(2011c) 'The Wars of Who Belongs Where: The Unstable Politics of Autochthony on Kenya's Mt Elgon', *Ethnopolitics* 10(3–4): 391–410.

——(2012) 'Becoming Indigenous in the Pursuit of Justice: The African Commission on Human and Peoples' Rights and the Endorois', *African Affairs* 111(442): 24–45.

Mafeje, A. (1971) 'The Ideology of "Tribalism"', *The Journal of Modern African Studies* 9(2): 253–61.

Mamdani, M. (1996) *Citizen and Subject: Contemporary Africa and the Legacy of Late Colonialism*, Princeton, NJ: Princeton University Press.

Marshall-Fratani, R. (2006) 'The War of "Who is Who": Autochthony, Nationalism, and Citizenship in the Ivorian Crisis', *African Studies Review* 49(2): 9–43.

Mbembe, A. (2001) *On the Postcolony*, Berkeley, CA: University of California Press.

Mitchell, J.C. (1956) *The Kalela Dance: Aspects of Social Relationships among Urban Africans in Northern Rhodesia*, Manchester: Manchester University Press.

Molteno, R. (1974) 'Cleavage and Conflict in Zambian Politics: A Study in Sectionalism', in W. Tordoff (ed.) *Politics in Zambia*, Manchester: Manchester University Press.

Mueller, S. (2008) 'The Political Economy of Kenya's Crisis', *Journal of Eastern African Studies* 2(2): 185–201.

Prunier, G. (1995) *The Rwandan Crisis, 1959–1994: History of a Genocide*, New York, NY: Columbia University Press.

Ranger, T. (1993) 'The Invention of Tradition Revisited: The Case of Colonial Africa', in T. Ranger and O. Vaughan (eds) *Legitimacy and the State in Twentieth Century Africa*, Basingstoke: Macmillan.

Scott, J. (1972) 'Patron-Client Politics and Political Change in Southeast Asia', *The American Political Science Review* 66(1): 91–113.

Thompson, E.P. (1978) 'Eighteenth-Century English Society: Class Struggle without Class?', *Social History* 3(2): 133–65.

Vail, L. (1989) 'Introduction: Ethnicity in Southern African History', in L. Vail (ed.) *The Creation of Tribalism in Southern Africa*, London: James Currey.

Willis, J. (1992) 'The Makings of a Tribe: Bondei Identities and History', *The Journal of African History* 33(2): 191–208.

9

AUTOCHTHONY AND THE POLITICS OF BELONGING

Peter Geschiere

The aim of this chapter is to explore the recent upsurge in various regions of Africa of the notion of 'autochthony' (literally 'from the soil itself') as a virulent political slogan that seems to imply, perhaps almost inevitably, a call for excluding strangers ('allogènes' or 'allochthons'). For the African continent, this intensification in the politics of belonging seems to be directly related to democratization and decentralization, the two main trends dominating the post-Cold War moment. However, it is important to place this in a wider, comparative perspective. Indeed the African cases fit in with a much broader, even global, concern with belonging that seems to be the flipside of intensified processes of globalization, a process seen also in wealthier parts of the world. The contrast with the parallel notion of 'indigenous' – also undergoing a recent renaissance, but following a strikingly different trajectory – can help to outline certain ambiguities in this volatile quest for belonging and for limiting the ranks of those who can claim to be 'real' citizens.[1]

The terms autochthony and indigenous go back to classical Greek history and have similar implications. Autochthony refers to 'self' and 'soil'. Indigenous means literally 'born inside', with the connotation in classical Greek of being born inside the house. Thus, both notions inspire similar discourses on the need to safeguard the 'ancestral lands' against 'strangers' who 'despoil' this patrimony; they uphold firstcomers' rights to special protection against later immigrants. Nonetheless, these two terms followed quite different trajectories and they impact differently on present-day issues of belonging. Over the last decades, the notion of 'indigenous peoples' acquired a new lease of life with truly global dimensions. This is especially so since the founding of the United Nations (UN) Working Group on Indigenous Populations in 1982, representing groups from all six continents. The spread of the notion of 'autochthony' remained more limited. During the 1990s it became a burning issue in many parts of Africa, inspiring violent efforts to exclude 'strangers', especially in Francophone areas but with a spillover into Anglophone countries.[2] At the same time it became a key notion in debates on multiculturalism and immigration problems in several parts of Europe, notably Flemish Belgium and the Netherlands.

The spread of the notion in Western contexts is of particular interest. While most Westerners think of 'indigenous peoples' as 'others' who live in distant regions and whose cultures can only 'survive' if they receive special protection, the epithet of 'autochthon' is claimed by important groups in the West itself. This term thus reinforces the preoccupation with belonging and the exclusion of strangers, which have become major issues in everyday politics throughout the world, in the North as much as in the South.

The new dynamics of autochthony discourse on a global scale can therefore serve as a strategic entry point for understanding the enigmatic intertwinement of globalization with intensified struggles over belonging and exclusion. The New World Order, announced by President Bush, Sr, and others at the end of the Cold War, seems to be less marked by freely circulating cosmopolitans than by explosions of communal violence and fierce attempts towards exclusion. Appadurai (1996) already signalled some years ago that globalization and the under-mining of the nation-state inspire a vigorous 'production of locality'. Meyer and Geschiere (1999: introduction) characterized globalization as 'a dialectic of flow *and* closure'. For Southeast Asia, Tania Murray Li (2002) speaks of a 'current conjuncture of belonging' that poses 'deep dilemmas'. It is clear that this conjuncture takes on global forms – widely different trends all over the world converging towards a growing concern with belonging. Neo-liberal economics inspiring new development policies of bypassing the state and decentralization; democratization turning questions like 'who can vote where?' into burning issues; the global concern with ecological degradation inspiring a celebration of local knowledge and a preoccupation with disappearing cultures; popular concerns over immigrants who refuse to integrate: all these trends seem to work towards a defence of local roots. It is also clear that this conjuncture creates great uncertainty that can have violent effects. Belonging promises safety, yet raises fierce disagreements in practice over who *really* belongs.

This global conjuncture of belonging may express itself in different forms between regions, yet two common points stand out, although regional differentiations are manifest. First of all, notions such as 'autochthony' or 'indigenous' appear to defend a return to the local, but in practice are more about access to the global. This point is made most explicitly for Africa by Achille Mbembe (2001: 27) and AbdouMaliq Simone (2001: 25). It may seem logical to equate autochthony with a celebration of the local and of closure against global flows, yet in practice it is often directly linked to processes of globalization. Simone (2001: 25) is right to insist that 'the fight is not so much over the terms of territorial encompassment or closure, but rather over maintaining a sense of "open-endedness"'. What is at stake is often less a closer definition of the local than a struggle over excluding others from access to the new circuits of riches and power.

A second point is the surprising elasticity of autochthony discourses, allowing for constant shifts and re-definitions, which can also make this discourse a somewhat hollow one. It is striking that similar discourses, inspiring almost identical slogans, can have great mobilizing power in highly different contexts, from present-day Africa to Europe. Studies that place the notion in a longer historical perspective show how easily autochthony discourses can switch from one 'Other' to the next without losing their credibility (Geschiere and Nyamnjoh 2000). This may explain their great resilience in the face of modern developments, easily adapting to the constant re-drawing of borders that seem to be inherent to processes of globalization. The flipside is a certain diffuseness. In a given situation it may appear to be self-evident who can claim autochthony. Yet, any attempt to define the autochthonous community in more concrete terms gives rise to fierce disagreements and nagging suspicions of 'faking'. Indeed, autochthony discourse is of a segmentary nature: belonging tends to be constantly redefined in increasingly narrow circles. It is an identity with no particular name and no specified history, merely a claim to have come first, which can of course constantly be contested. Precisely these vagaries can give it highly violent implications.

Below, I will briefly discuss the genealogy of 'autochthony' in Africa, notably its role in the imposition of French colonial rule, a crucial link to its present-day upsurge on the continent. Next I discuss its new dynamics in post-colonial Africa in the 1990s, in the context of what can be termed the new politics of belonging, using Cameroon and Côte d'Ivoire as specific examples. A brief comparison with its manifestations elsewhere on the continent can help to bring out a common pattern – notably the aforementioned paradox between apparent security and a practice of deep uncertainty.

Colonial roots: autochthony and French rule in the Sudan

The term 'autochthony', which is now current in Francophone Africa in particular, was introduced in Africa by French military, researchers, and administrators immediately after the colonial conquest at the end of the nineteenth century. It was meant to play a vital role in categorizing the new subjects in order to make the administration of the vast, newly conquered areas possible. For instance, for Maurice Delafosse (1912), administrator-cum-ethnographer, and a towering figure in the imposition of French rule in West Africa, autochthony was a first criterion in his influential book *Haut-Sénégal-Niger*. He used the notion as a basic categorization within the dazzling variety of *indigènes:* some *indigènes* were autochthons, whereas others were definitely not (Delafosse 1912; Arnaut 2004: 207).

The background to the emphasis on this distinction was the *politique des races*, a fixed principle for setting up a colonial administration during the early decades of French rule (Suret-Canale 1964: 103). Whereas the British with their policy of Indirect Rule were preoccupied with finding 'real' chiefs, French policy was (at least initially) to bypass chiefs (who might be troublesome) and instead form homogeneous *cantons*, populated by the same *race*, hence the need to separate ruling immigrant groups from true *autochtones*. In practice, however, things were not that different: the French also soon began to involve local chiefs in the administration of the vast territories they had conquered (Crowder 1964). It is characteristic, therefore, that Delafosse, despite his search for *autochtones* in line with the *politique des races*, was clearly much more interested in mobile groups that had created larger political units. For instance, in his book on *Haut-Sénégal-Niger* the Peul get nearly 40 pages – clearly the author is deeply interested in their peregrinations throughout West Africa and their reputation as empire builders – while most 'autochthonous' groups only get a brief mention (Triaud 1998). Striking is also that Delafosse refers to the latter in quite condescending language, describing them, for instance, as *les malheureux* (ibid.: 230).

This paradox of looking for autochthons as an anchor for the administration, but at the same time treating them as some sort of humble group became more pronounced as the autochthon/ non-autochthon distinction became canonized under French rule. In many societies in the Senegal-Niger area described by Delafosse, local patterns of organization were indeed dominated by a complementary opposition between 'people of the land' and 'ruling' groups that claimed to have come in from elsewhere. Thus, 'the chief of the land' formed (and still forms) a kind of ritual counterpoint to the chief of the ruling dynasty. To the French, the term 'autochthony' proved to be an obvious one to describe this opposition. A good example is the vast literature on the Mossi (the largest group in present-day Burkina Faso). For generations of ethnologists this opposition between what they termed *autochtones* and 'rulers' became the central issue inspiring highly sophisticated, structuralist studies (Izard 1985; Zahan 1961). In this context the notion of autochthony again acquired somewhat condescending overtones. Luning (1997: 11), for instance, indicates that in the prevailing discourse of the Mossi Maana, the *tengabiise* (now translated as autochthons) were characterized as some sort of 'pre-social' terrestrial beings, who had only became classified as a human society since the coming of the *naam*, their foreign rulers. She also notes that in practice *naam* power was in all sorts of ways limited by the *tengabiise*. Still, the *naam*, as foreign rulers, were formally at the top of the prestige scale, decidedly above the autochthons.[3] This stands in striking contrast with how the distinction between autochthon and stranger came to be seen in later phases of post-colonial rule.

Autochthony in the post-colony

In many parts of Francophone Africa, the autochthony notion was initially appropriated by the local populations, becoming an important categorizing principle. Yet after independence (for most countries around 1960) its role seemed to decline, at least formally. During the first decades after independence in Cameroon, for instance, it was not done to talk about *autochthons* or *allogènes*, at least not openly. 'We are all citizens of Cameroon' would be the inevitable, politically correct rejoinder. However, this changed dramatically in the 1990s following the end of the Cold War and the demise (at least formally) of one-party authoritarianism on the African continent. Under political liberalization, the seemingly matter-of-fact categorizations of colonial administrators according to the autochthons/non-autochthons divide turned out to be highly explosive. In the 1990s and 2000s Côte d'Ivoire made headlines because of the fierce hatred behind the violence with which self-styled *autochtones* tried to expel immigrants, but similar outbursts have been reported from elsewhere. One factor behind this was clearly the practical effect of the wave of democratization that overran the continent. Democratization as such was certainly welcomed, but several authors have stressed how the reintroduction of multi-partyism inevitably turned questions like 'who can vote where?' and, crucially, 'who can stand as a candidate where?' – in other words, questions of where one belongs – into red-hot issues (see Geschiere and Nyamnjoh 2000; Socpa 2003).[4] Particularly in more densely settled and urban areas, the locals' fear of being outvoted by more numerous 'strangers' – often citizens of the same nation-state – ran so high that the defence of autochthony seemed to take prevalence over national citizenship. A striking complication was that in many countries incumbent regimes encourage such strife over belonging: the old slogans of nation-building and reinforcement of national citizenship give way rapidly to a support of localist movements with the clear aim of trying to divide the opposition.

A more hidden factor was an equally dramatic switch in the policies of the development establishment during the 1980s, from a decidedly statist approach (emphasizing nation-building as a prerequisite for achieving development), to an emphasis on decentralization, bypassing the state and reaching out to civil society and non-governmental organizations (NGOs). Several authors emphasize that this, again, almost inevitably triggered fierce debates about belonging over who could or could not participate in a 'project-new-style' (Chauveau 2000; Geschiere 2004).

Yet, most importantly, nearly all authors warn that upsurges of autochthony during the 1990s were not simply triggered by political manipulations from above, but equally carried by strong feelings from below. Some authors discuss the proliferation of funeral rituals, turning the burial 'at home' (that is, in the village of origin) into a key moment in the contest over belonging (Geschiere and Gugler 1998; Monga 1995; Vidal 1991). Others point to land (see Lentz 2003 on Ghana and Burkina Faso) or ritual associations (see Austen 1992 on Duala) as crucial issues in popular movements to defend autochthony. The themes outlined above will be elaborated for two specific examples, Cameroon and Côte d'Ivoire, with shorter examples from other regions.

Cameroon: autochthony versus national citizenship

The upsurge of autochthony as a virulent issue in Cameroon during the 1990s must be understood in relation to the determined, sometimes even desperate, struggle of President Paul Biya, the leader of the former one-party, to remain in power. Probably under direct pressure of then-President of France François Mitterrand, Biya permitted freedom of association only towards the end of 1990. This immediately brought a proliferation of opposition parties. However, Biya refused to give in and after 1992 the opposition petered out. The crucial presidential elections of 1992 became a scandal since it was quite clear that Biya obtained his narrow victory (38 per cent against 35 per cent) over his main rival, John Fru Ndi, due to massive rigging. However, in subsequent years Biya held out against all pressure and his party won all subsequent elections.

Biya's capacity for political survival is, indeed, impressive – all the more so since this took place in the midst of a deep economic crisis. This begs the question of how he and his team succeeded nonetheless in completely outmanoeuvring the opposition, which seemed to be in such a promising position in the early 1990s. An obvious answer is the regime's success in playing the autochthony card. Indeed, Cameroon offers a prime example of the effectiveness that autochthony slogans can acquire in national politics. Geschiere and Nyamnjoh (2000) show how the regime used the growing fear among 'autochthons' in the Southwest Province and Douala city, the country's core economic areas. Their concern was that they would be outvoted under the new and increasingly democratic constellation by more numerous immigrants from the highlands of the northwest and West Province. After the 1996 municipal elections, the government actively supported large-scale and quite violent demonstrations by 'autochthons' in Douala to protest against the fact that in four of the six *communes* of the city politicians who identified themselves as 'Bamileke' had been elected as mayor on an opposition ticket. The demonstrators' slogans were all too clear: the *came-no-goes* (the Pidgin term for immigrants) should go home and vote where they really belonged. The government defended its support for this viewpoint with reference to the new Constitution of 1996, which emphasized the need to protect the rights of 'minorities' (i.e. *indigenes*).

There is a telling contrast here with the earlier Constitution of 1972, at the high tide of nation-building, which emphasized the right of any Cameroonian to settle anywhere in the country. Nyamnjoh and Rowlands (1998) show that the regime's support for newfangled elite associations created another arena for struggles over belonging and autochthony. Again, there was a striking reversal of former policies. Under one-party rule any form of association outside the party was severely discouraged, but after the onset of democratization, the regime even obliged regional elites (mostly civil servants and therefore in the pay of the government) to constitute their own associations. These associations often had ostentatious cultural aims, but in practice there was an underlying obligation to go home and campaign for the president's party. Such regional associations offered, therefore, a welcome channel to mobilize votes and to neutralize the effects of multi-partyism. This was all the more so since they also served to exclude elites who were not really autochthonous to the area and thus blocked the political participation of *allogènes* who mostly supported the opposition parties.[5] Konings (2001) discusses how effective the regime has been in dividing the Anglophone opposition, which in the early 1990s still seemed to form a solid front. They achieved this through a tactical mix of support to elite associations and minority groups, coupled with a general emphasis on belonging. In subsequent years the southwest's autochthons (Anglophones) – fearing, like the (Francophone) Douala, that they would be overwhelmed by *come-no-go* immigrants – became the regime's staunchest supporters (see Konings and Nyamnjoh 2003).

These events triggered a fierce debate among academics and other intellectuals over the rights of *autochtones* versus *allogènes*. The Cameroonian review *La Nouvelle Expression* offered a seminal overview of various perspectives in its May 1996 issue. While several contributors such as Ngijol Ngijol, Bertrand Toko, and Philip Bissek warned against the dangers of the political use of discourses on autochthony, the contribution by Roger Nlep was to attain a central position in the debates in Cameroon. With his 'theory' of *le village electoral*, Nlep takes a different view, arguing that 'integration' is the central issue in Cameroonian politics, and people can only be fully integrated in the place where they live if there is not *un autre chez soi* (another home). Therefore, if a person runs for office in Douala and still defends the interests of his village elsewhere, this must be considered as 'political malversation'. The relation to the regime's manipulation of voters' lists, telling people to go 'home' and vote there, is quite clear.[6]

However, other notions on belonging, less directly linked to the vicissitudes of national politics, also emerged in these debates. A crucial statement, as seminal as it is succinct, came from Samuel Eboua, an *éminence grise* of Cameroonian politics, in an interview in the review *Impact Tribu-Une*:

> Every Cameroonian is an *allogène* anywhere else in the country … apart from where his ancestors lived and … where his mortal remains will be buried. Everybody knows that only under exceptional circumstances will a Cameroonian be buried … elsewhere.
>
> *(Interview with Samuel Eboua in* Impact Tribu-Une *1995: 5, 14)*

Such statements emphasize how strongly the Cameroonian version of autochthony opposes the very idea of a national citizenship and the principle that every Cameroonian 'has the right to settle in any place', celebrated by the earlier Constitution of the time of nation-building. Geschiere and Nyamnjoh (2000) highlight the growing emphasis, in the context of autochthony politics, on the place of funeral as the ultimate test of belonging. Protagonists of autochthony repeat time and again that as long as immigrants, even if they are Cameroonian citizens, still want to be buried back home in the village, it is clear that this is their home and therefore where they should return to vote (see also Geschiere 2004; Monga 1995).

Similar arguments play a central role in the confrontations between autochthons and *allogènes* studied by Socpa (2003) in two very different parts of the country: the capital Yaoundé and the Logone area, where the first explosion of violence erupted after democratization. In both areas autochthony has a long history. In Yaoundé it was mainly the issue of land, the supposed tricks with which Bamileke immigrants succeeded in appropriating the land from the Beti auto-chthons. This created animosity between the groups ever since the French made the town the capital of the colony in 1921, but it was the new-style elections that made these tensions acute. Socpa shows that when Bamileke succeeded in buying a plot for building they continued to address the former owner as their 'landlord' (*bailleur*), while former owners talked about their 'tenants' (*locataires*) even though they had sold the land' (ibid.: 117). Significantly, this implies in the latter's view that these 'tenants' should behave as good 'guests' and not vote for the opposition – that is not try and rule in their 'landlord's house'. Socpa also highlights the elusive nature of the notion despite all the emphasis it receives. In the competition for political posts, autochthons take it for granted that they should rule in their own area, but some are apparently more autochthonous than others (ibid.: 208). After Biya's party won the 1996 municipal elections in Yaoundé, furious fighting broke out between different local clans who each claimed the mayoral position on the grounds that they were the 'real' autochthons. Thus it is in Yaoundé, which remains a bastion of autochthony in the Cameroonian context, that the discourse shows its 'segmentary' character, subject as it is to a constant tendency to redefine the 'real' autochthon at ever-closer range.

The vicissitudes of autochthony in a very different part of the country – the sparsely popu-lated forest area of the southeast – highlight other factors that can exacerbate these issues of belonging: the impact of globalization and the new style of development politics that empha-sizes decentralization and 'bypassing the state'. With the dramatic fall of world market prices for Cameroon's main cash crops (cacao, coffee, and cotton), and the threatening depletion of its oil reserves, timber has become a crucial export product. Thus the southeast, long seen as the most backward part of the country, became a region of central interest because of its rich forest resources. However, there was vehement opposition from global ecological movements, strongly supported by the World Bank, against the further plundering of this 'lung of the world'. The result was the new forest law of 1994, which the Cameroonian government only accepted under heavy pressure from the Bank and the International Monetary Fund.

As is typical in the new approach to development, the law emphasizes the role of local 'communities' – unfortunately not further defined – as central stakeholders in the exploitation of the forest, advocating moreover far-reaching financial decentralization. Consequently, municipalities of a few thousand inhabitants were to receive almost half of the taxes on logging in their areas. This no doubt well-intentioned insistence on redistribution and protecting the 'community' immediately triggered fierce contestations over belonging in this sparsely populated area. Local communities here are notoriously diffuse, constantly splitting up according to malleable oppositions between lineage branches. In practice, the village committees that are supposed to manage the new 'community forests' are constantly divided over accusations that some people do not 'really' belong. Even kin can be unmasked as *allogènes* who belong in another village and should therefore join the new development project there. Clearly the segmentary tenor of the autochthony discourse is perpetuated, hence its violent implications. Even within the intimacy of these close-knit villages that seem lost in vast tracts of forest it has become possible to unmask one's neighbour or relative as a stranger.

Côte d'Ivoire: autochthony and the difficult birth of a 'new' nation

The trajectory of the autochthony notion in Côte d'Ivoire during the same troubled period of democratization is markedly different, notably in its relation to the nation. In Cameroon, autochthony seems to be some sort of rival for citizenship, denying the formal equality of all citizens and defending special forms of access to the state. In Côte d'Ivoire, by contrast, it refers to efforts to redefine or even 'save' the nation.

In this country, the concept of autochthony, again introduced by French colonials, was quickly appropriated by local spokesmen. One of the first signs of a new local vigour was the foundation, already in 1934, of an association that baptized itself *Association de défense des intérêts des autochtones de Côte d'Ivoire* (Arnaut 2004: 208; Dozon 2000a: 16). In those days, Senegalese and Dahomean clerks occupying the lower ranks in the colonial administration were the main targets for Ivorian autochthony, although other 'strangers' were soon to replace them. From the 1920s, cocoa production in the southern part of the colony attracted ever greater numbers of immigrants from the north who first came as labourers, but soon managed to create their own farms. Especially after Independence in 1960, this immigration became one of the mainstays in the *miracle ivoirien*, the spectacular flowering of the country's economy. Both Dozon (2000b) and Arnaut (2004) mention the role of President Houphouët-Boigny's pan-African ideas in his conscious encouragement of immigrants to push the 'frontier' of cocoa production ever further in the country's southern areas. Local communities were encouraged to grant land to enterprising immigrants.

Chauveau (2000: 107) demonstrates that the autochthons' main chance to continue to profit from their original rights was to hang on to their role as *tuteurs*, which allowed them to ask for regular 'gifts'; over time, with the value of land rising, this 'tutorship' became a 'permanent and conflict-ridden negotiation'. Immigrants came mainly from both the northern parts of the country and neighbouring countries (Mali and, especially, Burkina Faso). However, Dozon (2000b) emphasizes that southerners hardly distinguish between Ivorian citizens and others among these northerners. Commonly called 'Dyula', whether Ivorians or non-Ivorians, they all shared similar characteristics – many are Muslims – and this created an idea of *le grand Nord* from which all these people came.

However, towards the end of the 1980s Houpouët-Boigny's miracle seemed to stagnate: the scarcity of land led to increasing tensions; world market prices for cocoa collapsed; and, because of the crisis, the return of young urbanites to the village increased rural tensions. This gave rise to a *réactivation de l'idéologie de l'autochtonie* (Chauveau 2000: 114). After the 1990 elections, the southern opposition parties openly accused Houphouët-Boigny of owing his re-election to the votes of 'strangers', and even alleged that he himself was some sort of 'allochthon' (Arnaut 2004: 216; Dozon 2000a: 16). The developments after his death in 1993, particularly since 2000, have confirmed the fears of several authors that such tensions would result in the consolidation of a cleavage between a bloc of self-proclaimed southern autochthons and the north (Chauveau 2000; Dozon 2000b; Losch 2000).

It is important to signal that this broad trajectory, which in retrospect appears almost inevitable, involved all sorts of twists and turns and may still involve a variety of different trajectories. Chauveau (2000) highlights, for instance, that the definition of the *autochtone* keeps shifting together with the moving frontier of the cocoa zone. Production began in the southeast of the country and expanded from there gradually to the southwest and the west. In earlier phases, Baule (from the centre of the southern part of the country) were the main migrants. They moved first into the southeast when cocoa production took off there. Later on, cocoa entered their own region, but they continued to expand, following the frontier into the western and southwestern parts of the country. Thus in the 1960s the claim to autochthony was mainly raised by groups in the southwest and west (notably the Bete and Dida) against Baule 'immigrants'. Now, terms like *allogène* or immigrant are nearly synonymous with northerners. However, Chauveau warns that the Baule are very conscious of the fact that 'real' autochthons may at any time redirect their grievances against them (ibid.: 121). Since Houphouët-Boigny, the Baule may have been highly represented in the national centres of power and they may have been at the forefront of defending the autochthony of the southerners against northern immigrants, but they are increasingly reminded by the 'true' locals, especially in the southeast, that they are also immigrants and could therefore be marked as 'fake' autochthons.

After 1993, the defence of autochthony was couched in more ideological terms when Houpouët-Boigny's successor, Henry Konan Bedié, launched the notion of *ivoirité*. He introduced this notion in order to oust one of his main rivals for the presidency, Alassane Ouattara, from the electoral competition on the grounds that both the latter's parents came from Burkina Faso. Dozon (2000a) and, in rich detail, Arnaut (2004), show that this was part of a broader ideological offensive, trying to justify the need to distinguish *Ivoiriens de souche* (of the trunk) from others. Dozon speaks of an *aéropage* of intellectuals and writers around Bedié, brought together in the journal *Curdiphe*.[7] Similarly, *Politique Africaine* published part of the Acts of a colloquium of this institute in which, for instance, Professor Niangoran-Bouah (the country's first anthropologist, as director of the *patrimoine culturel* of the Ministry of Culture) proposed a 'regrouping' of 'the ancestors of Ivorians, or Ivorians *de souche*' (Curdiphe 2000). On the basis of this, he describes 'the autochthons with a mythical origin' and then *les autochtones sans origine mythique*. He insists – and this is clearly very important to him – that all these groups were already settled in the country on 10 March 1893 when 'Ivory Coast was born' (ibid.: 66).[8] This tendency to develop ever-finer distinctions on very shaky basis (how can the learned anthropologist distinguish between groups who claim a mythical origin and those who do not?) is a striking example of the dangerous, 'segmentary' tendency of discourses of autochthony.

In such enumerations *ivoirité* seems to coincide with the notion of a southern autochthony, but Dozon (2000a) warns that, again, there are sub-texts hidden in Bédié's celebration of *ivoiriens de souche*. At a deeper level it highlights the special vocation of the Baule (the group to which both Bédié and Houphouët-Boigny belonged) as some sort of super-autochthons. As part of the broader Akan group (which also includes the neighbouring Ashanti in Ghana), Baule see themselves as blessed with state-forming talents that distinguish them from other southern groups (like the more 'segmentary' Bete). The idea of *Ivoiriens de souche* therefore implies a double exclusion: on the one hand of northern immigrants, and on the other of certain southerners, supposedly less capable because of their cultural heritage to lead the nation.

Arnaut highlights that the discourse shifts not only per region but also over time. In 1999, Bédié was pushed aside by a military coup under general Guéï. In 2000, Laurent Gbagbo, another southern politician (but a Bete from the southwest), won the elections from which Ouattara, the candidate of the north, was excluded. However, in September 2002 a military insurgency in the north effectively split up the country between north and south, 'the kind of geographical framework within which the discourse of autochthony flourishes so well in Côte d'Ivoire' (Arnaut 2004: 240). Under Gbagbo the idea of *ivoirité* acquired a new lease of life, one in which there were new aspects: the *ivoirité* of Gbagbo had a more global outlook and it set up the 'frontier' in Bete land (rather than any Baule element) as a symbol of the nation, but now a new, emerging nation of Ivorians (ibid.: 242, 252). As Arnaut concludes, 'Autochthony is … also a powerful discourse for a regional minority to reinvent itself as a "national" majority' (ibid.: 247).

Thus, while autochthony in Côte d'Ivoire may remain more closely linked to the nation, albeit in purified form, it shows similar segmentary tendencies as elsewhere. Who the 'real' autochthon is remains an object of deep controversies, just as 'the Other' takes on constantly new guises.

Other African settings

Another hotbed of autochthony is the Great Lakes Region, notably Rwanda, Burundi, and the adjacent parts of the Democratic Republic of Congo (DRC, specifically North and South Kivu). Stephen Jackson's recent thesis (2003) on 'War-Making' in Goma, the capital of North Kivu, is based on research from the late 1990s when Congolese 'rebels', backed by Rwandan and Ugandan troops, conquered this part of the DRC. He speaks of 'a breakneck chase to exert control over fluctuating identity categories' (Jackson 2003: 247). His second chapter, on 'Making History and Migratory Identities', evokes a dazzling vortex of identities with constantly changing names and historical claims. However, a recurring dividing line in all this is apparently the opposition between autochthons and allochthons, and a fixed point of reference in defining the latter are the much-resented Banyarwanda – 'Rwandophones' who are constantly suspected of plotting to deliver the region to neighbouring Rwanda.

Yet, even this more-or-less fixed beacon has its ambiguities: it can refer to recent Hutu refugees (who fled to the DRC after the 1994 genocide of Tutsi in Rwanda and the subsequent takeover by Kagame and his Tutsi army); but it can also refer to their arch-opponents, the Banyamulenge, whom autochthons often call 'Congolese Tutsi'. Jackson's study highlights both the surprising resilience of the idea of a Congolese nation among the 'autochthons' of this remote part of the country and the fierce debates over history in this context: Where do these Banyamulenge come from? When did they settle in Congo? How can they claim to belong here as well? Jean-Claude Williame (1997) similarly highlights an important factor behind all these uncertainties. Former President Mobutu's volatile manipulations of national citizenship initially promised the Banyamulenge recognition of their Congolese citizenship when he needed their support, which he subsequently denied when he required the support of other groups.

Liisa Malkki's (1996) references to 'autochtonisation' as a central trait in the construction of a group history among Hutu refugees from Burundi similarly highlight the narrow link – albeit with a somewhat different tenor – between autochthony claims and the struggle over national citizenship. The Hutu historical claim for autochthony is essential to their hope of being liberated from their domination by Tutsi with their false pretence of superiority. However, Malkki also shows that such claims to being autochthonous have additional consequences: Hutu have to share their autochthony with Twa (often termed 'pygmies' and who constitute around 1 per cent of the population). This indicates how easily the notion of autochthony can be associated with an idea of 'primitive', as though in the first stage of development. There are similarities here with the term as it was originally conceived when it was first introduced in western Sudan by French civil servants, when almost 'pre-human' autochthons were seen as only being socialized by incoming foreign rulers. Malkki is certainly right to emphasize that for the Hutu refugees 'autochthony can be a double-edged sword' (ibid.: 63).

Various authors highlight the centrality of preoccupations with autochthony in recent political developments in other parts of Africa. Carola Lentz (2003) emphasizes the long history of these tensions, going back to pre-colonial times, in Burkina Faso and neighbouring parts of Ghana. However, she also notes that autochthony became a powerful political slogan, particularly in the 1990s, in the competition for posts, but even more so in struggles over access to land. The language of autochthony also seems to penetrate into Anglophone parts of the continent, not only in Cameroon (see above), but also in areas of northern Ghana that border on Burkina Faso and Togo (Wienia 2003). Yet even where the notion is not current or even explicit, similar discourses prove to be highly mobilizing. Comaroff and Comaroff (2001) are certainly right to compare the threatening upsurge of xenophobia in South Africa against the *makwere-kwere* (African immigrants from across the Limpopo) to the autochthony obsession elsewhere on the continent. In reverse, their analysis of the 'zombification' of these *makwere-kwere* – the tendency to de-personalize immigrants – is highly relevant for the autochthony examples discussed above.[9] Catherine Boone's (2003) challenging comparison of developments in Senegal, Côte d'Ivoire, and Ghana shows how easily similar discourses, again centring on access to land, cross-cut the border between Anglophone and Francophone Africa. Achim von Oppen's recent *Habilitationsschrift* (2003) on Bounding Villages in Zambia similarly highlights the paradox of exclusionist discourses on locality and belonging that manage at the same time to remain open-ended and tuned in to globalization.

In general it might be useful to emphasize that this upsurge of autochthony in Africa is cause for surprise. Historians and anthropologists used to characterize African societies as oriented towards 'wealth-in-people' in contrast to conceptions of 'wealth-in-things' prevailing elsewhere (see Miller 1988; Guyer 1993, 2004). Africa would be characterized by its open forms of organization with special arrangements for incorporating people into local groups. This naturally encompasses elements such as very broad kinship terminology, adoption, and forms of clientelism. The current emphasis on autochthony and local belonging seems, therefore, to be quite a dramatic turn towards closure and exclusion. However, the examples presented here demonstrate that such apparent closure may deceive in view of the extreme malleability of autochthony discourse. It is doubtful whether one can simply characterize it as a 'retraditionalization' and a return to the village. Its exclusionary propensity is rather about limiting access to the state and new global circuits.[10] Autochthony can present itself as a rival to national citizenship, but it can also pretend to reinforce the nation (often by 'purifying' it). Despite its appeal to local belonging as a self-evident criterion, its segmentary proclivity creates nagging uncertainties: one always risks being unmasked as 'not really' autochthonous. Indeed, the elusiveness of who is 'really' an autochthon gives it an ambiguous quality. African examples of recent autochthony movements suggest that the quest for belonging is a never-ending one, simultaneously promising safety yet raising basic insecurities.[11]

Conclusion

From the variations discussed above, autochthony clearly emerges as a perpetual mirror game (but certainly not an innocent one). Its apparent 'naturalness' hides a constant flux of redefining a kind of belonging that just as constantly seems to slip away. Its highly variable implications for the nation-state are quite striking. In Cameroon it presents itself as an alternative to the very idea of national citizenship. In Côte d'Ivoire, by contrast, it defines itself as the nation, albeit in a renovated, purified form. For the Athenians, long ago, it implied a kind of inborn propensity towards democracy. In modern times it seems more to express a deep disappointment about what democracy has become.

Despite these differences, however, there exist some general trends. A crucial one is highlighted by the classical glorification of autochthony in early Athens, in the challenging interpretation of Nicole Loraux (1996). She evokes the paradoxical instability of a discourse that celebrates stability. Autochthony may invoke staying-in-place as some sort of norm, but for historians movement is rather the norm: any history starts with a migration. Even the Athenian families that were so proud of their autochthony had myths of origin from elsewhere. Similarly, the Beti, who have now become the arch-autochthons of Cameroon, express their unity by a myth of an only partially successful crossing of the majestic Sanaga river on the back of a huge python. Autochthony needs movement as a counterpoint to define itself, and it is precisely this basic instability that makes it a potentially dangerous discourse.

The paradox between a promise of primordial security and a practice of basic insecurity seems to be of all times and places, whenever autochthony or similar notions (like 'sons of the soil') become current. Yet it is clear that the force of such notions and their emotional appeal can differ greatly. An obvious question remains why, especially during the 1990s, such discourses on belonging and exclusion became suddenly so strong that they began to dominate politics, not only in many parts of Africa but also elsewhere in the world. It is clear that there is a link with intensified processes of globalization, albeit one with varying outcomes. For Africa democratization and the new style of development policies were mentioned above as specific factors in this context. In Europe the growing concern about migrants, who supposedly refuse 'cultural integration', seems to play a big role. Clearly we need to follow much more closely the different historical trajectories in the articulation of globalization and the preoccupation with belonging which always has exclusion as its flipside.

Notes

1 This text contains elements from my book (Geschiere 2009), notably from the Introduction and chapters 2, 3 and 4. *Cf.* also a text I published with Bambi Ceuppens (Ceuppens and Geschiere 2005).
2 This is further complicated by the fact that since 2000 the UN working group began to use the term *autochtone* as the official translation in French of 'indigenous', which created considerable confusion in areas where this French term had been used with quite different meanings. See Gausset *et al.* (2012).
3 There is an intriguing similarity between forms of 'diarchy' between land-chief and ruler (usually coming from elsewhere) described by anthropologists for Southeast Asia; for an overview article see Schefold (2001).

4 This was certainly not limited to Francophone Africa. A notorious case was the ousting in Zambia of former President Kenneth Kaunda from political competition by his successor Frederick Chiluba on the grounds of Kaunda's descent from foreigners.

5 See Geschiere and Nyamnjoh (2000) and Konings (2001) on the 'Assocation of the Elites of the Tenth Province', an imagined province (Cameroon has only nine provinces), proclaimed by elites who feel excluded from belonging anywhere else.

6 For an overview of more extreme voices (for instance on the supposed 'ethnofascism' of Bamileke), see Geschiere and Nyamnjoh (2000).

7 This stands for *Cellule universitaire de recherche et de diffusion des idées et actions du président* Konan Bédié.

8 See Arnaut (2004) for a discussion of similar texts.

9 On Ghanaian immigrants in Botswana see also van Dijk (2003).

10 *Cf.* Mbembe's and Simone's emphasis, quoted above, on the open-endedness of these discourses.

11 For reasons of space we can not address here the relation with alternative notions of belonging that seems to feed on people's perception that the continent is in crisis. Notably a comparison with the upsurge of Pentecostalism would be of interest since it clearly offers a different sense of belonging from autochthony. Most authors (*cf.* Meyer 1999) signal Pentecostalists' deep distrust of 'the village' and 'the family' equated with the Devil; instead they belong to a (global?) community of 'born-agains'. However, for Malawi, Englund (2004) emphasizes the close links urban Pentecostalists retain with their village of origin. Apparently in the relation between autochthony and Pentecostalism, as seemingly opposite discourses on belonging, varying contradictions and articulations are possible.

Bibliography

Appadurai, A. (1996) *Modernity at Large, Cultural Dimension of Globalization*, Minneapolis, MN, and London: University of Minnesota Press.

Arnaut, K. (2004) 'Performing Displacements and Rephrasing Attachments: Ethnographie Explorations of Mobility in Art, Ritual, Media and Politics', unpublished PhD thesis, University of Ghent.

Austen, R.A. (1992) 'Tradition, Invention and History: The Case of the Ngondo (Cameroon)', *Cahiers d'etudes africaines* 32(126): 285–309.

Boone, C. (2003) *Political Topographies of the African State: Territorial Authority and Institutional Choice*, Cambridge: Cambridge University Press.

Ceuppens, B. and Geschiere, P. (2005) 'Autochthony: Local or Global? Struggle over Citizenship and Belonging in Africa and Europe', *Annual Review of Anthropology* 34: 385–409.

Chauveau, J.-P. (2000) 'Question foncière et construction nationale en Côte d'Ivoire', *Politique africaine* 78: 94–126.

Comaroff, J. and Comaroff, J. (2001) 'Naturing the Nation: Aliens, Apocalypse and the Postcolonial State', *Journal of Southern African Studies* 27(3): 627–51.

Crowder, M. (1964) 'Indirect Rule, French and British Style', *Africa* 33(4): 293–306.

Curdiphe (2000) 'L'Ivoirité, ou l'esprit du nouveau contrat social du Président H.K. Bédié', *Politique Africaine* 78: 65–69.

Delafosse, M. (1912, reprinted 1972) *Haut-Sénégal-Niger*, Paris: E. Larose.

Dozon, J.-P. (2000a) 'La Côte d'Ivoire au péril de l'ivoirité – Génèse d'un coup d'Etat', *Afrique contemporaine* 193: 13–23.

——(2000b) 'La Côte d'Ivoire entre démocratie, nationalisme et ethnonationalisme', *Politique africaine* 78: 45–63.

Englund, H. (2004) 'Cosmopolitanism and the Devil in Malawi', *Ethnos* 69(3): 293–316.

Gausset, Q., Gibb, R. and Kenrick, J. (eds) (2012) 'Indigenous or Autochthonous', *Social Anthropology*, forthcoming.

Geschiere, P. (2004) 'Ecology, Belonging and Xenophobia: The 1994 Forest Law in Cameroon and the Issue of "Community"', in H. Englund and F.B. Nyamnjoh (eds) *Rights and the Politics of Recognition in Africa*, London: Zed Books.

——(2005) 'Funerals and Belonging: Different Patterns in South Cameroon', *African Studies Review* 48(2): 45–64.

——(2009) *Perils of Belonging, Autochthony, Citizenship and Exclusion in Africa and Europe*, Chicago, IL, and London: University of Chicago Press.

Geschiere, P. and Gugler, J. (eds) (1998) 'The Politics of Primary Patriotism', *Africa* 68(3): 309–19.

Geschiere, P. and Nyamnjoh, F.B. (2000) 'Capitalism and Autochthony: The Seesaw of Mobility and Belonging', *Public Culture* 12(2): 423–53.

Guyer, J. (1993) 'Wealth in People and Self-realisation in Equatorial Africa', *Man* 28(2): 243–65.

——(2004) *Marginal Gains: Monetary Transactions in Atlantic Africa*, Chicago, IL: Chicago University Press.

Izard, M. (1985) *Gens du pouvoir, gens de la terre: Les institutions politiques de l'ancien royaume du Yatenga (Bassin de la Volta blanche)*, Cambridge: Cambridge University Press.

Jackson, S. (2003) 'War Making – Uncertainty, Improvisation and Involution in the Kivu Provinces, DR Congo, 1997–2002', unpublished PhD thesis, Princeton University.

Konings, P. (2001) 'Mobility and Exclusion: Conflicts between Autochtons and Allochthons during Political Liberalization in Cameroon', in M. de Bruijn, R. van Dijk and D. Foeken (eds) *Mobile Africa: Changing Patterns of Movement in Africa and Beyond*, Leiden: Brill.

Konings, P. and Nyamnjoh, F.B. (2003) *Negotiating an Anglophone Identity: A Study of the Politics of Recognition and Representation in Cameroon*, Leiden: Brill.

Lentz, C. (2003) '"Premiers arrivés" et "nouveaux venus": Discours sur l'autochtonie dans la savane ouest-africaine', in R. Kuba, C. Lentz and C.M. Somda (eds) *Histoire du Peuplement et Relations Interethniques au Burkina Faso*, Paris: Karthala.

Li, T.M. (2002) 'Ethnic Cleansing, Recursive Knowledge, and the Dilemmas of Sedentarism', *International Social Science Journal* 54(173): 361–71.

Loraux, N. (1996) *N'e de la Terre: Mythe et Politique à Athènes*, Paris: Le Seuil.

Losch, B. (2000) 'La Côte d'Ivoire en quête d'un nouveau projet national', *Politique africaine* 78: 5–26.

Luning, S. (1997) *Het Binnenhalen van de Oogst: Ritueel en samenleving in Maane, Burkina Faso*, Leiden: CNWS publications.

Malkki, L. (1996) *Purity and Exile: Violence, Memory, and National Cosmology among Hutu Refugees in Tanzania*, Chicago, IL: Chicago University Press.

Mbembe, A. (2001) 'Ways of Seeing: Beyond the New Nativism – Introduction', *African Studies Review* 44(2): 1–14.

Meyer, B. (1999) *Translating the Devil: Religion and Modernity among the Ewe in Ghana*, Edinburgh: IAI/ Edinburgh University Press.

Meyer, B. and Geschiere, P. (eds) (1999) *Globalization and Identity: Dialectics of Flow and Closure*, Oxford: Blackwell.

Miller, J.C. (1988) *'Way of Death': Merchant Capitalism and the Angolan Slave Trade 1730–1893*, Madison, WI: Wisconsin University Press.

Monga, C. (1995) 'Cercueils, orgies et sublimation: Le coût d'une mauvaise gestion de la mort', *Afrique 2000* 21: 63–72.

Nyamnjoh, F.B. and Rowlands, M. (1998) 'Elite Associations and the Politics of Belonging in Cameroon', *Africa* 68(3): 320–37.

Schefold, R. (2001) 'Vision of the Wilderness on Siberut in A Comparative Southeast Asian Perspective', in G. Benjamin and C. Chou (eds) *Tribal Communities in the Malay World*, Singapore: Institute of Southeast Asian Studies.

Simone, A. (2001) 'On the Worlding of African Cities', *African Studies Review* 44(2): 15–41.

Socpa, A. (2003) *Démocratisation et autochtonie au Cameroun: Variations régionales divergentes*, Münster: LIT.

Suret-Canale, J. (1964) *Afrique noire occidentale et centrale II: L'Ere coloniale 1900–1945*, Paris: Éditions Sociales.

Triaud, J.-L. (1998) '"Haut-Sénégal-Niger", un modèle positiviste? De la coutume à l'histoire: Maurice Delafosse et l'invention de l'histoire africaine', in J.-L. Amselle and E. Sibeud (eds) *Maurice Delafosse – Entre orientalisme et ethnographie: Itinéraire d'un africaniste (1870–1926)*, Paris: Maisonneuve et Larose.

van Dijk, R. (2003) 'Localisation, Ghanaian Pentecostalism and the Stranger's Beauty in Botswana', *Africa* 73(4): 560–83.

Vidal, C. (1991) *Sociologie des Passions: Rwanda, Côte d'Ivoire*, Paris: Karthala.

von Oppen, A. (2003) *Bounding Villages: The Enclosure of Locality in Central Africa, 1890s to 1990s*, unpublished PhD thesis, Humboldt University of Berlin.

Wienia, M. (2003) *The Stranger Owns the Land but the Land is for Us: The Politics of a Religious Landscape in Nanun, N. Ghana*, Leiden: Institute of Social and Cultural Studies.

Willame, J.-C. (1997) *Banyarwanda et Banyamulenge: Violences ethniques et gestion de l'identitaire au Kivu*, Paris: L'Harmattan.

Zahan, D. (1961) 'Pour une histoire des Mossi du Yatenga', *L'Homme* 1(2): 5–22.

10

RELIGION AND POLITICS

Stephen Ellis and Gerrie ter Haar

Politics, however it is defined precisely, is a way of conceiving and organizing relations of power. In modern times it has become closely identified with the sovereign states that, since 1945, have been the building blocks of the international system of diplomacy and law. Yet in most of Africa sovereign states of the modern type have only a short history, so much so that, according to the historian John Lonsdale (1981: 139), 'the most distinctively African contribution to human history could be said to have been precisely the civilized art of living fairly peaceably together *not* in states'.

It is when one considers how people in so many parts of Africa were able to live together for countless centuries in coherent societies, but without states in the conventional sense, that the deep-seated importance of religion in sub-Saharan Africa becomes apparent. In Africa, religion has historically been considered a form of power, and it is this above all that makes it the Siamese twin of politics in modern times. As Michael Schatzberg notes, most Africans:

> ... understand that 'politics' and 'religion' are parts of the same terrain: that power flows between the visible material world and the invisible spiritual world; and that the political kingdom contains a politically significant spiritual terrain. Moreover, intelligent and gifted politicians know the contours of this terrain and are comfortable traversing it in either its material or spiritual manifestations. They understand that in their culture power is unitary and cannot be divided into separate boxes.
>
> *(Schatzberg 2001: 74)*

In considering this observation, it immediately becomes clear how important it is to define what precisely is meant by religion. This is not best done by choosing a favourite definition of religion from among the many dozens on offer. Many of the definitions of religion popular among social scientists are derived from classical sociologists such as Durkheim and Weber, yet these are generally not the most conducive to understanding the relation of religion and politics in Africa. It is therefore most useful to formulate a definition that emerges from the context under study. It is to this end that we have elsewhere proposed a working definition of religion in Africa as 'a belief in the existence of an invisible world, distinct but not separate from the visible one, that is home to spiritual beings with effective powers over the material world' (Ellis and ter Haar 2004: 14). This is a working definition, elaborated with a view to incorporating the entire range of religious practices and ideas in Africa. It follows in the tradition of the nineteenth-century anthropologist E.B. Tylor (1958: 8) in its insistence on the spiritual element of religion.

Three aspects of our working definition make it particularly well suited for present purposes. First, it is not only Africans who are religious inasmuch as they believe it is possible to communicate with a perceived world of spirits, but people in many other parts of the world too. Considering religion in this way therefore emphasizes some of what Africa has in common with other places rather than drawing attention to its uniqueness – the latter being a feature of so much writing on Africa. Second, our definition incorporates practices often referred to as 'magic' or 'superstition' or in similarly value-laden terms, the use of which excludes certain forms of religious expression from qualifying as religion at all. A third, related advantage of defining religion in the way we do is that it avoids attributing a moral value to any particular type of belief. Our definition does not imply that religion is always in pursuit of that which is noble or good. Religion, in the sense we define it, may include both socially constructive and destructive practices. It is hard to understand its relation to politics in Africa without appreciating this point.

Throughout Africa's known history, people have generally perceived all power to have its ultimate origin in the spirit world. This is often not immediately apparent, however, as many Africans may normally devote rather little time to religious matters. A person may spend virtually all of his or her time dealing with mundane matters yet still believe that these are ultimately determined in the invisible world. Rather as the driver of a car knows that his vehicle depends utterly on petrol but does not generally spend more than a few minutes taking on fuel, so people might give regular attention to the spirit world in order to maintain their wellbeing, but only for short periods. This emphasis on the invisible world as a source of power, and religious practice as a means of accessing it, stands in marked contrast to a common tendency in Europe and North America to define religion primarily in terms of a search for meaning in life.

Notwithstanding the closeness of their relationship, religion and politics in Africa are not identical. Some of Africa's billion people are determined secularists in the sense of holding that society should be governed by institutions that have no connection with any perceived spirit world. In fact, there are indications that people in Africa are more indifferent to religion today than in the past (Messi Metogo 1997; Shorter and Onyancha 1997). However, as one expert tells us, 'even those who claim to be atheist, agnostic, or anti-religion, of whom there is a growing number, often have no option but to participate in extended family activities, some of which require the invocation of supernatural powers' (Moyo 2001: 299).

The imposition of intellectual categories

The idea that politics and religion form two distinct fields is not common to all societies, nor has every language had exact equivalents for these two terms in their vocabularies. Ideas about the nature of religion and politics (especially their identification as distinct and separate fields) have evolved in particular ways in Europe and in societies heavily influenced by European emigration to such an extent that they have become a key shared element of the otherwise disparate collection of countries known as 'the West'. Over time, European authors, ethnographers, missionaries, and officials have introduced to Africa ideas emanating from their own history that they have assumed to be universal or, at any rate, to be essential to any project of development or progress. One of the keys to understanding the history of power relations in Africa is to appreciate the way in which indigenous ideas and those introduced by colonial officials and missionaries have influenced one another to produce the situation as it obtains today (see Erdmann, this volume).

So deeply embedded in history are specific European ideas about religion and politics that they can be traced back to classical antiquity. It is illuminating briefly to consider the history of theorizing about religion in Christian Europe in order to elucidate some of the problems inherent in applying the term 'religion' to Africa.

For the ancient Romans, *religio* was an organized and controlled activity of the patrician class that could be distinguished from *superstitio*, the religious practice of the lower orders of Roman society, which was associated with perceived social and intellectual disorder (Momigliano 1977: 141–59). In regard to the twin concepts of *religio* and *superstitio*, Italo Ronca (1992: 43) has observed that 'neither the terms themselves nor their negative correlation are cross-cultural universals to be reckoned with in all cultures or at all times: in many areas not influenced by Christianity there is no equivalent to such conceptual terminology'. The meaning of these terms is historically conditioned, as are their correlative semantic fields. Early Christian authors, of whom the most influential was Augustine of Hippo (CE 354–430), drew on this classical model of higher and lower forms of religion to define Christianity as true religion, considering other types of belief or practice as being of a lesser order. Furthermore, the circumstances of early Christian Europe after the fall of the Roman Empire in the West were such as to emphasize the separation of the Catholic Church as the bastion of official religion from the institutions of the state (Brown 1996). Formed by this history and drawing on these traditions, European writers in mediaeval and early modern times considered there to be four types of religious observer in the world: Christians, Jews, Mohammedans (as Muslims were then known), and 'the rest', meaning all others deemed to be attached to some form of idolatry (Masuzawa 2007: 181) or, indeed, superstition – terms used in regard to beliefs of a supposedly lower order (Pagden 1986: 168–69).

As Europe's influence in the world expanded, and its traders, soldiers and administrators came into sustained contact with distant parts of the globe, it became apparent to writers that a more complex classification was necessary, not least in order to accommodate the sophisticated beliefs enshrined in Buddhism, which possessed all the hallmarks of what a European intellectual of the time could regard as a 'real' religion as opposed to a mere superstition. However, the degree of respect shown to religions with sacred texts and extensive theological traditions hardly extended to indigenous African religious practices until quite recent times, and these remained consigned by writers to a residual category that included – to use the vocabulary of the nineteenth century – polytheists, animists, and idolaters.

In regard to the study of religion in Africa, it is, broadly speaking, possible to identify two phases (Platvoet 1996). The first of these can be described as 'Africa as object', referring to an early period in which religious data were studied by scholars from outside Africa, many of them amateur ethnographers. The cohort of early foreign collectors, antiquaries, and observers established many of the basic approaches, methods, concepts, and labels used by later scholars. A second phase is that of 'Africa as subject', when similar data were also being studied by professionally trained specialists, African scholars among them, eventually including those based in the universities that were established in Africa from the mid-twentieth century. Accompanying this change of phase from Africa-as-object to Africa-as-subject was a change in the moral value that observers ascribed to religion in Africa. In the high Victorian period, missionaries and colonizers generally considered indigenous African religious practices to be more or less uniformly contemptible because they did not constitute 'true' religion, with a partial exception being made only for Islam. John Peel (2000: 12) has noted in regard to Nigeria, for example, how early Christian evangelists often considered indigenous religious practices as 'a kind of absence'. In other words, they were not perceived to have any real substance.

In general, it was only well into the colonial period that opinions like these tended to change. Some colonial officials, spending long periods in Africa, came to appreciate the complexity and subtlety of African religious ideas. If only for administrative purposes, they had to learn to understand the relationship of indigenous religion to justice, land tenure, and other matters affecting the social and political order which, as time went by, were increasingly likely to be glossed as 'politics'. Moreover, the colonial period witnessed the arrival of professional anthropologists in Africa, who in the mid-twentieth century were inclined to view African religious ideas and practices in functional terms, as the cultural epiphenomena associated with specific social and political complexes bearing an ethnic label. Thus was the concept of ethnic religions formed, with a plethora of books on Zulu religion, Yoruba religion, and many others. It was characteristic of European administrators and scholars until quite late in the colonial period that Africa was best understood as being divided into thousands of discrete ethnic communities, each having its own culture and its own religion. Towards the end of the colonial period there also emerged the first texts from African intellectuals trained in European methods, who were able to describe in the academic vocabulary of their day religious and cultural systems that they knew from within.

The ways in which certain ideas and practices were construed by writers, clerics, politicians, and officials during colonial times as 'religion', 'superstition', or politics was of enduring importance. This was a process that had a great bearing on local perceptions of power and on the moral value attached to attempts to access it. While Europeans may have made sharp intellectual and practical distinctions between religion, public administration, and commerce, it was by no means clear that Africans did the same, being more likely to view these as different facets of the demonstration of prosperity and the exercise of power. During the heyday of European global expansion and empire, Christian religious ideas and practices in particular became associated with factors of material significance, including the import of manufactured goods, exposure to new patterns of consumption, new political arrangements and new practices of power more generally. It has been estimated that by the 1930s, colonies or ex-colonies covered no less than 84.6 per cent of the land surface of the globe (Loomba 1998: xiii).

The identification by European thinkers and administrators of certain practices as being religious or otherwise in nature had a deep and lasting impact on societies not only in Africa but in many other parts of the world as well. Some of the effects have been well described by the Korean scholar Chin Hong Chung (2007), who notes that before the late nineteenth century the Korean language had no equivalent to the word 'religion'. It was an alien term that entered the country as part of a more general process of modernization, in this case transmitted via Japan. According to Chung:

> ... [t]he concept of religion never succeeded in incorporating our experience fully, and it has been utilised as an inappropriate measure and criterion in the description and understanding of our traditional belief culture. It is unavoidable, therefore, to reach the point where the empirical reality of traditional religious experience and its expression is distorted, devalued, and confused by such a newly enforced word as 'religion'.
>
> *(Chung 2007: 206)*

Similarly in Africa, where many or probably most languages appear to have had no ready translation for the word 'religion' prior to evangelization by Christian missionaries, existing practices of communication with an invisible world were changed by the manner in which they were variously described as either 'religion' or 'superstition'. A new vocabulary and conceptual order gave a new meaning to ideas and practices in African societies concerning the manipulation of power generally, cutting across existing categories and thereby distorting the empirical reality of indigenous religious experience as well as its various expressions.

The introduction of a new vocabulary concerning the invisible world was part of a far more widespread imposition of new administrative arrangements and practices of power of Western origin or inspiration, most particularly during the colonial period, when European officials were at liberty to introduce administrative techniques that they not only found useful, but considered to be necessary for instituting the type of government structure that African societies would have to adopt if they were to make progress. Among the novelties introduced at this time was the identification of religion and politics as two distinct realms, which should properly be subject to institutional and intellectual separation. When early ethnographers wrote about power in African societies, they initially tended not to use the vocabulary of politics, so intimately bound up with European notions of statecraft, but rather to consider the matter in terms of culture and custom. In this regard, a landmark was reached with the publication in 1940 of *African Political Systems* (Fortes and Evans-Pritchard 1940), a series of case studies of social organization and the principles of traditional government in a number of African societies, conceived explicitly as political institutions. Just as the experts of the colonial period were becoming able to appreciate the nuances of African ideas concerning the invisible world, and to describe these in terms of religion rather than mere superstition, so too were they becoming aware of the relationship between indigenous practices of power over the material world and wider patterns of governance, reflected in the vocabulary of politics.

The nationalist effect

Dispositions of power in general were rearranged with extraordinary speed by the movement towards decolonization. In the case of Nigeria, the most populous of all African countries, before the Second World War the academic Margery Perham (1962: xi) had, like just about every other observer, detected 'an atmosphere of almost unlimited time in which to carry on the task, regarded then as hardly begun, of building a new Nigeria from the bottom up'. Three decades later, looking back on what had actually happened, it seemed incredible to her that Nigeria had in fact been constructed from above by the new party organizations that emerged with such amazing speed after 1945 (ibid.).

As one country after another south of the Sahara acquired sovereign status, enthusiasts both African and foreign believed that this represented a rupture in Africa's history, to the extent that the continent was experiencing a new beginning (Davidson 1970: 266–68). Those like the historian Joseph Ade Ajayi, who perceived a great element of continuity in local ideologies and practices that transcended the colonial period, were rather spurned (Ade Ajayi 2000: 158). However, with the passage of time the degree to which African nationalists had assimilated many items of colonial ideology and colonial administrative practice has now become rather more apparent. Both colonialists and nationalists believed that Africa had previously lagged behind Europe in a variety of ways but that it could catch up by adopting the techniques of social engineering that were in vogue worldwide after 1945. Among all the colonial categories of thought to which new meaning was attributed by nationalist ideologues from the mid-twentieth century, politics took pride of place. Like the colonialists who had established colonial administrations using bureaucratic techniques similar to those in European metropoles, African nationalists conceived of the state as 'the ultimate, most civilized form of organizing social and political life', the necessary vector for all historical change (Soares de Oliveira 2007: 30). This way of thinking was incorporated into slogans of nation-building and development. It was generally assumed that African political life would henceforth revolve around the state and other formal institutions in much the same way as it had come to do since the seventeenth century in Europe. Among the raft of ideas taken over wholesale by nationalists was that states should be secular and bureaucratic in nature and that certain types of religion were more advanced than others. Even the handful of African countries that at a later stage were to declare themselves to be Islamic republics nevertheless retained many of the administrative techniques originally instituted by colonial rule (see Villalón, this volume).

Only with the passage of time did it become clear just how much continuity existed between colonial rule in its last phase and the early years of nationalist rule once African countries had acquired sovereign status. Post-colonial regimes that were presided over by Africans rather than Europeans continued to make abundant use of the practices, routines, and mentalities of their colonial predecessors. In fact, post-colonial states at first implemented colonial techniques and policies more intensively than ever, using them as a platform for a more ambitious form of political monopoly than anything to which their colonial predecessors could aspire (Young 2004). The former colonial metropoles were also pleased to make use of the continuities between colonial and nationalist rule for purposes of their own.

Like their counterparts in other fields, the African theologians and writers on religion who emerged in the mid-twentieth century also tended to assimilate colonial ideas, most often by turning colonial prejudices on their heads. African theologians articulated what may be called a 'theology of continuity' (Westerlund 1985: 89), by which African religious ideas and practices – far from being seen as inferior as they had been portrayed by earlier European writers – were interpreted in such a way as to identify elements of African indigenous religions that appear to resemble or anticipate aspects of Christian belief. Typical of this enterprise was the construction of African Traditional Religion – in the singular, and with capital letters – as a system of belief comparable to other major religions. One result of this change of perspective was to suggest that the African sub-continent is not divided into autonomous areas, each with its own distinctive religion corresponding to an ethnic identity, as earlier generations of Europeans had often supposed. Instead, commentators now tended to discern some of the similarities between religious ideas and practices over wide tracts of Africa, for example in regard to healing, noting that certain cults may mobilize people over very wide areas, creating a religious geography that transcends political boundaries (Ranger 1991).

New realities

Looking back from the twenty-first century, it is increasingly clear that the actual workings of African states have come to differ in significant ways from the classical models of European origin, which remain the basic currency of formal statehood. Post-colonial governments in most of Africa were undermined in the first instance by the profound changes in the global context in the 1970s, especially in regard to finance. However, since the 1990s there have been various attempts to describe the ways in which power has come to be actually manipulated or located in African societies, giving rise to talk of 'collapsed', 'failed', or 'fragile' states. Several writers have resorted to images of shadows to evoke the ways in which Africa is now governed and how it is integrated into world affairs (e.g. Reno 1995: 2–3). The state, they imply, is like a solid object that casts a shadow. Analysts who deploy this image do so in an attempt to explain why concentrating on the official institutions and ideologies of the state deflects attention from some important relationships and institutions that, from an official point of view, have only an insubstantial existence. Actually, the metaphor of a shadow is rather misleading, as the shadow cast by official institutions often has more real substance than the formal structures of the state. One could better describe the state as a hologram, discernible amid the complex of relationships by which African societies are actually governed. Whatever solidity official institutions have often derives only from the fact that they enjoy legal recognition. In these circumstances, political power has become increasingly located in the gap between the official structures of the state and the law on the one hand, and everyday reality on the other. Successful politicians make use of the material provided by their societies.

In no field is this truer than in regard to religion. In many African countries, political leaders have taken to patronizing various types of religion and have become highly sensitive to the potential offered by spiritual power in general. Many countries have witnessed the rise of prophetic movements, which can emerge with astonishing speed from the most obscure corners of society. Sometimes, new prophets can attract massive followings with formidable political and even military consequences. In the most extreme cases, religious leaders have assumed political or even military roles, such as in the case of Alice Lakwena, the Ugandan prophetess who in the 1980s made common cause with a group of officers from a defeated army to create an important military movement (Behrend 1999).

The eruption of religious activity into the field of politics poses problems to students of both religion and politics. Labelling it a 'revival' or 'resurgence' in some ways conveys the misleading impression of a trend that previously existed but which had gone underground, whereas in fact many of today's most visible religious movements have been publicly active for a long time, even if they have become subject to academic scrutiny only rather recently. In the case of Africa, both Christianity and Islam have been present in parts of the continent for a thousand years or more, and so their recent growth throughout the continent cannot be considered simply as a break with tradition. Similarly, the revival of African traditional religions is not a simple return to the past, but rather a reconfiguration for modern times. The current dynamism of religion as a political force in so many countries is a phenomenon with historical roots that extend into pre-colonial times. Nowadays, however, even movements that claim to be traditional in nature operate with an unprecedented awareness of global forces. Communities adopt religious beliefs and practices that emphasize their connection to, or difference from, other groups in ways that have to be considered in both global breadth and historical depth.

Taking account not only of the importance of religion but of a whole range of informal practices, it has become increasingly apparent that any comprehensive study of politics in Africa cannot be restricted to the formal workings of the state, particularly in situations where the state is notable more by its absence than its presence. Accordingly, many analysts have set off in search of politics 'from below' (Bayart 1981), to be found in the words and deeds of ordinary people and not only the formal activities of elected representatives or ministers of state. It is indeed here that the interaction between politics and religion is easiest to apprehend, at the point where religious belief motivates people to action. However, both political scientists and anthropologists seem to experience difficulty in getting to grips with religion in Africa. The main reason for this is that some fundamental aspects of religion in Africa do not easily fit into the core assumptions of academic disciplines that descend from a literary and theological tradition 2,000 years old, which represents religion within African societies in cultural terms rather than as the locus of substantive ideas. Even the spectacular rise in adherence to the universal religions of Islam and Christianity has not changed this tradition of viewing religious practice in Africa as an essentially cultural matter. Quite a few writers on politics exclude religion from their scope of analysis altogether, regarding religion as something divorced from the material world and the world of politics.

An accurate analysis of the relation between religion and politics has to take account of the extent to which, in time-honoured fashion, the invisible world is perceived to be the place of origin of all power – not only political power in the conventional sense, but the very ability to live and to prosper. The South African theologian Allan Anderson summarizes the idea, widespread in Africa, that all forms of sickness and misfortune are related to a lack of power as a whole. 'Our life, our very existence is inextricably tied up with power. To live is to have power, to be sick or to die is to have less of it', he writes (Anderson 1991: 67). It is in order to achieve a condition of wholeness that people feel the need to consult religious specialists for purposes of what we may call self-empowerment. Spiritual power, for this reason, is described by Anderson as 'enabling power,' which allows people to take control of situations they are otherwise unable to master. It is worth noting in passing that the ability of power in the most general sense to shape people's lives is recognized in many parts of the world, and indeed many definitions of political power include some consideration of its ability to transform those over whom it is exercised (Schatzberg 2001: 38–40). In the case of Africa, the search for power from the invisible world is common to the bulk of the population, from the highest to the lowest. This produces an atmosphere of intimacy in the spiritual domain in spite of the vast gulf in wealth and lifestyle that distinguishes Africa's upper classes from the very poor.

The fact that power in Africa has ceased to be located primarily in the formal apparatus of the state and the whole range of institutions and practices introduced in colonial times makes it still more urgent for people to search for power that will effectively protect them. Many people easily turn to the spirit world for effective remedies for their troubles and insecurities, notably in the form of medicines that can protect and heal them. In this regard the concept of medicine implies more than just a medium for curing a physical ailment. A medicine is an instrument for channelling power from the spirit world, which may be either harmful or protective according to the ambivalent nature of the spirit world itself. There are 'good' medicines designed to cure illness and amulets to ward off danger, but also 'bad' medicines that are intended to transmit harmful forces, sometimes referred to as 'magical charms', *juju*, and so on, used for offensive purposes.

A typical circumstance calling for closer contact with the spirit world could be, for example, a serious illness, infertility, or impotence, but it could also be something as mundane as long-term unemployment or other forms of 'bad luck' – anything that diminishes the quality of life. By the same token, 'good luck' may be sought from the spirit world actively, such as for safe travel or success in school exams. African footballers routinely pray when they take to the field for a match, and have been known to take a range of other spiritual measures intended to secure victory. Riots have occurred when a team or its supporters find evidence of counter-measures by the opposing team, such as burying *juju* (i.e. power objects) under the goalmouth with the aim of attracting the ball into the net (Schatzberg 2001: 121–29). Entire sports teams may consult healers before matches. Likewise, politicians, too, may seek spiritual power in order to succeed in elections or in other aspects of their struggle for position and influence.

Getting access to spiritual power is deemed to be a field in which women excel. At the heart of women's perceived spiritual qualities is the belief that they are by nature closer than men to the spirit world due to their ability to produce new life. As in many other parts of the world, there is evidence that people think there to be a connection between women's fertility and a dimension of spiritual knowledge from which men are excluded, causing them to respect and fear women at the same time (King 1989: ch. 4). This is probably one reason why women are more likely than men to be accused of witchcraft. The capacity of women to produce new life in the form of children is shared by deities, which in some traditions are also considered able to reproduce by creating new versions of themselves that can be transported from a 'mother' shrine to a new site (e.g. Rattray 1923: ch. 16).

Women are prominent as leaders of the thousands of independent churches in Africa that are known particularly for their healing activities. West Africa even has female Muslim sheikhs (Coulon and Reveyrand 1990). One new religious movement in Ghana, Zetaheal Mission, combines elements of both Christianity and Islam and is led by a woman (Atiemo 2003). Typically, such movements start when a person, male or female, is recognized as being called by a powerful spirit, and then goes on to become established as a religious specialist. In Christian belief, such a calling is seen as the work of the Holy Spirit. The historical mainline mission churches – those that emerged from the experience of European mission – tend to accord a far less prominent role to this spirit than African indigenous churches, more familiar with spirit belief, generally do. In mainline churches the power of the spirit is usually mediated by professional male functionaries, who may doubt the legitimacy of any unregulated vocation. Women leaders are therefore not easily accommodated into these churches, as the continuing debate on women's ordination in the Catholic Church indicates. Hence, women are more likely to establish their own independent congregations.

Spiritual insecurity

Africans today are confronted with a formidable range of problems, from economics to epidemics. To judge from the popular literature sold on the streets of African cities, stories on the radio and in the newspapers, sermons preached in the astonishing variety of churches, and rumours swapped through the oral communication known in African French as *radio trottoir*, many people consider these matters in a spiritual idiom. Although people are well aware of the material reasons for many of their difficulties, many also think about problems – from AIDS to food shortages to corruption – as having their deepest explanation in the actions of powerful people who manipulate the spirit world (Ellis and ter Haar 2004: chs 1 and 2). This is not in the first instance because of a lack of technical information, as most people seem well aware of the ways in which AIDS is transmitted or the techniques by which public monies are embezzled. However, public education campaigns about safe sex do not necessarily change popular ideas about the origins of AIDS, and nor do campaigns for good governance always prevent corruption.

Popular literature circulating in Africa suggests a widespread preoccupation with evil and its manifestations in daily life. There are numerous accounts of a spiritual underworld where people may make money through contracts that promise worldly riches in return for a pact with the Devil. Stories of witches and sinister ghosts and spirits are popular in television soap operas and video fictions and are discussed in radio phone-ins. They are a common topic of conversation. Yet the spiritual dimension does not displace more prosaic explanations for Africa's problems, such as poor governance or an unjust world order. Rather, many people merge religious and secular modes of explanation, so that secular forces like imperialism or neo-colonialism are assumed to have a spiritual component.

Although there is evidence that Africans have thought about the world in terms of a spirit idiom throughout recorded history, they have not always had such a bleak view as in recent years. The old techniques for managing the spirit world do not work any longer, and the traditional spirit world itself has increasingly come to be seen as inherently evil. There are at least three reasons why people have come to see the traditional spirit world this way. First, there has been a gradual demonization of the spirit world over a long period, dating back to the nineteenth century evangelization of Africa by foreign missionaries. As a result, the traditional spirit world has lost much of its original morally neutral character. Second, the traditional religious specialists who used to have the authority to regulate relations between the human and the spirit worlds have lost much of their influence as a result of developments during the twentieth century. Factors that have eroded it include: the institution of a secular state apparatus; social changes that undermine the standing of the village elders and notables who officiate in traditional religious cults; and Western education, secular or Christian. Traditional experts today are often ridiculed by younger people and despised by adherents of new religious movements, including Islamists and 'born-again' Christians. There are raging debates between advocates of a return to tradition and those, including the more radical Pentecostals, who maintain that indigenous practices, or indeed any religious actions not based on explicit scriptural authority, are evil. Third, since the spirit world is to some extent a reflection of the material world, it is not surprising that it mirrors the adverse conditions that so many African countries have undergone in recent decades. After a century of rapid and profound change, there is considerable confusion about what precisely constitutes good and evil, including in such important matters as making war, while in many countries there is no consensus on which authorities are competent to pronounce on such matters.

As a result of this situation, people have lost the means to resolve the great number of problems that are nowadays often attributed to evil spirits and witches. This has been widely noted by Western anthropologists, among others, who have in recent years produced a series of works on witchcraft in Africa (e.g. Comaroff and Comaroff 1993; Geschiere 1997), and on the theologies of evil in charismatic churches (e.g. Meyer 1999). People who are believed to manipulate the spirit world for selfish purposes include politicians and plutocrats, certainly. Above all, though, witchcraft accusations concern neighbours and family members.

Concerns about evil spirits and witchcraft accusations have been addressed extensively by African academics too, especially theologians and scholars of religion. Their work has received rather little attention from European and North American scholars (ter Haar 2007). In part, the reason for this neglect may be that African authors have published work locally, and not always in forms that are easily accessible internationally. A good deal of the literature produced in Africa may not immediately appear to Western scholars to be of academic relevance as it emerges from theological debates, often assumed by social scientists to have little or no bearing on their own work. Over the years, African theologians have been concerned particularly with pastoral approaches to spiritual problems, including problems of evil and witchcraft (Lagerwerf 1987 provides a bibliography of some older works), and many clerical intellectuals have addressed the same issues (e.g. Hebga 1982; Milingo 1984). More recent African writers include Elizabeth Amoah (1986) and Seratwa Ntloedibe-Kuswani (2007) on witchcraft accusations against women. Similarly, the Circle of Concerned African Women Theologians is a network of female authors who have published on aspects of religious and social life in Africa and their effects on women. Other contemporary African writers on witchcraft include Thias Kgatla (1995, 2003) on South Africa, Elom Dovlo (2007) on Ghana, Augustine Musopole (1993) on witchcraft terminology and hermeneutics, and Elias Bongmba (2001) on the moral aspects of witchcraft, to mention only a few.

Conclusion

The resilience of religion the world over has been one of the greatest surprises of recent decades. Many classic works of social science considered the 'disenchantment' of the world – to use Weber's phrase – as an inevitable accompaniment of the rise of modern states and modern economies. Classic theories of development paid no attention to religion, simply because it seemed irrelevant to the processes they were analysing other than, perhaps, as an obstacle to modernization (ter Haar and Ellis 2006). The fact that many African countries are now enjoying high rates of economic growth (Ellis 2011) should not be interpreted as a sign that the importance of religion will now decline. On the contrary, religion and politics, subject to institutional separation in colonial times, are likely to be increasingly connected.

Bibliography

Ade Ajayi, J. (2000) 'Continuity of African Institutions Under Colonial Rule', in T. Falola (ed.) *Tradition and Change in Africa: The Essays of J.F. Ade Ajayi*, Trenton, NJ: Africa World Press.

Amoah, E. (1986) 'Women, Witches and Social Change in Ghana', in D. Eck and D. Jain (eds) *Speaking of Faith: Cross-Cultural Perspectives on Women, Religion and Social Change*, London: Women's Press.

Anderson, A. (1991) 'Pentecostal Pneumatology and African Power Concepts: Continuity or Change?' *Missionalia* 1: 65–74.

Atiemo, A. (2003) 'Zetaheal Mission in Ghana: Christians and Muslims Worshipping Together?' *Exchange* 32(1): 15–36.

Bayart, J.-F. (1981) 'Le politique par le bas en Afrique noire: Questions de méthode', *Politique africaine* 1: 53–82.

Behrend, H. (Mick Cohen, trans.) (1999) *Alice Lakwena and the Holy Spirits: War in Northern Uganda, 1986–97*, Oxford: James Currey.

Bongmba, E. (2001) *African Witchcraft and Otherness: A Philosophical and Theological Critique of Intersubjective Relations*, Albany, NY: SUNY Press.

Brown, P. (1996) *The Rise of Western Christendom: Triumph and Diversity AD 200–1000*, Oxford: Blackwell.

Chung, C.H. (2007) 'Religion-before Religion and Religion-after Religion', in G. ter Haar and Y. Tsuruoka (eds) *Religion and Society: An Agenda for the 21st Century*, Leiden: Brill.

Comaroff, J. and Comaroff, J.L. (eds) (1993) *Modernity and its Malcontents: Ritual and Power in Postcolonial Africa*, Chicago, IL: Chicago University Press.

Coulon, C. and Reveyrand, O. (1990) *L'Islam au féminin: Sokhna Magat Diop, cheikh de la confrérie mouride (Sénégal)*, Talence: Centre d'étude d'Afrique noire.

Davidson, B. (1970) *Old Africa Rediscovered*, second edition, London: Longman.

Dovlo, E. (2007) 'Witchcraft in Contemporary Ghana', in G. ter Haar (ed.) *Imagining Evil: Witchcraft Beliefs and Accusations in Contemporary Africa*, Trenton, NJ: Africa World Press.

Ellis, S. (2011) *Season of Rains: Africa in the World*, London: Hurst.

Ellis, S. and ter Haar, G. (2004) *Worlds of Power: Religious Thought and Political Practice in Africa*, London: Hurst.

Fortes, M. and Evans-Pritchard, E.E. (eds) (1940) *African Political Systems*, London: Oxford University Press.

Geschiere, P. (1997) *The Modernity of Witchcraft: Politics and the Occult in Postcolonial Africa*, Charlottesville, VA: University Press of Virginia.

Hebga, M.P. (1982) *Sorcellerie et prière de délivrance: réflexion sur une expérience*, Paris: Présence Africaine; Abidjan: INADES.

Kgatla, S.T. (1995) 'Beliefs About Witchcraft in the Northern Region', *Theologia Viatorum* 22: 53–79.

——(2003) *Crossing Witchcraft Barriers in South Africa: Exploring Witchcraft Accusations: Causes and Solutions*, Utrecht: Utrecht University (SANPAD Research Report).

King, U. (1989) *Women and Spirituality: Voices of Protest and Promise*, London: Macmillan.

Lagerwerf, L. (1987) *Witchcraft, Sorcery, and Spirit Possession: Pastoral Responses in Africa*, Mambo Press: Gweru.

Lonsdale, J. (1981) 'States and Social Processes in Africa: A Historiographical Survey', *African Studies Review* 24(2–3): 139–225.

Loomba, A. (1998) *Colonialism/Postcolonialism*, London: Routledge.

Masuzawa, T. (2007) 'Theory Without Method: Situating a Discourse Analysis on Religion', in G. ter Haar and Y. Tsuruoka (eds) *Religion and Society: An Agenda for the 21st Century*, Leiden: Brill.

Messi Metogo, E. (1997) *Dieu peut-il mourir en Afrique? Essai sur l'indifférence religieuse et l'incroyance en Afrique noire*, Paris: Karthala; Yaoundé: UCAC.

Meyer, B. (1999) *Translating the Devil: Religion and Modernity Among the Ewe in Ghana*, Edinburgh: Edinburgh University Press.

Milingo, E. (ed.) (1984) *The World In-Between: Christian Healing and the Struggle for Spiritual Survival*, London: Hurst; Maryknoll, NY: Orbis Books.

Momigliano, A. (1977) *Essays in Ancient and Modern Historiography*, Oxford: Basil Blackwell.

Moyo, A. (2001) 'Religion in Africa', in A.A. Gordon and D.L. Gordon (eds) *Understanding Contemporary Africa*, third edition, Boulder, CO, and London: Lynne Rienner Publishers.

Musopole, A.C. (1993) 'Witchcraft Terminology, the Bible and African Christian Theology: An Exercise in Hermeneutics', *Journal of Religion in Africa* 23(4): 347–54.

Ntloedibe-Kuswani, G.S. (2007) 'Witchcraft as a Challenge to Batswana Ideas of Community and Relationships', in G. ter Haar (ed.) *Imagining Evil: Witchcraft Beliefs and Accusations in Contemporary Africa*, Trenton, NJ: Africa World Press.

Pagden, A. (1986) *The Fall of Natural Man: The American Indian and the Origins of Comparative Ethnology*, second edition, Cambridge: Cambridge University Press.

Peel, J. (2000) *Religious Encounter and the Making of the Yoruba*, Bloomington, IN: Indiana University Press.

Perham, M. (1962) *Native Administration in Nigeria*, second edition, London: Oxford University Press.

Platvoet, J.G. (1996) 'The Religions of Africa in Their Historical Order', in J.G. Platvoet, J.L. Cox and J.K. Olupona (eds) *The Study of Religions in Africa: Past, Present and Prospects*, Cambridge: Roots and Branches.

Ranger, T.O. (1991) 'African Traditional Religion', in S. Sutherland and P. Clarke (eds.) *The Study of Religion, Traditional and New Religion*, London: Routledge.

Rattray, R.S. (1923) *Ashanti*, London: Oxford University Press.

Reno, W. (1995) *Corruption and State Politics in Sierra Leone*, Cambridge: Cambridge University Press.

Ronca, I. (1992) 'What's in Two Names: Old and New Thoughts on the History and Etymology of *Religio* and *Superstitio*', in S. Prete (ed.) *Republica Literarum: Studies in the Classical Tradition* XV(1).

Schatzberg, M. (2001) *Political Legitimacy in Middle Africa: Father, Family, Food*, Bloomington and Indianapolis, IN: Indiana University Press.

Shorter, A. and Onyancha, E. (1997) *Secularism in Africa. A Case Study: Nairobi City*, Nairobi: Paulines Publications.

Soares de Oliveira, R. (2007) *Oil and Politics in the Gulf of Guinea*, London: Hurst.

ter Haar, G. (1992) *Spirit of Africa: The Healing Ministry of Archbishop Milingo of Zambia*, London: Hurst; Trenton, NJ: Africa World Press.

——(ed.) (2007) *Imagining Evil: Witchcraft Beliefs and Accusations in Contemporary Africa*, Trenton, NJ: Africa World Press.

ter Haar, G. and Ellis, S. (2006) 'The Role of Religion in Development: Towards a New Relationship between the European Union and Africa', *European Journal of Development Research* 18(3): 351–67.

ter Haar, G. and Tsuruoka, Y. (eds) (2007) *Religion and Society: An Agenda for the 21st Century*, Leiden: Brill.

Tylor, E.B. (1958) *Religion in Primitive Culture* (first published 1871 under the title *Primitive Culture*) New York, NY: Harper Torchbooks.

Westerlund, D. (1985) *African Religion in African Scholarship: A Preliminary Study of the Religious and Political Background*, Stockholm: Almqvist & Wicksell International.

Young, C. (2004) 'The End of the Post-Colonial State in Africa? Reflections on Changing African Political Dynamics', *African Affairs* 103(410): 23–49.

11

MUSLIM POLITICS IN WEST AFRICA

Leonardo A. Villalón

Taken as a whole, continental West Africa is roughly evenly divided between Muslims and non-Muslims. Religious demography, however, varies significantly across the 15 countries: Mauritania – officially the Islamic Republic of Mauritania – is effectively 100 per cent Muslim; five others are overwhelmingly (at least 85 per cent) Muslim; another five might be categorized as religiously divided countries, with Muslim populations ranging from 40 per cent to 60 per cent; and finally, four countries of coastal West Africa include significant (10–25 per cent) Muslim minorities (see Table 11.1).

Simple demography helps explain certain patterns, as well as account for the diversity of Muslim politics in the region. The constitution of the Islamic Republic of Mauritania prescribes *sharia* (Islamic law) as the country's 'organic law'. Muslim politics in the country have at times involved discussion on what this label of 'Islamic Republic' might require of successive governments, and there are some tensions and ambiguity in the relationship between political and religious authorities. However, demography has its limits: as a point of cultural commonality religion has been rather marginal in Mauritania's tumultuous domestic politics.

In the five countries where Muslims comprise large and dominant majorities, the central political debate on religion and politics might be characterized as a discussion about how and to what extent political and legal systems should reflect or accommodate the religious beliefs of the majority. Interestingly, however, in all five of these countries this debate has been framed in the context of the need to ensure the full citizenship rights of non-Muslim minorities.

In the religiously divided countries there is an obvious potential for rivalry for control of the state, although there is significant variation in terms of whether the religious divide in fact emerges as a political cleavage. When struggles for dominance do occur, they tend to resemble raw identity politics with rather limited religious content. Such dynamics have been notably central to politics in Nigeria. To a more limited extent, religion emerged as one element of the identities framing politics over the decade of crisis in Côte d'Ivoire. Nevertheless, it is also striking to note the *lack* of significant politicization of the religious cleavage in other divided cases: Burkina Faso, Sierra Leone, and Guinea-Bissau.

Finally, in the countries in which Muslims comprise a clear minority, Muslim politics have tended to focus on demands for full religious freedom for minorities and at times for religious autonomy in such crucial social arenas as education and family law. These dynamics have marked countries such as Benin and Ghana (Galilou 2002; Weiss 2008).

Table 11.1 Religious demography of West Africa

Country	Estimated population (millions)	Estimated Muslims (%)
Mauritania	3.2	100
Senegal	12.3	94
Mali	13.8	90+
Niger	15.9	90+
Gambia	1.8	90
Guinea-Conakry	10.3	85
Sierra Leone	5.2	60
Nigeria	150.0	50
Guinea-Bissau	1.5	50
Burkina Faso	16.2	50
Côte d'Ivoire	21.0	40
Benin	9.0	24
Togo	6.6	20
Ghana	24.3	16
Liberia	3.7	12

Note: Estimates for population size and for religion vary significantly among various sources. Reliable censuses in Africa are rare, and even when carried out many do not ask about (or release information on) religion due to the political sensitivity of religious demographics. Additionally, in various countries, the question of whether people should be categorized as 'Muslim' based on self-declaration or on observed practice produces rather different estimates. The population numbers provided in this table are primarily from the CIA World Factbook (www.cia.gov/library/publications/the-world-factbook/index.html); religious estimates have been adjusted from other sources.

The chapter cannot pretend to offer a full account of these varied countries with strikingly diverse patterns of Muslim politics. Rather, in what follows I will discuss some of the more important dimensions of religious politics in the region, with particular attention to the cases where Islam has taken a central political role. These include the overwhelmingly Muslim countries of the Francophone Sahel – Senegal, Mali, and Niger – and Nigeria, a religiously divided country but one with a population alone that is approximately the same as all other 14 countries combined.

Situating Muslim politics

There is a long history of 'Muslim politics' across West Africa – in the sense of political action rooted in religious ideas, mobilized around religious symbolism, and pursuing policies rooted in religious values – but three important preliminary points must be made in situating religious politics in the region.[1]

As elsewhere, Muslim politics in Africa are nothing more than a variant of politics more broadly and must be understood in the context of other political dynamics, to which religion is in fact often marginal. Thus across West Africa major national political debates are primarily focused on such burning questions as the status of constitutionally prescribed presidential term limits, increases in the costs of basic food staples, government shortcomings in the provision of public services and utilities, and corruption scandals – that is, the everyday stuff of African politics across the continent. Religion may or may not colour such debates, but raw politics remains primary.

Second, while situated in the broader world of Islam, African Muslim politics are constrained and shaped by local factors. Transnational religious movements and the increasingly globalized discourse on religion have been fully felt in the region – and increasingly so since the events of

11 September 2001 and the US-led wars in the Muslim world that followed them. However, the impact of external factors is filtered through local social institutions and political dynamics. Even in the interconnected countries of the region, issues that become central in one place may well prove to be irrelevant in another as local actors choose among available symbols and tools to pursue local political goals. Thus even the appeal of, say, Salafist movements, and the specific role they might play in politics, is contingent and shaped by local dynamics (Østebø 2008).

Third, the terrain of Muslim politics lies in the public sphere and is thus rooted in public debate and the popular sentiments of Muslim populations. Too often in contemporary discussions of Islam and politics in the African context there is an implicit assumption of the vulnerability of the Muslim masses to the sway of outside (especially 'radical' or 'extremist') religious ideologies. Analyses attempting to measure the spread of any given religious ideology ('radical' or other) often underestimate the role of individual deliberation and agency in the adoption of ideological stances. However, what Cruise O'Brien (1986) long ago labelled 'the people's voice in West African Muslim politics' remains central. In the everyday lives of Muslim societies, in families, friendships, and social relations, religious ideas are discussed, debated, and accepted (or not) in accordance with local preferences and prevailing values.

The state context

While in practice colonial policies often deviated significantly from the declared norms, both the official French and British colonial policies, and the specific forms that those policies took in given locales, had a major impact and have continued to shape the parameters of Muslim politics in postcolonial West African states.

With the only partial exception of Mauritania (where the 'Islamic republic' was adopted at independence primarily to attempt to unite an otherwise diverse population), religion was almost completely absent from the mobilizing discourses of independence. The mostly young and Western-trained nationalist intellectuals who led West African independence movements had little patience for religious (or ethnic) identities, with their potential divisiveness and their implications of 'tradition' and backwardness. Rather, the independence leaders were over-whelmingly secular in spirit and ideologically focused on the rapid 'modernization' of societies, premised on the notion that primordial ties of ethnicity, language, or religion would soon fade. Obviously this was not always to be, and to varying degrees these factors have persisted – or emerged – as elements of national politics.

The official French policy of 'assimilation', however limited in its effective application, produced a political elite imbued in French conceptions of politics and of the state, and the resulting political orientations have continued to dominate across the Francophone countries. The persistence of French colonial educational policies after independence and the fact that the intellectual elite in the region continued to be trained in French institutions contributed significantly to this ongoing impact. Of particular note in terms of Muslim politics is the persistence of the principle of secularism, *laïcité*, as a core element of the state. The ongoing commitment in the Francophone countries of the region to *un état laïc*, and the ongoing debate about what this implies for policies and symbolic politics, is intertwined to this day with the unresolved debate in France about the role of religion in public life.

As elsewhere in Africa, the first governments of the post-colonial Francophone Sahel often gave way to authoritarian regimes of various sorts. These regimes, such as those growing out of the military coups in Mali (1968) and Niger (1974), had no more religious credentials or inspiration than their predecessors. As authoritarian regimes focused on social control, however, they were keenly aware of the mobilizational potential of religion and anxious to suppress alternative sources of authority and incipient challenges to their rule. Given the tenuous social bases of military regimes, however, many also sought to harness religion as a source of legitimation. These governments thus tended to try simultaneously to limit and control the power of religious figures, while also extending patronage to religious groups in an effort to enhance their own legitimacy. In the corporatist state structures that came to characterize Mali and Niger until the early 1990s this led to the creation of single, officially sanctioned national Islamic associations under government patronage and tutelage: the *Association Malienne pour l'Unité et le Progrès de l'Islam* (AMUPI) and the *Association Islamique du Niger* (AIN). Until the advent of democracy in the early 1990s, then, Muslim politics in Mali and Niger were carefully circumscribed within these limited state channels, in states that remained officially secular in orientation.

Senegal, the other important Francophone Sahelian country, was long considered a political exception, and the role of religion in maintaining the country's relative stability and its civilian and even quasi-democratic system has been much discussed. The colonial period saw the development of a system of symbiotic relations between the religious and political elite that survived largely intact into the independence era, and which made possible an officially secular state that benefited directly from the conferred legitimacy of the country's religious elite (Villalón 1995). The system was built on the strength of the Sufi orders in Senegal, of which two are particularly important: the indigenous and highly centralized Mouride order, and the more widespread but less cohesive Tijaniyya. After an initial period of suspicion and fear, the French were eventually to find 'paths of accommodation' (Robinson 2000) with the Sufi religious elite. These relations in turn helped to strengthen the Senegalese Sufi system itself, which developed as a far more structured, socially anchored, and hierarchical form of religious organization than elsewhere in the region.

Senegal's first president, Léopold Sédar Senghor (1960–80), although a Catholic himself, built the bases of the post-colonial regime on the continuation of close collaborative ties with the Muslim elite. By contrast with much of the region, Senegal maintained a system of regular elections and constitutionally enshrined a multi-party system in the mid-1970s, just as other neighbouring countries were consolidating single-party rule. The Sufi religious elite were closely implicated in this system, lending support to Senghor and often pronouncing themselves publicly in his favour at election time, thus gaining a reputation as kingmakers. In retrospect it is hard to decipher the exact power of the religious elite in determining outcomes, given that the electoral system was carefully circumscribed, but clearly they were an important stabilizing force. Under Senghor's successor Abdou Diouf (1980–2000), the collaborative ties were to continue, but as the legitimacy of Diouf's rule was eroded by the increasingly difficult economic conditions of the 1980s and simmering dissatisfaction about a lack of political change, the religious elite took a more cautious stance. Thus the last major religious directive on elections was that pronounced by the Mouride Caliph in favour of Abdou Diouf in the elections of 1988. In the tumultuous period that began with those elections and continued on through the 1990s, the religious elite remained politically influential but carefully cultivated their independence from politicians (Villalón 1999).

In 2000 the defeat of Diouf and the election of Abdoulaye Wade in the country's first electoral transition signalled a new epoch in many ways, but relations between the religious and the political elite remain central. Wade's first and highly controversial gesture upon his election was to go to the Mouride holy city of Touba and to be photographed bowing before the Caliph of the order. He was to repeat this act in the company of his entire government following legislative elections the following year. This gesture and subsequent actions sparked sharp criticism of Wade and much controversy about the relationship between the religious and the political elite, but clearly religion remains highly influential in Senegalese political life. There is no religious bloc, however, capable of defining political outcomes.

A striking legacy of the colonial period in the Francophone Sahel is thus the persistence of officially secular states in the context of negotiated ties with the representatives of deeply religious Muslim societies. Despite some initial challenges to this system in the epoch of democratization, it appears to remain well entrenched. An additional legacy, and one that has been carefully nurtured in the postcolonial context, is a lack of significant religious conflict and a solicitous respect for the non-Muslim minorities – mainly Catholics.

This Francophone context is in sharp contrast to the legacy of British indirect rule in the other zone of significant Muslim politics in West Africa, namely the northern states of Nigeria. In very direct ways, the impact of colonial policies continues to shape Muslim politics in that country (Sanusi 2007). Under the colonial administrator Lord Frederick Lugard, the policy of 'indirect rule' applied in the region explicitly maintained and in many ways even reinforced the power of local emirs, whose political legitimacy was deeply rooted in Islam. The Sokoto Caliphate which dominated the region at the time of the British conquest was a singularly successful political entity, born of the *jihad* that swept the region in the early nineteenth century, and which had established a theocratic state under Islamic legal principles of *sharia*.

When Lugard proclaimed the Protectorate of Northern Nigeria in 1900, he explicitly pledged not to interfere in the religious affairs of the Muslim population, and in fact Christian missionaries were banned for most of the colonial period. The colonial concessions to religion allowed for the continued application of *sharia* in various domains. Thus, Islamic personal law was left under the jurisdiction of the emirs. While the British gradually circumscribed Islamic penal law and banned various Islamic corporal punishments (the *hudud* penalties), various aspects of colonial criminal law remained inspired by *sharia*.

The amalgamation of northern and southern Nigeria in 1914 did not produce any uniform policies in the colony, and in fact the two regions continued to be governed quite differently. The continued reliance on the emirs to implement and enforce colonial rule in the north both reinforced their positions and simultaneously undercut their historical religious legitimacy, forcing them to rely more on repression and less on patronage. This must be seen as an important contributing factor to the subsequent history of controversy and conflict about the right to claim religious authority in the region. Indirect rule also intentionally curtailed the expansion of Western-style education in order to limit the development of an intellectual elite capable of challenging colonial rule, as had occurred in the southern portions of colonial Nigeria. The result of these policies was that at independence northern Nigeria – in contrast to the south – was 'educationally backward, politically reactionary, socially hierarchical, and deeply steeped in a dependent mind-set' (Sanusi 2007: 182).

Of particular salience in terms of Muslim politics, the legal differences between the northern and southern portions of Nigeria have never been reconciled and continue to be problematic. Attempting to minimize the contradictions shortly before independence, a Northern Nigeria Penal Code was implemented in 1959 to create a uniform and largely secular criminal law for the north, but which nevertheless made several concessions to Islamic concerns, and which remained distinct from the common-law criminal code prevailing in the south. Far from resolving the issue, however, this was to lead to the 'unending sharia debates' of independent Nigeria (Suberu 2005: 215). These debates have been particularly intense at the various moments of attempting to transition to civilian and constitutional rule in the country. Thus there was a major debate on the place of *sharia* courts in the period leading up to elections and a return to democracy in 1979 (Laitin 1982), and again in the period leading up to the failed transition of the early 1990s.

Most significantly, when Nigeria again embarked on a return to democratic civilian rule in 1999, a reinforced federal structure allowed the northern states to strike out on their own.

Beginning with the small state of Zamfara, 12 Muslim-majority states of the north eventually declared that they were returning to a *sharia* penal code, and took quick measures to do so. The constitutional status of these state decisions at the federal level has not been clarified, and within each state the move sparked significant debates about the meaning of returning to *sharia* (Ostien *et al.* 2005). While portrayed by some observers as the product of a new Islamic fundamentalism in the country, in fact the Nigerian *sharia* re-implementation process beginning in 1999 must be seen as a continuation of an unresolved contradiction bequeathed to the country by the colonial system.

Muslim politics in Nigeria are therefore played out at multiple levels: at the federal level in terms of the place of the Islamic legal system within the constitution; at the national level in terms of often difficult relations between Muslims and non-Muslims; and within the north in terms of competing claimants to religious authority, with multiple and often conflicting interpretations of Islam. The roots of all of these political confrontations must be situated in the colonial experience, and the form they take today is largely shaped by Nigeria's difficult post-colonial history.

The politics of religious change

While historical state legacies are clearly central, the political role of Islam in West Africa is also shaped by dynamics internal to religion and which are in part influenced by broader tendencies in the Muslim world, as mediated through local contexts.

West African Islam historically has been overwhelmingly Sunni, and the Maliki school of Islamic law is almost universally followed in the region. As in much of Africa, the dominant practice of Islam has been shaped by Sufism. The Sufi focus on mysticism over legalism, and the central role of religious leaders or guides (known variously as *shaykhs*, marabouts, and other local terms) facilitated an historical accommodation of the religion to local cultures and societies in a process that might be labelled the 'Africanization of Islam' (Robinson 2004; see also Brenner 2000; Sanneh 1997). Echoing colonial discourse, much contemporary analysis has tended to portray Sufi Islam in West Africa as distinctive and uniquely 'peaceful' or 'tolerant', in sharp contrast to a seemingly more 'militant' and 'rigid' Islam from the Arab world. This is reflected in scholarly distinctions between Sufism and Reformism, sometimes labelled 'African Islam' versus 'Islam in Africa' (Westerlund and Rosander 1997). This distinction reflects real social and political tensions, but it is important to note that these are embedded in much more fluid debates about correct religious practice. There is a long history in the region of attempts to purify and reform Islamic practice, of which the most important may be the various *jihads* that swept much of West Africa in the late eighteenth and nineteenth centuries. Notably, however, those militant reform movements were launched by leaders closely affiliated with Sufi orders, but seeking to correct what they portrayed as deviations from Islamic orthodoxy.

While the distinction between Sufis and Reformists must thus be nuanced, most countries in the region have indeed been marked by the gradually increasing importance of explicitly anti-Sufi religious movements, often calling themselves simply 'Sunnites' but frequently labelled by others as 'Wahhabis' or 'Salafists' (Loimeier 2003, 2005; Miles 2007; Sani Umar 1993). In most cases organized reformist movements had their genesis in the late colonial period, frequently appealing in particular to people with a Western education in the 'modern' sector, and often as an alternative to the perceived quiescence to colonial rule of traditional Islamic leaders and the 'backwardness' of rural religious practice. Throughout most of West Africa these movements stayed small and with very limited popular appeal until the 1980s, devoted primarily to critiques of religious practice to an audience of urban intellectuals.

In the context of the apparent worldwide 'Islamic revival' of the 1970s and 1980s, however, reformist movements began to experience a new dynamism and to take on more explicitly political orientations in West Africa. Given the disillusionment both within the Muslim world and in Africa about the failure of the promises of independence, there was a new receptivity to arguments about the need for local alternatives to Western models of 'modernization'. Economic stagnation and the implementation of structural adjustment programmes that marked the end of assured state employment for university graduates also fed social change, stimulating new reflections on the social and political role of Islam (Brenner 1993). Although its impact was limited and in retrospect rather brief, the Iranian revolution of 1979 sparked some unprecedented – if limited – efforts to organize explicitly political movements based on religion in the region. In the effervescence of the period, various new religious movements emerged and small inroads were made by Muslim groups from outside the region, including Shi'a Islam and the South Asian Ahmadiyya movement, particularly present in Ghana, Benin, and other coastal countries.

Contacts between sub-Saharan Africa and the Arab world, carefully circumscribed under colonial rule, increased with independence (Hunwick 1997). In many countries, informal or private schools teaching at least partially in Arabic proliferated as an alternative to the official state schools, and these gradually channelled students to the Arab world for advanced study. The questioning of the local practices of Islam was further fed by the returning graduates of Arabic universities, influenced by their stays abroad and often frustrated by constrained employment opportunities at home given their limited mastery of the official European languages. Such *arabisants*, as they are known in the Francophone countries, added new voices, with new religious authority, to the critiques of traditional Sufi Islam, thus strengthening the reformist movements.[2]

In northern Nigeria, the rise of particularly strong tensions between Sufis and anti-Sufis intersected with debates about the religious authority of the emirs (Sani Umar 1993). In this context a movement known as 'Izala' (from its full name *Jama't izalat al bid'a wa iqamat as-Sunna* – the 'Society for the removal of innovation and re-establishment of the Sunna'), founded in 1978, was to emerge as the first really serious challenge to the dominance of Sufism in the region. Izala was widely described as a rising 'fundamentalist' force as it grew into the largest reformist Muslim movement in sub-Saharan Africa over the course of the 1980s (Kane 2003). Tellingly, though, its energies were directed more towards the socio-religious than the political. As Loimeier has noted, while Izala came to represent the 'most important Muslim movement of religious, social and educational reform in contemporary northern Nigeria, and a major force of religious opposition to the Sufi brotherhoods', it never became 'a revolutionary Islamist organization in political terms' (Loimeier 1997: 54).

The evolution of Izala illustrates two notable dynamics in the Sufi-Reformist tensions in the region: the importance of local context, and the potential for religious change and influences across ideological divides. Despite its stated universal critiques about appropriate Muslim religious practice, in fact Izala's activities are shaped primarily by a Nigerian national agenda, and its very organization reflects the Nigerian federal state (Kane 2003: 235–37). Underlining the importance of local political contexts to religious dynamics, branches of Izala established in neighbouring countries have adapted their discourse and activity to the political realities in those countries. Second, given the growing rivalry between Muslims and Christians in Nigeria as efforts at democratization resurfaced in the early 1990s, the violent opposition between Izala and the Sufi orders was gradually downplayed in the 1990s as Muslims in the north came to make common cause against Christian 'crusaders' (Loimeier 1997: 60–62). In the strong ethno-regional cleavages that define Nigeria, this has led to periodic violent conflict between Muslims and Christians since the late 1980s.

The liberalization of social life that accompanied the efforts at democratization across the region in the early 1990s was to open up new possibilities for religious movements, and led to a proliferation of new voices. The advent of democracy has thus further blurred distinctions between Sufis and reformists and led to a range of new religious debates with political implications. As was the case across the Muslim world, public debate about religion was to increase even further following the terrorist attacks in the United States on 11 September 2001. Contemporary Muslim politics in West Africa were thus heavily shaped by these two major transformations in the local and the global context, to which we now turn.

Muslim politics and democratization

The wave of demands for democratization across Africa in the early 1990s, however mixed the outcomes, nevertheless brought a significant liberalization that led to an explosion of associational life across the continent, including in the religious sphere. In much of Muslim Africa, this has led to the emergence of an 'Islamic public sphere' and the rise of what we might call an 'Islamic civil society' (Holder 2009; Tayob 2007). The proliferation of varied religious voices has reflected in part the debates between Sufism and its critics, but it has also led to new dynamics and indeed in many ways to a 'democratization' of religion itself, in the sense of new possibilities for individual voices to challenge established authorities. As democratization has put policy issues on the public agenda, debates about the appropriate Islamic position on any given issue leads naturally to interpretation and thus opens the door to religious change driven by these public discussions.

In the Francophone Sahel this process has led to wide-ranging debates on policy issues, but few fundamental conflicts on religion.[3] Religious voices have, however, certainly made themselves heard more loudly than ever before in the political domain, leading to some tensions with secularists. In Nigeria the transformations of the Islamic public sphere in the new era of democratization starting in 1999 has led to a great degree of conflict and controversy, both in the Muslim north and especially at the national level given the religiously divided context. In the Muslim states of northern Nigeria, however, there has also been a gradual accommodation of public religion and support for democracy.

In much of Francophone Africa, democratization in the early 1990s came via 'national conferences', convened to chart a transitional path to the inauguration of new regimes. In the Muslim Sahel the two most important countries to follow this path were Mali and Niger. The overthrow of the military regime in Mali and the marginalization of the much-weakened one in Niger in 1991 led to transitional governments, elections, and finally the inauguration of new regimes. While the Malian democratic experiment has been widely considered a major success, Niger's experience has been much more difficult and marked by various setbacks. In both countries, however, there has been real and substantial liberalization of political life and an ongoing commitment to the democratic system. In Senegal the point of departure was somewhat different and the process therefore more gradual, but in that country as well the early 1990s were marked by a series of negotiations between government and opposition, a series of fundamental reforms, and finally the country's first democratic alternation of power in 2000.

Two aspects of the democratization process in the Francophone Sahel are crucial to understanding the evolution of Muslim politics in those countries. First, the pro-democracy movements, while fed by popular frustration and economic grievances, were in fact led by the small educated elite of people with formal French-language education – Francophone 'intellectuals' as they are known in the region. Students, teachers, lawyers, journalists, and human rights activists were consequently among those at the forefront of the new 'civil society' demanding change. In the international enthusiasm for democracy of the early post-Cold War years, there was a wave of outside support for such groups, further strengthening their positions. Second, these pro-democracy activists took their inspiration for the design of new regimes from the model they knew best, namely the French Fifth Republic. Crucially, their normative approach to the democracy they sought to build suggested the need to focus on social transformation so as to build cultures compatible with their vision of democracy, rather than the elaboration of institutions to reflect local values in public policy. The question the pro-democracy activists tended to ask themselves was not, 'how do we build a democracy that reflects an African Muslim society?' but rather, 'How do we transform an African Muslim society so that it is compatible with democracy?'

Not surprisingly, this approach led rather quickly to clashes with representatives of Muslim groups. In Mali and Niger an ideologically and religiously diverse array of new Muslim associations – dozens in each case – were quickly formed and officially recognized following the demise of the corporatist single association system. In Senegal the weight of the Sufi hierarchy and the more gradual political opening resulted in slower evolutionary religious change, but which nonetheless parallels the other countries. While there was initially an important element of rivalry and occasional conflict among different religious groups, they also rather quickly learned to make common cause in opposition to the agenda of the secular pro-democracy forces. The 1990s thus saw a number of conflicts and protests between Muslim groups and new governments on both substantive and symbolic moral issues such as the holding of fashion shows or the opening of bars during Ramadan. These conflicts were often coloured by critiques of the very notion of democracy by religious groups, given the normative content with which it was proposed. The most significant feature of Muslim politics in the region, however, is the fact that religious society quickly came not only to accept the idea of democratization, but to learn to play the democratic game to their advantage. This was facilitated by the demographic advantage of Islamic associations in the confrontation with the secular 'civil society' forces, given the much broader appeal of those groups to popular sentiment in deeply religious countries.

As politics have evolved in the era of democracy, then, there has been an increased presence of religion in public life in the form of participation in debates, but also in protests and public pressuring on policy issues of concern to religious sensibilities. There has, however, been very little direct electoral involvement by religious movements and no serious efforts by religious groups to seek direct power. Explicitly religious parties (like ethnic or regional ones) are officially banned in all of these countries, but tellingly even those few that have made implicit appeals on religious grounds have had little electoral success. Rather the rise of religion in the public sphere in the context of democratization has moved from a series of confrontations between secular 'pro-democracy' activists and Islamic actors to a much more fluid and wide-ranging debate about what democracy should entail in Muslim societies. These debates have taken place within both the political and the religious arenas. So public issues such as the acceptability of polygamy, or whether the death penalty should be allowed, also become debates within religious society and carried out in religious terms, with different voices claiming varying 'Islamic' positions. Of particular importance in these debates has been the rise of Francophone Muslim intellectuals, often organized into new associations, who share a commitment to democracy and the capacity to engage in public policy debate, but who also argue that in a democracy these policy issues should reflect popular (religious) sentiment. In addition these debates have led to new forms of Muslim women's politics and even to forms of 'Islamic feminism', as Muslim women's associations have weighed in on debates (see Alidou 2005; Augis 2005; Masquelier 2009).

Given the colonial heritage, much of the debate has been couched in terms of the meaning of secularism, *laïcité*, in a democratic system. The anti-religious French connotations of the term made it the source of explicit attacks at first, and in both the Malian and the Nigerian national conferences there were demands that the term be excluded from the new constitutions. Even in Senegal, the first draft of the new constitution published in 2001 eliminated the term 'laïc' in favour of a statement about the 'non-confessional' character of the state. In Niger, in fact, this replacement was to take place in a subsequent constitution, and now remains. On this issue as well, what is striking is that there is no longer a serious discussion about whether the state should be secular, but rather a debate about the appropriate limits of religion in a secular state. The term has been reinterpreted from its French connotations of anti-religiosity to a rather American conception of the limits of religious freedom. As a result, we find debates about whether in *un état laïc* it is acceptable for the state to allow, or build, mosques on university campuses or other public spaces; about whether it is acceptable to allow elected officials to take the oath of office on a religious text; and about whether state schools should provide religious education. Not surprisingly in a democratic context of deep religiosity, the answers have tended to accommodate religion. Thus the ceremony to inaugurate a newly elected president and return Niger again to democratic rule on 7 April 2011 began with the invocation of the *Fatiha* prayer, and the new president took the oath of office with his hand on a copy of the Qur'an. Such symbolic gestures that would have been hotly contested as religious assaults on democracy in the early 1990s, are now an unquestioned aspect of Niger's democracy.

Unsurprisingly, agreement on the limits of religion in public policy has not been resolved in many areas, and some have proven rather intractable. This is particularly the case on issues that concern clashes between what secular activists present as 'international' and 'universal' values that cannot be compromised, and prevailing local values. These conflicts occur over whether a given position is an inalienable element of democracy, regardless of what the majority might want, or whether it is subject to democratic majority rule. The most noteworthy and difficult policy issues have been those concerning family law and issues regarding the status of the sexes more broadly. In each of the Francophone countries there have been long, intense, and ultimately unresolved debates about 'family codes' (Villalón 1996; Soares 2009; Schulz 2003; Brossier 2004). While these debates often have been portrayed as struggles between democrats and anti-democratic forces, their parallels with American debates on abortion or gay marriage suggest that it is more useful to frame them as intrinsic characteristics of the functioning of democracy in religious societies.

The adoption of *sharia* by 12 states of northern Nigeria was undoubtedly the most significant entry of religion into the public sphere in West Africa in the 1990s. As elsewhere in the region, this was a direct product of democratization. Following the collapse of the particularly repressive military regime of Sani Abacha, democratization and the elections of 1999 brought new possibilities for the states in Nigeria's federal system to assert their autonomy. At the national level the southern Christian candidate Olusegun Obasanjo was elected president, ending years of northern dominance under military regimes. In this context, a gubernatorial candidate in the small northern state of Zamfara seized the opportunity during the campaign to promise an adoption of *sharia* law, and quickly moved to do so once he was elected. The move was widely publicized and received enormous popular support in the north of the country, and other states quickly followed suit so that by 2002, 12 northern states (of Nigeria's 36) had declared that they would adopt *sharia* – or more specifically *sharia* penal codes. While the constitutional status of these actions within Nigeria remains unresolved, the states have moved to establish *sharia* courts to try criminal cases, presenting the reforms as a 'return' to the Islamic penal codes that had been abolished by the British on the eve of independence. There is significant variation among the states in how this was done, but in all cases these courts are parallel to (rather than replacing) existing magistrate courts, which still maintain jurisdiction over cases involving non-Muslims, and under some conditions even Muslims (Ostien *et al.* 2005).

The ultimate outcomes of these ongoing experiments with democratic *sharia* implementation, in many ways unprecedented in the Muslim world, remain to be seen, but a number of trends have clearly emerged. While the principle of *sharia* has maintained wide popular support in the region, the decade following its implementation saw significant internal debates about the actual meaning of *sharia*, and a consequent evolution in how it is understood. The dramatic initial cases that attracted much attention and outcry both within Nigeria and internationally – such as the sentencing of several women to the *hudud* punishment of death by stoning for adultery – were in fact eventually overturned by *sharia* courts of appeal, on Islamic grounds. What instead has remained at the official level are ongoing social policy debates on the need to 'sanitize' society, by banning or restricting alcohol, policing sexual practices, and censoring 'immoral' electronic media. Strikingly, however, the debate on *sharia* has also increasingly empowered popular criticisms of political corruption and demands for good governance, critiques levelled in the name of the need to establish a just Islamic social order. In part, *sharia* has thus been converted into a useful instrument for pursuing popular goals and limitations on the arbitrary exercise of power within a democratic context. The adoption of *sharia* has therefore been a major factor in the legitimation of the principle of democracy in northern Nigeria (Kendhammer 2010).

In addition, rather than the radicalization that was originally feared by many, the implementation of *sharia* in the democratic context has also tempered Muslim politics. Suberu (2005: 223) argues that 'the implementation of *shari'a* in Nigeria within a constitutional federal democratic framework has probably contributed to the moderation of Islamic religious fundamentalism in the country'. To be sure, this should not obscure the fact that *sharia* implementation has been accompanied also by significant violence. Especially in the states with important Christian minorities, the *sharia* controversy at the national level has fed the long-standing religious tensions in Nigeria, with periodic explosions of intense violence. In addition, the perceived shortcomings of *sharia* and its accommodation to democracy has opened the door to new forms of radical Muslim sects, such as the so-called 'Boko Haram', which rejects schooling and all forms of 'Western' modernity. Boko Haram's actions have been met with severe repression by the state, producing other cycles of violence. It is important to note, however, that both of these sources of violence have been persistent characteristics of the Nigerian political landscape and so cannot be attributed to *sharia* implantation per se. Nigeria's difficult politics pose the more significant threat to the future of democracy in the country. As Kendhammer (2010: 35) concludes, 'While the sharia debate has been a source of support for democracy in Northern Nigeria, whether democracy as it is practiced in Nigeria can sustain this support remains an open question'.

In Nigeria as in the Francophone Sahel, then, much research strongly supports the findings of Afrobarometer polls which show strong support for democracy among Muslims across West Africa (Bratton 2003). These cases point to the fact that it is precisely because democracy accommodates religion that it enjoys this support. We thus find that across the region popular sentiment simultaneously expresses support for religious tenets – including *sharia* – and democracy. The tension often expressed in the West between public religion and democracy appears to be largely absent in the African context, a fact strikingly demonstrated in a major survey of religion in Africa conducted by the Pew charitable trusts (Pew Research Centre 2010).[4] This seeming paradox is rooted in notions of the compatibility of religion with specific conceptions of democracy. The fact that it has allowed religious groups to advocate policies that are more accommodating of local cultural values than had ever been the case in Africa since the colonial period has strengthened support for democracy.

The 'war on terror'

The terrorist attacks of 11 September 2001 provoked intense debates about religion across the Muslim world, and in many ways much soul-searching about the place of Islam in the modern state system and about the relations between Muslims and the West. In Africa, as elsewhere, this has led simultaneously to the erasure of some historical distinctions, but also to the emergence of new or renewed religious perspectives. Across the region – and despite some appeal at the popular level of Osama bin Laden as a sort of folk hero – Muslim leaders from both Sufi and Reformist groups tended overwhelmingly to condemn the attacks and to distance themselves from them. Both, however, were also quickly angered by the American response to the events, especially by the launching of the Iraq war in 2003. Anger at the subsequent policies of the Bush Administration led to periodic protests in various countries of the region, and often to common cause among otherwise varied Muslim groups.

The search to identify a 'correct' Islamic response to such difficult events has further fed the new respect and public role for *arabisants* and other Muslim intellectuals, as well as a new willingness to reinterpret Sufi tradition in light of the earlier history of Sufi militancy in the region. Pointing to the *jihad*s of the nineteenth century, some intellectuals in the region have identified Sufism as an ideology with potential for militant mobilization against aggression. Interestingly, it has also led in some areas to a renewed assertion of a Sufi Muslim identity as an indigenous African way of being Muslim, distinct from Arab 'extremism'. After having been largely on the defensive, Sufism thus seems to be both rapidly evolving and experiencing a resurgence in West Africa, in the same context in which reformists have adopted more explicitly political stances.

In the face of this fluid religious situation, fears of 'radicalization' of 'traditionally peaceful' African Islam are the hallmarks of much Western debate about contemporary Muslim politics in West Africa. Often posed as the likely outcome of the 'spread of extremist ideologies', some have identified a 'terrorist threat' (Lyman and Morrison 2004; ICG 2005). These fears intensified following a number of highly publicized kidnappings of Westerners and other targeted attacks in the West African Sahara, especially in Niger and Mali. These attacks have been claimed by a group which, since 2007, calls itself 'al-Qaeda in the Islamic Maghreb' (AQIM), but which is a transformation of the earlier 'Salafist Group for Preaching and Combat' (GSPC), itself an outgrowth of the Algerian 'Islamic Armed Group' (GIA). The origin of these militant movements is rooted directly in Algerian politics and their original impetus springs from the refusal to allow the Islamic party that was poised to come to power in Algeria through democratic elections to take office.

This 'terrorist threat' is of very specific North African origin and in fact it has shown very little potential for action south of the Sahara (*cf.* Menkhaus, this volume). While they clearly have some capacity for disruption, these movements seem to have virtually no popular traction capable of translating into sustained political action in the region. The few incidents of violence that have been linked to AQIM in Nigeria represent familiar iterations of the long history of violence in Nigeria, and the label appears to be opportunistic at best. Only in Mauritania does AQIM appear to have gained a toehold in terms of popular recruitment, but even in the context of that country's more established Islamist movement, one keen observer notes a process of 'deradicalization', both as 'political programme and a strategic option' (Ould Ahmed Salem 2012).

While little in the history of Muslim politics or in the current dynamics under liberalized regimes would suggest the likelihood of significant religiously based terrorism in West Africa, the question of whether al-Qaeda could 'turn African in the Sahel' haunts current policy debates (Filiu 2010). This fear has driven a militarization of Western and especially American policy in the region, and the unanswered question is whether policies based on such fears could prove to be self-fulfilling prophecies. The Algerian case strongly suggests that denying democracy may be a prescription for the violent transformations of Muslim politics. The dynamics of the ongoing democratization of West Africa, by contrast, show all signs of being the most effective counterforce to radicalization, though it is indeed likely to bring increased religious influence in politics and increased importance to Muslim politics in shaping the future.

Notes

1 A thorough discussion of what 'Muslim politics' entail (intentionally framed as an alternative to discussing 'Islam and politics') is provided by Eickelman and Piscatori (1996).
2 For a number of studies of this phenomenon in different countries, see Otayek (1993).
3 A longer discussion of the issues described below in Francophone Africa is available in Villalón (2010).
4 In a survey of 600 university students in Senegal, Mali, and Niger, which the author carried out in 2008, these young and educated Francophone intellectuals avowed strikingly similar sentiments. Overwhelmingly in each country, students expressed strong support for democracy, while majorities also answered that they were in favour of the adoption of *sharia* in their country.

Bibliography

Alidou, O. (2005) *Engaging Modernity: Muslim Women and the Politics of Agency in Post-Colonial Niger*, Madison, WI: University of Wisconsin Press.

Augis, E. (2005) 'Dakar's Sunnite Women: The Politics of Person', in M. Gomez-Perez (ed.) *L'Islam politique au sud du Sahara: Identités, discours et enjeux*, Paris: Karthala.

Bratton, M. (2003) 'Briefing: Islam, Democracy and Public Opinion in Africa', *African Affairs* 102: 493–501.

Brenner, L. (ed.) (1993) *Muslim Identity and Social Change in Sub-Saharan Africa*, Bloomington, IN: Indiana University Press.

——(2000) 'Sufism in Africa', in J.K. Olupona (ed.) *African Spirituality*, New York, NY: The Crossroad Publishing Company.

Brossier, M. (2004) 'Les Débats sur la reforme du Code de la Famille au Sénégal: La Redéfinition de la laïcité comme enjeu du processus de démocratisation', unpublished D.E.A. thesis, Université Paris I.

Cruise O'Brien, D. (1986) 'Wails and Whispers: The People's Voice in West African Muslim Politics', in P. Chabal (ed.) *Political Domination in Africa: Reflections on the Limits of Power*, Cambridge: Cambridge University Press.

Eickelman, D.F. and Piscatori, J. (1996) *Muslim Politics*, Princeton, NJ: Princeton University Press.

Filiu, J.P. (2010) 'Could Al-Qaeda Turn African in the Sahel?' Carnegie Middle East Program Papers No. 112, Washington, DC: Carnegie Endowment for International Peace.

Galilou, A. (2002) 'The Graduates of Islamic Universities in Benin: A Modern Elite Seeking Social, Religious and Political Recognition', in T. Bierschenk and G. Stauth (eds) *Islam in Africa*, Yearbook of the Sociology of Islam, Vol. 4, Münster: LIT Verlag.

Gomez-Perez, M. (ed.) (2005) *L'Islam politique au sud du Sahara: Identités, discours et enjeux*, Paris: Karthala.

Holder, G. (ed.) (2009) *L'Islam, nouvel espace public en Afrique*, Paris: Karthala.

Hunwick, J. (1997) 'Sub-Saharan Africa and the Wider World of Islam: Historical and Contemporary Perspectives', in D. Westerlund and E.E. Rosander (eds) *African Islam and Islam in Africa: Encounters Between Sufis and Islamists*, London: Hurst.

ICG (International Crisis Group) (2005) 'Islamist Terrorism in the Sahel: Fact or Fiction?' Africa Report No. 92, www.crisisgroup.org/en/regions/africa/west-africa (accessed 9 April 2011).

Kane, O. (2003) *Muslim Modernity in Postcolonial Nigeria: A Study of the Society for the Removal of Innovation and Reinstatement of Tradition*, Leiden: Brill.

Kendhammer, B. (2010) 'Framing Sharia and Democracy: How Public Debate about Islamic Law Implementation Shapes Mass Beliefs about Democracy in Northern Nigeria', paper presented at the annual meeting of the African Studies Association, San Francisco, CA, 18–21 November 2010.

Laitin, D. (1982) 'The Sharia Debate and the Origins of Nigeria's Second Republic', *Journal of Modern African Studies* 20(3): 411–30.

Loimeier, R. (1997) *Islamic Reform and Political Change in Northern Nigeria*, Evanston, IL: Northwestern University Press.

——(2003) 'Patterns and Peculiarities of Islamic Reform in Africa', *Journal of Religion in Africa* 33(3): 237–62.

——(2005) 'De la dynamique locale des réformismes musulmans. Etudes biographiques (Sénégal, Nigeria et Afrique de l'Est)', in M. Gomez-Perez (ed.) *L'Islam politique au sud du Sahara: Identités, discours et enjeux*, Paris: Karthala.

Lyman, P.N. and Morrison, J.S. (2004) 'The Terrorist Threat in Africa', *Foreign Affairs* 83(1): 75–86.

Masquelier, A. (2009) *Women and Islamic Revival in a West African Town*, Bloomington, IN: Indiana University Press.

Miles, W.F.S. (ed.) (2007) *Political Islam in West Africa: State-society Relations Transformed*, Boulder, CO: Lynne Rienner Publishers.

Østebø, T. (2008) 'Localising Salafism: Religious Change Among Oromo Muslims in Bale, Ethiopia', unpublished PhD thesis, Stockholm University.

Ostien, P., Nasir, J.M. and Kogelmann, F. (eds) (2005) *Comparative Perspectives on Shari'ah in Nigeria*, Ibadan: Spectrum Books Ltd.

Otayek, R. (ed.) (1993) *Le radicalisme Islamique au sud du Sahara: Da'wa, arabisation et critique de l'Occident*, Paris: Karthala.

Ould Ahmed Salem, Z. (2012) 'The Paradoxes of Islamic Radicalisation in Mauritania', in G. Joffé (ed.) *Islamist Radicalization in North Africa: Politics and Process*, Abingdon: Routledge.

Pew Research Centre (2010) 'Tolerance and Tension: Islam and Christianity in Sub-Saharan Africa', Pew Forum on Religion and Public Life, Washington, DC: Pew Research Centre, www.pewforum.org/uploadedFiles/Topics/Belief_and_Practices/sub-saharan-africa-full-report.pdf (accessed 10 April 2011).

Robinson, D. (2000) *Paths of Accommodation: Muslim Societies and French Colonial Authorities in Senegal and Mauritania, 1880–1920*, Athens, OH: Ohio University Press.

——(2004) *Muslim Societies in African History*, Cambridge: Cambridge University Press.

Sani Umar, M. (1993) 'Changing Islamic identity in Nigeria from the 1960s to the 1980s: From Sufism to Anti-Sufism', in L. Brenner (ed.) *Muslim Identity and Social Change in Sub-Saharan Africa*, Bloomington, IN: Indiana University Press.

Sanneh, L. (1997) *The Crown and the Turban: Muslims and West African Pluralism*, Boulder, CO: Westview Press.

Sanusi, S.L. (2007) 'Politics and Sharia in Northern Nigeria', in B.F. Soares and R. Otayek (eds) *Islam and Muslim Politics in Africa*, New York, NY: Palgrave Macmillan.

Schulz, D.E. (2003) 'Political Factions, Ideological Fictions: The Controversy over Family Law Reform in Democratic Mali', *Islamic Law and Society* 10(1): 132–64.

Soares, B.F. (2009) 'The Attempt to Reform Family Law in Mali', *Die Welt des Islams* 49: 398–428.

Suberu, R. (2005) 'Continuity and Change in Nigeria's Shari'a Debates', in M. Gomez-Perez (ed.) *L'islam politique au sud du Sahara: identités, discours et enjeux*, Paris: Karthala.

Tayob, A. (2007) 'Muslim Publics: Contents and Discontents', *Journal for Islamic Studies* 27, Thematic Issue: 'Islam and African Muslim Publics': 1–15.

Villalón, L.A. (1995) *Islamic Society and State Power in Senegal: Disciples and Citizens in Fatick*, Cambridge: Cambridge University Press.

——(1996) 'The Moral and the Political in African Democratization: The *Code de la famille* in Niger's Troubled Transition', *Democratization* 3(2): 41–68.

——(1999) 'Generational Changes, Political Stagnation, and the Evolving Dynamics of Religion and Politics in Senegal', *Africa Today* 46(3/4): 129–47.

——(2010) 'From Argument to Negotiation: Constructing Democracies in Muslim West Africa', *Comparative Politics* 42(4): 375–93.

Weiss, H. (2008) *Between Accommodation and Revivalism: Muslims, the State, and Society in Ghana from the Precolonial to the Postcolonial Era*, Helsinki: Finnish Oriental Society.

Westerlund, D. and Rosander, E.E. (eds) (1997) *African Islam and Islam in Africa: Encounters Between Sufis and Islamists*, London: Hurst; Athens, OH: Ohio University Press.

12

WOMEN IN POLITICS

Amina Mama

During the first decade of the twenty-first century, several of Africa's 54 nations have seen dramatic increases in the number of women in politics. This change can be attributed to several factors. Women's political activism increased during the 1990s, both within and beyond the formal political sphere. The mobilization of women's movements within national political transitions has become much more effective. The internationalization of feminism globally – which has put women's demands for greater representation on the international stage – as evidenced in the World Conferences convened by the United Nations (UN) and by increasingly vocal transnational feminist networks, has also empowered women's activism at local levels. The countries with increased women's political representation are all electoral democracies, many of which have undergone transitions from various forms of authoritarian rule (van de Walle, this volume).

These transitions have been diverse. The end of apartheid brought the African National Congress (ANC) to power in South Africa in 1994; the military victory of the National Resistance Movement (NRM) over the government of Uganda led to a new government, the institution of a 'one-party democracy', and a new constitution that included an affirmative action strategy for women in 1986; and post-genocide Rwanda elected 48.8 per cent women to the House of Representatives in September 2003. Five years later, this rose even further when women won 45 out of 80 parliamentary seats in the 2008 election, making Rwanda the first country in the world to elect a majority of women representatives. These highly celebrated examples remain exceptions to the general rule, which sees men continue to significantly outnumber women and dominate political power and influence in most of the world. In this global context, the low average for the percentage of female elected representatives in sub-Saharan Africa at 19.1 per cent is on par with the global scenario, in which 19.2 per cent of the world's elected representatives are women (IPU 2011). Comparatively, the United States lags behind other Organisation for Economic Co-operation and Development (OECD) nations, ranking 67th in the world with only 16.6 per cent women elected – far less than many African nations.

It is important to keep in mind that while some African countries have an impressive number of female members of parliament (MPs), gender equality is more problematic the higher one goes up the political ladder. There were no democratically elected female heads of state until Ellen Johnson Sirleaf was elected in Liberia in 2004. Indeed, the historical record only makes her election more impressive. Throughout the whole of the twentieth century Africa had no democratically elected female heads of state, and only three women monarchs. Empress Zauditu ruled Ethiopia from 1917 to 1930, and Queen-regents Dzeliwe Shongwe (1982–83) and Ntombi Thwala (1983–86) ruled the Kingdom of Swaziland. President Jean-Bédel Bokassa appointed Africa's only female prime minister, Elizabeth Domitien, in the Central African Republic (CAR), but she only served for one year (1975–76). Africa's first female head of state was Ruth Perry, selected as interim chair of Liberia's Council of State during the mid-1990s. It is thus clear to surmise that women's marginalization has been a deeply entrenched feature of African political cultures and institutions.

Sadly, these complexities and the efforts of women's movements to promote female political participation have often gone unnoticed because many mainstream studies of African politics still neglect changing gender configurations. Van Allen (2001) observes that most research continues to focus on the contestations arising between male elites, with insufficient attention to the important role played by labour and other social movements – such as international women's movements – in advancing women's political equality. As this chapter illustrates, further attention to the role of women and a gender analysis of African politics can contribute to a deeper understanding of broader democratization processes.

Attention to gender exclusions and the masculinized quality of political cultures illuminates both the formal and informal character of political institutions and processes that clearly involve far more than the obvious contestations between ruling men. Indeed, it is often argued that the equitable participation of women gives a good indication of just how democratic a given regime is. The Inter-Parliamentary Union (IPU) states:

> The advancement of women goes hand in hand with the overall development of society and contributes to better and more effective governance. A stronger presence of women in parliament will allow new concerns to be highlighted on political agenda; and new priorities to be put into practice through the adoption and implementation of policies and laws. The inclusion of the perspectives and interests of women is a prerequisite for democracy and contributes to good governance.
>
> *(IPU 2008: 6)*

However, given that most of the world's democracies exhibit severe under-representation of women, taking gender equality as a definitive criterion implies that no nation has yet attained democratic governance. That feminist political theorists uphold this definition while it has less currency in mainstream political studies indicates that different conceptualizations of 'politics' and 'democracy' are at play within the literature.

Although well-intentioned, the tendency of qualitative research on gender and politics in Africa to focus on 'best case' scenarios, combined with a lack of in-depth research, has had the effect of focusing attention away from the under-representation of women and on to a small number of success stories, most notably post-apartheid South Africa, post-1989 Uganda, and post-genocide Rwanda – all countries that are in the top 25 globally in terms of women's numerical representation. As home of Africa's first democratically elected woman president, Liberia is now generating wide interest. Ghana, Nigeria, South Africa, Uganda, and Zimbabwe have strong scholarly communities carrying out significantly more local research than much less-studied nations, like Mauritania, Burkina Faso, Mali, and the Seychelles. Similarly, some conflict-affected countries – Liberia, Sierra Leone, Democratic Republic of Congo (DRC), and Rwanda – have generated studies on gender and security, while other conflict zones, such as Chad, Sudan, or Morocco, have not.[1]

Nevertheless, it is also these countries that have generated a larger body of research, wherein both local and international scholars have begun to debate and theorize the political possibilities of having women in office, and what it will take to make them more effective political actors in political institutions. Scholars must grapple with the challenges arising from the fact that the national histories of women, gender, and politics are in continuous flux, being influenced by local dynamics and by the complex interplays between local and international influences. Researchers have shown a deepening interest in investigating challenging questions about the quality of women's political participation and their effectiveness. How much political influence do women actually have? Do they exercise influence as women, or do they simply perform in the same ways as men? Women's movements in the countries with the highest numbers of women in the legislature are increasingly concerned about the extent to which women in structures of power and policymaking do actually translate their hard-won and increasing presence into the delivery of gender-just policies – that is, policies that lead to real advances in the lives and prospects of women in the society at large. Qualitative studies go further than surveys to answer these questions and explore some of the conditions under which women participate, the normative gendered assumptions that prevail in the institutional cultures, the procedures and practices of government and political institutions, and the gendered inequalities in economic status that so often curtail women's participation.

This chapter draws on this literature to review the changing gender configurations in contemporary African politics, and the critical role that African women and women's movements have played in regional political development in the post-Cold War period. It supports the view that democracy cannot be fully understood without attention to the various social forces involved in bringing it about – what Saul (1997) refers to as 'democratization from below'. It argues that many of the constraints to women's political participation lie within the gendered construction of political institutions and processes, so that women are faced with the dual task of entering and working within male-dominated arenas, while also working outside of them to promote reform.

The global picture

The broad global scenario of gender politics has emerged following several decades during which women's movements made important inroads at many levels of international governance and politics. The latter years of the twentieth century saw women's movements participate in the UN Decade for Women, Development and Peace (1975–85), the main feature of which was the emphasis on integrating women into development. The concern that women and their interests be taken more seriously by male-dominated governments was specifically addressed in the call for governments to establish official structures (described in UN parlance as the 'national machinery' for women) in order to integrate women into development planning and policymaking. African nations pursued this ahead of other regions in the world, so that by the 1990s the majority of nations had some institution dedicated to this task. However, an independent review – carried out 25 years after the third Global Women's Conference, held in Nairobi in 1985, inspired a surge of gender activism – reveals that these were largely under-resourced, with limited capacity to effect change.

The initial government responses to the post-Nairobi demands for women's fuller participation in development were limited and instrumental, and can be characterized as liberal rather than transformative, in the sense that they did not challenge the basic features of women's subordination (such as the gender division of labour, economic disparities, or women's political marginalization). Instead, the emphasis was on integrating women into development (the Women in Development or WID approach). WID was implemented largely through supplementary projects for women, which were themselves small-scale and did not challenge unequal power dynamics. Over time, awareness of the limits of the 'add women' approach gave rise to a more strategic focus on power relations, articulated in the increasingly assertive demand for the inclusion of women in political power and decision making. These were manifest in the Beijing Platform for action, formulated at the 1995 World Conference a decade after Nairobi, amidst the 1990s upsurge in global feminist networks and women's movement activism (Basu 1995; Naples and Desai 2002).[2]

The last two decades have seen local and transnational feminist activism bear fruit in local and global governance arenas, respectively. An array of UN resolutions, declarations, legal reforms, and policy instruments has been implemented, with varied levels of uptake in member countries. Women's political participation has been a particular focus of international feminist activism since the Beijing Conference of 1995. In 2010, the vigorous engagement of women's movements around the world culminated in the establishment of a new global governance structure for women, UN Women, whose head, former Chilean President Michelle Bachelet, reports directly to the UN Secretary-General.

Contemporaneous positive changes in Africa include the African Union's (AU) unequivocal policy commitment in 2003, under the leadership of former Malian President Oumar Konare, that no less than 50 per cent of future AU commissioners would be women. This was followed by a Gender Working Group convened to begin strategic planning for a special session on gender during the 2004 Heads of State Summit, which resulted in a Solemn Declaration on Gender Equality in Africa signed by all heads of state. At the sub-regional level, the Southern African Development Community (SADC) has taken the lead in Africa in adopting its Protocol on Gender and Development, which commits to attaining gender parity in political decision making by 2015.

Women in African nationalist politics

African politics has seen many changes since the attainment of political independence. During the nationalist era, women's movements contributed to decolonization and political development in many countries. However, very few women were afforded leadership roles in the main political parties or movements. Furthermore, the fact that women contributed significantly to the struggles for political independence and national liberation across Africa was for a long while neglected in mainstream studies of African politics. It has largely been left to feminist scholars to unearth and document women's participation in these historic processes. Women contributed to national political movements in a multiplicity of ways, often transgressing local gender norms in order to do so, and often at some cost to themselves and their families.

One of the best-known cases can be found in the region that makes up Nigeria's southern states, where there is a long history of militancy by women's movements. These include the Nwaobiala dancing women's movements of the 1920s and the Women's War, quelled by a colonial army that shot and killed 53 women protesters (Mba 1982). During the 1940s and 1950s women's political activism in southern Nigeria continued, including the many actions led by prominent socialist feminist Ransome Kuti, who campaigned tirelessly for women's political inclusion (Johnson-Odim and Mba 1997). It was women who came together across regional and ethnic colonial divisions to form a national organization (the Nigerian Women's Union) and to lobby for the extension of suffrage to all Nigerian women, instead of excluding women in the Muslim-dominated northern parts of the country.

Similarly, women participated actively in Guinea-Bissau's national liberation war against the Portuguese (Urdang 1979). In Eritrea's 30-year struggle for independence from Ethiopia, as many as 30 per cent of fighters were reportedly women (Wilson 1991). In Algeria, women also performed multiple roles in both the political and the armed struggles against the French, a factor that led the French to mount specialized programmes to educate women in the hope of preventing their recruitment by the National Liberation Front (FLN) (Lazreg 2009). High levels of women's involvement were also evident in the liberation struggles waged in Southern Africa, Namibia, Angola, Mozambique, and Zimbabwe.

It is worth noting that many of the above-mentioned movements were inspired by socialism and reflected the influence of the relatively progressive gender politics that characterized leftist politics and socialist methods of struggle. According to the basic Marxist tenets espoused by Samora Machel and other revolutionary African leaders of the 1980s and 1990s, the emancipation of women was fundamental to the success of the revolution. That this went against indigenous cultural norms was a matter for education and consciousness-raising in the movement. The extent to which women's participation can be attributed to the exigencies of war has been a subject of some debate, because movement victories have not translated into the significant and sustained participation of women in national politics that international feminists – perhaps romantically – anticipated.

In contexts where the struggle for independence involved the growth of political parties and movements, rather than liberation wars, women were extensively involved in political mobilization and anti-colonial activism. African women were often already organized through various networks and organizations that embraced political activism as the nationalist movement took shape. In Ghana, the mobilization of women across the class spectrum contributed to the victory of the Convention People's Party, led by Kwame Nkrumah, forming the first independent government in 1957 (Manuh 1991). In Guinea, women engaged actively alongside veterans, labour, and student movements in the political processes that saw the *Rassemblement Démocratique Africain* (RDA, African Democratic Rally) form the first independent government under the leadership of Sekou Toure. In East Africa, too, women were actively involved in national party politics, as well as through women's organizations such as the Sudanese Women's Union, Maendeleo ya Wanawake in Kenya, and the Tanzanian Women's Union. Taken together, these examples demonstrate that women were highly motivated and effective political activists during the nationalist struggles that took place in many parts of Africa. For the most part, they mobilized in support of otherwise male-dominated political movements and parties.

Political independence

Political independence marked a new level of democratization, expanding the possibilities for African political leadership and participation. All of the party leaders were men, but some made definite efforts to include women, although their involvement remained largely restricted to highly gendered roles as men's help-mates and party supporters. Early studies argue that women were therefore unable to play a major role in African statecraft (Parpart and Staudt 1989). Yet, it is clear that political independence marked a significant advance from colonial rule. Ghana offers an example, as Nkrumah readily acknowledged the contribution of women to his success (Manuh 1991). The fact that there were no women in his cabinet led Nkrumah to introduce the first ever quota system in African politics, in the form of the Representation of the People (Women Members) Bill, passed into law on 16 June 1960. Thereafter, 10 women were elected unopposed as MPs, setting Ghana ahead of the rest of the continent and indeed much of the Western world in women's representation in politics.

The case of Tanzania under Julius Nyerere offers another example in which the Tanzanian Women's Union played a prominent role in national politics, and female political leaders like Bibi Titi came to prominence working for the party (Geiger 1997). Like Tanzania, other socialist-inspired governments, such as Guinea, Angola, Mozambique, and Guinea-Bissau, also sustained mass national organizations for women after independence. These gave women a gender-specific political space to play roles that remained largely supportive, in contrast to the more autonomous women's movements that were later to develop in civil society and advocate more assertively for women's rights (see below).

The early democracies of the 1960s and 1970s nevertheless saw women minimally represented in government, and expected to support mainstream agendas rather than engaging in feminist advocacy. The exceptions were those countries that developed socialist-style mass national women's organizations (e.g. Ethiopia under Mengistu Haile Meriam), or those countries in which political parties established women's wings in the service of the party and its leaders. Not long after, many of Africa's new nations began to display levels of authoritarianism and instability that in some instances – Sudan and Nigeria were the first – deteriorated into the bloody conflicts and a series of military coups d'état that dominated the grim landscape of the 1980s, imposing extreme limitations on women's political participation in particular.

Gender politics under authoritarian regimes

By the mid-1970s more than half of Africa's nations were under military rule, characterized by limited public involvement in the political sphere, widespread political repression, human rights abuses, and a tightly managed political strategy of unconditional co-optation (Cheeseman, this volume). Neither military rulers nor civilian dictatorships allowed any significant level of representation for women in government. In all cases, military or civilian, political power was monopolized by a male elite, with deep and lasting effects on political culture.

Systematic repression of civil society and dissent eroded civilian capacity for pro-democracy activism, provoking numerous struggles to expand democratic spaces, many of them involving women. Military leaders occasionally appointed individual women to political office, usually to address traditionally feminine areas of government, such as social welfare and education. The gender politics of military rule were somewhat more complex than mere tokenism, because a number of authoritarian regimes developed strategies that involved elite women in high-profile ways, while reinforcing the conservative gender ideologies of African militaries. These are addressed in discussions of 'first lady syndrome' and 'wifism' in Nigeria (Ajayi 2010) and Ghana (Manuh 1993). Women's highly visible public presence on terms directed by their military husbands can be understood in part as a state response to the internationalization of feminism that took place during the 1980s. However, the various manifestations of 'state feminism' that arose under authoritarian regimes in African nations have been hostile towards independent women's organizing, and in actuality are anti-feminist in their restoration of conservative gender politics.

Beyond this, military elites shared the public eminence and spoils of office with their wives. In 1980s Nigeria, for example, successive military leaders' wives launched high profile pro-grammes and mobilized military wives across the Federation to run them, placing elite wives in the public spotlight as never before. Nana Agyeman Rawlings, wife of Ghanaian military ruler Jerry Rawlings, established the 31st December Women's Movement, which served the ruling regime by mobilizing women and creating international credibility for a regime that was very rapidly abandoning its revolutionary pretensions (Aubrey 2001). The 31st December Women's Movement later metamorphosed into a party support wing, mobilizing women for Rawlings's subsequently elected People's National Democratic Convention. Later it became more like a non-governmental organization (NGO) and pursued women's agendas in civil society (Tsikata *et al.* 2005).

Some ostensibly all-male military regimes established national political machinery for women – the official structures advocated by the UN under the Women in Development rubric. So it was that Nigerian military ruler General Ibrahim Babangida established the National Women's Commission in 1985, the year of the Nairobi Conference. Ironically, women's activists returning from the same conference were arrested and briefly detained by the regime for allegedly bringing Nigeria into disrepute. After a brief period in which the National Women's Commission existed as a government body and developed its own programmes, the leadership was arrested and control of the commission was subsequently taken over by Mrs Babangida. A decade later, General Abacha's wife attended the 1995 Beijing Conference with a 200-person delegation; that same year, her husband inaugurated the Federal Ministry for Women's Affairs and Social Welfare. However, these formal structures for women were largely devoted to housing the pet programmes of the successive first ladies, who thus left the business of government to their husbands.

As Sisulu *et al.* (1991: 9) observe, 'state feminism serves ultimately to maintain the status quo of the public life of politics, and to repress women's engagement in civil society'. Africa's authoritarian regimes therefore consolidated the patriarchal character of the state, and the accompanying militarization of political life ensured that the majority of women remained relative outsiders to politics and decision making during the 1980s and 1990s. As a result, the democratization movements that emerged to challenge authoritarian governments largely fell short of seriously addressing women's marginalization within their ranks, mostly regarding feminist causes as a distraction from the real business of politics.

Women in Africa's democracies

During the wave of democratization in the 1990s, women's political activism resurged and significantly greater numbers of women began to contest for office amidst these political transitions. At the highest level, women ran for president in Kenya and Liberia, and sought party nominations for the presidency in Angola, Burkina Faso, the CAR, Guinea-Bissau, Kenya, Nigeria, São Tomé and Príncipe, and Tanzania. None, however, succeeded in their campaigns. It was thus a remarkable development when Agathe Uwilingiyimana was elected to serve as Rwanda's prime minister in 1992. Killed with her family at the outset of the genocide, she was a strong advocate of women's rights and set a new standard for women in high public office. Neighbouring Burundi also elected a woman prime minister, Sylvie Kinigi, in 1993. In 1994 President Yoweri Museveni of Uganda appointed Wandera Specioza Kazibwe as his second in command, making her Africa's first female vice-president, albeit in a 'no-party', multi-tiered system that reserved seats for women. In West Africa, Senegal became the first country to have a woman prime minister when Mame Boye was appointed by President Abdoulaye Wade in 2001. By the end of the 1990s, legislative bodies in Ethiopia, Lesotho, and South Africa had all appointed female house speakers, while those in Uganda, Zimbabwe, and South Africa had female deputy speakers, giving women a great deal more visibility and presence in the political arena.

Similarly, Mauritius is a signatory to two important protocols that aim to improve the representation of women in parliament, namely the Convention on the Elimination of All Forms of Discrimination Against Women and the 1997 SADC Declaration on Gender and Development. Yet despite its relative economic stability and success, it has the lowest representation of women in politics among the SADC countries, at just 5.7 per cent. The 'invisibility' of women in politics has been described as 'a grave democratic deficit', and blamed on the present electoral system, which 'will never do justice to the true role of women in society and will never enhance the empowerment of women' (Bunwaree and Kassenaly 2005: 29).

Botswana's parliamentary system provides another example of a stable and peaceful democracy, in place since independence from the British in 1966. Like Mauritius, Botswana has seen sustained economic growth; wealth from diamond mining has been utilized for development, including social, educational, and health infrastructure. An active and highly effective women's movement led by Emang Basadi ('Women Stand Up') successfully pursued legal reforms to equalize women's citizenship rights. Re-elected President Festus Mogae subsequently appointed 10 women to top positions in government and the public service, including the ministers of local government and of health, assistant ministers of local government and of the Office of the President, and head of the National Bank. The ensuing years have seen the women's movement continuing to support women's entry into politics, lobbying for better representation in political parties, transforming women's wings, carrying out training among women, and advocating for political reforms that would enable further progress for women in political life. However, women's participation has increased slowly, and institutional constraints in the political system have been identified as the major obstacle to further progress.

In Tanzania, the transition from a one-party state to a multi-party democracy has delivered very limited gains to women: men dominate emergent political parties and women candidates have difficulty winning support. Two years after the ruling party Chama Cha Mapinduzi (CCM) initiated a multi-party democratic transition in 1992, women comprised only 21.6 per cent of party membership in the eight parties for which data were available. Among these, just one party, Chama Cha Demokrasia na Maendeleo (CHADEMA), achieved gender parity, although several others surpassed the 30 per cent quota set by the Beijing Platform in 1995. The active lobbying and advocacy work of a vocal women's movement and other women's NGOs has kept gender equality on the political agenda, though progress has remained slow.

In contrast to the gradual progress of multi-party democracies, there are also contexts in which increased levels of authoritarianism and political repression have hampered progress for women. Zimbabwe is a case in which women's participation in the liberation war was followed by some modest gains under the Zimbabwe African National Union (ZANU) government. A national machinery was established and, for the first time, women from all racial groups were able to campaign and contest for seats in the national legislature. However, these gains were not sustained. The national machinery was downsized and under-resourced, and political participation remained low and ineffective in pursuing women's rights. By the early 1990s an independent women's movement had formed, partly in response to the ZANU government's 'clean-up' campaigns, which led to the mass arrests and victimization of women. Popular media humiliated former fighters in a public debate over the question of whether freedom fighters could make good wives. The challenges facing women within Zimbabwe's political arena have given rise to a women's movement that plays a leading role in Zimbabwe's beleaguered civil society, consistently working to increase women's participation through continuous activism, advocacy, training, and outreach activities.

The political crisis in Zimbabwe that has developed since the 1990s has seen women's groups establish a broad coalition and play a leading role in the constitutional reform process. The National Constitutional Assembly (NCA) was chaired by long-term feminist activist Thoko Maatshe. However, this process was overtaken by other developments, as the Mugabe government has continued toward authoritarianism, monopolizing power, detaining and arresting critics, and actively suppressing the opposition Movement for Democratic Change (MDC). High levels of political violence deter many women from campaigning for office, and it is well known that those who do dare to run for office are often subjected to abusive and humiliating treatment. It is not surprising that the number of women elected to office declined during the 1990s. In the 1995 election, women won 22 per cent of parliamentary seats, but by 2000, although more women than ever before were contesting, only a small proportion (14 per cent of the 55) were elected, to make up just 9.3 per cent of the total 150 seats.

Even without making reference to the wider crisis of democracy, Gaidzanwa notes that:

> In Zimbabwe, the electoral system places a great burden on women since membership in a political party is a prerequisite for election into parliament. Membership in political parties is a strongly gendered process based on the availability of one's time, energy, resources and skills to participate in the public domain. Political parties hold meetings, rallies, and workshops and require their members to devote time to relationships with other party members to enhance their chances of attaining electoral office. These requirements therefore rule out the participation of large numbers of women, especially those of childbearing and child-caring ages who also shoulder domestic responsibilities.
>
> *(Gaidzanwa 2004: 11)*

Male party leaders obstruct women's participation when they select only male candidates, and influence the selection at constituency and provincial levels. Women are also constrained by their limited exposure to the complex systems and procedures, and by the fact that they generally lack the funding to protect themselves during campaigns. Electoral dynamics between political parties also have negative effects on women's chances of election, as does the fact that decisions are often determined by deals cut between men, while women remain outsiders in a situation that has been only worsened by the struggle between the two main contenders for power, ZANU and the MDC, which entered a precarious power-sharing arrangement after the 2008 election.

In South Africa, representation of women has steadily increased since the end of the apartheid regime which had upheld racial and gendered exclusions for decades. The successful mobilization of women under the Women's National Congress guaranteed constitutional equality to all citizens of the new South Africa. It also led the victorious African National Congress to introduce a quota system, thus dramatically increasing women's representation. By 2008, women constituted 42.8 per cent of ministers – a 200 per cent increase from 1997. Women have not only controlled portfolios traditionally associated with their gender roles, but also several key cabinet portfolios that have tended to remain under the purview of men, notably foreign affairs, public works, land and agriculture, and justice and constitutional development. By 2008, women were also holding 40 per cent of deputy minister positions, including defence. South Africa is a clear case in which women have mobilized successfully in the context of a transition toward democratic governance.

In addition to increased political representation, significant gains have been made in the legal and policy status of women, partly due to the high level of mobilization by women during the transition. Women in the parliament formed a cross-party parliamentary caucus in an effort to maintain the sense of unity around women's rights. The remarkable legislative achievements of the Parliamentary Standing Committee on the Quality of Life and the Status of Women under the leadership of ANC MP Pregs Govender demonstrates how the combination of affirmative action and strategic organization by women in political institutions can be effective, even in a political culture that is still male-dominated.

It also shows the fragility of women's gains, as the significance of particular individuals raises uncertainty about the extent to which they can be sustained over time (Gouws 2005). Similarly, some local analysts remain critical of the fact that even with the relatively favourable scenario that shaped the South African transition and its first few years of majority rule, women's significant legislative and political gains have not translated into real social and political transformations in the wider society (Friedman 1999). Thus, for example, although South Africa's legislation on termination of pregnancy is among the most progressive in the world, a range of additional factors – such as ensuring that health services apply the law, and that women have the resources and confidence to access and make use of the legal provisions – continue to limit its implementation.

Overall, Africa's democracies see women's equality still hampered by the patriarchal and sometimes violent political cultures that still bear the legacy of authoritarian regimes. Structures and processes continue to advantage men, and economic disparities mean few women have the resources to campaign. Thus, while women have embraced the new range of possibilities that have opened up with the transition from authoritarian rule to multi-party politics, a range of new challenges have limited and hampered their equitable participation. Some of these can be understood as the highly undemocratic and often misogynistic political cultural legacies of patriarchal and authoritarian rule. These have permeated civil society, women's movements, and emergent party systems, and produced a mistrust of political institutions, discouraging many women from putting themselves forward as candidates. As Goetz and Hassim note:

> Party systems, and the ruling party, may be insufficiently institutionalised for women to challenge rules which exclude women – simply because there are no firm rules and rights, only patronage systems and favours. Alternatively, where a military or theocratic power structure bolsters ruling parties, there is little scope for women's engagement because the rules of these institutions explicitly deny women's full right of participation.
>
> *(Goetz and Hassim 2003: 11)*

In addition to the continued dominance of single parties in many states, transfers of power through electoral processes have often been marred by electoral malpractice and electoral violence in which women are attacked in gender-specific ways that are often deeply personal, as demonstrated by recent events in Kenya in 2007–08 and Côte d'Ivoire in 2011. Instances of political disorder and civil war are particularly significant for women because they tend to create particular difficulties for female political participation. Indeed, war and conflict have negative effects on women's lives as well as on gender relations: in addition to hunger, death, and the loss of loved ones, women living in conflict zones have been subjected to widespread rape and sexual violence (particularly in the DRC, Liberia, and Sierra Leone). Partly because of this, post-conflict contexts have been enthusiastically discussed as heralding a post-war window that might offer women new opportunities for political participation (see Clark, and Curtis, both this volume). However, the experience of countries that have attempted to build democracy out of conflict since the end of the Cold War suggests that this is not necessarily so.

While female participation has increased in countries such as Rwanda due to the use of quotas, as discussed below, the picture is very different in Liberia and Sierra Leone. Liberia, despite having the region's first woman president, still has only 12.5 per cent women elected representatives, well below the regional average. Despite President Johnson Sirleaf's appreciation of the active support of the women's movements in both the peace and the electoral processes, the Liberian case indicates that it will take a great deal more than a woman president to overcome the enduring effects of years of misogynistic, militaristic rule, and violent conflict. Whereas the various militias that waged the war involved as many as 30 per cent women combatants, the new national army displays the conventional exclusion of women. Women have also remained politically marginalized in post-conflict Sierra Leone, where they make up only 13.2 per cent of the legislature, despite the activities of women's organizations seeking to increase this participation.

Affirmative action

The effectiveness of quotas in facilitating women's numerical representation has been well established, as countries without quota systems have largely failed significantly to increase numbers. The fact that the average number of women in parliament is higher in sub-Saharan Africa than in the rest of the world can largely be attributed to quotas (see Table 12.1). The top 10 nations with regard to women's political representation are Burundi, Lesotho, Mozambique, Namibia, Rwanda, Senegal, South Africa, Tanzania, Tunisia, and Uganda. Seven of these have constitutional quotas for national parliaments, some of which are also combined with legislative quotas for lower levels of government. At the time of writing, 29 of Africa's 54 countries have quotas, the majority of which have been voluntarily introduced by political parties, rather than as constitutional requirements. Their implementation thus remains contingent on election outcomes. In South Africa, for example, the closed list system adopted by the ANC includes a proportional representation requirement, under which the 'zip' or 'zebra' system requires that alternative male and female candidates be included on the party list for each seat.

The combination of quotas and the pressure brought to bear by international and domestic women's movements has supported an increase in the percentage of women elected to office in sub-Saharan Africa, from 12.2 per cent at the end of 2001 to 19.1 per cent in 2011. However, it is important to note that this continental trend has not been evenly distributed within Africa (Table 12.2), and that its impact has not been uniformly positive.

Consider Uganda, which instituted mandatory reserved seats, whilst other countries have adopted a combination of these two systems. Ahikire (2003) investigates the effectiveness of women in local government, noting that the quota system yielded as many as 10,000 women in local political office around Uganda in 1998 – a dramatic change in the level of representation, which might have been expected to lead to more substantive and qualitative changes. Instead, the impact has been contradictory, as the increased number has been accompanied by a lack of legitimacy and women are often accused of not having secured their positions on merit. She concludes that women in electoral office would be more effective if there were a strong civil society support system.

Ugandan MP Miria Matembe argues that women in Uganda 'have been trapped and have become hostages to the quota system, which was originally introduced to liberate them' (Matembe 2006: 8). However, arguments against the reserved seats option do not take cognizance of the fact that without it women fared far worse. In Matembe's view, Ugandan women have perceived women's seats in parliament as a privilege bestowed by a benevolent president, and this has clearly limited the extent to which they have challenged the status quo and pursued gender equality agendas.

Table 12.1 Regional percentage of women in elected office

Region	Percentage of women in office
Global	19.2
Americas	22.4
Europe	21.9
Nordic	41.2
Sub-Saharan Africa	19.0
Asia.	18.3
Pacific	12.4
Arab states	11.4

Source: IPU, March 2011.

Table 12.2 Percentage of women elected representatives in Africa

Country	Lower house (%)	Upper house (%)
Rwanda	56.3	34.6
South Africa	44.5	29.6
Mozambique	39.2	–
Angola	38.6	–
Tanzania	36.0	–
Burundi	32.1	46.3
Ethiopia	27.8	16.3
Sudan*	25.6	10.9
Namibia	24.4	26.9
Lesotho	24.2	18.2
Senegal	22.7	40.0
Mauritania	22.1	14.3
Eritrea	22.0	–
Cape Verde	20.8	–
Malawi	20.8	–
Mauritius	18.8	55.0
Burkina Faso	15.3	–
Zimbabwe	15.0	24.2
Gabon	14.7	17.6
Zambia	14.0	–
Cameroon	13.9	–
Djibouti	13.8	–
Swaziland	13.6	40.6
Sierra Leone	13.2	–
Liberia	12.5	16.7
Madagascar	12.5	11.1
Togo	11.1	–
Benin	10.8	–
Morocco	10.5	2.2
Mali	10.2	–
Equatorial Guinea	10.0	–
Guinea-Bissau	10.0	–
Kenya	9.8	–
Côte d'Ivoire	8.9	–
DRC	8.4	4.6
Ghana	8.3	–
Botswana	7.9	–
Algeria	7.7	5.1
Libya	7.7	–
Gambia	7.5	–
Congo	7.3	12.9
Nigeria	7.0	8.3
Somalia	6.8	–
Comoros	3.0	–

Source: IPU, March 2011.
Note: *Before the independence of South Sudan.

Thus, in terms of effectiveness, the challenge is not whether quotas lead to an increase in the number of women representatives, but the extent to which women representatives can effectively pursue substantive changes that advance gender equality beyond the legislature itself. The evidence indicates that having more women in the legislature contributes to a change in the public attitudes concerning the acceptability of women in politics (Tripp *et al.* 2006: 129). It can also lead to significant progress in policies pertaining to women and gender equality, as has been the case in South Africa and Uganda. However, the extent of women's effectiveness at actually transforming the gendered culture of politics remains the subject of much debate.

Overall the evidence points to women's effectiveness being highly contextual, relating to local and international dynamics that cannot be read from statistical data on numbers alone. Qualitative research points to various aspects of the national political cultures that constrain women's participation. Key among these are the level of democracy, manifest in the rule of law and general respect for human rights that goes disregarded in authoritarian regimes (VonDoepp, this volume). Other aspects of the political culture that limits the extent to which quotas for women can be effective in advancing women's rights includes the persistence of misogyny, male backlash, and the subversion of quota systems by men manipulating individual women to pursue their own agendas.

In sum, while the emphasis on affirmative action and quotas may have generated some change, overall it does little to take the wider social, economic, and cultural conditions of gender inequality into account. Quota systems fall short of advancing the deeper changes that would make equal participation in political arenas possible. Goetz and Hassim (2003) distinguish feminine presence from political effectiveness, calling numerical and substantive representation 'feminine presence' and 'feminist activism', respectively. However, as others have noted, the various efforts to break down the barriers to women's equal political participation 'signal that there is room for women's agency to shape politics, and that formal political rights are an important precondition for advancing equitable social policies' for women (Hassim and Meintjes 2005: 4).

Women's movements and political change

In addition to their rising profile in formal political institutions, women have played key roles opposing corrupt and repressive regimes through civil society engagement in many countries. Public demonstrations, nationwide manifesto processes, and other militant actions have seen women engage with the challenges of political participation in numerous ways. In Kenya, the early 1990s saw women at the forefront of often violent protests in support of imprisoned human rights activists, and more recently, protesting against the 2008 post-electoral violence and its targeting of women. In Sierra Leone, too, women actively advocated for peace during the war years, and openly defied soldiers to demonstrate for a free vote when it was rumoured that the military government might postpone the February 1996 elections. The sub-regional Mano River Women's Peace Network in Guinea, Liberia, and Sierra Leone, was instrumental in the regional peace process, strong women advocates were involved in the Truth and Reconciliation Commission, and women have continued to agitate for greater inclusion of women in democratic governance with a 50:50 campaign supported by various non-governmental networks and organizations.

In Nigeria, though women continue to face challenges in making gains in formal representation, the women's movement mobilized independently across the country during the 1990s. A key achievement of this period was *A Political Agenda for Nigerian Women*, coordinated by Gender and Development Action (GADA) (GADA 1998) working with other women's organizations across the country. The political summits that generated the agenda gave a high profile to women's opposition to military rule, as women called for an end to the violent, corrupt, and monetized political culture that had come to prevail during 30 years of military rule.

In Uganda, the Forum for Women in Democracy (FOWODE) has worked tirelessly to increase and facilitate women's political participation. In 2010 they coordinated the national consultative process that gave rise to the Ugandan Women's Agenda, which reiterates national commitments to gender equality, identifies obstacles hindering women from full and equal participation, and demands a series of measures which would overcome these to facilitate women's political engagement. Ghana has also seen significant independent mobilization of women outside the auspices of the government and ruling party, led by NGOs and networks that advocate for women's rights and strengthened political participation. Led by the ABANTU network, the women's movement organized a highly successful Ghanaian Women's Manifesto that involved nationwide outreach and awareness building in the run up to the 2004 elections (Mama 2005). In Tanzania, women have organized themselves into the Feminist Activist Coalition (FEMACT), a broad coalition dedicated to pursuing women's empowerment and political participation. A Women's Manifesto was ratified by FEMACT members in 2011 and an active '50:50' campaign is ongoing. Women's movements in Ethiopia, South Africa, and Uganda have also produced manifestos that prioritize the increased political participation of women and list measures that would facilitate this in and beyond the formal political sphere.

These examples all illustrate a change that goes beyond numbers. Men's domination of African political arenas is being challenged by women's movements at many levels. At the national level the picture is still very diverse, but women's movements are active in even the most beleaguered and unstable contexts. Women's activism has been most effective at shifting the political terrain when other conditions have also made this possible, as was the case in South Africa during the mid-1990s, but there is also ample evidence that strong women's movements have been key actors in the transitions to peace and democracy.

Conclusion

Africa's feminists have long argued that there can be no democracy without the full and equal participation of women. Left-leaning male political leaders and nationalists have often concurred and made significant gestures toward the inclusion of women in politics at key moments of change. The evidence confirms the value of affirmative action mechanisms to redress numerical inequality as a first step, but highlights the need for other positive interventions that can address long-standing political cultures of exclusion. The African nations with larger numbers of women in office, where gender inequality is still very much in evidence within and beyond the political arenas, demonstrate that even equal numbers are a minimal condition for fuller equality, not an end point. Overall, the continental shift toward democratization has made it more possible to increase women's representation in public office and to make inroads in ensuring that this translates into more effective pursuit of women's interests. The growing strength and capacity of women's movements correlates closely with women's formal political participation. Yet, women continue to face challenges at every stage and must be prepared to pursue a great deal more than mere numbers and legal reforms to bring about the level of gender justice and democratization that African women are now demanding.

Notes

1 These include the work of the IPU and several African networks including Electoral Institute of Southern Africa (EISA) and the Council for the Development of Social Research in Africa (CODESRIA).

2 Examples include *iKnow*, a virtual network linking women across the world to inform, exchange information and experiences, and develop collaborative projects that will advance women in politics. Within the African region, the Violence Against Women in Politics (VAWiP) initiative is part of a larger Africa regional project by UN Women, with aims to set up structures that can respond to the prevalence of electoral violence against women. Independent activism includes the international '50:50' campaign launched in 2000 by a well-established non-governmental organization (NGO), the Women's Environment and Development Organization (WEDO). There are also active 'Get the Balance Right!' campaigns in several African countries (Sierra Leone, Tanzania, South Africa).

Bibliography

Ahikire, J. (2003) 'Gender Equity and Local Democracy in Contemporary Uganda: Addressing the Challenge of Women's Political Effectiveness in Local Government', in A.M. Goetz and S. Hassim (eds) *No Shortcuts to Power: African Women in Politics and Policy Making*, London: Zed Books.

Ajayi, K. (2010) *The Concept of First Lady and Politics in Nigeria*, Dakar: CODESRIA.

Aubrey, L. (2001) 'Gender, Development, and Democratization in Africa', *Journal of Asian and African Studies* 36(1): 87–111.

Basu, A. (ed.) (1995) *The Challenge of Local Feminisms: Women's Movements in Global Perspective*, Boulder, CO: Westview Press.

Bunwaree, S. and Kassenaly, M. (2005) *Political Parties and Democracy in Mauritius*, Johannesburg: Electoral Institute of South Africa.

Creevey, L. (2006) 'Women's Access to Political Power in Senegal', in G. Bauer and H. Britton (eds) *Women in African Parliaments*, Boulder, CO: Lynne Rienner Publishers.

Friedman, M. (1999) 'Effecting Equality: Translating Commitment into Policy and Practice', *Agenda* 15(s1): 2–17.

GADA (Gender and Development Action) (1998) *A Political Agenda for Nigerian Women*, Lagos: Gender and Development Action.

Gaidzanwa, R. (2004) *Gender, Women and Electoral Politics in Zimbabwe*, Johannesburg: Electoral Institute of South Africa.

Geiger, S. (1997) *TANU Women: Gender and Culture in the Making of Tanganyikan Nationalism, 1955–1965*, Oxford: James Currey.

Goetz, A.M. and Hassim, S. (2003) 'Introduction: Women in Power in Uganda and South Africa', in A.M. Goetz and S. Hassim (eds) *No Shortcuts to Power: African Women in Politics and Policy Making*, London: Zed Books.

Gouws, A. (ed.) (2005) *(Un)thinking Citizenship: Feminist Debates in Contemporary South Africa*, Cape Town: University of Cape Town Press.

Hassim, S. and Meintjes, S. (2005) 'Overview Paper', prepared for the 'Expert Group Meeting on Democratic Governance in Africa: Strategies for Greater Participation of Women, Arusha (Tanzania), 6–8 December 2005', New York, NY: United Nations, Office of the Special Adviser on Africa.

IPU (Inter-Parliamentary Union) (2008) *Equality in Politics: A Survey of Women and Men in Parliaments*, Reports and Documents No. 54, Geneva: IPU, www.ipu.org/pdf/publications/equality08-e.pdf (accessed 9 June 2012).

——(2011) 'Women in National Parliaments', Situation as of 31 March 2011, www.ipu.org/wmn-e/arc/world310311.htm (accessed 9 June 2012).

Johnson-Odim, C. and Mba, N. (1997) *For Women and the Nation: Funmilayo Ransom-Kutin*, Chicago, IL: Chicago of University Press.

Lazreg, M. (2009) *Torture and the Twilight of Empire: From Algiers to Baghdad*, Princeton, NJ: Princeton University Press.

Mama, A. (ed.) (2005) 'Women Mobilised', *Feminist Africa* (Special Issue) 4.

Manuh, T. (1991) 'Women and their Organizations during the Convention People's Party Period', in K. Arhin (ed.) *The Life and Work of Kwame Nkrumah*, Accra: Sedcoe Books.

——(1993) 'Women, the State and Society Under the PNDC', in E. Gyimah-Boadi (ed.) *Ghana Under PNDC Rule*, Dakar: CODESRIA.

Matembe, M. (2006) 'Participating in Vain: The Betrayal of Women's Rights in Uganda', paper presented to the Reagan-Fascell Democracy Fellows, 16 May, Washington, DC.

Mba, N.E. (1982) *Nigerian Women Mobilized: Women's Political Activity in Southern Nigeria, 1900–1965*, Berkeley, CA: Institute of International Studies, University of California.

Naples, N. and Desai, A. (2002) *Women's Activism and Globalization: Linking Local Struggles and Transnational Politics*, New York, NY: Routledge.

Parpart, J.L. and Staudt, K.A (1989) *Women and the State in Africa*, Boulder, CO: Lynne Rienner Publishers.

Saul, J.S. (1997) 'Liberal Democracy vs. Popular Democracy in Southern Africa', *Review of African Political Economy* 24(72): 219–36.

Selolwane, O. (2004) 'Profile: The Emang Basadi Women's Association', *Feminist Africa* 3.

Sisulu, E., with Imam, A. and Diouf, M. (1991) 'Report on the Workshop on Gender Analysis and African Social Science, held in Dakar, 16–21 September 1991', *CODESRIA Bulletin* 4: 2–14.

Tripp, A.M. (2000) *Women and Politics in Uganda*, Kampala: Fountain Publishers.

Tripp, A.M., Konaté, D. and Lowe-Morna, C. (2006) 'Sub-Saharan Africa: On the Fast Track to Women's Political Représentation', in D. Dahlerup (ed.) *Women, Quotas and Politics*, London: Routledge.

Tsikata, D., Mensah-Kutin, R. and Harrison, H. (2005) 'The Ghanaian Women's Manifesto Movement. In Conversation', *Feminist Africa* 4: 124–39.

Urdang, S. (1979) *Fighting Two Colonialisms: Women in Guinea-Bissau*, New York, NY: Monthly Review Press.

van Allen, J. (2001) 'Women's Rights Movements as a Measure of African Democracy', *Journal of African and Asian Studies* 36(1): 40–63.

Wilson, A. (1991) *The Challenge Road: Women and the Eritrean Revolution*, Trenton, NJ: Red Sea Press.

PART III

The politics of conflict

13

CIVIL WAR

Philip Roessler

The prevalence and persistence of large-scale conflict has been one of the most significant obstacles to political and economic development in post-colonial Africa. Since 1956, when Sudan became one of the first sub-Saharan African countries to obtain its independence, more than one-third of the world's civil wars have been in Africa, directly affecting one out of every two countries in the region.[1] The average civil war endures for more than eight years, killing thousands,[2] displacing tens of thousands, reducing economic growth, stifling democracy, and spreading conflict into neighbouring countries. Moreover, these conditions often trap countries in a cycle of violence that is difficult to break. Half of the war-affected countries have experienced two or more civil wars.

What explains this deadly phenomenon? Over the last 15 years a robust research programme has emerged to study the onset, duration, and termination of civil war. Global in scope, but with particular relevance to Africa, a first wave of civil war scholarship emphasized the structural determinants of large-scale political violence. A series of studies found that populous, low-income countries, with weak states and rough terrain, and war-affected neighbours are most vulnerable to civil war (Collier and Hoeffler 2004; Fearon and Laitin 2003; Hegre and Sambanis 2006; Salehyan 2007). These conditions, the authors conclude, foment civil war by increasing the 'feasibility' of insurgency (Collier *et al.* 2009) while hamstringing the government's counter-insurgency capabilities (Fearon and Laitin 2003: 75). As war further erodes state capacity and undermines economic development, many of these countries become caught in a 'conflict trap' (Collier 2007).

While this first wave of scholarship has advanced our understanding of global variation in civil war risk (e.g. why Chad is more likely to experience civil war than Qatar), it tells us less about *why* and *how* civil war occurs – that is, the dynamic process by which bargaining over power and wealth ends in large-scale violence. To understand this part of the puzzle we must shift our focus from underlying structural determinants to the *politics of civil war*. Remarkably, in the vast civil war literature, this critical dimension has been understudied. This chapter helps to address this gap in the civil war research programme, while advancing a new analytical perspective on some of Africa's most devastating conflicts.

The chapter makes two broad points. First, it argues that civil war risk in sub-Saharan Africa is mediated by political alliances or networks, especially the institution of ethnic accommodation.[3] While low income and state weakness increase the likelihood of large-scale political violence, these factors are not deterministic. Rulers can still secure social peace by striking bargains with members of other ethnic groups and maintaining ethnically inclusive regimes.[4] This is the predominant strategy that African rulers have followed (Rothchild 1997). According to data from the Ethnic Power Relations dataset,[5] in any given year 55–60 per cent of politically relevant ethnic groups are included in the central government.[6] At the same time, however, this suggests that exclusion along ethnic lines has been a regular feature of politics in many African countries (Lynch, this volume), leaving the central government more vulnerable to societal rebellion.

The second section of the chapter seeks to explain ethnic exclusion. After reviewing more familiar theses about the effects of colonialism and resource scarcity, I suggest an alternative logic that posits that ethnic exclusion is a function of strategic uncertainty – in particular the difficulties of sharing power in the shadow of the coup d'état. Ethnic exclusion reduces this uncertainty but at the cost of increasing the risk of civil war.

Securing social peace in weak states

Over the last decade a consensus has emerged in the civil war literature that the outbreak of large-scale political violence is most likely in poor countries with large populations, incongruent authority structures, and neighbours at war (Hegre *et al.* 2001; Collier and Hoeffler 2004; Salehyan 2007). These factors are posited to increase civil war risk by contributing to 'weak states' that lack the capacity to police and control their peripheries, thus increasing the feasibility of rebellion while undermining the government's counter-insurgency capabilities. The 'weak state' hypothesis has attracted a great deal of interest in the civil war literature as scholars have sought to unpack what some have described as a nebulous analytical framework (Kocher 2010) and better to specify how different dimensions of state capacity affect civil war risk (Hendrix 2010).

Within this growing literature, studies have tended to focus on the importance of formal institutions – such as government bureaucracy and the military – as key pillars of state capacity and therefore civil peace (Fearon and Laitin 2003; Hendrix 2010). Less attention within the civil war research programme, however, has been paid to the informal institutions – namely neopatrimonialism, or clientelism – that rulers in weak states employ to supplant and often subvert an autonomous bureaucracy and military.[7] While these informal institutions are deleterious for state-building and economic development over the long run (Reno 1998; van de Walle 2001), they are the principal mechanisms by which regimes in weak states exert control over society in the short run (Lemarchand 1972; Rothchild and Foley 1988). Unable to rely on their bureaucracies, the ruling elite leans on its brokerage networks to help extract taxes, distribute state resources, address local grievances and demands, and manage dissent. Accordingly, in weak states we would expect state control and civil war to be mediated by the institutions of elite accommodation and ethnic brokerage (Snyder 1998). As Englebert and Ron (2004: 76–77) conclude in a case study of Congo-Brazzaville, 'Neopatrimonialism can promote either political stability or violent conflict, depending on its level of inclusiveness'.

One empirical regularity consistent with this idea is that African rulers almost never face civil wars from their co-ethnics (see Roessler 2011). This correlation could be a function of sub-national variation in state capacity, particularly if the ruler's ethnic group 'inherited' the state at independence (and benefited from skewed state development during the colonial period). However, what is striking is that it holds even for rulers and groups who historically were marginalized and come from the poorest and weakest states, wherein we would expect the central government's bureaucratic quality and military capacity to be extremely low.

I posit that the institutions of elite accommodation and ethnic brokerage account for the absence of intra-ethnic rebellions. Substantial qualitative and quantitative evidence suggests that rulers tend to have stronger political ties and networks with their co-ethnics, especially from their home area, than with members of other ethnic groups. Three prominent examples are the regimes of Juvenal Habyarimana of Rwanda (Prunier 1995), Samuel Doe in Liberia (Berkeley 2001), and Mwai Kibaki in Kenya (Wrong 2010). These ties are not limited to elite circles; there is evidence that they also extend to the local level. Kasara (2007) finds that African rulers tend to impose higher taxes on agricultural crops grown in their home areas than those located in other parts of the country. She attributes this to the information advantages that rulers derive from having strong brokerage networks in their homelands. Franck and Rainer (2012) note the reciprocal nature of these exchanges. While co-ethnics may endure higher taxes, they also benefit from better health and education services. Overall, then, networks of exchange between rulers and their co-ethnics facilitate the more efficient extraction and allocation of resources, which should reduce the underlying grievances that fuel rebellion while equipping the government with the tools necessary to prevent or contain it effectively.

Additional evidence suggests that the pacifying effects of elite accommodation and brokerage networks are not limited to within the ruler's ethnic group but can extend across society. Englebert and Ron (2004) attribute the end of the 1997 civil war in Congo-Brazzaville to the 'patrimonial peace' Denis Sassou-Nguesso secured by co-opting elites from various ethno-regional militias into the government and public sector. Across sub-Saharan Africa, a systematic relationship between ethnic inclusion and stability appears to exist. Controlling for a country's income level and population size, groups included in the central government at the junior partner level or above are significantly less likely to start a civil war than excluded groups (see Roessler 2011). This suggests that even in the face of unfavourable structural conditions, rulers are able to avoid large-scale political violence through the institution of ethnic accommodation, or political alliances with members of other ethnic groups.

The economic logic of ethnic exclusion

Consistent with earlier waves of scholarship on neopatrimonialism, especially that of Donald Rothchild (see Rothchild 1997; Rothchild and Foley 1988; Lemarchand 1972), systematic evidence from across the region suggests that African rulers have employed ethnic accommodation to help resolve the 'strong societies, weak states' problem (Migdal 1988) that they faced in the post-independence period. Such 'ethnic federations' (Azam 2001) have served as the modal regime type. Nonetheless, exclusion along ethnic lines has remained a regular feature of African politics. In fact, in any given year between 1966 and 2005, 40–45 per cent of politically relevant ethnic groups have been excluded from the central government. Given the associated costs with ethnic exclusion, such as weaker political control and increased risk of group rebellion, this section seeks to account for the phenomenon of ethnic exclusion and outlines a set of possible factors that increase the likelihood of exclusion along ethnic lines.

Colonial legacies

Of the 128 ethno-regional groups to experience some exclusion from the central government between 1955 and 2005, 47 of these groups (36 per cent) were excluded at the time of independence. For most of these groups, we can trace political marginalization to colonial government policies, in particular the uneven recruitment patterns used to fill positions in colonial institutions, including schools, bureaucracy, and the military. Though European administrators favoured the use of indirect rule and local intermediaries to control the indigenous majority and undermine nationalist sentiments, as the colony grew they lacked the foreign capacity to administer key institutions and had to rely more heavily on locals. Given the locus of colonial activity in the capital and the geographic concentration of ethnicity, however, not all groups benefitted equally from educational, employment, and business opportunities provided by the colonial government (Horowitz 1985). Consequently, those ethnic groups with homelands in close proximity to the capital were more likely to emerge from colonialism better educated, wealthier, and more active in nationalist movements, and thus better positioned to inherit the state at independence. On the other hand, many from the hinterland, such as the Somalis in Kenya, Highlanders in Madagascar, Southerners and Darfurians in Sudan, Northerners in Chad, Kabre in Togo, and Tuaregs in Niger and Mali, found themselves on the outside looking in at the inaugural governments.

The regional inequalities produced by colonialism have had lasting effects on ethnic political configurations. For example, the ethno-regional groups that were excluded from the central government at independence remained excluded for the next 30 years, on average. Some 45 per cent of these groups became involved in a large-scale rebellion during the post-colonial period. Prominent examples include Southerners in Sudan, Arabs and Muslim Sahel Groups in Chad, Zulu and Xhosa in South Africa, and Africans in Zimbabwe.[8]

While colonialism has had a decisive effect on post-colonial ethnic accommodation and civil war, there are clear limitations of its explanatory power. First, while colonial policies disproportionately benefited some groups, there was nothing deterministic about the power imbalances to emerge from colonialism. Whether these were remedied or not rested in the hands of post-colonial governments. Second, almost two-thirds of the incidents of ethnic exclusion began after independence, and are thus cases in which groups are represented in the central government in one year but then are purged or barred in the next. To account for both the prevalence and onset of ethnic exclusion, we need a more dynamic theory that specifies the incentives and constraints rulers face as they bargain with their co-ethnics, other power holders, and members of excluded groups. We now turn to the ways in which economic and strategic factors may structure ethnic bargaining and political configurations.

Wealth accumulation

One of the defining features of Africa's political economy is that the state often has been the primary means of accumulating wealth (Joseph 1987). Inheriting statist economies developed under colonialism, African rulers leveraged them as a means to build and maintain power. Rulers manipulated their economies in order to generate economic rents that they then disbursed for political purposes (Boone 1992). This system of political rule, which scholars refer to as neopatrimonialism (Erdmann, this volume), helped rulers of weak states to consolidate their personal power but at the cost of retarding long-run economic production and development (van de Walle 2001) and undermining inclusive, stable states. To maximize their economic rents, ruling elites have an incentive to limit the number of groups and powerbrokers with access to the central government.

Why, though, do ruling coalitions form along ethnic lines rather than based on ideology or party affiliation? Fearon (1999) suggests that ethnicity's ascriptive quality, in which it cannot be easily chosen or changed by individuals, makes it a superior cleavage because it makes it more difficult for those outside the winning coalition to 'switch' their identity to gain access to state spoils. In other words, as Caselli and Coleman write, 'Ethnicity provides a technology for group membership and exclusion which is used to avoid indiscriminate access to the spoils of conflict. Without such a technology groups become porous and the spoils of conflict are dissipated' (Caselli and Coleman 2006: 30). According to this view, then, ethnic exclusion is driven by economic considerations as the ruling coalition seeks to maximize its wealth and retain a monopoly on economic rents. Broadly, this hypothesis resonates with the history of African states from South Africa to Sudan, wherein small groups of ruling elites have reaped tremendous economic advantages from their ethnocratic rule.

Resource constraints

Following from the above, we would expect that rulers face constant pressure from those inside the regime to narrow the size of the ruling coalition to maximize their spoils. Moreover, we would anticipate that the size of the ruling coalition and the number of groups with access to the central government are contingent on the size of the economy. Put simply, larger economies should provide rulers with the ability to build larger political coalitions. Consistent with this point, Arriola (2009) finds that cabinet sizes in Africa – one observable measure of the ruling political coalition – are strongly correlated to gross domestic product (GDP) per capita. All else equal, he estimates that a US$100 increase in per capita income is associated, on average, with an additional cabinet appointment.

Similarly, economic contraction or expansion would be expected to affect political coalitions. One prominent example often cited is the case of Côte d'Ivoire.[9] The country's first president, Félix Houphouët-Boigny, built a multi-ethnic political coalition to stave off potential opposition and strengthen his hold on power. One region that he reached out to was the north, through political appointments and investment of state resources in development projects in the northern region. However, in the 1980s, in the face of declining revenues after a prolonged economic crisis, the government found it difficult to continue to commit to this redistribution strategy and, after the death of Houphouët-Boigny in 1993, the coalition was more or less abandoned, opening the door for political conflict.

Information problems and the logic of ethnic exclusion

Economic factors are posited to be key pressures that push rulers to exclude along ethnic lines, but, of course, ethnic exclusion is a costly policy – it reduces societal control, undermines extractive capacity, and in some cases increases the risk of civil war. Thus rulers have to be strategic in their use of ethnic exclusion. While they prefer to maximize spoils, they prefer to do so 'without precipitating a reaction (such as violent protest or rebellion) from the ethnic group that would be even more costly to suppress' (Cetinyan 2002: 649). Thus, the ruler's optimal strategy would be one in which he makes the minimal concessions (e.g. resource transfers and political appointments) necessary to co-opt key members of a rival group and prevent the outbreak of armed rebellion. However, in line with an extensive bargaining literature, these types of transactions are often undermined by information and commitment problems, leading to suboptimal outcomes (Fearon 1995).

As rulers bargain with members of other ethno-regional groups over patronage and political appointments, they are reluctant to offer more than the minimal concessions necessary to win the group's support and secure social peace. Overpaying eats into the spoils available to the ruling coalition and wastes resources that could be used to buy off other groups. The problem for the ruler is that it is difficult to gauge a group's mobilizational capabilities.

Rulers face several constraints in this regard. One is that information asymmetries create incentives for parties to misrepresent their true capabilities to win greater concessions (Fearon 1995). Consequently, regimes tend to dismiss a group's demands and threats at face value and discount the patronage and political appointments it offers. A second constraint is the organizational challenge of collecting and processing information. While all governments and large organizations face this problem, it is especially difficult for weak states that depend on informal political networks to monitor society. Weak states face coverage problems: those areas where the regime is most in need of information, such as ethnic enclaves excluded from the central government, is where the regime has the least penetration and fewest brokers. To compensate, the ruler may rely on nearby regional contacts or co-ethnics and other 'foreign' agents deployed to monitor the excluded group. However, these outside brokers often are not enmeshed in the ethnic networks of the excluded group and possess little genuine information about the group's capabilities and demands. Moreover, as these agents tend to come from rival groups, it is not always in their interest to accurately convey information to the central government, particularly if it means it will lead the central government to adopt new policy concessions that could cut into their own share of spoils.

We would expect these types of information problems to undermine ethnic bargaining and contribute to more exclusive regimes, but over time, as new information is generated – often due to violent mobilization by the marginalized group – we would expect the central government to adjust the minimal concessions it offers in an effort to prevent the conflict from becoming a full-scale civil war. Accordingly, information problems alone cannot account for sustained ethnic exclusion. Commitment problems on the other hand are less forgiving. Even as the costs of exclusion are revealed and conflict escalates, rulers cannot change course and adopt a more accommodative policy if the underlying constraints contributing to ethnic exclusion remain in place.

Political bargaining in an environment of uncertainty

In economic-based models of ethnic bargaining the ruling coalition faces a trade-off between maximizing spoils and social peace. Expanding the coalition to include all politically relevant groups reduces the risk of rebellion but at the cost of diluting the ruling coalition's share of spoils. The essence of politics is then the bargaining that takes place between the ruling group and other groups over patronage and political appointments. In deciding how to allocate resources, the ruler weighs the costs of accommodation versus the costs of repression.

An important dimension is missing, however, from these economic models: the ruler's hold on power is not fixed or guaranteed. In fact, this is one of the defining characteristics of post-colonial politics in Africa – the prevalence of irregular transfers of power (Goldsmith 2001). Between 1956 and 2001, coups d'état represented the primary source of regime instability in Africa, accounting for more than 40 per cent of all leadership changes.[10] In addition to 80 successful coups, there were 108 failed coups during this period (McGowan 2003). According to the Archigos dataset, since 1960 no region has experienced a higher percentage of irregular transitions of power than sub-Saharan Africa.[11]

The threat of an irregular transfer of power changes the nature and stakes of the political game. Politics is not merely about relative shares of spoils but absolute control – to lose power is to lose everything. Such strategic concerns are as powerful a motivating force as economic rents and can severely constrain rulers in their bargaining with elites inside and outside their ruling coalition. Rulers cannot commit to accommodative policies that will increase their vulnerability to being ousted from power. This section theorizes how the strategic environment has structured ethnic bargaining and contributed to more exclusive configurations.

Ethnic bargaining as a two-level game

Ethnic bargaining in Africa can be seen as a two-level game (Putnam 1988). On one dimension rulers are bargaining with members of other societal groups – 'rivals' – who seek their fair share of access to state resources and representation in the government. On another dimension they are bargaining with those inside the ruling coalition – 'allies' – who want to preserve their privileged position and share of spoils. As discussed above, with complete information we would expect rulers to make the minimal concessions necessary to rivals to stave off rebellion and to avoid the costs of civil war. However, without buy-in from their allies, who would bear the costs of such a policy, we would expect the promises of accommodation not to be credible.

Burundi and Rwanda in the early 1990s illustrate this dynamic. In Burundi, after decades of exclusive Tutsi rule and episodic outbreaks of mass violence against Hutus – including massacres in 1988 that killed an estimated 20,000 people – in the late 1980s Burundi's President Pierre Buyoya started to change course.[12] In the face of acute international pressure following the 1988 massacres, and as it became increasingly clear 'that a strategy of rule based solely on oppression could not continue indefinitely' (Uvin 1999: 266), Buyoya built a more ethnically balanced cabinet and promised a series of political reforms. Despite facing pressure from within the military, including several abortive coups, Buyoya pushed forward and multi-party presidential and parliamentary elections were held in 1993.

In the landmark elections, Buyoya and his National Unity and Progress (UPRONA) party were thoroughly defeated by Melchior Ndadaye and the Front for Democracy in Burundi (FRODEBU). Buyoya accepted the results, making way for the first Hutu-led government since the country's independence. In the months after the election, however, the Tutsi-dominated military, apprehensive about the transition, struck twice, first in July and then again in October. Though both attempts technically failed, in the second coup the mutinous soldiers assassinated Ndadaye and effectively derailed the political transition. The putsch preserved the military's political dominance and quashed the new ethnic equilibrium that the elections brought, but at the cost of precipitating a new round of bloodletting and a civil war that would not end until 2006.

While Tutsi military elites sabotaged ethnic accommodation in Burundi in 1993, in Rwanda it was a powerful group of Hutu political extremists, known as the Akazu, who served as the key spoilers. This group, who had strong ties to Rwanda's President Juvenal Habyarimana and his wife, was motivated by an ideology of Hutu Power that viewed Tutsi as a '*race* alien to Rwanda, and not an indigenous *ethnic group*' (Mamdani 2001: 190, emphasis in original). Its members vehemently opposed the August 1993 power-sharing accords in Arusha that Habyarimana signed with the Rwandan Patriotic Front (RPF), a predominantly Tutsi rebel movement that invaded Rwanda from Uganda in October 1990. To pre-empt the implementation of the Arusha Accords, and 'preserve the gains' made since the 1959 revolution when power was taken from the Tutsi, the Akazu, led by Colonel Théoneste Bagosora, seized *de facto* control of the government after the death of Habyarimana in a plane crash on 6 April 1994. The Hutu extremists immediately murdered the prime minister, who should have taken over the reins of the government. As Mamdani notes, 'the death of the president and the killing of the prime minister removed precisely those leaders who had publicly championed an agenda for "ethnic reconciliation" between Hutu and Tutsi' (Mamdani 2001: 215).

Ethnic bargaining and the commitment problem

The Burundi and Rwanda cases illustrate how insiders' veto power can undermine accommodative policies pursued by their leaders, but they also illuminate how the strategic environment in Africa's weak states structures ethnic bargaining. The biggest fear hardliners in Burundi and Rwanda had was that their rivals would convert political concessions into absolute power. In Burundi, the Tutsi-dominated military feared Ndadaye would harness the executive authority he gained through democratic elections to entrench Hutu control and disband the army, leaving Tutsi powerless and defenceless. In Rwanda, members of the Akazu feared that the Arusha Accords – which granted the RPF control of 50 per cent of the officer corps, the ministry of interior, and the right of return of refugees who fled after the 1959 revolution – would open the door for the rebels to seize power and reinstitute Tutsi hegemony (Mamdani 2001).

In theoretical terms, the strategic environment that prevailed in Burundi and Rwanda in the early 1990s aroused fears that adoption of accommodative policies would set in motion a large, rapid, and irreversible shift in the distribution of power.[13] With no guarantees that their rivals will not exploit ethnic accommodation to seize absolute power and persecute, or even worse, annihilate, the previous ruling group, incumbents cannot credibly commit to an inclusive policy and instead pursue ethnic exclusion as an inefficient way to protect one's hold on power. The following two sections explore the conditions in which we would expect the commitment problem to arise and whether it produces ethnic exclusion as predicted.

Regime change and the commitment problem

In Burundi and Rwanda history casts a dark shadow over political bargaining, as events in the past colour how parties read their rivals' motivations and intentions in the present. In Rwanda, members of the Akazu emphasized that they had to 'preserve the gains' made since the 1959 'social revolution' or else the RPF would 'restore the dictatorship of the extremists of the Tutsi minority', as one pamphlet published in 1991 described it (Des Forges 1999: 64). Thus, the history of the Tutsi monarchy and fears that Tutsi politicians would try to restore it contributed to the commitment problem the ruling Hutu elite believed they faced in their strategic interactions with the RPF.

The implication of this is that the commitment problem contributes to the reproduction of exclusive regimes – the overthrow of one ethnically dominant cabal merely leads a new one to take its place. While a new ruler recognizes that cutting a deal with his 'enemies' and allowing them to retain a share of power in exchange for their political support would help to legitimize his ascension to power and promise to put an end to the cycles of ethnic hatred and conflict, he cannot credibly commit to this because of fears that the old ruling group is intent on reclaiming its political supremacy and will exploit any concessions they receive to achieve this end.

One could argue that this is the predicament in which the RPF found itself after stopping the genocide and seizing Kigali on 4 July 1994. It sought to build a broad-based, post-ethnic state, but it calculated the security situation remained too critical to allow potentially disloyal agents to control the key levers of power and finance. Thus, though the national cabinet included a diversity of figures, real power was concentrated in the hands of a small coterie of RPF elites whose bonds of trust were cemented over time spent together in refugee camps in Uganda, attending the same schools, and in combat, first as part of Yoweri Museveni's National Resistance Army and then in the RPF. Over time this led to an attrition of opposition figures, who felt their appointments were merely cosmetic, and contributed to the RPF's monopolization of power and the reproduction of a politically exclusive regime (Reyntjens 2004).

The political strategy that the RPF pursued is not uncommon in post-colonial Africa. Regimes that capture the state by force frequently exclude the ruling group they oust from power (see Roessler 2011). Other prominent cases include Nigeria in 1966 and Uganda in 1971. In Nigeria, the July 1966 counter-coup led by northern officers 'permanently reversed the ethnic composition of the army. Virtually all of the Igbo soldiers were killed, permanently incapacitated or forced out of their positions. After eliminating Igbos from the army, Northern soldiers consolidated their supremacy at all levels' (Siollun 2009: 147–48). Similarly in Uganda, after Idi Amin's rise to power in 1971, co-ethnics of former president Milton Obote in the military were violently purged (Omara-Otunnu 1987).

Co-conspirators and the commitment problem

That irregular transfers of power produce ethnically exclusive regimes is not surprising. After all, by the time of the transfer of power mistrust is already extremely high because of the violent interactions leading up to the regime change, as the cases of Rwanda, Nigeria, and Uganda exemplify. What is more surprising, and what better demonstrates the destabilizing power of the commitment problem in an uncertain strategic environment, is that it not only divides enemies, but also allies, especially *co-conspirators* – those violent specialists who worked together to forcibly seize power and who assume the most critical and sensitive positions in the new regime.

After seizing power, co-conspirators have much to gain from working together to preserve their control of the state and prevent members of the *ancien régime* from reclaiming power. However, they also have a lot to lose if any faction among them defects from this bargain and exploits their privileged position to unilaterally usurp power at the expense of others within the regime. Trust built up during their struggle for power often helps to reduce fears of betrayal, but tends to be eroded over time as comrades-in-arms compete for power and economic rents in the new regime. Co-conspirators, who formerly placed their very survival in each other's hands, can no longer take it for granted that their allies will reciprocate cooperation.

As mistrust deepens, the commitment problem dominates strategic interactions. Fearful of being permanently displaced from the regime or, even worse, killed, the opposing sides man-oeuvre to neutralize others' first-strike capabilities by grabbing hold of strategic ministries, stacking the military and security organs with co-ethnics, and strengthening alliances within the regime. Such manoeuvring, however, tends to increase uncertainty, elevating fears that one's allies-turned-rivals are preparing to make a bid for power. As the conflict spirals, the rivals calculate that the only way to preserve their political survival is by eliminating the other side, and violent rupture becomes inevitable. When ethnicity structures such elite conflicts, the regime often breaks down along ethnic lines.

Classic examples of this dynamic include the collapse of the Alliance of the Democratic Forces for the Liberation of Zaire (AFDL) a mere 15 months after disposing of Mobutu Sese Seko; the violent falling out in the early 1980s between the group of non-commissioned officers in Liberia who had brought an end to the 133-year rule of the Americo-Liberians; and the breakdown of the political alliance between Hissene Habre and his Zaghawa backers, including Hassan Djamous and Idriss Deby, who conspired to take power from Goukoni Oueddei in 1982 and to subsequently wrest northern Chad from Libyan control in 1986 and 1987. In each of these cases the falling out ended with the ruler resorting to ethnic exclusion – Kabila targeting Tutsi, Doe the Gio and Mano, and Habre the Zaghawa – as a means to insulate his hold on power and neutralize his co-conspirators' coup-making capabilities.

Substituting civil war risk for coup risk

Overall, ethnic exclusion is conceived as an inefficient strategy that rulers choose to manage the commitment problem they face when sharing power in an uncertain strategic environment. It is designed to deny ethnic rivals' proximity to and partial control of the key levers of the state in order to prevent them from effecting a sudden and decisive shift in the balance of power. While such a strategy mitigates the risk of a coup d'état from the targeted group, though, the cost is that it destroys the institutional basis of social peace in Africa – ethnic accommodation – and increases the risk of a societal-based rebellion.

In other words, ethnic exclusion serves as a *threat substitution strategy* – it forces rivals to shift their technology of resistance from the coup to the insurgency. In contrast to coups, in which dissidents use the state apparatus itself to usurp power (Luttwak 1968), insurgencies require a significant mobilization of resources to mount a credible challenge to the central government (Collier *et al.* 2009). Rather than using extant state institutions, the dissidents have to build and finance their own rebel army, and then cover large swaths of territory to reach the capital and forcibly capture the state. This provides the ruling regime with the time and opportunity to contain the threat from society. In line with this expectation, major insurgencies have proven to be more difficult to organize and much less effective as a technology of capturing power than coups d'état in post-colonial Africa.

Conclusion

This chapter challenges the conventional wisdom on civil war in Africa. It shifts the focus from the material and institutional capacity of the state, to the inter-ethnic bargains that are critical to social peace. Understanding the breakdown of ethnic bargaining is fundamental to understanding civil war in Africa. This chapter has reviewed familiar theses about colonial legacies of societal inequality and the pathologies of neopatrimonialism to argue that the strategic environment in which ethnic bargaining plays out – in particular the low barriers to using force as a means to permanently shift the balance of power in one's favour – also significantly shapes ethnic political configurations. Ethnic exclusion is theorized to be a function of the commitment problem that rulers face as they share power in the shadow of the coup d'état. Ethnic exclusion insulates the ruling group's hold on power, though at the cost of forfeiting its societal control and leaving it vulnerable to civil war. This model speaks to the resurgence of devastating violence in Burundi and Rwanda in the early 1990s, but also informs a number of other important cases, including Africa's Great War, which broke out in the Democratic Republic of Congo in August 1998, the Darfur civil war, and the civil war in Chad in the late 1980s.

Overall this strategic theory of civil war makes two important contributions to the study of armed conflict in Africa. First, it brings the study of politics back in. In contrast to prevailing structuralist accounts that tend to see civil war as a predominantly rural or peripheral phenomenon that hinges on state reach and local dynamics (Kalyvas 2008), the model views civil war as rooted in conflict over the distribution of power and wealth at the centre which then becomes strategically displaced to the periphery.

A second important implication is that if the strategic environment in Africa changes, we would expect the phenomena of ethnic exclusion and civil war to decline. Since the end of the Cold War there has been a dramatic transformation in the nature of political change across sub-Saharan Africa, in which elections have surpassed coups and rebellions as the dominant mode of transfer of power. Coupled with this, the African Union (AU) since 1997 has started to take seriously the threat that unconstitutional changes of government pose to political stability. Article 30 of the constitution of the AU, which superseded the Organization of African Unity (OAU) in 2002, states, 'Governments which shall come to power through unconstitutional means shall not be allowed to participate in the activities of the Union'.

The shifting strategic environment should facilitate political bargaining, as it helps to mitigate the commitment problem and reduce the risk of ethnic accommodation. However, while coups have declined since the OAU and AU adopted anti-coup measures, it is not clear to what degree this is a consequence of higher costs to seizing power in a coup or unparalleled economic growth during the same period allowing African rulers to consolidate their hold on power. Political strategies by African rulers suggest that they are not taking it for granted that their rivals and enemies have internalized anti-coup norms. As long as rulers fear the shadow of the coup d'état and other sudden challenges to their hold on power, they will continue to fall back on exclusionary political strategies.

Notes

1 The civil war data are from Fearon and Laitin's (2003) updated civil war dataset.
2 According to the Battle Deaths Dataset from the International Peace Research Institute in Oslo, there were about 1,750,000 battlefield deaths due to civil wars in Africa between 1956 and 2005 (Lacina and Gleditsch 2005). This does not include war-related deaths due to disease, malnutrition, etc., which would increase the figure into the tens of millions.
3 This chapter focuses on ethnic cleavages – that is, when individuals with shared ancestry and culture (e.g. language, customs, religion, and sense of homeland) collectively organize and coordinate their behaviour – as opposed to other potential divisions (such as religion, ideology, or region), because of its political salience in many African countries. Ethnicity matters because it is seen to structure more than motivate political action (Hale 2008). In-group norms of reciprocity among co-ethnics facilitate cooperation (Habyarimana *et al.* 2009), which is critical in the high-stakes game of African politics. This is not to suggest that ethnicity is fixed or represents the only coordination mechanism, but it does assume that it represents one of the principal mechanisms in most countries in the first five decades of independence.
4 Wimmer *et al.* (2009) and Cederman *et al.* (2010) demonstrate that ethnic inclusion significantly decreases the risk of civil war at both group and state level.
5 The Ethnic Power Relations (EPR) dataset was constructed by Wimmer *et al.* (2009). It provides information on ethnic political configurations in all countries in which ethnicity is deemed politically salient between 1946 and 2005. Derived from a survey of 100 scholars of ethnic politics, the EPR codes each politically relevant ethnic category 'according to the degree of access to central state power by those who claimed to represent them' for a given year (Wimmer *et al.* 2009: 326). Access to power is coded as a seven-point categorical variable: *monopoly, dominant, senior partner, junior partner, regional autonomy, powerless,* or *discriminated.* Throughout the chapter, I consider groups coded as junior partner to monopoly in a given year as 'included' in the central government, and groups coded as regional autonomy to discriminated as 'excluded'.
6 The figure of 55–60 per cent represents the average across all sub-Saharan African countries between independence (or 1955) and 2005. Of course important variation exists across countries. Some countries such as Malawi and Zambia have always had 100 per cent of politically relevant ethnic groups included in the central government, whereas in Sudan only one group, riverine Arabs, has dominated the central government, representing less than 8 per cent of all politically relevant ethnic groups.
7 Much has been written about neopatrimonialism in the African politics literature, including an important body of work that has linked the system of rule to violent conflict (e.g. Reno 1998, 2000; Chabal and Daloz 1999; see also Erdmann, this volume). However, these theories have not been systematically incorporated into the civil war literature, despite the prevalence of civil war and neopatrimonial rule in low-income countries.
8 Names correspond to ethnic categories as defined by EPR.
9 See Bates (2008), who summarizes the work of Boone (2003) and Azam (2001).
10 This figure is calculated using data from Goldsmith (2001) and McGowan (2003).
11 Calculated by the author; for the Archigos dataset, see Goemans *et al.* (2009).
12 For a political history of this critical period in which the Hutu-Tutsi, intra-Tutsi, and intra-Hutu dynamics are all explored up through the 1993 elections, see Lemarchand (1994).
13 Powell (2006) proffers that this mechanism is at the root of all commitment problems.

Bibliography

Arriola, L.R. (2009) 'Patronage and Political Stability in Africa', *Comparative Political Studies* 42(10): 1339–62.
Azam, J.-P. (2001) 'The Redistributive State and Conflicts in Africa', *Journal of Peace Research* 38(4): 429–44.
Bates, R.H. (2008) *When Things Fell Apart: State Failure in Late-Century Africa*, New York, NY: Cambridge University Press.
Berkeley, B. (2001) *The Graves Are Not Yet Full: Race, Tribe, and Power in the Heart of Africa*, New York, NY: Basic Books.
Boone, C. (1992) *Merchant Capital and the Roots of State Power in Senegal, 1930–1985*, New York, NY: Cambridge University Press.
——(2003) *Political Topographies of the African State*, Cambridge: Cambridge University Press.
Caselli, F. and Coleman, W.J. (2006) 'On the Theory of Ethnic Conflict', National Bureau of Economic Research Working Paper No. 12125.

Cederman, L.-E., Wimmer, A. and Min, B. (2010) 'What Makes Ethnic Groups Rebel? New Data and New Analysis', *World Politics* 62(1): 87–119.

Cetinyan, R. (2002) 'Ethnic Bargaining in the Shadow of Third-Party Intervention', *International Organization* 56(3): 645–77.

Chabal, P. and Daloz, J.-P. (1999) *Africa Works: Disorder as Political Instrument*, Oxford: James Currey.

Collier, P. (2007) *The Bottom Billion: Why the Poorest Countries Are Failing and What Can Be Done About It*, New York, NY: Oxford University Press.

Collier, P. and Hoeffler, A. (2004) 'Greed and Grievance in Civil War', *Oxford Economic Papers* 56(4): 563–95.

Collier, P., Hoeffler, A. and Rohner, D. (2009) 'Beyond Greed and Grievance: Feasibility and Civil War', *Oxford Economic Papers* 61(1): 1–27.

Des Forges, A. (1999) *'Leave None to Tell the Story': Genocide in Rwanda*, New York, NY: Human Rights Watch.

Englebert, P. and Ron, J. (2004) 'Primary Commodities and War: Congo-Brazzaville's Ambivalent Resource Curse', *Comparative Politics* 37(1): 61–81.

Fearon, J.D. (1995) 'Rationalist Explanations for War', *International Organization* 49(3): 379–414.

——(1999) 'Why Ethnic Politics and "Pork" Tend to Go Together', paper presented as part of conference on 'Ethnic Politics and Democratic Stability', University of Chicago, 21–23 May 1999.

Fearon, J.D. and Laitin, D.D. (2003) 'Ethnicity, Insurgency, and Civil War', *American Political Science Review* 97(1): 75–90.

Franck, R. and Rainer, I. (2012) 'Does the Leader's Ethnicity Matter? Ethnic Favoritism, Education and Health in Sub-Saharan Africa', *American Political Science Review* 106(2): 294–325.

Goemans, H.E., Gleditsch, K.S. and Chiozza, G. (2009) 'Introducing Archigos: A Dataset of Political Leaders', *Journal of Peace Research* 46(2): 269–83.

Goldsmith, A. (2001) 'Risk, Rule and Reason: Leadership in Africa', *Public Administration and Development* 21(2): 77–87.

Habyarimana, J., Humphreys, M., Posner, D.N. and Weinstein, J.M. (2009) *Coethnicity: Diversity and the Dilemmas of Collective Action*, New York, NY: Russell Sage Foundation.

Hale, H. (2008) *The Foundations of Ethnic Politics: Separatism of States and Nations in Eurasia and the World*, New York, NY: Cambridge University Press.

Hegre, H., Ellingsen, T., Gates, S. and Gleditsch, N.P. (2001) 'Toward a Democratic Civil Peace? Democracy, Political Change, and Civil War, 1816–1992', *American Political Science Review* 95(1): 33–48.

Hegre, H. and Sambanis, N. (2006) 'Sensitivity Analysis of Empirical Results on Civil War Onset', *Journal of Conflict Resolution* 50(4): 508–35.

Hendrix, C.S. (2010) 'Measuring State Capacity: Theoretical and Empirical Implications for the Study of Civil Conflict', *Journal of Peace Research* 47(3): 273–85.

Horowitz, D.L. (1985) *Ethnic Groups in Conflict*, Berkeley, CA: University of California Press.

Joseph, R. (1987) *Democracy and Prebendal Politics in Nigeria: The Rise and Fall of the Second Republic*, New York, NY: Cambridge University Press.

Kalyvas, S.N. (2008) 'Civil Wars', in C. Boix and S.C. Stokes (eds) *The Oxford Handbook of Comparative Politics*, New York, NY: Oxford University Press.

Kasara, K. (2007) 'Tax Me If You Can: Ethnic Geography, Democracy, and the Taxation of Agriculture in Africa', *American Political Science Review* 101(1): 159–72.

Kocher, M.A. (2010) 'State Capacity as a Conceptual Variable', *Yale Journal of International Affairs* 5(2): 137–45.

Lacina, B. and Gleditsch, N.P. (2005) 'Monitoring Trends in Global Combat: A New Dataset of Battle Deaths', *European Journal of Population* 21(2–3): 145–66.

Lemarchand, R. (1972) 'Political Clientelism and Ethnicity in Tropical Africa: Competing Solidarities in Nation-Building', *American Political Science Review* 66(1): 68–90.

——(1994) *Burundi: Ethnocide as Discourse and Practice*, Washington, DC: Woodrow Wilson Center Press.

Luttwak, R. (1968) *Coup d'Etat: A Practical Handbook*, London: Penguin Press.

McGowan, P.J. (2003) 'African Military Coups D'état, 1956–2001: Frequency, Trends and Distribution', *Journal of Modern African Studies* 41(3): 339–70.

Mamdani, M. (2001) *When Victims Become Killers: Colonialism, Nativism, and the Genocide in Rwanda*, Princeton, NJ: Princeton University Press.

Migdal, J. (1988) *Strong Societies and Weak States: State-Society Relations and State Capabilities in the Third World*, Princeton, NJ: Princeton University Press.

Omara-Otunnu, A. (1987) *Politics and the Military in Uganda, 1890–1985*, New York, NY: St. Martin.

Powell, R. (2006) 'War as a Commitment Problem', *International Organization* 60: 169–203.

Prunier, G. (1995) *The Rwanda Crisis: History of a Genocide*, New York, NY: Columbia University Press.

Putnam, R.D. (1988) 'Diplomacy and Domestic Politics: The Logic of Two-Level Games', *International Organization* 42: 427–60.

Reno, W. (1998) *Warlord Politics and African States*, Boulder, CO: Lynne Rienner Publishers.

——(2000) 'Internal Wars, Private Enterprise, and the Shift in Strong State-Weak State Relations', *International Politics* 37(1): 57–74.

Reyntjens, F. (2004) 'Rwanda, Ten Years On: From Genocide to Dictatorship', *African Affairs* 103(411): 177–210.

Roessler, P. (2011) 'The Enemy Within: Personal Rule, Coups, and Civil War in Africa', *World Politics* 63 (2): 300–46.

Rothchild, D. (1997) *Managing Ethnic Conflict in Africa: Pressures and Incentives for Cooperation*, Washington, DC: Brookings Institution Press.

Rothchild, D. and Foley, M.W. (1988) 'African States and the Politics of Inclusive Coalitions', in D. Rothchild and N. Chazan (eds) *The Precarious Balance: State and Society in Africa*, Boulder, CO: Westview Press.

Salehyan, I. (2007) 'Transnational Rebels: Neighboring States as Sanctuary for Rebel Groups', *World Politics* 59(2): 217–42.

Siollun, M. (2009) *Oil, Politics and Violence: Nigeria's Military Coup Culture (1966–1976)*, New York, NY: Algora Publishers.

Snyder, R. (1998) 'Paths out of Sultanistic Regimes: Combining Structural and Voluntarist Perspectives', in H.E. Chehabi and J.J. Linz (eds) *Sultanistic Regimes*, Baltimore, MD: Johns Hopkins University Press.

Uvin, P. (1999) 'Ethnicity and Power in Burundi and Rwanda: Different Paths to Mass Violence', *Comparative Politics* 31(3): 253–71.

van de Walle, N. (2001) *African Economies and the Politics of Permanent Crisis, 1979–1999*, Cambridge: Cambridge University Press.

Wimmer, A., Cederman, L.-E. and Min, B. (2009) 'Ethnic Politics and Armed Conflict: A Configurational Analysis of a New Global Dataset', *American Sociological Review* 74(2): 316–37.

Wrong, M. (2010) *It's Our Turn to Eat: The Story of a Kenyan Whistle-Blower*, New York, NY: Harper Perennial.

14

OIL POLITICS

Ricardo Soares de Oliveira

This essay explores the politics of oil in Africa. Section one provides the historical background of the oil industry and surveys the momentous transformation since the discovery in West-Central Africa of major ultra-deepwater oil reserves in the mid-1990s. This resulted in a continent-wide race for African oil acreage, including onshore and in frontier countries not previously thought of as oil-rich. These changes are discussed in the context of the oil price boom of the current decade as well as growth prospects for oil across Africa.

Section two outlines the relationship between the major players in the political economy of oil, including the international oil companies, the oil-producing states, and the industrial importers of oil in the West and, more recently, in Asia. This entails an analysis of the pattern of state-society relations, the so-called 'resource curse', and the type of state structures created by dependence on oil. Section three focuses on the long-term governance failures in oil-rich countries and surveys the normative challenge to 'business as usual' as articulated by Western and African civil society groups in the past 15 years in matters of human rights, corruption, and the environment. Despite some improvements, the essay concludes that the oil-and-politics nexus is likely to exacerbate conflict and produce non-developmental outcomes in the new oil states, with existing patterns of domestic and international relations prevalent in the established producers being replicated.

Oil development in the 1990s

Since the mid-1990s, the African oil sector has gone through momentous changes. In a short span of time, the oil-rich Gulf of Guinea region became one of the world's petroleum investment hotspots, with companies from China, India, Brazil, Norway, and Russia – amongst many others – joining the still-predominant Western oil majors in the race for acreage.[1] In addition to increased production in established oil states such as Angola and Nigeria, this period has witnessed massive new investments in adjacent states, including Ghana, Equatorial Guinea, Chad, and a number of states in East Africa. These dynamics have already drastically changed, or are set to change, the political economy and exercise of power of a number of important states. Despite these recent upheavals, it is important to note that the political economy of oil extraction in West and Central Africa is much older, often having roots in the late colonial era. This history is important in its own right when dealing with the older oil producers, but it also reveals much about the institutional and political economy impacts of oil in post-colonial Africa, its effect on the calculus of power, and the likely results of oil wealth for a number of up-and-coming oil states.

In some cases, oil exploration started in the first half of the twentieth century, and by the late 1950s, several states, such as Angola and Nigeria, were modest producers. Companies present in these countries in late colonial or early post-independence days remain the leading players across the region. Even in today's diversified investment context, around 80 per cent of oil production is by, or involving state partnerships with, just five firms: ExxonMobil, Chevron, Royal Dutch/ Shell, Total, and ENI. These companies, as well as others they have absorbed over the past decades, have proven remarkably resilient in the tough political and economic environment of the Gulf of Guinea, braving large-scale warfare, regime changes, and all sorts of logistical challenges. They have laboured under the imperative of continued engagement with the region on account of its oil endowment, the access provided to foreign oil corporations and the very favourable investment conditions.

An important feature is the pragmatism at the heart of long-standing relationships between oil investors and foreign oil firms. While resource nationalism in 1960s–1970s North Africa, the Middle East, and Latin America led to the expropriation or diminishment of Western oil corporations' interests and political clout, in the Gulf of Guinea this had but a slight impact on operators, even in Nigeria where there were substantial contract renegotiations. The reason for this more cautious leadership by oil-rich governments is straightforward: they had neither the capital nor the technical and managerial expertise to extract the oil themselves. Nigeria's and Angola's notable human resources were primarily so at the level of negotiations: NNPC and Sonangol, respectively, could never match the ambitions of such developing world counterparts as PEMEX, PDVSA, or SONATRACH.

In the Nigerian case, attempts at indigenization of the economy and gaining membership to Organization of the Petroleum Exporting Countries (OPEC) were laced in 1970s nationalist rhetoric, but the role of Western corporations was left intact (Biersteker 1987). In the Francophone *chasse guardée*, France's national oil company (NOC), Elf-Aquitaine, retained a dominant position both in conservative states, such as Gabon, and the nominally socialist Congo-Brazzaville. In Angola, this pragmatism was even more surprising in view of the country's embrace of socialist economics and Eastern Bloc assistance. On account of the total destruction of the non-oil economy following civil war and foreign invasion in 1975, the *Movimento Popular de Libertação de Angola – Partido do Trabalho* (MPLA, The People's Movement for the Liberation of Angola) government understood that the oil sector would be its fiscal lifeline. To that effect, it proceeded to woo back the foreign oil corporations (with emphasis on Gulf Oil, later bought by Chevron) that had been responsible for oil production in the late colonial years. Moreover, Angola's leaders created national oil company Sonangol, which was deliberately insulated from the predominant logic of the Angolan economy and allowed to mature into a competent representative of the state's interests. The Angolan oil sector thus thrived, in spite of Cold War politics and internal conflict. The bizarre scenario of Cuban troops protecting US oil companies from US-backed guerrilla attacks became commonplace (Soares de Oliveira 2007b).

An assessment of the Gulf of Guinea's worth for the global economy of oil in the early 1990s would have been lukewarm, and at this stage, no other African sub-region was a major producer. It contained one world-class oil power – Nigeria – and a number of medium-sized producers. Companies active across the Gulf of Guinea and in possession of the relevant geological data knew that the region had great potential (as did some companies interested in Sudan), but for many it still paled in comparison with oil provinces opening up elsewhere. Aside from French interests, the region did not rank high in geopolitical considerations. This received wisdom abruptly changed in the mid-1990s.

The introduction of seismic research and ultra-deepwater technology suddenly opened up a new offshore frontier to foreign investors. The enthusiasm for the Gulf of Guinea's oil potential was such that a global suspension in investment in the late 1990s, when oil prices dipped below US$10 giving oil firms no incentive for capital expenditures, did not affect the investment frenzy in the region. Over the next decade, tens of billions of dollars-worth in oil sector investment poured into the Gulf of Guinea. Despite some misgivings, international financial institutions (IFIs) have contributed to this and were even the lead actors in opening up Chad, one of the new petro-states in the region, through support of the Chad–Cameroon pipeline to bring the crude oil to world markets.

The geopolitical importance of this region soon followed its promising commercial reassessment. Eager to diversify energy supplies outside of the Persian Gulf, the United States defined the Gulf of Guinea as an area of 'national strategic interest'[2] and resultantly sees securing energy supply routes to be one of the key missions of the newly created Africa Command (AFRICOM). In tandem with an exponential increase in its Africa presence, China's interest in African oil has grown considerably (Alden *et al.* 2008). The same applies to other Asian states, such as India, Malaysia, South Korea, and Japan as well as investors from Norway, Russia, and Brazil and the myriad small companies interested in frontier locations. By the mid-2000s, this enthusiasm for African oil poured out of the Gulf of Guinea in all directions, with East Africa in particular witnessing a stampede of investors (Anderson and Browne 2011). Such a massive escalation of foreign direct investment (FDI), together with the increase in oil production and, most importantly, the jump in oil prices to an unprecedented $147 per barrel in July 2008, resulted in record levels of gross domestic product (GDP) growth and international interest, with the treasuries of Africa's oil-rich states expected to earn hundreds of billions of dollars in oil rents.

Oil states, oil companies, and oil importers

Since the late 1950s, the political economy of oil, and its character, have been structured around three sets of empowered players and their three-way relationship. They are: the oil-producing state itself, in the form of its governing elite; the foreign (mostly Western) oil companies; and the oil-importing states in the industrial world, which until the 1990s essentially meant the West.

Oil states

The seven oil-rich states in West and Central Africa include Nigeria, Cameroon, Angola, Gabon, Congo-Brazzaville, Equatorial Guinea, and Chad; Ghana began oil production in 2010, bringing it to eight countries. Other neighbouring states are either engaging in serious oil exploration or have started to produce modest but growing amounts of oil. The Gulf of Guinea's oil states are heterogeneous in size, population, colonial legacy, and resource endowment, but they share three key factors. The first is their dependence on foreign technology to extract oil; second is an overwhelming dependence on oil revenues for the fiscal sustenance of the state; and third is a consistent record of poor use of oil revenues, high corruption, and low human development indicators. These common characteristics mean that oil-rich states, while unique in their own right, can be studied within a general framework and are amenable to a degree of generalization regarding their post-colonial trajectories. This is particularly so when comparing their character during the pre-oil, oil-boom, and post-oil boom eras.

The first common element concerns the pre-oil character of their political economies. Although there were differences in economic development, availability of skilled personnel, timing and manner of decolonization, and so on, all of the states mentioned above faced important deficiencies at the time of independence that did not augur well for productive use of oil revenues. Their economies were commodity-based (sometimes on just one major agricultural commodity) and therefore highly dependent on world market shifts (Williams, this volume). Their institutions were shallow and their bureaucracies inefficient. Their politics were despotic and uncivil. Strictly speaking, none of the states in the region had ever experienced what is now termed 'good governance', and a 'developmental elite' was everywhere absent. Many analysts have rightly emphasized the impact of the so-called 'resource curse' – the paradox whereby mineral resource endowment in developing countries tends to lead to the deepening of poverty and strife rather than development, however defined – on oil-rich states in the Gulf of Guinea and elsewhere, as well as of other closely related phenomena, such as 'Dutch Disease' (Gelb 1988; Auty 1995). That said, it is important to recognize that these states had none of the preconditions that have led to at least ambivalently positive results in other oil-rich states. Post-independence governance challenges made it highly unlikely from the outset that oil would be a force for good in the Gulf of Guinea.

The second shared element is the character of boom-era policies during the 1970s and early 1980s. Visions for the state that held sway during this period were statist and high-modernist, with emphasis on the need to import the hardware of industrial advanced societies – in the form of infrastructure and heavy industry – and a concomitant neglect of previously predominant (i.e. agricultural) economic activity. Even at this stage, Gulf of Guinea states did not resemble the Weberian model of a modern bureaucracy exercising a monopoly of violence over a given territory. Still, the oil-fuelled, nationalist rhetoric of state elites was premised on mimicking the industrial world and achieving such an end-product through state intervention in society. In practice, however, such dreams of modernization were trumped by patrimonial politics, corruption and mere incompetence, the undermining of labour-intensive economic activity, non-pursuit of economic diversification, and the failure to construct a viable non-oil fiscal foundation for the state. All of this was compounded by the serial resort to foreign lending. When oil prices fell in the 1980s, the oil states saw a precipitous fall in their revenues and the near impossibility of repaying their quickly escalating debts. The very viability of the state was at stake amidst the debris of white elephant projects, half-finished infrastructure, and social unrest.

The third element is the manner in which the Gulf of Guinea's oil-rich states tackled the political and economic decay of the post-boom era. Essentially, they have done so through the following trends: state abandonment; state 'privatization' or discharge of functions; and the tailoring of state tools around core matters with which it is still concerned. State abandonment is the simplest. Areas previously under the scope of state intervention were no longer defined as the state's own and were therefore neglected. This contains a policy-specific dimension (for example, the abandonment of welfare, health, and educational provisions), and a geographical dimension (the retreat from economically useless areas). The result was the implosion of human development indicators throughout the region.

State privatization meant more than the sale of state assets to private entities. It included the passing of former state responsibilities to non-state actors from security and education sectors (to private companies, militias, mercenary outfits; and to the churches, respectively), to disease control and food provision (to the UN system and non-governmental organizations – NGOs – see Jennings, this volume). These trends have remained constant in most of the region's petro-states, even after oil revenues and investor interest soared again in the 1990s and beyond. The contradiction is apparent in the appellation of these countries as 'successful failed states', wherein both segments of the population – the oil-rich and the extremely poor – amount to one half of the political and economic makeup of the Gulf of Guinea states.[3]

The empirical element of failure is undeniable. A veritable basket case of dysfunctional state experiences, the Gulf of Guinea brings together the pathologies of the colonial and post-colonial African state with the ailments of petro-statehood studied by political economists the world over (Karl 1997; Chaudhry 1997). However, the presence of oil deposits *changes the calculus of state survival* by preserving oil states in the region from Somalia-type demise. Because they do not need money to the same extent as other oil-poor African states, oil states are guaranteed considerable freedom from international financial institutions. They also possess solidly long-term, legal engagement with the international economy through the sale of the fuel that powers industrial civilization. Oil ensures that whatever the domestic political conditions of these states, there will be an interest by multiple external and internal actors in maintaining a notional central structure, and that enough resources will be available to prop up incumbents, guarantee their enrichment, and coerce or co-opt enemies. This allows these ruling elites to build and maintain a political order that is violent, arbitrary, and exploitative, but fairly reliable. The resulting political process is and will be unstable and fragmentary, but the structure of politics itself will be stable and viable, while oil lasts. This political and material success of the elite does not cancel out the decay around itself but, as Prunier and Gisselquist (2003: 103) note, an analysis of failure must allow for the fact that certain forms of governance can be 'successful as measured against its own parameters and judged by the standards of its political program'.

Provided two conditions are in place, the relationship between oil states and oil companies will work in a mutually beneficial way despite the surrounding chaos. The first is a prerequisite for foreign involvement in the oil sector: the creation of a parallel economic system that insulates oil companies from the unreliability of local conditions, with its own acceptable legal framework and logistical efficiency. In such enclave contexts, companies can operate freely and do not face the rent-seeking, contractual uncertainty, or threat of expropriation that are widespread outside the oil sector. The second condition – essential for elite survival and enjoyment of revenues – is the creation and maintenance of two kinds of state organizations that are spared the decline evident elsewhere. The first pertains to the instruments of coercion, in the form of armed forces, numerous police and paramilitary outfits, and more informal instruments of repression, such as private militias. There is substantial variation across the region, from the warfare of the Niger Delta to the more controlled environments elsewhere, but trends are similar throughout. The second is an entity that can articulate state interests in the oil sector with comparative prowess, bringing together its scarce human resources and enabling success in negotiations and joint ventures, as well as access to oil-backed loans. This function is normally performed by the NOC, with Angola's Sonangol as the best example, but can also be performed informally by consultants close to the executive.

Although there is no space here to discuss the subject of elite politics in the oil state in-depth (see Soares de Oliveira 2007a), a brief comment is in order. A dependency theory type of approach to the political economy of the region – one that gives the key explanatory role to the evils of the world economy and very little or none to the character of domestic empowered political actors – fails to address the role of elites in the oil partnership. While they are indeed constrained by their specific position in the world economy and the feeble character of the polities over which they preside, they are well-endowed, consequential actors in their own right. Any investigation of African oil will find them at the centre of political and economic outcomes in the post-colonial era, especially at a time of unparalleled revenues.

Oil companies

A close study of corporate involvement in the oil sector dispels a number of misconceptions about foreign investment in Africa. While some decently run African states have found it hard to attract FDI, some of the worst-governed states on the continent are the site of a large-scale, long-term corporate presence. In this context, oil companies are best understood as integral parts of the local power structure and co-creators of the political economy of oil, rather than passive entities accepting pre-existing methods and structures. They are intensely networked with local decision makers and understand the nature of the business-and-politics nexus in the oil states. The technically capable, vital role in oil extraction played by these firms is underpinned by a vast array of associated foreign businesses that perform useful roles in the functioning of the political economy of oil, including assorted consultants, oil services companies, auditors, and the international banking industry, which has played the role of creditor and money launderer for decades. The latter in particular is central to understanding the character of oil money flows from Africa into the core of the world economy.

Although corporate reactions to the governance of oil states has evolved in recent years, a core perception still holds sway: oil firms act under the geological imperative of going where the oil is and the political imperative of going where they are welcomed by sovereign authorities. What oil-rich sovereign governments do or do not do with the revenues they earn is a different matter altogether and, from the corporations' point of view, not their responsibility. Leaving aside the fact that this apolitical discourse is often contradicted by intensely political actions (e.g. lobbying in Western capitals in favour of the governments of oil-rich states), it goes without saying that the policy choices of Africa's petro-elites could not possibly be implemented in the absence of the resources that these companies make available to them. Furthermore, the lack of diversification of oil economies means that a handful of corporations are by far the largest taxpayers and that there is barely any fiscal activity outside the oil sector. Any comparative fiscal history, or a specific comparison with the political role of the NOCs of oil-rich countries from Iran, to Venezuela, or Mexico, shows that entities that bestow upon the state such a disproportionate amount of the resources that allow it to exist and function are endowed with significant political clout and are constitutive of the governance outcomes of the state.

Oil-importing states

The third and final category of players in the oil partnership is that of the oil-importing states in the industrial world, which until recently meant the Organisation for Economic Co-operation and Development (OECD) economies, but has now come to include emerging Asian economies as well. For decades the political economy of oil was based on the exchange of political support and prosperity for local dictators, and reliable provision of oil for industrial states and their consumers. While there were other factors at work, including the generally accommodating attitude towards post-colonial states in their early years and the sidelining of normative concerns during the Cold War, the existence of a smooth-running and mostly positive oil partnership played a key role in facilitating authoritarian rule.

There were, of course, difficulties in doing business in such an unstable region as the Gulf of Guinea. Civil wars, like the attempted secession of Biafra, could close down production, and wider political dynamics, such as a Nigeria–UK diplomatic tussle, could result in investor casualties. Generally, though, the region proved a reliable source of oil imports, with Cold War inclinations on the African side tempered by the desire for oil revenues. Even today, oil companies still find it to be lucrative, on balance, to persevere amidst conditions as disabling and violent as those prevalent in the Niger Delta. Indeed, new companies keep coming to the region. It can be argued that the issues now at the forefront of all discussions of oil in Africa – the governance, environmental, and human rights record, and corruption and the failure to bring forth a development dividend for the majority – were non-issues until a decade ago.

The dramatic commercial and geopolitical reassessment of African oil in the mid-1990s, discussed above, was eventually matched by a normative reassessment. There were long-term trends at stake, both in the West and in Africa. In the former, this included the end of the Cold War and the emergence of 'ethical' foreign policies promoting democracy and free markets. The West had less willingness to partner with questionable regimes, and civil society agendas increasingly challenged corruption, environmental exploitation, and the use of natural resources to underpin war efforts. In Africa, especially in the impoverished and highly polluted Niger Delta region, vocal and occasionally violent grassroots protest emerged, confronting the corporation-state nexus and the tragic implications of oil production for surrounding communities. Jointly, these trends amounted to a searing critique of the oil partnerships of the previous decades, and led to the politicization of its governance record. The speed with which this critique burst into international policy debates nonetheless took many by surprise.

The international 'progressive agenda'

While the progressive agendas matured rapidly in the early 1990s, a tragic event in late 1995 was the precipitating cause of their near-complete mainstreaming in the subsequent years. Despite high-level international opposition and pleading, Nigeria's military ruler Sani Abacha ordered the execution of Ken Saro-Wiwa and eight other anti-oil activists. Saro-Wiwa, a writer, was the leader of a protest by his fellow Ogoni against perceived exploitation by the government and oil firms. Royal Dutch/Shell, the biggest oil operator in Ogoniland and in Nigeria, was dubbed an accomplice in the executions, as well as in the long-term destruction of lives and the ecosystem across the Niger Delta. Oil companies were put on the defensive as Human Rights Watch, Global Witness, Transparency International, and other international organizations shed light on their role in the region.

Other developments raised uncomfortable questions about the oil industry's record in Africa. In France, long-simmering scandals regarding Elf-Aquitaine finally erupted and a vast Gabon-centred regional strategy of corruption and influence-peddling was unmasked. At the IFIs, received wisdom on the beneficial impact of extractive industries was questioned by research that showed an inverse connection between mineral resource endowment and broad-based development. Indeed, research seemed to show that oil- and mineral-rich states in the developing world were more likely to suffer from heightened political competition, corruption, and civil war than non-resource-rich states, and were also more likely to be poorer in the long run (see Gelb 1988). The lifting of the taboo around discussions of corruption at the IFIs also facilitated international scrutiny over oil-related malfeasance in Africa.

There are three dimensions to the subsequent pursuit of a 'progressive agenda' in Gulf of Guinea oil politics (Soares de Oliveira 2007a). While they vary in their impact and are not the only such developments to have taken place, they encapsulate the dynamics of reform in the late 1990s and the early part of the last decade. The first call for change pertains to the lack of transparency of business transactions, and the attendant corruption and siphoning off of oil revenues. Though colossal graft in developing nations and the role of multinational corporations in facilitating it had been a concern for decades, the broad-based recognition that it needed to be tackled is relatively recent (until the mid-1990s, the 1977 US Foreign Corrupt Practices Act was one of the few pieces of legislation to target such occurrences). Aided by strong civil society campaigning and such developments as the 1997 OECD anti-corruption convention and G8 pronouncements on the evils of corruption, international efforts to address this gathered speed in the mid- to late 1990s. This new emphasis was part of a broader concern with corruption, but had particular implications for resource-rich countries. These were not only states where the discrepancy between available resources and dire poverty was most glaring; there was also a clear link between illicit revenue flows and war-making – especially by insurgent groups – which fuelled high-profile campaigns, such as that against 'blood diamonds'. Crucially, this focus soon transcended the usual reformist constituencies and came to include institutions like the International Monetary Fund (IMF), which became interested in the huge gaps in oil-rich member-state accounts.

In addition to the persistent work of the international NGOs mentioned above, two attempts to address corruption should be mentioned. The first was the Publish What You Pay (PWYP) campaign, which started in 2002 with the support of civil society organizations around the world. The campaign argued for hard regulation of financial transactions between states and companies, with timely and disaggregated publishing of accounts made a precondition for firms listing in Western stock exchanges and respecting accounting standards. Unsurprisingly, support for a regulatory approach was very thin beyond the core activist groups. A second campaign, launched by British Prime Minister Tony Blair and now having its own secretariat in Oslo, was the Extractive Industries Transparency Initiative (EITI), which called on both governments and companies to publish their transactions on a voluntary basis. EITI was loudly embraced by stakeholders across the oil nexus, including not just oil-importing states and oil firms but also many oil states.

While some were genuine in their embrace of EITI, three aspects were pivotal from the viewpoint of recalcitrant players in the oil game. First, this 'reform-light' option allowed them to buy into the now-unavoidable reformist discourse at little cost. Second, it helped stave off the threat of hard regulation, for which there was no constituency outside civil society groups. Third, its vague and loophole-ridden character meant that constraints to long-standing behaviour would either not materialize or be phased in slowly enough that alternative routes for similar behaviour could be explored. As to genuine reformists, who urged less patient 'hard regulators' to accept slow and incremental approaches, they assumed that the reformist turn was irrevocable and its deepening inexorable. The possibility that the very international climate allowing for the blossoming of reforms could change fast in a contrary direction was not taken into account.

The second call for change pertained to the responsibilities of corporations themselves. The dismissive approach of most oil companies could not withstand the challenges to their actions. The private sector concocted a discourse on corporate social responsibility (CSR). It appeared as an essentially reactive endeavour by companies to both deflect criticism on the environmental and social impact of their activities, and to prevent the creation of putative transnational regulatory frameworks to tackle these problems. Eventually, most firms adopted non-binding, voluntary codes of good corporate behaviour and are now more capable of dealing with external criticism of operations with less awkwardness. The most important development amidst the upsurge in oil company philanthropy entailed by CSR was the outpouring of resources across the Niger Delta. The killing of Saro-Wiwa provided oil companies with a wake-up call, at least from the perspective of improving their dismal public relations record. Royal Dutch/ Shell, for instance, went from a measly $100,000 in social spending in 1991, to $69 million in 2002 (Soares de Oliveira 2007a: 243–53). A Niger Delta Development Commission was created with partial financing by the oil companies, although it soon became infested with networks linked to the ruling party. While this shows an increased commitment on the corporate side, there is scarcely a positive impact in the region and the evermore sophisticated and criminalized insurgency has continued to expand.

A third progressive agenda was, when first put forth, potentially the most intrusive of all suggestions to improve the record of the political economy of oil in the Gulf of Guinea. This was the idea that in order to bring about the desired developmental outcomes for oil-producing states, important aspects of public policy – especially at the level of oil revenue management – should be supervised by the international community. This approach was implemented in landlocked Chad. The project was reminiscent of nineteenth-century attempts at controlling the public finances of bankrupt states, such as Greece, Egypt, and the Ottoman Empire, and appropriately dubbed an instance of 'shared sovereignty' by Krasner (2004). After years of reluctance on account of the security situation, a consortium headed by Exxon-Mobil got the crucial support of the World Bank in 2000. In exchange for the financing and political support for building the oil and pipeline project, the Chadian government had to sign up to agreements that, among other things: environmental standards would be high throughout the project; 80 per cent of oil revenues would be used for social purposes; part of the revenues would be kept in a future generations fund; and government spending decisions would be followed and, if necessary, vetoed by a revenue oversight committee partly staffed by civil society representatives (Gary and Reisch 2005). Chad's President Idriss Deby was never enthusiastic about the agreement but played along while the project was being built. Once it was up and running, Deby reneged on important sections of the agreement and, after almost three years of acrimonious relations with the World Bank, the agreement was quietly dropped in 2008 (*The Economist* 2008).

Contemporary challenges to reform

By 2004, the governance and oil debates were seemingly over. While the reformist agendas meant different things to different people, no serious public voice was arguing that such matters were irrelevant, not a matter for corporations, or best addressed by a laissez-faire approach. Actors diverged on the urgency of specific reforms, but the character of governance outcomes in oil-rich African states was the subject of tacit agreement. Even violent dictatorships, such as Equatorial Guinea, scrambled to sign up to EITI in hope of not falling foul of the new reformist consensus. However, the apparent victory of the reformist agenda was overshadowed by two facts. First, that rhetorical acceptance of reforms was not actually materializing into different policies on the ground. Second, that a massive shift then underway in international oil markets led to record oil prices and a concomitant move away from the more austere economic conditions that had enabled the reformist drive to take place initially.

In the four years to 2012, several factors have militated against progress in addressing the deep-seated problems of oil states. As always, the rise of oil prices (this time, to an historically unprecedented $147 per barrel in July 2008) meant that policymakers in industrial states again embraced the default realpolitik approach to relations with major energy producers. The chancelleries of even the most reformist northern European states are now wary of antagonizing states from which they badly need oil and gas.

In addition to high oil prices, other factors have played a role in taming the West's reformist enthusiasm. Oil provinces expected to provide big opportunities to foreign investors – from Mexico and Venezuela, to Russia and assorted Middle Eastern states – either did not open up or, in fact, became more difficult to access. This made access to Africa's oil fields even more precious. Additionally, major competitors from Asia's oil-hungry economies – such as China's CNOOC, PetroChina, and Sinopec, Malaysia's Petronas, and India's ONGC – engaged with Africa's oil elites without the pretence of a reformist impulse. While the differences between big 'Western' and 'Eastern' oil companies is overemphasized, Western corporations have had to contend with strong challenges to the realpolitik approach, whereas Eastern companies have more or less unproblematically embraced it. The enabling role of Asian companies for the Khartoum regime is a high-profile example of this.

Another factor is that the commitment to reform was always timid and biased towards the incremental and voluntary, as opposed to the forceful and regulatory. Oil companies, even when they seemed to jump on the reformist boat, were more often than not engaging on damage limitation exercises. What is now deemed corrupt practice never decidedly affected the bottom line of these companies, and their engagement with African oil states has always been highly profitable. In fact, the clearest danger for oil firms was the damage to relations with power-holders in the oil-rich states if reform was pursued too strenuously. It is thus not surprising that oil companies were amongst the first to desert the reformist agenda as soon as the debates shifted.

The final and perhaps most important factor in accounting for the lack of success of the reformist agenda is that there was never a strong enough reformist constituency in oil-producing countries themselves. Despite protest by mainline churches, NGOs, and the media, where there was space to do so, and the occasional armed rebellion in countries such as Angola, Chad, Congo-Brazzaville, and Nigeria, the arrangements that are dismissed by those outside of the oil elite as abhorrent were and remain highly rewarding for those on the inside. Few, if any, realistic competitors to the oil incumbents think very differently about the state or the economy, and those who do are not at the present time within reach of decision-making positions. In fact, the clearest trend across the region is the consolidation and growing sophistication of these oil-fuelled regimes, to the detriment of better alternatives. In some countries there was a partial engagement with the reformist agenda but ultimately no schism occurred at the elite level. The political economy of oil in Africa is a joint, transnational creation of numerous local and foreign actors. It cannot be changed from the outside alone, and as made clear in this essay, the outside's willingness to enact change was always ambivalent anyway.

Developments in this arena are not consistently negative. There is ground for cautious optimism that Ghana, the continent's newest oil state and a democratic one with a free press, will be capable of managing its resources better than its neighbours have. At the international level, the US Dodd-Frank Act of 2010, which makes it compulsory for companies to disclose payments and other data in a disaggregated manner, brings on board many of the suggestions of the PWYP campaign, and money laundering and capital flight are slowing entering the mainstream of discussions on the world economy. This nascent transparency is not a panacea to decades of disappointing outcomes at the domestic level of established oil states. In addition to fundamental continuities in those cases, the dynamics in up-and-coming oil states, such as Uganda and South Sudan, do not point to a stronger regulatory framework, the institutionalization of revenue management, respect for local communities, or the suppression of rentier appetites. Moreover, there is a worrying degree of cross-border complexity and potential for dispute (especially but not only between Khartoum and Juba) that has been secondary in West and Central African oil development. In short, change to the patterns outlined in this essay needs to be based on reform at the level of the oil states, even if necessarily grounded in an international setting that incentivises benign choices instead of rewarding malfeasance. For the time being, this is an unlikely prospect in the old, and many of the new and up-and-coming, oil states.

Notes

1 For further discussion of many of the themes in this chapter, see Soares de Oliveira (2007a).
2 Assistant Secretary of State for Africa Walter Kansteiner, quoted in *The Economist* (2002).
3 The idea of a 'failed state' that can be 'successful' because it continues to provide for the prosperity of elites and because it benefits from resource flows that allow it to go on standing is derived from Prunier and Gisselquist (2003). See also Soares de Oliveira (2007a).

Bibliography

Alden, C., Large, D. and Soares de Oliveira, R. (eds) (2008) *China Returns to Africa: A Rising Power and a Continent Embrace*, London: Hurst and Co.

Anderson, D.M. and Browne, A.J. (2011) 'The Politics of Oil in Eastern Africa', *Journal of Eastern African Studies* 5(10): 369–410.

Auty, R. (1995) *Sustaining Development in Mineral Economies: The Resource Curse Thesis*, London: Routledge.

Biersteker, T.J. (1987) *Multinationals, the State and the Control of the Nigerian Economy*, Princeton, NJ: Princeton University Press.

Chaudhry, K. (1997) *The Price of Wealth*, Ithaca, NY: Cornell University Press.

The Economist (2002) 'Black Gold', *The Economist*, 24 October 2002.

——(2008) 'Breaking the Bank: A Vaunted Development Project Goes Awry', *The Economist*, 25 September 2008.

Gary, I. and Reisch, N. (2005) *Chad's Oil: Miracle or Mirage? Following the Money in Africa's Newest Petro-State*, Washington, DC: Catholic Relief Services and Bank Information Centre.

Gelb, A. (1988) *Oil Windfalls: Blessing or Curse?* New York, NY: World Bank and Oxford University Press.

Karl, T.L. (1997) *The Paradox of Plenty: Oil Booms and Petro-States*, Berkeley, CA: University of California Press.

Krasner, S. (2004) 'Sharing Sovereignty: New Institutions for Collapsed and Failing States', *International Security* 29(2): 85–120.

Prunier, G. and Gisselquist, R. (2003) 'The Sudan: A Successfully Failed State', in R. Rotberg (ed.) *State Failure and State Weakness in a Time of Terror*, Washington, DC: Brookings Institution.

Soares de Oliveira, R. (2007a) *Oil and Politics in the Gulf of Guinea*, London: Hurst and Co.

——(2007b) 'Business Success, Angola-Style: Postcolonial Politics and the Rise and Rise of SONANGOL', *Journal of Modern African Studies* 45(4): 595–619.

15

POWER-SHARING

Andreas Mehler

The principal means of conflict termination since the end of the Cold War has been negotiated settlement rather than military victory. This is true not only globally (Hartzell and Hoddie 2007: 10), but particularly in Africa, where few wars over the past two decades have ended with an outright military victory. This is remarkable in itself and reflects a new trend: today only between one-fifth and one-third of all wars end in military victory. Yet not all negotiated settlements to violent conflicts are sustainable. Many stakeholders seek to avoid 'losing the peace' even at the cost of starting a new war. In response to this challenge, another trend has emerged: in negotiated conflict settlements, power-sharing devices have become more prominent (Mehler 2009).

Power-sharing may be defined as an elite pact between representatives of political or military parties on the division of responsibility in different fields of political and economic life. It has become an attractive solution to severe political crises because it aims to avoid future armed confrontations by minimizing the security concerns of rival groups. It is in this context that classic debates regarding the appropriate division of power – or more specifically the necessary curtailing of presidential power – have been revived. The spill-over of crisis-solving approaches into fundamental debates over the appropriate systems of government in post-conflict countries hints at the multi-dimensionality of power-sharing. Accordingly, one might distinguish between: short-term and medium- to long-term intentions and effects on one axis; and the spheres in which power is shared, most notably the different branches of government and the military, economy, and territory of a given polity.

Consociational democracy and post-conflict power-sharing

The academic debate on power-sharing is strongly influenced by the problem of how to make democracy work in divided societies. Given that the main characteristic of democracy is majority rule, minority groups may find themselves constantly dominated by the majority and unable to defend their vital interests. They may become alienated from the general polity and seek violent solutions to accommodate their grievances. Classical power-sharing theory therefore proposes strategies to make democracy work in plural societies. Most prominent among this group of scholars is Arend Lijphart (1977), whose concept of 'consociational democracy' may be summarized as follows:

- A broad-based grand coalition, including political parties not needed to form a majority;
- A minority veto in essential decisions;
- Proportional representation in allocating all major political and administrative positions and in the distribution of public goods; and
- Group autonomy, that is, while decisions of national interest are taken at state level by the grand coalition, those issues of particular concern to autonomous groups are dealt within territorially delimited entities (and can be best implemented in a federal system).

An influential school of thought represented by Donald Horowitz and others opposes Lijphart's view with its own 'integrative approach' to power-sharing. Indeed Horowitz (1985: 566) has warned that Lijphart's standard recipe could easily cement ethnic identities and consequently provide disincentives for elites to moderate their discourse and behaviour. While both consociationalists and integrationists address the same core problem, the remedy they identify is radically different: whereas integrationists advocate institutional mechanisms that provide incentives for cooperation across the main dividing lines of plural societies, consociationalists follow a strategy of minority empowerment. This debate has evolved and gained new prominence as a result of the aforementioned trends. In contrast to the classic debate between Lijphart and Horowitz, the contemporary post-conflict power-sharing literature focuses less on the quality of democracy than on the role played by power-sharing in the preservation of fragile peace.

Again, there are both staunch supporters and opponents to power-sharing as a key element in peacebuilding strategies. Supporters base their argument on the 'security dilemma' evident at the point of conflict termination. Disarmament of the various parties to a conflict is rarely the key to resolving a crisis of mutual trust, particularly when a government retains – or regains over time – control of the state's security forces (Curtis, this volume). Power-sharing arrangements typically seek to resolve this dilemma in the immediate pre- and post-conflict termination periods by providing guarantees regarding the uses of state power, thus rendering commitments to peace more credible. The main arguments in favour of post-conflict power-sharing are therefore that they reduce uncertainty in the immediate post-conflict era, and accommodate entrenched grievances through the introduction of appropriate power-sharing institutions. The main arguments against post-conflict power-sharing resemble the integrationists' critique of consociational democracy – namely, that post-conflict power-sharing offers rewards to rebels, thereby providing incentives to take up arms, and deals with identities as primordial and thus incentivises individuals to portray themselves as group members, in the process cementing societal cleavages.

A second discussion touches on the nexus between post-conflict power-sharing and democracy. Again, the views on the matter diverge substantially. Proponents of power-sharing expect a transitional power-sharing phase to be beneficial in facilitating the transition to democracy (Hartzell and Hoddie 2007; for a critical view see Roeder and Rothchild 2005). Former rivals learn to live and work with each other, develop mutual trust and esteem; a government of national unity may work as a 'school of democracy'. Moreover, former adversaries take the 'risk of democracy', as they have guarantees of at least minimal representation in power-sharing institutions. The opposite view argues that even established civilian parties are sidelined in power-sharing deals, which are likely to impact negatively on democratic transitions. Power-sharing could also be argued to result in the effective abandonment of democracy, given that the rule of the majority has lost significance. Furthermore, critics suggest that once in government, rebel movements are likely to be less disposed to relinquish power at elections than civilian movements, given that they have paid a 'higher price', or to cooperate with other armed movements for the same reason (Spears 2000).

Important refinements to these arguments have been put forward over the last decade or so. Walter (2002) has proposed a so-called 'credible commitment theory' to explain the success or failure of peace agreements. One central element of this argument is that by making 'costly signals' that demonstrate their genuine commitment to the process, parties can enhance their credibility, which may result in the incumbent government being willing to cede important positions of power to other actors. This thinking suggests that we need to include further dimensions of power-sharing in our analysis. Whereas Lijphart focused on the political dimension only, Hartzell and Hoddie (2007; also Hoddie and Hartzell 2003) have proposed an influential distinction between political, territorial, military, and economic forms of power-sharing. A political dimension is nearly always part of a power-sharing deal; the other dimensions are only variably included, but can be greatly relevant in practice.

Alongside these debates, an expanding quantitative literature on post-conflict power-sharing has focused predominantly on the inclusion of power-sharing provisions in the text of a peace agreement (e.g. Pearson *et al.* 2006; Derouen *et al.* 2009), and has only rarely addressed their actual implementation (e.g. Jarstad and Nilsson 2008). The findings of this literature are often contradictory and inconclusive, perhaps unsurprisingly, given the many problems that one faces when coding complex treaties and their haphazard implementation. By contrast, qualitative studies often focus on single cases and lead to largely positive or largely negative results. A recent comprehensive effort by Sriram (2008), for instance, covers 25 cases in Europe, Latin America, Asia, and Africa and comes to a rather sceptical general conclusion with regard to the value of power-sharing. However, qualitative approaches always face the risk of selection bias, which may support the preconceived opinions of their authors.

Africa's experience with consociational democracy

African states have often employed some, but rarely all, elements of the consociational model. Governments of national unity, very familiar to Africa from independence onward, come immediately to mind when thinking about grand coalitions (Rothchild and Foley 1988). The African experience with this form of government is ambivalent; it may have avoided severe conflicts in some states but also precluded democracy in others. Oversized governments have been common but problematic, most notably the forced inclusion of smaller parties within unified parties in the 1960s. Significantly, coalition agreements were rarely enacted by party congresses, but were instead signed by party leaders with little attempt to include supporters. More recent attempts at governments of national unity have explicitly followed the power-sharing model, albeit in countries such as Kenya and Zimbabwe, which did not experience full-fledged civil war (see Cheeseman and Tendi 2010).

By contrast, the minority veto is rarely an established feature in African constitutions. Yet this does not necessarily dictate against its *de facto* employment. Lijphart (1977: 38) himself writes that the minority veto can be an informal and unwritten understanding. In the case of Burundi, the Tutsi minority had for decades enjoyed the 'ultimate' veto in the form of a monopoly on military power (Sullivan 2005: 88). As Sullivan notes, it was 'the threat of losing that ultimate veto which caused it to be used, thus ending the attempt at peace' (ibid.). This could be an argument for more explicit, formal veto rights. Transparency on the option and procedures of a veto can only be achieved by formally acknowledging those veto rights in peace agreements or (interim) constitutions.

Proportional representation has also rarely made its entry into an African constitution as the guiding principle in the distribution of senior positions within the government and bureaucracy. However, some ethnically polarized countries have recurrently experienced near-to-proportional representation in higher offices. One country in which the media constantly counts and compares the ethnic proportions of newly appointed governments, or a new higher military command, is Cameroon. However, this did not make the country any more of a consociational democracy (or any other form of democracy for that matter). The record is more balanced with regard to proportional representation at national elections. A good number of African countries have experienced proportional representation (PR) in legislative elections, such as South Africa and Namibia (pure PR systems), Burkina Faso (since 2002) and Mozambique (PR in medium and large multi-member constituencies), and Burkina Faso (1992–97) and Guinea-Bissau (PR in small constituencies).[1] However, PR has not always prevented the concentration of power within one party as the comparative literature would suggest: even in democratic South Africa and Namibia proportional voting systems have proved compatible with one-party dominance rule.

Finally, the continent has not experienced many federal experiments and those that have been introduced have not met with great success (Suberu, this volume). Currently, Comoros (since 2002), Ethiopia (since 1994; earlier period 1952–62), Nigeria (since 1954/1960), South Africa (since 1996), Sudan (since 2005–11; earlier period 1972–83) and Tanzania (since 1964) exhibit federal systems. In Ethiopia (Ethiopia and Eritrea in the earlier period), Sudan (Northern and Southern part), and Tanzania (Tanganyika and Zanzibar), only two states constituted the federation, so these systems were far from ideal cases of how to accommodate group interests in a multi-ethnic setting. Nevertheless, in all cases it was hoped that the introduction of a federal system would mitigate conflict.

There are persuasive arguments for and against what Bunce and Watts (2005: 136) call 'ethnofederalism'. On the one hand, it may counter two typical temptations in multi-ethnic settings: of minorities to defect and of majorities to dominate. It may also legitimize difference and empower minorities, thereby creating trust. Conversely, ethnofederalism may unnecessarily cement differences and identities, undermining commonality. Such a system may also undermine cooperation and give minorities the institutional prerequisites for later secession. The South African case is usually seen as a success (as are India and Canada), while all other African cases are much more contested. The Comoros case exemplifies the pattern of lengthy negotiations with many setbacks, facilitated by external help. In recent years there has been a strong tendency to establish a degree of decentralization, sometimes in the name of conflict prevention and power-sharing (Spears 2000: 115; Crawford and Hartmann 2008). Only a few of the many decentralization reforms that have been introduced across the continent were comprehensively conceived and implemented by ruling elites. Taken together, we can hardly say that the four main elements of consociational democracy have had uniformly positive effects on African countries. Indeed, most have a decidedly mixed track record.

Africa's (recent) experience with post-conflict power-sharing

One of the best-known peace agreements in Africa is the Arusha agreement meant to end the civil war in Rwanda in 1993. It contained a good number of power-sharing mechanisms designed to include both the Hutu-dominated government and the Tutsi-dominated rebels. One of the problematic effects of the agreement was the refusal of regime hardliners to accept the outcome (i.e. the loss of substantial power); as a consequence of the peace deal and a number of other processes there followed a period of political radicalization among extreme Hutu factions which ultimately led to the genocide in which over 800,000 Tutsi lost their lives. After the spectacular failure of the Arusha agreement, more complex negotiations have taken place in Africa's severest crises. If one concentrates on the time span between 1999 and 2010, 18 of 19 peace agreements concluded in Africa had at least one power-sharing element. Not all were inclusive in nature.

At least in name, the peace agreement between the central government and southern rebels in Sudan is a comprehensive one. However, in reality the agreement did nothing to stop the new bloody conflict in Darfur, and some would argue that it even contributed to the violence (Woodward 2006: 177). The apparent irrelevance of the agreement to other conflict zones in Sudan (and other local rebel movements) proved problematic as the 'national cake' (that is, oil from South Sudan and top positions in the state apparatus) was shared between only two partners.[2] Equally problematic was the fact that the very title 'Comprehensive Peace Agreement' masked the continuing heterogeneity of the South Sudanese rebels. Yet the 'paradox of inclusion' is not specific to Sudan. In numerous cases in Africa, the inclusion of one rebel group in a peace agreement and subsequently in a power-sharing government has left others excluded, who then face incentives to strengthen their war efforts in order to demonstrate that they merit inclusion at a later stage. Limited inclusion may therefore undermine the sustainability of peace.

Burundi

Burundi is rightly presented as the most complex and complete case ever of power-sharing in Africa. Different reasons are invoked to explain this. One is the Belgian experience with consociational democracy, given Burundi's history as a UN mandate territory under Belgian rule after the First World War. Another is the role of South African mediators, who drew on their own experiences with elements of consociational democracy. A third argument, advanced by Vandeginste (2009), is that Burundi's complete form of power-sharing is best explained with reference to the country's trial-and-error approach to finding lasting solutions to a recurrent and extremely violent conflict pattern that has claimed around 200,000 lives between 1993 and 2005, and has accounted for maybe double that number of deaths since independence. Both the war and the peace processes impacted on the main actors: the Hutu rebels were weakened militarily as a result of combat, while the Tutsi establishment was politically weakened through years of inconclusive negotiations. These factors certainly carried as much weight as the substance of the agreement shaping the outcome of the negotiations, which was a complex and sophisticated architecture of institutions and rules.

Based on the assumption that societal cleavages, and in particular the main Hutu–Tutsi divide, is a constant in public life, the main provisions for peace were fixed within the country's constitution. Significantly, a strong emphasis on minority rights for the Tutsi (approximately 14 per cent of the population) was already encapsulated in the Burundian Constitution of 1992 and the preceding Charter of National Unity (1991). This had major effects on the behaviour of political actors, but it did not have positive consequences for any of the political parties that participated in the process. The winner of the first multi-party elections in 1993, the *Front pour la Démocratie au Burundi* (FRODEBU, the Front for Democracy in Burundi), lost its leader with the assassination of President Melchior Ndadaye (the first Hutu president) in a bloody coup attempt in 1993 and was entirely removed from power in a second military coup d'état in 1996. Although FRODEBU subsequently re-entered the peace process, it never regained a dominant position. FRODEBU's old rival, the *Union pour le Progrès National* (UPRONA, the Union for National Progress), fared little better, losing political weight (and ultimately ministerial positions and parliamentary seats) to a number of more extremist parties and (ex-)rebel organizations.

In the wake of the civil war that raged following Ndadaye's assassination until 2005, progress at the negotiation table was at first extremely slow. This can be explained by the tactical moves and material motives of some stakeholders, but also by the antagonistic positions that they held. The power-sharing deal reached on 8 October 2003 in Pretoria contained provisions on territorial power-sharing and reinforced the significance of the provincial level of government through the introduction of 'political' governors. Significantly, rebels were given a share of the posts of governor and municipal administrator positions in the 2003 peace negotiations. Additionally, the Burundian peace agreement, which was later codified in the constitution, fixed the ethnic quota for the distribution of governmental seats. A Constitutional Referendum was held in February 2005, and the resulting document enshrined a new set of power-sharing rules regulating access to positions of power. Accordingly, parliament must be 60 per cent Hutu and 40 per cent Tutsi. In the Senate, each of the 17 provinces must be represented by a Hutu and a Tutsi. Moreover, the cabinet must also feature a 60:40 Hutu/Tutsi split. Similar provisions were fixed for all other public positions.

Burundi's first post-war parliamentary elections, in July 2005, were won by the former rebel movement *Conseil National pour la Défense de la Démocratie-Forces pour la Défense de la Démocratie* (CNDD-FDD, National Council for the Defence of Democracy – Forces for the Defence of Democracy), but both UPRONA and FRODEBU obtained substantial parts of the vote and thereby gained their share of power. Pierre Nkurunziza, the leader of the most important rebel movement CNDD-FDD, was indirectly elected president thereafter and all three parties formed a coalition government. The second rebel movement, *Forces Nationales de Libération* (FNL, the National Forces of Liberation), joined the peace process belatedly in 2006, and those four parties/(ex-)rebel movements were expected to become the main building blocks of the party system, with smaller parties excluded from parliament as a result of the adoption of a 5 per cent threshold. However, this was not what materialized.

Elections are obviously critical to the viability of this architecture. In 2010, a new series of elections was held, and both the electoral process and outcome risked jeopardizing the peaceful transition. The party of President Nkurunziza (CNDD-FDD) won municipal elections (held prior to national elections) by a large margin and other parties cried foul.[3] However, while reports of widespread intimidation against opponents of the regime are indisputable, the complaints of opposition parties were not supported by local and international observers. Subsequently, most parties opted to boycott both presidential and parliamentary elections.[4] This had major consequences, as parties not contesting the polls were barred from joining a broad-based coalition government. Following the election, no major party other than the former single-party UPRONA (associated with Tutsi minority rule in the 1970s and 1980s) and the ruling CNDD-FDD was represented in parliament. A split-off from FRODEBU (FRODEBU Nyakuri) under former party president Jean Minani received five seats and one ministerial position in government, but neither FRODEBU nor the FNL – both credited with substantial Hutu support – gained seats. UPRONA obtained three positions in the cabinet. Indirect senatorial elections were even more problematic with UPRONA being able to win only the two Tutsi seats in the capital Bujumbura and Bururi province. The boycott and the warped outcome of the elections created a crisis of Burundi's post-conflict democracy, and at the time of writing it was difficult to predict whether or not also it would lead to a new civil war. However, some features of Burundi's consociational system may mitigate this risk: ethnic power-sharing in Burundi is organized not only between parties, but also within. If CNDD-FDD and UPRONA can represent within their structures – and thus within the different layers of government – both Hutu and Tutsi communities, it may help to prevent the inequalities underpinning party competition in the country from exploding into fresh violence.

Côte d'Ivoire

On 19 September 2002 a rebel attack on different sites in the metropolis of Abidjan by former government soldiers of northern origin started a low-intensity civil war. The rebellion did not achieve its aim to take over power from President Laurent Gbagbo, but the government also failed to roll back the rebels beyond the southern part of the country. Former student leader Guillaume Soro became the leader of the rebels, claiming to represent the marginalized north of the country. After lukewarm support for the government in the first weeks of the confrontation, French troops stationed in Côte d'Ivoire stabilized the situation. This was the starting point for a drawn-out power-sharing process.

The list of negotiations and negotiators is long. After a first round under the aegis of the Economic Community of West African States (ECOWAS), a complex attempt was made by Côte d'Ivoire's former colonial power France, leading to the much-cited agreement of Linas Marcoussis, signed on 23 January 2003. Participants of the negotiation were all political parties represented in parliament or government plus the three rebel organizations of the time. The agreement addresses the majority of the most salient political problems of the country, including questions of citizenship, which have implications for electoral eligibility, human and civil rights and land ownership. The deal ultimately proved unsuccessful, in part because the proposed reforms would have required a change of constitution and this was not popular with the ruling *Front Populaire Ivoirien* (FPI, Ivorian Popular Front). However, just as important to the failure of the agreement was the role of France as mediator, and the power-sharing formula subsequently imposed (during a second Paris summit immediately after the Linas Marcoussis agreement). The government, and particularly the army leadership, found it simply unacceptable that the rebels should get the defence and interior portfolios, ministries that would give them preponderance in all security issues.

As a result, some concrete details regarding the formation of the government of national unity were left to a new summit in Accra (Ghana) on 7 March 2003 when the rebel groups, now united under the label *Forces Nouvelles* (FN, New Forces), obtained two senior ministries (territorial administration and communication). Additionally, a 15 member-strong National Security Council was established, in which all parties were represented. The Accra developments could be interpreted as a second layer of power-sharing (within the military), building on the first layer that was put forward in Paris (the sharing of government positions). Subsequently, the consensually elected Prime Minister Seydou Diarra was able to build a grand coalition that included 10 ministries for the FPI, seven each for the two other main political parties – *Rassemblement des Républicains* (RDR, Rally of the Republicans) led by former Prime Minister Alassane Ouattara, and *Parti Démocratique de la Côte d'Ivoire* (PDCI, the Democratic Party of Côte d'Ivoire) led by former President Henri Konan Bédié – while nine went to the FN and six to smaller parties. The earlier impasse regarding the interior and defence ministries was resolved via a compromise that saw them assigned to technocrats.

However, the country remained geographically divided and this division was entrenched by the presence of ECOWAS and UN peacekeepers. The territorial division was in no way the result of the power-sharing agreement, but nonetheless had some of the same effects as a formal system of decentralization or regional autonomy, as the northern part of the country was no longer under the command of the central administration. Even essential commercial flows were controlled by rebel leaders for at least four years.

In the period that followed one camp refused to disarm; the other refused to change the constitution to allow for fair elections. This led to two Pretoria summits in 2005, which were attended by Gbgabo, Soro, Ouattara, Bédié and Diarra: minor political parties were no longer part of the game. The most important aspect of these meetings concerned details of article 35 of the Ivorian Constitution concerning eligibility for political office: the refusal of incumbents to allow rival leaders to contest the presidency had been an important source of political tension. South Africa's Thabo Mbeki identified a way to avoid a constitutional referendum by interpreting article 48 of the Ivorian Constitution (on the exceptional rights of the president) as an instrument through which President Gbagbo, after consultation with the president of the National Assembly and the Constitutional Court, could authorize the candidatures of personalities that would be presented by those individuals who had signed the agreement of Linas-Marcoussis. This looked like an apt juridical way out of the deadlock that had been caused by Gbagbo's insistence that the constitution must be followed.

However, new confrontations of a smaller scale continued to take place and neither the disarmament of the rebels and of pro-government militias, nor other preconditions for elections, were fulfilled in time to allow them to take place in 2005. In turn, the South African mediation effort lost credibility when the calendar of the peace process could not be kept. At the same time, a new prime minister was imposed on Gbagbo. Konan Banny, the ambitious former director of the regional central bank and PDCI member, was believed to be a true challenge to Gbagbo's rule, but Gbabgo succeeded in curtailing Banny's influence and 2006 proved to be a year of deadlock. Things changed in 2007. After a month of intense negotiations in what was called 'direct dialogue' between Gbagbo and Soro, the Agreement of Ouagadougou was signed on 4 March 2007. The agreement represented a much more viable power-sharing arrangement. The mediator and third signatory, President Blaise Compaoré of Burkina Faso, was an 'insider' in contrast to the mediators of all preceding agreements. He was very close to the rebels, but gradually became aware of the nefarious effects of the Ivorian crisis on his country and so had good reason to seek a permanent settlement to the dispute. Under his guidance a so-called 'permanent consultation framework' was established which consisted of Gbagbo, Soro, Compaoré, Bédié and Ouattara, and was significant because it gave all of the main players a function during times of crisis. The content of the agreement was rather specific and gave an indication of how two of the major bones of contention should be resolved: the issuing of identity papers was to occur after the holding of special decentralized registration sessions (which then formed the basis of the electoral registration), and the creation of a unified army was to be advanced via the creation of an integrated military command centre in which the government's and the rebels' chiefs of staff held joint authority. This represented an important step in building trust between the rival parties. However, the elite power-sharing deal between President Gbagbo and rebel leader – and by this point Prime Minister – Soro was not made part of the agreement, although it was clearly related and a pre-condition for securing Soro's signature. This created a situation whereby Soro was explicitly rewarded for taking up arms.

The permanent consultation framework proved useful during a series of political crises in 2010. Gbagbo first dissolved the government and the Electoral Commission in February, provoking an outcry from the opposition. Thanks to the established consultative procedure, however, it was possible quickly to form a new broad coalition government and a new Electoral Commission.[5] The consultation framework also proved instrumental to resolving disputes when, after lengthy disagreement, discussions between the four key leaders mediated by Compaoré led to an agreement to accept a final voters' list on 6 September 2010. As the identification of voters and citizens were parallel processes, and the marginalization of certain communities within both economic and political life was one of the main reasons for the rebellion of 2002, this touched at the heart of the Ivorian crisis.

Despite the progress made after 2007, the power-sharing arrangement was not sufficiently resilient to withstand the controversy that followed the contested presidential elections on 28 November 2010. According to the Electoral Commission, opposition candidate Ouattara won in the second round, securing 54.5 per cent of the votes against Gbagbo's 45.5 per cent (first round Gbagbo 38 per cent, Ouattara 32 per cent, Bédié 25 per cent). Subsequently, the Constitutional Council (the highest court in the land, which consisted mainly of Gbagbo supporters) invalidated the results in a couple of northern constituencies so that the president would retain power with 51.5 per cent of the vote.

Almost all international actors and bodies responded by siding with Ouattara and demanding Gbagbo's resignation. The UN even went so far as to 'certify' the figures provided by the Electoral Commission, conferring legitimacy on Ouattara's claim to be the rightful president of Côte d'Ivoire. The standoff between Gbagbo and Ouattara sparked armed incidents leading to several dozen casualties, mainly in Abidjan. Ouattara responded to Gbagbo's intransigence by naming a shadow cabinet under Soro and seeking to take control of the various government institutions. Violence escalated in Abidjan and western Côte d'Ivoire (which probably cost more lives than the original civil war). Ultimately, with the support of French troops, Ouattara's forces were able to surround and then capture the former president.

The Ivorian power-sharing process shows some interesting characteristics: all governments since the first major peace agreement in Linas-Marcoussis in January 2003 were broad based and included a strong majority of non-FPI ministers. However, Gbagbo's party managed to secure some of the key portfolios and the share of FPI ministers in the cabinet rose from about one-quarter to one-third between 2003 and 2010, to the detriment of the RDR and PDCI. This may have given the impression that Gbagbo was less and less willing to share power with others. However, consecutive prime ministers (Diarra, Banny and Soro) were distinctively non-FPI. Moreover, non-Gbagbo factions secured substantial concessions: Ouattara was ultimately allowed to contest elections and his supposed supporters were registered to vote and given the necessary identity papers, while the Election Commission was placed under non-FPI rule. This did not prevent the post-electoral crisis, however, perhaps because too few provisions to secure the fate of electoral losers and ensure them an ongoing role in the political process were included in the relevant agreements.

Liberia

Liberia's first experience with power-sharing was meant to end the country's first civil war, which had begun in 1989. In August 1995 the main warring factions signed an agreement brokered by Ghana's then-President Jerry Rawlings, in Abuja. Charles Taylor, leader of the strongest military organization, agreed to a ceasefire. A ruling council of six members was formed, including three main warlords (Taylor, Alhaji Kromah, and George Boley). Other factions were included in the government, which could not, however, effectively run the affairs of the country as they continued to work against each other. Hostilities continued and only ceased after a further agreement in Abuja, Nigeria later that year. The viability of the agreement was not tested over a long period. Instead, Liberia rushed to hold presidential and parliamentary elections in 1997, leading (after widespread intimidation) to the clear victory of Charles Taylor.

Amos Sawyer (2004: 451), a prominent Liberian intellectual who led a governance reform coalition in 2010, criticized the peace settlement and in particular its power-sharing content. Sawyer argues that the power-sharing government was 'substantially, if not totally, controlled by armed groups whose leaders could hardly find in such arrangements sufficient incentive to blunt their greed and ambition'. Indeed, the peace thus brokered proved unsustainable. Taylor's election enabled him to continue his warlord politics, now in the guise of a elected president. In 1999 war broke out again after the emergence of a Guinean-backed rebel group, the Liberians United for Reconciliation and Democracy (LURD). This rebellion was later joined by a second military group, the Movement for Democracy in Liberia (MODEL), operating from Côte d'Ivoire.

The renewed civil war ended in 2003, with the LURD rebels close to a decisive military victory; Charles Taylor handed power to his vice-president, Moses Blah, and left the country.

The three warring parties and 18 civilian party representatives met in Akosombo and Accra, Ghana, from 4 June 2003 to 18 August 2003 within the framework of the ECOWAS Peace Process for Liberia and under the auspices of ECOWAS Chairman and Ghanaian President John Kufour. The talks were mediated by General Abdulsalami Abubakar, former head of state of Nigeria. The Accra Agreement contained some clear power-sharing elements. At the military level, all of the warring parties contributed representatives to the newly established National Commission for Disarmament, Demobilization, Rehabilitation and Reintegration. The Accra Agreement determined that state forces could be drawn from the ranks of the present government of Liberia forces, the LURD and the MODEL, 'as well as from civilians with appropriate background and experience' (Article VII, 1 (b) of the Accra Agreement). No territorial power-sharing was provided for in the Accra Agreement, although economic power-sharing was regulated in annex 4 to the agreement, with each of the three warring parties being given four positions at state corporations and two positions in national agencies (and 10 state corporations/ 14 national agencies attributed to the collectivity of 'political parties and civil society').

At the political level, while Taylor's vice-president was allowed to run government affairs for a short period until October, the transitional institutions that were developed were clearly designed according to standard power-sharing prerequisites. Significantly, it was agreed that no representative of a warring faction could hold the position of chairman or vice-chairman in the transitional government. Thus, independent businessman Gyude Bryant became head of the executive branch of government. However, 15 out of 21 cabinet posts were allocated between the two rebel movements and the former Taylor government – in other words, once again the warring factions were given a strong majority. Taylor's faction retained internal affairs, defence, planning and economic affairs, health and social welfare, and post and telecommunications, which meant that Taylor's defence minister was thereby allowed to continue in his job. LURD received transport, justice, labour and finance, and the ministry of state, while MODEL secured agriculture, commerce, foreign affairs, public works, and land, mines and energy.

The problem of rebel leaders with dubious intentions gaining control over civilian posts was replicated in the legislature. The National Transitional Legislative Assembly was composed of the three warring parties (with 12 seats each), political parties (18 in total), civil society and special interest groups (7), plus one representative each of the different counties (15 in total) (Article XXIX, 4). Moreover, a controversial LURD leader was made the interim speaker of the Legislative Assembly. This was meant to be an interim arrangement but nonetheless reveals what motivated those who signed the agreement: jobs, cars, and money. The heavy involvement of peacekeepers subsequently enabled early national elections, held at the end of 2005 under a new constitution. However, although these polls allowed for the transition to a civilian government, they also permitted several key figures of Taylor's regime and warlords of the type of the notorious Prince Johnson to become elected legislators and thereby acquire immunity. Taylor, by contrast, was indicted by the UN-sponsored Special Court for Sierra Leone, and finally ended up behind bars in The Hague.

The Accra Agreement has been heavily criticized. In the view of Amos Sawyer (2004: 454), 'fixing the central state is important but insufficient … Authority must be constitutionally shared at other levels of government and local people must become empowered participants.' The alternative security architecture envisaged by Sawyer would have been organized across national borders and would have involved, where appropriate, religious bodies and community militia units. This is a useful suggestion, given that numerous locally based ethnic disputes have fuelled the civil war at the national level. Furthermore, Sawyer's insistence on the need for international involvement in maintaining the peace makes sense given that for all of the externally brokered power-sharing agreements in Liberia's history only the strong and active presence of international peacekeepers achieved a respectable degree of stability and security.

The experiences of Burundi, Côte d'Ivoire, and Liberia with power-sharing arrangements exhibit both similarities and differences. Liberia is an example of an agreement driven by material interests that worked to some extent because of the strong presence of peacekeepers. Côte d'Ivoire is an example of an iterative approach that led to a partially viable agreement and dealt with some of the important causes of conflict, but failed to produce a set of rules that bound actors in the long term. Burundi is the only example of a case in which actors sought to use constitutional devices and the over-representation of a minority group to regulate a long-enduring confrontation.

On the basis of this summary a general lesson may be drawn. In all three examples, power-sharing provisions operated in tension with established electoral practice; in other words, we need to think about the implications of power-sharing both on (short-term) conflict mitigation and (long-term) democratic consolidation in plural societies. The choice of institutions can have an impact on whether actors choose peace or conflict, but may also shape formation, competitiveness and survival of political parties. Rewarding or banning parties for being dominantly mono-ethnic, choosing an electoral system that guarantees former militia leaders will remain within the political elite (and that others will not), and representing regional interests via a newly introduced Senate may undermine the position of existing civilian political movements with significant – although often unintended – consequences for democracy.

Conclusion

There are a number of issues that warrant closer inspection: the question of the 'amount' of power-sharing, the local-national nexus, the appropriate negotiation of power-sharing, and the idea of power-sharing as a process constituted by a series of episodes. Walter (2002) has claimed that the more power-sharing, the better, but what is more? Should we understand this to mean that more dimensions are included (political, military, territorial and economic power-sharing if we follow Hoddie and Hartzell's distinction)? That more (relevant) actors are included? Or that more substantive power is shared between the government and its contenders? All three aspects are likely to be important.

How inclusive an agreement is depends on the structure of the formal process of peace negotiations. We have seen that the mediation practice is rather heterogeneous. 'More inclusive' does not always mean 'more effective'. Yet to exclude some of the main players is always problematic. Quite frequently, part of the leadership of a rebel movement agrees to the terms of a peace agreement while others, who do not feel accommodated, initiate a split within the organization, in many cases sparking new violence. Now leading rebel movements in their own right, such 'spoilers' often emerge from renewed conflict with a stronger claim to a place at the table in the next round of negotiations.

Measuring and evaluating other aspects of power-sharing agreements is also complex. Scholars could better define what it means for an agreement to be successful; it seems somewhat arbitrary to simply state that a deal 'worked' because it was followed by X months of peace. Similarly, determining the extent or degree of power-sharing is a complicated exercise. A first step would be to identify the 'real' positions that confer power on actors in a given society, as this may not be the same across countries and cultures. Revisiting the classical literature on power in Africa may therefore be appropriate to find out whether the most fundamental power relations are touched at all by power-sharing deals. To be more explicit, as long as the president of the republic remains the one that hands out the sinecures and makes the most important decisions with regard to appointments to 'juicy' positions, redistributing ministries or administrative posts will not result in a fundamental change in the rules of the neopatrimonial game.

The dominant assumption in the existing literature is that the sharing of national power leads to a territorially uniform and locally meaningful peace process – the level of analysis on which scholars operate is more or less systematically the nation-state. However, this assumption is not grounded empirically. Studies that look more specifically at sub-national arenas particularly affected by violence would permit us to advance more far-reaching conclusions with regard to the contribution of power-sharing agreements to peace on the ground. National elites cannot simply determine how politics is played at the local level. A more realistic assumption is that national peace and power-sharing accords are unlikely to act as the foundation for countrywide peace if they ignore local constellations of actors and their interests.

The relative prominence of negotiators may also merit greater scrutiny. In some cases, mediators are more active than in others: at times, they sign the document themselves and represent a 'power guarantor' capable of lending legitimacy to the agreement, but may also be discreet to the point of not being mentioned. One potential explanation may lie in the different post-agreement roles that mediators are assigned to play. However, we must then ask who assigns them a specific role? The more informal aspect of such processes also needs to be considered. The realm of African peace negotiators is growing. Some of the continent's leaders are – or were – frequently invited to engage in peace talks, such as Gabon's Omar Bongo Ondimba until his death in 2009. When mediating negotiations, many drew on their own country's experience with power-sharing (such as Presidents Mandela and Mbeki in South Africa), while others enjoyed a close relationship to some participants, putting them in a unique position in relation to the conflict concerned (see the above discussion of Compaoré in Côte d'Ivoire).

Path-dependency is an equally important concept to consider. Initial power-sharing agreements rarely resolve all problems; further agreements are frequently needed after new outbursts of violence. It is often the case that the development of effective power-sharing deals comes only after many years of 'trial and error'. Historical institutionalism – the search for 'critical junctures' in peace processes – thus merits more attention. By working within this framework scholars may be able to develop an account of power-sharing that would enable key actors to value past, better understand apparently 'failed' peace agreements, and develop best practices.

Notes

1 For more on these variations see Erdmann and Basedau (2008: 248). Note that the level of disproportionality between the distribution of voters and the distribution of seats in the legislature grows, the smaller the constituencies.

2 The failure of peace negotiations for Darfur is well described by an insider in Alex de Waal's 'I Will Not Sign', *London Review of Books*, www.lrb.co.uk/v28/n23/waal01_.html (accessed 22 December 2010).

3 CNDD-FDD received 62 per cent, FNL 15 per cent, UPRONA 8 per cent, and FRODEBU (the clear winner of the first free elections in 1993) only received 6.4 per cent.

4 Nkurunziza as the sole candidate obtained 91 per cent of the votes. In parliamentary elections CNDD-FDD obtained 81 seats, UPRONA 17 and the FRODEBU Nyakuri splinter group five seats. Indirect senatorial elections produced 32 CNDD-FDD senators and two UPRONA senators.

5 Soro was again named prime minister and could present a full government on 4 March. Most instrumental was the nomination of a PDCI member at the helm of the Electoral Commission, replacing another PDCI representative accused by the presidential camp of rigging the registration process.

Bibliography

Bunce, V. and Watts, S. (2005) 'Managing Diversity and Sustaining Democracy: Ethnofederal versus Unitary States in the Postcommunist World', in P. Roeder and D. Rothchild (eds) *Sustainable Peace: Power and Democracy after Civil Wars*, Ithaca, NY: Cornell University Press.

Cheeseman, N. and Tendi, M. (2010) 'Power-Sharing in Comparative Perspective: The Dynamics of "Unity Government" in Kenya and Zimbabwe', *Journal of Modern African Studies* 48(2): 203–29.

Crawford, G. and Hartmann, C. (eds) (2008) *Decentralisation in Africa: A Pathway out of Poverty and Conflict*, Amsterdam: Amsterdam University Press.

Derouen, K., Lea, J. and Wallensteen, P. (2009) 'The Duration of Civil War Peace Agreements', *Conflict Management and Peace Science* 26(4): 367–87.

Erdmann, G. and Basedau, M. (2008) 'Party Systems in Africa: Problems of Categorising and Explaining Party Systems', *Journal of Contemporary African Studies* 26(3): 241–58.

Hartzell, C. and Hoddie, M. (2007) *Crafting Peace: Power-Sharing Institutions and the Negotiated Settlement of Civil Wars*, Pennsylvania: Pennsylvania State University Press.

Hoddie, M. and Hartzell, C. (2003) 'Civil War Settlements and the Implementation of Military Power-Sharing Arrangements', *Journal of Peace Research* 40(3): 303–20.

Horowitz, D. (1985) *Ethnic Groups in Conflict*, Berkeley, CA: University of California Press.

Jarstad, A.K. and Nilsson, D. (2008) 'From Words to Deeds: The Implementation of Power-Sharing Pacts in Peace Accords', *Conflict Management and Peace Science* 25: 206–23.

Lijphart, A. (1977) *Democracy in Plural Societies: A Comparative Exploration*, New Haven, CT: Yale University.

Mehler, A. (2009) 'Peace and Power Sharing in Africa: A Not So Obvious Relationship', *African Affairs* 108(432): 453–73.

Pearson, F.S., Lounsbery, M.O., Walker, S. and Mann, S. (2006) 'Rethinking Models of Civil War Settlement', *International Interactions* 32: 109–28.

Roeder, P.G. and Rothchild, D. (2005) 'Power Sharing as an Impediment to Peace and Democracy', in P. Roeder and D. Rothchild (eds) *Sustainable Peace: Power and Democracy after Civil Wars*, Ithaca, NY: Cornell University Press.

Rothchild, D. and Foley, M. (1988) 'African States and the Politics of Inclusive Coalitions', in D. Rothchild and N. Chazan (eds) *The Precarious Balance: State and Society in Africa*, Boulder, CO, and London: Westview.

Sawyer, A. (2004) 'Violent Conflicts and Governance Challenges in West Africa: The Case of the Mano River Basin Area', *Journal of Modern African Studies* 42(3): 437–63.

Spears, I.S. (2000) 'Understanding Inclusive Peace Agreements in Africa: The Problems of Sharing Power', *Third World Quarterly* 21(1): 105–18.

Sriram, C.L. (2008) *Peace as Governance: Power-sharing, Armed Groups and Contemporary Peace Negotiations*, New York, NY: Palgrave Macmillan.

Sullivan, D. (2005) 'The Missing Pillars: A Look at the Failure of Peace in Burundi through the Lens of Arend Lijphart's Consociational Theory', *Journal of Modern African Studies* 43(1): 75–95.

Vandeginste, S. (2009) 'Twenty Years of Trial and Error', *Africa Spectrum* 46(3): 63–86.

Walter, B. (2002) *Committing to Peace: The Successful Settlement of Civil Wars*, Princeton, NJ: Princeton University Press.

Woodward, P. (2006) 'Peacemaking in Sudan', in O. Furley and R. May (eds) *Ending Africa's Wars: Progressing to Peace*, Aldershot: Ashgate.

16

POST-CONFLICT PEACEBUILDING

Devon Curtis

The last decade has seen a decrease in the number of violent conflicts in sub-Saharan Africa. While violence in parts of the Democratic Republic of the Congo (DRC), Sudan and South Sudan, Somalia, Mali, and Nigeria show that many areas of Africa remain highly insecure, the overall extent and severity of conflict in Africa has decreased since the end of the Cold War. The *Human Security Report* argues that international peacemaking and peacebuilding policies are an important part of the explanation for the overall decline in conflict in the 1990s and 2000s (Human Security Report Project 2011).[1]

Post-conflict peacebuilding programmes and initiatives have, indeed, become much more prominent in the last two decades, and many of these programmes are targeted towards countries in sub-Saharan Africa. The United Nations Peacebuilding Commission (UNPBC) was established in 2005, and so far all the countries on its agenda have been in Africa, including Burundi, Central African Republic (CAR), Guinea, Guinea-Bissau, Liberia and Sierra Leone. Many bilateral donor agencies have established peacebuilding and post-conflict reconstruction units and programmes. In 2006, the African Union (AU) adopted a Post-Conflict Reconstruction and Development Policy Framework (AU-PCRD) and some African sub-regional organizations have also developed peacebuilding units and initiatives. Similarly, the number of international non-governmental organizations (INGOs) with peacebuilding and post-conflict reconstruction programming in Africa has also increased. Peacebuilding in Africa – as both policy and concept – seems to be in its heyday.

Nonetheless, this chapter argues that alongside the proliferation of peacebuilding institutions, there is no consensus about the role, aims, and effects of international post-conflict peacebuilding programmes and initiatives in Africa. While it is clear that the local, regional, and global spaces for peace in Africa have been altered through discourses and practices of peacebuilding, these practices play out differently in different locales. Post-conflict peacebuilding ideas and initiatives are at various times reinforced, questioned, subverted, or re-appropriated and redesigned by different African actors. The results, therefore, do not follow a single script towards a condition called 'peace'. Instead, the trajectories of post-conflict peacebuilding programmes and initiatives tend to be messy and multifaceted, and only very rarely correspond to the cheerful statements in policy documents and institutional reports.

This chapter briefly traces the rise of post-conflict peacebuilding in sub-Saharan Africa and the types of activities and practices that typically fall under its purview. It then analyses four different perspectives on post-conflict peacebuilding in Africa, along with related criticisms. Finally, the chapter argues that post-conflict peacebuilding may be best thought of as a contest between multiple shifting ideas and practices, where the stakes are high and where continued violence is often a very real possibility. In other words, post-conflict peacebuilding in Africa is contested politics.[2]

The concept and practices of post-conflict peacebuilding

Post-conflict peacebuilding is not a new phenomenon. The questions of how to ensure security, how to govern, and how to distribute resources after violent conflict have been addressed in many different ways across Africa and across the world over time (Murithi 2008; Curtis 2012: 4–5).

At the end of the Cold War, post-conflict peacebuilding came to be seen as a *distinctive* or specific area of international policy intervention. *An Agenda for Peace*, published in 1992 by then-UN Secretary-General Boutros Boutros-Ghali, provided a coherent conceptualization of post-conflict peacebuilding, defining it as 'action to identify and support structures which will tend to strengthen and solidify peace in order to avoid a relapse into conflict' (Boutros-Ghali 1992: para. 21). For Boutros-Ghali, post-conflict peacebuilding was seen as integrally related to, but distinct from, preventive diplomacy, peacemaking, and peacekeeping. While peacekeeping was the deployment of a UN presence in the field to expand the possibilities for the prevention of conflict and the making of peace, peacebuilding included efforts to consolidate peace and advance a sense of confidence and wellbeing among people (ibid.: para. 55).

The early 1990s was a time of great optimism and belief in the possibilities of post-conflict peacebuilding, and in the ability of the UN to take the lead in these interventions (Sabaratnam 2011: 14). At the time of the publication of *An Agenda for Peace*, the number of UN peacekeeping operations was rapidly expanding. Nearly half of UN peacekeeping operations since the end of the Cold War have been in Africa. When this volume went to press, seven out of the 16 UN peacekeeping operations currently deployed were in Africa.

Although a reinvigorated UN was seen as the key institution to promote post-conflict peacebuilding through peace missions coordinated by the Department of Peacekeeping Operations (DPKO), other institutions followed suit. For instance, in 1997, the Organisation for Economic Co-operation and Development (OECD) created the *Conflict Prevention and Post-Conflict Reconstruction Network* to help coordinate aid agencies' peacebuilding activities. Also in 1997, the World Bank adopted *A Framework for World Bank Involvement in Post-Conflict Reconstruction*, and established the Post-Conflict Fund (PCF) to make fast loans and grants to conflict-affected countries (van Houten 2007; World Bank 2004). Other UN agencies and units also took on peacebuilding roles. For instance, the UN Development Programme (UNDP) created the Bureau for Crisis Prevention and Recovery in 2001 to 'provide a bridge between the humanitarian agencies that handle immediate needs and the long-term development phase following recovery'. The establishment of the UNPBC in 2005 was meant to provide even greater support to countries undergoing post-conflict transitions. Its goal is to bring together relevant actors and propose integrated strategies for post-conflict peacebuilding in specific countries.[3]

African-level institutions and programmes also developed post-conflict peacebuilding units and frameworks. The New Partnership for Africa's Development (NEPAD) developed a post-conflict reconstruction framework in 2005 and the AU developed one in 2006. In 2008 the Economic Community of West African States (ECOWAS) adopted a *Conflict Prevention Framework*, to strengthen efforts to 'prevent violent conflicts within and between states, and to support peacebuilding in post-conflict environments' (ECOWAS 2008: section II, para. 5). To date, the

AU and African regional organizations have mounted peacekeeping operations in Burundi, Comoros, Côte d'Ivoire, Guinea-Bissau, Liberia, Sierra Leone, Somalia, and Sudan, which often included peacebuilding elements (for more on regional organizations see Khadiagala, this volume). Therefore, since the publication of *An Agenda for Peace* in 1992, the number of institutions involved in post-conflict peacebuilding in Africa has expanded. Several other broad changes to peacebuilding are also notable.

First, Boutros-Ghali and others had conceptualized peacebuilding as part of a linear progression, starting with humanitarian relief and conflict management, then peace settlement, then peacebuilding and reconstruction, and finally development. Increasingly in the 1990s and 2000s, however, scholars and practitioners acknowledged that transitions from conflict rarely follow such a linear path. The very term 'post-conflict' may be a misnomer since violent conflict often continues at various levels of intensity even after the end of formal hostilities. Peacebuilding activities can therefore take place before, during, or after conflict. Likewise, 'peace' and 'war' may exist simultaneously in different parts of the same country. For instance in Sudan, even after the Comprehensive Peace Agreement formally ended the conflict between the North and the South in 2005, the conflict in Darfur escalated (Flint and de Waal 2005). Recent violence in disputed regions of Sudan and South Sudan is a result of what is often labelled as a 'successful peace process'. Uganda is typically viewed as a 'peaceful' country since the National Resistance Army won the war and brought President Museveni to power in 1986. However, this obscures the years of continued conflict involving the Lord's Resistance Army (LRA) in the northern part of Uganda and across its borders. Rwanda is often described as a peaceful country that has embarked on an ambitious developmental path, yet repeated controversies over the role of Rwanda in contributing to violence in the neighbouring DRC raise questions about the nature of peace in that country. Compared to the early 1990s, therefore, there is widespread belief that peacebuilding programmes and initiatives may be useful at various points in time, not only in the immediate aftermath of violent conflict.

Second, there has been a broadening of the notion of peacebuilding, and a corresponding expansion in the number and kinds of activities that are considered under the rubric of post-conflict peacebuilding initiatives. Peacebuilding occurs when security is, at best, unevenly distributed, and virtually all understandings of peacebuilding include ideas about how best to reduce insecurity. Often, reducing insecurity in countries emerging from conflict involves a reorganization of the security sector. Security sector reform (SSR) as well as disarmament, demobilization, and reintegration (DDR) programmes tend to be seen as important components of peacebuilding, but this is not always the case. Eboe Hutchful criticizes African security sector reform for its emphasis on 'effective' security systems rather than on accountable systems, thereby contributing to militarization on the continent (Hutchful 2012). In Sierra Leone, Humphreys and Weinstein (2007) found little evidence that internationally funded DDR programmes facilitated successful demobilization or reintegration of combatants.

As the issue of 'failed' and 'failing' states increasingly gained prominence on the international security agenda, particularly after the terrorist attacks of 11 September 2001, many conceptions of peacebuilding expanded to include state-building or the establishment of legitimate forms of political authority. Indeed, by the early 2000s most multilateral peacebuilding institutions endorsed the view that durable peace depended on the construction or strengthening of state institutions. The goal is typically to ensure a regime is in place that is accountable to international norms, that has internal legitimacy, and that has 'earned' its sovereignty. Yet, as discussed below, there are some real dilemmas and questions involved in incorporating state-building into conceptions of post-conflict peacebuilding. What happens when locally specific ways of conducting politics do not conform to international normative expectations? This is especially important in Africa, where there is great diversity in terms of governance structures, patrimonial relationships, and hybrid mechanisms, and where there are significant border areas that fall outside of the state's coercive reach.

The 2000 Brahimi Report on Peacekeeping Reform illustrates a broadened conception of peacebuilding. The Report explains that peacebuilding consists of activities to 'provide the tools for building on those foundations something that is more than just the absence of war' (UN 2000). By 2004, the UN Secretary-General's High-Level Panel on Threats, Challenges and Change identified poverty, infectious disease, and environmental degradation as major threats to security, along with armed conflict, terrorism, organized crime, and weapons of mass destruction, thus further expanding the scope of peacebuilding activities (UN 2004).

This expansion of activities reflects a change in emphasis from negative peace (the absence of war), towards positive peace (the absence of structural violence) (Ali and Matthews 2004: 7; see also Galtung 1969). Proponents of positive peace argue that focusing on negative peace as the desired outcome of peacebuilding is insufficient, since this ignores the multiple ways that people suffer. A narrow focus on negative peace puts efforts and resources into reaching cease-fires between belligerent groups, and guaranteeing these agreements through peacekeeping missions, whilst leaving other forms of insecurity, inequalities, and vulnerabilities unaddressed. A wide range of new issues have been placed on the broadened post-conflict peacebuilding agenda, such as addressing the unequal status of women, unequal access to education, and uneven development.

Third, there has been a deepening of peacebuilding activities. Peacebuilding no longer targets only the state, its institutions and its military, but also individuals and their local communities. For some, peacebuilding involves the reconstitution of individual identities and the re-forging of individual and community relationships. Social transformation may become an object of peace-building concern and intervention, including initiatives to improve individual psycho-social wellbeing. Since violent conflict affects the social fabric of communities in terms of population dislocation, mistrust, identity formation, and the erosion and creation of new social bonds, these issues have made their way onto the peacebuilding agenda. The role of ethnicity, the question of land distribution and reform, the consequences of population displacement, and issues of transitional justice and human rights are often seen as central to post-conflict peacebuilding.

The broadening and deepening of peacebuilding activities and the increased tendency to view these activities in a non-linear fashion have amplified the conceptual confusion associated with the term. Peacebuilding usually involves questions of how to ensure a secure environment, how to establish legitimate political authority, how to generate sustainable livelihoods, and how best to manage societal relations, yet within these broad categories there exist many trade-offs and ambiguities. The way in which these questions and tensions are resolved (or unresolved) varies from case to case in Africa.

Four perspectives on post-conflict peacebuilding

The field of post-conflict peacebuilding is therefore replete with tensions, contradictions, and conceptual confusion. A growing body of multi-disciplinary academic work has attempted to make sense of peacebuilding efforts and their consequences in different contexts. Often, this work contains important normative assumptions about the nature of peace and about the motivations of peace-builders. While there are significant areas of overlap, it is helpful to distinguish between four main perspectives on peacebuilding. These four positions are both analytical frameworks for under-standing peacebuilding, as well as normative positions. Indeed, there is frequent slippage between normative and descriptive categories in the academic and policy literature on peacebuilding.

Peacebuilding as liberal governance

Perhaps the most widespread view of post-conflict peacebuilding sees peacebuilding as part of a global project of liberal governance. Much of the policy and academic literature describes peacebuilding in this way, and adopts normative positions either in favour or against it.

It is not difficult to find policy documents and donor statements that put forth the notion of peacebuilding as liberal governance. *An Agenda for Peace* described political and economic liberalization as key elements in the transformation of war-torn societies.[4] The 2005 UN report *In Larger Freedom* said that: 'Humanity will not enjoy security without development, it will not enjoy development without security, and will not enjoy either without respect for human rights.' The central message in the 2011 'World Development Report' is that 'strengthening legitimate institutions and governance to provide citizen security, justice, and jobs is crucial to break cycles of violence' (World Bank 2011: 2).

This view of peacebuilding as liberal governance is based upon the idea of a 'liberal peace', with its roots in European Enlightenment thinking. Multi-party electoral democracy and a market economy are seen as inherently peaceful and desirable. Post-conflict peacebuilding therefore consists of activities and initiatives to help bring about and facilitate this desired liberal end. This includes promoting the rule of law, constitutional democracy, human rights, a pro-market economy, and neoliberal development. Once these processes take hold with the support of international peacebuilders, it is believed that they will become self-reinforcing.

Liberal peacebuilding is based upon a number of universalist assumptions. There is a shared belief in ideas of progress and rationality. Despite their different configurations and particularities, all societies will benefit from political and economic liberalization. That means that peacebuilding lessons, techniques, and programmes applied in one part of the world are relevant to other parts of the world. A standardized approach to peacebuilding that includes the promotion of multi-party elections and institution building, constitutional and legal reform, and economic pro-market reform are universally appropriate, with only limited adaptations to suit the 'local' context. An approach that works for El Salvador should therefore also work in the DRC, with only limited adjustments. This approach assumes that peacebuilding is authored primarily by outsiders, perhaps with the assistance and input of enlightened locals. All actors in conflict-affected countries are identified *vis-à-vis* their position on liberal peace. Those who violently disagree with liberal peacebuilding are labelled as 'spoilers' who must be socialized or marginalized (Heathershaw and Lambach 2008: 285). Peace, development, and governance are seen to go hand in hand and reinforce one another in this liberal framework.

The widely shared conviction in peacebuilding as liberal governance coincided with the end of the Cold War. The perceived success of (liberal) war-to-peace transitions in Namibia in 1989–90 and in Mozambique in 1992–94 reinforced these ideas. The problem, however, was that many of the peacebuilding efforts in the 1990s did not lead to their intended outcomes. In Rwanda, a carefully crafted peace settlement and power-sharing agreement in 1993 failed to prevent – and arguably may have contributed to – the genocide in 1994 (Clapham 1998). In Angola, notwithstanding a peace agreement in 1991, a UN peacekeeping mission, and multi-party elections in 1992, hostilities resumed when the losing presidential candidate Jonas Savimbi disputed the results. Even those countries that are often judged as peacebuilding successes, such as Namibia and Mozambique, have experienced high rates of inequality and persistent insecurity among some communities. In the late 1990s and 2000s as UN missions took on a larger set of peacebuilding goals, the results remained mixed. In Liberia, new rounds of fighting occurred after the elections of 1997. In Sierra Leone, conflict continued even after the Lomé Peace Accord of 1999 and its power-sharing provisions. Peacebuilding in Sudan may have contributed to the reduction of hostilities between the North and South, but triggered further conflict in Darfur. The disputed election in Côte d'Ivoire in 2010 followed a 2007 peace agreement, but resulted in further violence.

For proponents of peacebuilding as liberal governance, peacebuilding failures such as these do not represent the limits of liberal peace, but rather the flawed implementation of policies and initiatives grounded in liberal ideas. Thus, post-conflict peacebuilding failures in Africa had more to do with improper sequencing, a lack of coordination, or insufficient commitment by outsiders, not problems with the liberal idea itself. In a widely cited argument, Roland Paris (2004, 2010) notes that rapid political and economic liberalization in post-conflict countries can trigger a renewal of conflict instead of a reinforcement of structures of peace. Paris does not criticize economic and political liberalization per se; he simply argues that it cannot be done too quickly in the immediate aftermath of violent conflict. Rapid political liberalization can exacerbate tensions since elites may use violence to gain electoral support; and rapid economic liberalization can generate tensions through increased unemployment and economic uncertainties. Paris argues in favour of 'institutionalization before liberalization', meaning building state institutional capacity first in order to enable liberal values and practices to take hold over time.

This argument, and others like it, do not fundamentally question the content of liberal post-conflict peacebuilding, but suggest ways in which the international peacebuilding community may improve practices to get to their desired outcomes (Jarstad and Sisk 2008). These improvements may include more local buy-in and local participation, more reliance on African continental and regional organizations, or deeper and more intrusive peacebuilding engagement. For proponents of peacebuilding as liberal governance, academic knowledge is an important tool for peacebuilding, which can help practitioners identify and better understand the local obstacles to liberal peace, and help develop better mechanisms to promote and support peacebuilding. Unsurprisingly, many policy practitioners, through lessons learned units and evaluations divisions, have adopted similar conclusions about post-conflict peacebuilding failures and possible remedies. The UN High-Level Panel on Threats, Challenges and Change, for instance, makes a case for greater policy coherence and donor coordination and more careful attention to sequencing (UN 2004).

The criticisms of peacebuilding as liberal governance are diverse. Some critics disagree that contemporary peacebuilding practices can be characterized as liberal. Many others agree with the peacebuilding as liberal governance descriptive framework, but criticize it as a normative project and believe that peacebuilding's failures can be attributed to its liberal underpinnings. These critics put forth alternative normative positions on peacebuilding, discussed below.

Peacebuilding as stabilization

A second perspective on post-conflict peacebuilding shares the liberal concern with order, but rather than focusing attention on order within states, this view sees peacebuilding as being primarily concerned with maintaining the international status quo. Like the peacebuilding as liberal governance perspective, peacebuilding as stabilization is both a descriptive framework as well as a normative position.

While this view acknowledges the multitude of activities conducted under the post-conflict peacebuilding umbrella, the rationale for these activities is to maintain global security and stability. Authors that describe peacebuilding in this way do not see peacebuilding as transformative or emancipatory. Instead, peacebuilding is a disciplinary tool that serves to regulate and stabilize the global South (Duffield 2002).

The view of peacebuilding as stabilization has become increasingly important since the 9/11 attacks on the United States and the subsequent global 'war on terror'. The recent conflation, for instance, of anti-terrorism measures with peacebuilding shows that this view may be gaining currency (Stepanova 2003). The UN peace operation in the DRC changed its mission and its name from United Nations Organization Mission in the Democratic Republic of the Congo (MONUC) to the United Nations Organization Stabilization Mission in the Democratic Republic of the Congo (MONUSCO) in 2010. A central part of MONUSCO's mandate is to assist the Congolese government in strengthening its military capacity, and to support the Congolese government in consolidating state authority. In Uganda, peacebuilding has been re-fashioned to focus on the military defeat of the LRA, particularly as it has become active in the CAR and DRC (Branch 2011).

There are therefore signs that the more expansive and multi-faceted liberal peacebuilding may be giving way to a more limited view of peacebuilding. In part, this may be a response to the perceived failings of peacebuilding as liberal governance with its transformational agenda. As China becomes increasingly involved in areas of Africa emerging from conflict, this view of peacebuilding as stabilization may continue to rise in importance. China has been reluctant to engage with an expansive peacebuilding agenda, and instead has emphasized win-win development on the one hand, and stabilization or security on the other. Other international actors may retreat to this more limited agenda.

Peacebuilding as stabilization is a descriptive framework for understanding contemporary peacebuilding practices, yet it also raises different moral claims. For some, limiting the objectives of peacebuilding programmes in Africa is justifiable due to the difficulties in achieving success with a more expansive agenda. Peacebuilding as stabilization reflects more traditional realist concerns. Other authors are much more critical of an emphasis on stability and the maintenance of the global status quo (Pugh *et al.* 2008; Chandler 2006; Duffield 2002), with some authors claiming that peacebuilding is disguised imperialism covering for the political and economic interests of the West (Schellhaas and Seegers 2009). Indeed, the peacebuilding as stabilization perspective focuses on the interests and motivations of external peacebuilders and asks 'whose peace' is served by peacebuilding programmes and activities. In contrast to advocates of the peacebuilding as liberal governance view who believe in the shared benefits of liberalism, a stabilization perspective implicitly acknowledges that the benefits of post-conflict peacebuilding may be unequal and selective. While much of the peacebuilding as liberal governance literature focuses on African elites and their identities and interests as being the main obstacles to overcome and re-shape through peacebuilding, the stabilization literature puts the interests of external peacebuilders at the forefront. It highlights that global powers and institutions are not disinterested actors or neutral vessels, and that their post-conflict peacebuilding programmes are not divorced from other political interests.

Contrary to peacebuilding as liberal governance, this stabilization view holds less faith in the possibilities of transformation and socialization. If part of failure of post-conflict peacebuilding in Africa is perceived as Africans' stubborn attachment to parochial identities, peacebuilding as stabilization seeks to control the expression of those identities, without transforming them. Low-intensity conflict and localized violence or repression may be acceptable or perhaps inevitable under this view, so long as it does not affect international order and stability. Paradoxically then, increased militarization comes to be seen as peacebuilding.

Peacebuilding as stabilization and peacebuilding as liberal governance share a concern with order. For some critics, they are both part of a strategy to maintain the global status quo, with its inequalities and selective privileges intact. These intentions may be obscured by the universalist language of peacebuilding, but like similar concepts of human security, the 'responsibility to protect', and development, the aim is to subvert radical challenges to the global distribution of power and resources. While stabilization relies more heavily on external coercion and on building the coercive apparatus of the state, and liberal governance relies more extensively on building institutions and markets, both share a preoccupation with stability.

Peacebuilding as social justice

A third perspective on post-conflict peacebuilding emphasizes social justice. The peacebuilding as liberal governance framework would see an initiative to end discrimination against minority groups as a step towards order, and therefore peace. A social justice perspective would see the same initiative as a step towards justice, and therefore peace.

Under a peacebuilding as social justice framework, post-conflict peacebuilding can and should address structural violence, and not only the threat of direct physical violence (Francis 2002). Post-conflict peacebuilding therefore involves programmes to encourage inclusive access to resources and institutions, to empower marginalized groups, to end discrimination against women and other disadvantaged groups, and to redistribute income and land ownership. Peacebuilding is thus a powerful agenda and rallying cry through which deeply rooted inequalities and vulnerabilities can be addressed.

This perspective therefore provides a framework for understanding post-conflict peace-building activities and initiatives, but also makes moral claims about the purpose and desired outcomes of these activities. Advocates of peacebuilding as liberal governance believe that questions of social justice can and have been addressed within liberal frameworks. Critics, however, believe that liberal governance privileges order and the interests of the interveners, rather than justice. Thus peacebuilding as social justice has emerged as a substantive critique of peacebuilding programmes and initiatives that are based on geopolitics and donor self-interest. Advocates of peacebuilding as social justice focus their attention both on inequalities between Africa and the rest of the world, and inequalities within Africa.

For instance, many authors who take a social justice approach believe that peacebuilding cannot be divorced from a discussion of global capitalism and the distribution of the world's resources. Liberal peacebuilding tends to focus on how to restructure economies internally so that countries can attract foreign investment and be better integrated into the global economy. However, the networked economies in the DRC, Sierra Leone, Nigeria, Angola, Sudan, and South Sudan show that both violent conflict and peace are compatible with markets that are well integrated internationally, albeit unevenly. An emphasis on social justice raises questions about these networks and about unequal international economic relations. According to a social justice view, seeing uneven global capitalist structures as the indisputable and inevitable context for post-conflict peacebuilding severely limits possibilities.

In calling for a redistribution of resources both within countries and internationally, post-conflict peacebuilding as social justice echoes earlier claims made by dependency theorists such as Samir Amin, who believed that underdevelopment in Africa was linked to global capitalism. However, as Mahmood Mamdani (1997) points out, a social justice approach to peacebuilding also requires a focus on state structures, including the de-racialization of power, the redressing of systemic group disadvantage, and the formation of an inclusive, redefined political community at the level of the state.

Peacebuilding as local participation and ownership

The three previous perspectives see post-conflict peacebuilding as a series of activities and initiatives to help reach certain predetermined goals: liberal governance, stability, and social justice. A fourth perspective on post-conflict peacebuilding differs from the previous three in that it focuses on process rather than outcomes. Often, this is framed in terms of local participation and ownership.

The starting point for advocates of this view is the disjuncture between the peacebuilding requirements of African local communities and the goals of external peacebuilders. Thus, rather than being guided by external models and by the disciplining power of external norms, post-conflict peacebuilding gains meaning and value from within African countries and locales. This resonates with calls for local ownership and participation, which is believed to lead to more sustainable outcomes and institutions that are more widely accepted by local communities. This view of post-conflict peacebuilding opens up the space for participation by a broader range of actors, including faith-based leaders, representatives of ethnic communities, and others who may fall outside the parameters of the liberal peace.

This view therefore tends to reject the universalist assumptions of liberal peace and the presumed distinction between the liberal peacebuilder and illiberal 'other' underpinning the peacebuilding as stabilization approach. Likewise, it may raise questions about who determines the content of social justice, and indeed about the very premise that outside intervention can be characterized as peacebuilding.

Yet within this perspective there exists significant disagreement. A key question is whether continental and regional African institutions are better informed about the possibilities for post-conflict peacebuilding than their international counterparts, and whether they are the appropriate vehicles for local participation and ownership. The experiences of the AU, NEPAD, the African Development Bank (AfDB), and African sub-regional organizations suggest that these institutions tend to adopt similar peacebuilding logics to their international counterparts, relying heavily upon liberal governance and stabilization packages.

Devolving responsibility to post-conflict governments will not resolve ambiguities or satisfy the transformative aspirations of other local groups. Domestic elites tend to revert to strategies that reproduce their positions of power, and there is nothing to indicate that there is any more of a consensus on peacebuilding priorities among inhabitants within a country than outside.

Finally, it is notoriously difficult to discern who is the 'local' in local peacebuilding. Sometimes, local is used to mean the national country in which a post-conflict peacebuilding intervention takes place. Yet a national actor from the capital city may be an outsider when entering into another specific local community (Pouligny 2009: 175). The question of who is involved and who decides on process and priorities in post-conflict peacebuilding cannot be settled with a mere appeal to local participation and ownership.

The contested politics of post-conflict peacebuilding

The literature on the political economy of conflict in Africa suggests that peace and war often have much in common (Keen 2001; Richards 2005; Mwanasali 2000). During armed hostilities, belligerents and those associated with the conflict near and far have a diverse set of aims and interests, which do not always have to do with winning the war. Likewise, a post-conflict peace involves the negotiation and re-negotiation of interests and values without necessarily finding common ground or consensus. Gaining profits, sustaining livelihoods, promoting honour, and maintaining power can be aims pursued in both war and in peace. Since conflict and peace are often situated in internationalized networks, the large numbers of beneficiaries and losers to any programme, change, or intervention typically stretch beyond national borders.

The four different perspectives on post-conflict peacebuilding described above are not necessarily mutually exclusive, and institutions such as the UN and the AU use the language of all four. Furthermore, it is possible for the same actor or agency to hold a normative commitment toward social justice and local participation, but to encourage stabilization and/or liberal governance. In practice, however, certain goals and processes are prioritized and privileged over others by different actors, at different times, and in different places. Despite the common use of the language of peacebuilding, different institutions show important variation in the way that they conceptualize and operationalize peacebuilding. In a survey of 24 governmental and intergovernmental bodies active in peacebuilding, Barnett *et al.* (2007) show that there are great divisions among these bodies regarding the specific approaches to achieve peace, often depending on prevailing organizational mandates and interests.

These different approaches lead to tensions in peacebuilding programming and unintended consequences on the ground. Post-conflict processes and goals are fragmented, contradictory, and contested. For instance, in 2001 the Rwandan government instituted the *gacaca* jurisdictions to hear and judge the cases of genocide suspects (Clark, this volume). Supporters saw this as a home-grown, historically rooted way of achieving post-conflict reconciliation and justice in Rwanda. Critics saw it as the reinvention of tradition with the aim of further extending the power of a repressive Rwandan state. In Uganda, *mato oput* ceremonies have been discussed as a locally appropriate way to address community reconciliation in northern Uganda. Yet critics say that the emphasis on *mato oput* represents a convergence of interests between some foreign aid organizations and older male Acholi who want to reinforce their diminishing power. It is not something that is universally accepted among the Acholi (Allen 2007). Claims to universality should be suspect in any post-conflict peacebuilding programme or initiative.

Similarly, the very logic of a negotiated peace agreement can be very different for international peacebuilders and for local political competitors. Some international actors may view a peace agreement as a binding commitment between different belligerents that sets out a common vision for a post-conflict future, whereas the parties themselves may see it in instrumental and contextual terms. This happened in both the DRC and Sudan, where political elites adjusted their strategies to a changed context. Elites that were included in the peace agreements as well as elites that were excluded maintained the use or the threat of violence as a parallel tool in what Alex de Waal (2009) calls the political marketplace. In Burundi there have been repeated tensions between the government and the donor community over post-conflict peacebuilding priorities. Using the language of sovereignty, the Burundian government has tried to assert full control over the agenda, while at the same time ensuring the continuation of donor funds. Leaders in the DRC, Sierra Leone, and Liberia have made similar claims.

Post-conflict peacebuilding in Africa is therefore not solely a product of hegemonic external forces or a failed example of peacebuilding elsewhere. Africans are not passive recipients of post-conflict frameworks, policies, and programmes. Instead, they have at times adjusted, re-shaped, implemented, and subverted international peacebuilding strategies. In some cases, the large amounts of foreign aid that accompany post-conflict peacebuilding have been used by holders of state power as an additional rent that can be used for decidedly non-peaceful purposes (Englebert and Tull 2008: 123). When conflict ends through military victory as in Ethiopia, Rwanda, and Uganda, peacebuilding power dynamics are often different than in cases where conflict ended through a negotiated settlement. Different state-society relations in various African countries inevitably lead to different post-conflict political configurations.

Post-conflict peacebuilding is thus not a single script, but a set of ideas and practices, mediated by interactions between local communities, national, regional, and international actors. Rather than being viewed in terms of a specific goal, outcome, or process, post-conflict peacebuilding is the expression of continued contested politics. There is no independent perspective that can adjudicate between competing perspectives and normative commitments to post-conflict peacebuilding. All actors with a stake in post-conflict structures bring their own ideas, interests, norms and practices to a situation that is highly political and that may alter the local and international landscapes in expected and unexpected ways. Recent work on hybridity in peacebuilding, focusing on the interactions between multiple groups, practices, and worldviews, better captures the diverse agendas at play in any post-conflict arena (Mac Ginty 2011). Thinking of peacebuilding as contested ideas and practices opens the possibility that there may be multiple manifestations of peace within African societies and politics, and alternatives to peacebuilding as liberal governance. Oliver Richmond proposes unscripted conversations between local actors (Richmond 2009: 326, 328–29). Still, any conversation cannot be separate from relations of power, and the different conceptions of a post-conflict normative order have significant consequences. Much is at stake with peacebuilding in Africa, and continued violence often remains a very real possibility.

Conclusion

This chapter has highlighted the rise of post-conflict peacebuilding in sub-Saharan Africa, and the different activities and approaches commonly associated with it. In different ways and in different places, post-conflict peacebuilding engages with questions of security, political authority, economy, and society. Various approaches to post-conflict peacebuilding in Africa as elsewhere carry with them certain assumptions about how best to resolve these questions, and indeed which questions and whose interests take precedence over others. The result is a necessarily fragmented, contradictory, and polyvalent set of practices seeking to shape the nature and exercise of power in African countries emerging from conflict.

Ultimately post-conflict peacebuilding is a political contest, where peace is not a universally recognized object to discover or impose, but a set of contested ideas and practices. These contests play out differently in various parts of Africa and are contingent upon a wide set of factors. Across Africa, the political meanings of peace and peacebuilding are subject to continued negotiation and renegotiation between international, regional, and local actors. Masking the subjective nature of post-conflict peacebuilding disguises ideology and may obscure the various ways in which peace is understood and experienced in different African contexts.

Notes

1 The '2006 Human Security Brief' stated that the greatest decline in armed conflict around the world was in sub-Saharan Africa, and that sub-Saharan Africa was no longer the world's most conflict-affected region (Human Security Centre 2007: 26–31).
2 The chapter draws extensively from Curtis (2012), which presents an extended version of the argument here.
3 For more information visit the UNPBC website, www.un.org/en/peacebuilding/ (accessed 2 June 2012); see also Bellamy (2010).
4 Paragraph 9 sees new opportunities for peace now that 'many States are seeking more open forms of economic policy'; paragraph 56 talks of social and economic development; and paragraph 59 recommends the strengthening of new democratic institutions, the rule of law, and good governance (Boutros-Ghali 1992).

Bibliography

Ali, T. and Matthews, R.O. (eds) (2004) *Durable Peace: Challenges for Peacebuilding in Africa*, Toronto: University of Toronto Press.
Allen, T. (2007) 'The International Criminal Court and the Invention of Traditional Justice in Northern Uganda', *Politique Africaine* 107: 147–66.
Barnett, M., Kim, H., O'Donnell, M. and Sitea, L. (2007) 'Peacebuilding: What is in a Name?' *Global Governance* 13: 35–58.

Bellamy, A.J. (2010) 'The Institutionalisation of Peacebuilding: What Role for the UN Peacebuilding Commission', in O.P. Richmond (ed.) *Palgrave Advances in Peacebuilding: Critical Developments and Approaches*, London: Palgrave Macmillan.

Boutros-Ghali, B. (1992) *An Agenda for Peace: Preventive Diplomacy, Peacemaking and Peacekeeping*, New York, NY: United Nations.

Branch, A. (2011) *Displacing Human Rights: War and Intervention in Northern Uganda*, New York, NY, and Oxford: Oxford University Press.

Chandler, D. (2006) *Empire in Denial: The Politics of State-building*, London: Pluto Press.

Clapham, C. (1998) 'Rwanda: The Perils of Peacemaking', *Journal of Peace Research* 35(2): 193–210.

Curtis, D. (2012) 'The Contested Politics of Peacebuilding in Africa', in D. Curtis and G.A. Dzinesa (eds) *Peacebuilding, Power and Politics in Africa*, Ohio: Ohio University Press.

de Waal, A. (2009) 'Mission Without End? Peacekeeping in the African Political Marketplace', *International Affairs* 85(1): 99–113.

Duffield, M. (2002) 'Social Reconstruction and the Radicalization of Development Aid as a Relation of Global Liberal Governance', *Development and Change* 33(5): 1049–71.

ECOWAS (Economic Community of West African States) (2008) 'The ECOWAS Conflict Prevention Framework', MSC/REG 1/01/08.

Englebert, P. and Tull, D.M. (2008) 'Postconflict Reconstruction in Africa: Flawed Ideas about Failed States', *International Security* 32(4): 106–39.

Flint, J. and de Waal, A. (2005) *Darfur: A Short History of a Long War*, London: Zed Books.

Francis, D. (2002) *People, Peace and Power: Conflict Transformation in Action*, London: Pluto Press.

Galtung, J. (1969) 'Violence, Peace, and Peace Research', *Journal of Peace Research* 6(3): 167–91.

Heathershaw, J. and Lambach, D. (2008) 'Introduction: Post-Conflict Spaces and Approaches to Statebuilding', *Journal of Intervention and Statebuilding* 2(3): 269–89.

Human Security Centre (2007) 'Human Security Brief 2006', Vancouver: Liu Institute for Global Issues, University of British Columbia.

Human Security Report Project (2011) *Human Security Report 2009/2010: The Causes of Peace and the Shrinking Costs of War*, New York, NY: Oxford University Press.

Humphreys, M. and Weinstein, J. (2007) 'Demobilization and Reintegration', *Journal of Conflict Resolution* 51(4): 531–67.

Hutchful, E. (2012) 'Security Sector Governance and Peacebuilding', in D. Curtis and G.A. Dzinesa (eds) *Peacebuilding, Power and Politics in Africa*, Ohio: Ohio University Press.

Jarstad, A. and Sisk, T. (eds) (2008) *From War to Democracy: Dilemmas of Peacebuilding*, Cambridge: Cambridge University Press.

Keen, D. (2001) 'War and Peace: What's the Difference', in A. Adebajo and C.L. Sriram (eds) *Managing Armed Conflicts in the 21st Century*, London: Routledge.

MacGinty, R. (2011) *International Peacebuilding and Local Resistance: Hybrid Forms of Peace*, Basingstoke: Palgrave.

Mamdani, M. (1997) 'From Justice to Reconciliation: Making Sense of the African Experience', in C. Leys and M. Mamdani (eds) *Crisis and Reconstruction*, Uppsala: Nordisk Afrikainstitutet.

Murithi, T. (2008) 'African Indigenous and Endogenous Approaches to Peace and Conflict Resolution', in D. Francis (ed.) *Peace and Conflict in Africa*, London: Zed Books.

Mwanasali, M. (2000) 'The View from Below', in Mats Berdal and David Malone (eds) *Greed and Grievance*, Boulder, CO: Lynne Rienner Publishers.

Paris, R. (2004) *At War's End: Building Peace After Civil Conflict*, Cambridge and New York, NY: Cambridge University Press.

——(2010) 'Saving Liberal Peacebuilding', *Review of International Studies* 36: 3337–65.

Pouligny, B. (2009) 'Local Ownership', in V. Chetail (ed.) *Post-Conflict Peacebuilding: A Lexicon*, Oxford: Oxford University Press.

Pugh, M., Cooper, N. and Turner, M. (eds) (2008) *Whose Peace? Critical Perspectives on the Political Economy of Peacebuilding*, Basingstoke: Macmillan.

Richards, P. (ed.) (2005) *No Peace No War: An Anthropology of Contemporary Armed Conflict*, Oxford: James Currey.

Richmond, O.P. (2009) 'Becoming Liberal, Unbecoming Liberalism: Liberal-Local Hybridity via the Everyday as a Response to the Paradoxes of Liberal Peacebuilding', *Journal of Intervention and Statebuilding* 3(3): 324–44.

Sabaratnam, M. (2011) 'The Liberal Peace? An Intellectual History of International Conflict Management 1990–2010', in S. Campbell, D. Chandler and M. Sabaratnam (eds) *A Liberal Peace? The Problems and Practices of Peacebuilding*, London: Zed Books.

Schellhaas, C. and Seegers, A. (2009) 'Peacebuilding: Imperialism's New Disguise?' *African Security Review* 18(2): 1–15.

Stepanova, E. (2003) 'Anti-Terrorism and Peace-Building During and After Conflict', Stockholm: SIPRI.

UN (United Nations) (2000) 'Report of the Panel on United Nations Peace Operations (Brahimi Report)', A/55/305-S/2000/809.

——(2004) 'A More Secure World', Report of the Secretary-General's High Level Panel on Threats, Challenges and Change.

——(2005) 'In Larger Freedom', Report of the Secretary-General of the United Nations, September 2005.

van Houten, P. (2007) 'The World Bank's (Post)-Conflict Agenda: The Challenge of Integrating Development and Security', *Cambridge Review of International Affairs* 20(4): 639–57.

World Bank (2004) 'The Role of the World Bank in Conflict and Development: An Evolving Agenda', Washington, DC: World Bank Conflict Prevention and Reconstruction Unit.

——(2011) 'World Development Report 2011: Conflict, Security and Development', Washington, DC: The World Bank.

17

TRANSITIONAL JUSTICE AFTER ATROCITY

Phil Clark

Since the mid-1990s, transitional justice has become part and parcel of international and domestic responses to mass conflict and repressive rule in Africa. Incorporating a wide range of processes – including war crimes tribunals, truth commissions, reparations programmes, and community-based reintegration rituals – transitional justice is central to efforts to usher African societies from violence and authoritarianism to stability and democracy. Nearly all peace negotiations today involve calls for accountability for perpetrators of atrocities on the basis that dealing with the past is critical to securing the future.

As a broad field, transitional justice combines pragmatic and lofty aims, seeking to rebuild the physical, political, and judicial infrastructure of recovering societies, as well as reconciling fractured communities, reshaping contested memories, and healing emotional and psychological wounds. This combination of pragmatic and profound objectives reflects the enormous ambitions of transitional justice. It also highlights the wide range of societal concerns and actors that are captured by this field, with processes aimed at the regional, national, community, and individual levels.

The ubiquity, variety, and scope of transitional justice in Africa has generated considerable controversy. This chapter explores four key debates concerning the politics of transitional justice in Africa. First, it examines the ill-defined objectives of transitional justice. This opening section highlights that, while transitional justice mechanisms are commonly advocated to address the legacies of a divided past, their precise aims are rarely clear. Second, tensions between the specific aims of peace and justice have generated heated debates in a wide range of African transitional settings. This issue is especially prevalent following the advent of the International Criminal Court (ICC) and the growing expectation that transitional justice processes should operate during ongoing conflict and delicate peace negotiations. Third, this chapter examines issues of neo-colonialism and problems of external transitional justice interventions, including questions of power, domination, agency, and ownership. Such issues are paramount in Africa, given that most of the societies in question have long histories of colonial rule and fraught interactions with foreign donors, multilateral financial institutions, peacekeeping missions, and multinational corporations. Finally, the chapter explores tensions inherent in attempts to combine international, national, and community-level approaches to transitional justice. This final section highlights recent trends toward 'holistic' responses to conflict, which propose combinations of these different levels of processes. In Africa, such approaches have so far proven highly problematic, necessitating clearer thinking about the possible coordination of different types of actors and mechanisms.

Unclear objectives

There is no doubting the vastness of transitional justice aspirations. The immense challenges faced by societies recovering from conflict or draconian rule have not dampened the enthusiasm for transitional justice in Africa or the expectations of what these processes can achieve. Such ambitions, however, have rarely coincided with clarity about the objectives of these mechanisms. Transitional justice has tended to emphasise the importance of particular institutions – for example, a widespread belief in the need for prosecutions of atrocity perpetrators – without coherently articulating their ultimate purposes. This lack of clarity manifests in two forms: confusion over the meaning of common transitional justice objectives; and uncertainty over which objectives are best pursued by which transitional processes.

First, in scholarly and policy debates over justice, peace, truth, reconciliation, healing, and other concepts, it is not always clear what these terms mean. Both the South African Truth and Reconciliation Commission (TRC) and the International Criminal Tribunal for Rwanda (ICTR), for example, claim to pursue 'reconciliation' – the former through exchanging amnesty for truth about apartheid crimes, the latter through the prosecution of the most senior genocide suspects (UN 1995). In the TRC case, punishment and reconciliation were deemed to be incompatible, while the ICTR holds that punishment is a prerequisite of reconciliation. Such examples highlight that different transitional institutions often aim for different political, social, or legal outcomes. However, even when institutions claim to pursue the same objectives – as in the South African TRC's and the ICTR's stated pursuit of reconciliation – they (often unconsciously) define these objectives, and the means for achieving them, in very different ways. Judging such institutions according to their own stated aims and comparing them mean-ingfully when they claim to pursue similar objectives requires greater theoretical precision and clearer conceptions of key terms.

Second, transitional justice is replete with institutional 'toolkits', 'toolboxes', 'menus', and 'templates' (Franke 2006; Hamber 2009; ICTJ n.d.), proposing universal methods of addressing past atrocity. This tendency to implement certain ready-made models has precluded careful consideration of the *needs* of particular transitional settings, the *aims* they engender, and *which processes* are most appropriate to pursue particular objectives. The toolkit approach to transitional justice begins with institutions and appears to work backwards through questions of needs and objectives.

Regarding the justifications for transitional justice templates, their short-term objectives are often overly ambitious and their ultimate objectives are rarely explicit. In the short term, there is still major disagreement among transitional justice scholars and practitioners over what particular 'toolkit' institutions can feasibly achieve. Should international courts and tribunals aim only to prosecute suspects of serious crimes, or pursue more ambitious ends such as reconciliation? Can truth commissions feasibly aim to recover the truth about the past as well as facilitate healing, reconciliation, and some form of catharsis? Can single institutions realistically pursue multiple objectives and are those objectives themselves compatible? Connected to the earlier concern over conceptual clarity in transitional justice, the field still struggles to elucidate the precise purposes of common transitional processes. Expectations of such processes are often too high, necessitating clearer understandings of what particular approaches to transitional justice can practicably achieve.

Frequently, the broader aim of transitional justice is assumed to be democratization, facilitating the transition of societies toward governance and institutional structures that reflect liberal democratic concerns for individual freedoms, the protection of human rights, and the rule of law. This tendency no doubt derives from prevailing modernization and democratization theories in the early years of transitional justice. The close linkage between transitional justice and democratization, however, makes a teleological assumption that all societies should be encouraged toward similar forms of democracy. Such a view proves problematic when translated to the diverse political, social, cultural, and historical settings in which transitional justice takes place. Furthermore, it emphasizes forward-looking over backward-looking concerns, holding that redress for past wrongs should always contribute to future democratic entrenchment. The implied objective of democratization also privileges – with insufficient justification – society-wide concerns over the harm done to discrete individuals and groups. These concerns regarding objectives highlight important conceptual weaknesses at the heart of the entire transitional justice agenda. As argued below, these theoretical problems substantially affect the practice of transitional justice in Africa.

Peace versus justice and the role of human rights advocates

A symptom of under-developed transitional justice theory is a tendency toward binary debates: accountability versus amnesty, justice versus forgiveness, punishment versus reconciliation, retributive versus restorative justice, law versus politics, international versus local. In most cases, these terms are not mutually exclusive and conceiving them as such prevents the possibility of combining different objectives and approaches. It narrows the options and generates unhelpfully polarized discussions.

A central transitional justice debate in Africa concerns the tension between justice and peace. The conundrum of 'peace versus justice' has possessed the field from its earliest years, with scholars and practitioners debating whether justice – and especially punishment through international criminal proceedings – will contribute to peace by deterring potential perpetrators or impede it by prosecuting the same political and military leaders who are essential for viable negotiations. The debate pits 'realists', who believe the quest for peace and security should take precedence over justice, against 'idealists' and 'legalists', who argue that justice is both a good in and of itself, and necessary for long-term stability.

Such tensions were apparent in the early years of transitional justice processes in Africa. The South African TRC, drawing heavily on the experience of truth commissions in Central and South America during the 1980s and 1990s, held that attempts to prosecute those responsible for egregious crimes would only increase the likelihood of further violence. The political compromises that were central to the post-apartheid transition in South Africa barred the prosecution of apartheid leaders, provided they fully disclosed their political crimes. In the South African case, amnesty was seen as crucial to long-term stability and reconciliation. In contrast, the ICTR held that punishment of high-level Rwandan *génocidaires* was essential for reconciliation and durable peace, especially in terms of eradicating the culture of impunity that was considered a key enabler of the genocide in Rwanda.

While used by advocates on both sides of the 'peace versus justice' debate to support their respective positions, the South African and Rwandan examples say more about the impact of different types of political transitions on the choice of transitional justice mechanisms. In the South African case, amnesty was considered a necessity and justice a virtual impossibility during a negotiated transition characterized by political compromise. In the Rwandan case, where an outright military victory by the Rwandan Patriotic Front (RPF) had ended the genocide and facilitated transition to a new government, punishing the previous regime was viable and indeed desirable for both the RPF and the United Nations (UN), still smarting from its embarrassing failure to intervene militarily during the genocide. In these instances, decisions regarding peace or justice were determined more by political exigencies during transition than by high principle normative considerations.

The political scenario that has most energized the international field of transitional justice in recent years – and which has been definitive in the language of 'peace versus justice' – was the Juba peace talks between the Ugandan government and the Lord's Resistance Army (LRA) in 2006–08 (Waddell and Clark 2008). Advocates of 'retributive justice' through the ICC claimed that law should supersede politics and that any attempts to defer or remove the ICC indictments of the LRA leadership would contravene international law. On the other side, supporters of 'restorative justice' advocated the use of community cleansing and reintegration rituals for LRA combatants returning from the bush, and claimed that support for the ICC elevated abstract legal norms over the practical necessity of achieving peace in northern Uganda. Confined by the narrow conceptual architecture of the debate, the parties continually talked past each other, undermining the potential for creative solutions to the serious problems on the table in Juba.

These examples highlight the problems of the binary framing of debates such as 'peace versus justice'. Such a conceptualization suggests stark choices between polarized policy options. It precludes the possibility of sequencing, for example negotiating a lasting ceasefire before considering justice. It also presupposes that justice must entail punishment rather than other forms of accountability, such as perpetrator apologies, public acknowledgement of harm, and material reparation. During the Juba talks, these alternative formulations garnered some attention – principally among northern Ugandan civil society actors – but were stymied by the polarized debates among the negotiators and their principal interlocutors.

A key generator of this polarization at Juba was the influence of human rights organizations, which prescribed narrow legal responses to the northern Ugandan conflict. A constant stream of advocacy reports and press releases from Amnesty International (AI), Human Rights Watch (HRW), and others throughout the negotiations proclaimed the ICC as the only justifiable response to crimes committed during the conflict and rejected outright other potential approaches, including local reintegration rituals, reform of the national civilian and military courts, and national reparations programmes (AI 2008a, 2008b; HRW 2008). Such claims were made on the basis of generalized legal principles and obligations, rather than the specific political and social circumstances in Uganda.

This points to a larger problem in transitional justice. The field balances uneasily between analysis and advocacy, which is further complicated by the fact that many academics and practitioners engage in both processes. Human rights actors have been powerful in transitional justice from the outset, providing many of its intellectual, institutional, and financial resources. Advocacy organizations such as AI and HRW play a central role in many transitional justice debates. The influence of such advocates, however, has not been universally positive. Human rights ideology – a firm belief, for example, in the need for international judicial responses to human rights violations – has often trumped finer-grained theoretical and empirical analysis, leading to 'faith-based' rather than 'fact-based' prescriptions (Thoms *et al.* 2008: 5). These ideologically based influences undermine the ability objectively to question certain assumptions. In particular, what if the advocated responses to massive violations diverge from particular conditions and context-specific needs within transitional societies? The fervent certainty of much human rights advocacy has generated unnecessarily polarized debates and often hampered the tasks of impartial research and informed policymaking.

Neo-colonialism and challenges of foreign transitional justice interventions

A further criticism of the ICC and international justice generally emanating from the Juba talks was that such approaches represent the neo-colonial imposition of external force on African societies. Such critiques proliferated following the ICC's indictment of Sudanese President Omar al-Bashir in July 2008. Critics of the ICC – including the leadership of the African Union (AU) – viewed this as a violation of the principles of national sovereignty and sovereign immunity. By this reckoning, as an attempt at regime change via international law, the Bashir indictment was rendered even more egregious by the fact that Sudan was not a signatory to the Rome Statute and therefore had not formally recognized the legitimacy of the Court.

The ICC and ICTR have not always responded effectively to accusations of neo-colonial interventions. International transitional justice institutions have often displayed hubris and expressed a civilizing mission toward African societies recovering from conflict or authoritarian rule. Based in The Hague and Arusha, respectively, far from the immediate sites of conflict, such institutions have often treated Africa as a blank canvas for their judicial artistry, seemingly unaware of the continent's history of fraught engagement with myriad external powers and the impact of this on their own legitimacy. As discussed further in the final section, international courts and tribunals have also rarely sought to coordinate their operations with domestic transitional processes or expressed coherently how they contribute meaningfully to affected communities. These tendencies have fuelled claims of neo-colonial arrogance and political meddling. Concerns over criticisms of lofty detachment are a key reason for the recent trend in creating 'hybrid' tribunals, such as the Special Court for Sierra Leone, which are located inside conflict-affected countries and employ both international and national personnel (Kelsall 2009).

Depictions of all-powerful international institutions interfering with fragile domestic states and populations, however, are too stark. The ICC and ICTR have typically struggled to investigate and prosecute cases without the cooperation of African states, which in turn have proven highly effective at using international justice to their own ends (Clark 2011; Peskin 2008). When then-ICTR chief prosecutor Carla del Ponte threatened in 2002 to investigate post-genocide revenge attacks committed by the RPF, the Rwandan government responded by barring the travel of ICTR investigators to Rwanda, and Rwandan witnesses to Arusha, effectively halting the Tribunal's operations.

In the case of the ICC, the Office of the Prosecutor entered into lengthy negotiations with the Ugandan and Congolese governments before those states agreed to refer their situations to the Court. Having 'chased' these state referrals, the ICC was forced to negotiate the terms of its investigations with those governments (Clark 2011). This largely explains why, to date, the ICC has not charged any Ugandan or Congolese government officials, despite the widely acknowledged complicity of state actors in atrocities. In Sudan, Bashir has stymied the ICC's operations by refusing to allow the Court's investigators on the ground. In the meantime, he has often succeeded in generating domestic sympathy in the face of the Court's 'Western intervention', thus bolstering his domestic legitimacy. These examples highlight the ability of African states to instrumentalize international justice for their own political gain. This critical agency of African governments is often overlooked in debates over neo-colonialism and the legitimacy of international transitional justice interventions.

Hybridity and holism: linking international, national, and community-based approaches

Hybridity is an increasingly common theme in the study and practice of transitional justice. In recent years, a growing trend has emerged in institutional responses to complex conflict situations that advocates 'legal pluralism', or hybrid structures in which 'two or more legal systems coexist in the same social field' (Merry 1988: 870). Today, legal pluralism usually involves some type of international criminal tribunal and a locally directed truth commission, as in the cases of Sierra Leone and Burundi. The primary purpose of such hybridity is to facilitate holism. A holistic approach to transitional justice provides that multiple political, social, and legal institutions, operating concurrently in a system maximizing the capabilities of each, can contribute more effectively to the reconstruction of the entire society than a single institution. Holistic approaches cater to the various physical, psychological, and psychosocial needs of individuals and groups during, as well as after, conflict.

The trend toward hybrid systems coincides with the greater legitimacy afforded to and more regular use of localized methods of accountability and conflict resolution, which are often designed to augment international and national processes. In 2004 then-UN Secretary-General Kofi Annan stated that in the context of transitional societies, 'due regard must be given to indigenous and informal traditions for administering justice or settling disputes to help them to continue their often vital role and to do so in conformity with both international standards and local tradition' (UN Secretary-General 2004: 12).

It is becoming increasingly popular in Africa to employ forms of local or traditional dispute resolution in response to serious atrocities. In many cases, traditional mechanisms have been co-opted by political elites and modified so that they bear only a cosmetic resemblance to their antecedent institutions, calling into question the legitimacy of referring to these institutions as 'indigenous' or 'traditional'. The impetus for community-level transitional justice emanates from various sources, including: the need for faster and cheaper mechanisms to handle enormous backlogs of community-level perpetrators; a frustration with international approaches to transitional justice, especially war crimes tribunals, which focus only on high-level suspects in conflicts that involve multiple levels of actors; and a desire for local ownership in situations where a wide range of external political, social, and economic interventions have constrained domestic agency.

In the last decade, the Great Lakes region, in particular, has witnessed various forms of customary or revived traditional practices designed to deal with questions of mediation, justice, and reconciliation after mass atrocity. Between 1999 and 2004, the *Barza Inter-Communautaire* in the eastern Democratic Republic of Congo (DRC) assembled the cultural leaders of the nine major ethnic groups in North Kivu to mediate ethnic-based disputes. Over those five years, the Barza ensured there was no major outbreak of violence in its sphere of influence. In Rwanda since 2001, the community-level *gacaca* jurisdictions became the principal instrument for dealing with the country's backlog of genocide cases: by the time the courts closed on 18 June 2012, they had prosecuted nearly 400,000 genocide suspects. In 2006, in the midst of the Juba peace talks, a Ugandan parliamentary committee was established to consider whether local, particularly Acholi, rituals could be codified and nationalized, similar to Rwanda's reform and formalization of the *gacaca* courts. Not all Ugandan government or civil society advocates of local rituals in the context of serious crimes, however, believed they should be codified and nationalized. Some actors argued that different ethnic groups should employ their specific ritual methods, and that attempts to codify a nationwide system of rituals would suppress much of their cultural specificity and thus undermine their popular legitimacy.

Increasingly in African states, international, national, and community-level transitional justice processes coincide and frequently clash. Advocates of 'holism' often support this multi-level approach to transitional justice. Such approaches, however, are typically the product of accident rather than design, with different actors creating different levels of institutions at different times, with little coordination among them. The Great Lakes region, in particular, has become the focus of multi-tiered transitional justice: in the case of Rwanda through the ICTR, the Rwandan national courts, and *gacaca*; and in the cases of Uganda and the DRC through the ICC, the national military and civilian courts, and a range of community-level accountability and reconciliation mechanisms.

The ICTR and the ICC are founded, respectively, on the principles of 'stratified-concurrent jurisdiction' and 'complementarity', which assume close coordination with, and respect for, domestic transitional institutions. However, in practice these international institutions have tended to compete with domestic institutions for popular legitimacy and for jurisdiction over particular criminal cases. There has often been bad blood between the ICTR and Rwandan transitional institutions, as exemplified by the issue of RPF crimes discussed above. The concurrent operation of the ICTR, the Rwandan national courts, and *gacaca* has also on several occasions led to clashes over whether international or domestic bodies have jurisdiction over particular suspects (Gourevitch 1996: A15; Mutagwera 1996: 17–36). In recent years, the ICTR, under pressure from the UN to halt its operations because of the Tribunal's enormous expense, has nevertheless refused to transfer its residual cases to the Rwandan courts, claiming that the national jurisdictions do not meet international judicial standards and therefore genocide suspects would not receive a fair trial in Rwanda. These developments suggest an antagonistic rather than holistic relationship between international and domestic institutions.

Similarly, there has been little interaction between the ICC and domestic processes in countries such as Uganda and the DRC. Where there has been interaction, it has tended to be competitive. The example of the DRC, where all of the ICC's operations have so far focused on Ituri province, is salient in this regard. Ituri provided the ICC with a simpler judicial task than other provinces. Of the conflict-affected provinces of the DRC, Ituri has the best-functioning local judiciary, which has already proven adept at investigating serious crimes (Clark 2011). Since July 2003, the European Commission's (EC) Ituri-centred investment of more than US $40 million towards reforming the Congolese judiciary has seen considerable progress in strengthening local capacity. The EC funded the purchase of new judicial offices and equipment, and provided training and salaries for investigators and magistrates. Since 2003 the UN Organization Mission in the Democratic Republic of the Congo (MONUC) has provided around-the-clock protection to all judges in Bunia, the provincial capital. These developments have contributed greatly to the increased efficiency of the Bunia judiciary.

In 2006 the military tribunal in Bunia prosecuted the case of Chef Mandro Panga Kahwa, a senior member of the UPC and later founder and president of the *Parti de l'Unité et la Sauvegarde de l'Intégrité du* Congo (PUSIC, Party of Unity to Safeguard the Integrity of Congo). Kahwa, found guilty of crimes against humanity, including the murder of villagers in Zumbe in 2002, was sentenced to 20 years in prison and ordered to compensate 14 of his victims up to $75,000 each (see Trial Watch). Among other serious cases before the Bunia courts, in 2008 the same military tribunal convicted a Congolese army lieutenant and sergeant for the use of rape and threats of violence against civilians in Fataki and Nioka (UN 2008: section 34).

That the Bunia courts have been able to investigate and prosecute such serious cases, involving rebel leaders and senior Congolese military personnel, highlights the substantial increase in domestic judicial capacity since the start of the EC reform programme. It is therefore unclear whether the ICC can adequately justify its involvement in Ituri, given the capacity of domestic institutions to investigate and prosecute major crimes. This has led some observers to question the validity of the ICC's strategy in Ituri, asking why a global court has focused its energies where the judicial task is more straightforward due to substantial local capacity, while mass atrocities continue in provinces where judicial resources are severely lacking. The domestic impact of the ICC's interventions in Ituri has been widespread disappointment among local judicial actors that despite the major legal reforms of the last seven years, they will not be able to prosecute major atrocity suspects in local courtrooms. This has important ramifications for the long-term legitimacy and efficacy of the domestic judiciary. It also leads some domestic judicial actors to believe they are receiving mixed messages from the international community, which has invested heavily in legal reform but maintains that such reforms are insufficient to warrant domestic trials of high-profile suspects (Clark 2011).

The examples of the ICTR and ICC highlight that while international transitional justice institutions employ the language of coordination and cooperation, in practice they tend to function unilaterally and often perceive domestic institutions as falling short of global standards of justice. This underscores a key problem for attempts at holistic, multi-level approaches to transitional justice, which require trust among foreign and domestic actors, and clear divisions of jurisdiction. Such issues are exacerbated by the problem of unclear objectives, discussed above, as effective coordination of different institutions first requires an articulation of the purposes of different types of processes. Thus, to date, multi-level transitional justice processes have tended to operate separately rather than systematically.

Conclusion

This chapter has not been an exhaustive analysis of transitional justice in Africa but rather an overview of the key theoretical and policy tensions in this field. Its aim is to highlight the need for greater clarity when identifying and conceptualizing the objectives of transitional justice, determining which types of processes best pursue those aims, and navigating complex politics when international, national, and community-level actors and institutions intersect.

Certain human rights and legal discourses have often hampered transitional justice endeavours in Africa by advocating narrow judicial responses to atrocity and paying insignificant attention to power relations between foreign and domestic agents. For the field of transitional justice to provide meaningful redress to the legacies of conflict and authoritarianism, it must identify more feasible objectives and tailor policy responses more carefully to the specific needs of affected populations. It must also guard against the tendencies of international legal actors toward hubris and detachment from local circumstances, and of domestic governments to instrumentalize transitional processes for their own ends. Thus the grand ambitions of transitional justice may be gradually turned into more tangible benefits for communities affected by atrocity.

Bibliography

AI (Amnesty International) (2008a) 'Government Cannot Negotiate Away International Criminal Court Arrest Warrants for LRA', 20 February 2008, AI Index: PRE01/056/2008.

——(2008b) 'Uganda: Agreement and Annex on Accountability and Reconciliation Falls Short of a Comprehensive Plan to End Impunity', 1 March 2008, AI Index: AFR 59/001/2008.

Clark, P. (2010) *The Gacaca Courts, Post-Genocide Justice and Reconciliation in Rwanda: Justice without Lawyers*, Cambridge: Cambridge University Press.

——(2011) 'Chasing Cases: The ICC and the Politics of State Referral in Uganda and the Democratic Republic of Congo', in C. Stahn and M. El Zeidy (eds) *The International Criminal Court and Complementarity: Theory and Practice*, Cambridge: Cambridge University Press.

Franke, K. (2006) 'Gendered Subjects of Transitional Justice', *Columbia Journal of Gender and Law* 15(3): 813–28.

Gourevitch, P. (1996) 'Justice in Exile', *The New York Times*, 24 June 1996: A15.

Hamber, B. (2009) *Transforming Societies after Political Violence: Truth, Reconciliation, and Mental Health*, New York, NY: Springer.

HRW (Human Rights Watch) (2008) 'Benchmarks for Justice for Serious Crimes in Northern Uganda: Human Rights Watch Memoranda on Justice Standards and the Juba Peace Talks', www.hrw.org/news/2008/09/01/benchmarks-justice-serious-crimes-northern-uganda (accessed 28 February 2012).

ICTJ (International Center for Transitional Justice) (n.d.) 'What is Transitional Justice?' http://ictj.org/about/transitional-justice (accessed 7 February 2012).

Kelsall, T. (2009) *Culture Under Cross-Examination: International Justice and the Special Court for Sierra Leone*, Cambridge: Cambridge University Press.

Merry, S.E. (1988) 'Legal Pluralism', *Law and Society Review* 22(5): 869–901.

Mutagwera, F. (1996) 'Détentions et Poursuites Judiciaires au Rwanda', in J.-F. Dupaquier (ed.) *La Justice Internationale face au Drame Rwandais*, Paris: Karthala Editions.

Peskin, V. (2008) *International Justice in Rwanda and the Balkans: Virtual Trials and the Struggle for State Cooperation*, Cambridge, and New York, NY: Cambridge University Press.

Thoms, O., Ron, J. and Paris, R. (2008) 'The Effects of Transitional Justice Mechanisms: A Summary of Empirical Research Findings and Implications for Analysts and Practitioners', Centre for International Policy Studies Working Paper, University of Ottawa.

Trial Watch (n.d.) 'Yves Mandro Kahwa Panga', www.trial-ch.org/en/trial-watch/profile/db/legal-procedures/yves_mandro-kahwa-panga_576.html (accessed 3 March 2012).

UN (United Nations) (1995) 'Statute of the International Criminal Tribunal for Rwanda', www.un.org/ictr/statute.html (accessed 2 March 2012).

——(2008) 'Human Rights Monthly Assessment: March 2008', Section 34.

UN Secretary-General (2004) 'Report of the Secretary-General on the Rule of Law and Transitional Justice in Conflict and Post-Conflict Societies', 12, UN Document No. S/2004/616, 23 August.

Waddell, N. and Clark, P. (eds) (2008) *Courting Conflict? Justice, Peace and the ICC in Africa*, London: Royal African Society.

PART IV

Democracy and electoral politics

18

ELECTORAL AUTHORITARIANISM AND MULTI-PARTY POLITICS

Nicolas van de Walle

The wave of democratization that swept through sub-Saharan Africa in the early 1990s brought about substantial political change (Lindberg 2006; Bratton and van de Walle 1997). Within a decade of independence, all but a small handful of African states had evolved into military and police dictatorships. Through the 1970s and 1980s, Botswana and Mauritius were the only countries in the region to hold regular competitive multi-party elections, and incumbent governments lost power only in the latter. The other African states generally either suspended all political party activity, or promoted a single party, closely tied to the state. Elections were neither regularly convened nor competitive. Most allowed only a single party to compete and constituted little more than participatory rituals. This all changed with the wave of democratization in the early 1990s, and by the end of the first decade of the twenty-first century, most sub-Saharan African countries had held multiple multi-party elections. Most now formally recognize the legitimacy of various political and civil rights, even if the exercise of competitive politics often falls far short of democratic ideals, and even if the same rights constitutions promised on paper are rarely practised with much conviction or consistency. Between 1989 and 2010, some 43 different African countries held 164 multi-party legislative elections and 132 presidential elections. Although incumbents won most of these elections, they did result in a significant number of power alternations, and opposition parties enjoyed ample representation in a range of legislatures.

In other words, multi-party politics has become the norm in the region over the course of the last two decades (see Lindberg, this volume). This chapter attempts to make sense of this period by focusing on the nature of party competition in the region and its relationship with the quality of democracy that is being practiced. The evidence suggests that party competition in Africa continues to be marked by the dominance of the incumbent party, and that most of the countries in the region are better understood as electoral autocracies than democracies, even if it would be wrong to underestimate the democratic progress that has been made. The chapter suggests that political parties play a critical role in the consolidation of democracy, so a lot can be learned by assessing their role in Africa today. Perhaps not surprisingly, given the continuing importance of political clientelism in the region, incumbent parties dominate politics, usually thanks to the discretionary utilization of state resources for political ends. The modal party system in the region combines a dominant party in power with a large number of relatively small and weak opposition parties. Nonetheless, a process of institutionalization has begun, and the strength of opposition parties is positively correlated with both the level of democracy and the duration of democratic politics. The chapter starts with a description of Africa's range of regimes today. It then examines the dominant form of political regime in the region, electoral autocracy. The next section then analyses the impact of electoral authoritarianism on the kinds of party systems emerging in the region. A concluding section offers some tentative predictions for the future.

Africa's range of regimes

The generalization of multi-party politics in the region disguises the considerable variation in the level of democracy actually being practised. The 2010 Freedom House scores help underscore the political variation present today on the continent. Freedom House rates nine countries in Africa as 'free' in 2010, followed by 23 as 'partly free' and 16 as 'not free' (see Table 18.1). The overwhelming majority of these states convene regular elections, but in fact, only the nine countries in the 'free' category appear to be in the process of consolidating fairly robust democratic institutions, with genuine checks and balances, a free press and a reasonably independent judiciary.

Virtually all African states continue to be characterized by presidentialism, in the sense that the formal and informal powers of the presidency and the president himself (as of publication, Africa has had only one female president, Ellen Johnson-Sirleaf in Liberia) have been preponderant (van de Walle 2003). Before the recent democratization, the region's 'big man' politics meant

Table 18.1 Freedom House scores, Africa, 2010

Free	Partly free	Not free
Cape Verde (1,1)	Lesotho (3,3)	Angola (6,5)
Ghana (1,2)	Senegal (3,3)	Congo-B (6,5)
Mauritius (1,2)	Sierra Leone (3.3)	Côte d'Ivoire (6,5)
Benin (2,2)	Comoros (3,4)	Gabon (6,5)
Namibia (2,2)	Liberia (3,4)	Mauritania (6,5)
São Tomé & Príncipe (2,2)	Malawi (3,4)	Rwanda (6,5)
South Africa (2,2)	Mozambique (4,3	Cameroon (6,6)
Botswana (3,2)	Tanzania (4,3)	Congo-K (6,6)
Mali (2,3)	Zambia (3,4)	Swaziland (7,5)
	Burkina Faso (5,3)	Zimbabwe (6,6)
	Guinea Bissau (4,4)	Chad (7,6)
	Kenya (4,4)	Guinea (7,6)
	Burundi (4,5)	Equatorial Guinea (7,7)
	Niger (5,4)	Eritrea (7,7)
	Nigeria (5,4)	Somalia (7,7)
	Togo (5,4)	Sudan (7,7)
	Uganda (5,4)	
	CAR (5,5)	
	Djibouti (5,5)	
	Ethiopia (5,5)	
	Gambia (5,5)	
	Madagascar (6,4)	

Source: Freedom House, www.freedomhouse.org.
Note: Numbers in parentheses are the 2010 Freedom House scores for political rights and civil liberties, respectively, where 1 indicates the most free or democratic and 7 the most repressive.

that the president could be quite literally above the law, with substantial discretion over the resources of the national budget, the irrelevance of terms of office, and with unchecked powers of appointment (Bayart 1989; Bratton and van de Walle 1997). Even in the most democratic states of the region, this presidentialism persists to this day. Botswana, Mauritius, South Africa and Lesotho have parliamentary systems, and several Francophone states have semi-parliamentary systems; in addition, recent power-sharing agreements in Zimbabwe and Kenya include semi-presidentialism. Otherwise more than 40 of the 48 countries in the region have presidential constitutions. Moreover, the formal powers of the presidency tend to be quite expansive relative to the other branches of government. These include limits on legislative prerogatives, the presidency's powers of decree, discretion over civil service and judicial appointments, control over key revenue sources, such as natural resource parastatals, and general budgetary discretion.

One key dimension of democratization is thus necessarily the circumscription of presidential power, largely through the development and strengthening of institutions of accountability. Elections and political parties provide the main institutions of vertical accountability and are discussed below. Here, the institutions of horizontal accountability – the legislature and judiciary – deserve a brief mention.

Across the region, legislatures have become stronger, thanks to the efforts of a more independent, younger and better-educated cadre of legislators and, in some cases, the pressures of the opposition. Donor-funded efforts to build capacity within specific legislatures have also borne fruit, but the formal and informal powers of most African legislatures remain very much subordinated to the presidency, which continues to dominate the legislature, through some combination of constitutional power, a substantial presidential majority within the house, the president's appointment powers and a culture of deference to the executive that is hard to overcome (Barkan, this volume). Much the same could be said about judiciaries across the region (Prempeh 1999), where if anything, issues of low capacity and professionalism are even more pressing. Although the apex of the judicial sector has played an often brave and proactive role in promoting the consolidation of democracy, the routine work of the judicial sector is undermined by under-qualified judges, inadequate resources and various forms of corruption.

The emergence of electoral authoritarianism

Most of the countries in the 'partly free' and 'not free' categories in Table 18.1 combine more or less competitive regular elections with more traditional authoritarian practices to ensure that the incumbents never face real political challenges. Democratic government, with regular elections, has become a kind of political default, because of its widespread legitimacy both within Africa and in the donor community. At the same time, the pressures for further democratization do not appear irresistible, and incumbents have many instruments and resources at their disposal to maintain the various advantages that tilt the playing field in their favour.

A multitude of terms have been used to characterize these 'hybrid' regimes (Diamond 2002; van de Walle 2001), which combine democratic institutions and authoritarian practices, from 'façade' democracies (Joseph 1998), to 'competitive authoritarianism' (Levitsky and Way 2002, 2010). This chapter will use the expression 'electoral authoritarianism' because it best conveys the sense that these regimes remain authoritarian in nature despite the convening of regular multi-party elections. Can all these states be viewed as a single, distinctive regime, as Levitsky and Way have argued? Such a regime type seems problematic for two reasons. First, the category is essentially unstable; indeed, instability is one of its defining characteristics, because it is difficult to remain at the same level of semi-democracy for very long. Incumbents become more tolerant of dissent when they feel secure, or they increase repression levels when their rule is threatened. The example of Zimbabwe over the course of the last 20 years is compelling in this respect: has the fundamental nature of the Mugabe regime changed, or has Mugabe since 2000 exhibited the various anti-democratic tendencies of his regime that were always there, as his grip on power has weakened? Many observers of the regime would argue the latter (for instance, see Kriger 2005). Much the same could be said of such regimes as Gabon, Angola or Cameroon, in which the degree of repression has oscillated over time as a function of the political needs of regimes that appear quite stable.

Second, the category covers a very wide variety of regimes, from electoral regimes that fall just short of adequate political and civil rights, to thuggish dictatorships with a thin veneer of electoral respectability. One solution is to sub-divide the category into a more precise classification, but the gain in precision is probably offset by the loss of generalizability. Ultimately, the 'electoral autocracy' terminology is heuristically useful to designate a common general kind of political system, but it does not approach the analytical precision of a taxonomic category.

The predominance of electoral autocracies in the region leads to a key question: is Africa's wave of democratization over? In our assessment of democratization, how much should we weigh the authoritarian reversals, such as the one in Congo-Brazzaville, which brought back to power another wily old strongman, Sassou Nguesso, at the end of a brutal civil war (Clark 2007)? What should we think of countries like Cameroon, Gabon or Tanzania, in which the old guard remain very much in power despite regular elections? Are these regimes still, slowly but surely, moving towards democratization or not?

Two distinct theoretical responses have been made to these questions. The first, pessimistic, response can be identified as the 'end of the transition paradigm' view and is associated with Thomas Carothers, who argues that these countries are mostly condemned to alternate between unstable and imperfect democratic periods and more autocratic phases, as they lack the structural requisites of full-fledged democracy, are undermined by some combination of ethnic conflict, inconsistent economic growth and weak institutions (Carothers 2002). There is certainly evidence from Africa to support the Carothers view. With empirical support, Prempeh (2008) argues that throughout the region, even in the more democratic countries, the president remains 'untamed', and endowed with all sorts of legal and administrative privileges that make him less accountable to voters and to the other branches of government. Rakner and van de Walle (2009) point to the continuing weakness of opposition parties across the region, and the rarity of incumbent defeats, to suggest that in most countries, alternation in power remains highly unlikely. Joseph (2008) also laments low levels of presidential accountability and emphasizes the lack of progress over the course of the last 10 years in most African countries.

The other, more optimistic view is what Lindberg (this volume) has called the 'electoral path to democratization'. This view suggests that democracy has become the only legitimate form of government, and that every electoral competition advances the prospects for democracy. In part, democracy is a learning process: with every election, the democratic machinery (ballot counting and reporting, election monitoring, party organization and so on), gains strength. Yet the evidence that elections have advanced democracy over the course of the last several decades is mixed. The different contributions in Lindberg (2009) advance evidence for and against it, though with a slight tilt on its behalf. The analysis of elections in Africa suggests their quality is, if not rapidly improving, certainly not worsening in democratic quality (Lindberg 2006). Posner and Young (2007) argue that democracy is in the process of being institutionalized in the region, pointing to the increasing tendency of Africans to institute democratic safeguards such as term limits or independent electoral commissions.

However, term limits are only likely to have a significant impact if they promote transfers of power. Following Huntington (1991), most scholars agree that alternation of the executive is both the ultimate test of democracy and the best way to move democratization forward. What factors account for alternation? Maltz (2007) and Cheeseman (2010) have shown that an open-seat election is the single best predictor of an opposition victory. Much alternation on the continent is thus possible because a sitting president decided to respect term limits and/or to retire, and his party's choice to succeed him was unable to get elected.

The ability of the opposition to defeat the incumbent president who decides to run is of course itself a measure of the democratic quality of the political system. Such African presidents as Laurent Gbagbo in Côte d'Ivoire, Robert Mugabe in Zimbabwe and Paul Biya in Cameroon remained in power, despite having almost certainly lost an election, because the opposition is not able to force the president's ouster.

In addition, however, it is useful to examine the factors that enhance the possibility of alternation, at a given level of democratic quality. A standard argument is that opposition cohesion is a necessary pre-requisite for opposition success. Clearly, the ability of presidents to divide the opposition typically has been key in allowing them to stay in power. Most notoriously, Daniel arap Moi won the Kenyan elections in 1992 with a small plurality of the vote, because the opposition could never agree on a single candidate. Presidents Bongo in Gabon and Biya in Cameroon have also proved brilliant at this game, which has reduced the need for them to engage in outright repression. Presidential control over patronage and state resources suggests that this strategy is often available to the executive. One factor that does seem to facilitate alternation is a two-round majority voting system because the period between the two rounds of voting facilitates negotiation between the candidates of the opposition (van de Walle 2007).

In the end, the death or retirement of the incumbent president appears to represent an important watershed for Africa's electoral autocracies and provide perhaps the most likely pathway for political reform for many of these countries. Revealingly, in countries like the Democratic Republic of Congo (DRC), Gabon, and Togo, the death of the president resulted in a dynastic evolution, with sons taking over executive power, assuring the stability of the status quo. Additionally, in the case of Djibouti, the 1999 retirement of Hassan Gouled resulted in the presidency of his hand-picked nephew, Ismaïl Omar Guelleh. However, the exit from power of long-standing presidents brought about significant democratic breakthroughs in such countries as Kenya (2002), Ghana (2001) and, more problematically, Guinea (2008). In general, electoral autocracies appear to be threatened by power transfers, in part because their democratic failures undermine their long-term legitimacy, and in part because political power has been centralized around individual strong men, who were typically loathe to name a successor. The death or retirement of these long-standing presidents places strong pressures on the political systems to increase the institutionalization of political dynamics, unless the political elite can agree on a clear heir.

Emerging party systems

Having described the electoral autocracies that predominate in the region, this chapter turns its attention to the key role of political parties in shaping national political dynamics. Political parties typically play a key role in democratic political systems because they aggregate citizen preferences and give them voice and coherence. When effective, opposition parties in particular can use their organization and ability to mobilize voters and promote mass political participation that serves as a check on state power (Sartori 1976). Moreover, citizens are more likely to feel politically efficacious when they believe that strong parties represent their views effectively. Similarly, well-represented and robust parties in the legislature can constitute an effective check on presidential power. Thus, a number of scholars have argued compellingly that the stability of party systems and the strength of opposition parties are particularly important for the success of democratization in low-income countries, where other structural factors favourable to democracy are likely to be weaker (Linz and Stepan 1996; Randall and Svasand 2002).

The halting and inconsistent consolidation of democratic rule in Africa is in part characterized by the weakness of political parties, particularly those in the opposition. Even in the more democratic states, parties remain weak and poorly institutionalized, though the evidence suggests a small, positive correlation between democratic consolidation and party strength (Kuenzi and Lambright 2005; Rakner and van de Walle 2009). The institutionalization of party systems in the region has been disappointing, at least given the high hopes brought about by democratization almost two decades ago. The African parties that compete in elections today remain relatively young and inexperienced, and have not always proved able to survive more than one or two electoral cycles, fragmenting or consolidating with other parties. Thus, Kuenzi and Lambright report that the average age of parties in their data set of 33 African cases that had managed to win at least 10 per cent of the seats in a national parliamentary election was just 21.5 years, well under half of the mean age of parties in a similar sample of Latin American cases (Kuenzi and Lambright 2005: 431).

The weakness of opposition parties is in part a reflection of experience and in part a structural problem of funding. Experience plays a role in the sense that it takes time to develop effective party organizations. Because elections usually occur only every four or five years, and multiple electoral cycles are needed to master the technology of campaigning, voter registration and mobilization, and electoral monitoring, the performance of political parties improves only slowly. Reassuringly for the future of democracy in the region, Kuenzi and Lambright (2005) find that countries with a greater experience of electoral politics tend to have more stable party systems, but this process is likely to prove slow and incremental.

In addition, moreover, a tremendous disparity is likely to remain between the funding available to African opposition and incumbent parties. Opposition parties lack the resources to contest presidential power effectively, and presidential resources can and have been used effectively to undermine them. The incumbent party can tap into a wide variety of state resources. Not only can the incumbent obtain support through timely public spending, but party cadres can be given jobs in the administration and campaigns can be supported with the resources of the state administration, as when campaign workers use state transportation, or the police are used to discourage opposition rallies and hassle opposition party activities, and the state media is used to discredit the opposition.

For their part, opposition parties usually cannot rely on the membership fees of party rank and file, an important source of funding for political parties in the Organisation for Economic Co-operation and Development (OECD) democracies. Perhaps as many as a dozen countries in the region, including South Africa, have legislated public support for political parties (Mathisen and Svasand 2002). In some cases, public funding initiatives have been undertaken by incumbents in order to increase the number of parties and fragment the opposition, rather than to promote democracy. For instance, when President Omar Bongo promised roughly US$35,000 and a four-wheel drive car for any registered party in 1990, some 70 parties registered. Many appear to have simply disappeared before the election, but seven parties managed to win seats in the October 1990 parliamentary elections, helping Bongo's incumbent Gabonese Democratic Party win a comfortable majority. In some of the richer and bigger countries of the region, state and local government offices can provide significant support for opposition parties if and when they can win these sub-national elections (Conroy-Krutz 2006), but this source of resources is not available to many parties in the region. As a result, opposition parties are usually reliant on the resources of individuals for their funding. Either opposition candidates typically have to fund their own campaigns, which tends to undermine party discipline and cohesion, and/or parties rely on the funding of businessmen (see Bryan and Baer 2005; Pottie 2003).

The historical pattern in the Western democracies suggests that parties can compensate for the advantages of incumbent parties through the development of organization and ideological resources, a pattern that was particularly effective for the emergence of mass left-wing parties in Europe, for instance (Shefter 1994). However, there are few signs of such a trend emerging in Africa. Party organizations remain thin and transient. Most parties are loose coalitions dominated by a small number of prominent individuals and lacking cohesion or discipline. Between electoral competitions, they remain mostly dormant, and maintain few links with citizens.

Too many parties remain focused on clientelistic linkages to voters and rely on ascriptive ties, such as ethnicity. Few mobilize voters effectively on policy issues of importance to them (Bleck and van de Walle 2011), and instead rely on vague promises of patronage rewards to core constituencies. This is puzzling because various surveys suggest African voters have a number of material and ideological concerns that politicians could invoke in order to mobilize constituencies. For instance, Bleck and van de Walle (2011) show that in six multi-party systems of West Africa, voters care deeply about such issues as the public role of Islam or the public management of national resources, yet political parties hardly mention these issues in their campaign rhetoric. Bleck and van de Walle give the example of the nearly unanimous passage in the 2009 Malian legislature of a deeply unpopular bill reforming Mali's Family Code; passage of this bill, long sought by western donors and non-governmental organizations (NGOs), brought about massive popular protests orchestrated by grassroots Muslim civil society groups. They argue that the Westernized elites that shape party platforms are often too dependent on the donors and external actors, as well as inexperienced and out of touch with common citizens, to effectively mobilize voters on issues they care about.

Resnick (2012) argues that populist parties are starting to emerge in some countries, given the rapid levels of urbanization in the region, and the electoral incentives parties have to cater to poor urban voters. She argues that the Popular Front of Michael Sata in Zambia represents a kind of model of African populism, which is likely to become more common over time (see also Larmer and Fraser 2007; Cheeseman and Hinfelaar 2010). Populist dynamics can be gleaned in recent campaigns in such diverse other countries as Senegal (Resnick 2011), Ghana (Nugent 2001), and Madagascar (Razafindrakoto and Roubaud 2002). Nonetheless, attempts to mobilize voters through programmatic campaigns still remain the odd exception, as most parties rely on a mixture of non-programmatic appeals to co-ethnics, and broad valence-issue rhetoric linked to vague promises of service and infrastructure delivery to core constituencies.

Perhaps it is not surprising in this context, that the Afrobarometer attitudinal surveys suggest that opposition parties are little trusted by voters; in the fourth round of surveys recently completed, close to 60 per cent of voters said they did not trust opposition parties 'at all or just a little' (Resnick 2011: 18). In part, the notion of 'loyal opposition' as a legitimate function of political parties appears to remain foreign to African voters socialized in the era of the single party. In part, as well, in the absence of either coherent policy programmes or viable organizations, parties appear to voters as opportunistic and transient, interested in votes to gain power rather than to advance the common interests of citizens.

These different factors help explain two clear trends present in Africa since the return of electoral politics. First, opposition parties have only rarely been able to effectively contest incumbents in elections, even in the most democratic countries of the region. At the presidential level, very few incumbents have competed and lost an election since the early 1990s. In the less democratic countries, there has been little to no regime change, so stable is the political personnel in power. In no fewer than 10 countries (Angola, Burkina Faso, Cameroon, Chad, Congo-Brazzaville,

Equatorial Guinea, Ethiopia, Sudan, Uganda, and Zimbabwe), the leader in power in 1989 has remained in place. In each case, the old single party has adapted, more or less gingerly, to multi-party politics, but retains various advantages that protect it from competition.

In a handful of other, relatively democratic states (Botswana, Mozambique, Namibia, Tanzania, South Africa), strong single parties have survived the movement to the multi-party era, and maintained a virtual stranglehold on the presidency, despite turnovers of individual presidents. Thus, in Tanzania, for instance, Chama Cha Mapinduzi (CCM), the party created by Julius Nyerere in 1979 dominates national politics, despite its adherence to term limits for its leaders since Nyerere retired in 1985. The country is today officially committed to pluralism, but CCM's historic role and incumbency advantages means it has comfortably won successive elections, at least in part with the help of gerrymandering, election day fraud and intimidation of the opposition (Tripp 2000). Adding to this list the countries mentioned above that have witnessed dynastic turnovers further narrows the set of countries in which democratization has brought about a real political turnover to a small handful of countries. Moreover, in countries like Zambia, Malawi, or Benin, the initial turnover of power that occurred at the founding election in the early 1990s has not been repeated, as incumbents have won every election they have competed in since.

This political continuity is also evident for political parties at the legislative level. The leading opposition party has averaged only a quarter of the vote in African elections since 1989 and fewer than 20 per cent of the seats (author's database), compared to 57 per cent and 65 per cent for majority parties. Only 15 elections during this time did not lead to a winning party with a simple majority of seats, and most of those could in fact count on a stable parliamentary majority because of other subservient parties and independents. By way of comparison, it is very unusual in the democracies of Western Europe for the leading party to win an outright majority of votes and seats (Lijphart 1999), which typically implies the need for political coalitions and compromise for the biggest party, and consequently increases the number of political parties with a genuine chance of joining a governing coalition.

The second central characteristic of party systems in the region is the combination of dominant parties with a low number of effective parties in most African countries (van de Walle 2003; Kuenzi and Lambright 2005). Reflecting the many advantages of incumbency just discussed, the winning party in the legislative elections is the party of the sitting president in the overwhelming majority of cases. Moreover, the presidential majority often grows in the weeks following an election, as different legislators choose to join the incumbent's party. This phenomenon is often particularly pronounced in the case of small parties and the large number of independents that have won seats in many recent elections. Circumstances vary across countries and elections, of course, but this swelling of the winning party's ranks seems to reflect the reality that being in the majority affords material advantages. Some opposition parties are clearly lured into the majority with formal promises from the president of lucrative and powerful positions in the cabinet and state apparatus. Individual legislators may be convinced that joining the presidential majority is advantageous for their constituencies, as many believe the more or less explicit threats that opposition districts will receive less priority in terms of social services and infrastructure.

The extent to which presidential resources and patronage condition electoral and party dynamics is best illustrated in cases like Benin (2006) or Mali (2002), where the winning presidential candidate ran as an independent without party support, and then constructed a fairly stable legislative majority once in power, by promising cabinet positions to leading politicians of the parties that had competed in the election (on Benin, see Seely 2007; Mayrargue 2006; on Mali, see Baudais and Chauzal 2006). Given the low popularity of parties, the electoral campaigns of both Yayi Boni in Benin and Amadou Touré in Mali willingly emphasized their independence from partisan politics, and then once elected, resorted to tried and true clientelist strategies to construct a governing coalition with these same party leaders.

This dynamic also helps to explain the fact that despite the large number of political parties that fledgling African democracies have the reputation of encouraging, the typical African legislature actually features a relatively low number of 'effective parties' (a measure of parties that takes into account their size and the disparity between large and small parties; see Laakso and Taagepera 1979). Thus, while it is not unusual for well over two dozen political parties to participate in elections, on average just over six parties are represented in the typical African legislature, and because of the small size of many opposition parties the effective number of parties is around three (Rakner and van de Walle 2009).

Is this pattern of presidential dominance related to the quality of democracy? Compared to older democracies, the weakness of African opposition parties is striking, even in the region's most democratic countries. Nonetheless, the evidence does suggest that the level of democracy and the length of the democratic experience does have a positive effect on the strength of the opposition. For instance, Rakner and van de Walle (2009) find that the second biggest party, in principle the leading party of the opposition, wins on average 75 per cent more seats in the legislature in 'free' regimes compared to those in the 'not free' category. Similarly, they find that opposition parties gain strength as countries convene more elections. Although the winning party remained as strong from the first multi-party elections to the fourth and fifth ones, the second biggest party went from winning under a fifth of the seats in the first election to winning over a quarter of the seats in fourth and fifth elections.

Conclusion

This chapter has focused on the weakness of political parties and the deficiencies of democracy in sub-Saharan Africa. With the wholesale shift to multi-party electoral politics in the 1990s and the new democratic rhetoric espoused by many erstwhile dictators, it is important to realize the limits of the transitions that have occurred in the region. The generalized move to multi-party electoral politics does not equal the triumph of democracy, albeit with a handful of exceptions. For the latter to occur, the region's current electoral autocracies will need further reform that reduces the current abuses of political and social rights, makes governments more accountable and responsive to their citizens, and reins-in the centralized power currently in the hands of individual presidents, still largely above the law.

This chapter has also argued that these reforms will almost certainly require and be accompanied by stronger, better-organized and more institutionalized political parties, which play a key role in democratic consolidation. The chapter has shown that most opposition parties remain too weak to promote the greater accountability of governments. In fact, the nature of party systems in the region seems largely tributary of the level and quality of democratic practice. In particular, I have sought to demonstrate that the modal pattern of a large presidential party dominating a bevy of small, volatile and transient parties is a direct result of the presidentialism and clientelism of these regimes.

In closing, it is nonetheless worth stressing how much democratic progress has been achieved in Africa since the late 1980s. As Posner and Young (2007) and others have argued, democratic politics is now the only form of legitimate government in the region, to which all politicians now pay homage, however hypocritically. Political participation and competition has increased significantly in the vast majority of states, and the evidence suggests that governments and politicians are more responsive to the needs of citizens as a result. Thus, Stasavage (2005) finds a significantly positive relationship between democratization in Africa and social spending.

A further cause of optimism can be found in the apparent fact, underscored above, that democratic performance improves over time and with experience of multi-party electoral politics. Thus, though parties are weak and party systems favour incumbents, the passage of time and the greater experience it affords is likely to serve to promote party institutionalization and improved party performance. To be sure, this is a slow and uneven process, and increased competition and political participation can unleash dangerous demons in ethnically divided political systems, as argued by scholars like Paul Collier (2009). Still, it suggests that in many countries, the current evolution favours greater democracy over time.

Bibliography

Baudais, V. and Chauzal, G. (2006) 'Les partis politiques et "l'indépendance partisane" d'Amadou Toumani Touré', *Politique Africaine* 104: 61–80.

Bayart, J.-F. (1989) *L'Etat en Afrique: la politique du ventre*, Paris: Fayard.

Bleck, J. and van de Walle, N. (2011) 'Parties and Issues in Francophone West Africa: Towards a Theory of Non-Mobilization', *Democratization* 18(5): 1125–45.

Bratton, M. and van de Walle, N. (1997) *Democratic Experiments in Africa: Regime Transitions in Comparative Perspective*, New York, NY: Cambridge University Press.

Bryan, S. and Baer, D. (eds) (2005) *Money in Politics: A Study of Party Financing Practices in 22 Countries*, Washington, DC: National Democratic Institute.

Carothers, T. (2002) 'The End of the Transition Paradigm', *Journal of Democracy* 13(1): 5–20.

Cheeseman, N. (2010) 'African Elections as Vehicles for Change', *Journal of Democracy* 21(4): 139–53.

Cheeseman, N. and Hinfelaar, M. (2010) 'Parties, Platforms, and Political Mobilization: The Zambian Presidential Election of 2008', *African Affairs* 109(434): 51–76.

Clark, J.F. (2007) 'The Decline of the African Coup', *Journal of Democracy* 18(3): 141–55.

Collier, P. (2009) *War, Guns and Votes: Democracy in Dangerous Places*, New York, NY: Harper Collins.

Conroy-Krutz, J. (2006) 'African Cities and Incumbent Hostility: Explaining Opposition Success in Urban Areas', paper presented at the annual meeting of the African Studies Association, San Francisco, CA, November 2006.

Diamond, L. (2002) 'Thinking about Hybrid Regimes', *Journal of Democracy* 13(2): 21–36.

Huntington, S.P. (1991) *The Third Wave: Democratization in the Late Twentieth Century*, Norman, OK: University of Oklahoma Press.

Joseph, R. (1998) 'Africa, 1990–97: From Abertura to Closure', *Journal of Democracy* 9: 3–17.

——(2008) 'Progress and Retreat in Africa: Challenges of a "Frontier" Region', *Journal of Democracy* 19(2): 94–108.

Kriger, N. (2005) 'ZANU(PF) Strategies in General Elections, 1980–2000: Discourse and Coercion', *African Affairs* 104(414): 1–34.

Kuenzi, M. and Lambright, G. (2005) 'Party Systems and Democratic Consolidation in Africa's Electoral Regimes', *Party Politics* 11(4): 423–46.

Laakso, M. and Taagepera, R. (1979) 'The "Effective" Number of Parties: A Measure with Application to West Europe', *Comparative Political Studies* 12(1): 3–27.

Larmer, M. and Fraser, A. (2007) 'Of Cabbages and King Cobra: Populist Politics and Zambia's 2006 Election', *African Affairs* 106(425): 611–37.

Levitsky, S. and Way, L.A. (2002) 'The Rise of Competitive Authoritarianism', *Journal of Democracy* 13(2): 51–65.

——(2010) *Competitive Authoritarianism: Hybrid Regimes After the Cold War*, Cambridge: Cambridge University Press.

Lijphart, A. (1999) *Patterns of Democracy*, New Haven, CT: Yale University Press.

Lindberg, S. (2006) *Democracy and Elections in Africa*, Baltimore, MD: Johns Hopkins University Press.

——(ed.) (2009) *Democratization by Elections: A New Mode of Transition?* Baltimore, MD: Johns Hopkins University Press.

Linz, J.J. and Stepan, A. (1996) *Problems of Democratic Transition and Consolidation: Southern Europe, South America, and Post-Communist Europe*, Baltimore, MD: Johns Hopkins University Press.

Maltz, G. (2007) 'The Case for Presidential Term Limits', *Journal of Democracy* 18(1): 128–42.

Mathisen, H. and Svåsand, L. (2002) 'Funding Political Parties in Emerging African Democracies: What Role for Norway?' Report R 2002: 6, Chr. Michelsen Institute Development Studies and Human Rights, Bergen, Norway.

Mayrargue, C. (2006) 'Yayi Boni, Un President Inattendu? Construction de la figure du Candidat et Dynamiques Electorales au Benin', *Politique Africaine* 102: 155–72.

Nugent, P. (2001) 'Winners, Losers and Also Rans: Money, Moral Authority and Voting Patterns in the Ghana 2000 Elections', *African Affairs* 100(400): 405–28.

Posner, D.N. and Young, D.J. (2007) 'The Institutionalization of Political Power in Africa', *Journal of Democracy* 18(3): 126–40.

Pottie, D. (2003) 'Party Finance and the Politics of Money in Southern Africa', *Journal of Contemporary African Studies* 21: 5–28.

Prempeh, H.K. (1999) 'A New Jurisprudence for Africa', *Journal of Democracy* 10(3): 135–49.

——(2008) 'Presidents Untamed', *Journal of Democracy* 19(2): 109–23.

Rakner, L. and van de Walle, N. (2009) 'Opposition Parties and Incumbent Presidents: The New Dynamics of Electoral Competition in Sub-Saharan Africa', in S. Lindberg (ed.) *Democratization by Elections*, Baltimore, MD: Johns Hopkins University Press.

Randall, V. and Svasand, L. (2002) 'Political Parties and Democratic Consolidation in Africa', *Democratization* 9 (3): 30–52.

Razafindrakoto, M. and Roubaud, F. (2002) 'Le scrutin presidential du 16 décembre 2001', *Politique Africaine* 102: 18–43.

Resnick, D. (2011) 'Are Electoral Coalitions Harmful for Democratic Consolidation in Africa?' UNU-WIDER Working Paper No. 2011/07, Helsinki: WIDER.

——(2012) 'Opposition Parties and the Urban Poor in African Democracies', *Comparative Political Studies*, forthcoming.

Sartori, G. (1976) *Parties and Party Systems: A Framework for Analysis*, Cambridge: Cambridge University Press.

Seely, J. (2007) 'The Presidential Election in Benin, March 2006', *Electoral Studies* 26: 196–231.

Shefter, M. (1994) *Political Parties and the State: The American Historical Experience*, Princeton, NJ: Princeton University Press.

Stasavage, D. (2005) 'Democracy and Education Spending in Africa', *American Journal of Political Science* 49(2): 343–58.

Tripp, A.M. (2000) 'Political Reform in Tanzania: The Struggle for Associational Autonomy', *Comparative Politics* 32(2): 191–214.

van de Walle, N. (2001) 'The Impact of Multi-Party Politics in Sub-Saharan Africa', *Forum for Development Studies* 28(1): 5–42.

——(2002) 'Africa's Range of Regimes', *Journal of Democracy* 13(2): 66–80.

——(2003) 'Presidentialism and Clientelism in Africa's Emerging Party Systems', *Journal of Modern African Studies* 41(2): 297–321.

——(2007) 'Meet the New Boss, Same as the Old Boss? The Evolution of Political Clientelism in Africa', in H. Kitschelt and S.I. Wilkinson (eds) *Patron, Clients and Policies: Patterns of Democratic Accountability and Political Competition*, Cambridge: Cambridge University Press.

19

THE POWER OF ELECTIONS

Staffan I. Lindberg

The role of elections in processes of democratization was not analysed in any depth until a few years ago when a vigorous debate emerged on whether the holding of elections in authoritarian regimes furthered democracy or was simply a way for dictators to prolong their stay in power,[1] if 'early' elections risked plunging complex societies into chaos and civil war, and whether liberalizing reforms had to be sequenced in a certain way to support democratic consolidation. In this chapter I wish to pursue a bold claim. For the first time in Africa's history, multi-party elections have become the only game in town. As a result, the conditions of 'the art of ruling' have changed and the continent is entering a new era. What is happening in these 48 countries today is naturally linked to the past, yet it is also different because incumbents have to deal with a fresh set of political challenges and incentives. We are only at the very beginning of understanding this change, and its consequences.

Let me give a few examples. Mali is almost 100 per cent Muslim and one of the world's poorest countries, yet has reasonably democratic politics and boasts a higher female political representation than the United States and most European countries. The multi-ethnic, multi-religious, low-income country Benin has held an uninterrupted series of four multi-party elections that have been accompanied by three alternations in power. In December 2008, the National Democratic Congress (NDC), the former ruling party in Ghana, won back power by a margin of less than one per cent, thus adding the country to the short list of African states that have passed the 'two-turnover test' (Huntington 1991). In a conversation I had with the former dictator of Lesotho, Major-General Justin Lekhanya, he acknowledged that even if he himself and many of his supporters wanted to take over again, the national and international conditions made it plainly impossible.

Young Andry Rajoelina in Madagascar has come to learn a similar lesson, just like President Mwai Kibaki in Kenya. The latter tried the old trick of fabricating election results at the electoral commission's headquarters, holding an unconstitutional swearing-in ceremony, and deploying the police to intimidate the opposition. Yet, this failed and the ensuing process eventually produced a power-sharing arrangement. Apparently, this cable never reached incumbent president Laurent Gbagbo in Côte d'Ivoire, who tried to steal the presidential run-off election that should have ended a long period of civil war. He and his supporters in the army apparently failed to anticipate the UN Secretary-General, the US president, European Union (EU) member states, and even the regime's own friends in ECOWAS refusing to recognize him as the legitimate head of state. Other coup leaders such as Ely Ould Mohamed Vall, who took power in Mauritania on 8 December 2005, have caught the drift towards more open and competitive politics and intervened to reignite the democratization process, much like the Turkish military has done in the past.

This is not to say that democratic politics are perfectly functioning in these countries; rather the key point is that the politics are different. Of course, there remain a number of countries that have been bogged down in civil conflict, such as Sudan, Central African Republic (CAR), the Democratic Republic of Congo (DRC), Somalia, Eritrea, and Swaziland. Moreover, in a few places, such as Equatorial Guinea, Cameroon, and Gabon, oil riches help sustain lingering authoritarian regimes. Similarly, American, EU, French, and NATO (North Atlantic Treaty Organization) strategic interests help undemocratic regimes in Djibouti, Ethiopia, and the Republic of Congo stay in power. Nonetheless, almost all of these governments today also feel the need to subject themselves to holding multi-party elections and nowhere on the continent is it simply business as usual.

Elections in the New Africa

A series of recent publications have detailed some of the empirical manifestations of the recent watershed of political reform in Africa.[2] Almost all countries in Africa are now holding *de jure* multi-party elections. The point of multi-party elections is that even if they are held in non-democratic settings, they have the potential to lead to real political competition and meaningful participation – that is, to lead to democracy. It has been shown empirically that dictators in Africa who continue holding an unbroken series of elections typically lose their grip on power. Iterations of electoral contests also tend to unleash a series of self-reinforcing sub-processes making politics become less authoritarian. This is the 'power of elections' (Di Palma 1993: 85).

Table 19.1 gives a snapshot of the pattern of elections and democracy in Africa as of 1 January 2010. It shows that 33 of the countries in Africa have held at least three successive elections without a coup, civil war, or other interruption. More than 20 countries have held four elections or more in a row and 12 have completed an uninterrupted sequence of at least five multi-party elections. Among countries that have held at least three successive elections, we find no fewer than 15 relatively democratic regimes, whilst another four or five countries are competitive electoral authoritarian regimes with relatively good prospects of becoming democratic in the future: Kenya, Mozambique, Tanzania, Uganda, and perhaps Gambia. We must remember that processes of democratization are typically non-linear, unfolding in a zigzag-like pattern. It was no different in the now established democracies where the shift from strong, often personal, monarchies to popular democracies took decades and in some cases centuries. In Africa, a majority of countries are still 'on the road'. Some may not become democracies in any real sense of the word for a long time. The critical point, however, is that they have begun their journey: the nature of politics on the continent has changed.

My own work analysing 282 elections showed that not only are more and more countries holding elections and doing so successfully without a coup, civil war or other major interruption (which is crucial), but an increasing share of these elections are also substantively free and fair. In 1989–2007 only 54 per cent of first ('founding') presidential elections in Africa and 49 per cent of second elections were free and fair, yet fully 82 per cent of fourth and later elections received the same judgment. Political participation is steadily high in Africa with average turnout rates hovering around 65 per cent, and as more elections are held, old autocratic rulers are leaving the electoral scene in increasing numbers. Indeed, political competition usually increases as countries hold more elections. The winner's share of votes in presidential

Table 19.1 Snapshot of a New Africa, 1 January 2010

No elections	PR	Founding elections	PR	Second elections	PR	Third elections	PR	Fourth elections	PR	Fifth+ elections	PR
Eritrea	7	Angola	6	Burundi	4	Cameroon	6	Burkina Faso	5	Benin*	2
Somalia	7	CAR*	5	RoC	6	Chad	7	Cape Verde*	1	Botswana	3
Swaziland	7	DRC	6	Guinea Biss*	4	Comoros*	3	Equatorial Guinea	7	Gabon	6
		Guinea	7	Rwanda	6	Djibouti	5	Ethiopia	5	Ghana*	1
		Côte d'Ivoire	6	Sierra Leone*	3	Gambia	5	Kenya*	4	Mali*	2
		Liberia	3			Lesotho*	3	Malawi*	3	Mauritius*	1
		Mauritania	6			Nigeria	5	Mozambique	4	Namibia	2
		Madagascar*	6			Niger*	5	Sao Tome*	2	Senegal*	3
						Sudan	7	South Africa	2	Seychelles	3
						Uganda	5	Tanzania	5	Togo	6
										Zambia*	3
										Zimbabwe	6
Mean PR	7.0		5.6		4.6		5.1		3.8		3.2

Notes: * Indicates a country that has experienced an executive and/or legislative turnover. PR refers to Political Rights Score by Freedom House, 2010 rankings.

contests goes down from an average of over 60 per cent in most first elections, to less than half (47 per cent on average) in fourth and later elections. This is crucial, as many countries employ a presidential run-off if no candidate secures more than 50 per cent of the vote, and thus have experienced fierce competition for the highest office. Even if opposition parties in many countries are still weak and/or divided, over 30 per cent of countries in Africa have seen alternations in executive power and/or legislative majorities – not counting turnovers seen in founding elections.

The improvements that come with an iteration of the electoral process can also be seen in terms of legitimacy. In elections that were free and fair, losers accepted the outcome in almost two-thirds of the fourth and subsequent polls, compared to only 47 per cent of the first and second. The ultimate indicator of the new dispensation's legitimacy – survival of the electoral regime – presents even stronger evidence. Breakdowns almost always occur shortly after 'founding' elections are held. If the military or militarized factions decide to abort the process, this is almost exclusively done before the electoral regime has become institutionalized. Once more firmly in place, it seems that the perceived costs of a full and radical autocratization are simply too high (Lindberg 2009a: 28–37).

Overall, the pattern in Africa points to what Schedler (2009: 291) calls the regime-subverting potential of elections in authoritarian countries. Another indication of this is that improvements in individual rights, the rule of law, associational rights, and freedom of expression and beliefs, typically occur around elections (Lindberg 2009a: 38). This suggests that elections facilitate challenges to authoritarian rule. Over several iterations of this process, a gradual democratization by elections has taken place in many African countries.

The democratizing power of elections in Africa over the past two decades has an explanatory power that also stands up to alternative explanations featuring factors such as the level of development, socio-cultural modernization, level of education, natural resource-wealth, ethnic/linguistic fractionalization, religion, and government performance and economic crises. I have tested the power of elections thesis repeatedly in standard regression models alongside all of these factors and consistently find that the number of successive elections held without interruption is by far the strongest predictor of the level of democracy in contemporary Africa (e.g. Lindberg 2009a: 42–44). There is nothing tautological about this finding. While regimes in the Middle East and in Latin America have held long series of multi-party elections without any significant effects, in Africa each successive electoral cycle has tended to have democratizing effects.[3]

Let me mention one more aspect of this process. Women's representation has improved with each electoral cycle across different electoral systems, although proportional representation, especially in combination with large parties, also leads to better representation by women in Africa, as in the rest of the world (Lindberg 2004). A series of countries have also adopted national or party-specific women's quotas that further improve the cause of women's equal representation; at the time of writing, Rwanda holds the world record with 56 per cent women in the legislature (e.g. Tripp and Kang 2008; Yoon 2004). Thus, African politics is no longer an exclusively male affair, and Ellen Johnson-Sirleaf's taking of the oath to become the 24th president of Liberia on 16 January 2006 is perhaps the ultimate proof of this. Without multi-party elections, this shift would have been unimaginable.

The key: costs of repression and toleration

Authoritarian rulers in the Middle East have held long series of elections and yet stand largely uncontested today, orchestrating games of 'competitive clientelism' through elections (Lust-Okar

2008; Gandhi and Lust-Okar 2009). Latin American dictators also used to hold elections without allowing them to threaten their hold on power (McCoy and Hartlyn 2009). Although 'electoral revolutions' led to democracy in most Eastern European countries (Bunce and Wolchick 2009), the current situation in Russia and many old Soviet republics display 'autocratization by elections'. Why have authoritarian regimes in Africa been particularly sensitive to processes of democratization by elections?

At this point, consider Dahl's dictum: 'The more the costs of suppression exceed the costs of toleration, the greater the chance for a competitive regime' (Dahl 1971: 15). As I have discussed in more detail elsewhere (Lindberg 2009b), the basis of his thinking was simple but elegant and remains valid today. While acknowledging that costs are subjective, it is clear that any author-itarian government will have to confront two interrelated issues. First, whether the high costs of oppression (in terms of deaths, economic loss, and the impact of issues such as legitimacy and donor assistance, intra-elite splits, defections, and so on) are acceptable. Second, to what extent, or at what point, do the potential costs of allowing increasing competition and inclusion become tolerable in terms of their implication for power, wealth, status, protection, and so on? Figure 19.1 depicts this reasoning graphically. The curved lines, indicating when various regime types are more likely, are based on the idea that both the costs of repression and of reform are important factors shaping whether or not regime change occurs. A dictator facing increasing costs of repression *should* liberalize but is unlikely to do so if the costs of toleration are still

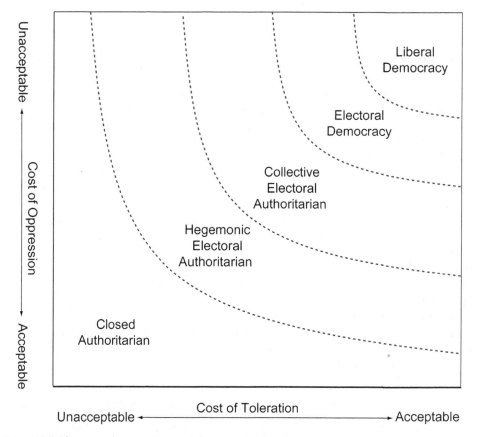

Figure 19.1 The cost of oppression and the cost of toleration

intolerably high (if it would lead to the death of the ruler, his family, and cronies, for example). Conversely, even if the costs of toleration are drastically reduced, autocrats will have no need of democratization as long as the costs of repression are acceptably low.

Yet, there is a blind spot in Dahl's reasoning. For Dahl, electoral rights, institutions, and processes were only indicators of polyarchy, and this is how they have continued to be used in the literature ever since.[4] What has not been acknowledged until recently is how the holding of elections can contribute to changing the costs of oppression and toleration. This is why elections play such an important role as causal factors in both democratization and autocratization.[5] Each election becomes a nested 'sub-game' to the overall macro-game of regime-transition. Although they appear to be simply about winning votes, they have serious implications for the costs of repression and toleration. With this in mind we can now return to the question why the repetition of elections in so many African countries has had such a democratizing impact over the last few decades.

The end of the Cold War was certainly important (Roessler and Howard 2009), as were the demonstration effects provided by the collapse of authoritarian rule following the colour revolutions in Eastern Europe and the symbolic democratization of South Africa. Diffusion is no illusion, as Coppedge (2006) put it. What is believed to be true, is true in its consequences (Thomas and Thomas 1928),[6] and the most powerful diffusion effect was to change the perceptions of both rulers and opposition leaders of what is possible and what cannot be avoided. That 41 countries in Africa suddenly came to hold some kind of multi-party elections in the short period from 1990–94 can hardly be explained without reference to this phenomenon. The shift in the international community towards a stronger emphasis on democracy promotion, heralded by the Clinton Administration, was another important factor that raised the costs of oppression – even if the pressures were and are applied unevenly. As the pivotal event when the most basic rights and institutions of citizenship and liberty are tested, elections became the driving force through which donors could leverage their interests in order to promote democracy.

In a small number of cases, international factors led to elections becoming a tool of autocratization because strategic interests in either natural resources (e.g. Republic of Congo) or in security (e.g. Ethiopia) trumped other concerns. However, in the majority of cases, the gradual institutionalization of multi-party elections strengthened political parties, civil society, and think-tank institutions, developing ever-stronger competencies in organizing and advocating for the expansion of political rights. It is during the campaign and in the immediate post-election period that domestic and international pro-reform forces tend to put all their resources to work to defend key electoral rights and institutions. When these groups succeed in mobilizing support, the costs of repression are radically increased for autocrats. Similarly, media actors typically focus on the flurry of events thrown up by electoral contests and thus typically raise the costs of oppression. These twin processes may not lead to dramatic regime changes immediately, but they change the longer-term calculations and prospects for everyone involved.

A gradual transition in which autocrats stay in power for one or two terms as elected governments (even if by fraudulent means), lowers their fear of elections and so lowers the perceived cost of toleration significantly, thus making democratic reforms more likely. Former abuses of power can be forgiven or tactically 'forgotten' by opposition groups and international actors alike, in return for reforms and the spectre of alternation in power in the future. Meanwhile, while foreign donors and scholars may frown upon lingering autocrats who are able to use state resources to co-opt the opposition during transitional periods in order to stay in office, this can nevertheless facilitate a pragmatic approach on behalf of the incumbent and increase the governing capacity among opposition leaders. We are now beginning to realize that through this process an extended period of democratization by elections has led to the moderation of opposition groups in a number of countries, further lowering the cost of toleration for the incumbent regime. With greater experience and successively more effective collective action, opposition groups may subsequently be able to campaign for the respect of political rights and civil liberties, increasing the costs of repression and hence the prospects of a real democratic breakthrough. When the balance of power starts to shift, defections from a coalition of authoritarian forces become more likely. This process has already materialized in a number of African countries as former autocrats have sought to reinvent themselves as born-again democrats and opposition leaders. This is what happened in Kenya and although the outcome there is far from certain, I suspect that the long-term outcome will be successful democratization. Thus, instead of the fatal split in the authoritarian regime occurring before 'founding' elections as famously formulated by O'Donnell and Schmitter (1986), repetitive elections in Africa mean that such schisms often occur after the initial transition, further increasing the costs of oppression.

In parallel to this, we have witnessed how the reintroduction of elections has led actors in important state institutions to change their own calculations in a number of countries. With *de jure* multi-party elections, institutions such as the electoral commission, human rights bodies, the police and courts, and even the military are given a formal role in protecting new democratic rights. Defending the interests of the ruling government is no longer necessarily the default option (Lindberg 2006, 2009b). Bratton and van de Walle (1997) found that the militaries in Africa intervened more often to facilitate democratization than to keep autocrats in power. This trend has continued and the repetition of elections has further lowered the cost of toleration for bureaucrats and the like, thus making it more likely that they will look to further their own careers by acting to promote democracy and defend citizens' rights to fair and just processes.

These are some of the main causal mechanisms whereby the repetition of multi-party contests has led to a process of democratization by elections. However, the increasing importance of polls for the distribution of power in Africa has also had another equally important impact: it has increased the role of ordinary citizens in African politics significantly.

African politics: from elites to institutions and citizens

A standard conception about the art of ruling in Africa has been that 'big man' politics dominate. In different variants of this broad argument, patronage rather than policy is seen to drive choice and behaviour (e.g. Bates 1981; Hydén 2006; Lemarchand 1972; van de Walle 2001). The consequence, most seem to agree, has been one or the other type of privatization of the state and its resources leading to a series of 'lost decades' (Bates *et al.* 2007). Even the basic notion of sovereignty has been appropriated and distributed to sustain loyalty in countries strapped of resources (Englebert 2009). This expresses itself also in the manifestation of informal institutions, i.e. the prevalence of face to face-based networks that may support or undermine, complement or disregard formal institutions (Helmke and Levitsky 2006; Bratton 2007). What this older literature cannot grapple with is the greater dependence of elites on the consent of the people of Africa in the last 20 years. As scholars we now have to uncover what the 'demand side' of African politics looks like. What do citizens want and therefore push to get from political leaders? Do such demands translate into changes in political leaders' behaviour, and if so how? We know very little about how these things play out in Africa today.

As research on voting behaviour in the United States and Europe confirms, these questions are crucial to understanding in what way and to what extent democratic institutions and citizen-representative relationships make a difference to political outcomes. If the principal-agent relationship suffers from too severe problems of moral hazard[7] and information deficits,[8] the prospects for accountability are undermined and it is less likely that representatives will behave in ways that reflect the principal's interests. On the other hand, even if the accountability relationship is strong, collective action problems among the principals are solved, and information deficits compensated by efficacious proxies, political outcomes may be less than optimal from the perspective of collective and club good provision.[9] For example, citizens may simply demand private goods rather than club or collective goods either because of poverty or as a result of path-dependent expectations. In either case, we would expect politicians to seek to satisfy such demands in order to secure re-election. The problem is that we do not know much about the principals: citizens as voters.

Vote buying is more likely to occur in poor areas and countries because the marginal utility of one vote is a constant in any given context while the cost of buying a vote varies. More affluent citizens are less likely to sell their votes for a small inducement than very poor people. Yet, in very competitive settings the value of one extra vote can potentially make all the difference between winning and losing, especially in majoritarian systems. As a result, one would expect vote-buying activities to be directed primarily towards independents, or swing voters as described by Nichter (2008). On the other hand, elections can also be won by 'getting out the vote' of core supporters, which would suggest that candidates should direct their efforts more to their core constituents to ensure that they actually show up at the polls (e.g. Stokes and Dunning 2008).

There is certainly considerable evidence that supporters expect to be well rewarded for their efforts and that leaders do their best to meet these expectations when they capture office. When a southerner was elected president of Malawi in 1994 the electorate in that region began to expect that they would receive preferential treatment from the government (Kamwambe 1994). In a survey of voter attitudes in the 1991 gubernatorial election in Akwa Ibom State in Nigeria, Ikpe (2000: 148–50) shows that a larger percentage of poor (65 per cent) than well-off voters (39 per cent) viewed elections as occasions in which they could derive benefits from parties and candidates. Yet, much of what passes as knowledge about African voters is still assumed rather than empirically proven. Afrobarometer surveys provide some insights, but it would be premature to draw definite conclusions from an attitude survey that does not specifically target citizens at the time of elections.[10] Valuable efforts have been made to try to infer conclusions about the African voter from Afrobarometer data (e.g. Bratton and Kimenyi 2008; Bratton and Logan 2006; Cheeseman and Ford 2007; Eifert *et al.* 2007; Kramon 2009; Logan 2008; Moehler and Lindberg 2009), but without questions specifically designed to explain voting behaviour, these conclusions are tentative at best. Systematic research on voting behaviour is only now beginning to emerge (e.g. Erdmann 2007; Fridy 2007; Kuenzi and Lambright 2005; Lindberg and Morrison 2005, 2008; Mattes and Piombo 2001; Mulenga 2001; REDET 2004; Wantchekon 2003). Compared to what we know about voting behaviour and alignments in other regions of the world, the African voter remains perhaps not anonymous, but certainly known only in a diffuse manner. In the context of studying the extent to which democracy is being consolidated in Africa, this is a research frontier.

The 'demand-side' of private and public goods in Ghana

As a final contribution, allow me to illustrate with recent survey data ($N = 1,600$) from Ghana some trends that are likely to be replicated in other African countries. The survey focused on elections of legislators (MPs) in Ghana's single-member districts and was carried out in 10 purposively selected constituencies, with a random selection of 160 respondents in each constituency.[11] Table 19.2 reports how respondents answered two related questions: 'What was the

Table 19.2 Relationship between reported rationale and expectations on MPs

| Reported voting rationale (2004) | Main expectation on incoming MP? | | | | Total |
	Personal support	Constituency service	Lawmaking/ oversight	Other issues	
Personal support	26.2%	61.9%	2.4%	9.5%	100.0%
N	11	26	1	4	42
Constituency service	12.2%	73.4%	8.4%	5.9%	100.0%
N	35	210	24	17	286
Lawmaking/oversight	18.6%	63.8%	10.4%	7.2%	100.0%
N	59	203	33	23	318
Other issues	13.2%	71.6%	4.6%	10.6%	100.0%
N	55	298	19	44	416
Total	15.1%	69.4%	7.3%	8.3%	100.0%
N	160	737	77	88	1062

Source: Author's survey, August 2008.
Notes: Sign.: Chi2 26.539, df. 9, $p=.002$.

main reason you voted for "X" in the legislative election in your constituency?'; and 'What was the main thing you hoped or expected that the elected MP would do, when you voted in the last election?'

First, when asked for their voting rationale, very few (less than 4 per cent) respondents acknowledged individual patronage as a reason for voting, and relatively large shares (roughly 30 per cent and 27 per cent, respectively) gave politically correct answers regarding national law making and executive oversight. Let us contrast this with what we interpret as the more genuine indicator – answers to the question regarding what respondents expect the candidate to do if and when elected. Roughly 70 per cent responded that they primarily wanted their MP to provide their community with development projects, in other words 'club' goods. This indicates that in the Ghanaian case legislative elections are primarily about local development for voters. This finding echoes what Barkan (1979) and Hydén and Leys (1972) found in East Africa some 35 years ago. However, whereas much of the literature conflates the provision of club or collective goods with clientelism and the creation of long-lasting personal bonds, the survey here suggests that a vast majority of voters put the main emphasis on collective goods that are understood in rational-evaluative (i.e. non-clientelistic) terms. Almost regardless of what voters say was their 'rationale' for voting for a particular candidate, around 70 per cent of them first and foremost want their MP to deliver collective goods to their local community (a relatively 'large' club good if you like).

Do voters punish incumbents if they fail to deliver better development? If so, this could indicate support for the 'economic voting' thesis famously set out by Downs (1957), which adopts a classic rational choice approach to the behaviour of citizens.[12] However, it is also possible that voters in Africa punish incumbents for bad economic performance not because of any Downsian economic rationality but instead because they perceive the failure of their leaders to represent a breach of reciprocal norms in a moral economy (see Hydén 1983; Berman 1998). In other words, voters could be acting on the basis of either dispassionate policy evaluations or culturally embedded understandings of political legitimacy. We can start to develop an explanation of which motivation is the more important through a survey question that asks voters if they punish incumbents if their own economic situation or the economic situation of the country becomes worse.

Table 19.3 Perceptions of economy and vote choice

Economy at present compared to 1 year ago?	Reported vote choice in upcoming election 2008?					Total
	NPP (government)	*NDC (opposition)*	*Other (not government)*	*Don't know*	*Will abstain*	
Much worse/worse	40.3%	69.9%	59.3%	50.3%	59.0%	53.4%
N	226	281	70	77	46	700
About the same	18.7%	11.4%	20.3%	18.3%	21.8%	16.8%
N	105	46	24	28	17	220
Better/Much better	41.0%	18.7%	20.3%	31.4%	19.2%	29.9%
N	230	75	24	48	15	392
Total	100.0%	100.0%	100.0%	100.0%	100.0%	100.0%
N	561	402	118	153	78	1,312

Source: Author's survey, August 2008.
Notes: Sign.: Chi2 97.284, df=8, p=.000.

In Table 19.3 we tabulate voters' assessment of the present state of the economy in Ghana compared to one year ago, with their self-reported projected vote choice for the upcoming elections (7 December 2008). Citizens who thought that the economy over the last year had become 'worse' or 'much worse' were far more likely to say that they would vote for the main opposition party, or any of the smaller non-ruling parties, while citizens with a positive evaluation of the economy were more than twice as likely to vote for the then-ruling party, the New Patriotic Party (NPP), than other voters. The results are highly statistically significant and remain essentially the same if we substitute the evaluation of the economy with individuals' evaluation of their own personal financial situation. In short, in this broad sense, the economic voting thesis seems to have something important to say about electoral behaviour in Africa. Yet, there is a catch. An analysis of each party's core voters' evaluation of the economy shows that the opposition's core voters are much more likely to have a negative evaluation of the economy than the core supporters of the ruling party. It is thus very difficult to tell if the evaluation of the economy is endogenous to party affiliation, and so simply reflects the distribution of voters, or is actually based on individuals' independent analyses of the state of the economy, and directly affects voting behaviour. This question should be the focus of further study.

Conclusion

The forms of personal rule common in colonial and post-colonial times have changed fundamentally as a result of the processes of democratization by elections over the past two decades. While we need to remember that transitions to democracy often take a generation or more, a new landscape in which leaders are more dependent on citizens is nevertheless emerging. The underlying drivers of voter behaviour in Africa thus represent a new research frontier. Understanding why politicians act as they do requires us to uncover how politicians understand the incentives facing them, especially with regard to for what citizens hold their political representatives accountable. Data from Ghana indicate that rational politicians in the era of free and fair elections gain many more votes by seeking to further constituency development (a narrow collective/club good) than they lose by disengaging from personalized clientelism. There is therefore some hope that democratic African states will start to see the alleviation of poverty, creation of sustainable economic growth, and production of public goods after 50 years of failure.

Notes

1 With one significant exception: Hermet *et al.* (1978).
2 A long list of contributions to various aspects of this new era could be mentioned, but space limitations prevent me from doing so. However, Barkan, Bratton, and van de Walle similarly reflect these aspects in their respective chapters in this *Handbook*.
3 The differences should perhaps not come as a surprise. The countries in Latin America have been independent for 200 years and many had experienced prolonged periods of multi-party elections and democracy before the third wave. Many regimes in the Middle East have built their grip on power on the basis of control over natural resource rents and clan-based distributive politics, which served to stabilize the social and political situation – at least for a time.
4 See, for example, O'Donnell and Schmitter (1986), followed by scholars such as Diamond (1996), Diamond and Plattner (1999), and Günther *et al.* (1995). Linz and Stepan (1996) even use the date of the first election as the day when the transition process ended; Bratton and van de Walle (1997: 195) adopted their approach. The number of elections, voter turnout, competitiveness, and turnovers have been used to indicate the degree of democratization (e.g. Barkan 2000; Herbst 2000; van de Walle 2001); the level of democracy (e.g. Altman and Pérez-Linán 2002; Foweraker and Landmann 2002); and the consolidation of democracy (e.g. Diamond 1999; Huntington 1991). Cross-national measures also use election-related indicators (Freedom House; Przeworski *et al.* 2000).
5 See Schedler's (2002) work on electoral routes to democracy as 'nested two-level games' involving strategic dilemmas in the context of structural uncertainty.
6 Thomas's theorem's original formulation was 'If men define situations as real, they are real in their consequences' (Thomas and Thomas 1928: 571–72). See also Merton (1995).
7 The term 'moral hazard' originates from the insurance industry and refers to the problem that by protecting their clients from risks (like fire), insurers might inadvertently encourage clients to behave in riskier ways (like smoking in bed).
8 'Information deficits' refers to situations in which voters have too little relevant information on the intentions and actions of elected politicians to be able to make meaningful decisions. According to economists this is the ultimate source of moral hazard problems, but this has been disputed.
9 Public goods are non-excludable and non-divisible goods such as clean air – they can be enjoyed by all. 'Collective goods' are non-divisible within a defined group (such as citizens of a particular country). The term 'club goods' is typically used to denote that the group enjoying a particular good is rather small and that there are significant barriers of entry to the community in question (in the context of this chapter, think of voters in a particular constituency or village). Private goods are perfectly divisible and excludable, such as cash, a bag of rice, a paid hospital bill, and so on.
10 The Afrobarometer round three survey for the first time asked about voting using the question: 'If (presidential) elections were held tomorrow, which party's candidate would you vote for?' Based on studies in other regions, we know that this hypothetical is a highly imperfect measure of actual behaviour and that measurement error increases with the length of time to the upcoming election. In the Afrobarometer's case, this becomes a huge problem since the length of time to the next election in most cases was more than one year.
11 The aim was to get a representative sample of constituents in each district, rather than a nationally representative sample. The strategic selection of constituencies was done in a larger project tracking citizens' opinions in a series of surveys covering elections from 1996 to 2008.
12 Downs assumes that voters support the party closest to their ideal policy position and so punish parties that do not represent their favoured policy positions.

Bibliography

Altman, D. and Pérez-Linán A. (2002) 'Assessing the Quality of Democracy: Freedom, Competitiveness and Participation in Eighteen Latin American Countries', *Democratization* 9(2): 85–100.
Barkan, J.D. (1979) 'Legislators, Elections, and Political Linkage', in J.D. Barkan and J. Okumu (eds) *Politics and Public Policy in Kenya and Tanzania*, New York, NY: Praeger.
——(2000) 'Protracted Transitions Among Africa's New Democracies', *Democratization* 7(3): 227–43.
Bates, R.H. (1981) *Markets and States in Tropical Africa*, Berkeley and Los Angeles: University of California Press.
Bates, R.H., Coatsworth, J.H. and Williamson, J.G. (2007) 'Lost Decades: Post-independence Performance in Latin America and Africa', *The Journal of Economic History* 67(4): 917–43.

Berman, B.J. (1998) 'Ethnicity, Patronage, and the African State: The Politics of Uncivil Nationalism', *African Affairs* 97(388): 305–41.

Bratton, M. (2007) 'The Democracy Barometers: Formal Versus Informal Institutions in Africa', *Journal of Democracy* 18: 96–110.

Bratton, M. and Kimenyi, M.S. (2008) 'Voting in Kenya: Putting Ethnicity in Perspective', Working Paper No. 95, Michigan State University: Afrobarometer.

Bratton, M. and Logan, C. (2006) 'Voters but not yet Citizens: The Weak Demand for Vertical Accountability in Africa's Unclaimed Democracies', Working Paper No. 63, Michigan State University: Afrobarometer.

Bratton, M. and van de Walle, N. (1997) *Democratic Experiments in Africa: Regime Transitions in Comparative Perspective*, New York, NY: Cambridge University Press.

Bunce, V.J. and Wolchick, S.L. (2009) 'Oppositions versus Dictators: Explaining Divergent Electoral Outcomes in Post-Communist Europe and Eurasia', in S.I. Lindberg (ed.) *Democratization by Elections? A New Mode of Transition*, Baltimore, MD: Johns Hopkins University Press.

Cheeseman, N. and Ford, R. (2007) 'Ethnicity as a Political Cleavage', Working Paper No. 83, Michigan State University: Afrobarometer.

Coppedge, M.C. (2006) 'Diffusion is No Illusion: Neighbor Emulation in the Third Wave of Democracy', *Comparative Political Studies* 39(4): 463–89.

Dahl, R.A. (1971) *Polyarchy: Participation and Opposition*, New Haven, CT: Yale University Press.

Diamond, L. (1996) 'Democracy in Latin America: Degrees, Illusions, and Directions for Consolidation', in T.J. Farer (ed.) *Beyond Sovereignty: Collectively Defending Democracy in the Americas*, Baltimore, MD: Johns Hopkins University Press.

——(1999) *Developing Democracy: Toward Consolidation*, Baltimore: Johns Hopkins University Press.

Diamond, L. and Plattner, M. (eds) (1999) *Democratization in Africa*, Baltimore, MD: Johns Hopkins University Press.

Di Palma, G. (1993) *To Craft Democracies: An Essay on Democratic Transitions*, Berkeley, CA: University of California Press.

Downs, A. (1957) *An Economic Theory of Democracy*, New York, NY: Harper Collins.

Eifert, B., Miguel, E. and Posner, D.N. (2007) 'Political Sources of Ethnic Identification in Africa', Working Paper No. 89, Michigan State University: Afrobarometer.

Englebert, P. (2009) *Africa: Unity, Sovereignty, Sorrow*, Boulder, CO: Lynne Rienner.

Erdmann, G. (2007) 'Ethnicity and Voter Alignment in Africa: Conceptual and Methodological Problems Revisited', in S. Gloppen and L. Rakner (eds) *Globalization and Democratization: Challenges for Political Parties*, Bergen, Norway: Fagforlaget.

Foweraker, J. and Landmann, T. (2002) 'Constitutional Design and Democratic Performance', *Democratization* 9(2): 43–66.

Fridy, K.S. (2007) 'The Elephant, Umbrella and Quarrelling Cocks: Disaggregating Partisanship in Ghana's Fourth Republic', *African Affairs* 106(423): 281–306.

Gandhi, J. and Lust-Okar, E. (2009) 'Elections Under Authoritarianism', *Annual Review of Political Science* 12: 403–22.

Günther, R., Nikiforos Diamandouros, P. and Puhle, H.-J. (1995) *The Politics of Democratic Consolidation: Southern Europe in a Comparative Perspective*, Baltimore, MD: Johns Hopkins University Press.

Helmke, G. and Levitsky, S. (eds) (2006) *Informal Institutions and Democracy in Latin America*, Baltimore, MD: Johns Hopkins University Press.

Herbst, J. (2000) *States and Power in Africa: Comparative Lessons in Authority and Control*, Princeton, NJ: Princeton University Press.

Hermet, G., Rose, R. and Rouquié, A. (1978) *Elections Without Choice*, New York, NY: Wiley.

Huntington, S.P. (1991) *The Third Wave: Democratization in the Late Twentieth Century*, Norman and London: University of Oklahoma Press.

Hydén, G. (1983) *No Shortcuts to Progress: African Development Management in Perspective*, Berkeley, CA: University of California Press.

——(2006) *African Politics in Comparative Perspective*, Cambridge: Cambridge University Press.

Hydén, G. and Leys, C. (1972) 'Elections and Politics in Single-Party Systems: The Case of Kenya and Tanzania', *British Journal of Political Science* 2(4): 389–420.

Ikpe, U.B. (2000) *Political Behaviour and Electoral Politics in Nigeria: A Political Economic Interpretation*, Lagos: Golden Educational Publishers.

Kamwambe, N. (1994) *Post-Mortem of 1994 Elections in Malawi*, Limbe, Malawi: Manifest Press.

Kramon, E. (2009) 'Vote-Buying and Political Behavior: Estimating and Explaining Vote-Buying's Effect on Turnout in Kenya', Working Paper No. 114, Michigan State University: Afrobarometer.

Kuenzi, M. and Lambright, G.M.S. (2005) 'Who Votes in Africa? An Examination of Electoral Turnout in 10 African Countries', Working Paper No. 51, Michigan State University: Afrobarometer.

Lemarchand, R. (1972) 'Political Clientelism and Ethnicity in Tropical Africa: Competing Solidarities in Nation-Building', *American Political Science Review* 66(1): 68–90.

Lindberg, S.I. (2004) 'Democratization and Women's Empowerment: The Effects of Electoral Systems, Participation and Repetition in Africa', *Studies in Comparative International Development* 38(1): 28–53.

——(2006) *Democracy and Elections in Africa*, Baltimore, MD: Johns Hopkins University Press.

——(2009a) 'The Power of Elections in Africa Revisited', in S.I. Lindberg (ed.) *Democratization by Elections? A New Mode of Transition*, Baltimore, MD: Johns Hopkins University Press.

——(2009b) 'A Theory of Elections as a Mode of Transition', in S.I. Lindberg (ed.) *Democratization by Elections? A New Mode of Transition*, Baltimore, MD: Johns Hopkins University Press.

Lindberg, S.I. and Morrison, M.K.C. (2005) 'Exploring Voter Alignment in Africa: Core and Swing Voters in Ghana', *Journal of Modern African Studies* 43(4): 1–22.

——(2008) 'Are African Voters Really Ethnic or Clientelistic? Survey Evidence from Ghana', *Political Science Quarterly* 123(1): 95–122.

Linz, J.J. and Stepan, A. (1996) *Problems of Democratic Transition and Consolidation: Southern Europe, South America, and Post-Communist Europe*, Baltimore, MD: Johns Hopkins University Press.

Logan, C. (2008) 'Rejecting the Disloyal Opposition? The Trust Gap in Mass Attitudes Toward Ruling and Opposition Parties in Africa', Working Paper No. 94, Michigan State University: Afrobarometer.

Lust-Okar, E. (2008) 'The Politics of Jordanian Elections: Competitive Clientelism', in E. Lust-Okar and S. Zerhouni (eds) *Political Participation in the Middle East and North Africa*, Boulder, CO: Lynne Rienner Publishers.

McCoy, J. and Hartlyn, J. (2009) 'The Relative Powerlessness of Elections in Latin America', in S.I. Lindberg (ed.) *Democratization by Elections? A New Mode of Transition*, Baltimore, MD: Johns Hopkins University Press.

Mattes, R. and Piombo, J. (2001) 'Opposition Parties and the Voters in South Africa's General Election of 1999', *Democratization* 8(3): 101–28.

Merton, R.K. (1995) 'The Thomas Theorem and the Matthew Effects', *Social Forces* 74(2): 379–424.

Moehler, D. and Lindberg, S.I. (2009) 'Narrowing the Legitimacy Gap: The Role of Turnovers in Africa's Emerging Democracies', *Journal of Politics* 71(4): 1448–66.

Mulenga, C.L. (2001) 'The Attitudes and Aspirations of the Main Political Parties and the Voters in Zambia: Case of the 2001 Elections and Implications for Democratic Consolidation', University of Zambia: Institute of Economic and Social Research.

Nichter, S. (2008) 'Vote Buying or Turnout Buying? Machine Politics and the Secret Ballot', *American Political Science Review* 102(1): 19–31.

O'Donnell, G. and Schmitter, P.C. (1986) *Transitions from Authoritarian Rule: Tentative Conclusions about Uncertain Democracies*, Baltimore, MD: Johns Hopkins University Press.

Posner, D.N. and Simon, D.J. (2002) 'Economic Conditions and Incumbent Support in Africa's New Democracies: Evidence from Zambia', *Comparative Political Studies* 35(2): 313–36.

Posner, D.N. and Young, D.J. (2007) 'The Institutionalization of Political Power in Africa', *Journal of Democracy* 18(3): 126–40.

Przeworski, A., Alvarez, A., Cheibub, J.A. and Limongi, F. (2000) *Democracy and Development: Political Institutions and Well-Being in the World, 1950–1990*, Cambridge: Cambridge University Press.

REDET (2004) 'The 2005 General Elections: Voters' Opinions and Preferences', Working Paper, University of Dar es Salaam: Research and Education for Democracy in Tanzania, September.

Roessler, P. and Howard, M. (2009) 'Post-Cold War Political Regimes: When Do Elections Matter?' in S.I. Lindberg (ed.) *Democratization by Elections? A New Mode of Transition*, Baltimore, MD: Johns Hopkins University Press.

Schedler, A. (2002) 'The Nested Game of Democratization by Elections', *International Political Science Review* 23(1): 103–22.

——(2009) 'The Contingent Power of Authoritarian Elections', in S.I. Lindberg (ed.) *Democratization by Elections? A New Mode of Transition*, Baltimore, MD: Johns Hopkins University Press.

Stokes, S. and Dunning, T.C. (2008) 'Clientelism as Persuasion and as Mobilization', paper presented at the Annual Meeting of the American Political Science Association, Boston, Massachusetts, 31 August 2008.

Thomas, W.I. and Thomas, D.S. (1928) *The Child in America: Behavior Problems and Programs*, New York, NY: Knopf.

Tripp, A.M. and Kang, A. (2008) 'The Global Impact of Quotas: On the Fast Track to Increased Female Legislative Representation', *Comparative Political Studies* 41(3): 338–61.

van de Walle, N. (2001) *African Economies and the Politics of Permanent Crisis, 1979–1999*, Cambridge: Cambridge University Press.

——(2007) 'Meet the New Boss, Same as the Old Boss? The Evolution of Political Clientelism in Africa', in H. Kitschelt and S.I. Wilkinson (eds) *Patrons, Clients, and Policies: Patterns of Democratic Accountability and Competition*, Cambridge: Cambridge University Press.

Wantchekon, L. (2003) 'Clientelism and Voting Behavior: Evidence from a Field Experiment in Benin', *World Politics* 55: 399–422.

Yoon, M.Y. (2004) 'Explaining Women's Legislative Representation in Sub-Saharan Africa', *Legislative Studies Quarterly* 29(3): 447–68.

20

EMERGING LEGISLATURES

Joel D. Barkan

A puzzling gap in the literature on democratization in Africa is the paucity of work on the emergence of the legislature. Yet, the rise of the legislature in several African countries is proving to be important for the consolidation of democracy in those states. This chapter seeks to fill this gap by asking the question: when and why has the legislature evolved into a significant political institution in some emerging African democracies, but not in others?[1]

Why legislatures are essential for democracy

Two decades since the resumption of multi-party politics in Africa, Terry Karl's observation that 'elections alone do not a democracy make' is truer today than ever before (Karl 1986). All but two African countries have now held multi-party elections – some for the fifth time – and a number of these countries are fledgling or consolidated democracies, yet most are not. Indeed, a review of the 2011 Freedom House ratings for political rights and civil liberties suggests that only six African countries could be classified as 'democracies' (Freedom House 2012).

What distinguishes the countries that score highest on indices of democracy, such as the Freedom House rankings, from those falling in the middle or below is not whether they hold multi-party elections at regular intervals, or even whether they have experienced an alternation in government, but whether they have developed, or are in the process of developing, strong and independent political institutions. This is especially true with respect to the development of *institutions of countervailing power* – those institutions that contain and limit the power of the executive branch, particularly executives associated with neopatrimonial or 'big man' rule (see Erdmann, this volume). Institutions of countervailing power are important because they have the potential to neutralize and perhaps end what is arguably the primary source of 'bad governance' across Africa: authoritarian rulers who perpetuate their own power via a web of patron-client relationships that are financed by the looting and hollowing out of the state. Institutions of countervailing power curtail neopatrimonial influence because they substitute institutions for personal rule. Not surprisingly, their development is fiercely resisted by neopatrimonial leaders striving to retain power.

One such institution is the legislature, *provided* it develops the capacity to perform all four of its core functions. Other institutions of countervailing power include the judiciary, special offices or commissions (such as an independent electoral commission or independent public service commission), ombudsman's offices, civil society, and the press. Though different in the functions they perform, all of these organizations extract a measure of vertical and/or horizontal accountability from the executive branch when performing well. Most importantly, they force the executive to be accountable during the periods between elections. Conversely, without such institutions, the executive invariably becomes unaccountable and exercises its authority to achieve its own preferences.

The four core functions of the modern legislature

Legislatures in democracies perform four core and unique functions that distinguish the legislature from other political institutions and highlight why they are an essential institutional component of *all* democracies. First, legislatures are the institutional mechanism through which societies realize representative governance on a day-to-day basis. Regardless of the type of electoral system through which members of the legislature gain their seats, the main function of individual legislators and the body to which they belong is to *represent* the varied and conflicting interests extant in society as a whole. The legislature is the institutional arena in which competing interests articulate and seek to advance their respective objectives in the policy-making process. While the president in a democratic presidential system is also expected to 'represent the people', she or he is not expected to articulate the diverse and competing interests of particularistic constituencies on a continuous basis. Rather, presidents are expected to synthesize, balance, and aggregate interests, and, as the head of the executive branch, to implement public policy.

Second, legislatures obviously *legislate* and they must do this at two levels. At a minimum they pass laws, but such activity may merely rubber stamp legislation handed down by the executive. More significantly, legislatures contribute to the making of public policy by crafting legislation in partnership with or independent of the executive, and then pass such legislation into law. It is important to remember that legislating in this broader sense is a process of collective action involving all members of the legislature (although those in leadership positions often play more prominent roles than others). It is thus a process that often requires intense bargaining and compromise between rival claimants for government action (or inaction).

Third, legislatures exercise *oversight* of the executive branch, to ensure that policies agreed upon and passed into law are in fact implemented by the executive. Oversight is an essential function for any democratic legislature because it ensures both vertical accountability of rulers to the ruled and horizontal accountability of all other agencies of government to the one branch whose primary function is representation. For the same reason, effective oversight requires a measure of transparency about the substance of governmental operations.

Fourth, legislatures – or more accurately, legislators acting individually rather than as members of a corporate organization engaged in collective decision making – perform the function of *constituency service*. In countries where members of the legislature (MPs) are elected from single or multi-member districts, and especially in Africa where most societies remain agrarian despite continuous migration to urban areas, constituency service takes one of two forms. First, MPs regularly visit their districts to meet constituents and assist some with their individual needs. Second is MP involvement in small- to medium-scale development projects that provide various forms of public goods – roads, water supply systems, schools, health clinics, meeting halls, and so on – to the residents of their district. In countries where MPs are elected by proportional representation (PR), constituency service is less important because members do not represent citizens on the basis of a shared place of residence.[2]

Although the performance of *all* four of these functions defines the legislature and distinguishes it from other institutions, it is important to appreciate that another defining and inherent feature of legislatures is that these functions exist in tension with each other.[3] There is tension between providing representation and legislating, because representation requires members to advocate the particular concerns of their respective constituencies or political parties, while legislating requires bargaining and compromise across these and other interests. Similarly, there is a tension between legislating and providing constituency services, because in the first MPs seek to arrive at decisions that serve the entire nation, while constituency service is, by definition, addressed to a sub-community of society. Oversight may or may not exist in tension with representing, legislating, and providing constituency services, depending whose interests are at stake.

The tensions between the four core functions become even more apparent with respect to how individual legislators – and by extension the legislature as a whole – choose to allocate their time across these responsibilities. MPs elected from single- and multi-member districts, especially in agrarian societies where political interests are often defined in local geographic terms, are under constant pressure from their constituents to service their districts. Parliamentary elections are largely referendums on incumbents' performance to meet this expectation. This in turn often leads MPs to spend far more time on this function than on legislating or oversight, the two functions that legislators perform on a collective basis. However, when members do not perform these functions and focus overwhelmingly on constituency service, the legislature exists in name only – as a conglomerate of elected officials from separate constituencies who rarely act as a whole.

Changing the incentives

Given these realities, a fundamental challenge to the development of stronger legislatures in Africa is restructuring the incentives facing MPs so that they will devote more time and effort to the functions of legislating in the broad sense and to oversight, while ensuring that MPs' reputations for constituency service are not compromised. This means changing the way African legislatures do business, which in many states will involve reshaping practices that became entrenched during lengthy periods of one-party rule.

Prior to the reintroduction of multi-party politics in the early 1990s, the legislature had either ceased to exist (as was often the case in countries under military rule), or existed simply to rubber stamp the decisions of the executive, where civilian rule continued. As such, African legislatures legislated only in the narrowest sense; they passed proposals handed down by the executive into law, but they did not participate meaningfully in the crafting of these proposals. Nor did they engage in oversight of the executive branch. To the extent that they were elected to represent diverse constituencies, as was the case in countries such as Kenya and Tanzania where a system of semi-competitive elections was maintained within the one-party format, members fulfilled the function of representation, albeit weakly (see Cheeseman, this volume).[4] The result was an asymmetrical allocation of effort to constituency services, the only function of the modern legislature that the regimes of the military and one-party era permitted MPs to perform.

MPs were both excluded from the decision-making process and encouraged by the executive – that is to say, the typical neopatrimonial president of the period – to engage in constituency service through a combination of very low salaries and the disbursement of patronage to MPs who toed the line. The scenario was nearly identical across the continent. More than one-third of all MPs were appointed to an ever-expanding number of positions as ministers or assistant ministers in what became bloated executives of between two and three dozen departments of cabinet rank. Others were appointed to the boards of state-owned enterprises. Becoming an MP was thus viewed as a way to secure patronage jobs, especially ministerial positions, rather than as a way to engage in policymaking for the nation. Those so appointed were well compensated. Equally importantly, MPs serving under intensely neopatrimonial regimes gained access to an array of state resources that could be steered to their constituencies back home. However, because their appointment and thus their ability to serve their constituencies was contingent on their loyalty to the regime and its leader, they rarely challenged the system to shift more responsibility to the legislature of which they were nominally members.

By contrast, those who remained on the backbenches were barely able to meet their basic financial obligations, including regular travel to and from their constituencies. As a result, they were often dependent on cash handouts by the regime to maintain their local political base and have any hope of winning re-election.[5] Unsurprisingly, backbenchers also aspired to executive appointments. Either way, there was no reward for expanding backbench involvement in either oversight or legislating in the broad sense.

The reintroduction of multi-party politics at the beginning of the 1990s changed the rules of the game in two respects. First, the legalization and legitimization of the opposition meant that there now existed a cadre of MPs whose power would increase from an expansion of the role of the legislature. Since members of the opposition do not shape public policy from within the executive branch, their only opportunity to effect change was to enhance the capacity of the legislature to legislate, and thereby to engage in effective oversight of the executive branch. Second, backbenchers of the ruling party were now motivated to support change for the same reason that members of the opposition did: they were poorly compensated and had little or no power *vis-à-vis* the executive. By entering into informal coalitions with the opposition they could expand both their terms of service and their power.

Building legislative capacity, however, was contingent on changes to the formal rules that structure legislative-executive relations and the provision of adequate resources to both the legislature as an institution and to its individual members. Indeed, without additional funds and expertise, MPs would be unable to take advantage of any changes in the rules. Not surprisingly, such changes were resisted by incumbent presidents and ministers.

The result in some countries – most notably in Kenya, but also in Uganda and to a much lesser extent in Ghana, Nigeria, and South Africa – has been the emergence of *coalitions for change* within the legislature. These are informal groupings of MPs who seek to alter the formal balance of power between the executive and the legislature, and to increase the flow of resources to the institution and its members in order to improve the performance of the legislature in all four of its core functions. Both changes are critical if MPs are to devote more time to the collective responsibilities of crafting legislation and providing oversight.

Changing the rules

Changing the formal rules that specify the nature of executive-legislative relations requires either a constitutional amendment, the passage of specific legislation, or some combination of the two. These include but are not limited to:

- Whether the legislature is defined as a separate and independent branch of government by the constitution;
- Whether the executive can dissolve the legislature and call for new elections, or members of legislature are elected for a fixed term;
- Whether the executive can suspend the sitting of the legislature;
- Whether the legislature can pass legislation without the assent of the president and whether it can override a presidential veto;

- Whether senior presidential appointments, such as cabinet ministers, the head and senior members of the judiciary, heads of special commissions (such as the electoral commission), and ambassadors must be confirmed by the legislature;
- Whether the legislature can require senior members of the executive branch to testify before the legislature about executive actions, and whether the legislature can require official documents from the executive branch;
- Whether the legislature can set its own budget, including salaries for members and professional staff;
- Whether the legislature can recruit and maintain its own parliamentary service, or is dependent on the provision of staff from the public service;
- Whether the legislature can amend the national budget or is restricted to merely approving or rejecting the budget, and whether there is a process through which the legislature can negotiate the preparation of the final budget with the Ministry of Finance;
- Whether members of the legislature are elected from single- or multi-member districts, PR or some combination of the two; and
- Whether there is a constituency development fund (CDF) to facilitate the provision of basic services on a constituency-by-constituency basis.

The cumulative effect of these 11 sets of formal procedures is to tip the balance of power toward, or away from, the legislature *vis-à-vis* the executive branch. Of these, the seventh and ninth are arguably the most important and controversial in terms of blocking the emergence of an omnipotent executive. Where the legislature has a free hand in setting its own budget, it is in a position to raise salaries for both its members and staff, as well as to make other expenditures required to support the institution. Where the legislature can amend the national budget, it becomes a full partner in the governing process.

Increasing resources

In order to perform the four core functions effectively, African legislatures require substantially more resources – financial, human, and physical – than they received during the era of neopatrimonial rule. To keep their monopoly on power, executives historically starved their countries' legislatures of cash. In addition to revising the formal rules governing the scope of legislative action, legislatures must therefore also secure adequate funding. This has become a highly controversial area of reform, because at the very time that some African legislatures are becoming meaningful actors in the policymaking process and a counterweight to the executive branch, there have been examples of overreaching for the purpose of personal enrichment by members in several countries.

MPs in some countries – most notably Kenya, Nigeria, Uganda, and South Africa – have raised their salaries and other perks, including health insurance, pensions, and allowances for travel to and from their constituencies. In Nigeria, the total package of 'official' emoluments has risen to US$224,000 per annum, while in Kenya, members' salaries and benefits now exceed $165,000.[6] Given that these pay packages match or exceed those for parliamentarians in most developed countries, it is not surprising that they have evoked severe criticism in the Nigerian and Kenyan press. Opinion polls in Kenya indicate that the public perception of the National Assembly is low. Indeed, 72 per cent of the members of the Ninth Parliament were not re-elected to the 10th in December 2007, a significantly higher proportion than in prior elections, when roughly half were defeated. The percentage of incumbents of the House of Representatives in Nigeria who were defeated in elections held in April 2011 was the same. Whether these high levels of incumbent defeat are evidence of a public backlash against the level of compensation for MPs is unclear, but in these countries (which, it should be noted, are outliers in Africa) the issue is no longer one of insufficient salaries, but salaries that are deemed excessive.

That said, higher salaries appear to have facilitated greater productivity on the part of MPs with respect to legislating and providing oversight. Since 1999, the Kenya National Assembly has implemented a broad series of constitutional and internal reforms, including the strengthening of its committee system, the revision of the Standing Orders (the internal rules of the legislature), and the establishment of a parliamentary budget office.[7] In the process, the Ninth Parliament arguably became one of the most effective legislatures on the continent. The 10th Kenyan Parliament has continued the trend, passing enabling legislation that produced a new constitution which substantially increased the powers of the legislature *vis-à-vis* the executive branch. Similarly, in Nigeria the development and competence of the committee system and the level of legislative oversight of the executive increased markedly during the Third Assembly, which served from 2007 to 2011 (Lewis 2009).

In addition to monetary resources, African legislatures face a shortage of human resources. Significantly, the two go hand in hand. The number of professional staff (those with administrative, parliamentary, and/or policy experience) is small – often not more than one to two dozen individuals – compared to the large number of secretaries, messengers, drivers, sweepers, and other support staff, who often number in the hundreds. In this, the staff at most African legislatures resembles African bureaucracies prior to civil service reform: bloated and often staffed by individuals who obtained their posts through patronage rather than merit.

Restructuring and professionalizing the staff of the legislature, however, requires not only the will to reform, but also sufficient funds to be devoted to the task. First, the members of the legislature must decide that such restructuring is essential if they and their institution are fully to perform the four functions of the legislature. Second, they must take control of existing staff by creating a separate parliamentary service, for example, thereby separating legislative staff from the government's civil service. Knowledgeable professionals must be recruited, especially as support staff for the evolving system of portfolio (i.e. ministerial) and oversight committees – the heart of the modern legislature. Competent managerial staff must be recruited at the level of the chief clerk and senior deputy clerks to guide this expansion. Finally, to the extent that resources permit, competent staff must be assigned to individual MPs both at the legislature itself and back in their constituencies, where members are beginning to establish local offices.

In addition to the dearth of adequate legislative staff, most African legislatures are woefully short of physical infrastructure. In Ghana, for example, the National Assembly does not have enough rooms for the legislative committees to meet regularly. Most African legislatures cannot provide offices for their members other than for the few who occupy leadership positions. Constituency offices are almost non-existent, yet are important if MPs are to maintain sustained direct or indirect contact with those they represent. All this requires a rapid expansion of the legislature's budget, an expansion invariably resisted by the executive for the obvious reason that the building of such capacity comes at the expense of presidential power. Only South Africa, and to a lesser extent Kenya and Nigeria, provide adequate staff and physical infrastructure for their MPs. In the case of South Africa, this is largely a reflection of the country's relative wealth and government resources, and a continuation of the level of support provided for MPs during the apartheid era. It is also a reflection of the commitment of the leadership of the ruling African National Congress (ANC) to competitive politics. Notwithstanding former president Thabo Mbeki's reputation as a 'centralizer', his government lavishly funded the South African National Assembly and regularly sang its praises as 'one of the cornerstones of our democracy'. This policy has continued under his successor, Jacob Zuma.

In Kenya and Nigeria, where the provision of individual offices to all MPs and the professionalization of staff is a more recent development, the explanation is quite different. In these cases, the increase in resources to support the legislature is the direct result of MPs taking control of the parliamentary budget to provide for their needs. The Kenya National Assembly has also benefited from more than a decade of technical assistance from the US Agency for International Development (USAID) and the UK Department for International Development (DfID), which has been marked by a strong working relationship between these aid agencies and the leadership of the Assembly. All three cases illustrate that without adequate resources the building of modern legislatures in Africa will be difficult. Yet as the case of South Africa demonstrates, financing alone does not guarantee a strong legislature.

Constituency service and campaign finance

The transformation of the legislature also requires that some attention be given to the overlapping issues of constituency service and campaign finance. As noted above, African MPs are under intense pressure to service their constituencies and their re-election often depends on it. They are therefore on a never-ending quest for funds to support trips to their home areas and to provide assistance to their local communities in the form of public goods. This not only consumes much time, at the expense of time that might be spent on legislating and oversight, but it also makes MPs vulnerable to blandishments of patronage from the executive, which in turn limits the degrees of freedom MPs have to perform their other legislative roles. It is therefore not surprising that legislators in some countries have begun to devise new mechanisms for both financing constituency service and for reducing their dependence on patrons and other supporters who have provided them with cash to fulfil their constituency obligations in the past. The increase in allowances for travel back to the constituency and funds for the establishment of constituency offices are best understood in this context.

The most significant of these efforts is the establishment of constituency development funds or CDFs. CDFs are an annual programme of unconditional transfers of funds from the central government to all parliamentary constituencies based on allocation formulas – usually population adjusted for poverty – specified by law. The funds are then given to local development projects and programmes prioritized by each constituency's MP and/or a constituency development committee established for this purpose. CDFs were first established in Kenya in 2003, where they have proved immensely popular amongst both MPs and the public. Under current legislation, the government of Kenya is required to allocate 2.5 per cent of its annual budget to CDFs. During the 2010–11 fiscal year, this disbursement averaged $1,077,000 per constituency – enough to repair or construct a substantial number of classrooms, health clinics, water systems, and other infrastructure desired by rural communities. Not surprisingly, Kenyan MPs want more. MPs in Nigeria, Tanzania, Uganda, and Zambia have since established their own CDFs. A variation of this funding mechanism has also been established in Ghana, where 5 per cent of that country's Regional Development Fund is set aside for reallocation to each parliamentary constituency within its respective region. Most legislators regard this as terribly inadequate. Other African countries, including Malawi, are considering the establishment of CDFs.

Notwithstanding the popularity of CDFs, the emergence of these funds has not resulted in an automatic advantage for incumbent MPs seeking re-election to the legislature. The impact has proven quite the contrary. Where they have been closely involved in the allocation of the funds, MPs have often found themselves mired in controversy, or the object of allegations that they have engaged in corrupt practices or otherwise steered the funds into activities that benefit them politically. Where, on the other hand, the procedures for allocating the funds have been revised to prevent such abuses, as in Kenya, MPs find that they have little influence over the allocation of the funds and thus gain minimal or no political advantage from their creation. Indeed, in both Kenya and Nigeria, the establishment of CDFs has occurred at the same time as the rate of MP re-election has plummeted to just over 20 per cent.

The emergence of 'coalitions for change'

The size, composition, and influence of the coalitions for change that have formed in many African legislatures varies greatly from one country to the next, but the following characteristics stand out. First, in terms of 'committed activists', the number of MPs involved in these coalitions remains small – no more than 30 to 50 MPs in the legislatures considered for this chapter, sometimes as few as a dozen. Given that the size of these legislatures ranges from a low of 222 in Kenya, to 400 in South Africa, this means that no more than a fifth to a quarter of all members, and usually far fewer, join such coalitions.[8] Despite their small numbers, their impact can be profound. Second, as previously noted, the demand for change is articulated most forcefully by members of the opposition in alliance with a portion of backbenchers of the ruling party. Third, and perhaps most important, these coalitions include both *reformers* and *opportunists*. That is to say, they are led by MPs who seek certain changes and reforms to enhance the institutional capacity and power of the legislature so that it can perform its core functions and advance the process of democratization generally, but are also joined by other members whose main motivation is to improve their own personal situation.

The issue of MPs' salaries nicely illustrates this distinction. Reformers want higher salaries for MPs and staff because they recognize that it is an important first step in professionalizing the legislature. Higher salaries make MPs less susceptible to the blandishments of patronage by the executive, while enabling legislators to perform their entire portfolio of duties. Higher salaries also attract better-qualified candidates who desire to strengthen the institution. By contrast, opportunists are interested in higher salaries for their own sake and because greater resources will help them to deal more effectively with the expectations of their constituents. They are not particularly interested in strengthening the legislature as an institution, but they do not oppose this goal either. Thus, they join reformers for their own ends, but often provide the crucial number of votes required to make the changes reformers seek. Whereas reformers are never more than an activist minority within the legislature, opportunists often include most members of the opposition and a significant number of ruling party backbenchers. Reformers rarely achieve their objectives without the presence and support of opportunists.

Which conditions or variables determine the size and power of these 'coalitions for change' and what conditions determine the size of its core component of reformers? The answer is hard to specify quantitatively from the available evidence. However, six variables are clearly important.

1. The changing membership of the legislature

African legislatures have historically been composed of individuals whose levels of income, occupation, and especially education, are substantially higher than those of the rest of the population. This is not surprising given that MPs are members of society's elite. Moreover, these demographic characteristics do not seem to distinguish 'reformers' from 'opportunists', nor reformers from opponents of reform. Instead, what distinguishes this group of MPs from their peers is their *attitude and values* – a combination of their genuine commitment to the goal of democratization, their familiarity with and sensitivity to global norms of political and economic governance, and their general 'savvy'. Put differently, these MPs are *outward looking* rather than inward looking, in that they analyse their society and its political institutions from a comparative and global perspective. One indication of this orientation is that nearly all reformers are also computer literate and use the internet, skills almost non-existent among MPs of the previous political generation that sustained neopatrimonial rule. Many are also private sector entrepreneurs. They place a greater emphasis on performance than on loyalty cemented by patronage. They therefore constitute a new political generation of African legislators – not necessarily younger in terms of chronological age, although many are young, but different in terms of their *outlook and approach.*[9]

2. Voter expectations for constituency service

Notwithstanding these characteristics, reformers must overcome the challenge that their re-election depends on their records of constituency service rather than their ability to legislate or oversee the executive branch, and the fact that half or more are likely to be defeated when seeking re-election. Reformers are consequently a group marked by high turnover, the number of which in most countries becomes smaller over successive elections. Reformers face a basic dilemma: the more time they devote to building the capacity of the legislature, and to legislating and oversight, the less time they are able to devote to constituency service, and thus the less likely their prospects for re-election.

3. Urbanization and the size of civil society

The number of reformers also reflects the relative strength and size of civil society. The more urbanized and economically developed a country, the greater the size of its civil society and the more likely it is that the legislature will be populated by reformers seeking to expand the powers of the institution to which they belong. This largely explains why a powerful and sustained coalition for change emerged in the Kenya National Assembly, while such a coalition has not emerged in the legislatures of Benin, Ghana, Senegal, and Uganda. It may also explain why civil society organizations, professional associations, and businesses in Kenya and South Africa have developed the practice of lobbying the legislature, approaching relevant committees to a greater extent than what the author has observed in other African countries.

4. Parity between government and opposition

The emergence of a coalition for change is more likely where the number of seats controlled by the ruling and opposition parties approach parity. The reason should be obvious: when the ruling party and opposition hold a nearly equal number of seats, a majority coalition for strengthening the legislature can be formed by the opposition in alliance with a small-to-modest number of backbenchers from the ruling party. This is especially true where party identity and party discipline are weak. Thus, in Kenya during the Eighth Parliament (1997–2002) and in Ghana during the Third Parliament (2001–04) reformers were able to organize themselves effectively and commence the process of reform, whereas this was not possible before parity. Conversely, where the ruling party commands an overwhelming majority, as in South Africa and Senegal, the prospects for expanding the powers of the legislature are limited. Moreover, in countries where the leadership of the ruling party enforces party discipline to retain executive power – as in Uganda – the emergence of a viable opposition may complicate, and in some instances reverse, the expansion of legislative authority (Kasfir and Twebaze 2009).

5. Role and persona of the presiding officer and the chief administrative officer

During the period of one-party rule, the role of the presiding officer (the speaker) and the chief administrative officer (the clerk) conformed to the patronage-based systems of that era. Presidents handpicked loyalists for these positions. Their mandate was to keep the legislature compliant and contain any mavericks seeking to enhance its powers, *de facto* or *de jure*. Rather than being genuinely elected by their colleagues, these speakers were imposed. Rather than seeking to expand the array of services provided to MPs, clerks and their staffs were kept on a short leash by the executive and provided with few resources. After the return to multi-party politics in the early 1990s, the executive expected that the speaker and clerk would continue to run the legislature as before. This created a measure of friction in some legislatures, including the National Assemblies in Kenya and Tanzania, where reformers sought to expand the capacity of the legislature but were repeatedly frustrated by the presiding officer. In Tanzania, the speaker retained his position for three terms before eventually retiring after the 2005 elections. In Kenya, the incumbent speaker also retained his position for three terms, but was defeated in his bid for a fourth term when the newly elected House convened after the 2007 elections. In both cases, the speaker sought to transform his role – and thus retain his job – from the watchdog for the executive tasked with blocking change, to the spokesperson for reform, albeit on the government's timetable. In the South African National Assembly, the role of the first speaker in the post-apartheid era was different, yet similar insofar as she was expected to serve the leadership of the ruling party and the executive first, and the MPs second.[10] Following the 1994 election, which brought the first African-led government to power, the speaker was faced with the challenge of organizing and presiding over a new legislature with 400 members, of which less than 20 per cent had ever served before. In this role, she was highly supportive of members, particularly younger and less-educated members, of the ruling ANC. She also had the delicate task of assuming authority over a highly competent yet holdover staff from the apartheid era, a transition she managed well. Yet she was also expected to ensure that members of the ANC toed the party line as laid down by its leadership, with the result that many – including several committee chairs, all of whom were members of the ANC – chafed under her control. A variation of this scenario occurred in Ghana where an independent speaker who sought to strengthen the legislature in the Third Parliament (2000–04) was subsequently pushed aside by then-President John Kufuor when he sought to retain the speakership in the Fourth Parliament (Lindberg and Zhou 2009).

6. The type of electoral system used to elect MPs

Unlike the rules specifying the relationship between the executive and the legislature, the rules specifying how votes are translated into seats determines support for a 'coalition for change', especially amongst backbenchers of the ruling party. Where proportional representation based on lists of candidates nominated by the party is employed, as in South Africa, Mozambique, and Namibia, the likelihood of backbenchers joining a reform movement to challenge the executive is much less than where MPs are elected from single- or small multi-member districts. Party discipline within the legislature is generally much stronger in legislatures elected via PR than from single-member districts, as the leadership can threaten MPs who challenge the executive with removal or demotion on the party list for the next election. Moreover in South Africa, where the ruling ANC periodically 're-deploys' (i.e. reassigns) its members to different positions in government, renegade members have been removed from the National Assembly in the middle of their terms.[11] The impact of PR also suggests that contrary to conventional wisdom, cohesive and highly disciplined political parties are not necessarily 'good' for the development of the legislature and whether it performs its core functions effectively.[12]

Measuring legislative performance

Measuring the performance and impact of legislatures is a challenging task and space does not permit more than a cursory discussion here. It is nonetheless essential to develop at least some rudimentary measures of legislative performance lest there be no way to measure their development over time or to compare and explain why some have developed while others have not.

To date, five methods have been used to measure legislative power or performance. The first is a relatively straightforward assessment of the formal powers of the legislature to measure its independence from the executive branch. This is the approach taken by Steven Fish and Michael Kroenig in their construction of the Parliamentary Powers Index (PPI) (Fish and Kroenig 2009). Fish and Kroenig identify 32 such measures and then, based on the responses to their survey by a panel of at least five experts per country, compute the percentage of items scored 'yes' for each country by the panels. The more items scored 'yes' by the panel, the stronger the legislature.

Although the PPI helps to explain some variations in Freedom House scores and demonstrates a clear relationship between the level of legislative power and the level of democracy, the index does not directly consider the extent to which legislatures perform any of the four core functions discussed above. Such a series of functional assessments, however, could be constructed via the same panel approach used by Fish and Kroenig. This would reveal more about actual legislative performance than the PPI because it would highlight the tensions and tradeoffs arising from the performance of the four functions. For example, one would expect that any given legislature might score high on the index for one or two functions – say, representation and legislating – but not for the others.

Yet another approach, and one also preferred by this author, would be an assessment of the quality of key components and actors in the legislative process. For example, a number of measures can and are being developed to assess the capacity and practice of the committee system. This area of inquiry was surprisingly ignored or avoided by Fish and Kroenig, yet most observers agree that a strong committee system is central to the development of a powerful and effective legislature – that is, how well it performs the core functions, especially legislating in the broad sense, and oversight. Other components of the legislative process, such as the involvement by the legislature in the formation of the budget, could also be assessed. Indeed, the Kenya National Assembly is one of the most powerful legislatures in Africa on these dimensions, but Fish and Kroenig (wrongly, in the opinion of this author) rank it among the least powerful for the PPI.

A fourth approach often employed by students of the US Congress is to measure the extent and manner to which the legislature legislates by assessing the frequency and content of bills passed. While this approach attempts directly to measure the productivity of the legislature, it becomes mired in a host of methodological questions, including, but not limited to, the question of how to 'weight' individual pieces of legislation. Not all bills passed into law are in fact individual pieces of legislation, but omnibus laws that need to be disaggregated in order to be properly measured. Not all disaggregated measures, however, are of equal significance. Many are simply amended versions of earlier legislation. How does one assess the relative significance or ultimate impact of these pieces of legislation? The approach is fraught with difficulties, yet is perhaps still worthwhile, given that the crafting and passage of legislation is a defining function of the legislature.

Fifth, and finally, there are variations of the reputational approach, assessments by either experts or citizens about how well they believe the legislature is performing its core functions.

Such measures, however, are subjective assessments that may tell us more about those giving their opinions than the performance of the legislature itself.

Conclusion

Although legislative performance with respect to the four defining functions is uneven across the African continent, the legislature is emerging as a key player in some countries. It has begun to initiate and modify legislation to a degree never seen during the era of neopatrimonial rule, nor during the early years following the return of multi-party politics. It sometimes exerts meaningful oversight over the executive. In Kenya, Malawi, Nigeria, and Zambia (but not Uganda), it has blocked presidents from changing the constitution to repeal the limit on presidential terms. Where the legislature must ratify key appoints by the president, as in Kenya, it is also beginning to reject such nominations. Put simply, the institution is emerging as a check on the executive – a true institution of countervailing power – in some countries.

Because of its emerging power, the legislature is also becoming the object of lobbying by civil society and, increasingly, the business community in some countries. In short, African legislatures are beginning to 'matter'. That said, there is no uniformity across Africa, and we are only beginning to understand and explain the variations. If the legislature is a defining institution of liberal democracy, then clearly more attention must be given to explaining its development and nurturing its growth.

Notes

1 Portions of this chapter appeared in an earlier article (Barkan 2008).

2 It is therefore noteworthy that in South Africa, a country that employs proportional representation, the ruling party found it necessary to establish a 'shadow' system of single-member districts to which it assigns its MPs for the purpose of maintaining contact with the grassroots.

3 I am indebted to Shaheen Mozaffar for this insight.

4 In these elections, two or more candidates of the ruling party competed for office much as they do for party primary elections or non-partisan elections in the United States. Such elections, which occurred between 1965 and 1990, never resulted in the alternation of government, but did result in a high turnover of MPs.

5 In a typical parliamentary election in Africa, between 60 per cent and 75 per cent of incumbents fail to win re-election. Not surprisingly, the turnover rate for assistant ministers and ministers is much lower. Between 50 per cent and 65 per cent of assistant ministers win re-election while the percentage for ministers runs as high as 75 per cent.

6 Unofficial payments are widely reported to raise the total package paid to Nigerian MPs to over $1 million annually.

7 Formally known as The Office for Fiscal Analysis and Management.

8 The National Assembly of Benin, which is included in our study, has only 87 members. Regrettably, no identifiable group of reformers nor a 'coalition for change' has emerged in that body, with the result that it has been excluded from these estimates of the proportion of MPs who press for reform. We also found no such coalition in Senegal. These data come from a larger study in which a group of researchers studied the legislatures of Benin, Ghana, Kenya, Senegal, Tanzania, Uganda, and South Africa.

9 The perspective and motivations of this group are not hard to explain. Most view the world including politics and the economy through a new lens for the simple reason that they want to make money.

10 She was also an ANC loyalist who aspired to a cabinet post.

11 In 2000 the ANC chair of the Standing Committee on Public Accounts was removed from the chairship and ultimately forced to resign after his committee became too aggressive in investigating alleged corruption in the granting of procurement contracts by the Ministry of Defence.

12 As noted by Nelson Kasfir, the conventional wisdom about the desirability of cohesive and strong parties is also tested in Uganda. Prior to the parliamentary elections of February 2006, when Uganda operated under the 'Movement' system and all MPs were members of the National Resistance Movement, the lines

between government and opposition were highly fluid. During this period, a coalition for change emerged in the National Assembly which adopted several significant reforms, including a significant rise in MP compensation and the passage of legislation that provided for the scheduled involvement of the Assembly in the budgetary process. The committee system was also strengthened, especially the Public Accounts Committee, the principal mechanism by which the National Assembly scrutinizes executive performance. Although they were not enthusiastic about these developments, President Museveni and his government went along with this expansion of legislative power. However, following the adoption of 'multi-partyism' in 2005, several MPs who had been prominent in the coalition for change that lobbied for these reforms morphed into the opposition, thus drawing Museveni's ire and his determination to bring the legislature to heel.

Bibliography

Barkan, J.D. (2008) 'Legislatures on the Rise', *The Journal of Democracy* 19(2): 124–37.
——(ed.) (2009) *Legislative Power in Emerging African Democracies*, Boulder, CO: Lynne Rienner Publishers.
Calland, R. (2006) 'Parliament: The Good, the Bad and the Simply Irrelevant', in R. Calland (ed.) *Anatomy of South Africa: Who Holds Power?* Cape Town: Zebra Press.
Fish, M.S. (2006) 'Stronger Legislatures, Stronger Democracies', *Journal of Democracy* 17(1): 5–20.
Fish, M.S. and Kroenig, M. (2009) *The Handbook of National Legislatures: A Global Survey*, New York, NY: Cambridge University Press.
Freedom House (2012) 'Freedom in the World 2012', New York, NY, and Washington, DC: Freedom House.
Karl, T. (1986) 'Imposing Consent, Electoralism and Democratization in El Salvador', in P. Drake and E. Silva (eds) *Elections in Latin America*, San Diego, CA: University of California.
Kasfir, N. and Twebaze, S.H. (2009) 'The Rise and Ebb of Uganda's No-Party Parliament', in J.D. Barkan (ed.) *Legislative Power in Emerging African Democracies*, Boulder, CO: Lynne Rienner Publishers.
Lewis, P.M. (2009) 'Rules and Rents in Nigeria's National Assembly', in J.D. Barkan (ed.) *Legislative Power in Emerging African Democracies*, Boulder, CO: Lynne Rienner Publishers.
Lindberg, S. and Zhou, Y. (2009) 'Co-optation Despite Democratization in Ghana', in J.D. Barkan (ed.) *Legislative Power in Emerging African Democracies*, Boulder, CO: Lynne Rienner Publishers.
Salih, M.A.M. (ed.) (2005) *African Parliaments*, New York, NY: Palgrave Macmillan.

21

POLITICAL PARTIES

Matthijs Bogaards

Modern democracy is party democracy. Even modern authoritarianism cannot do without parties – witness the rise of electoral authoritarian or competitive authoritarian regimes, of which Africa has its fair share (van de Walle, this volume). There are still countries without political parties. Eritrea has no political parties, and in the Kingdom of Swaziland, whilst political parties are now able to register thanks to pressure from the High Court, they are not allowed to contest elections. In addition to these party-less states there are anti-party states with 'regimes that have suppressed pre-existing parties, take an anti-party stand, or profess an anti-party doctrine' (Sartori 1976: 40). The most instructive examples come from Ghana and Uganda.

No-party democracy

The best-known experiment with no-party democracy comes from Uganda. In 1986 Yoweri Museveni's rebels secured power in Uganda. Building on the Resistance Councils that had been set up in the areas under the control of the National Resistance Army, Museveni outlined his vision of a political system without the political parties that he identified as a root cause of many of the country's troubles. Political party activity was outlawed, all Ugandans were represented through the National Resistance Movement, and elections were held on the basis of 'individual merit'.

Carbone's (2008) study of the last 40 years of Ugandan politics shows the tension between the ideas of 'no-party' or movement democracy, and how the movement in the end assumed many of the functions of a political party in the electoral and parliamentary process. At the same time, the legal restrictions on party activity prevented the National Resistance Movement (NRM) from becoming a more effective political organization. These contradictions were only resolved in 2006, when the ban on party activities was lifted. It should come as no surprise that the first multi-party elections were won by the ruling 'movement'.

Less well-known but perhaps even more instructive is the case of Ghana. The idea of a no-party government in Ghana was first mooted around 1966, when a Constitutional Commission was preparing the groundwork for the Second Republic. After the experience with Nkrumah's one-party state (1964–66), there seemed to be widespread support for the idea of a 'no-party state'. Two arguments were advanced in favour of no-partyism. First, that there was some sort of affinity between the no-party state and traditional authority, a claim that was strongly pushed by the Ghanaian chiefs. Second, that foreign models of party politics were unsuitable to the Ghanaian context. Owusu (1979: 97), for example, argued that one could 'eliminate political parties without damage to the representational principle'.

In general, party politics was thought to be elitist; to encourage bribing and corrupting voters; to exploit regional, ethnic, and other primordial sentiments to the detriment of the nation; to degenerate into one-party tyranny; to have lost the faith of most people; and not to be based on real differences between parties (Owusu 1979: 100–1). This is the same diagnosis that led to the widespread adoption of one-party states across the continent in the late 1960s and early 1970s.[1] However, the multi-party system found a staunch defender in the form of the supposedly impartial chairman of the Constitutional Commission, Ghana's Chief Justice. In the end, the proponents of the traditional Westminster-type parliamentary democracy carried the day.

After the rapid demise of the Second Republic (1969–72), the idea of a no-party state resurfaced, this time with the strong backing of the military. Toward the end of 1976, the Supreme Military Council initiated a proposal for Union Government. A committee composed of legal scholars, academics, and representatives of key professional groups reviewed past constitutions, received scores of depositions, and conducted several public hearings. The 1977 *Report of the Ad Hoc Committee on Union Government* proposed a no-party political system (Chazan and Le Vine 1979).

The following year, the people of Ghana were asked in a referendum whether the drafters of the new constitution should follow the principle of 'Union Government'. The majority vote in favour was widely understood to have been rigged, but head of state General Acheampong proceeded to ban the main opposition movement and incarcerate its leaders nonetheless. As public hostility toward these government actions grew, a coup occurred. Under a new leadership, and under a new constitution approved by referendum in 1979, multi-party elections were to be held. However, before this could happen flight-lieutenant Jerry Rawlings came to power through a coup against the military government, promising a revolution and issuing a ban on party politics. 'Rawlings was strongly opposed to a pluralist political system because he considered that it was merely a front for the corrupt and self-serving behavior of politicians' (Haynes 1995: 101). Instead, some government representatives advocated the development of an indigenous system of democracy without parties, which they argued would return Ghana to the consensual methods of local decision making which they claimed had been destroyed by colonialism.[2]

In 1990 and 1991 the government stage-managed public discussions on the country's political future. The outcome was a proposal to introduce district assemblies without parties. Whatever the possible intrinsic merits of this policy, the 'plan was too much like the vilified UNIGOV proposal of the late 1970s to elicit much popular support. Rawlings' support of the "no-party" option was to many Ghanaians unfortunately reminiscent of the attempt in 1978 to legitimize the breathtakingly corrupt military regime of General Acheampong', writes Haynes (1995: 97). This helps to explain the high levels of opposition to the plan. Moreover, the re-launch of the idea of no-party government in Ghana was poorly timed, for it came at the very moment that the third wave of democratization reached Africa.

Thus, in 1991 Rawlings unexpectedly embraced the idea of conventional, multi-party elections for the national parliament. No-party democracy survived at the local level. The 'revolutionary' organs at the local level were reorganized into a no-party District Assembly structure. In the words of Crook, 'the decentralized administration and District Assembly system created in 1988–89 was based on a theory of community-level, participatory, no-party democracy which idealized the consensual character of "traditional" Ghanaian village life' (Crook 1999: 133). The underlying idea was that 'ordinary people' all have a common and obvious interest in development and the provision of basic services and infrastructure. Political competition is therefore about the qualities of the individuals who wish to take responsibility for these matters, and their fitness to work for or represent their communities. Parties are superfluous. The new constitution was approved with an overwhelming majority in a referendum in 1992.

The idea of non-partisan local councils has also found favour with some political scientists (see Kasfir 1992). However, it is difficult to see how such a combination of no-party elections at the district level and multi-party elections at the national level could have worked in the long run.

The no-party and the one-party state rests on negative conceptions about the role and impact of political parties. They are seen to distort representation, thwart nation-building, and imperil political stability. Even if this evaluation were correct, it does not follow that elections without parties produce a polity free from these evils. Like the one-party states, Uganda and Ghana both returned to multi-party politics and while Uganda remains an electoral-authoritarian regime, Ghana is now seen as a model of responsible electoral politics (but see Jockers *et al.* 2010).

The study of parties in Africa

It is only a slight exaggeration to say that the last systematic study of political parties in Africa – in all their facets, including organization and ideology – was published almost half a century ago (Coleman and Rosberg 1964). However, much of the early scholarship is of limited relevance today. In the pre-independence period the focus was on the nationalist movements that helped to end colonialism, whereas after independence, the emphasis quickly shifted to the different types of one-party states (Hodgkin 1961; Morgenthau 1961) and the role of 'machine politics' (Zolberg 1966; Bienen 1971). Early typologies of African parties were largely simplifications of the European literature from the 1950s that sought to distinguish between mass and elite parties. This endeavour was handicapped by conceptual confusion and the absence of genuine mass parties in Africa (Dudley 1967; Sartori 1976). The spread of authoritarianism on the continent resulted in 'lost decades' for political party scholarship.

Parties perform a variety of functions (Bartolini and Mair 2001). First, they have a representative function, in that they represent societal interests within the political system. Second, parties perform a variety of institutional functions, including the recruitment of political leaders and the organization of parliament and government. However, 'no matter what roles parties have been assigned, almost everywhere in tropical Africa – whether in single-party, multi-party, or non-party states – they perform few (of them)' (Rotberg 1966: 571). What Carothers (2006: 4) calls 'the standard lament' about parties sounds eerily familiar to observers of African party politics: parties are corrupt, only active around election time, and do not stand for anything, while party leaders are selfish and preoccupied with squabbling instead of governing the country. Explanations have focused on social structures, economic development, presidential forms of government, weak rule of law, authoritarian legacies, and problems of state and nation-building (Randall and Svåsand 2002; McMahon 2004; Carothers 2006).

Already in 1966, Lapalombara and Weiner had cautioned in their classic study on parties and development that in emerging nations the conditions for party development were wanting. They were careful to note that 'many of the so-called political parties in Africa are not political parties as we are using the term' (Lapalombara and Weiner 1966: 29). That is to say, African party organizations normally lacked at least one of the following features: continuity, extension from the national to the local level, active pursuit of followers at the polls or popular support in general, or leaders determined to capture and hold decision-making power. Hydén (2006) therefore suggests thinking of some of these organizations as political movements rather than parties. For comparative purposes, the minimal definition of Sartori is probably most helpful.

Sartori (1976: 64) defines a party as 'any political group that presents at elections, and is capable of placing through elections, candidates for public office'.

There is consensus, although a waning one, about the importance of ethnicity for party politics in Africa. The first analyses of political parties in Africa had already noted how a lack of social differentiation led to the formation of parties the primary reference group of which was traditional. Today, it is commonplace to refer to African parties as ethnic parties. This does not imply the assumption of a simple one-to-one relationship between ethnic group and political party. Mozaffar (2006: 239) has stressed that the relationship between party and ethnicity is 'strategic and contingent'. Posner's (2005) influential case study of Zambia shows that ethnicity was a key factor during both one-party and multi-party politics. The change from dictatorship to democracy did not lessen or intensify the role of ethnicity in politics, but it did change the type of ethnicity: from local affiliations in one-party elections, to the building of regional coalitions in multi-party elections. However, most of the studies on ethnic parties are not so much about the parties themselves – how they are organized, their leaders and members, how they appeal to voters – but about voting behaviour. The logic being that if people from one group vote disproportionately for one party, the party must be ethnic (Basedau *et al.* 2011). Research that examines how parties appeal to voters reaches a more nuanced conclusion (Elischer 2012).

Ethnic politics is commonly linked to clientelism and neopatrimonialism. Following Erdmann and Engels, the distinguishing feature of neopatrimonialism is the 'mixture of two co-existing, partly interwoven, types of domination: namely, patrimonial and legal-rational bureaucratic domination' (Erdmann and Engel 2007: 105). Under neopatrimonialism the distinction between public and private exists, but is not always observed (see Erdmann, this volume). Following van de Walle (2007), a change can be observed in the nature of state capture by political parties. In the decades following independence, prebendalism was common. Prebendalism means that 'an individual is given a public office in order for him/her to gain personal access over state resources' (ibid.: 51). Resources were mediated by the state rather than parties. With the advent of multi-party elections, clientelism has democratized as well, changing from elite-centred prebendalism to a more responsive form of patronage with a bigger role for parties. A good illustration of this logic is the size of cabinets, which has increased over time (Arriola 2009). Several studies provide evidence of clientelism in election campaigns (Lindberg 2003; Wantchekon 2003).

Many donor organizations in the last 20 years have invested heavily in ways to assist parties in new democracies. This includes Western political parties, party foundations or institutes affiliated with parties, specialized aid organizations that work closely with political parties, as well as a growing number of multilateral organizations (Carothers 2006). Nonetheless, some would say political science is ill-prepared to give meaningful advice to donors, due to a lack of knowledge of party politics in new democracies outside Europe (Erdmann 2010).

Surprisingly, interest in party politics has been slow to pick up again since the advent of democratization. There is a dearth of case studies of individual political parties, and systematic comparisons are even more rare. In the words of Carbone, '[i]n spite of recent progress, however, research into African party politics is still unsatisfactory. Neither side of the balance – the elaboration of theoretical frameworks and the detail of empirical knowledge – has achieved adequate levels of development as yet' (Carbone 2007: 18–19). The 'renaissance' of political party and party research in Africa predicted by Tetzlaff (2002) has only recently gained momentum. A good example is the comparative study of the strength of opposition parties in Southern Africa by LeBas (2011). Finally, little is known about the party in parliament, something that will change, it is hoped, with the recent interest in parliaments in Africa (Barkan, this volume).

African parties in comparative perspective

Is there a specific model of a prototypical African political party and do we need a separate typology of African parties? Erdmann answered both questions in the negative, arguing that 'a universal typology of parties that includes the differentiated experience of western Europe but is enlarged by non-European types provides a basic tool for party research in Africa' (Erdmann 2004: 81). Gunther and Diamond (2001) provide such a typology. They first differentiate between what could be called democratic and non-democratic settings, and then group parties operating in a democracy into five broad types, each with their own sub-types: elite parties, mass-based parties, ethnicity-based parties, electoralist parties, and movement parties. Party types are distinguished through four criteria: goals, electoral strategy, organizational structure and linkages, and social base. Both Erdmann (2004) and Carbone (2007) suggest that Gunther and Diamond's typology may be a good starting point for charting contemporary African parties. However, although widely cited, this party typology has not been used systematically in empirical research, whether in Africa or elsewhere.

Moreover, there is reason to believe that there is something particular about parties in third-wave democracies in general and Africa in particular. Compared to European parties, the trajectory of third-wave parties is unusually compressed. First, right from the start these parties have revolved around winning elections, not having accumulated the roles that European parties acquired and fulfilled over time, such as social mobilization and political integration. Carothers (2006: 54) calls this 'electoralist-from-the-start'. Second, third-wave parties appeared in a very different era which was characterized by the rise of mass electronic communication. By consequence, they could rely on the mass media to reach and mobilize voters and supporters and they did not have to invest heavily in party organization. In Africa, clientelism is a functional equivalent. In other words, third-wave parties skipped some of the stages that Western parties went through, decisively shaping 'patterns of party development' (Carothers 2006: 56).

Unfortunately, there is 'little systematic empirical knowledge about the various new types of political parties that emerged during the third wave of democratization outside Europe' (Erdmann 2010: 1288). It is no excuse that 'party organisations are often so weak that, in a sense, there appears to be little to observe' (Carbone 2007: 10).[3] Nor has multi-party politics in Africa spurred theorizing on the subject. In the final section of this chapter, I will sketch the contours of a research programme on African political parties that combines Carothers's (2006) insights about the peculiarity of third-wave parties with the state-of-the-art literature on parties in Western industrialized countries. In line with the counsel of Erdmann (2004) and Carbone (2007), this approach seeks to give the African experience a place in a broader framework of analysis. Concretely, I will highlight the usefulness of the cartel party model for the study of African parties. While this model has never been applied outside the Western world, upon closer scrutiny I hope to demonstrate the cartel party model's hidden potential for explaining the position of African parties in relation to state and society and for examining the consequences of this relationship.[4]

The cartel party is presented by the inventors of the term, Katz and Mair (1995, 2009), as the last in a long line of party models that have defined party politics in the Western world since the emergence of effective parliaments. First there was the elite party of the nineteenth century. Suffrage was restricted and parties were little more than small clubs of fellow members of the local elite. With the advent of mass politics came the mass party. The mass party had a distinct ideology, class, or religious constituency, a highly developed organization, close ties with ancillary organizations in society, and active and paying members. The mass party was the dominant form of party from the 1880s to the 1960s, when it was succeeded by the catch-all party. The transformation of the mass party into catch-all parties was reflected in a weaker ideological profile, more reliance on external sources of finance, a more hierarchical type of party organization, and a less important role for party members.

From the 1970s on, the catch-all party in turn began to morph into what Katz and Mair term the 'cartel party'. This type of party relies increasingly on the state for its income, uses modern communication techniques to reach supporters and voters, creates autonomy for the party leadership within the party organization, has less and less need for members, and competes on the basis of managerial competence rather than policy positions. If the party is seen as an intermediary between society and the state, the evolution of parties over time resembles a move away from society and towards the state. Whereas the mass party still fulfilled the linkage function that many observers deem so important (Hill 1980), the cartel party has become part of the state, rather than part of society. Moreover, as the name suggests, the cartel party does not exist in isolation. To safeguard their position within the state and share its resources amongst each other, cartel parties form a cartel that tries to make it more difficult for new entrants. Clearly, then, the features of the individual cartel party plus their collective behaviour have provoked a new, critical, look at the functioning of political parties today.

The cartel party thesis has been highly influential and the model has been applied in a range of countries in North America, Western Europe, and Eastern Europe, despite theoretical and empirical critiques (see especially Koole 1996). The driving force behind the emergence of cartel parties is the self-interest of politicians and the collective interest of the political class (Blyth and Katz 2005). Although the promise of the cartel party thesis for an analysis of party politics in Africa has been noted (Kopecký and Mair 2003), no such study exists.

The question is therefore how well the cartel party thesis describes party organization and behaviour in Africa and what can be learned from such an analysis. From the start, we should be prepared to find a more complex picture. First, not all parties will follow the cartel party model; other party types may co-exist. For example, those ruling parties in southern Africa that started out as liberation movements are expected to show organizational legacies of mass mobilization. The same holds for parties that have their origin as rebel movements (Manning 2002) or Marxist-Leninist revolutionary organizations. Second, individual parties may be more 'cartelized' in some respects than in others. This is one of the lessons of recent research on cartel parties in Western Europe (Detterbeck 2005). We would expect the same pattern in Africa, where levels of party system institutionalization, although generally low, show remarkable variation (Kuenzi and Lambright 2001).

The cartel party thesis makes much of the dependence of contemporary parties on the state for its finances. Africa is no exception, as data on direct and indirect state subsidies to parties collected by Pinto-Duschinsky (2002) and International IDEA (2004) show (see also Lodge 2001). The need for money is expected to be high in Africa as 'old-fashioned, face-to-face politicking costs more than the new mass-marketing, media-heavy approach' (Pinto-Duschinsky 2002: 83). Following Southall and Wood (1998), three stages in party funding can be identified. Whereas the early mass-based political parties were said to be funded in considerable part by members, the ruling parties after independence utilized state resources. After the return of multi-party politics, ruling parties continue to rely on their control of state resources, whereas challengers look for grassroots financing and foreign donors. One insight from the application of the cartel party thesis to Africa is that attempts to strengthen parties through party finance reform in Africa may end up making parties even more dependent on the state, further weakening the incentive for building up party organizations with active membership and roots in society.

The second driving force behind the cartel parties is the trend toward the constitutionalization of parties (Bogaards 2008). In Africa, almost all constitutions now mention political parties. In a recent count, 35 countries had a law on political parties (Moroff 2010). Internationally, Africa stands out for its far-reaching bans on ethnic parties (Bogaards *et al.* 2010). Worldwide, regulations on disclosure of donations, bans on foreign donations, campaign spending limits and, to a much lesser degree, other restrictions on political finance are increasingly common (Pinto-Duschinsky 2002). In contrast, 'political financing is relatively under-regulated in Africa', which is explained with reference to the partisan interests of ruling parties and the weakness of opposition parties (Saffu 2003: 21). Another difference is that in Western Europe state regulation of political parties occurred in tandem with state funding for parties, whereas in Africa party laws have been adopted irrespective of, and often prior to, subsidies to parties.

Looking inside political parties, Katz and Mair (2009: 759) observe three tendencies: the rise of the party in public office, the centralization and professionalization of the party bureaucracy, and the 'disempowering of activists'. Subsequent empirical research by other scholars has made progress in specifying the indicators of internal party cartelization: composition of national party executives, candidate selection, national party leadership selection, internal policy decision making, rights and obligations of members, and number of party staff. In Africa, in light of the persistent complaints about the weakness of parties there, their dependence on individual leaders, and their lack of internal democracy, we would expect to see strong signs of internal party cartelization. Of special interest to Africa, where dominant parties prevail (Bogaards 2004), is that organizational weakness may be linked to one-party dominance. Another prediction – that cartel parties cut their ties with social associations – has not been corroborated in Western Europe (Poguntke 2002). For African political parties the question is whether it pays off at all to establish links with identity groups. According to Widner (1997), this depends on the make-up of civil society and especially the presence of large and encompassing associations.

According to the cartel party thesis, party competition has changed because fiscal crisis and globalization have limited the policy space. Parties have reacted by emphasizing competence over content and by deliberately taking issues out of politics through a delegation of authorship to lower or higher levels of government (Blyth and Katz 2005). In Africa, where programmatic competition is in any case seen as rare, this should be even more true. The end of the Cold War and neoliberalism have constrained policy choices, and the big political questions have changed from those of 'what', to questions of 'how' (Carothers 2006: 61–63). Moreover, the scope of decision making in many countries is restricted by financial dependence on donors and international organizations.

The most controversial aspect of the cartel party thesis is undoubtedly that cartel parties form a cartel party system (see Koole 1996). Cartel parties collude to protect their collective interests. They use the state as 'an institutionalized structure of support, sustaining insiders while excluding outsiders' (Katz and Mair 1995: 16). In a democracy, it is parties themselves that decide on state funding and state regulation of parties, providing them with a unique opportunity to manipulate the rules of the game to their advantage. However, this is not what Bowler *et al.* (2006) found looking at all Organisation for Economic Co-operation and Development (OECD) countries in the period 1960–2000. In contrast, the trend was for requirements to be relaxed for new and small parties. Again, in Africa this question assumes particular importance in the presence of dominant parties and concern about their impact on democratic consolidation (Giliomee and Simkins 1999).

Pushing back the frontier

Against the background of the cartel party thesis, van Biezen and Kopecký (2007) propose a framework for the study of the party-state relationship that also holds promise for Africa. It focuses on the public funding of parties, the public regulation of parties, and their rent-seeking behaviour in the form of clientelism, patronage, and corruption. They suggest that a 'particular type of party-state linkage may be prevalent in Africa, which is one where the sizeable benefits that parties amass from the state are almost solely derived from patronage and clientelistic practices and corruption' (ibid.: 245). However, empirical evidence for this claim is lacking and Africa may be less exceptional than is often assumed in light of the role that party patronage plays in contemporary Europe. Clearly, then, while research on political parties in African has much to gain from a grounding in the contemporary European literature in general, and the cartel party thesis in particular, scholars should shy away from easy generalizations as well as equally superficial references to African particularities.

Nor is the cartel party the only modern party type that can be fruitfully applied to Africa. Marcus and Ratsimbaharison quote a joke about President Ravalomanana in Madagascar, in which the self-made millionaire is said to have 'decided to enter politics in 1999 by running for mayor because there was too much red tape for him to conduct his business unfettered' (Marcus and Ratsimbaharison 2005: 506). This is not much different from standard interpretations of Silvio Berlusconi's motivation to go into politics and it would be interesting to compare the structure of Forza Italia, classified as a 'business-firm type of party' (Krouwel 2006), with Ravalomanana's party, *Tiako-i-Madagasikara*. Ideally, the insights from such application of theory to practice could then filter back into the general literature on parties, to further the integration and accumulation of our knowledge on party development and its consequences.

Notes

1 Shaw (1986) provides a particularly insightful account of the different arguments that were used by Mugabe in Zimbabwe but which resonate across the continent.
2 The same argument has been made to justify the idea of 'one-party democracy', which Tanzanian president Julius Nyerere defended by asserting that 'where there is one party, and that party is identified with the nation as a whole, the foundations of democracy are firmer than they can ever be where you have two or more parties, each representing only a section of the community' (Nyerere 1967: 196).
3 Moreover, Cheeseman and Hinfelaar (2010) clearly demonstrate the importance of intra-party politics.
4 This approach will be further developed in my current research on cartel parties in Africa.

Bibliography

Arriola, L. (2009) 'Patronage and Political Stability in Africa', *Comparative Political Studies* 42(10): 1339–62.
Bartolini, S. and Mair, P. (2001) 'Challenges to Contemporary Political Parties', in L. Diamond and R. Gunther (eds), *Political Parties and Democracy*, Baltimore, MD: Johns Hopkins University Press.
Basedau, M., Erdmann, G., Lay, J. and Stroh, A. (2011) 'Ethnicity and Party Preference in Sub-Saharan Africa', *Democratization* 18(2): 462–89.
Bienen, H. (1971) 'One-Party Systems in Africa', in S. Huntington and C. Moore (eds) *Authoritarian Politics in Modern Society: The Dynamics of Established One-Party Systems*, New York, NY: Base Books.
Blyth, M. and Katz, R. (2005) 'From Catch-All Politics to Cartelisation: The Political Economy of the Cartel Party', *West European Politics* 28(1): 33–60.
Bogaards, M. (2004) 'Counting Parties and Identifying Dominant Party Systems in Africa', *European Journal of Political Research* 43(2): 173–97.
——(2008) 'Comparative Strategies of Political Party Regulation', in B. Reilly, E. Newman and P. Nordlund (eds) *Political Party Regulation in Conflict-Prone Societies*, Tokyo: United Nations University Press.

Bogaards, M., Basedau, M. and Hartmann, C. (eds) (2010) 'Ethnic Party Bans in Africa', *Democratization* 17(4): 599–617.

Bowler, S., Carter, E. and Farrell, D. (2006) 'Changing Party Access to Elections', in B. Cain, R. Dalton and S. Scarrow (eds) *Democracy Transformed: Expanding Political Opportunities in Advanced Industrial Democracies*, Oxford: Oxford University Press.

Carbone, G. (2007) 'Political Parties and Party Systems in Africa: Themes and Research Perspectives', *World Political Science Review* 3(3): 1–29.

——(2008) *No-Party Democracy? Ugandan Politics in Comparative Perspective*, Boulder, CO: Lynne Rienner Publishers.

Carothers, T. (2006) *Confronting the Weakest Link: Aiding Political Parties in New Democracies*, Washington, DC: Carnegie Endowment for International Peace.

Chazan, N. and Le Vine, V. (1979) 'Politics in a "Non-Political" System: The March 30, 1978 Referendum in Ghana', *African Studies Review* 22(1): 177–201.

Cheeseman, N. and Hinfelaar, M. (2010) 'Parties, Platforms, and Political Mobilization: The Zambian Presidential Elections of 2008', *African Affairs* 109(434): 51–76.

Coleman, J. and Rosberg, C. (1964) 'Introduction', in J. Coleman and C. Rosberg (eds) *Political Parties and National Integration in Tropical Africa*, Berkeley, CA: University of California Press.

Crook, R. (1999) '"No-Party" Politics and Local Democracy in Africa: Rawlings' Ghana in the 1990s and the "Ugandan Model"', *Democratization* 6(4): 114–38.

Detterbeck, K. (2005) 'Cartel Parties in Western Europe?' *Party Politics* 11(2): 173–91.

Dudley, B.J. (1967) 'On the Classification of African Political Parties', *Nigerian Journal of Economic and Social Studies* 9(1): 81–97.

Elischer, S. (2012) 'Measuring and Comparing Party Ideology in Nonindustrialized Societies: Taking Party Manifesto Research to Africa', *Democratization* 19(4): 642–67.

Erdmann, G. (2004) 'Party Research: Western European Bias and the "African Labyrinth"', *Democratization* 11(3): 63–87.

——(2010) 'Political Party Assistance and Political Party Research: Towards a Closer Encounter?' *Democratization* 17(6): 1275–96.

Erdmann, G. and Engel, U. (2007) 'Neopatrimonialism Reconsidered: Critical Review and Elaboration of an Elusive Concept', *Commonwealth & Comparative Politics* 45(1): 95–119.

Giliomee, H. and Simkins, C. (eds) (1999) *The Awkward Embrace: One-Party Domination and Democracy*, Amsterdam: Harwood Academic Publishers.

Gunther, R. and Diamond, L. (2001) 'Types and Functions of Parties', in L. Diamond and R. Gunther (eds) *Political Parties and Democracy*, Baltimore, MD: Johns Hopkins University Press.

Jockers, H., Kohnert, D. and Nugent, P. (2010) 'The Successful Ghana Election of 2008: A Convenient Myth?' *Journal of Modern African Studies* 48(1): 95–115.

Haynes, J. (1995) 'Ghana: From Personalist to Democratic Rule', in J. Wiseman (ed.) *Democracy and Political Change in Sub-Saharan Africa*, London: Routledge.

Hill, F. (1980) 'People, Parties, Polities: A Linkage Perspective on African Party-States', in K. Lawson (ed.) *Political Parties and Linkage: A Comparative Perspective*, New Haven, CT: Yale University Press.

Hodgkin, T. (1961) *African Political Parties*, London: Penguin.

Hydén, G. (2006) *African Politics in Comparative Perspective*, Cambridge: Cambridge University Press.

International IDEA (2004) 'Political Finance Database', www.idea.int/parties/finance/db/ (accessed 14 November 2011).

Kasfir, N. (1992) 'Popular Sovereignty and Popular Participation: Mixed Constitutional Democracy in the Third World', *Third World Quarterly* 13(4): 587–605.

Katz, R. and Mair, P. (1995) 'Changing Models of Party Organization and Party Democracy: The Emergence of the Cartel Party', *Party Politics* 1(1): 5–28.

——(2009) 'The Cartel Party Thesis: A Restatement', *Perspectives on Politics* 7(4): 753–66.

Koole, R. (1996) 'Cadre, Catch-All or Cartel? A Comment on the Notion of the Cartel Party', *Party Politics* 2(4): 507–23.

Kopecký, P. and Mair, P. (2003) 'Political Parties in Government', in M. Salih (ed.) *African Political Parties: Evolution, Institutionalisation and Governance*, London: Pluto Press.

Krouwel, A. (2006) 'Party Models', in R. Katz and W. Crotty (eds) *Handbook of Party Politics*, London: Sage.

Kuenzi, M. and Lambright, G. (2001) 'Party System Institutionalization in 30 African Countries', *Party Politics* 7(4): 437–68.

Lapalombara, J. and Weiner, M. (1966) 'The Origin and Development of Political Parties', in J. Lapalombara and M. Weiner (eds) *Political Parties and Political Development*, Princeton, NJ: Princeton University Press.

LeBas, A. (2011) *From Protest to Parties: Party-Building and Democratization in Africa*, Oxford: Oxford University Press.

Lindberg, S. (2003) 'It's Our Time to "Chop": Do Elections in Africa Feed Neo-Patrimonialism Rather Than Counteract It?' *Democratization* 10(2): 121–40.

Lodge, T. (2001) 'How Political Parties Finance Electoral Campaigning in Southern Africa', *Journal of African Elections* 1(1): 53–60.

McMahon, E. (2004) 'Catching the "Third Wave" of Democratization? Debating Political Party Effectiveness in Africa Since 1980', *African and Asian Studies* 3(3–4): 295–320.

Manning, C. (2002) *The Politics of Peace in Mozambique*, Westport, CT: Praeger.

Marcus, R. and Ratsimbaharison, A. (2005) 'Political Parties in Madagascar: Neopatrimonial Tools or Democratic Instruments?' *Party Politics* 11(4): 495–512.

Morgenthau, R.S. (1961) *Political Parties in West Africa*, Oxford: Clarendon Press.

Moroff, A. (2010) 'Party Bans in Africa: An Empirical Overview', *Democratization* 17(4): 618–39.

Mozaffar, S. (2006) 'Party, Ethnicity and Democratization in Africa', in R. Katz and W. Crotty (eds) *Handbook of Party Politics*, London: Sage.

Nyerere, J. (1967) *Freedom and Unity, A Selection from Writings and Speeches, 1952–1965*, London: Oxford University Press.

Owusu, M. (1979) 'Politics Without Parties: Reflections on the Union Government Proposals in Ghana', *African Studies Review* 22(1): 89–108.

Pinto-Duschinsky, M. (2002) 'Financing Politics: A Global View', *Journal of Democracy* 13(4): 69–85.

Poguntke, T. (2002) 'Zur Empirischen Evidenz der Kartellparteien-These', *Zeitschrift für Parlamentsfragen* 33(4): 790–806.

Posner, D. (2005) *Institutions and Ethnic Politics in Africa*, Cambridge: Cambridge University Press.

Randall, V. and Svåsand, L. (2002) 'Political Parties and Democratic Consolidation in Africa', *Democratization* 9(3): 30–52.

Rotberg, R. (1966) 'Modern African Studies: Problems and Prospects', *World Politics* 18(3): 566–78.

Saffu, Y. (2003) 'The Funding of Political Parties and Election Campaigns in Africa', in R. Austin and M. Tjernström (eds) *Funding of Political Parties and Election Campaigns*, Stockholm: International IDEA.

Sartori, G. (1976) *Parties and Party Systems: A Framework for Analysis*, Cambridge: Cambridge University Press.

Shaw, W. (1986) 'Towards the One-Party State in Zimbabwe: A Study in African Political Thought', *Journal of Modern African Studies* 24(3): 373–94.

Southall, R. and Wood, G. (1998) 'Political Party Funding in Southern Africa', in P. Burnell and A. Ware (eds) *Funding Democratization*, New York, NY: Manchester University Press.

Tetzlaff, R. (2002) 'Zur Renaissance der Politischen Parteienforschung in Afrika', *Afrika Spectrum* 37(2): 239–57.

van Biezen, I. and Kopecký, P. (2007) 'The State and the Parties: Public Funding, Public Regulation and Rent-Seeking in Contemporary Democracies', *Party Politics* 13(2): 235–54.

van de Walle, N. (2007) 'Meet the New Boss, Same as the Old Boss? The Evolution of Political Clientelism in Africa', in H. Kitschelt and S. Wilkinson (eds) *Patrons, Clients, and Policies: Patterns of Democratic Accountability and Political Competition*, Cambridge: Cambridge University Press.

Wantchekon, L. (2003) 'Clientelism and Voting Behavior: Evidence from a Field Experiment in Benin', *World Politics* 55(3): 399–422.

Widner, J. (1997) 'Political Parties and Civil Societies in Sub-Saharan Africa', in M. Ottaway (ed.) *Democracy in Africa: The Hard Road Ahead*, Boulder, CO: Lynne Rienner Publishers.

Zolberg, A.R. (1966) *Creating Political Order: The Party-states of West Africa*, Chicago, IL: Rand McNally.

22

PUBLIC OPINION AND DEMOCRATIC CONSOLIDATION

Michael Bratton

More than 20 years have passed since the Berlin Wall came down, an event followed in sub-Saharan Africa by pressures for political liberalization and transitions to multi-party rule. In addition, more than 10 years have elapsed since the Afrobarometer embarked (in Ghana in 1999) on a pioneering effort to conduct surveys of public opinion about these changes. The Afrobarometer Network – an international consortium of researchers[1] – has since accumulated interviews with over 100,000 Africans in four rounds of surveys in up to 20 countries.[2]

The time is ripe, therefore, to assess the current state of political development in these countries from a citizen's perspective and to track changes in public attitudes that have occurred over the first decade of this century (1999–2008).[3] The central question concerns the fate of democracy. Do Africans say they *want* democracy, a preference that we call the 'popular demand' for democracy? Do they think they are *getting* it – that is, do they perceive that their leaders are providing a supply of democracy? Moreover, if citizens see evidence of democratic development in Africa, to what extent are these regimes established, stable, or *consolidated*?

Of course, it would be a mistake to view African politics exclusively through the lens of democracy. After all, most African countries have had limited experience with a form of political regime more commonly associated with the mature polities of the West. For this reason, we wish to keep an open mind about whether political regimes in Africa are best characterized as democracies or as some other regime configuration. After all, regimes may survive in various forms, including as autocracies or as hybrid regimes that are neither fully authoritarian nor completely democratic.

With reference to particular countries, this chapter arrives at three conclusions:

- Africa is characterized by a *diversity of political regimes*;
- Most political regimes in Africa are *unconsolidated hybrid systems*; and
- Some political regimes are *consolidating*, but not always as democracies.

Evidence in this chapter is derived from face-to-face interviews in the languages of the respondents' choice with more than 25,000 Africans in 2008 and 2009. This unique dataset gives voice to ordinary people whose views about democracy and development are all too often overlooked by ruling political elites. In focusing analysis on individual attitudes and behaviours, the Afrobarometer seeks both to provide a counterweight to the elite-centred focus of many political studies of Africa and systematically to achieve a measure of scientific precision and generalization that is unavailable from most anthropological and historical case studies. In the decade that Afrobarometer data have been available, scholars have generated scores of articles, working papers and monographs on popular attitudes towards democracy, governance, leadership, and corruption, as well as on everyday practices of economic livelihood and political participation, and many other topics (see the bibliography).

The meaning of 'democracy'

Before attempting to measure popular attitudes to democracy, we must ensure that respondents to Afrobarometer surveys have a similar object in mind. We offer evidence to suggest that Africans regard democracy in reasonably standard fashion. When asked in 1999 and 2005, 'what, if anything, does democracy mean to you?' three-quarters of those surveyed could offer a definition. Respondents in almost all countries ranked personal liberty in first place, with a consistent average of 41 per cent mentioning liberty in both surveys. The next most common substantive meaning was 'government by the people', which was mentioned by 16 per cent and 10 per cent, respectively, in 1999 and 2005. Significantly, the rank order of meanings was virtually identical across all countries.[4]

To test further for shared meanings in 2008, we asked respondents to compare two hypothetical African regimes. Is Country A (with free speech, multi-party competition, and electoral turn-over of leaders) more or less democratic than Country C (with restricted speech, a dominant party and regular re-election of incumbents)? Some 71 per cent of respondents ranked Country A as more democratic and only 3 per cent as less democratic than Country C.[5] To be sure, popular understandings of democracy are not yet universal, but these results suggest that Africans share enough of an emergent consensus on what democracy is to allow valid and reliable comparisons of mass attitudes to political regimes.

Popular demand for democracy

Do Africans say they *want* democracy? To start investigating this question the Afrobarometer asks a standard question, the wording of which is given at the bottom of Figure 22.1. Respondents who say that 'democracy is preferable to any other kind of government' are deemed to support democracy.

In 2008, an average of 70 per cent of Africans interviewed in 19 countries expressed overt support for democracy.[6] However, there was considerable cross-national variation around this mean value, ranging from 85 per cent support in Botswana to 39 per cent support in Madagascar. This distribution of opinion accords with each population's political experience: Batswana apparently derive their regime preferences from more than 40 years of stable multi-party rule, whereas Malagasy convey concern over a recent history of irregular elections, mass protests and non-constitutional power grabs.

A critic might complain that public opinions are unreliable because citizens lack knowledge about democracy or easily acquiesce to a socially approved symbol. After all, it is as easy to express a favourable opinion about motherhood as it is to claim support for democracy. However, the substance of democratic preferences is affirmed by the fact that less than 7 per cent of Afrobarometer respondents in 2005 said they support democracy without being able to offer a definition of its meaning.[7]

Moreover, we probe whether professed democrats are willing to countenance alternative authoritarian regimes. Figure 22.2 compares the proportions of those interviewed across

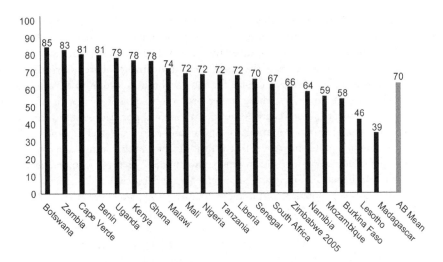

Figure 22.1 Support for democracy, 2008

* Mean excludes Zimbabwe

"Which of these three statements is closest to your own opinion?

A. Democracy is preferable to any other kind of government;

B. In some circumstances a non-democratic government can be preferable;

C. For someone like me, it doesn't matter what form of government we have."

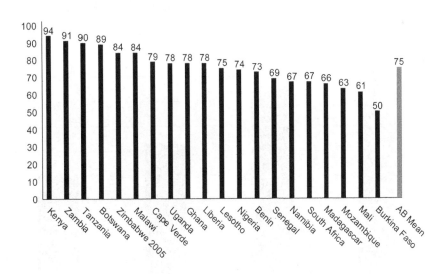

Figure 22.2 Rejection of military rule, 2008

* Mean excludes Zimbabwe

"There are many ways to govern a country. Would you disapprove or approve of the following alternative: The army comes in to govern the country?"

Afrobarometer countries that express disapproval of military rule. A higher mean proportion of respondents state opposition to this form of authoritarian governance (75 per cent) than profess pro-democratic sentiments (70 per cent), suggesting that Africans remain clearer about the kind of government they *don't* want than the kind they affirmatively desire. Reflecting strong commitments to civilian rule, Kenyans display the most vigorous rejection of an army takeover (94 per cent). Burkinabe, however, whose leader first rose to power by means of a military coup, are more ambivalent (50 per cent). Majorities of national populations also roundly reject two other authoritarian regimes common to Africa: one-party rule and personal rule by a strongman (not shown). Note, however, that a majority of Mozambicans barely rejects one-party rule (51 per cent), suggesting either popular wistfulness for a pre-democratic past or a genuine, if mistaken, belief that one-party arrangements are democratic.

A tougher test of deep popular commitment to democracy, however, is whether citizens *both* support democracy *and* reject a range of authoritarian alternatives (including one-party and one-man rule). We measure this composite attitude with an index of *demand for democracy*. Figure 22.3 indicates that in 2008 almost all Africans interviewed rejected at least one form of autocracy (90 per cent). However, far fewer rejected two or three such alternatives, and less than half of all respondents (45 per cent) expressed a robust demand for democracy that was unqualified by any kind of authoritarian nostalgia. In other words, the commitments of most Africans to democratic ideals remain quite shallow.

What has happened to demand for democracy over time? Figure 22.4 shows trend data for the 11 countries for which we have four survey observations between 1999 and 2008.[8] On average, popular support for democracy was initially quite high in the aftermath of the regime transitions of the 1990s (68 per cent), though it began to dissipate by 2005 (62 per cent). In the last three years of the period covered, however, we discern a sharp upsurge in the mean level of expressed support for democracy (to 72 per cent). The reasons remain unclear. Perhaps

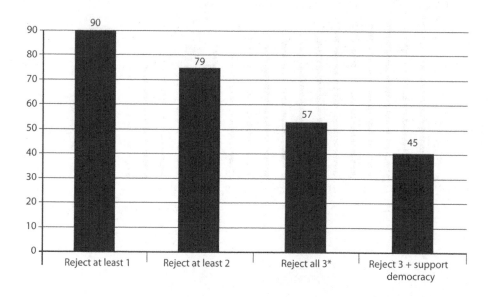

Figure 22.3 Demand for democracy, 2008
* Military rule + one-party rule + personal dictatorship

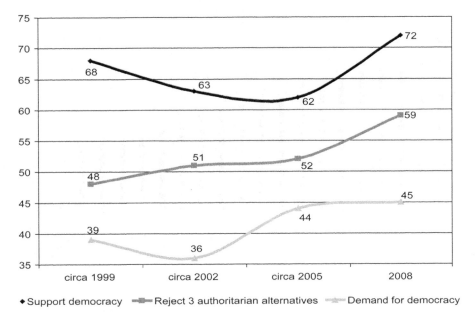

Figure 22.4 Demand for democracy, 2002–08. Average trends, 11 African countries
Percentage approving democracy or rejecting three authoritarian political regimes (military + one-party + one-man rule). Countries covered are Botswana, Ghana, Lesotho, Malawi, Mali, Namibia, Nigeria, South Africa, Tanzania, Uganda, and Zambia.

economic recovery spurred by a commodity price boom has encouraged growing confidence in the political regime. However, support for democracy in 2008 is only weakly correlated with perceptions of improvements in macroeconomic conditions over the previous 12 months. More likely, citizens perceive that political reforms are taking root; after three or four rounds of competitive elections, including several turnovers of ruling parties, they are gaining confidence in the institutionalization of their right to choose leaders (see Lindberg, this volume).[9]

We also discern a steady upward trajectory of anti-authoritarian sentiments. Each time an Afrobarometer survey has been conducted, more and more Africans report that they reject all three forms of authoritarian regime, which suggests that one-party, military, and one-man rule are becoming less appealing over time. This trend is consistent with the diminished frequency of military coups in Africa over the past 20 years and the growing unwillingness of the international community, including even the African Union, to recognize such illegal transfers of power.

As expected, demand for democracy echoes the arcs of its component attitudes, moving up from 39 per cent to 45 per cent between 1999 and 2008. However, before we prematurely celebrate the consolidation of democracy in Africa, we must note that on average robust demand for democracy remains a minority sentiment in the countries we have studied.

The perceived supply of democracy

On the supply side, the key question we need to ask is, do ordinary people think that they are *getting* democracy? One way to generate an answer is to ask everyone, 'how much of a democracy is (this country) today?' Response categories for this item range on a four-point scale from 'a full

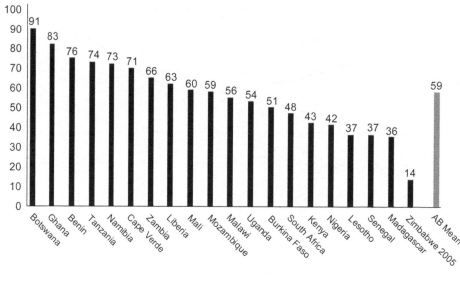

■ Percent saying full or almost full democracy
■ Afrobarometer mean*

Figure 22.5 Perceived extent of democracy, 2008
* Mean excludes Zimbabwe
"In your opinion, how much of a democracy is (your country) today?"

democracy', through 'a democracy with minor problems' and 'a democracy with major problems', to 'not a democracy'.

Sceptics might again argue that non-literate people in the developing world are insufficiently knowledgeable or experienced about democracy to offer meaningful responses. However, in 2005 less than 10 per cent of respondents who had an opinion on the extent of democracy were unable to define the term. While this uninformed group was slightly more prone innocently to perceive 'a full democracy', their views on the extent of democracy otherwise resembled the opinions of those who better understood the nature of the regime.

By 2008, an average of 59 per cent of all Africans interviewed considered that they lived in a full or almost full democracy. The reader should recall, however, that because Afrobarometer surveys are conducted in Africa's more open societies, this figure does not necessarily apply to the continent as a whole. The range of responses in Figure 22.5 is wider for the perceived extent of democracy than for any other item of opinion considered here.

While the citizens of Botswana again lead the pack (at 91 per cent), with Ghanaians close behind (at 83 per cent), Zimbabweans trail far below (at a dismal 14 per cent in 2005). With regard to the perceived extent of democracy, countries can be roughly divided into three groups of roughly equal size:

- In six countries (from Botswana to Cape Verde), at least seven out of 10 citizens think they have extensive democracy;
- In seven other countries (from Zambia to Burkina Faso) citizens see moderate levels of democratic development; and
- In a last group of seven countries (from South Africa[10] to Zimbabwe), less than half think they live in a full or almost full democracy.

It is within this last group that we discern regimes at risk, for example in Kenya, Nigeria, Senegal, Madagascar, and Zimbabwe.

To check our measurements we offer two tests. First, to be externally valid, African public opinion should be consistent with judgements about the level of democracy made independently by international experts. Figure 22.6 compares the Afrobarometer's extent of democracy with the well-known status of freedom score published annually by Freedom House. The scatter-plot shows that in 2008 experts and citizens converged on assessments of the level of democracy for countries like Kenya, Mozambique, Mali, and Benin. To be sure, the experts think that South Africa is more democratic than do its citizens, and Tanzanians think they have more democracy than professionals would grant. However, all told, the fit of the country cases to the shared regression line is good.

Second, as a test of internal validity, we would expect popular perceptions of the extent of democracy to be closely correlated with expressed satisfaction with 'the way democracy works'. Figure 22.7 shows that, on average, less than half (49 per cent) of all Africans interviewed were satisfied (either 'fairly' or 'very') with democracy in 2008. However, the cross-country distribution for satisfaction closely resembles that for the extent of democracy; for example, democracy is again at risk in exactly the same group of countries. Moreover, satisfaction with democracy is closely associated with the perceived extent of democracy, not only at the country level, but also at the individual level.

As Figure 22.8 shows, fully 81 per cent of those who are satisfied with democracy also perceive extensive democracy.

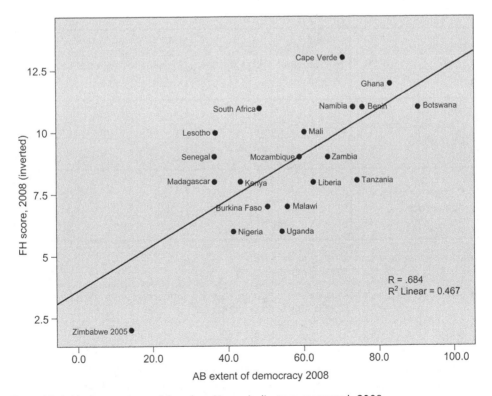

Figure 22.6 Afrobarometer and Freedom House indicators compared, 2008

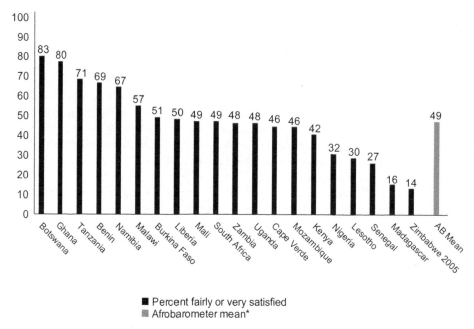

Figure 22.7 Satisfaction with democracy, 2008
* Mean excludes Zimbabwe
"Overall, how satisfied are you with the way democracy works in (your country)?"

	Not satisfied with democracy	Satisfied with democracy
Don't see extensive democracy	63%	19%
Perceive extensive democracy	37%	81%

Measures of association: Ordinal: Gamma = .763
Interval: Pearson's r = .451

Figure 22.8 Cross-tabulation of extent of democracy by satisfaction with democracy, 2008 (weighted n = 22,800 AB R4 respondents)

Because of the coincidence of these measures, we combine the indicators for satisfaction with democracy and perceptions of the extent of democracy into an additive construct of the *supply of democracy*. It measures whether individual Africans are *both* satisfied with democracy *and* perceive it to be extensive in their country. The evolution of this indicator, along

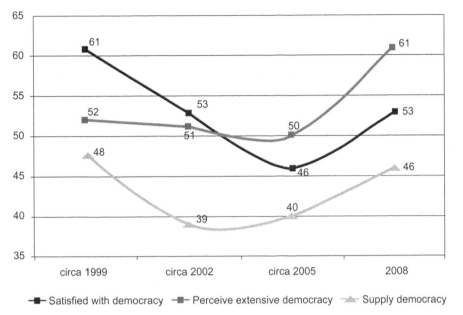

Figure 22.9 Supply of democracy, 2000–08. Average trends, 11 African countries
Percentages (a) satisfied with "the way democracy works", (b) perceiving that country has "full" or "almost full" democracy. Countries covered are Botswana, Ghana, Lesotho, Malawi, Mali, Namibia, Nigeria, South Africa, Tanzania, Uganda, and Zambia.

with its component attitudes, is shown in Figure 22.9, which illustrates several noteworthy trends:

- On average, satisfaction with democracy was lower in 2008 than 10 years earlier (by 8 percentage points);
- By contrast, the perceived extent of democracy had risen between 1999 and 2008 (by 9 percentage points); and
- All indicators, including the perceived supply of democracy, were on an upward path over the three-year period from 2005 to 2008.

It would appear, therefore, that the Africans we interviewed think that they have more democracy today than earlier in the decade. Most importantly, we note that the perceived extent of democracy has risen even as satisfaction has dropped. This unexpected result suggests an adjustment of mass expectations. People are recognizing a measure of democratic progress even as they realistically conclude that actual democratic practice is falling short of their dreams.[11]

A model of regime consolidation

So how many African regimes are democracies, at least in the eyes of their citizens? Which regimes in Africa are consolidating? In Figure 22.10 we suggest a schema for addressing both the nature and the stability of various political regimes. It builds upon the political indicators of supply and demand that we have already described. The logic of the model is that in consolidated regimes demand and supply are in equilibrium (or balance), a condition represented by the diagonal intercept that dissects the space in Figure 22.10.

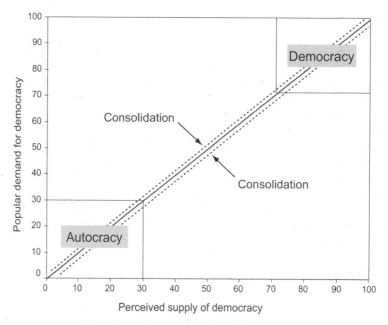

Figure 22.10 Consolidation of political regimes
Assumptions:
1. Intercept line represents consolidated regime (equilibrium of demand and supply)
2. Dotted lines represent margin of sampling error around survey point estimates
3. Equilibrium at 70 per cent or higher represents consolidated democracy
4. Equilibrium at 30 per cent or lower represents consolidated autocracy
5. Points off intercept line represent unconsolidated regimes

As Rose and colleagues argue:

> What happens to a new democracy is the outcome of a continuing process of inter-action between what elites supply and what the populace demands … Uninterrupted progress towards the *completion* of a new democracy will occur if popular demands for reforms to improve the regime are met by political elites. This positive *equilibrium* is often described as a stable or established democracy.
>
> *(Rose et al. 1998: 14, emphasis added)*

We extend this argument about the consolidation of new democracies to claim that a sustained balance between mass demands and institutional supply signals the consolidation of *any* type of regime. Whereas a high-level political equilibrium connotes the consolidation of democracy, a low-level equilibrium signals the consolidation of autocracy.

For *democracies*, how high must a political equilibrium be? Let us assume that the consolidation of democracy minimally requires that for a sustained period of time, 70 per cent or more of the adult population wants this type of political regime and a similar proportion thinks they are getting it (Diamond 1999: 68). When these circumstances occur, the probability that democracy will break down declines considerably. In Figure 22.10, *democracies* are found in the upper-right bloc and are consolidated to the extent that they approach, or lie on, the equilibrium line within this space.

At the opposite end of the spectrum (in the lower-left segment) lie *autocracies*. In these regimes the populace neither demands democracy nor perceives its supply by the state elite (scoring 30 per cent or lower in each case). Because strong initiatives for democratization do not emanate from above or below, the regime is caught in a low-level equilibrium trap. The closer that actual regimes approach the equilibrium line, and do so over successive surveys, the more that autocracy is consolidated.

Regimes that lie elsewhere in the property space are *hybrid regimes*; that is, regardless of their formal characteristics, their citizens perceive neither democracy nor autocracy but something in between. Hybrid regimes may consolidate at intermediate levels, lending permanence to forms like electoral democracy, electoral autocracy, or other semi-formed systems (see van de Walle, this volume).[12] Indeed, the greatest risk to the consolidation of new democracies in Africa is that the architecture of the regime hardens prematurely – that is, before democratic institutions or beliefs have had a chance to take root.

Regimes that fall far from the equilibrium line can be considered *unconsolidated*. Where demand exceeds supply, citizens will pressure their governments for ongoing democratic reforms. Where supply exceeds demand, we should suspect that elites have room to manipulate the rules of the democratic game. Moreover, because of the imbalance between political demand and supply, hybrid regimes are prone to instability.

Regime consolidation in Africa

We can now enter Afrobarometer data for 2008 into the regime consolidation model. Figure 22.11 reveals several interesting results.

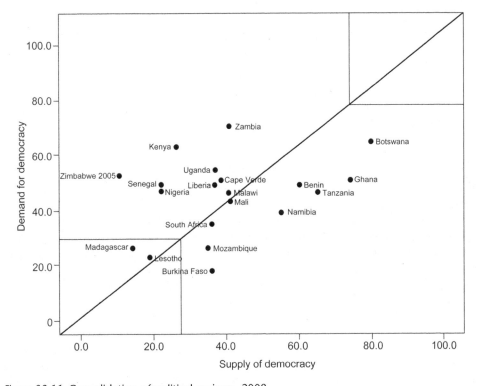

Figure 22.11 Consolidation of political regimes, 2008

First, by our standards, there are *no consolidated democracies* among Afrobarometer countries. Botswana comes closest, where 65 per cent of adults demand democracy and 80 per cent think that democracy is institutionalized. To the extent that supply exceeds demand, however, Botswana's democracy is not yet consolidated. Second, and by contrast, Lesotho is apparently caught in a low-level trap: in 2008, it could even be classified as a *consolidated autocracy* by our standards.[13] Only 23 per cent of Basotho demand democracy and 18 per cent perceive a supply. Despite a façade of parliamentary institutions, the country's political culture seemingly still manifests monarchical and military legacies inherited from the past.

Third, all other countries possess *hybrid political regimes*. Democratic demand and the perceived supply of democracy reach intermediate levels in Benin, Malawi, Mali, and South Africa. The coordinates for these cases fall close to the equilibrium line. We infer from their spatial location that their regimes are consolidating as hybrids that fall short of full democracy. Moreover, with supply and demand in balance, there is no political force propelling major political changes in these countries in the foreseeable future.

Fourth, *most hybrid regimes are unconsolidated*, but in distinctive ways. On the one hand, citizens demand more democracy than elites are willing to supply in places like Kenya and Zambia. Indeed, Zimbabwe in 2005 displayed high demand (56 per cent) but the lowest supply (10 per cent) of any Afrobarometer country, which suggests that Zimbabwe could register quick democratic progress if ever a new government were installed as a result of a free and fair election. Because demand is twice as high as supply in Nigeria and Senegal, one can also predict continued popular pressures from below for further democratic reforms in these countries.

Conversely, political regimes like those in Tanzania and Namibia are unconsolidated for other reasons. Citizens in these places report that their governments provide more democracy than they really want. In Burkina Faso, the supply of democracy (36 per cent) exceeds demand (18 per cent) by a factor of two to one. With this profile of opinion, the general public in this group of countries is predisposed to easily acquiesce to strong leaders who control dominant political parties or originate from the armed forces. Unless these autocratic elites reform themselves, any change in these countries is likely to move away from, rather than toward, consolidated democracy.

Diverse trajectories

A major result of this analysis is that *African political regimes are diverse* along at least two dimensions. With regard to the nature of the regime, some are nearly democratic, a few seem autocratic (at least in the eyes of the citizenry), while most fall into an inter-mediate hybrid category. A common African regime type is electoral democracy, meaning democratic in institutional form (e.g. elections), but lacking essential attributes of rights availability or leadership accountability. With regard to the likelihood of change, some regimes – including some hybrids – have attained a stable equilibrium, but more are unconsolidated.

With Afrobarometer data it is possible to track the political evolution of particular African countries over recent years. Selecting the countries that have undergone the most change, we distinguish autocratizing from democratizing regimes according to their movement away from or toward consolidated democracy. In the interests of brevity, we simply report trends and leave the informed reader to interpret them and identify causal events. Again, the main theme is the *diversity of regime trajectories*.

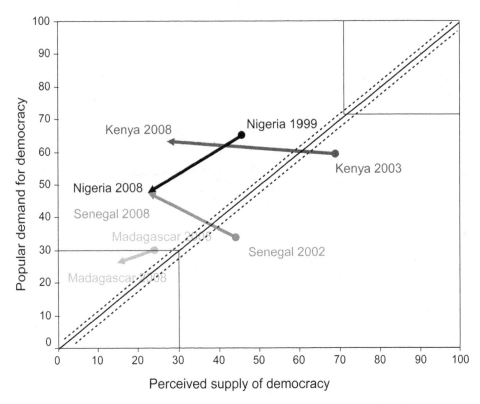

Figure 22.12 Declining regimes in Africa, selected cases

Figure 22.12 illustrates four autocratizing regimes:

- In Kenya, demand for democracy has risen slightly, but the perceived supply dropped over 40 percentage points, more than in any other country we have examined. As a consequence, a promising new democratic regime in 2003 had unravelled (or 'deconsolidated'?) by 2008.
- Over the same period, Senegal followed a similar trajectory to Kenya, but its citizens have always displayed lower levels of democratic attitudes. While perhaps more consolidated, the Senegalese regime is currently a lower-quality semi-democracy than even Kenya.
- The quality of political regime in Nigeria also declined between 1999 and 2008, but this country experienced setbacks on *both* the demand *and* supply sides. Indeed, the drop-off in popular demand for democracy (18 percentage points) is the largest that has occurred in any country.
- The quality of democracy was never high in Madagascar. Even in 2005 it teetered on the brink of consolidated autocracy. By 2008, prior even to the civilian coup of March 2009, citizens reported declining levels of both demand for, and supply of, democracy.

By contrast, Figure 22.13 selects four democratizing regimes:

- In Ghana, demand for democracy has held pretty steady (between 56 per cent and 51 per cent) between 1999 and 2008, but the general public has substantially revised its opinion of the supply of democracy, which they see as rising dramatically (by 30 percentage

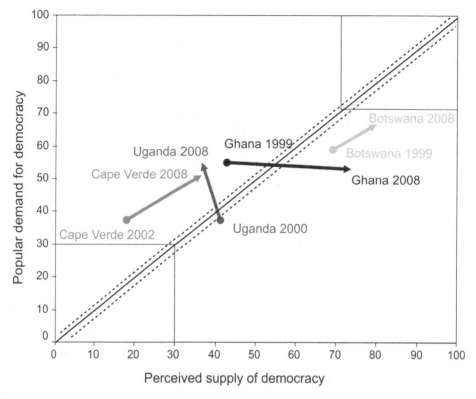

Figure 22.13 Advancing regimes in Africa, selected cases

points over 10 years), perhaps due to a series of well-conducted elections and two peaceful alternations of ruling party.

- Uganda displays an opposite pattern of political development. While the perceived supply of democracy has slipped somewhat, popular demand for democracy has risen substantially (by 19 percentage points) during a period when the country transited from no-party to multi-party rule.

- According to our data, Botswana gradually deepened its democracy over the past 10 years. Both demand and supply rose marginally. However, since there is no evidence of a high-level convergence of these two attitudes (and because demand lags behind supply) we conclude that consolidation remains elusive.

- Even though it began from an unexpectedly modest start-point, Cape Verde is the only country in the Afrobarometer where demand and supply are both growing substantially (up 13 and 19 points, respectively). Moreover, these public attitudes are converging on the equilibrium line, which we take as evidence of a process of regime consolidation.

Conclusion

At the risk of obscuring the above diversity of regime trajectories, we end with general observations. Figure 22.14 traces the overall trends in popular demand for democracy and the perceived supply of democracy from 1999 to 2008. The referent is a 'typical' Afrobarometer polity (as if there were such an abstract entity).

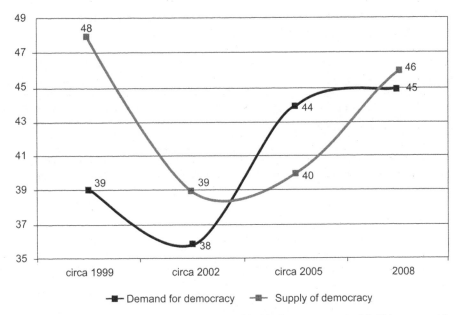

Figure 22.14 Democratic demand and supply, 2000–08. Average trends, 11 African countries
Percentages (a) satisfied with "the way democracy works", (b) perceiving that country has "full" or "almost full" democracy. Countries covered are Botswana, Ghana, Lesotho, Malawi, Mali, Namibia, Nigeria, South Africa, Tanzania, Uganda, and Zambia.

At the outset, in 1999, the Africans we interviewed perceived that on average, the provision of democracy by new multi-party regimes exceeded the level of popular demand. While 48 per cent felt supplied, demand stood at just 39 per cent. At this time, people were unsure about the virtues and vices of a democratic dispensation and therefore hedged their bets. They offered tentative support to democracy but at the same time retained residual loyalties to older, authoritarian alternatives.

By 2005, however, demand for democracy (which rose to an average 44 per cent) had outstripped the perceived supply (which by then had fallen to 40 per cent). We interpret this juxtaposition to mean that Africans began to appreciate the virtues of democracy, especially civil liberties and electoral participation, and so began to put authoritarian attachments behind them. Simultaneously, the experience of living under democratic regimes that rarely performed up to expectations led to increasingly sceptical judgements about how much freely elected governments were likely to achieve.

By 2008, as political rights became institutionalized, demand and supply came into alignment, at least in terms of gross averages across more than 25,000 respondents in 19 countries. Some 45 per cent demanded democracy and 46 per cent perceived a supply. However, it would be a mistake to interpret this result as evidence of an underlying consolidation of Africa's existing array of regimes. There is too much political diversity across African countries – not only of regime type, but also in terms of the degree of institutional stability – to allow any such conclusion.

We can note both good and bad news. The good news is that democratic attitudes are generally on the rise among the African populations we have surveyed. If sustained, this increase – measured prior to the onset of the global financial crisis in late 2008 – is a promising portent for further democratization. However, the bad news is that less than half of all Africans interviewed demand democracy and perceive its supply when these indicators are measured rigorously. As such, the project of democratization still has a long way to go.

Notes

1 The Afrobarometer is a joint enterprise of the Centre for Democratic Development (CDD-Ghana), the Institute for Democracy in South Africa (Idasa) and the Institute for Empirical Research in Political Economy (IREEP, Benin). Fieldwork, data entry, preliminary analysis, and the dissemination of survey results are conducted by National Partner organizations in each African country. Michigan State University and the University of Cape Town provide technical and advisory support services. Several donors support Afrobarometer's research, capacity building and outreach activities, including SIDA, the UK Department for International Development (DfID), CIDA, the US Agency for International Development (USAID) and the Royal Danish Ministry of Foreign Affairs. For more information see: www.afrobarometer.org.
2 Fieldwork for Round 4 Afrobarometer surveys was conducted in 19 African countries between March and December 2008. Due to political unrest, a Round 4 survey could not be conducted in Zimbabwe during 2008; instead this paper refers to results from the Round 3 survey in Zimbabwe of October 2005.
3 Afrobarometer surveys can only be conducted in the continent's most open societies. Hence the results do not represent the continent – or all Africans – as a whole.
4 Note, however, that the second most common response was 'don't know', suggesting that Africans still have much to learn about this unfamiliar form of government.
5 Some 11 per cent said 'equally democratic' and 14 per cent said 'don't know'. Country B was a middle category, not reported here.
6 All mean scores for 2008 exclude Zimbabwe.
7 Of those who could not offer a definition (the 28 per cent who said they 'don't know' any meaning of democracy in 2005), more than half (52 per cent) also said they 'don't know' whether they support democracy and a further fifth (20 per cent) said that the type of regime 'doesn't matter' to them.
8 Botswana, Ghana, Lesotho, Malawi, Mali, Namibia, Nigeria, South Africa, Tanzania, Uganda, and Zambia.
9 Citizen preferences for elections as a means of choosing leaders and their judgements about the availability of civil and political rights are strongly and significantly related to demand for democracy.
10 The position of South Africa, often considered a democratic success story, reflects the instrumental conception of democracy held by many of its citizens. More so than other Africans, they equate democracy with the delivery of social and economic goods rather than the availability of equal political opportunity. This orientation may well be a by-product of the totalizing deprivations of apartheid.
11 To confirm, we note that the proportion of *dissatisfied democrats* (i.e. those who demand democracy but are dissatisfied with its performance) has risen from 34 per cent to 41 per cent. The latter figure would be even higher if Zimbabwe were included in the 11-country sample for which we have trend data.
12 An electoral democracy holds competitive elections, but respect for civil liberties is incomplete. An electoral autocracy holds sham elections that the opposition can almost never win.
13 Moreover, Lesotho has sustained this status since 1999 (see Bratton *et al.* 2005: ch. 13).

Bibliography

Bratton, M. and Mattes, R. (2001) 'Support For Democracy in Africa: Intrinsic or Instrumental?', *British Journal of Political Science* 31: 447–74.
Bratton, M., Mattes, R. and Gyimah-Boadi, E. (2005) *Public Opinion, Democracy and Market Reform in Africa*, New York, NY: Cambridge University Press.
Diamond, L. (1999) *Developing Democracy*, Baltimore: Johns Hopkins University Press.
Eifert, B., Miguel, E. and Posner, D. (2010) 'Political Competition and Ethnic Identification in Africa', *American Journal of Political Science* 54(2): 494–510.
Evans, G. and Rose, P. (2007) 'Support for Democracy in Malawi: Does Schooling Matter?' *World Development* 35(5): 904–19.
Levi, M., Sacks, A. and Tyler, T. (2009) 'Conceptualizing Legitimacy, Measuring Legitimating Beliefs', *American Behavioral Scientist* 53(3): 354–75.

Moehler, D. (2009) 'Critical Citizens and Submissive Subjects: Election Losers and Winners in Africa', *British Journal of Political Science* 39: 345–66.

Rose, R., Mishler, W. and Haerpfer, C. (1998) 'Democracy and Its Alternatives: Understanding Post-Communist Societies', Baltimore, MD: Johns Hopkins University Press.

Schedler, A. and Sarsfield, R. (2007) 'Democrats with Adjectives: Linking Direct and Indirect Measures of Democratic Support', *European Journal of Political Research* 46(5): 637–59.

Stasavage, D. (2005) 'Democracy and Education Spending in Africa', *American Journal of Political Science* 49 (2): 343–58.

PART V

Political economy and development

23

AID, TRADE, INVESTMENT, AND DEPENDENCY

Martin Williams

This chapter discusses how external economic forces – aid, trade, and investment – affect politics and policy in African countries. It proceeds in two parts. The first half is historical and descriptive, narrating a stylized but common progression of economic policies in Africa from post-colonial developmentalism to crisis, structural adjustment, and liberalization. This short history culminates with a survey of the opportunities and challenges posed by the global economy and the current workings of the international aid system. A key theme is that the impacts of aid, trade, and investment on African countries cannot be considered in isolation, as policy responses to each of these forces usually affect the other as well, and so any potential policy change requires African policymakers to juggle a complex set of considerations.

The second half of the chapter builds on this foundation to address two key topical debates. First, what is the relationship between these global forces and domestic politics and policy? This includes a discussion of the incentives and constraints created by global forces for economic policymaking in Africa, as well as how policymakers and elites can manipulate aid, trade, and investment to their political advantage. The second topic revisits the dependency debate in light of the preceding discussion. It seeks to avoid stale dichotomies by asking not only how much policy space African governments have to make economic policy, but also what influences how well they are able to use it.

Aid, trade, and investment are each enormous topics in their own right. To limit the scope, the chapter focuses on the politics, policies, and choices of African governments, rather than those of donors or international institutions, and on how global forces create incentives and constraints for governments, rather than on whether these forces are 'good' or 'bad' for Africa. The focus is on aid delivered by multilateral institutions and bilateral (government-to-government) donors rather than non-governmental organizations (Jennings, this volume, discusses NGOs).

Economic policy in post-independence Africa

Post-independence economic policy in most African countries followed a pattern that can generally be divided into three phases: progression from state-led developmentalism to crisis (independence through the 1970s); structural adjustment and stagnation (1980s and early 1990s); and the era of globalization and 'partnership' (from the mid-1990s). Each country's path is unique, of course; the aim of this section is to synthesize some common themes without obscuring this diversity of experience.

From developmentalism to crisis (independence through the 1970s)

At independence most African economies were largely rural and agrarian. Domestic economies and government revenues were heavily dependent on a handful of primary commodity exports, mainly minerals and cash crops. This meant that African producers missed out on the potential economic gains from processing and adding value to these commodities, and were vulnerable to global price volatility. As a result of mercantilist colonial economic policies that saw Africa as a source of raw materials and a captive market for manufactured products from Europe, industrial capacity was extremely weak and infrastructure was limited to the minimum necessary to get commodities to port.

The overriding economic priority of most post-colonial governments was therefore to industrialize their economies as rapidly as possible. Mainstream economic thought of the day emphasized that 'modernization' – the transition from rural agricultural economies, to urban industrial ones – would not happen on its own. Rather, the state needed to lead a 'big push' to get industrial growth to the point where it could be self-sustaining. Evidence for this view was provided by the rapid, state-led industrialization of the USSR in the previous decades and the accomplishments of the Marshall Plan in rebuilding post-war Europe. There was also an overlap between these statist economic theories, the nationalist political projects of post-independence leaders, and the narrow social and economic foundations of the inherited colonial states.

The industrialization imperative gave rise to the package of economic policies known as import substitution industrialization (ISI). Tariffs and quotas on imports were used to create a protected domestic market for local 'infant' industries, which would need time to compete with much larger and more advanced European firms. Furthermore, governments would heavily tax their existing export commodities (often by using monopsonistic marketing boards to pay producers much less than the world market price) and use the proceeds to invest in infrastructure and fund industrial promotion efforts. Importantly, industrial policy was usually selective, in that governments would choose particular industries to actively support and develop, either through targeted subsidies or state-owned enterprises (SOEs). African governments were not unique in their approach. Much of Latin America and Asia had also adopted similar strategies, and many large-scale industrial projects were supported by World Bank loans and aid from other donors.

Initially it seemed to be working, and in the decade after independence much of Africa experienced strong economic growth. By the late 1960s, however, cracks began to appear. In too many cases, SOEs were inefficient and corruptly managed; grand investment projects were unviable, unrealistic, or poorly executed; infant industries failed to become more competitive over time; and existing commodity export sectors were being severely squeezed for revenue so that production fell or was diverted into black markets.

There was also a political component to these failings. In theory, ISI was supposed to be implemented by rational, impartial technocrats motivated only by the national interest, but in practice personal and political considerations often dominated. In addition to more general instances of corruption and clientelism, it was argued that governments exhibited 'urban bias' in their policies, systematically favouring politically powerful urban workers over less visible but more numerous rural farmers (Lipton 1977). Even when they had developmental motivations, governments were often too politically and administratively weak to coordinate diverging political interests and properly plan and implement interventions. By the late 1960s, state weakness was increasingly erupting into full-blown political crisis in many countries, further undermining economic performance and increasing the necessity for rulers to use economic policy and projects to prop up clientelist networks and maintain political stability.

These internal challenges were soon compounded by external events, beginning with the Arab oil embargo in 1973. This episode triggered a series of shocks to Africa's terms of trade, as

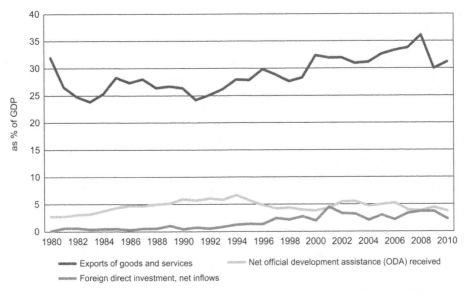

Figure 23.1 Terms of trade and GDP per capita growth in sub-Saharan Africa, 1962–95

shown in Figure 23.1, both by increasing the price of oil (which most countries imported) and by reducing the prices of its commodity exports as a result of global economic recession and hence reduced demand. This accelerated the downward spiral of economic weakness and political crisis in much of Africa. As the 1970s drew to a close, an increasing number of African countries were beset by stagnant or collapsing economies, high inflation, overvalued currencies, and bankrupt and unstable governments. With the situation untenable and few viable options, governments began to turn to the International Monetary Fund (IMF) and World Bank for help.

Structural adjustment and stagnation (1980s and early 1990s)

The IMF and World Bank were founded in the wake of the Second World War to help govern the international economy and, initially, to rebuild Europe. The IMF was intended to focus on macroeconomic issues, acting as a lender of last resort to governments that were experiencing foreign exchange and balance of payment crises, while the World Bank mostly financed specific projects. When African governments needed money to stabilize their crisis-stricken economies, the IMF and World Bank were the natural place to turn – often the only place, since most other lenders viewed engagement with these institutions as a prerequisite to their own involvement.

The IMF and World Bank would loan money to governments on concessional terms, with below-market interest rates and long repayment periods, but in return they insisted that the recipient government undertake a set of policy reforms. This combination of stabilization loans paired with policy reforms came to be known as a Structural Adjustment Programme (SAP). During the 1980s, 36 African countries took 241 different adjustment loans (van de Walle 2001: 7), and this rate of borrowing continued into the 1990s. The idea of putting conditions on loans was not novel, but under SAPs conditionality began to take on a more deeply transformational role aimed not just at coping with the crisis at hand but at liberalizing the entire economy. Prior to this new paradigm of 'policy-based lending', foreign aid to Africa in the 1960s and 1970s had mostly consisted of governmental transfers which were often politically motivated (especially in the context of the Cold War), directed to specific large-scale infrastructure projects, or in the form of technical assistance.

The conditions imposed by SAPs can be divided into two categories: macroeconomic targets, such as cuts in government expenditure, exchange rate devaluation, and reductions in money supply to bring inflation under control; and policy reforms aimed at liberalizing the domestic economy. The latter category included the abolition of many statist economic policies, such as price controls, import restrictions, monopolistic commodity marketing boards, and restrictions on foreign investment. It also included extensive privatization of SOEs, many of which were perennially loss-making and required government subsidies to continue operating, as well as the curtailment of social service provision and introduction of user fees. The combination of the contraction in government expenditure, the privatization of SOEs, and the exposure of previously protected industries to international competition typically forced both the public sector and the formal private sector into large-scale lay-offs. Indeed, this was often an explicit goal of SAPs.

The IMF and World Bank believed that imposing these harsh conditions had both economic and political justifications. Economically, African economies were perceived as being burdened by price distortions that prevented efficient resource allocation. Financial and human resources were being poured into badly run SOEs that were unlikely ever to become competitive, consumers and businesses were forced to purchase expensive, poor-quality local manufactures, and traditional commodity exports (often the only internationally competitive sector of the economy) were being taxed to the point of collapse. If only all these economic distortions could be eliminated in order to 'get the prices right', the private sector would ensure that resources were efficiently allocated and economic growth would spontaneously follow. Williamson's (1990) 10-point 'Washington Consensus' is perhaps the most widely cited summary of the policies being espoused by the IMF and World Bank at this time.

It was also believed that these same reforms would have beneficial effects on African countries' politics. This was informed by an analysis of the corruption, mismanagement, and clientelism that had often characterized implementation of state-led development strategies in the 1960s and 1970s (e.g. Bates 1981). If import licenses and subsidized credit were being allocated based on political favouritism or opportunistic rent-seeking, it was thought easier to simply eliminate these and other policy tools that created opportunities for corruption than to improve their administration. Shrinking the state might also reduce the ability of regimes with authoritarian tendencies to use their control of state resources to suppress political competition. It was hoped that conditionality would provide greater leverage for reform-minded policymakers inside the government.

This reform project was as ambitious as it was controversial. For better or worse, though, the reality of structural adjustment rarely matched its lofty ambitions. In large part this was because countries often did not implement the conditions to which they had agreed. Many African governments managed to maintain aspects of their economic policies that they viewed as politically important, or twist the reforms to their political advantage, and so economic liberalization was rarely as complete as the IMF and World Bank would have wished (van de Walle 2001). Privatization efforts also met with limited success, as divestiture procedures were often marred by corruption and cronyism, and in some cases simply served to replace public monopolies with *de facto* private monopolies. In addition, the withdrawal of the state from many areas of the economy did not necessarily lead to spontaneous growth and investment in the private sector. Indeed, the presence of market failures and attendant supply-side limitations was part of the original developmentalist justification for state intervention in the economy. In the absence of either decisive reforms or economic take-off, most countries spent the better part of this period muddling through and taking multiple loans, sometimes just to pay off previous ones.

Did structural adjustment work? The answer is not obvious. Certainly the 1980s and much of the 1990s were a period of poor economic performance – sub-Saharan Africa's gross domestic product (GDP) declined by an average of 1 per cent annually from 1980 to 1997 (Collier and Gunning 1999). Proponents of SAPs argue that countries that adopted policy reforms somewhat improved their growth rates and that the problem was poor implementation of reforms. Opponents point out that these growth rates were still too small to make a difference to poverty reduction, and cited the obvious hardships imposed on large parts of the population by expenditure cuts and price changes (e.g. Cornia *et al.* 1987).

Adjudicating between these claims is problematic, however, since the effects of SAPs are difficult to distinguish from the effects of the economic crises that invariably preceded the programmes. Even where loan conditions explicitly required expenditure cuts, it can be argued with some justification that the depth of the economic crisis would have imposed fiscal contraction in any case. The partial nature of conditionality implementation also limits the extent to which SAPs can be said to have 'caused' poverty and stagnation (see Rodrik 1995).

Although there was disagreement about whether structural adjustment went too far or not far enough, by the 1990s both sides of the debate increasingly agreed that it was not achieving its objectives. Even the World Bank's own evaluation department rated half of all Bank adjustment loans in Africa as having failed to meet their objectives (Dollar and Svensson 2000). While stabilization had clearly been necessary, there was an increasing recognition that conditionality was not working, that SAPs had undermined social development, and that more attention needed to be paid to governance and the role played by state institutions in enabling growth. Some of these critiques gradually began to be taken on board by donors in the 1990s, precipitating yet another shift in the aid paradigm.

Globalization and 'partnership' (from the mid-1990s)

If the dominant theme of economic policy in Africa during the 1980s had been response to domestic crises through structural adjustment, in the 1990s the main challenge facing newly liberalized African economies was how they would fare in the world's increasingly globalized economy. The spread of the Washington Consensus as a blueprint for national economic policies was accompanied at the global level by the increasing importance of international flows of goods and capital. At the same time as enthusiasm grew regarding the potential of trade and investment, the frustrations of the structural adjustment era had led to greater scepticism about aid from both the right and the left. This intellectual shift gained popular expression in the phrase 'trade, not aid'.

It also gained legal and institutional underpinnings, most notably with the founding of the World Trade Organization (WTO) in 1995. The WTO was created as a result of the Uruguay Round of trade negotiations with a mandate to enforce countries' existing multilateral trade liberalization commitments and provide a permanent negotiating framework for further liberalization. The early 2000s saw the advent of a number of explicitly 'pro-development' trade agreements (or negotiations directed toward agreements), partially in response to criticisms of the global trade system by developing countries and NGO campaigners. The most visible was the (still un-concluded) Doha Round of WTO talks launched in 2001, optimistically marketed as the 'Development Round' since it was intended to address some issues of concern to developing countries, such as rich-country agricultural subsidies, while also pushing for deeper liberalization of other trade barriers.

In addition to the multilateral WTO, the new global trade architecture included a growing web of bilateral and plurilateral treaties that go deeper than the requirements of the WTO and are aimed (at least nominally) at supporting development. These include trade preference schemes that give tariff-free treatment in rich-country markets to exports from certain developing countries, such as the United States' African Growth and Opportunity Act and the European Union's (EU) Everything But Arms scheme. Since the Cotonou Partnership Agreement of 2000, the EU has been attempting to convert these unilateral preferences into Economic Partnership Agreements (EPAs) with groups of African, Caribbean, and Pacific countries. The EPAs are meant to be free trade agreements that would go beyond WTO levels of integration, beginning with trade in goods but eventually extending to other areas, such as services and investment. Although they would impose more restrictions on policy than the WTO, EPAs are intended to be 'pro-development' and thus include some favourable provisions and leniency for African countries, as well as financial aid. EPA negotiations have been slow, however, and are currently stagnant with different African countries at different stages of the process.

Despite all this attention to trade's role in development, the shift in emphasis from aid to trade was not as abrupt as the rhetoric made it seem. Aid flows did decrease somewhat in the 1990s, as shown in Figure 23.2, but were still very significant for Africa. The IMF and World Bank continued to give structural adjustment loans and promote economic liberalization, even if the term 'structural adjustment' gradually fell out of favour and faded into new aid modalities. More importantly, the concern with trade was not new. A primary goal of SAPs was to re-orient African economies toward production for export markets rather than the domestic market, so trade was seen as a successor to structural adjustment, not an alternative. From a more historical perspective, international trade was nothing new for African economies, which have for centuries been profoundly influenced by global economic linkages. Even the 'trade, not aid' mantra actually dates from the 1968, when developing countries called for a more equitable global trade regime at the second meeting of the United Nations Conference on Trade and Development (UNCTAD).

These qualifications notwithstanding, promoting exports and attracting foreign investment did take on a new importance for African economies in the 1990s and 2000s. In part this was inspired by the success of export-led growth in East Asian economies. Producing for export would allow African firms to take advantage of economies of scale in production and the size of the global market. More practically, economic liberalization had left African countries with little alternative but to turn to exports and investment for economic growth and job creation, as the

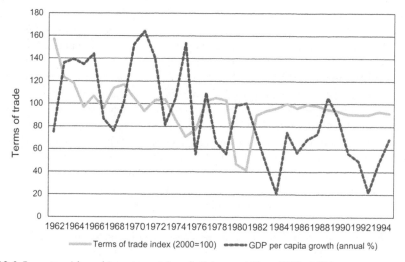

Figure 23.2 Exports, aid, and investment in sub-Saharan Africa, 1980–2010

dismantling of protective tariffs and import controls had taken away the option of using protected domestic demand to incubate new industries. Neoclassical economists emphasized that African countries could successfully compete in the world economy by focusing on their comparative advantage – goods they could produce relatively efficiently. In effect this usually meant traditional commodity and resource exports, with the intention that foreign investment and domestic entrepreneurship could help Africa gradually diversify its exports and develop agro-industry as a base for industrialization.

Again, though, the supply-side response of African economies was underwhelming. The latter half of the 1990s did witness a gradual return to growth in many countries, but this growth tended to be based on traditional commodity exports rather than economic diversification and structural transformation. Foreign investment in non-extractive sectors was also not as forthcoming as had been hoped. It was becoming increasingly clear that economic development in Africa was being hindered by a factor that was not economic, but political: poor governance.

The concern with governance arose from the recognition that the state was a critical part of growth, not simply an obstacle. The efficient operation of markets required (at a minimum) a state that could effectively and impartially protect property rights and enforce contracts. This recognition stemmed from practitioner experience but also from the growing academic literature on institutions and the historical determinants of development, and was gradually integrated into the canon of development orthodoxy. The 'good governance' paradigm soon expanded from protection of property rights to encompass a wide array of state functions and character-istics, such as corruption, citizen voice, effective service delivery, and stable macroeconomic policy. The concept's rapid rise was in large part because it was vague and flexible enough to accommodate perspectives from across the political spectrum, from the minimalist and technocratic neoliberal vision of government to more redistributive and participatory ideologies. The gov-ernance agenda expanded the scope of what donors expected of African governments to include new outcomes and process conditions – *how* the government did its business, not just what it did.

A further change in aid practice was also underway in the 1990s. Conditionality had become unpopular with everyone, albeit for opposing reasons. In Temple's (2010: 4468) apt formulation, 'views differ on whether [conditionality] should be criticized for the clear success in securing policy change, or the equally clear failure to do so'. The discourse that grew to replace it was one of 'partnership' and recipient government 'ownership' of the aid process. 'Ownership' promised to solve the conditionality problem and was also seen as a solution to the problem of donor coordination, a challenge that was increasing as a result of the growing number of international institutions, bilateral donors, and NGOs trying to aid and influence governments (Whitfield 2009).

This rhetoric gradually led to the creation of new aid delivery mechanisms that sought to get away from the model of structural adjustment lending with externally driven *ex ante* policy conditionality. The Poverty Reduction Strategy Papers (PRSPs) of the early 2000s were one such attempt. The widespread reliance on foreign borrowing throughout the 1980s and 1990s had seen the creation of a group of Highly Indebted Poor Countries (HIPCs), mostly in Africa, with economies weighed down by large external debts and interest payments. The IMF and World Bank coordinated an international debt relief effort, but required countries to produce PRSPs in order to qualify. PRSPs were intended to be comprehensive, prioritized national development plans drafted by the government (but in intensive consultation with donors and civil society). In theory, donors could then formulate their aid programmes based on this document and the use of HIPC funds could be tracked. Other new delivery mechanisms included the United States' Millennium Challenge Corporation (MCC), which would give money only to countries that exhibited good governance according to a pre-defined set of indicators; and the use of outcome targets for determining aid awards, with the idea that these *ex post* conditions would allow governments to decide how best to achieve these goals and make prescriptive *ex ante* conditions unnecessary.

However, the practice of 'ownership' has not been as transformative as its discourse. New governance and planning process conditions were simply layered on top of existing types of economic and policy conditions, with no overall decrease in the use of 'hard' conditionality. Rather than implying greater control for the recipient government over the aid process, Fraser and Whitfield argue:

> The World Bank and the IMF define ownership as commitment to the reforms and policies which they think governments should implement. They hope that they can convince recipients to see it their way, and to believe that the ideas are their own. If not, they retain conditionality.
>
> *(Fraser and Whitfield 2009: 92)*

In addition to new delivery mechanisms, aid took on new focuses in the 1990s and early 2000s, again often as a reaction to criticisms of SAPs. Poverty alleviation and social development gained new emphasis, most obviously with the Millennium Development Goals (MDGs) created in 2000. These established a set of human development targets for 2015 and became a common benchmark for allocating and evaluating aid. A variety of aid programmes grew out of the good governance agenda, including civil service reform and capacity building, administrative and judicial reforms for the protection of property rights, and reforms aimed at the ease of doing business. The challenges of economic globalization led to 'aid for trade', which aims to help countries improve their infrastructure and productive capacities to take advantage of the export opportunities provided by global market access. Going beyond the economic liberalization required by SAPs, bilateral and multilateral donors alike have also provided technical and financial support for countries to reform their investment laws and domestic regulatory frameworks to attract foreign investment and deepen their integration into the global economy.

Even as this aid system was evolving, however, new trends were altering the issues facing African countries and the balance of power with donors. In the 2000s, a number of African countries began to experience strong and sustained economic growth and receive higher levels of investment (Figure 23.2 and Figure 23.3), which has increased governments' self-confidence

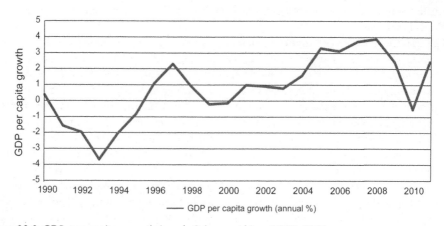

Figure 23.3 GDP per capita growth in sub-Saharan Africa, 1990–2011

and arguably also their leverage with donors. This growth has been driven in large part by high global commodity prices and demand for natural resources, which is mainly due to the economic success of emerging economies (e.g. Brazil, India, and especially China). The recent emergence of these countries as aid donors in their own right has also decreased African countries' dependence on the traditional donors (see Alden, this volume). For new donors like China, aid is even more closely linked to trade and investment, with impacts for Africa that will only become fully clear over time.

Global forces, national politics

Studies of the politics of economic policy are dominated by attempts to explain why governments often do not choose policies that are thought to maximize long-run aggregate social welfare (e.g. open markets, public good provision, balanced budgets, and long-term investment). Although the literature contains many such hypotheses, it is only a slight oversimplification to think of them as variations on a theme: governments use economic policy to benefit specific individuals or interest groups at the expense of the wider population, either for the purpose of personal enrichment or to build political support through patronage and clientelism. Examples include Bates's (1981) analysis of post-independence economic policies and van de Walle's (2001) study of the partial implementation of SAP-era reforms.

A more optimistic alternative to the rent-seeking approach to state-business relations is that business associations can be part of 'reform coalitions' or 'growth coalitions' that lobby and work with governments to correct market failures, such as under-provision of public goods (Bräutigam *et al.* 2002). In practice, however, the distinction between lobbying to solve market failures (to enable industry growth) and lobbying to create market failures (to capture rents) is blurry at best. The potential of these coalitions to promote diversification into new industries is also limited because (by definition) a non-existent industry has no constituency to lobby for provision of the public goods and infrastructure needed to bring it into existence, so policy will naturally tend to favour existing industries.

The incentives for rent-seeking are arguably greater in Africa than elsewhere because state power and wealth historically have been based on control over external economic ties, as opposed to internally oriented control of territory and taxation of the population (Herbst 2000). The insecurity and consequent short time horizon of many African regimes also accentuates the incentives for opportunistic predation and discourages public good provision, protection of property rights, and long-term investment. Weak or inconsistent rule of law encourages political insiders to seek informal favours and exceptions rather than to lobby for changes in formal policies, which benefits politically connected firms and undermines the potential for socially beneficial state-business relations.

Other authors approach aid, trade, and investment as resources and investigate how competition for control of these resources affects politics. The most extreme form of this is the hypothesized relationship between natural resource revenues and conflict (see Roessler and Soares de Oliveira, both in this volume). Large flows of aid and investment (especially in natural resources) would be expected to raise the stakes of political competition since governments exercise substantial discretion in directing fiscal spending and also potential commercial benefits, as investors are often required to enter into partnerships with politically connected elites. Alternatively, aid and investment flows could facilitate political compromise, since they provide the means to buy off political opponents and can give elites an incentive to maintain political stability. A vibrant private sector might also provide alternative means of accumulation for elites and therefore make them more likely to accept being out of power.

There is also commonly thought to be a negative relationship between revenues from aid and natural resources on the one hand, and domestic taxation and productive sector investment on the other. Large external transfers (such as revenue from aid and natural resources) cause exchange rate appreciation, which shifts resources into the non-tradable sector of the economy (that which produces exclusively for domestic consumption) and shrinks the tradable sector (exports and import-competing industries). This is often referred to as 'Dutch disease'. Since tradable industries are generally thought to have greater long-term growth potential, external windfall revenues can therefore lower the economy's long-term growth rate even while creating a boom in present consumption.

External revenues are also hypothesized to affect governments' accountability to their populations by reducing the need for domestic taxation. This has potentially two negative effects. First, domestic taxation requires a functional administrative apparatus, so aid can undermine the development of state capacity. Second, domestic taxation is thought to bind governments into a social contract with their populations, where governments provide public goods and accountability in exchange for the population's acceptance of taxation. This argument is largely based on the fiscal sociology literature on state development in Western Europe, and there exists a debate whether the same mechanism transfers to contemporary Africa (Bräutigam *et al.* 2008).

This leads to the question of how aid, trade, and investment affect the dynamics of political liberalization and democracy. During the 1980s and 1990s, democratization became a common demand of donors and sometimes an explicit condition for aid flows (see Brown, this volume). Although the evidence is mixed, Bratton and van de Walle (1997) sum up the mainstream opinion that international pressure can sometimes have a positive effect, but that it is secondary to domestic factors. Likewise, van de Walle (2001: 17) observes that donor-induced political liberalization was often only cosmetic, and in fact rather than democratization the two modal responses to structural adjustment-era reform pressures were: state decay, and even collapse, as the existing order is undermined; and further centralization of power and authoritarianism as regimes manipulate the reform process to consolidate their power.

Fraser and Whitfield (2009: 75) note another way in which aid might affect the relationship between African governments and their populations: while African governments frequently denounce aid conditionality, they nevertheless 'continue to use conditionality as an explanation of their unpopular policy choices and a buttress against internal dissent'. Aid also has been accused of de-politicizing economic policy in African countries by casting policymaking as a fundamentally technocratic – as opposed to political – activity and restricting the range of policies available to African governments (Ferguson 1990). A tangible example of how the aid process can create 'choiceless democracies' (Mkandawire 1999) is illustrated by the overlap between PRSPs and electoral cycles: even when governments change after elections, donors expect the new government to continue policies and projects initiated by the previous regime (Fraser and Whitfield 2009: 86).

Aid is not the only restriction on African countries' policy choices. The footloose nature of global capital may also act as a homogenizing force on economic policies, forcing countries to compete with each author by complying with investors' demands and encouraging a 'race to the bottom' in regulation and taxation. Such pressure is hardly unique to African countries, however; nor is it entirely new. Nonetheless, this possibility leads into the debate discussed in the next section: given the effects of aid and the global economic system, how much control do African countries really have over their own economic policies?

Dependency and policy space

The debate over whether African countries actually have control over their economic destinies has been raging since independence. In the colonial era, the orthodox view was that African economies needed to integrate into the capitalist economy in order to develop, but radical Marxists like Rodney (1972) argued the reverse: the underdevelopment of former colonies was not the result of a lack of integration into the world economy, but rather the structurally subordinate way in which these countries had been integrated – too much capitalism, rather than too little. This 'dependency theory' analysis helped provide the intellectual rationale for nationalist economic policies like import substitution. It also strongly influenced 'externalist' explanations for Africa's economic crisis in the 1980s, which focused on global factors like terms of trade shocks. In contrast, the 'internalist' analyses that informed SAPs located blame primarily with the policy choices of African governments (e.g. World Bank 1981).

In the 1990s two factors began to change the terms of this debate. First, the rapid growth of several East Asian countries showed that the global economic system did not strictly prevent poor countries from industrializing. Both sides claimed the East Asian experience as support for their position. The World Bank focused on the major role played by exports in these countries to argue that embracing export-led growth and global markets was a winning strategy (World Bank 1993). Critics pointed out that rather than trusting in markets, these countries had made extensive use of the statist industrial policies that the Washington Consensus claimed were bad for growth (Wade 1990).

Second, a new architecture of global trade governance was developing. The trend was towards ever-lower tariffs and more open markets, but also the extension of global trade rules beyond trade in goods to areas like intellectual property, investment, services industries, and subsidies. In part this was occurring through the WTO, but gridlock in the Doha Round negotiations has meant that deeper integration has increasingly been pursued at the plurilateral or bilateral level. The EU's EPAs are one example of this, but while these talks have stagnated, Africa's regional organizations have been undertaking their own economic integration (see Khadiagala, this volume). Numerous bilateral investment treaties (BITs) have been signed also between African countries and (mostly) developed and emerging countries. Although lower profile than trade agreements, BITs create restrictions on host governments' treatment of foreign investments that go far beyond the WTO's investment provisions.

Tighter global economic integration in the last two decades thus has been synonymous with greater restrictions on national policy space. Critics point out that some of the policies that have been prohibited were the same ones that rich countries used to promote their industries at earlier stages of their development (Chang 2002). Such policies include: high levels of tariff protection; targeted industrial subsidies; performance requirements on foreign investment, such as mandatory levels of local content and technology transfer; and weak patent laws to enable local manufacturers to copy cheaply foreign technology.

The effects of these restrictions on trade policy are linked to the operation of the aid system. In some cases this relationship is direct, as with the coordinating role played by the WTO in the global Aid for Trade initiative. The aid component of the EPAs, which the EU has used as a 'carrot' to entice its negotiating partners and 'compensate' them for the adjustment costs of integration, is another example of this connection. In general, however, the link is indirect or unintended. Aid conditionality by donors (especially during the structural adjustment period) and the WTO both exert strong liberalizing pressure on African countries, but this is due more to coinciding ideologies and interests than to explicit coordination. Competition for global capital can also reinforce the pressure for liberalization in an uncoordinated but systemic way, since governments are desperate to attract investment and afraid that unorthodox policies could scare away investors. As well as signing numerous BITs, the past two decades have seen many African countries pass new national investment laws that grant broad legal protections and financial incentives to foreign investors. These mutually reinforcing constraints on African governments' policy choices are portrayed by some as undermining sovereignty and preventing governments from taking actions that are necessary for their development (Soludo *et al.* 2004).

How much policy space still exists for African governments? It is certainly true that current African governments can choose from a more limited set of feasible trade and investment policies than was formerly the case, and that in the past some of these now-restricted options had been successfully employed elsewhere. However, critics sometimes overlook the range of policies that are still available. Even if a certain policy is forbidden by the WTO, it does not necessarily follow that it is unavailable to African countries, since countries can comply in letter but not in spirit and WTO dispute settlement procedures are rarely invoked against small, poor countries. Defenders of the WTO also argue that a variety of 'special and differential treatment' provisions for developing countries are built into the agreements.

Supporters of state intervention also point out that the WTO still allows a variety of 'smart' industrial policies directed at innovation, infrastructure, and provision of public goods (Amsden 2005). In addition, the concept of policy space is much broader than just trade policy, and includes such issues as macroeconomic management (although many African countries are also subject to external disciplines on this front). Even where desirable policies have been taken off the table, it is arguable that institutional shortcomings in African countries are still a bigger constraint on effective policymaking. The benefits to African economies from improved implementation of existing policies could be substantially greater than the benefits that might accrue from using now-restricted trade policies like industrial subsidies.

In terms of the policy pressures imposed by investors and global market competition, the straitjacket of global capitalism also may not be as tight as it first appears. High levels of private investment and growth can coexist with illiberal practices on the part of governments, as evidenced by the recent experience of some East Asian countries (most notably China). Whether African countries can replicate this success is an open question, since it is less feasible for countries that are not already attractive destinations for foreign investment. The extent of a country's effective policy space therefore depends to some extent on structural economic factors, such as market size, natural resource base, and competitiveness.

It is also important to emphasize that African governments usually have some room for negotiation, even when aid donors and trade treaties make explicit demands of them. The strategies used to negotiate with donors range from confrontational approaches, such as refusal to negotiate and the politicization of conditions, to more evasive tactics, such as non-implementation and the reversal of reforms through 'backsliding' (Whitfield 2009). Donors have strong institutional incentives to disburse loans regardless of whether conditions have been met, and recipients can manipulate this to their advantage. Aid is also fungible to an extent, in that money given for a particular project frees up resources that the government can allocate to other uses that the aid donor does not want to support (Temple 2010).

Jones *et al.*'s (2010) study of developing-country trade negotiators finds that strong negotiation teams can win important concessions despite structural challenges and power inequalities. This brings out an important point: what matters is not only how much policy space countries have, but also how well they are able to use it. This is influenced by overall state capacity and political economy factors, but of greater interest is how it might be endogenous to the operation of the aid system. Some scholars argue that the overall effect of the aid 'ownership' reforms has been to undermine the ability of recipient governments to negotiate with donors, for several reasons: the deep entanglement of government institutions with those of donors; permanent negotiation of resources and policy choices; encouragement of apparent passivity on the part of the recipient government; and discursive convergence based on donor ideologies (Whitfield 2009).

These factors can make it difficult not only for governments to win negotiations but even to formulate negotiating positions. Jones *et al.* (2010) stress the importance of clear identification of interests as a prerequisite for success, yet too often this is the step where developing country negotiators are found lacking. The failure of many governments to even identify their own interests in such situations has major implications for thinking about policy space and the determination of economic policies, since the awareness and pursuit of self-interest by political agents is assumed by many approaches.

Conclusion

The forces of global aid, trade, and investment should be thought of as producing a complex and often contradictory set of incentives and constraints for national politics and policy. These incentives and constraints are both *de jure* and *de facto*, formal and informal, 'hard' and 'soft'. There are a few inviolable imperatives, but even most formal rules (such as aid conditionalities) can usually be negotiated, bent, or manipulated to some degree. This is not to say that governments have complete freedom, even within certain bounds. Global forces may not manifest themselves deterministically, but they clearly influence how easy and rewarding it is for political and economic agents to take different courses of action. Ultimately, political outcomes and policy choices are shaped by the interaction of many such agents, and it is this interaction that determines whether governments respond to external pressures by identifying and acting in the national interest – or not.

This approach explains why the same global forces can have such diverse impacts in different countries. How a political agent reacts to a set of incentives and constraints depends not only on the agent's own preferences and capabilities (keeping in mind that in many cases political agents are themselves groups) but also on those of other agents. It is natural, then, that countries with different constellations of elites and interest groups will have different reactions to global economic forces.

The same approach can also be brought to bear on debates about dependency and policy space. Countries' policy choices are subject to formal limits of varying rigidity, as well as a set of incentives that establishes a 'path of least resistance', which may or may not coincide with the national interest. Whether African governments take control of their economic destinies depends on these external incentives and constraints, on the outcomes of domestic political interactions, and on the connection between the two.

Bibliography

Amsden, A. (2005) 'Promoting Industry under WTO Law', in K. Gallagher (ed.) *Putting Development First: The Importance of Policy Space in the WTO and International Financial Institutions*, London: Zed Books.

Bates, R. (1981) *Markets and States in Tropical Africa*, Berkeley, CA: University of California Press.

Bratton, M. and van de Walle, N. (1997) *Democratic Experiments in Africa: Regime Transitions in Comparative Perspective*, New York, NY: Cambridge University Press.

Bräutigam, D., Fjeldstad, O.-H. and Moore, M. (eds) (2008) *Taxation and State-Building in Developing Countries: Capacity and Consent*, Cambridge: Cambridge University Press.

Bräutigam, D., Rakner, L. and Taylor, S. (2002) 'Business Associations and Growth Coalitions in sub-Saharan Africa', *Journal of Modern African Studies* 40(4): 519–47.

Chang, H.-J. (2002) *Kicking Away the Ladder: Development Strategy in Historical Perspective*, London: Anthem Press.

Collier, P. and Gunning, J.W. (1999) 'Why Has Africa Grown Slowly?' *Journal of Economic Perspectives* 13(3): 3–22.

Cornia, G., Jolly, R. and Stewart, F. (1987) *Adjustment with a Human Face, vol. 1, Protecting the Vulnerable and Promoting Growth*, Oxford: Clarendon Press.

Dollar, D. and Svensson, J. (2000) 'What Explains the Success or Failure of Structural Adjustment Programmes?' *The Economic Journal* 110(466): 894–917.

Ferguson, J. (1990) *The Anti-Politics Machine: 'Development,' Depoliticization, and Bureaucratic Power in Lesotho*, Cambridge: Cambridge University Press.

Fraser, A. and Whitfield, L. (2009) 'Understanding Contemporary Aid Relationships', in L. Whitfield (ed.) *The Politics of Aid: African Strategies for Dealing with Donors*, Oxford: Oxford University Press.

Herbst, J. (2000) *States and Power in Africa: Comparative Lessons in Authority and Control*, Princeton, NJ: Princeton University Press.

Jones, E., Deere-Birkbeck, C. and Woods, N. (2010) *Manoeuvring at the Margins: Constraints Faced by Small States in International Trade Negotiations*, London: Commonwealth Secretariat.

Lipton, M. (1977) *Why Poor People Stay Poor: Urban Bias in World Development*, Cambridge, MA: Harvard University Press.

Mkandawire, T. (1999) 'Crisis Management and the Making of Choiceless Democracies in Africa', in R. Joseph (ed.) *State, Conflict and Democracy in Africa*, Boulder, CO: Lynne Rienner Publishers.

Rodney, W. (1972) *How Europe Underdeveloped Africa*, London: Bogle-L'Ouverture Publications.

Rodrik, D. (1995) 'Trade and Industrial Policy Reform', in J. Behrman and T.N. Srinivasan (eds) *Handbook of Development Economics*, Vol. 3, Amsterdam: Elsevier.

Soludo, C., Ogbu, O. and Chang, H.-J. (eds) (2004) *The Politics of Trade and Industrial Policy in Africa: Forced Consensus?* Ottawa: IDRC.

Temple, J. (2010) 'Aid and Conditionality', in D. Rodrik and M. Rosenzweig (eds) *Handbook of Development Economics*, Vol. 5, Amsterdam: Elsevier.

van de Walle, N. (2001) *African Economies and the Politics of Permanent Crisis, 1979–1999*, Cambridge: Cambridge University Press.

Wade, R. (1990) *Governing the Market: Economic Theory and the Role of Government in East Asian Industrialization*, Princeton, NJ: Princeton University Press.

Whitfield, L. (ed.) (2009) *The Politics of Aid: African Strategies for Dealing with Donors*, Oxford: Oxford University Press.

Williamson, J. (1990) 'What Washington Means by Policy Reform', in J. Williamson (ed.) *Latin American Readjustment: How Much has Happened*, Washington, DC: Institute for International Economics.

World Bank (1981) *Accelerated Development in Sub-Saharan Africa*, Washington, DC: World Bank.

——(1993) *The East Asian Miracle: Economic Growth and Public Policy*, Oxford: Oxford University Press.

24

SOCIAL POLICY

Jeremy Seekings

In 1987 Iliffe described how the 'African poor' had throughout history been forced to rely on their own ingenuity because there were few other sources of support. Iliffe argued that colonial states had played a very limited role in social welfare. In the 1940s, colonial states developed policies for policing specific categories of the supposed poor (notably 'vagrants' and 'juvenile delinquents' in town), and in the 1950s they began to organize contributory insurance or provident schemes for small numbers of formal sector employees. Caring for the poor, however, was left to kin and charity (mostly church-based). The Great Depression and Second World War had pushed colonial officials towards 'development' as their primary strategy for reducing poverty, and little changed after independence. The family remained the 'first defence' against poverty. In Iliffe's account, at best, post-colonial states performed the functions of their predecessors. When civil war or famine resulted in prospective starvation, it was generally up to international relief agencies to limit mortality. South Africa was an exception to this general picture, with a variety of formal state interventions from the 1930s (Iliffe 1987).

Iliffe's implicit assessment that there were no 'welfare states' in Africa (with the possible exception of South Africa) was reiterated emphatically in a much more recent assessment by Bevan (2004), in a volume on 'welfare regimes' across the global South (Gough *et al.* 2004). Bevan was tasked with locating countries in Africa in a broader typology of 'welfare regimes', to use a term developed by the Scandinavian scholar Esping-Andersen (1990, 1999) in his analysis of the different worlds of 'welfare capitalism' in the global North. Bevan suggests that African states do so little to provide their citizens with any kind of economic security that most African countries should be understood in terms of 'informal security regimes', meaning that any income security is provided through informal, mostly kin-based, mechanisms. Pension programmes are the preserve of the middle class, the poor hardly benefit from public education, and public healthcare is even worse. Countries with violent, predatory states (such as Sudan or Sierra Leone in the 1990s) should be understood as 'insecurity regimes' because the state destroys livelihoods and deepens income insecurity (among other forms of insecurity).

Data on public expenditure, however, suggest a rather more complex picture. Detailed data on public finances are scarce or unreliable across much of Africa. Weigand and Grosh (2008) collated data from eight countries in sub-Saharan Africa (and another five in North Africa) as part of a cross-national study of social spending, i.e. public expenditure on social insurance, social assistance, education, and health. (Social insurance refers to contributory programmes that insure contributors against risks – including risk of illness, long life, and sometimes unemployment – that result in lowered income; social assistance refers to non-contributory, tax- or donor-financed cash transfer programmes, often targeted on the poor through means-testing. Weigand and Grosh include under 'social assistance' related programmes such as price subsidies and public works programmes). They found that social spending in the eight sub-Saharan countries in the early 2000s or late 1990s amounted to more than 13 per cent of gross domestic product (GDP). This was a lower proportion than in post-communist Eastern Europe and Central Asia (more than 17 per cent), but it was the same proportion of GDP as in Latin America and the Caribbean, and the Middle East (including the five North African countries), and was higher than in South or East Asia. In terms of spending as a share of GDP, these African countries certainly look like welfare states.

There are several reasons why these African welfare states have generally been overlooked. One is that, as we shall see, the big increases in spending were generally late in the twentieth century. Second, they have a distinctive pattern of expenditure. Spending on both social insurance and public health was low in these selected African countries, at less than 3 per cent of GDP each (although North African countries spend somewhat more on social insurance). Expenditure on public education, however, was high, and expenditure on social assistance was higher (in proportion to GDP) than in any other region – higher even than in the Organisation for Economic Co-operation and Development (OECD) countries. It might not be surprising that, by a long stretch, Mauritius is the highest spender on 'social assistance' as defined by Weigand and Grosh in the global South, or that South Africa is not far behind. However, Iliffe would probably not have anticipated that Djibouti, Ethiopia, and Malawi were the second, third, and fourth highest spenders on social assistance in the global South. Expenditures are high in these countries primarily because of donor-funded emergency employment programmes, food aid, and subsidies. In Ethiopia, expenditure on food aid reached 6 per cent of GDP in some drought years, prompting Ethiopia to introduce its Productive Safety Net Programme (PSNP). The PSNP, which reached about 8 million people, or 12 per cent of the population, entails public work programmes for people who can work, 'livelihood packages' to help people develop non-agricultural income-generating activities, and cash or food for people who are unable to work (Devereux and White 2010: 66–68).

The picture that emerges from Weigand and Grosh is only somewhat distorted by their selection of countries. The countries for which they have complete or almost complete data include (in addition to the five cases above) Senegal, Madagascar, Benin, Botswana, and Burkina Faso, as well as Algeria, Morocco, Egypt, and Tunisia in North Africa. Detailed data are unsurprisingly unavailable or unreliable for countries with very weak states and low spending. However, omissions from Weigand and Grosh's set include a number of countries that spend heavily on education (such as Kenya, Namibia, and Lesotho). They also underestimate expenditure in at least one important case – South Africa. In addition to spending almost 4 per cent of GDP on social assistance and about 1 per cent on social insurance, a much larger share (about 6 per cent) is spent on what might best be called 'semi-social' insurance (because many workers are required by law, indirectly, to join contributory, employment-linked, but privately run insurance schemes which serve the same function as social insurance in many other middle-income economies). If this is included, then a total of almost 20 per cent of GDP is spent on the welfare 'state' in South Africa.

By comparison, social spending in Britain passed 10 per cent of GDP only in the 1930s, in the aftermath of the Great Depression, and it was only after the Second World War that spending accelerated above the levels observed in many African countries today (Lindert 2004). In other words, public social expenditure across large parts of Africa is now comparable with public expenditures in Britain after about 50 years of welfare state-building there.

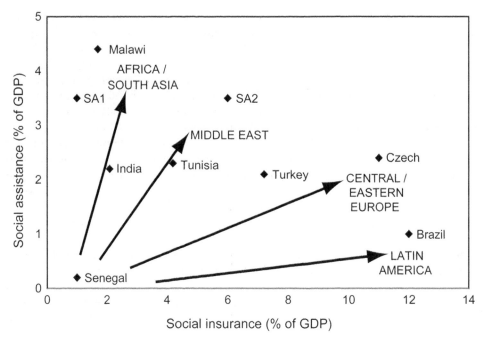

Figure 24.1 Social assistance and social insurance expenditures, selected countries and regional trajectories over time

Source: Constructed by the author using data from Weigand and Grosh 2008, and author's data on South Africa.

The Weigand and Grosh data on relative expenditure on social insurance and social assistance reveals that African welfare states have developed in a distinctive direction, rather than not at all. Figure 24.1 shows social insurance and social assistance spending as a percentage of GDP for a small number of countries,[1] together with a stylized version of the relative development of these categories of expenditure in Africa, South Asia, the Middle East/North Africa, Latin America, and Central/Eastern Europe. Whereas the Latin American and Central/Eastern European cases developed primarily through social insurance, the South Asian and African cases emphasized spending on social assistance. The Middle East/North African cases lay in between.

The origins of social policy and its post-war eclipse by 'development'

Not only do a significant number of African countries spend a substantial share of national income on public health, education, and social welfare programmes, but in some cases they have been doing so for a long time. British colonies in South Africa and Mauritius had poor laws, based on British precedents from the nineteenth century. The programmes associated with the 'modern' welfare state were first introduced in South Africa itself, where non-contributory, means-tested old-age pensions were introduced in 1927–28 for elderly people classified as 'white' or 'coloured'. Despite a conservative church-led backlash, programmatic provision was extended to the disabled, poor mothers with children, and the unemployed. By the late 1930s, South Africa had a well-developed welfare state for its white and coloured citizens. One sociologist exaggerated only somewhat when he proclaimed in 1937 that 'provision for [the] European population ... is scarcely less complete than that of Great Britain' (Gray 1937: 270). Similar non-contributory old-age pensions were introduced for white residents in Southwest Africa and

Southern Rhodesia. The construction of welfare states in these settler societies reflected a combination of elite ideology (which simultaneously entailed both racist and progressive elements) and democratic politics (within the enfranchised white and coloured population) (Seekings 2007, 2008).

Whilst part of the motivation for these schemes was to uphold a racial income hierarchy, old-age pensions were later extended to African people: in South Africa in 1944 and in Namibia in 1973 (but not in Southern Rhodesia). African people were initially excluded on the flawed grounds that 'traditional' systems of informal reciprocity protected them from poverty. The extension of pensions to African people in South Africa was driven by a combination of relatively progressive ideology (during the atypical circumstances of the Second World War) and recognition by both administrators and employers that rural poverty was pervasive and consequential (Seekings 2005). In Namibia, it has been suggested that the extension of coverage to vote-less African people was probably an attempt by the authoritarian regime to buy their quiescence and to improve the image of the South African army of occupation (Devereux 2007: 547–49).

South Africa was the first country in sub-Saharan Africa to extend social assistance pro-grammes to the non-voting poor. Soon after, Mauritius followed suit. Serious consideration was given to social insurance and social assistance in colonial Mauritius from the late 1930s, and non-contributory old-age pensions were finally introduced in 1950. The impetus in Mauritius initially came from colonial officials' modernizing ideology and concern with poverty within the Indo-Mauritian population, but combined with pressure from Indo-Mauritian workers (especially through riots in 1937 and 1943) and from the emerging Indo-Mauritian political elite, which itself embraced social democratic ideas. The colonial government dragged its heels for more than a decade, however, and it was only when substantial powers were transferred to a legislature elected with a broad franchise that pensions were finally introduced (Seekings 2011).

In the early 1940s it briefly seemed that reforms of these sorts might be introduced on a wide scale across British colonies and dominions. The word 'welfare' had been inserted into British colonial legislation in the 1940 Colonial Development and Welfare Act, which promised metropolitan funds for ill-defined categories of social and economic expenditure in the colonies. Debates over the 1941 Atlantic Charter fuelled concern with the welfare of colonial popula-tions. At the end of 1942, the publication in London of the Beveridge Report 'stirred public opinion' in a number of colonies, resulting in 'a considerable and growing interest ... in the question of social security or social insurance' (in the words of an anxious Colonial Officer). Faced with the suggestion that British colonial subjects should qualify for the kinds of pro-grammes being promised to the citizenry in Britain itself, the Colonial Office quickly moved to ward off reforms. It advised colonial governments that the 'more sophisticated forms of social insurance' were appropriate only in the 'more advanced', wage-earning economies. In societies 'in early stages of development', redistributive obligations were seen as generally still accepted by 'the tribal or family group', or the 'self-contained rural community'. In such cases, therefore, according to the colonial office 'the first consideration should be to support, for the time being at least, the existing social structure which ensures this traditional provision'. The most pressing priorities in rural areas were measures to stabilize the prices received for agricultural produce, and other interventions to develop agriculture and thereby 'raise the general standard of living'. These were seen as potentially needing to be supplemented by basic public health and education facilities, but not by the 'more sophisticated' kinds of welfare programme (all quotes from colonial archives cited in Seekings 2010a).

The new policy formed a core pillar of post-war British colonial strategy. Most colonies should be 'developed' economically, through the deployment of agricultural officers, experts in soil conservation and human nutrition, and public health and education advisers (Cooper 1997). Social order in rural and urban societies was to be upheld through the deployment of social welfare officers (Lewis 2000; Fourchard 2006). Expensive poverty-relief programmes were considered neither desirable nor feasible (e.g. Eckert 2004). A clear distinction came to be drawn between the colonies, which would be developed by what were in practice (rather ineffective) 'developmental states', focused primarily on agricultural development, and Britain itself, which would have a 'welfare state'.

The origins of public social welfare policies in Africa thus lay in the replication of aspects of the British model, and the limits to this replication reflected, above all, the British Colonial Office's insistence that British colonies in Africa required a very different, and less expensive, developmental model. Only in exceptional cases – South Africa, Mauritius – did welfare state-building begin. In these cases and only in these, the first reforms were driven by combinations of reformist elites and enfranchised citizens. A broadly similar process seems to have begun in French Africa, where family benefits were introduced in Algeria, Tunisia, and Morocco in the 1940s (Gruat 1990: 405).

Social welfare policies in Africa contrasted starkly with the situation across much of Latin America. By the late 1940s in Uruguay, Chile, Argentina, Brazil, and Mexico, large numbers of formal sector workers were covered by contributory social insurance schemes, protecting workers against the risks of poor health, disability, and old age. The different trajectories of welfare state-building on the two sides of the Atlantic reflected sharp economic, social, and political differences. In the major economies of Latin America, urban workers in the early twentieth century were mostly European immigrants without supportive roots or kin in the countryside. They also brought with them radical political traditions. In the face of urban militancy, Latin American elites sought to incorporate urban workers through corporatist institutions. In Africa, in contrast, not only were cities smaller, but most urban workers (even on the South African Witwatersrand or the Zambian Copperbelt) had close connections to the rural hinterland, and their militancy was more often channelled into anti-colonial, nationalist, or even millenarian struggles. Colonial elites in Africa sought political stability primarily through indirect rule, anchored in the countryside.

The slow expansion of social spending in post-war Africa

In practice, the late colonial state was soon forced to introduce very selective social insurance programmes or their equivalent in an attempt to buy the quiescence of African workers in formal employment, primarily in the public sector (Cooper 1996). The International Labour Organization (ILO) pushed for reforms in 'dependent territories' (or colonies), as well as independent states in a 1944 'Recommendation', followed by a 1952 Convention, on 'minimum standards' on social welfare programmes. It also facilitated a series of Africa-wide conferences on labour and welfare policies. These initiatives encouraged both the British and French to introduce statutory programmes. Contributory programmes of family and maternity benefits were introduced in most French colonies in the mid-1950s. Most of the North African countries introduced contributory programmes protecting against old age and sickness. In the 1960s, after achieving independence, the major former British colonies introduced contributory provident funds, through which formal sector workers were required to save for their retirement (or unemployment) – but on terms that presumed that they might return to rural villages and prefer lump-sum payments rather than monthly pensions, perhaps even prior to retirement age.

The new contributory programmes paid out benefits only to people who were members of and had previously contributed to these programmes. Except in North Africa, the coverage of these programmes thus remained very limited – generally to public-sector workers and small numbers of workers in formal employment in large private firms. In Egypt and Tunisia, by the 1980s, more than one-fifth of the population was covered. In sub-Saharan African countries, however, coverage was rarely above 10 per cent, and was often below 5 per cent. Welfare programmes entailed little redistribution or risk pooling. This was especially the case in the provident funds, which served as compulsory individualized savings institutions. Selected, privileged groups – notably the military and some other public employees – were often exempted from having to contribute to their pension schemes, so that welfare programmes sometimes served to redistribute upwards to privileged groups, as was the case in many other parts of the world (Paukert 1968).

Social insurance programmes in Africa 'have always been too exclusive and inadequate for the needs of the continent's people' (Butare and Kaseke 2003: 3). Not only did coverage rarely extend beyond workers in formal employment (and their immediate dependents) in a continent where formal employment was scarce, but also, few post-colonial states had the reach or capacity to ensure that even workers in formal employment and their employers made the required contributions. By the 1970s, the ILO itself was retreating from its prioritization of contributory welfare programmes, focusing instead on meeting 'basic needs' through 'development'.

After independence, across most of Africa the priorities for social policy and expenditure were education and health, with dramatic consequences in some cases. In Tanzania, less than one-half of lower primary school-age children and less than one in 10 of the higher primary school-age children were enrolled in school. Few children completed more than four years of schooling, and a negligible proportion reached secondary school. The new government initially prioritized the expansion of secondary schooling (and the establishment of the University of Dar es Salaam), but after 1967 reverted to an emphasis on practical, primary education. 'Education for Self-Reliance' – instilling the new political philosophy of collective responsibility and social commitment – was an integral part of the strategy of 'socialism and self-reliance'. The number of pupils entering primary school tripled in a decade, as did the (lower) number of pupils completing primary school. In 1969 the government announced its intention to achieve universal primary education within 20 years. Rapid gains soon prompted the government to bring the target date forward from 1989 to 1977. Spending on education doubled as a share of GDP in a decade (Coulson 1982; Buchert 1994).

Similarly, in Botswana only half of primary school-age children were enrolled in school, and very few progressed to secondary school at independence in 1966. In the 1970s, the government invested heavily in primary schooling with donors' support. Primary school fees were reduced and then, in 1980, abolished. Investment was redirected to secondary schooling in the 1980s. Between 1970 and 1990, the number of primary schools more than doubled, whilst the number of secondary schools rose ten-fold. In many countries, slow improvements in public health services also contributed to dramatic improvements in health outcomes. In Botswana, child immunization rates rose from almost zero in the 1960s to 78 per cent in 1990. Infant mortality declined and life expectancy rose – from 46 years in 1965, to more than 62 years in 1990 (Duncan *et al.* 1997). Given that Botswana – and many other countries – achieved almost universal primary education as well as greatly improved health indicators in the 1980s, it is not surprising that Iliffe failed to recognize these dramatic changes in *The African Poor*, written at precisely this time.

Education and healthcare were integral to both modernizing elites' developmental ambitions and the aspirations for upward social mobility and improved economic opportunities of ordinary people. In the 1970s and 1980s, social welfare programmes generally expanded much more modestly. Most former British colonies converted their provident funds into risk-pooling social insurance institutions, but there were dramatic changes in coverage or expenditure in few countries. The two exceptions were Mauritius and South Africa, which continued to be pioneers of welfare state-building in Africa. Mauritius extended its non-contributory social assistance programmes (introducing family allowances) in 1962, and in the late 1970s introduced a comprehensive 'social security' system combining social assistance and contributory social insurance.

Mauritius was an overwhelmingly commodified economy, with limited possibilities for subsistence agriculture. Demographic pressures (including rising numbers of elderly people), strong economic growth, and sustained electoral competition provided both incentives and resources for reform. Close links to progressive policy advisers in the UK helped to steer welfare state-building in Mauritius along much the same trajectory as the UK.

South Africa, under apartheid, invested heavily in the 1950s and 1960s in public education for the white population. Thereafter white people provided for their own retirement and illness primarily through the market (with privately administered pension and medical aid funds), whilst the state began to divert public expenditures to the education, healthcare, and welfare of the poor, black population. By the end of apartheid education was almost universal up to the age of 16, and about one in every two children completed secondary school. Racial discrimination in old-age pensions and other social assistance programmes was reduced and then abolished, with benefits being paid at a much more generous level than anywhere else in the global South. Progressive income taxes and pro-poor public expenditure meant that, even prior to South Africa's first democratic elections in 1994, there was substantial redistribution of income from rich to poor (Seekings and Nattrass 2005). The incentive was in part political (to contain domestic dissent and to deflect international criticism), but was not electoral, because the poor lacked the vote prior to 1994. There was also a developmental incentive to produce the skilled workers required by employers.

Social change, democratization, and welfare state-building in the late twentieth century

A combination of socioeconomic and political changes provided further impetus for welfare state-building at the end of the twentieth century. The crucial socioeconomic change was de-agrarianization: rising populations and slow-growing (or stagnant) economies pushed people into rapidly growing towns and made it harder for kin to meet the social obligations recognized by earlier generations. At the same time, democratization in many countries, together with changing preferences among international agencies and donors, generated incentives for political elites to introduce policy reforms (Lindberg, this volume).

The impact of social change is evident across much of West, East, and Southern Africa. In many parts of Africa, people now acknowledge obligations to a much narrower range of kin than in the past – for example parents, but not aunts or uncles – and even obligations to close kin are conditional and negotiable. These changes are most obvious in urban areas, but affect rural areas also. In Eastern and Southern Africa, social and cultural change has been accelerated by HIV/AIDS and unemployment, which have raised dependency rates.

At the same time, a range of international agencies have diversified their emphasis away from only 'developmental' interventions to cover 'welfare' programmes also, in what has been called a 'new model of development' (Hanlon *et al.* 2010). The World Bank began enthusiastically to promote 'conditional cash transfers', along the lines of the *bolsa família* in Brazil, which provides cash grants to poor families with children on the condition that the children attend school and visit a health clinic. In conferences it promoted conditional cash transfers not only in countries such as Kenya or Malawi, but also in post-war Angola and Sierra Leone.[2] The ILO also recognized the limited reach of contributory programmes of social insurance and began to endorse non-contributory programmes for the poor. The adoption of the Millennium Development Goals (MDGs) put additional pressure on international agencies and African governments. The World Bank assessed that social policies were central not only to the first MDG, on poverty reduction, but also to MDG 2 (universal primary education), 3 (gender equality in education), and 4 through 6 (health): 'without appropriate social protection mechanisms the MDG targets for 2015 will not be achieved' (World Bank 2003: 3). Relevant policies included old-age and disability pensions, unemployment benefits, safety nets, transfers targeted to children or youth, social funds, and public employment programmes, social insurance programmes that protect poor households from shocks, and targeted (and conditional) social assistance. The shifting discourses of public policy are reflected in policy positions adopted by the African Union (AU) and Southern African Development Community (Wright and Noble 2010).

In practice, policy innovations have been inhibited by concerns, within both international organizations and national states, over both affordability and desirability. The World Bank equivocates on the import of affordability, suggesting that 'even in the poorest of countries, safety net programs have a role to play', at the same time as acknowledging 'major problems of affordability and administrative feasibility' (World Bank 2001: 36). Its enthusiasm for social protection was limited by its insistence that these be seen as developmental. Social protection programmes should not be viewed as 'relief or welfare handouts, but rather investments that prevent irreversible human development losses by the poor, thereby protecting their future productivity' (ibid.). In developmental terms, the elderly are a lesser priority than children (Kakwani and Subbarao 2005).

This wariness of 'welfare states' has been widely shared among African political elites. The Mozambican minister of women's affairs and social welfare called for reductions in the value of (already modest) cash grants to the elderly because the government should not be giving 'alms' to the poor (Hanlon *et al.* 2010: 7). In Ethiopia, the government promoted the PSNP based on employment on public works, rather than conditional cash transfers because of a concern with an 'entitlement culture' (Devereux and White 2010: 67). In South Africa, most (but not all) of the leadership of the governing African National Congress (ANC) condemn 'handouts' and endorse instead 'developmental' social policies and self-reliance (Seekings and Matisonn 2012). Devereux and White conclude that 'political elites across Africa exhibit a striking bias in favour of the economically active poor, who are considered "deserving," and a fear, despite evidence to the contrary, that "handouts" create "dependency"' (Devereux and White 2010: 63). Elites worry that grants are spent on alcohol, or that there is fraud, or that they allow children to renege on their responsibilities to their parents (Devereux 2007: 559).

There is little good evidence on what African people themselves think. In South Africa, where most social assistance programmes are old, have broad coverage, and are often taken for granted, public opinion favours the extension of social assistance, but not unconditionally. The poor say that the government should support poor people, but when faced with specific questions about precisely who they consider deserving, rich and poor alike oppose the government providing financial support for people who are poor as a result of their own behaviour (for example, because they lost their jobs due to drinking or theft). However, the public are more generous than elites in their identification of who is deserving, though their generosity is not universal (Seekings 2010b). Surrender *et al.* (2010) found no evidence that receiving a grant does deter people from work or inculcate dependent attitudes. South Africa's disability grants provide a telling case study. In the face of high rates of AIDS, many doctors and nurses certified that their HIV-positive patients were unable to work, allowing them to claim the generous disability grant. The government baulked at the cost and sought reforms to prevent claims from patients whose health was improving due to antiretroviral treatment. Getting cooperation from medical professionals and grant administrators, however, was no easy task and the number of grants paid did not drop by much (Nattrass 2006).

A range of countries did introduce major reforms in the last part of the twentieth century. Southern African countries, especially, expanded existing programmes or replicated their neighbours and introduced new ones. South Africa's first democratic government inherited non-contributory old-age pensions and other programmes and a partial system of semi-social insurance for better-paid workers in formal employment. In the late 1990s, in the context of necessary fiscal austerity, the government focused on making its social expenditures more 'developmental'. In the 2000s, however, expenditure rose significantly. The total number of grants paid monthly rose from less than 3 million in 2000, to more than 14 million by 2010 – in a country with a total population of fewer than 50 million people. Expenditure on social assistance rose from 2 per cent of GDP to 3.5 per cent. The increased numbers and expenditure reflected primarily the expansion of child support grants, which entail modest benefits to poor parents supposedly for the support of their children. The governing ANC has won a majority of the national vote in every election since 1994, but threats from opposition parties (including in 2009 a party that had broken away from the ANC) provided some incentive for the ANC to expand grants, and thereby reduce poverty rates. Reforms were accelerated also by litigation, with a series of cases contesting whether the exclusion of various categories of beneficiaries accorded with South Africa's progressive constitution (Seekings and Matisonn 2012).

In 1992 the new, democratically elected government of independent Namibia ended racial discrimination in benefits, but set benefits at a much lower level than in neighbouring South Africa. In 1999 the value of the pension became an electoral issue, with opposition parties pressing strongly for a big increase. Botswana's Democratic Party government introduced old-age pensions in 1996 soon after it failed to win a majority of the vote in the 1994 elections, although it did win a majority of seats. The introduction of old-age pensions in Lesotho in 2004–05 – and a subsequent increase in their value – also reflected electoral politics. In Swaziland, old-age pensions were introduced in 2005, not in response to electoral competition, but in the face of strong lobbying by civil society organizations (Pelham 2007: 4; Devereux and White 2010: 70–72; Devereux 2010).

There is evidence also of the role of electoral competition in driving the expansion of public education. In the Ugandan presidential campaign in 1996, the incumbent president, Yoweri Museveni, promised to abolish primary school fees for up to four children per family. He had previously resisted calls for the abolition of fees, but slipped the promise as a minor item in his manifesto. When it proved popular, he adopted it as a central plank in his campaign. Although his re-election was likely, the predicted margin of victory was uncomfortably small. Museveni ended up winning comfortably and then honoured his election promise. As one Ministry of Finance official told Stasavage, 'we won the election because of the [free education] pledge, so we have to come up with the money for it' (Stasavage 2005a: 61). Stasavage argues that the school fee reform was especially attractive to Museveni because he wanted to expand his support outside of specific regions and the reform was an issue of country-wide appeal. In the following 2001 election, Museveni emphasized his record on primary education, and data from a 2000 survey of public opinion in Uganda suggest that voters rated his performance best with respect to education.

Using time series cross-sectional data on 44 countries between 1980 and 1996, Stasavage (2005b) shows that the Ugandan case was not exceptional. Multi-party competition is associated with increased spending on education, especially on primary education. This finding is consistent with the results of similar studies in Latin America and elsewhere. Stasavage finds an overall effect despite the fact that multi-party competition seems to have a muted effect on education spending in some African countries (such as Malawi) where parties have sharply defined regional bases and hence a reduced incentive to implement country-wide programmes.

Competitive elections are not always an incentive to programmatic reform, as the Zimbabwean case illustrates. Like South Africa and Namibia, Zimbabwe inherited at independence an Old Age Pension Act. Unlike its neighbours, however, the legislation was racially exclusive. Rather than introducing equal benefits for black Zimbabweans, the new government decided to repeal the Act. Very limited assistance was later provided for the elderly and disabled under a Social Welfare Assistance Act, passed in 1988 (Kaseke 2002). Both rhetorically and in practice, the government emphasized land reform. Even when other countries in the region introduced old-age pensions, and even in the face of strong electoral competition within Zimbabwe, the government did not introduce programmatic welfare reforms for the general population. The government did, however, introduce pensions for one specific group of beneficiaries: veterans of the independence war. In 1992, disgruntled war veterans demanded both land and welfare benefits. When President Mugabe conceded discretionary lump-sum payments for 'disabled' war veterans, the Veterans Association leadership rubber-stamped applications without any medical examinations, and later began to count supposed post-traumatic stress as disability. In the face of further protests, Mugabe conceded a lump-sum payment and monthly pensions to all veterans, as well as healthcare and education benefits, and a share of land expropriated from white farmers. In the Zimbabwean case, the state's strained resources were allocated to providing patronage to a special interest group – war veterans – rather than clear programmatic benefits to the poor.

Incumbent elites seeking to maintain semi-discretionary control over patronage have been one source of opposition to reforms. Another source of opposition are international agencies and donors, whose enthusiasm for reforms proved to be uneven. In Lesotho, the International Monetary Fund (IMF) opposed the introduction of old-age pensions on the grounds that the pensions were unaffordable (Devereux and White 2010: 65). In Ethiopia, also, the government established the PSNP in the face of opposition from some donors. Donors initially supported the proposal to move beyond emergency food aid, but then shifted to a more critical position, primarily on account of scepticism about the state's capacity to implement a national public works programme. Donors promoted conditional cash transfers instead (ibid.: 67). In these cases, domestic political considerations overrode donor influence.

In other cases, however, donors have driven reforms. 'In the majority of African countries', Devereux argues, 'social protection has been, and remains, a donor-led agenda' (Devereux 2010: 12). Donors and international organizations vigorously promoted cash transfer programmes, including through 'providing technical assistance and direct financing to the design, implementation and evaluation of pilot projects and national programmes, building the capacity of government ministries, and even lobbying Parliamentarians' (ibid.). In Mozambique, the ILO and the United Nations Conference on Trade and Development (UNCTAD) together proposed a conditional cash transfer, called the Minimum Income on School Attendance (MISA) programme. The proposal was incorporated into Mozambican government documents in 2002 and a pilot project was initiated (Lavinas 2003). In Malawi, food and cash transfer schemes were designed and implemented by an international non-governmental organization (NGO) with funding from bilateral Irish and British donors. In Malawi, and Zambia also, the government itself prioritized subsidies for agricultural inputs such as fertilizers, and tolerated rather than embraced donor-driven welfare experiments (Devereux and White 2010; Devereux 2010).

Conclusion

Africa does not warrant its neglect in the comparative scholarship on welfare states. Recent studies of the comparative politics and political economy of welfare provision draw their case studies from Latin America, South and East Asia, and post-communist Eastern Europe (e.g. Haggard and Kaufman 2008; Rudra 2008), whilst studies that encompass Africa (such as Gough *et al.* 2004) tend to emphasize the lack of public provision across most of Africa, or even the ways in which predatory states undermine the wellbeing of citizens. Yet many states in Africa spend a considerable share of national resources on public education, poverty alleviation and, to a lesser extent, public health. Social insurance programmes are limited across much of Africa (with North Africa being the conspicuous exception), reflecting primarily the limits to formal employment. However, the limits to social insurance do not mean that there are no programmes for maintaining incomes. Indeed, the data of Weigand and Grosh suggest that Africa spends a larger share of GDP on social assistance than any other region in the global South.

The construction of welfare states in Africa has entailed three broad phases. In the first period, the settler societies of Southern Africa and the island colony of Mauritius pioneered public welfare provision, borrowing from the British model. Faced with growing interest in other colonies, the British Colonial Office firmly discouraged further replication of the British model, emphasizing instead rural 'development'. In the second period, from the 1950s, the late colonial and then post-colonial states began to invest more heavily, expanding public primary education and initiating contributory welfare programmes for selected formal sector workers. These efforts accelerated in the 1970s and 1980s. A third period coincided with, and was to some extent due to, the wave of democratization across Africa from the 1980s. States expanded both the reach of and spending on public education, and introduced new cash transfer (and related) programmes to mitigate poverty.

The politics of reform varied across these three periods, although in each case reforms reflected the interaction of domestic and international factors. In the first period, domestic political elites drew on ideas from Britain, introducing reforms that placated selected groups of voters or complied with their modernist and (selectively) progressive ideologies. The limits of reform in this period were imposed by generally hostile colonial authorities. In the second period, domestic political elites, encouraged by international agencies, sought to use social policy to 'modernize' their societies and contribute to the 'development' of their economies. In this phase, the stimulus to elite action seems to have lain in the prevailing ideologies of modernization, whether dressed up in more 'socialist' or more 'capitalist' garb. The limits to reform were set by the weakness of domestic political pressures for reform. In the third phase, the impetus to reform came from foreign donors, on the one hand, and groups of domestic voters, on the other. In this period, domestic elites were generally uncertain about welfare reforms, embracing them only if they seemed 'developmental'.

Few African countries have, until recently, had strong interest groups pushing for programmatic interventions. Even in post-apartheid South Africa, where trade unions use their considerable institutional and political power to protect their interests with regard to wages, conditions of employment, and pensions and medical benefits, they have rarely made social policy reforms their priority. Elections, however, do matter; although experience suggests that electoral competition is neither necessary nor sufficient for programmatic reform. Incumbent elites can choose to contest politics through dispensing patronage, whether narrowly to specific interest groups, or more broadly. It is possible that elections matter more in specific circumstances. Research in Brazil suggests that the diffusion of *bolsa família* between municipalities in Brazil was driven in part by the intensity of competition between the centrist Brazilian Social

Democratic Party and the left-wing Workers' Party. When elections pitted left-wing against right-wing parties, there was little impetus to build support through commitments to programmatic welfare reforms. In Africa, it is likely that welfare reforms are especially appealing when incumbent parties feel they need to install a safety net to mitigate the risks associated with drastic economic adjustments or chronic drought. Moreover, electoral competition remains muted across much of the continent (van de Walle, this volume).

Notes

1 SA1 and SA2 mark South Africa, depending on how one categorizes semi-social insurance expenditures.
2 Third International Conference on Conditional Cash Transfers, Istanbul, Turkey, 26–30 June 2006.

Bibliography

Bevan, P. (2004) 'The Dynamics of African Insecurity Regimes', in I. Gough and G. Wood, with A. Barrientos, P. Bevan, P. Davis and G. Room (eds) *Insecurity and Welfare Regimes in Asia, Africa and Latin America*, Cambridge: Cambridge University Press.

Buchert, L. (1994) *Education in the Development of Tanzania*, London: James Currey.

Butare, T. and Kaseke, E. (2003) 'Social Security in Africa: Inherited Burdens, Future Priorities', *International Social Security Review* 56(3–4): 3–9.

Cooper, F. (1996) *Decolonisation and African Society*, Cambridge: Cambridge University Press.

——(1997) 'Modernizing Bureaucrats, Backward Africans, and the Development Concept', in F. Cooper and R. Packard (eds) *International Development and the Social Sciences*, Berkeley, CA: University of California Press.

Coulson, A. (1982) *Tanzania: A Political Economy*, Oxford: Oxford University Press.

Devereux, S. (2007) 'Social Pensions in Southern Africa in the Twentieth Century', *Journal of Southern African Studies* 33(3): 539–60.

——(2010) *Building Social Protection Systems in Southern Africa*, Background Paper to the European Report on Development, Brighton: Institute of Development Studies.

Devereux, S. and White, P. (2010) 'Social Protection in Africa: Evidence, Politics and Rights', *Poverty and Public Policy* 2(3) Article 5: 53–77.

Duncan, T., Jefferis, K. and Molutsi, P. (1997) 'Botswana: Social Development in a Resource-rich Economy', in S. Mehrotra and R. Jolly (eds) *Development with a Human Face: Experiences in Social Achievement and Economic Growth*, Oxford: Clarendon Press.

Eckert, A. (2004) 'Regulating the Social: Social Security, Social Welfare and the State in Late Colonial Tanzania', *Journal of African History* 45(3): 467–89.

Esping-Andersen, G. (1990) *The Three Worlds of Welfare Capitalism*, Princeton, NJ: Princeton University Press.

——(1999) *Social Foundations of Postindustrial Economies*, New York, NY: Oxford University Press.

Fourchard, L. (2006) 'Lagos and the Invention of Juvenile Delinquency in Nigeria, 1920–60', *Journal of African History* 47(1): 115–37.

Gough, I. and Wood, G. (with A. Barrientos, P. Bevan, P. Davis and G. Room) (2004) *Insecurity and Welfare Regimes in Asia, Africa and Latin America*, Cambridge: Cambridge University Press.

Gray, J.L. (1937) 'The Comparative Sociology of South Africa', *South African Journal of Economics* 5(3): 269–84.

Gruat, J.-V. (1990) 'Social Security Schemes in Africa: Current Trends and Problems', *International Labour Review* 129(4): 405–21.

Haggard, S. and Kaufman, R.R. (2008) *Development, Democracy, and Welfare States: Latin America, East Asia, and Eastern Europe*, Princeton, NJ: Princeton University Press.

Hanlon, J., Barrientos, A. and Hulme, D. (2010) *Just Give Money To the Poor: The Development Revolution from the Global South*, Sterling, VA: Kumarian Press.

Iliffe, J. (1987) *The African Poor*, Cambridge: Cambridge University Press.

Kakwani, N. and Subbarao, K. (2005) 'Aging and Poverty in Africa and the Role of Social Pensions', World Bank Social Protection Discussion Paper No. 521.

Kaseke, E. (2002) 'Zimbabwe', in J. Dixon and R. Scheurell (eds) *State of Social Welfare*, Westport, CT: Greenwood Press.

Lavinas, L. (2003) 'Encouraging School Attendance in Mozambique by Granting a Minimum Income to Parents', *International Social Security Review* 56(3–4): 139–55.

Lewis, J. (2000) *Empire State-Building: War and Welfare in Kenya, 1925–52*, Oxford: James Currey.

Lindert, P. (2004) *Growing Public*, Cambridge: Cambridge University Press.

Nattrass, N. (2006) 'Trading Off Income and Health: AIDS and the Disability Grant in South Africa', *Journal of Social Policy* 35(1): 3–19.

Paukert, F. (1968) 'Social Security and Income Distribution: A Comparative Study', *International Labour Review* 98(5): 425–50.

Pelham, L. (2007) 'The Politics Behind the Non-Contributory Old Age Pensions in Lesotho, Namibia and South Africa', CPRC Working Paper No. 83, Manchester: Chronic Poverty Research Centre.

Rudra, N. (2008) *Globalization and the Race to the Bottom in Developing Countries: Who Really Gets Hurt?* New York, NY: Cambridge University Press.

Seekings, J. (2005) '"Visions and Hopes and Views about the Future": The Radical Moment of South African Welfare Reform', in S. Dubow and A. Jeeves (eds) *Worlds of Possibility: South Africa in the 1940s*, Cape Town: Double Storey.

——(2007) '"Not a Single White Person Should be Allowed to Go Under": Swartgevaar and the Origins of South Africa's Welfare State, 1924–29', *Journal of African History* 48(3): 375–94.

——(2008) 'The Carnegie Commission and the Backlash Against Welfare State-Building in South Africa, 1931–37', *Journal of Southern African Studies* 34(3): 515–37.

——(2010a) 'The Beveridge Report, the Colonial Office and Welfare Reform in British Colonies', unpublished paper.

——(2010b) 'Race and Class Discrimination in Assessments of Just Desert in Post-apartheid Cape Town', in M. Centano and K. Newman (eds) *Discrimination in an Unequal World*, New York, NY: Oxford University Press.

——(2011) 'British Colonial Policy, Local Politics and the Origins of the Mauritian Welfare State, 1936–50', *Journal of African History* 52(2): 157–77.

Seekings, J. and Matisonn, H. (2012) 'The Continuing Politics of Basic Income in South Africa', in M. Murray and C. Pateman (eds) *Basic Income Worldwide: Horizons of Reform: Basic Income Solutions around the World*, London: Palgrave Macmillan.

Seekings, J. and Nattrass, N. (2005) *Class, Race and Inequality in South Africa*, New Haven, CT: Yale University Press.

Stasavage, D. (2005a) 'The Role of Democracy in Uganda's Move to Universal Primary Education', *Journal of Modern African Studies* 43(1): 53–73.

——(2005b) 'Democracy and Education Spending in Africa', *American Journal of Political Science* 49(2): 343–58.

Surrender, R., Noble, M., Wright, G. and Ntshongwana, P. (2010) 'Social Assistance and Dependency in South Africa: An Analysis of Attitudes to Paid Work and Social Grants', *Journal of Social Policy* 39(2): 203–21.

Weigand, C. and Grosh, M. (2008) 'Levels and Patterns of Safety Net Spending in Developing and Transition Countries', Social Protection Discussion Paper No. 817, Washington, DC: World Bank.

World Bank (2001) *Dynamic Risk Management and the Poor: Developing a Social Protection Strategy for Africa*, Washington, DC: World Bank.

——(2003) *The Contribution of Social Protection to the Millennium Development Goals*, Washington, DC: World Bank.

Wright, G. and Noble, M. (2010) 'Recent Social Policy Developments in Africa', *Global Social Policy* 10(1): 111–19.

25

NGOs

Michael Jennings

Whilst the non-governmental organization (NGO) is today mostly understood in relation to its work and position in developing countries, including sub-Saharan Africa, its history has largely been told from the perspective of Europe and northern America where the sector first emerged. In sub-Saharan Africa, the story of the NGO is intimately bound up with, in the popular telling at least, that of the decline of the post-colonial African state. Initially supportive of state-led development, the small NGO sector (largely external, mostly European and North American-based organizations) was transformed in scale and activity in the 1980s, its expansion mirroring the gradual retreat of the state under attack from economic crisis and externally imposed structural reforms. By now consisting of an ever-growing proportion of 'national' (African) NGOs of a bewildering array of types, NGOs were once more transformed from service deliverers (replacing the state) into civil society actors (challenging the state) from the 1990s as the good governance agenda, new policy agenda reforms, and focus on poverty reduction strategies once again re-set the balance of power and nature of the relationship between the state and the NGO sector.

The reality is, of course, more complex. The (very real) growth of NGOs as development actors, service deliverers, advocacy organizations, and civil society actors was not a simple reflection of the decline of the state. Nor are NGOs, despite the way in which they are often presented, the sole or even, perhaps, the main non-state actors in development in Africa.

In much of the literature, and in the narratives provided by NGOs themselves, there is an assumption that the story of NGO engagement in sub-Saharan Africa is a new one. However, the 'NGO-ization' (Hearn 1998) of sub-Saharan Africa is actually part of a wider story of the emergence and rise of voluntary sector welfare and service provision. In addition to their own historical narrative, NGOs are a part of this broader history of non-state, non-voluntary sector engagement. Associational life in sub-Saharan Africa is a much more richly complex phenomenon than is often presented in the narratives of the 'NGO-ization' of, or even civil society in, Africa.

How then to justify a focus on the history of the NGO, rather than the voluntary sector more widely? Despite large numbers, the reach of NGOs is not necessarily deeper or more extensive than other organizations (subject, as they are, to the same tarmac bias of other international organizations and governments). Their contribution to total aid funding is limited: official development assistance (ODA) channelled through NGOs accounted for US$2.17 billion of a total ODA figure of $120 billion in 2009 (OECD 2009). Nevertheless, this is a chapter about the NGO specifically, not civil society more broadly, nor the voluntary sector in its entirety.

Whilst such a focus may not capture the rich texture of non-state, non-profit engagement, it does reflect the extent to which NGOs have inserted themselves into the development and political landscape of sub-Saharan Africa. They matter because donors, national governments, and international organizations believe they do. They have, through a blend of their own efforts, international policy directions, and the shifting balance of power between African governments and donors over the control of development and macro-economic policy, successfully transformed themselves from small-scale, often amateurish, organizations into highly professional, well-resourced and -connected major actors in the politics of development in Africa.

What is 'the NGO'?

Most definitions focus on three key elements: they are non-state, non-profit organizations working towards the relief of poverty, distress, and want. Given the large variety of organizations known as NGOs, from the transnational to the very local; from service providers through to those focusing on emergency relief; to those who see their primary task as advocacy and campaigning; organizations that take much (most, even) of their funding from official sources and those who rely largely on private charitable sources; how useful (or accurate) are attempts to define the NGO? For example, whilst both a large international NGO such as Action Aid or Oxfam, as well as a small, community-based organization working in a village in Tanzania might both be NGOs, the way they function, their organizational structure, and their engagement with development and relief may differ so much that understanding them through the definition above alone tells us little about what they do, how they do it, and how effective they might be.

Perhaps a more useful way of understanding the NGO is to consider key drivers and the level at which it operates. Three main drivers shape the strategy, objectives, and work of NGOs: underlying ethos, objectives, and approach.

Table 25.1 Types of NGO, by ethos, objective, and approach

Driver	Orientation	Examples
Underlying ethos	Religious values	An organization formed by a particular faith group; organizations that believe in promoting understanding between different faiths
	Secular values	An organization that consciously rejects any links to organized religion (or projects that involve such actors)
	Socio-political values	Organizations critical of neo-liberalism; organizations that actively promote market-based solutions
Objectives	Relief	Humanitarian aid; disaster relief; refugees, etc.
	Welfare	Broad 'development' objectives; health; water supplies; livelihoods, etc.
	Advocacy or campaigning	Human rights; pro-democracy; anti-corruption; changing international trade/aid policy
Approach	Service delivery	Delivering key services to communities (vertical delivery)
	Empowerment	Participatory approaches; building up capacity of communities (horizontal engagement)
	Willing to work with state actors	Extent to which they are prepared to accept official donor funds
	Operational or non-operational	Does the organization plan and manage its own interventions (operational); or work with partners, channelling funding to the organization managing the project?

Organizations are not necessarily confined to any one position and may straddle several simultaneously or over time. Another way to consider the NGO is to focus on the level of operation: is it a large, international NGO, working mostly at the international level; a national-based organization working in a specific country (and emerging from that country); or community-based and small scale? As with key drivers, an individual NGO might operate at different levels at the same time.

The creation of the voluntary sector and the rise of the NGO

Much analysis of the NGO in Africa focuses upon the post-colonial and, in particular, the post-1980s period. Writing in the mid-1990s, Salamon suggested the rise of 'a massive array of self-governing private organizations' was part of a 'global "associational revolution" that may prove to be as significant to the latter twentieth century as the rise of the nation-state was to the latter nineteenth' (Salamon 1994: 109). Central to this 'new' 'associational revolution' was the institution of the NGO. The rise of the voluntary sector in sub-Saharan Africa was linked, by many, to this new (or new to the region) organizational type. Fowler, for example suggested 'voluntary development organisations' were synonymous with NGOs (Fowler 1995: 53).

As a result, analysis of the NGO – its role in development, the nature of the relationship with donors, states, and communities, issues around accountability, the degree of independence of the NGO, and so on – have largely focused on the institution itself rather than the particular context in which it operates. However, NGOs did not create the voluntary sector; they moved into it alongside other pre-existing and newly emerging actors. In doing so, they inherited a set of pre-existing relationships, an already-formed space in which much of the challenges and issues that would face NGOs as relief and development actors had already been established by their forerunners.

The origins of the formal voluntary sector lay in the division of social welfare responsibility in many African colonies between state and mission actors during the first half of the twentieth century. In this period, social welfare provision was divided into state and voluntary sectors, with voluntary agencies (mostly missions) given responsibility for education, health, training, and other service provision, alongside those services provided by the state. Formally incorporated into the structures of colonial welfare provision, this voluntary sector, in place across much of the region by the end of the 1930s, led not only to the dominance of non-state actors in a range of what would become considered 'developmental' services in many colonial African societies, but also the dominant narrative across Africa of the privatization of social welfare for most of its post-1900 history.

During the colonial period, the relative paucity (in both financial and human capacity terms) of the colonial state meant that social welfare was largely left to non-state agencies in the first decades of colonial rule. In practice, for much of sub-Saharan Africa this meant the missionary organizations that had spread inwards from the littoral from the mid-nineteenth century in particular. In the Belgian Congo, for example, the colonial state relied upon a mix of state and voluntary healthcare providers. Amongst the latter, the *Service Auxiliaire de l'Assistance Médicale aux Indigènes* (SADAMI) was dominated by missions. Even the official *Fondation Reine Élisabeth pour l'Assistance Médicale aux Indigènes* (Foréami) was a mix of public and private, supported as it was by government, royal, and public donations (Hailey 1939: 1178–79). In British colonial Africa, primary school education was almost completely in the hands of missions, colonial governments having realized early on that they could not afford to establish a state system. In healthcare, where the British colonial state did provide medical services for Africans, mission providers remained dominant in many areas until the 1930s at least, and longer in some areas (Jennings

2008b: 28). Even in French colonies, where the state was to take a more pro-active role in direct service provision, missions formed a distinct voluntary sector and were important actors in this regard.

What turned the presence of non-state actors in colonial service provision into a formal voluntary sector was the gradual acceptance by colonial authorities that they ought to be providing funds for these services. The colonial state became in effect a contractor of services, building a public-private partnership in service provision and local development interventions. In Tanzania, the colonial government agreed that it should financially support mission-run education services in 1925 and mission health services from 1945 (although it had provided ad hoc grants to specific mission health providers for particular health campaigns from the 1920s) (Jennings 2008b: 44–45). In Uganda, Mengo Hospital – the mission hospital established by the Church Missionary Society physician Albert Cook – was formally supported by the colonial government, providing health services and medical training for Ugandans.

As a result of the particular formation of the formal voluntary sector in the colonial period – dominated, if not almost solely populated, by missionary organizations – it was made up of non-African organizations, rather than formal and informal African associations. The division of service provision across distinct, but linked, state and voluntary sectors meant that the latter was playing a more significant role in social service delivery than in the home nations of the colonial occupiers by the 1950s and 1960s. Moreover, the relationships of those voluntary actors – part of the colonial system, but not simple tools of the colonial state; enjoying close relationships with and even dependence on that state; and existing in a condition of mutual dependence – would continue to shape relationships between new non-state actors and the post-colonial state (and increasingly with donors) in the aftermath of independence. Before the rise to prominence of the NGO, therefore, the particular context in which NGOs operated had been established over the previous six decades. It was a legacy that would shape the interaction of NGOs with the state and donors, their perception of their role, and issues of power and independence of non-state actors certainly until the 1980s, and arguably beyond.

NGOs in the colonial period

The history of the NGO specifically began for most in the 1960s. Their presence in the colonial period, certainly until the late 1950s, was largely confined to local branches of organizations such as the British Legion, St John Ambulance Brigade, or voluntary organizations committed to particular causes such as the Lady Chelmsford League (dedicated to improving children's health), or the East African Women's League in Kenya. Whilst such organizations would have been considered archetypal small-scale, community-based NGOs from the 1960s, their roots lay more in nineteenth-century European and North American philanthropic traditions transplanted into the colonies. Often formed by the wives and daughters of European settlers and colonial officials (a history of whose engagement in charitable activity has still been mostly unwritten), they generally focused on education, maternal and child health, and small-scale relief of dire poverty.

Modern NGOs were still largely focused on their own immediate hinterland. In the late 1950s, some began to look to Africa as a potential theatre for their operations. Engagement was limited: generally donations to meet a specific need, rather than the active operations (and a physical presence) that would come to be the hallmark of the NGO in Africa in the following decades. Oxfam, for example, made contributions to help those suffering from the after effects of serious drought in central Tanganyika in 1955.

African engagement in this area was generally unrecognized by the colonial state, nor did it form part of the formal voluntary sector. The exclusion of formal and informal African associations, such as tribal and home-town associations, burial societies, and religious groups, meant the role they could have played in the formal voluntary sector was largely taken by externally based NGOs. From the 1960s, national governments, donors, and international organizations would look to the organizational type they recognized – the NGO – rather than the amorphous, complex world of African associational life as a new partner.

Development is politics: from relief to development

The 1960s and 1970s saw several parallel (at times apparently conflicting, at other times intersecting) trends evolve within the NGO community. The first was their shift from relief to development activity. The second was the establishment of a particular set of relationships with the governments of the countries in which they operated, characterized at this stage more by cooperation and conflict. Third, a growing focus on alternative, especially participatory and grassroots approaches to their activities. In all aspects, NGOs were to be as influenced by their experiences in sub-Saharan Africa (and the wider developing world) as they were from internal debates in the head offices of their home countries.

The Congo famine of 1960–61 was one of the first post-colonial African crises that would draw in a large number of NGOs that had previously focused on European operations. For the first time, relief was to be supervised directly by NGO staff rather than through local actors. Oxfam's Secretary Leslie Kirkley, for example, went to the Congo to supervise projects. The famine not only brought in NGOs in larger numbers, establishing them, perhaps for the first time, as a new major development actor in sub-Saharan Africa, but it also influenced their understanding of the causes of disaster. The famine in the Congo was no natural disaster, but rather hunger and starvation wrought by state collapse and the violent politics of decolonization.

If NGOs first became involved in sub-Saharan Africa through disaster relief programmes, their engagement in the complexities and politics of such interventions gradually shifted their focus to more explicitly developmental objectives (even if, as it would turn out, NGOs could never really escape from emergency relief work). Involvement in a series of disasters, and the interpretation of the underlying causes of those crises, was to serve as the key catalyst for their evolution into development actors. Biafra, in particular, reinforced the lessons first taught by Congo: famine and hunger were primarily political. Just as war in Europe had led to the formation of NGOs in the first half of the twentieth century, a new set of organizations were established in response to the new crises in sub-Saharan Africa. The Irish NGO Concern, for example, was created in 1968 (originally known as Africa Concern) to assist in the Biafran crisis.

If engagement in actual interventions reinforced the complexity of the nature of the problem, and the necessity to adopt a broader approach than the hitherto practice of palliative care through relief, shifts in international development theory and policy within academies and amongst international organizations was similarly reflected in the evolution of the NGO in Africa from relief to development actor. In 1960 the Freedom From Hunger Campaign (FFHC) was launched by the Food and Agricultural Organization (FAO), liaising with NGOs across Europe and North America to provide deeper-rooted and longer-lasting interventions designed to reduce the incidence of famine. Involvement in this programme led NGOs to see development (the prevention of disasters) as a better way of meeting their commitments to providing assistance to those most in need than reacting after the event.

If during the Biafran conflict NGOs had first explored the possibilities of bypassing the officially recognized state entirely, with all the political ramifications this entailed, the experience of most NGOs in their dealings with the African state in this period was more cooperative and collaborative (Jennings 2008a). With state-controlled development planning and intervention still an orthodoxy for international policymakers, NGOs' engagement in development in villages and districts across the region was to be through the government at central and especially local levels.

In establishing their relationships with the African state, NGOs were not, of course, forging them anew. In this, they entered the already established voluntary sector space and inherited (or perhaps 'shared', given the continuing influence and importance of former-missions-now-established-churches and other religious leaders welcomed into the corridors of State House following independence) the nature of the pre-existing set of relationships and linkages between that sector and the state.

As previously relief-focused NGOs began to redefine themselves as development organizations in this era of state-controlled development planning, this inevitably meant working with states in implementing projects designed to fit broader national planning priorities. Still small in size both individually and as a broader sector, NGOs nevertheless were given access to local officials, ministers, and presidents. During the 1970s this trend increased for larger NGOs as the popularity of regional development programmes spread, linking together a number of projects across a wider administrative unit (or group of units) under an over-arching strategy under the control of central or local government officials. NGO projects thus became part of these wider official plans, linking their own objectives to those of the state and harnessing the power and funds of the NGO to state-led and -directed development.

However, whilst NGOs were working closely with government officials, their projects incorporated into local and national development plans, at the same time they were working closely with community-based and sometimes radical or alternative models of development that reinforced a counter-tendency: an understanding that the poor themselves needed to be given greater power over their lives and more say in the policies and programmes that affected them. From these roots, participatory approaches would emerge, as well as the increasing divergence between NGOs and the state over objectives, priorities, and strategies.

By the end of the 1970s, NGOs were becoming an increasingly potent force in Africa, increasing in numbers but still overwhelmingly dominated by international (mostly European and North American) organizations. However, NGOs remained one (still relatively small) part of the formal voluntary sector space in sub-Saharan Africa, and just as NGOs had shifted in this period to emphasize development over relief activity and forged a particular set of relationships with the state, so too had the bulk of the voluntary sector. Faith-based organizations and religious institutions remained dominant in service delivery and from the 1960s had similarly adopted a development prism for defining their social mission. The relationships established by NGOs reflected those established in the colonial period by the faith-based voluntary sector and refined by these same actors in the post-colonial period. Although they were becoming more important, NGOs had yet to dominate the African voluntary sector and were still largely shaped by that space, rather than shaping it themselves as they would begin to from the 1980s.

'Contracted agents'? NGOs from the 1980s

Whilst growing in significance throughout the 1960s and 1970s, and seen as increasingly important actors by African governments, it was not until the 1980s that the NGO sector exploded, witnessing a huge transformation not only in scale of the sector, but in the power it enjoyed within Africa and in relation to donors and the myriad organizational types that emerged in this period. As with the factors underpinning the evolution of the NGO in the previous two decades, experiences in Africa, as well as external policy shifts, contributed to the re-framing of the NGO within the African voluntary sector space.

Whilst some have argued that the decline of the African state in the 1980s allowed NGOs to occupy the gaps left, especially in service provision (Ndegwa 1996: 21), NGOs were not innocent bystanders to the retreat of the state in this period, benefiting by default. They were complicit in the process, in that they allowed themselves to be used by donors as a means of bypassing the state. In doing so they moved away from their former dependence upon African governments to a more complex set of relationships reflective of the new power balances that emerged as a result of economic crisis and the implementation of the Washington Consensus across the region.

During the previous two decades, NGOs largely had relied on their own fundraising activity. As a result, their numbers remained dominated by Western European and North American organizations that were able to raise sufficient incomes. In the late 1970s, donors began to offer direct financial support for NGO development programmes, and during the subsequent decade official development aid was increasingly channelled through these organizations. Two key factors contributed. First, a growing disillusion with state-led development programmes amongst donors and an ideological shift away from public- to private-sector solutions (the rise of the Washington Consensus and New Policy Agenda). Second, a growing perception that NGOs were more flexible, more efficient, subject to less corruption and mismanagement, and better able to reach the poorest than their state counterparts.

As NGOs were discovering their own areas of potential competitive advantage, international development policy was undergoing a seismic shift. Donors and international organizations underwent a bitter divorce with the African state. Economic and political crises across Africa and other developing countries from the late-1970s led to a fundamental reappraisal of the role of the state. From being regarded as the driving force behind development, it became regarded as the chief obstacle. Reducing the role of the state, it was argued, eliminated needless bureaucracy and inefficient, corrupt public institutions, and development gains would inevitably follow. Just as NGOs were positioning themselves as independent actors, better able to implement development that reached the poorest of the poor, donors and international organizations were seeking to shift their attention away from the public realm to non-state (non-profit) actors. The new policy agenda promoted by international organizations and donors pushed governments in Africa to slim down the size of the state and contract out service delivery and development management to non-state providers. NGOs were ready to take on the challenge.

NGOs had already demonstrated, to the eyes of donors, their capacity to take on significant funding and run sensitive, large-scale programmes, most notably during the famine in Ethiopia in the mid-1980s. To donors, they appeared to be flexible, efficient, and able to bypass delays and potential distortions linked to state-run programmes. Having proven themselves, and having established credentials in delivering services such as health, education, and training through projects across sub-Saharan Africa, NGOs seemed ideal partners to advance the New Policy Agenda and privatize (albeit to non-profit actors) service delivery and development in the region. As a result, the proportion of ODA channelled through the NGO sector by donors accelerated throughout the 1980s. As well as contributing to an expansion in the scale of northern-based NGOs (international NGOs – INGOs – for example, increased from around 13,000 in 1981 to over 47,000 in 20 years) (Anheier and Themundo 2002: 194), the shift kick-started the emergence of the southern NGOs that could now access funding (either directly from donors or from northern INGOs seeking local partners). In Kenya, for example, the number of officially registered NGOs increased from 124 in 1975 to more than 400 by 1987. Within that figure, Kenyan NGOs increased from 57 to 133. In 1990 official aid to Kenyan NGOs stood at around $35 million (or 18 per cent of all ODA received by the Kenyan government) (Ndegwa 1996: 19–20). By 2000, the total number of NGOs registered in Kenya had reached 2,511. In Tanzania, there were 41 registered NGOs in 1990, but by 2000 this had risen to more than 10,000 (Reuben, cited in Hearn 2007: 1096). Of course, most of these would not have been active organizations, probably no more than 450 or so, and more NGOs existed in 1990 than were officially registered so the numbers are at best a rough impression rather than an exact guide to scale.

However, as NGOs expanded into areas previously seen as the preserve of the state, and (perhaps more crucially) as ODA was transferred from African governments to the NGO sector, the relationship between the two was altered. If cooperation largely characterizes the relationship in the 1970s, increased competition, if not conflict, became the hallmark of the late 1980s and 1990s. NGOs now competed directly with government departments for donor funds, making claims as to their ability to use such funds more effectively. As Bratton noted at the end of the 1980s, reflecting on the rapid expansion of the NGO sector in Africa, the 'new prominence of NGOs' carried with it the potential for 'conflict' with African governments as well as 'complementarity', with states seeking to reduce efforts to curtail their control and leadership over development processes (Bratton 1989: 570). A more recent study by the US Agency for International Development (USAID) on the role played by NGOs in education in Ethiopia, Guinea, Malawi, and Mali highlighted 'frictions' between NGOs and states, 'specifically when NGOs want to take on other activities that the government does not allow them to do' (USAID 2003: 2). NGOs highlight government inefficiency and inability to reach those most in need; governments respond by suggesting NGOs cannot meet the required standards and fail to operate within the official system.

In setting up as rivals to the court of the state (or being established by donors as such), NGOs became further estranged from the states with which they had previously enjoyed such close relationships. Insistence that NGOs were more efficient, could reach the poor more readily, could reflect better the demands and wishes of the poor, inevitably meant criticism of the state. It was a shift that influenced the next phase in the evolution of the NGO sector: the rise of NGOs as civil society actors.

Civil society actors and the state: NGOs from the 1990s

The emergence of the 'good governance' agenda in the 1990s signalled another paradigm shift in the conception of the NGO (most especially for the perceived role of the southern NGO). The perception of what it was that NGOs could do so well shifted from their developmental role (whether in relief, service provision, or small-scale projects) to a more politicized understanding of their role. NGOs, it was argued, were a vital component of civil society, capable of monitoring and holding governments to account, protecting and promoting human rights, and articulating the needs of the poorest in policy discussions.

The catalyst for this next phase of evolutionary shift came from outside of Africa, again most notably in the good governance agenda and how it defined the importance of civil society in ensuring governments remained open, transparent, accountable, and democratic, and in the framing and implementation of pro-poor growth. However, the shift also reflected the increasing distance NGOs and other components of the African voluntary sector placed between themselves and the state. Whilst the shift away from a more cooperative, dependent relationship with the state reflected the increased competition between NGOs and the state for official aid resources, as noted above, it was also a response to broader shifts within the voluntary sector. Faith-based actors, in particular, had become more vocal in their criticism of the state from the late 1980s, highlighting corruption, poor human rights records, and taking the lead in prodemocracy movements. Whilst INGOs (and their southern counterparts that relied on their bigger partners for funding) took their lead from changes in international policy, they were also constrained and shaped by the shifts within the voluntary sector space they occupied.

However, the colonization of the voluntary sector space by NGOs over the previous decade had implications for how civil society was perceived by donors and national governments. NGOs were able successfully to champion themselves as the core, if not the main, constituent of African civil society, a positioning reinforced by donor blinkers that saw NGOs in these terms. NGOs, rather than other actors within the formal voluntary sector, were not merely championed as the most important element: for many they were seen as the sole constituents.

NGOs in this period, and into the 2000s, became characterized by donors as forces for the promotion, and guarantors, of democratization. Following on from understandings of civil society and social capital as outlined by Putnam, and found in the writings of Ferguson and Alexis de Tocqueville, the existence of the NGO itself was characterized as inherently good (Mercer 2002: 9). Critics, meanwhile, countered the positivist accounts of NGOs, pointing to the culpability in undermining the state and promoting donor-led agendas through their partnership with donors, and the ways in which they excluded, through their own dominance, other non-state actors with potentially different agendas and alternative voices.

The consequence of this was to close down civil society space according to the parameters set by donor discourses: a forum in which acceptance of notions of democracy, respect for rights, political pluralism, and so on, could be taken for granted. What was excluded were more political ways of conceptualizing civil society, ways that focused more on inherent conflicts and ideological tensions within the civil society space, in which the cherished values and principles of donors might be more contested. The closing down of civil society on a select band of organizations that resembled the forms that had emerged in the creation of civil society in Europe and North America thus closed down avenues for political conversation, rather than opening it up (as the claims suggested).

Even within the parameters of donor-bounded civil society actors, the premise that civil society could better reflect the demands, views, and experiences of the most marginalized was highly problematic. The claims by INGOs to be able to represent and reach the poorest had always been contested, of course, but local civil society organizations, often looking like or actually being NGOs, have not necessarily proven any more capable in this regard. Elite-led, often based in urban areas, and with limited channels for real dialogue, civil society organizations (CSOs), whether NGOs or other types of actor, have been accused of being more interested in meetings with government officials and chasing donor funding than their core function of engaging with the poorest.

Nevertheless, the current iteration of the NGO – civil society actor, critic of the government, core component and defender of political pluralism – has been reflected at all levels. From INGOs seeking to influence policy at the international level, to local NGOs in their consultations on pro-poor development policies and programmes, the NGO sector in Africa sees defending the interests of the poor to be as important as providing services and projects within communities. Formally eschewing politics, NGOs have become more openly the political beasts they always were.

Case study: Oxfam in Tanzania[1]

Established in 1942 to provide relief for those affected by the Allied blockade of Greece during the Second World War, Oxfam typified the rise of the modern NGO from relief to development organization, and from an organization with close links to the host government, to a civil society actor with close links to donor organizations. Oxfam's transition to a development-focused NGO was driven largely through its involvement in the FFHC (Oxfam sought in the early 1960s to fund the establishment of national FFHC programmes in Botswana, Lesotho, and Swaziland), and from its experiences in the Congo famine of 1960–61. The FFHC suggested preventing disasters from occurring, rather than responding time and time again, was a better way of alleviating poverty. The experience of running operations in Congo suggested Oxfam should directly run and manage its own funded programmes.

Both these processes were to be seen in the NGO's engagement in Tanzania. From its first grant in 1955 for the provision of vitamins for drought-stricken central Tanzania, to an Oxfam-funded and -run research project on collective action by women producers in markets in the country in 2010–11 (Oxfam 2011: 11), its funding decisions and campaigns in Tanzania reflect the evolution of not just Oxfam, but the wider NGO sector over the past 60 years or so.

In the 1960s and 1970s, with the state very much in charge of development processes, Oxfam programmes (in common with most other international NGOs operating in the country) were specifically designed to support official development programmes and policy. Although Oxfam enjoyed particularly close relationships with the government (initially through its first field officer, Jimmy Betts, who came to know Tanzania's first president Julius Nyerere personally through his work at the Fabian Colonial Bureau), many NGOs operating in Tanzania had ready access to government officials and saw their role as supportive, rather than critical, of state-led interventions.

However, whilst Oxfam was committed to the Tanzanian state's vision of rural socialism, the NGO was also evolving in its own development thinking and theory. Paolo Friere's notion of 'conscientization' was influential within the organization (speaking, perhaps, to the long-dominant strains of Quakerism and Fabianism that suffused the NGO). Indeed, Tanzania was seen by Oxfam in the 1970s as the perfect place to put into practice the more community-focused and participatory bottom-up thinking that increasingly motivated the organization (a paradox given its engagement in a profoundly top-down autocratic process in the country, but a paradox that was seemingly not recognized at the time). Oxfam was increasingly moving into a critique of orthodox development policy and practice that characterized the evolution of NGOs into agents of alternatives, a process that was to shape the next phase of its engagement. As part of this process, Oxfam would increasingly look to campaigning for policy changes in the global north as a core part of its mandate: funding the radical *New Internationalist* magazine; critiquing Western government and donor policies; and campaigning for a stronger voice for the world's poorest.

The economic crises of the late 1970s and early 1980s, and the ceding of control over development from states to donors, meant NGOs such as Oxfam were increasingly funded by donors directly. However, if Oxfam was increasingly looking upwards to donors as it took an ever-larger proportion of its funding from them, it was also being shaped by the rise of local NGOs that rendered the traditional model of expatriate-dominated INGO increasingly old-fashioned. Oxfam would not transform itself into a southern NGO (as Action Aid sought to do in the 2000s by moving its headquarters to South Africa), but it could ensure its Tanzania office better reflected the new environment. From 1987, the Oxfam field director was a Tanzanian national, as were the majority of its local staff.

By the mid-1990s, and into the 2000s, Oxfam was continuing to promote local, bottom-up approaches (at odds, some might argue, with the vertical delivery systems that donors favoured) and engaged more fully with an openly political understanding of development. In doing so, it sought to engage and promote 'civil society' and its own role as a critical outsider defending the interests of the poor. However, the focus of where the NGO felt it could make the most difference was shifting. Campaigning became increasingly important, as did establishing closer links with donors, especially in the UK following the establishment of a separate Department for International Development (DfID) in 1997. The first minister for international development, Clare Short, invited British NGOs who were only too willing to cooperate in influencing the shape and content of British development priorities. In Tanzania, Oxfam continued to retain influence, but it was an influence built on the strength afforded by donor links, rather than the close links to Tanzanian officials and leaders that characterized relationships in the 1960s and 1970s.

Conclusion

The history of the NGO in sub-Saharan Africa is inextricably entwined with that of the non-state formal voluntary sector in the region, a sector of which the NGO is part and to which it has contributed in shaping. Whilst the voluntary sector consists of many actors, some of which are NGOs but many of which are not, the NGO nevertheless has retained its dominance in its dealings with the state, with donors, and with the academy. The greatest success of the NGO, perhaps, has been to become the institution to which many look first when considering non-state action in relief, welfare, and service delivery.

However, the NGO in Africa has not been static and its history has followed the contours of African post-colonial history more broadly. From collaborator and close partner with the African state in the first decades of independence, to a new reliance upon donors following economic crisis in the late 1970s and economic and political reordering in the 1980s, and finally to the perceived champion of civil society and democratization in the 1990s and beyond, the NGO has evolved and shifted according to the context in which it has been operating. The narrative of this change has certainly reflected events at the international level – policies, conceptualizations of the relative roles of market and state as mechanisms for economic and social change, levels in donor funding and policies over its disbursement – and the internal politics of NGO debates in central offices. However, it has also reflected the particular circumstances in which they operated, their experiences of working in the field, and the constraints, challenges, and opportunities that opened up.

If NGOs have contributed to shaping development, development policy, and the non-state, voluntary sector space in Africa, they have also been shaped by their presence there: a product of sub-Saharan Africa's story over the twentieth century and beyond. Their history over the next 50 years will similarly reflect the collision of the external and internal impulses that have shaped them to date.

Note

1 This section is drawn largely from Jennings (2008a). Oxfam was initially called the Oxford Committee for Famine Relief, adopting the name Oxfam in 1958. However, it will be referred to here throughout as Oxfam.

Bibliography

Anheier, H. and Themundo, N. (2002) 'Organizational Forms of Global Civil Society: Implications of Going Global', in H. Anheier, M. Glasius and M. Kaldor (eds) *Global Civil Society*, Oxford: Oxford University Press.

Bratton, M. (1989) 'The Politics of Government-NGO Relations in Africa', *World Development* 17(4): 569–87.

Fowler, A. (1995) 'NGOs and the Globalization of Social Welfare', in J. Semboja and O. Therkildsen (eds) *Service Provision Under Stress in East Africa: The State, NGOs and People's Organizations in Kenya, Tanzania and Uganda*, London: James Currey.

Hailey, W.M. (1939) *An African Survey: A Study of Problems Arising in Africa South of the Sahara*, Oxford: Oxford University Press.

Hearn, J. (1998) 'The NGO-isation of Kenyan Society: USAID and the Restructuring of Health Care', *Review of African Political Economy* 75: 89–100.

——(2007) 'African NGOs: The New Compradors?' *Development and Change* 38(6): 1095–110.

Jennings, M. (2008a) *Surrogates of the State: NGOs, Development and Ujamaa in Tanzania*, Bloomfield, CT: Kumarian Press.

——(2008b) 'Healing of Bodies, Salvation of Souls: Missionary Medicine in Colonial Tanganyika, 1870s-1939', *Journal of Religion in Africa* 38: 27–56.

Mercer, C. (2002) 'NGOs, Civil Society and Democratization: A Critical Review of the Literature', *Progress in Development Studies* 2(5): 5–22.

Ndegwa, S.N. (1996) *The Two Faces of Civil Society: NGOs and Politics in Africa*, Bloomfield, CT: Kumarian Press.

OECD (Organisation for Economic Co-operation and Development) (2009) 'ODA by Donor, 2009', http://stats.oecd.org/Index.aspx?DatasetCode=ODA_DONOR (accessed 28 January 2012).

Oxfam (2011) *Oxfam Annual Report and Accounts 2010–11*, Oxford: Oxfam.

Salamon, L.M. (1994) 'The Rise of the Nonprofit Sector', *Foreign Affairs* 73(4): 109–22.

USAID (United States Agency for International Development) (2003) 'Partnerships in Education: Key Findings on the Role of NGOs in Basic Education in Africa, Bureau for Africa', Washington, DC: USAID, http://pdf.usaid.gov/pdf_docs/PNACS082.pdf (accessed 16 June 2012).

26

THE ECONOMY OF AFFECTION

Göran Hydén

The purpose of this chapter is to define and discuss the economy of affection, which is at the root of how African countries are being governed through a mish-mash of formal and informal institutions. Following a brief introductory discussion of where the concept belongs in the field of political science analysis, the chapter offers a definition and a set of illustrations of how it operates. It argues that although the economy of affection is most prevalent in African societies, it is a phenomenon that exists elsewhere as well. A second part of the chapter shows how the economy of affection gives rise to a varying set of informal institutions, some positive, others negative, when it comes to development. The third and final part discusses the governance implications of the prevalence of these informal institutions. The chapter concludes by suggesting that although the economy of affection is an integral – and dominant – element in political governance in Africa, it is by no means impossible to tackle and overcome when it proves to have negative consequences.

Structure and agency in political analysis

Explanations in political science run the full gamut from structure, via institutions, to human agency. In examining the way scholars have studied African politics there is evidence that types of explanation have shifted over time. Thus, structuralist approaches prevailed in the 1960s and 1970s, while actor-based and institutionalist approaches came to dominate in subsequent decades.

Explanations based on structural variables acknowledge the role of history and assume that human behaviour is embedded in social and/or economic relations from which people cannot easily free themselves. Modernization theory that was influential in the 1960s presumed that the human capacity to plan and control their destiny was largely a product of such processes as urbanization, industrialization, education, and participation in the market economy. Rationalism and the ability to organize human activities on a large scale come incrementally as tradition gradually gives rise to modernity. Neo-Marxist explanations of development that replaced modernization theory in the 1970s were equally rooted in history but added the sense that progress can be accelerated through revolutionary collective action. Class struggles aimed at overthrowing backward and reactionary elites can overturn structural hindrances and pave the way for a rational and modern organization of society (see Freund, this volume). Politics – and especially the revolutionary vanguard – would spearhead this process.

The 1980s saw the rise of actor-based explanations in the form of rational choice theory. It was the polar opposite to structuralism. It started from the positivist premise that individuals are autonomous and capable of acting rationally in their own interest. Collective action occurs not as a response to structural constraints, but rather through positive aggregation of individual interests. The political arena is treated like a marketplace in which persons exchange values. This orientation was attractive to many scholars who could use it to design policies and reforms, thus making political science more prescriptive and policy-relevant. This prescriptive urge has prevailed in more recent years, although it is tempered by the addition of institutional types of analysis. 'Good' governance has been interpreted as the transfer of successful institutional practices, largely borrowed from the West, to countries that are described as suffering from a 'democratic deficit', regime instability, or a 'weak' or 'failed' state. Knowingly or unknowingly, political scientists studying these phenomena in a comparative perspective have yielded to the underlying premise that there is a single development track that begins with democracy or 'good' governance so defined. It has been the price paid for ensuring that Africa is not treated as an 'exceptional' case, but can be studied through the same lens as all other regions of the world.

This orientation, however, also carries its own limitations. It assumes a uniform model or theory for understanding complex phenomena that we know from history come in very different shapes. It relies on data sets that tell part of the full story and sometimes are nothing but stylized facts. These are real pitfalls, especially in the study of African politics, where official data are hard to come by and often unreliable. Objectification – turning individual persons into categories of people and organizing society accordingly – is only an incipient and yet to be fully institutionalized practice. Conclusions drawn from what is possible to know through the study only of formal institutions, therefore, are by necessity incomplete. There is a need to complement these studies with a focus on informal institutions, how they interact with formal ones, and what their consequences are for political governance. A useful start for such studies is an understanding of the economy of affection.

The economy of affection

The economy of affection as a concept has its origin in the theoretical contribution made by the Nigerian sociologist Peter Ekeh, who analyses the governance predicament in African countries (Ekeh 1975). His main argument is that African societies are characterized by two public realms: a civic and public realm that coincides with the institutional legacy of the colonial days; and a second, 'primordial' realm built around the local communities in which people live and work. The former is built around formal institutions, the latter around informal ones. Ekeh's point is that moral and political conduct favours the latter at the expense of the former. To be more specific, he argues that political leaders extract resources from the civic realm to strengthen the community-oriented realm. This process has a similarity with the politics of favouring special interests that is such a prominent part of American politics, the difference being that in the United States it is subject to regulation and enforcement of the law to an extent that limits and calls into question the influence of personalized relations. Yet the phenomenon under study here is by no means unique to Africa. To the extent that it amounts to taking advantage of public office for private purposes – what is generally called 'corruption' – it is a universal challenge.

The 'economy of affection' is the concept that I have coined and used in order to draw attention to this type of governance dilemma in African politics. It originates from my own studies in Tanzania and Kenya in the 1970s and early 1980s and was meant to question the extent to which mainstream explanations at that time did justice to what was going on in African countries (Hydén 1980, 1983, 1987). Thus, the economy of affection provided an alternative to explanations offered by neo-Marxist scholars who, without any real empirical evidence, used the concept of social class to explain politics and development in post-independence Africa. Being dogmatically wedded to such a theoretical apparatus, they 'saw' social categories in Africa that did not exist on the ground but happened to be an integral part of their analytical framework.

The economy of affection also became an alternative to the economistic, rational choice-based theory that emerged as part of the neo-liberal policies of the early 1980s. The explanation of utilitarian human behaviour provided by rational choice theory looked elegant and parsimonious when compared with the more complicated structural explanations of the previous decades. Bates (1981) comparison of agricultural policies in Kenya and Tanzania using a rational choice approach became a classic in the study of African politics. However, the notion that elites act in their own interest is no significant 'discovery' in political science, and rational choice proponents tend to overlook the social relations in which choice is so often embedded, not only in Africa but elsewhere as well.

The alternative explanation offered by the economy of affection rejects the assumption that individuals are autonomous social beings capable of maximizing their own interests without considering the consequences for other beings. People are born and socialized into group or community relations that they can only ignore at great expense. This happens everywhere but it is particularly significant in societies, like many of those in Africa, where most people still stand with only one foot in the marketplace. The moral code in these places is still 'I am because we are'.

The social logic that is associated with the economy of affection, therefore, can be described as a reverse collective action problem, i.e. collective rationality overrides and undermines individual interests. Rational choice theorists like Olson (1971) have argued that individuals do not join groups or organizations if they do not perceive an immediate benefit by doing so. Based on his study of American society, he criticizes those who had previously argued that Americans are 'joiners', ready to join associations for some altruistic reason. In contrast, wherever the economy of affection is present, people are born into and brought up in primary social organizations like the family, clan, village, or ethnic group. The bonds of these groups are the basic social facts that determine much of not only economic but also political behaviour. Their individual autonomy is extensively circumscribed by these norms.

The point here is not that the logic of the economy of affection is so overwhelming that it pre-empts all other considerations. It functions in a context-specific way with variable consequences. In rural areas, it may still be hegemonic in the sense of determining how things get done as a result of the lower levels of information and education available to rural residents. In such cases, collective action is likely to be largely driven by moral codes associated with the economy of affection. Significantly, such codes pose a special challenge to the activities of international non-governmental organizations (NGOs). Representatives of these organizations, seeking to promote development and fight poverty, typically apply a positivist approach to development that implies modern standards of planning and implementing projects on the basis of the assumed individual rationality of participants. Even in the context of participatory analysis and learning approaches, this becomes controversial because the local social logic calls for collective action in response to needs and crises and thus tends to be intermittent, while the NGO representatives advocate an approach that is meant to make collective action locally regular and permanent. Thus, when outside support comes to an end, there is a tendency for local communities to revert to the local logic with which they are familiar. Many NGOs have experienced this outcome and it is still not clear how they can withdraw and at the same time ensure that their effort is fully understood and embraced by the communities.

The economy of affection is not just a rural phenomenon. Its logic also stretches into urban areas and is present among the elite as much as among ordinary city dwellers. Remittances from urban residents to their rural brethren are one case in point. These days, such remittances often come from members of the African diaspora and are an integral part of the country's efforts at reducing poverty. Particularly critical is the presence of the economy of affection in government and politics. Government officials find it hard to defect or ignore obligations that are nested in reciprocal relations with people, most of whom are kinfolk from home. This has a bearing on how they perform in office. Politicians literally feed on this logic. They perform the welfare functions that in more developed states are carried out by government departments based on specific budgetary allocations (Barkan, this volume). The economy of affection does not know such boundaries or limitations. Its logic trumps the civic and public one, as Ekeh argued in his piece many years ago.

So, how is the concept best defined? The easiest way of describing the economy of affection is to suggest that it is constituted by personal investments in reciprocal relations with other individuals as ways of achieving goals that are seen as otherwise impossible to attain. Sought-after goods – whether material or symbolic, such as prestige and status – have a scarcity value. Because they may be physically available but not accessible to all, people invest in relations with others to obtain them. This economy differs from capitalism as well as socialism. Money is not an end in itself, nor is the state the primary redistributive mechanism. It relies on the handshake rather than the contract, on personal discretion rather than official policy, to allocate resources. It co-exists with capitalism or socialism, often helping individuals to get around the 'rough edges' of such systems. Exchanges within the economy of affection do not get officially registered. As such, it is an invisible economy for which conscientious policymakers have no taste and economists find no real way of effectively incorporating into their conventional forms of analysis.

Informal institutions

Informal institutions are the clearest manifestation of the economy of affection. The latter is not an expression of irrationality or altruism, nor does it have anything to do with romantic love. It is a practical and rational way of dealing with choice in contexts of uncertainty and in situations where place, rather than distanciated space, dictate and influence people's preferences. People engage in affective behaviour and create informal institutions for a variety of reasons. They may do so from a position of either strength or weakness. They may do it when faced with either an opportunity or a constraint. Four motives for engaging in affective behaviour will help illustrate it here: to gain status; to seek favour; to share a benefit; and to provide a common good. As a form of 'moral economy', the economy of affection is more diverse and produces a wider range of informal institutions than is acknowledged, for example in Scott's studies of the moral economy in Southeast Asia (Scott 1976, 1985). The latter tends to confine the understanding of the moral economy to how poor peasants defend their life-world against intrusion by capitalist and other outside values and norms.

Informal institutions are forms of regularized behaviour. They arise for a variety of reasons. They may complement formal institutions by adding moral and political strength to official policy measures. For example, a charismatic political leader may create enthusiasm about a policy initiative that otherwise would have been difficult to implement. Informal institutions may also substitute for formal ones. This happens when the latter are either absent or ineffective. An example would be when people take the law into their own hands because the police are not there or lack the means to maintain law and order. A third scenario is when formal institutions accommodate informal ones. The former are effective but sometimes their own effectiveness may raise issues of political legitimacy. They are simply pushing their agenda with too much insistence and to avoid a political crisis, they become accommodating of opinions

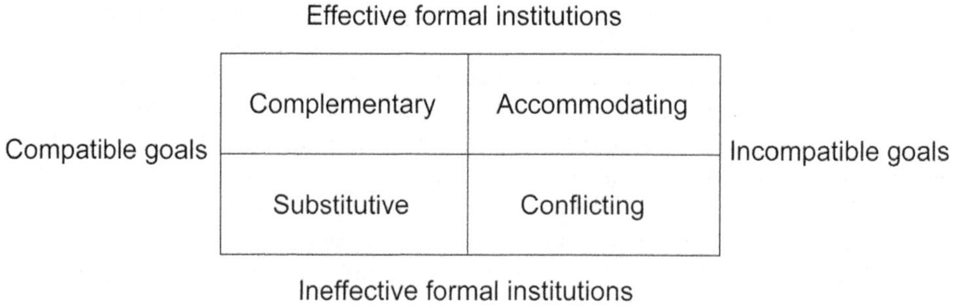

Effective formal institutions

	Complementary	Accommodating
Compatible goals		Incompatible goals
	Substitutive	Conflicting

Ineffective formal institutions

Figure 26.1 Different functions of informal institutions in relation to formal ones
Source: Helmke and Levitsky 2006.

expressed through informal means, such as an unofficial caucus group. A fourth scenario is when informal institutions undermine formal ones because their respective objectives are different. An obvious example would be when the habit of paying bribes has been institutionalized to the point where the law of the land is consistently broken. In their study of informal institutions in Latin American politics, Helmke and Levitsky (2006) offer a useful classification of these different scenarios, as shown in Figure 26.1.

The point that the authors make is that the functions of informal institutions vary according to two dimensions: whether formal institutions are effective or not, and whether the goals that are pursued are compatible or incompatible. Because formal institutions in most African countries remain weak, the most common scenarios there are associated with the boxes on the lower half of the diagram.

Substitutive institutions

There are plenty of examples of where informal institutions in Africa take on the role played by formal ones in other societies. Four types of informal institutions that have largely played a substitutive role are briefly discussed here.

Clientelism

Although clientelism is by no means a uniquely African practice, it is generally recognized as one of the prime hallmarks of politics on the continent. It is a way of conducting politics through patronage. Political leaders try to secure the support of underlings by distributing favours that cement relations of power. Although it is not gender-specific, it is typically associated with masculine power figures. Lemarchand (1972) rendered the first systematic account of clientelism in African politics. His treatment of this informal institution was quite appreciative: a political patron brought to the political centre a large following that facilitated national integration. In retrospect, one may argue that Lemarchand's treatment of clientelism is the informal equivalent of Lijphart's (1977) 'consociationalism' – the political order found in some multi-cultural countries in Western Europe. Even in these European countries, the political centre has been held together by a series of 'deals' among representatives of cultural groups sharing state power.

This positive account of clientelism has gradually become more critical, if not negative. 'Neopatrimonialism' – the ultimate form of clientelism in politics – has become the principal concept in Africanist political science (Erdmann, this volume). Political rulers treat the exercise of power as an extension of their private realm. The prevalence of clientelism in African politics is evidence that formal institutions are weak. The introduction of multi-party politics has tended to reinforce affective relations, because competition for power and resources has intensified in the new political dispensation (Bratton and van de Walle 1997). Although clientelism is therefore deemed problematic, especially in circles that are concerned with improving governance in African countries, there are some scholars who search for the seeds of a developmentally friendly patrimonialism (see Kelsall, this volume).

Pooling

The concept of pooling is sufficiently general to serve as a generic classification of all forms of cooperation in groups that are organized along voluntary and self-enforcing lines. These groups are not sanctioned by law; instead, they are constituted by adherence to unwritten rules. The family is the most basic social organization and it features, directly or indirectly, in many of the examples of lateral informal institutions that can be found around the world. Informal institutions in which the family is important prevail in societies where voluntary associations such as schools, clubs, and professional organizations, have yet to acquire influence in society. As Fukuyama (1995: 62–63) notes, cultures in which the primary avenue to sociability is family and kinship, rather than secondary associations, have a great deal of trouble creating large, durable economic organizations and therefore look to the state to support them (see also Putnam 1993).

The African family is typically extensive and generally open to cooperation with others. Cousins, even distant ones, are brothers and in each household it is not uncommon to find members of three or four generations living together. Kinship relations dominate, facilitating solidarity across family lines. This mode of organizing is also replicated outside the kinship network, but typically on a small scale. Rotating credit societies are one example; groups sharing labour another. Groups like these, however, are not necessarily as effective today as they used to be. Integration into the global economy means that gaining resources needed for one's livelihood involves transactions outside the local community. Instead, wealthier individuals in the community may become brokers with the outside world and use this role to build a position of power. Pooling gives way to clientelism.

Self-defence

Self-defence refers to informal institutions that mobilize support against a common threat or enemy, whether real or perceived. Affection is a powerful instrument to achieve this, as it binds people together across narrower organizational boundaries. In these instances, formal law enforcement institutions do not perform the role that they should. Modern African history is full of examples of how affection has been used to generate movements for defence of what is perceived as an African lifestyle. More recently, informal self-defence mechanisms have emerged in response to threats of violence. The *sungu sungu* vigilante groups in Tanzania are an example of such an informal institution that has a nationwide presence. The popularization of this institution has, by and large, led to greater security wherever they patrol. Instances of popular justice involving these groups have been reported but they are not the principal outcome.

The use of affection in self-defence is a more pronounced phenomenon in Africa than in Asia. A major reason is that Asian societies have generally been permeated by a single religion or philosophy. For example, Confucianism has defined social relations in China over 2,000 years. Even though its ethical principles have not been in the form of a national constitution, many Chinese, regardless of social status, have internalized these principles (Rozman 1991). By contrast, in Africa customary norms were never universal and were generally confined to small-scale societies. Although similarities did exist among these societies, usually they were not enough to form the basis for a national constitutional and legal framework. Instead, what has held the new nation-states together is a perceived need to guard against an enemy from within or without. Initially the enemy was the colonial power. After independence, there have been examples of internal enemies being fought in the name of getting rid of autocratic rulers. Ethiopia, Rwanda, and Uganda are cases in point. Although these campaigns or struggles have often been couched in ideological language, they have been sustained by close affective ties – in Ethiopia, centred on the Tigray group; in Rwanda on the Tutsi group; and in Uganda, the Hima.

Charisma

Charisma, one may argue, is the ultimate informal institution. 'Charismatic' leadership, according to Weber, is 'devotion to sanctity, heroism or exemplary character of an individual person, and the normative patterns or order revealed or ordained by him' (Weber 1947: 242). Weber applied it broadly to refer to all individual personalities endowed with supernatural, superhuman, or at least specifically exceptional powers or qualities. This included a great variety of people, like heroes, saviours, prophets, shamans, and even demagogues. Weber himself is not easy to understand on the issue of what charismatic authority really is, but, in short, his treatment of the concept is meant to capture the revolutionary moment in history. At the same time, he makes the point that charisma is not sustainable without routinization. In the study of law and administration, scholarship has treated the role of charisma as instrumental in transforming traditional or customary authority into a new type, called, in Weber's language, 'rational-legal' authority. In Africa, the story of charisma is different. It seems important especially in terms of filling the gap that exists between formal institutional structures on the one hand, and customary and informal institutions on the other.

The interesting thing about Africa is that charisma typically works to re-establish traditional, rather than rational-legal, authority. The affinity with the modern common or civil law that was brought to Africa by the colonial powers is virtually non-existent, except in professional legal circles. What counts are the principles of the past that a charismatic figure – a politician or a religious minister – can invoke in order to gain followers. By wishing to reinvent something genuinely 'African', these persons seek legitimacy based on the sanctity of age-old rules and powers. This is inevitably a process of informalization. Compliance in this scenario is not owed to enacted rules but to the persons who occupy positions of authority or who have been chosen for it by a traditional master. Galvan (2002) provides an intriguing and empirically rich case study of how this process works among the Serer in rural Senegal. Innovations or adaptations, even if they lead to 'syncretic' institutions – a merger of formal and informal norms – are legitimized by disguising them as reaffirmations of the past.

Charisma blurs the line between person and rule. It assumes a reciprocal exchange in which the authority of the charismatic figure is accepted without question. These exchanges are essentially affective in nature. No attempt is made to reflect on a particular principle before accepting authority because charisma makes such reflection superfluous. Many African nationalists were charismatic figures. No one succeeded more than Julius Nyerere in trying to disguise his modernist policies with reference to the sanctity of past rules. He developed socialist policies with a modern economy in mind, but legitimized every initiative he took in that direction with reference to recreating an ideal of the African past (*ujamaa*). The other more controversial side of Nyerere's policies is that the informal institutions he created inhibited a critical examination of his policies from within. Instead, they fostered conformity and compliance (Hydén 2006).

Conflicting institutions

While substitutive informal institutions may at times become controversial, they generally cause less controversy than those that are in outright conflict with formal institutions. The substitutive type of informal institutions often acquire a measure of political legitimacy that the formal ones do not have or have lost. In scenarios where the two types are in conflict, one of three outcomes is possible: collapse, stalemate, or reform.

Collapse

Collapse may occur in situations where the formal and informal institutions tear on each other until they both lose their legitimacy, and chaos or anomie replaces order. Violence, as occurred in Kenya after the December 2007 elections, is one example; what happened after the elections in Côte d'Ivoire in 2000 provides another. While in Kenya, credible formal institutions have been adopted and approved in a referendum in 2010, the violence in Côte d'Ivoire led to further and more widespread acts, and it is too early to say whether the 2010 election has served as a catalyst for change toward peace and order. What these cases indicate is that countries that are – or at least were – renowned for stability and relatively high levels of development may suffer heavily if informal and formal institutions are at loggerheads and thus undermine each other's legitimacy.

There are many other countries in Africa where such a scenario has played out but where the consequences have been even worse. The collapse of the state in Somalia is perhaps the most noteworthy, but the Democratic Republic of Congo (DRC), Central African Republic, and Chad are other equally worrisome cases. The humanitarian costs of the collapse – or near-collapse – of formal institutions in these countries are a big burden and one that is very difficult to remove. Informal institutions have been able to function only in local contexts and have failed to bring together political factions from different localities, as the failure to form an effective government in Somalia and the DRC indicates. Neopatrimonalism or clientelism has proved inadequate to overcome the political challenges caused by these collapses.

Stalemate

Stalemate is likely to happen in situations where formal and informal institutions live side by side in a competitive manner, but where the stakes are mainly individual rather than public. A case in point would be what happens in government offices where the principles of a legal-rational bureaucracy face the moral code of the economy of affection. Civil servants are expected to be impartial and make judgments based on meritocratic criteria. Such are the rules of the Weberian model of bureaucracy. Yet, most civil servants occupy their position fully aware that they cannot ignore demands from kinfolk and others with whom they have mutual obligations based on social criteria. Most occupants of government office in Africa know how to live with this conflict, but by paying attention to both, the delivery of public services and goods tends to suffer. An anthropological study of corruption in three West African countries – Benin, Niger, and Senegal – illustrates in great detail how these attempts to cope with both formal and informal institutions can lead to stalemate and poor performance (Blundo and Olivier de Sardan 2006). The reverse collective action problem is very much present in African civil services and, despite ambitious public-sector reform programmes, not much has changed since the 1980s when a study of civil servants in Southern Africa revealed a similar pattern (Montgomery 1987).

Reform

Reform is the scenario in which formal institutions prevail over informal ones, and the reverse collective action problem is solved in favour of a Weberian-type bureaucracy in which the norms of a legal-rational system of administration are institutionalized. Despite concerted efforts to reform the civil services in African countries, initially funded from local sources but in the past two decades financed almost exclusively by the World Bank and other donors, very little has been accomplished. A few countries, like Botswana and Mauritius, have the features of a Weberian bureaucracy and their civil services are deemed quite dependable and free from corruption. Reform efforts elsewhere in Africa have not really yielded significant improvements. Studying the initial reform efforts, Rweyemamu and Hydén (1975) conclude that politicization of the civil service, nepotism, and widespread red tape were the main reasons for poor performance. A review carried out over a quarter-century later identified the same factors among the most important explanations for performance shortcomings in African governments (Olowu 2003). As suggested above, civil services find it hard to break out of the hold that the economy of affection has over human choice and behaviour through its various informal institutional mechanisms. This persistent inability to reform African civil services with the help of measures that work elsewhere has led to a search for solutions from within. Rather than seeing the issue in terms of a 'governance deficit', there is a greater readiness to explore which aspects of indigenous institutions work well enough to constitute the basis for reform (see Kelsall, this volume). Although we know too little about the prospect for success of such an approach, Rwanda's reconstruction programme after the 1994 genocide is sometimes held up as a successful example of progress based on local institutions.

Political governance

The tensions between formal and informal institutions are at the core of how African countries are being governed. Patronage co-exists with policy as the driving force in politics; clientelism operates side by side with the rule of law; and autocracy occurs in tandem with democracy. Viewed through a Western democratic lens, virtually all countries in Africa are 'hybrid' states or, as Collier and Levitsky (1997) would describe them, 'diminished sub-types' of mainstream conceptualizations based on the Western experience. This description, however, does not imply that there is never any change in the political systems of these countries. It is there precisely because the tensions between formal and informal institutions keep these countries in perpetual movement, even if it is usually not clear whether these changes really are decisive and sustainable. Nor does hybridity mean that all countries are the same: it produces both positive and negative outcomes. Furthermore, the way informal institutions are applied varies from country to country depending on social context. A comparison between Kenya and Tanzania serves as an illustration of at least one significant variation in political governance.

The two countries make an interesting pair for comparison. They have similar colonial legacies: they are both located on the shores of the Indian Ocean with its unique Swahili culture; and both are multi-ethnic societies. After independence, however, they adopted different development policies: Kenya followed a more capitalist road (albeit in the guise of African socialism), while Tanzania experimented with moving forward on a socialist path. This distinction was for many years the principal criterion for comparing the two countries (e.g. Barkan 1994). More recently, following the wave of democratization in the 1990s, comparing the two has been much less common. Instead, they have been compared to other countries and placed on a global scale of democratization or good governance. This shift has encouraged a focus largely on the performance of formal institutions, with informal ones being treated as evidence of shortcomings. The result is that the mechanics of informal institutions have either been ignored or condemned. The campaign against what Westerners call political corruption is a case in point (*cf.* Olivier de Sardan, this volume).

Political governance in African societies is never fully understood without attention to informal institutions and how they operate. Kenya and Tanzania are again examples of two different modes. Although both countries are multi-ethnic, the make-up of ethnic relations is different. Kenya's ethnic map is dominated by a half-dozen large ethnic constellations, all of which still consider themselves occupants of their own homeland. Despite a high rate of urbanization – and an increasing rate of inter-ethnic marriage – the attachment to land in specific parts of the country prevails. The boundaries on Tanzania's ethnic map are much more blurred. First, the number of ethnic groups is large, and many of them are very small and often in some way related to their neighbours. Second, the widespread use of Kiswahili has meant that ethnic profiles have become less significant and are typically subordinated to a national identity. Finally, urbanization and inter-ethnic marriage have helped to further erase local identities based on ethnic group.

These different ethnic maps have also translated into two distinct forms of politics. In Kenya, ethnic boundaries have tended to be exclusionary, thus engendering the need for elite alliances or coalitions. In Tanzania, where ethnic boundaries have been less exclusionary and easier to transcend, a national political elite cadre has emerged that shares a similar normative outlook. The result is that the role of informal institutions in Kenyan politics has been especially prominent in cementing relations across ethnic boundaries. In Tanzania, on the other hand, the same institutions have been more often applied to secure popular support. In Kenya they have been applied horizontally, in Tanzania vertically. Political events in recent years illustrate this difference between the two countries.

Elections are especially significant mechanisms that offer great insight into how informal and formal institutions interact. Much power is at stake in these events and informal institutions, not only in African countries but elsewhere too, grow in importance as tools to gain advantages. The risk of fraud, violence, and other negative outcomes is particularly high. This proved to be the case in the 2007 Kenyan elections when ethnic competition erupted into violence after President Mwai Kibaki, the Kikuyu incumbent, was declared the official winner despite accusations from opposition leaders and some international observers of electoral manipulation. Kikuyus were attacked by other ethnic groups, especially in areas in which they constituted a minority, while pro-government police and militias were deployed in revenge attacks against their predominantly Luo and Kalenjin rivals (see also Lynch, this volume). In total, over 1,000 people were killed and hundreds of thousands made homeless. The events were a shock not only to Kenyans but to the outside world as well.

After a few weeks, during which other African leaders (including former UN Secretary-General Kofi Annan) played a role, Kenya's political leaders formed a government of national unity, bringing together key representatives of each ethnic group. Even though its operations were characterized by tension and the financial costs of creating a mega-government were high, the coalition has held together sufficiently well to steer the country in a new direction. The new government has even successfully completed the constitutional reform process, which had been repeatedly started and stalled since the reintroduction of multi-party politics in the early 1990s (Chege 2008). In 2010 a popular referendum supported by both President Kibaki and his main rival, Raila Odinga, overwhelmingly approved a new constitution that (among other things) limited the powers of the president, made him and his cabinet more accountable, and encouraged a degree of decentralization. Perhaps most important of all, a series of formal institutions were put in place to monitor the implementation of the constitution. In retrospect, one can argue that the misuse of informal institutions triggered the 'Kenya crisis', but it is also important to note that the very same institutions, notably ethnic networks and coalitions, subsequently supported the restoration of formal institutions in the name of the new constitution. Thus, the crisis created by the tensions between the two types of institutions was this time resolved in favour of the formal ones. Whether this is a reformative breakthrough it is too early to say, but Kenyans and others will follow with great interest how the country's political elite behaves.

If the political fissures in Kenya are primarily along ethnic lines, and informal institutions, notably clientelist patronage, are used to pre-empt or repair these cleavages, the most obvious division in Tanzania is between the elite and the 'masses'. Informal institutions are used by individual politicians to buy the support of ordinary people, a habit that was as evident in the 2010 election campaigns as in previous elections, despite laws limiting the amount a given candidate could spend and prohibiting bribery of the voters by offering gifts. The ruling party Chama Cha Mapinduzi (CCM) has never lost an election in a multi-party setting and takes its indispensability for the country's development and security for granted. Any challenge to its hegemony, therefore, is met with strong measures: some formal, such as use of the security forces; others informal, like trying to co-opt members elected to the opposition (Whitehead 2009). The camaraderie among the political elite in Tanzania is such that a 'brown envelope' – the symbol of a bribe – is often used to silence opposition or stopping its representatives from revealing uncomfortable political truths about how the country is being governed. The outcome of the 2010 election was no different from previous ones: CCM won big, although the opposition made significant gains in the wealthier northern parts of the country – an indication that the inclusionary character of Tanzanian politics is being challenged. Informal institutions may prove, as in Kenya, less effective than they have been in the past in maintaining peace, stability, and development in the country.

Conclusion

The economy of affection does not explain everything in Africa, but it does play its part in explaining how African countries are being governed as it generates the informal institutions that are so crucial to what happens – both positive and negative. Informal institutions are an integral part of the governance equation and their interaction with formal institutions is one of the most central fields of study in African politics. Far too much attention has been given by scholars and policy analysts alike to directly transferring formal institutional practices that are neither rooted in African social realities nor responsive to the social logic of the economy of affection. It is no surprise, therefore, that government reforms have fallen far short of expectations and that governance in most countries rests on a shaky foundation. At the same time, as the Kenyan example illustrates, Africans are ready to internalize new formal practices but want to do so on their own terms and in response to the challenges that they face internally, not in order to please the outside world and its conditionalities.

Bibliography

Barkan, J. (ed.) (1994) *Beyond Capitalism and Socialism in Kenya and Tanzania*, Boulder, CO: Lynne Rienner Publishers.

Bates, R.H. (1981) *Markets and States in Tropical Africa*, Berkeley, CA: University of California Press.

Blundo, G. and Olivier de Sardan, J.-P. (2006) *Everyday Corruption and the State: Citizens and Public Officials in Africa*, London: Zed Press.

Bratton, M. and van de Walle, N. (1997) *Democratic Experiments in Africa*, New York, NY: Cambridge University Press.

Chege, M. (2008) 'Kenya: Back from the Brink?' *Journal of Democracy* 19(4): 125–39.

Collier, D. and Levitsky, S. (1997) 'Democracy with Adjectives: Conceptual Innovation in Comparative Politics', *World Politics* 49(3): 430–51.

Ekeh, P. (1975) 'Colonialism and the Two Publics in Africa: A Theoretical Statement', *Comparative Studies in Society and History* 17(1): 91–112.

Fukuyama, F. (1995) *Trust: The Social Virtues and the Creation of Prosperity*, New York, NY: Free Press.

Galvan, D.C. (2002) *The State Must Be Our Master of Fire: How Peasants Craft Culturally Sustainable Development in Senegal*, Berkeley, CA: University of California Press.

Helmke, G. and Levitsky, S. (2006) *Informal Institutions and Democracy: Lessons from Latin America*, Baltimore, MD: Johns Hopkins University Press.

Hydén, G. (1980) *Beyond Ujamaa in Tanzania: Underdevelopment and an Uncaptured Peasantry*, London: Heinemann Educational Books.

——(1983) *No Shortcuts to Progress*, London: Heinemann Educational Books.

——(1987) 'Capital Accumulation, Resource Distribution, and Governance in Kenya: The Role of the Economy of Affection', in M. Schatzberg (ed.) *The Political Economy of Kenya*, New York, NY: Praeger.

——(2006) *African Politics in Comparative Perspective*, New York, NY: Cambridge University Press.

Lemarchand, R. (1972) 'Political Clientelism and Ethnicity in Tropical Africa: Competing Solidarities in Nation-Building', *American Political Science Review* 66(1): 91–112.

Lijphart, A. (1977) *Democracy in Plural Societies: A Comparative Exploration*, New Haven, CT: Yale University Press.

Montgomery, J.D. (1987) 'Probing Managerial Behavior: Image and Reality in Southern Africa', *World Development* 15(4): 518–44.

Olowu, D. (2003) 'African Governance and Civil Service Reforms' in N. van de Walle, N. Ball and V. Ramachandran (eds) *Beyond Structural Adjustment: The Institutional Context of African Development*, New York, NY: Palgrave.

Olson, M. (1971) *The Logic of Collective Action: Public Goods and the Theory of Groups*, Cambridge, MA: Harvard University Press.

Putnam, R. (1993) *Making Democracy Work: Civic Traditions in Italy*, Princeton, NJ: Princeton University Press.

Rozman, G. (ed.) (1991) *The East Asian Region: Confucian Heritage and Its Modern Adaptations*, Princeton, NJ: Princeton University Press.

Rweyemamu, A. and Hydén, G. (eds) (1975) *A Decade of Public Administration in Africa*, Nairobi: East African Literature Bureau.

Scott, J.C. (1976) *The Moral Economy of the Peasant: Rebellion and Subsistence in Southeast Asia*, New Haven, CT: Yale University Press.

——(1985) *Weapons of the Weak: Everyday Forms of Peasant Resistance*, New Haven, CT: Yale University Press.

Weber, M. (1947) *The Theory of Social and Economic Organization*, New York, NY: Oxford University Press.

Whitehead, R. (2009) 'Single-Party Rule in a Multiparty Age: Tanzania in Comparative Perspective', unpublished PhD thesis, Temple University.

27

THE POLITICS OF DEVELOPMENT

Tim Kelsall

For more than two decades donors have been trying to improve development in Africa by importing models of 'good governance' from the West – promoting multi-party elections, supporting civil society, implementing rule of law programmes, and encouraging an independent media, among other things. In spite of these efforts Africa continues to lag behind other developing regions on a number of indicators, notwithstanding the recent global commodity boom. This has prompted thinking in parts of the development community about possible alternatives to good governance – alternatives that harness local institutional resources instead of trying to transplant them from outside.

These efforts to think through Africa's current impasse are inspired by empirical evidence that most successful developers have built on the indigenous. European states, for example, developed step-wise from pre-modern foundations over long expanses of time: they did not adopt a raft of good governance reforms in advance of rapid development (Chang 2002). East Asian states have demonstrated that development can proceed extremely rapidly in the context of norms of governance that are generally regarded as a problem in an African context, and without the wholesale adoption of Western institutions (Khan and Sundaram 2000; Moore and Schmitz 2008). An explanation for why this is so can be found in theoretical literature that points to the high costs of 'retooling' culture, and to the comparative economy of adapting institutions from the past (Swidler 1986; Greif 2006). It can also be found in research that points to the positive impact of shared identities and moral solidarities in the solution of collective action problems (Tsai 2007), suggesting that development will work best by harnessing communal sentiments that have been built up over time. Tony Blair's Commission for Africa had similar ideas when it wrote that Africa needed 'workable hybrids' and that, 'outside prescriptions only succeed where they work with the grain of African ways of doing things' (Africa 2005: 35).

In 2007 an international consortium called the Africa Power and Politics Programme (APPP) with partner organizations in France, Ghana, Niger, Uganda, the UK, and the United States embarked on a five-year programme to investigate these issues in more detail.[1] For more than two decades conventional development policy in Africa has regarded African society and culture as a problem. It has been argued that African societies share a pre-scientific, pre-rational culture, in which the extended family forms the foundation for an 'economy of affection', presided over by a patriarch, 'big man', or chief. The norms generated therein have infected economic and political governance, where damaging forms of nepotism, patron-clientelism, and neopatrimonialism are the norm. Bureaucracies have become mere prebends, ill-suited to supplying public goods or services, while politicians view the economy largely as a source of rents for redistribution to political cronies, rather than a resource that should be nurtured and grown (Hydén 1983; Joseph 1987; Chabal and Daloz 1999).

Conventional donor assistance has tried to solve these problems by making African governments more like governments in the West, imposing a range of 'best-practice', 'good governance' modalities. These have ranged from 'supply-side' interventions, like privatization and public-sector reform programmes using 'New Public Management' techniques, to 'demand-side' interventions, including national multi-party elections, local government decentralization, and a variety of participatory approaches to service provision that attempt to harness client power and boost social accountability.

Generally speaking, the performance of these interventions has been disappointing. With the partial exception of financial management initiatives, public service reform programmes have gained very little traction, and most of the continent still suffers from poor civil service morale, professionalism, and capacity. In some countries multi-party democracy has taken root, and surveys reveal that it is generally popular with citizenries. However, a clear link between multi-party democracy and better development has not been convincingly established, and in certain countries electoral pluralism has been associated with increased ethnic tension, violence, and state breakdown. Documented successes with decentralization and social accountability are also rather few, and in most parts of the continent public goods provision at local level, ranging from road maintenance, to sanitation, health services, and security, is dismal (Crook 2010; Booth 2012). Facts such as these encouraged the APPP to investigate whether or not it was possible to find ways of doing development in Africa that, rather viewing African culture as a problem, worked successfully 'with the grain' of existing social, cultural, and economic institutions.

In 2008 I published an inaugural article entitled 'Going With the Grain in African Development?' It attempted to make sense of the 'grain' metaphor, fleshing out our hunch that development could be improved by building on indigenous resources, and detailing some areas where that process could already be observed. It also provided a number of purely speculative suggestions of ways in which extant notions of moral obligation and interpersonal accountability might be harnessed for development (Kelsall 2008). I revisit that article here. In the first section I provide a précis of the original argument. Next, I consider some objections, before proceeding in the third section to discuss what recent empirical research has told us about this debate.

Going with the grain: a précis

In my 2008 article I argued that several enduring features of the African social fabric, including the extended family, ethnicity, religion, and 'big man' rule, might conceivably provide the foundation for a new development strategy. Part of the reason these institutions had so much motivational force, I argued, was that they had their roots in pre-colonial times. Over much of pre-colonial Africa, the basic unit of economy and society was what anthropologists have called the 'lineage mode of production'. Under this mode older men used the institutions of marriage and bridewealth to accumulate wives, children, dependents, and resources. In some societies, the more successful became 'big men' or chiefs, establishing their authority over several extended families.

Often the chief was a proven warrior who could protect the community from external attack, or add to its wealth through warfare or raiding. Sometimes he oversaw the production of public goods, like bush clearing for settlement and agriculture, or the distribution of granaries during periods of famine. Very often he intermediated with the spirit world, influencing the weather, curing disease, and augmenting performance in battle. In other cases the chief was able to control trade with other communities, and in places this led to the development of kingdoms or even empires (Lonsdale 1981, 1986; Vansina 1990).

Commonly, this pattern of political economy was underpinned by an ideology of patriarchal rule, which emphasized the rights of older men over those of women and junior males, and which conceptualized the polity as an extension of the leader's household or family. A 'big man's' power was not absolute, however. Although having rights to accumulate wealth a leader was also expected to redistribute it, materially assisting clients in times of need and handing power to a new generation when the time was ripe. In many polities the chief was expected to consult with elders before making important decisions for the community, and if a leader failed in his responsibilities to bring health and welfare to his people he was vulnerable to usurpation. Sometimes this might take the form of dynastic competition, witchcraft attack, poisoning, outright rebellion, or more often simple migration. In most parts of Africa ethnicity was fluid, land was plentiful, and labour scarce, and dissatisfied subjects could often move to live under the protection of another chief or 'big man' (Feierman 1990; Kitching 1980; Koponen 1988; Lonsdale 1981, 1986; McCaskie 1995; Vansina 1990).

In the article I claimed that there was nothing intrinsically anti-developmental about the lineage mode of production, patriarchal governance, and patron-client politics: what was anti-developmental was the unfortunate way in which they had come to be institutionalized, at least in much of contemporary Africa. To grasp this it was necessary to appreciate that colonial rule changed these institutions in significant ways. To begin with, the bonds of accountability between a chief and his followers were weakened by the fact that chiefs were now agents of colonial power. Next, colonialism fixed ethnic categories in a way that made it more difficult for ordinary people to move and switch leaders. In addition, colonialism unleashed economic forces and developmental interventions that tended to increase inequalities, making it more difficult for 'big men' to fulfil their obligations to clients. New religions and opportunities for education also created a new class of men critical of chiefly power, often attacking them by reference to new ideas about public probity and corruption that were themselves imports from Europe. All of these factors combined to place the moral economy and 'moral ethnicity' that had once characterized pre-colonial polities under enormous stress (Berman 1998; Iliffe 1995; Lonsdale 1992, 1994).

To some extent independence, and the access to central state resources that this promised, was expected to ease the strain. In fact, in most cases the pressure intensified, since ethnic groups now found themselves in competition with others for government power. Aspiring politicians reacted by building clientelist machines. As part of this process they tended to style themselves as living embodiments of 'moral ethnicity', generous big-men who would lavish patronage on their political followers. To this end, they bought the support of local notables with jobs, contracts, and credit, while local electorates were promised developmental 'club goods' like roads, health centres, and schools (Allen 1995; Berman 1998).

Unfortunately most states did not possess sufficient resources to satisfy clientelist demands, and many descended into chaos shortly after independence. Those that survived normally did so by introducing some variant or other of authoritarian rule. The resulting regimes were 'neopatrimonial' in the sense that some of the substance and much of the ideology of pre-colonial patriarchy was combined with the modern institutions bequeathed by colonial powers. In the more successful neopatrimonial states, personalistic authority was melded with bureaucracy to good economic effect, a phenomenon to which we will return. For the less successful, however, the constant need to buy political support through patronage together with a lack of interest in sound economics made growth impossible (Allen 1995; Sandbrook 1985).

In the less successful regimes public offices tended to function as prebends. Either by default or design, officials were permitted considerable discretion to use their positions to extort money from the public. Often, a legitimating veneer was provided by the fact that in the pre-colonial period, public and private spheres had not been demarcated, but frequently a hefty dose of colonial-style tyranny and despotism was also involved. As economies shrank further in the 1980s, this situation tended to degenerate into a 'generalised informal functioning of the state' (Blundo and Olivier de Sardan 2006). It proved impossible to achieve much in the way of development goals. In most states this situation has continued, and in some cases it has even been exacerbated by the return to competitive politics in the 1990s.

In my article I argued that the combination of a Western-derived public–private divide together with competitive clientelist politics had driven distributional politics underground. Politicians needed to engage in money politics in order to win power, yet illegality made resource transfers opaque. This led to an information asymmetry and prisoner's dilemma situation in which 'even those groups and individuals who would prefer to co-operate in the responsible use of the nation's resources, feel impelled to act in selfish and damaging ways for fear of being left empty-handed' (Kelsall 2008: 636). However, this need not be an inevitable situation. If good governance reforms were not working, it was possible to imagine ways in which development might progress better by returning to African societies' historical grain.

Indigenous resources for African development

Contemporary Africa, I claimed, is home to a range of indigenous resources with pre-colonial roots that could conceivably act as foundations, not obstacles to development. In Africa today, I argued, the extended family represents the bedrock of social identity and moral obligation, much as in the pre-colonial period. This can be seen in a variety of spheres. Most Africans do not hesitate to contribute significant sums of money to committees created to celebrate life-cycle rituals, such as marriages and deaths. Wealthier or more fortunate family members often provide financial support for poorer extended family, especially in cases of ill-health or bereavement. Family elders devote considerable time to resolving conflicts. Indeed, anecdotal evidence suggests that these extended family institutions not only attract considerable commitment but that monies within them are much better managed than within the state, or other modern organizations like non-governmental organizations (NGOs). The question for development specialists was whether these moral imperatives could be harnessed for use in organizations that transcend the extended family.

One answer is that to some extent they already are. Based, like families, on the idea of kinship, clans and ethnic groups are among the most familiar features of the African institutional landscape. These groups – the precise boundaries to which often shift according to situation – have sometimes proved effective as a foundation for developmental or potentially developmental activities. For instance, in Somaliland they have acted as vehicles for natural resource conservation. In Nigeria and Benin they have provided a network for business transactions in sectors as diverse as drugs and automobiles. In Tanzania and Cameroon they have been a basis for hometown associations or district development trusts, which raise contributions in the national and international diaspora to fund development in the provinces. In many African societies they oversee land transactions and resolve land disputes (for further details see Kelsall 2008).

Ethnic groups acquire their efficacy by reproducing some of the moral adhesive that binds members of extended families, even though they transcend face-to-face levels. This can even be seen in the field of public administration. In many African countries, bureaucratic agencies have been so weakened by a combination of material dearth and informal pressures that citizen entitlements have failed. In their absence, some people secure services by appealing to kinship, as when one has a 'relative on the inside'. In my 2008 article I speculated that creating multi-purpose ethnic service ministries might be a means of tackling the chronic lack of commitment to service provision shown by many staff in African public administrations – although I was cautious to note that this was a risky option, which no African countries were currently in a position to undertake.

Another powerful and double-edged institutional resource in Africa is religion (see Ellis and ter Haar, and Villalón, both this volume). All over the continent, people evince high levels of spiritual belief and religious commitment, encompassing everything from credulity concerning witchcraft to high attendance at church and mosque. The former appears to be associated with all manner of anti-developmental behaviour, from a failure to appreciate etiology to a reluctance to discipline staff in the workplace. However, in the pre-colonial period witchcraft was often used as a means of holding leaders to account, and there is some evidence that ritual oathing and cursing could be more widely used as props to accountability in contemporary Africa (see the discussion of Rwanda below). High levels of commitment to organized religion appears to be more positive, since churches and mosques are among the major suppliers of social services in African countries, and their performance in this field is often equal to or better than what the state can provide. One hypothesis is that church workers feel an obligation to perform well because they are accountable to a higher power. Another is that the competition for religious adherents encourages good management in religious service providers (Leonard 2000).

My 2008 article also discussed the issue of African leadership. Hereditary leaders, including clan elders, chiefs, and kings remain influential at local level in many African countries. They often act as vital coordinators of collective action in activities such as bush clearing, path cleaning, and road maintenance, not to mention being intermediaries for interventions by NGOs and international agencies. They often also organize defence and security committees, and are frequently a vital part of the local justice system. In some African states, like Botswana and Somaliland, there has been a conscious decision to build on indigenous leadership. Some states, like Mozambique, where chieftancy had formally been abolished, have reintroduced it; in others, like Ghana, chieftancy has been given greater recognition through parliamentary 'Houses of Chiefs' at the national level. It seems probable that the role of hereditary leaders in development could be expanded in places where traditional legitimacy is strong, not least because traditional legitimacy provides a leader some leeway to make decisions concerning environmental health and public works that, although unpopular, are sometimes necessary. That being said, the performance and legitimacy of chiefs varies greatly across the continent, partly because in some countries they have never been anything other than a colonial invention. Trying to build on 'traditional' authorities in places where the foundations are shallow, then, would seem an unwise move.

It is notable that many African presidents, particularly in the immediate post-independence period, adopted some of the symbolism of traditional authority. In some cases, sycophantic followers were only too willing to bestow titles such as 'president for life'. Today that has changed with the introduction of two-term limits in most countries. This has undoubtedly reduced the incentives for political rivals to organize coups or armed rebellions and so is in one sense a positive thing. At the same time, though, it introduces a narrow time horizon into political-economic decision making that is not necessarily helpful to development. In my 2008 article I argued that discussion of increased term-times and limited franchise or indirect elections should not be considered taboo, especially given that the reverse seems to go against the grain of long traditions of hereditary rule.

Criticisms of going with the grain

Going with the grain immediately proved to be a controversial hypothesis, even within the APPP. Most notably, Jean-Pierre Olivier de Sardan argued that the approach should be sidelined in favour of a more broad-ranging investigation into what he called 'practical norms of real governance in Africa' (Olivier de Sardan 2008). The gist was that going with the grain risked institutionalizing a romanticized view of 'merrie Africa', a kind of structural-functionalism in which timeless communities used their own cultural resources to create harmony and development. There were a number of strands to this argument, which I will dissect below.

The first strand consisted of an objection to the use of various stereotypes like 'ethnicity', 'witchcraft', and 'neopatrimonialism' in Africanist social science. According to Olivier de Sardan, ethnicity and the occult, although often depicted as atavistic hangovers from a pre-colonial past, have actually been profoundly changed by the colonial and post-colonial periods, and are in fact modern responses to contemporary problems. Neopatrimonialism, on the other hand, while an undeniable element of African social reality, was a lazy, 'catch-all' concept, too often invoked to explain all of Africa's ills. In my view these objections do not represent a serious challenge to going with the grain. The original article was quite cognizant of the fact that ethnicity had changed considerably in the colonial and post-colonial periods, and even if it did not stress the same for witchcraft, this should have been obvious from the context. The point about neopatrimonialism also rings hollow, since part of the inspiration for going with the grain is that some types of neopatrimonialism may be better for development than others, suggesting that the concept is not monolithic, at least in my eyes.

More interesting for our purposes is whether or not these phenomena, though altered, have an identifiable link to the pre-colonial period, what the nature of the link is, and whether it makes a difference. For going with the grain, historical links can come in three broad kinds. The first is a concrete link, in the sense that it is possible to identify the historical threads that link a contemporary institution to a pre-colonial one, even though it may have evolved or transformed over time. For example, when clan elders in Tanzania meet to adjudicate land conflicts, it is possible to trace the threads of a practice that has existed since the nineteenth century at least, even though the context of land adjudication has changed significantly. A second type of link is a fictive one. In Kenya, when Kikuyu politicians mobilize their ethnic followers to 'defend the house of Mumbi', they draw in part on an imagined history that is actually a colonial invention; the link with the pre-colonial past here is in the minds of the ethnic membership. Finally, a third type of link is of the 'family resemblance' kind. When African leaders keep exotic religious or occult specialists as part of their entourages, they are not the direct descendants of pre-colonial leaders who frequently sought out itinerant occult practitioners to buttress their rule, but they do draw on shared understandings about the nature of politics, power, and the occult that have a definite resemblance to ideas that existed pre-colonially.

In all these cases the connection with the pre-colonial past has a special ability to motivate behaviour. In part this is about people knowing how to 'carry on' with practices really rooted in history, investing a little in modifying them slightly in response to changing circumstances, instead of investing a lot in creating or trying out entirely new and unproven institutions, with all the risk that entails (Greif 2006). In part it is because practices that bear a resemblance to ones in the past are familiar or – to borrow a term from Michael Schatzberg (2002) – 'thinkable' in ways that entirely new or imported practices may not be. Finally, it is because tradition, even if invented, is often its own source of legitimacy, with a curious capacity to elicit commitment from its followers. None of which is to say that it will be impossible to find ways of doing development in Africa which, while 'anchored in local realities', to use a phrase preferred by Olivier de Sardan, have only the shallowest historical roots. However, the peculiar power of the past does provide good reasons for thinking that a *significant proportion* of the solutions to African development problems will be found there. That being said, I should stress that my characterization of the types of historical resource that might prove useful to development was not meant to be exhaustive. Discovering which historically rooted institutions work should be an empirical matter: solutions cannot be read off from preconceptions of Africa, and the historical literature merely provides pointers.

Another of Olivier de Sardan's objections was that going with the grain placed too much emphasis on morality. I think the motivation for this point was that a focus on ethics might blind us to strategies and 'logics' that, while developmental, are not specifically moral. It is certainly true that rather few development solutions will be explained entirely by their ethical underpinnings. Nevertheless there is reason to think that ethics – by which I mean norms that, among other things, promote trust, honesty, reciprocity, and unselfishness and which discourage shirking, opportunism, and free-riding – will be pivotal in encouraging developmental behaviour in much of Africa, not least because external monitoring and rule enforcement tends to be weak. Support for this hunch comes from the burgeoning literature on common pool resources, social dilemmas, and collective action problems (Ostrom 2005). The APPP made a conscious choice to situate its research within this tradition, and since ethnic and religious sodalities seem to be obvious, if not unique, cradles for the growth of the aforementioned norms, the rationale for going with the grain appears justified (Booth 2008; Kelsall 2009).

It is true that some recent research suggests that the role of morality in these processes may have been exaggerated. Habyarimana *et al.* (2007) report that the positive relation between ethnic homogeneity and public goods provision in Kampala is better explained by the monitoring capability of ethnic groups than by 'shared values' or 'altruism' between members. Be that as it may, it is difficult to understand how monitoring systems for public goods provision can work without someone being motivated by more than material self-interest.

Another conceivable criticism concerns the potential danger of harnessing a set of essentially patriarchal institutions for development. However, going with the grain is a research agenda, not a normative position. It is an invitation to look afresh at the most successful arrangements for supplying public goods in Africa, and to ask whether or not there is a relationship between success and African societies' historical 'grain'. Whether or not the trade-offs involved in these solutions are worth accepting will depend on how one values democracy and development, and also on the empirical evidence regarding what actually works in practice. In fact, the original article was quite clear about the fact that the lineage mode of production is showing signs of decline in parts of the continent, and that Western ideas and practices attract a growing body of adherents. It is possible then that the more specifically patriarchal and gerontocratic aspects of Africa's institutional inheritance will not figure prominently in more successful development initiatives, an eventuality arguably borne out by some of the examples proffered below.

Developmental patrimonialism

As we saw in a previous section, neopatrimonial politics (a form of governance in which 'big-man' rule is combined with more modern bureaucratic elements) has often led to economic failure in Africa. In consequence, good governance orthodoxy has sought to reform or eradicate it, seeing the corruption, cronyism, and arbitrariness with which it is often associated as invariably negative. However, we at APPP were not convinced that eradicating neopatrimonialism is a realistic objective (for further details see Kelsall 2010; Kelsall *et al.* 2010). With these findings in mind, we decided to revisit the record of economic performance in Africa, as well investigating some contemporary scenarios.

We conducted research into seven roughly comparable 'middle-African' countries between independence and the present day, distinguishing between strong, weak, and reasonable economic performers. Of the 20 or so regimes we categorized, we found that four (Côte d'Ivoire 1960–75, Kenya 1965–75, Malawi 1963–78, and Rwanda 2000–10) had actually achieved strong economic performance for periods upwards of a decade, while another three could be described as reasonably strong (Uganda 1986–2000, Ghana 1981–92, Malawi 2004). This was in spite of the fact that these regimes showed definite neopatrimonial tendencies.

So what distinguished the strong neopatrimonial performers from the weak or merely average? We found that the key to strong economic performance was the success of leaders in centralizing the management of economic rents and gearing that rent-management to a lengthy time horizon. Certain mechanisms facilitated this. To begin with, the political leadership needed to acquire the means to protect key branches of the economic technocracy from political clientelism, and it needed to be able to discipline subordinate staff and supporters. This did not mean an end to corruption and cronyism, which were often essential to both political and economic strategy, but it did mean that the most egregious, wasteful, arbitrary excesses could be controlled. A competent, somewhat insulated technocracy was also important for the second criterion, long-horizon rent-management, since without sound policy advice economic performance was liable to be poor.

In practice, successful implementation of these mechanisms was associated with strong, personal leadership, usually by independence politicians considered 'fathers of their nations'. Such men did not hesitate to intervene forcefully against political rivals or incompetent staff, rarely respecting the rule of law or formal managerial procedures. Most of them banned multi-party politics, and there are reasons to believe that centralized, long-horizon rent-management is extremely difficult in conditions of vigorous multi-party competition, where short-term considerations predominate.

In fact, the only strongly performing multi-party democracy in our sample was contemporary Rwanda. Rwanda is, of course, a case of a dominant party in a constrained democracy, but the story does not end there. Our research has revealed that a key mechanism for managing rents in Rwanda has been the party holding company Tristar. Tristar has leveraged clientelist relations to provide capital for joint ventures in hitherto untapped areas of economic potential, channel funds to the ruling party for electoral purposes, and profits into politically important social infrastructure projects. Financial solvency has permitted the RPF to take a tough line on corruption in other areas of the administration, creating a virtuous circle of public goods creation and development.

In sum, research into business and politics has shown that in some country contexts, it is possible to work with neopatrimonialism, cronyism, and rent-seeking to advance economic development. A type of neopatrimonialism in which key areas of the economic technocracy are insulated from political interference and equipped to give high-quality advice, may be a good second-best solution for African conditions in which it is unrealistic to expect neopatrimonialism to disappear. It is important to note, however, that even in the most successful cases 'developmental patrimonialism' is subject to some limitations, and is probably not feasible for every African country (Kelsall 2010).

Practical hybrids

The compatibility between neopatrimonialism and strong development in contexts where some limitations have been placed on clientelism can be seen in other fields also. Although it is admittedly at an early stage, APPP research into the provision of public goods at local level has shown that these tend to be provided best when there is some maintenance of top-down performance discipline in local administration. This emerged most clearly in Rwanda, which appears to be making considerable progress in fields such as safe motherhood and sanitation, a trend that can be contrasted with countries like Niger where results tend still to be disappointing (Booth 2010). With respect to the former, APPP research found that Nyamagabe District has seen a significant increase in women attending pre-natal health checks and giving birth in health centres instead of at home. This allows women who experience complications with their pregnancies to be rapidly transferred to more specialist units, with the result that maternal mortality in the area has fallen below the Millennium Development target rate (Chambers 2010; Golooba-Mutebi *et al.* 2010).

A number of measures have helped to achieve this. To begin with, women who do not attend pre-natal checks within the first three months of pregnancy, and women who give birth at home, are fined. Second, most women are now members of a health insurance scheme, which helps defray the costs of modern healthcare, including a room where women can stay free of charge while waiting to deliver. Third, and very importantly, health workers, village authorities, and the population themselves are incentivized to provide these measures by what is known in Rwanda as the *imihigo*, a unique blend of a modern performance contract with a traditional oath of loyalty sworn by warriors in pre-colonial Rwanda to the king. According to our research, '[v]illage and sector-level imihigo ensure that these administrative units are held to account for their decisions and activities, encourage competition among sectors and districts to be the best performers in areas such as maternal health, hygiene and sanitation' (Chambers 2010: 18). However, if maternal health has in one way been improved by the injection of some 'neo-tradition' into health services, in another way the traditional aspects of maternal healthcare have been phased out. This can be seen in the role of traditional birth attendants, who were initially encouraged to participate by accompanying women to health centres, but then increasingly made redundant by the posting of maternal community health workers in villages, before finally being banned (Chambers 2010).

The successful merging of modern, professional standards with more indexical practices was also found in the local justice sector in Ghana (Crook *et al.* 2010). APPP research examined popular perceptions of three different levels of the justice system: common law courts, alternative dispute resolution mechanisms, and chiefly land tribunals. Perhaps surprisingly, the research showed that court-users rated the impartiality, authority, and finality of justice in the magistrates' courts most highly, a finding at odds with much of the legal anthropology of Africa, which argues that the formal adversarial nature of common law courts makes them less suitable than more informal forms of community-based, restorative justice. The conundrum is solved once it is realized that there has been a considerable adaptation of court procedure, which is notably informal, to local expectations. Chiefly courts, by contrast, were stiff, formal, intimidating, and tended to be rated poorly by users, while alternative dispute fora received middling reviews. The Ghana material bears out the thesis that development in Africa consists in successful adaptations of modern institutions to the grain of social practices and expectations, 'practical hybrids' in our terminology, while providing a clear warning that going with the grain does not imply a straightforward return to stereotypically assumed tradition (ibid.).

This can also be seen in the education sector in parts of the Sahel. For years, modern education there has received a poor uptake among some communities, worried about its secularizing effects. In recent years, the state has recognized or given support to what are known as Franco-Arabic schools, in which students learn both French and Arabic, with an emphasis both on modern subjects and studying the Qur'an. This is not a 'traditional' solution: pupils do not learn native languages and the subjects taught are importations to the Sahel of more or less recent provenance; however, it does go with the grain of local preferences for a religious component to education. The result is that school enrolment has increased impressively, especially amongst girls.

Local anchorage

More often than not, APPP fieldwork has uncovered evidence of public goods being poorly provided, even in areas where both governmental and non-governmental institutions have been created to address these issues (Booth 2010). Our findings chime with a growing body of literature that critiques the performance of the 'associational mode' in African contexts (Dill 2009; Swidler and Watkins 2009). The thrust of the findings is that the requirement to satisfy donor demands for formal procedures and financial accounting makes these organizations vulnerable to elite capture. They tend to evolve into externally oriented vehicles for the solicitation of donor funds, and they frequently have a divisive effect on the communities they are supposed to represent. Many collapse amid allegations of financial misuse. By contrast, some of the more successful examples of public goods provision that APPP has found have occurred where solutions are what we call *locally anchored*, in a double sense. First, they are contextual responses to *locally specific* collective action problems, and second, they make use of institutional elements inherited from the past (Booth 2010).

Perhaps the clearest of several examples to come from our field research is that of Malawian 'town chiefs'. These have emerged in many urban communities in response to the absence of traditional chieftaincy and the weakness of local government (Booth 2010: 29). Some are quite closely aligned with traditional chiefs while others are rooted more in democratic or party institutions. They are chosen for being 'of "good character", "respectable", and "quiet" people of "good standing" who know "how to stay with people"' (Cammack *et al.* 2009: 15). Some are retired civil servants, church leaders, or members of chiefly families in the places they were born. All stand outside the law and yet are widely recognized and valued in their communities, playing a variety of roles. Typically, they do a great deal of work in the maintenance of security and order, including in cases related to witchcraft, and also in the areas of justice and reconciliation. They also help create belonging and cohesion in urban areas where weak state capacity leads to unmet needs. They have also been known to have a positive impact in areas of infrastructure construction and social service delivery (ibid.: 31).

Town chiefs' success can be explained by three things: the first is a felt need for their services; the second is a repertoire of concrete sanctions that chiefs can apply to non-cooperators; and the third – which is most interesting from our point of view – is a resonant template of traditional authority transferred from the countryside into the town. Town chiefs are best described as 'hybrid governance nodes resulting from an indigenous adaptation of an existing hybrid institution to a modern environment' (Cammack *et al.* 2009: 31), exemplifying the 'constructive role of institutional elements inherited from the past' (Booth 2010: 30).

Conclusion

In the areas outlined above, as well as in recent research by the APPP and others, it has been demonstrated that better developmental results *can* be achieved by working with the grain of African societies, and what this practically entails. I have discussed above how successful examples of public goods provision in Africa tend to share one or more of three institutional features. They are developmental forms of neopatrimonialism, in which elements of clientelism and personal rule are combined with sound technical advice and bureaucratic discipline. They are practical hybrids that combine elements of real or fictive African tradition with more modern acquisitions, and they are locally anchored in that they build on pre-existing institutions to solve collective action problems that are contextually defined.

Naturally, interested readers will want to know more about the conditions in which these features are likely to be found or what can be done to bring them about. Here, Africa's relations with the external world and in particular the donor community seem to be important (see Brown; Mshomba; and Williams, all this volume). More research needs to be conducted in this area, but what seems clear is that development with the grain is most likely to emerge when donors are sensitive to the nature of in-country political settlements and systems of rule, appreciate their potentialities, and do not undermine them through conditionalities over elections or markets and competition. This does not mean that democracy must be sacrificed on the altar of development; it means simply that donors need to be more sensitive to the trade-offs and sequencing arrangements appropriate in different country contexts. In the same spirit, donor funding and projects should be continuous and unconditional enough to support local hybrid arrangements. Finally, government, donors, and NGOs should encourage local problem-solving and cultural borrowing, adapting to local agendas rather than prescribing associational forms or 'solutions looking for problems'. This does not mean that donors should not care about how their money is spent. On the contrary, it implies a thicker presence on the ground, understanding and assisting African governments headed generally in the right direction, on their chosen path.

Needless to say, another important enabling condition is a will on the part of African governments to develop, instead of living off aid or other unsustainable rent streams. The contexts in which such a will emerges are complex and variable, but we believe that change in the conditions under which aid is disbursed is an important first step to encouraging a genuinely developmental outlook in a greater number of African states.

Note

1 For more information please see: www.institutions-africa.org.

Bibliography

Allen, C. (1995) 'Understanding African Politics', *Review of African Political Economy* 22(65): 301–20.

Berman, B. (1998) 'Ethnicity, Patronage and the African State', *African Affairs* 97(389): 305–41.

Blundo, G. and Olivier de Sardan, J.-P. (2006) *Everyday Corruption and the State: Citizens and Public Officials in Africa*, London: Zed Books.

Booth, D. (2008) 'Choosing a Research Design that is Fit for Purpose', discussion paper, Draft 2, Africa Power and Politics Programme, London: Overseas Development Institute.

——(2010) 'Towards a Theory of Local Governance and Public Goods' Provision in sub-Saharan Africa', Working Paper No. 13, London: Africa Power and Politics Programme.

——(2012) *Development as a Collective Action Problem: Addressing the Real Challenges of African Governance*, London: Africa Power and Politics Programme, forthcoming.

Cammack, D., Kanyongolo, E. and O'Neil, T. (2009) '"Town Chiefs" in Malawi', Working Paper No. 3, London: Africa Power and Politics Programme.

Chabal, P. and Daloz, J.P. (1999) *Africa Works: Disorder as Political Instrument*, Oxford: James Currey.

Chambers, V. (2010) 'Maternal Health Services in Nyanza 1 and Kavumu Villages, Nyamagabe District, Rwanda', APPP Fieldwork Report, London: Africa Power and Politics Programme.

Chang, H.J. (2002) *Kicking Away the Ladder: Development Strategy in Historical Perspective*, London: Anthem Press.

Commission for Africa (2005) *Our Common Interest: The Report of the Commission for Africa*, Harmondsworth: Penguin.

Crook, R.C. (2010) 'Rethinking Civil Service Reform in Africa: "Islands of Effectiveness" and Organisational Commitment', *Commonwealth and Comparative Politics* 48(4): 479–504.

Crook, R.C., Asante, K. and Brobbey, V. (2010) 'Popular Concepts of Justice and Fairness in Ghana: Testing the Legitimacy of New or Hybrid Forms of State Justice', Working Paper No. 14, London: Africa Power and Politics Programme.

Dill, B. (2009) 'The Paradoxes of Community-based Participation in Dar es Salaam', *Development and Change* 40(4): 717–43.

Feierman, S. (1990) *Peasant Intellectuals: Anthropology and History in Tanzania*, Madison, WI: University of Wisconsin Press.

Golooba-Mutebi, F., Chambers, V., Munyabaranga, E., Habiyonizeye, Y. and Rwabukumba, C. (2010) 'Delivering Public Goods in Rwanda: Early Findings from Nyamagabe District', Draft Working Paper, London: Africa Power and Politics Programme.

Greif, A. (2006) *Institutions and the Path to the Modern Economy*, Cambridge: Cambridge University Press.

Habyarimana, J., Humphreys, M., Posner, D.N. and Weinstein, J.M. (2007) 'Why Does Ethnic Diversity Undermine Public Goods Provision?' *American Political Science Review* 101(4): 709–25.

Hydén, G. (1983) *No Shortcuts to Progress: African Development Management in Perspective*, London: Heinemann.

Iliffe, J. (1995) *Africans: The History of a Continent*, Cambridge: Cambridge University Press.

Joseph, R. (1987) *Democracy and Prebendal Politics in Nigeria*, Cambridge: Cambridge University Press.

Kelsall, T. (2008) 'Going with the Grain in African Development?' *Development Policy Review* 26(6): 627–55.

——(2009) 'Game-theoretic Models, Social Mechanisms and Public Goods in Africa: A Methodological Discussion', Discussion Paper No.7, London: Africa Power and Politics Programme.

——(2010) 'Rethinking the Relationship Between Neo-Patrimonialism and Economic Development in Africa', *IDS Bulletin* 42(2): 76–87.

Kelsall, T., Booth, D., Cammack, D. and Golooba-Mutebi, F. (2010) 'Developmental Patrimonialism? Questioning the Orthodoxy on Political Governance and Economic Progress in Africa', Working Paper No. 9, London, Africa Power and Politics Programme.

Khan, M.H. and Sundaram, J.K. (eds) (2000) *Rents, Rent-Seeking and Economic Development: Theory and Evidence from Asia*, Cambridge: Cambridge University Press.

Kitching, G. (1980) *Class and Economic Change in Kenya: The Making of an African Petite-Bourgeoisie*, New Haven, CT: Yale University Press.

Koponen, J. (1988) *People and Production in Late Pre-Colonial Tanzania*, Helsinki: Finnish Historical Society.

Leonard, D. (ed.) (2000) *Africa's Changing Markets for Health and Veterinary Services*, London: Macmillan.

Lonsdale, J. (1981) 'States and Social Processes in Africa: A Historiographical Survey', *African Studies Review* 24(2–3): 139–225.

——(1986) 'Political Accountability in African History', in P. Chabal (ed.) *Political Domination in Africa*, Cambridge: Cambridge University Press.

——(1992) 'The Moral Economy of Mau Mau: Wealth, Poverty and Civic Virtue in Kikuyu Political Thought', in J. Lonsdale and B. Berman (eds) *Unhappy Valley: Conflict in Kenya and Africa*, London: James Currey.

——(1994) 'Moral Ethnicity and Political Tribalism', in P. Kaarsholm and J. Hultin (eds) *Inventions and Boundaries: Historical and Anthropological Approaches to the Study of Ethnicity and Nationalism*, Roskilde: International Development Studies, Roskilde University.

McCaskie, T.M. (1995) *State and Society in Pre-Colonial Asante*, Cambridge: Cambridge University Press.

Moore, M. and Schmitz, H. (2008) 'Idealism, Realism and the Investment Climate in Developing Countries', Working Paper No. 307, Sussex: Centre for the Future State, Institute of Development Studies.

Olivier de Sardan, J.-P. (2008) 'Researching the Practical Norms of Real Governance in Africa', Discussion Paper No. 5, London: Africa Power and Politics Programme.

Ostrom, E. (2005) *Understanding Institutional Diversity*, Princeton, NJ: Princeton University Press.

Sandbrook, R. (1985) *The Politics of Africa's Economic Stagnation*, Cambridge: Cambridge University Press.

Schatzberg, M.G. (2002) *Political Legitimacy in Middle Africa: Father, Family, Food*, Bloomington, IN: Indiana University Press.

Swidler, A. (1986) 'Culture in Action: Symbols and Strategies', *American Sociological Review* 51(2): 273–86.

Swidler, A. and Watkins, S.C. (2009) '"Teach a Man to Fish": The Sustainability Doctrine and its Social Consequences', *World Development* 37(7): 1182–96.

Tsai, L.L. (2007) *Accountability Without Democracy: Solidary Groups and Public Goods Provision in Rural China*, Cambridge: Cambridge University Press.

Vansina, J. (1990) *Paths in the Rainforests: Towards a History of Political Tradition in Equatorial Africa*, London: James Currey.

PART VI

International relations

28

AFRICA AND THE GLOBAL ECONOMY

Richard E. Mshomba

What happens in the rest of the world affects Africa, directly or indirectly. For centuries Africa has been part of the global economy. Rural people today may seem concerned only with their personal daily needs and those of their immediate communities, yet most of them are just as closely connected to the world economy as those who work in the mining industries and those in the cities who work in the service and manufacturing sectors. Cotton produced by subsistence farmers in West Africa is mainly for export. Over 90 per cent of coffee produced by small farmers in East Africa is for export. Many pharmaceutical products come to Africa from developed countries, as do used clothes, which compete with the domestic textile and apparel industry in Africa. This chapter provides an overview of Africa's place in the global economy. It presents some key trade features of African countries and examines these countries' capacity to negotiate in the World Trade Organization (WTO). In addition, it provides a brief discussion of 'aid for trade' and agricultural policies in developed countries.[1]

Some anti-globalization activists describe African and other poor and/or developing countries as unable to compete and, thus, exploited by trade. What this viewpoint overlooks is that trade is mutually beneficial to trading partners in several respects. Most importantly, trade allows trading partners to increase their production according to their comparative advantage. Although a country may not have an absolute advantage in producing anything, it always has a *comparative* advantage in producing some things. For example, if, on average, a farmer in Senegal can produce 5 tonnes of cotton or 4 tonnes of peanuts, and a farmer in the United States can produce 10 tonnes of cotton or 15 tonnes of peanuts, the United States has an absolute advantage in producing both products. However, Senegal has a comparative advantage in producing cotton. That is, the opportunity cost of producing a tonne of cotton in Senegal is only 0.8 tonnes of peanuts, while the opportunity cost of producing a tonne of cotton in the United States is 1.5 tonnes of peanuts. Thus, both countries would benefit if Senegal exports cotton to the United States and the United States exports peanuts to Senegal.

Other benefits of trade include increased competition and increased varieties of products available to consumers. Trade also allows countries, especially small countries, to take advantage of economies of scale. Economies of scale are achieved when the average cost of production decreases as production increases. Some countries' markets are so small that they need access to the world market in order to take advantage of economies of scale. Thus, trade is an important tool for economic growth. Although economic growth does not guarantee development, it is certainly a prerequisite for it.

There is no doubt that African economies are small. Sub-Saharan Africa's gross domestic product (GDP) is only 1.5 per cent of world GDP. Sub-Saharan Africa's share of merchandise exports is only 2 per cent of world merchandise exports, with South Africa, Nigeria, and Angola contributing almost two-thirds of that share. Other countries' shares of world exports are negligible in size, as shown in Table 28.1. The small shares are directly related to the small size of the economies of African countries.

The level of Africa's integration in the world economy, however, is high. The level of a country's integration into the global economy is determined by the country's trade ratio, which is the sum value of exports and imports as a percentage of a country's GDP. It is a measure of a country's trade orientation, and these ratios are high for most sub-Saharan African countries. This is not surprising given that their major commodities, such as cocoa, coffee, fuels, and various minerals, are produced primarily for export. At the same time, Africa depends on the rest of the world for inputs, machinery, pharmaceuticals, and other manufactured goods. This dependence on trade is typical of small economies, developed and developing alike.

Table 28.1 shows that there is wide variation in the level of each country's trade with other sub-Saharan African countries.[2] A simple average would suggest that intra-regional exports in sub-Saharan Africa were as high as 20 per cent in 2009, but the weighted average, which takes into account the magnitude of each country's exports, is lower: about 12 per cent in the 2004–09 period. This is mainly because important exporters of oil, such as Angola, Equatorial Guinea, and Sudan, have very low intra-regional exports. While this is noticeably lower than the level of intra-regional exports for Asian countries, which is about 50 per cent, it is important to remember that increasing intra-regional trade is not an objective in itself. If it were, it could be achieved quite easily by shutting off trade with other parts of the world. Such trade diversion, which would blatantly neglect the dictates of comparative advantage, would make African countries worse off. Since regional economic integration is covered elsewhere (Khadiagala, this volume), it will be mentioned only in passing that intra-regional trade in sub-Saharan Africa is limited due to the high costs associated with trade in Africa, including transportation costs, inefficient border procedures, corruption, lack of transparency and predictability, and trade barriers (UNCTAD 2009).

Trade composition and patterns

The general trade composition and patterns developed and entrenched during the colonial era continue today, with African countries exporting unprocessed raw materials and importing manufactured products. Table 28.2 illustrates that African countries' major exports are still agricultural raw commodities, fuels, ores, and metals. Their main trading partners are still the European countries, as shown in Table 28.3. Most sub-Saharan African countries are still heavily dependent on one or only a few commodities for their export revenue, making their economies quite vulnerable. Table 28.4 shows the export concentration (Herfindahl) index for sub-Saharan African countries. The concentration index ranges from 0 to 1, with higher values indicating higher levels of concentration. About 80 per cent of sub-Saharan African countries had an export concentration index higher than 0.3 in 2000–09, while the average index was less than 0.15 for all developing countries and less than 0.08 for the world.

In the last 10 years there has been a steady, albeit slow diversification of exports by African countries that are not dependent on exports of oil and minerals. There has also been noticeable diversification in their trading partners. The explanations for the ongoing diversification in

Table 28.1 Sub-Saharan African countries' trade orientation

Country	Trade ratio 2005–08 (annual average)	Percentage share of world exports 2005–09 (annual average)	Percentage of exports destined to other African countries (2009)	Percentage of imports orginating from other African countries (2009)
Angola	96	0.317	4.1	5.4
Benin	38	0.007	32.7	7.9
Botswana	75	0.034	24.3	7.8
Burkina Faso	32	0.005	17.8	42.7
Burundi	45	0	8.5	27.5
Cameroon	36	0.028	13.1	19.5
Central African Republic	24	0.001	20.6	12.6
Chad	73	0.026	3.3	20.4
DRC	65	0.022	9.4	48.1
Congo, Rep. of	116	0.048	1.5	6.1
Côte d'Ivoire	76	0.068	30	28.7
Equatorial Guinea	114	0.074	0.1	10.5
Eritrea	44	0	20.4	17.7
Ethiopia	39	0.01	8.1	3.3
Gabon	76	0.044	3.2	11.6
Gambia	49	0	7.9	19.4
Ghana	80	0.034	10.7	25.4
Guinea	59	0.008	3.3	7.2
Guinea-Bissau	65	0.001	33.7	20.2
Kenya	51	0.031	37.9	13.6
Lesotho	156	0.006	1.3	13.3
Liberia	144	0.001	17.4	1.3
Madagascar	50	0.009	5.1	7.2
Malawi	64	0.006	25.3	56
Mali	52	0.001	17.2	30.2
Mauritania	98	0.01	15.3	8.6
Mauritius	85	0.017	14.3	12.3
Mozambique	71	0.017	16.5	36.6
Namibia	84	0.022	4.3	2
Niger	41	0.005	27.1	24.7
Nigeria	60	0.474	11.1	5
Rwanda	27	0.001	57	43.3
São Tomé and Príncipe	62	0	5.4	5.7
Senegal	57	0.014	45.3	18.9
Seychelles	133	0.003	6.9	11.6
Sierra Leone	41	0.002	9.4	25.2
South Africa	56	0.539	19.5	7.5
Sudan	39	0.058	2.3	14.5
Swaziland	157	0.017	15.4	22.4
Tanzania	44	0.018	19.1	17.9
Togo	77	0.005	59.6	16.9
Uganda	40	0.015	44.4	23.2
Zambia	67	0.03	29.9	66.2
Zimbabwe	92	0.016	50.6	73.6
Sub-Saharan Africa (SSA)	61	2.06	13.7	11.8
World	50			

Source: UNCTAD 2010b; World Bank 2007, 2008, 2009, 2010.

Table 28.2 African export and import structure, 2004–09

Product type	Exports (%)	Imports (%)
Manufactured goods	18	69
Ores, metals, precious stones, and non-monetary gold	12	3
Fuels	58	13
Agricultural raw materials and food items	12	15
Total	100	100

Source: UNCTAD 2010b.

Table 28.3 Africa's exports and imports by destination and source

	Destination of exports				Source of imports			
	Developed countries		Developing countries		Developed countries		Developing countries	
Year	Total	Europe	Total	Asia	Total	Europe	Total	Asia
1995	66.8	47.1	30.7	8.0	64.0	47.4	32.8	11.9
2005	69.7	42.4	28.7	12.2	51.5	39.8	44.0	18.6
2009	59.3	38.3	39.7	20.0	49.1	37.5	47.9	23.6

Source: UNCTAD 2010b.
Notes: 'Asia' refers to Eastern, Southern, and South-Eastern Asia. Total percentages do not add up to 100 because trade with countries of the former Soviet Union is not included.

exports vary from country to country, but in broad terms they include reductions in trade barriers by trading partners and reforms in domestic policies. For example, the growth of the textile industry in Kenya, Madagascar, Mauritius, Swaziland, and especially Lesotho, is explained largely by the African Growth and Opportunity Act (AGOA) (Seyoum 2007). AGOA is a 2000 US trade law that gives preferential tariff treatment to goods originating from sub-Saharan Africa. Lesotho has taken full advantage of AGOA by encouraging an inflow of foreign direct investment and increasing its production of apparel. It is currently the largest exporter of garments to the United States from sub-Saharan Africa, accounting for about 30 per cent of sub-Saharan African exports of garments to the United States in 2009 (USITC 2009). Between 2000 and 2009 Lesotho's exports of clothing to the United States increased by an annual average of about 13 per cent (UNCTAD 2010a). Of course, it is important for Lesotho not to rely heavily on AGOA for the growth of its textile industry, since the preferential treatment provided by AGOA will decrease over time.

Ironically, the rapid growth of the textile industry in Lesotho, relative to the growth in other sectors, has actually increased its export concentration index slightly, as shown in Table 28.4. This should underscore the importance of carefully examining the composition of a country's exports over an extended period of time, before drawing conclusions based on the export concentration index. A high index may indicate a country's vulnerability to production and price fluctuations of its major export product(s), as an increase in the value of the index may simply mean that the country has improved production of its major export product or that the world price of that product has increased. In fact, given that the Herfindahl index is calculated on the basis of an aggregated level of products, the index may not reflect increased diversification that has taken place within an industry, such as an increase in the variety of garments that a country exports. The same logic should follow that a decrease in the export concentration

Table 28.4 Export concentration index (Herfindahl*)

Country/region	2000	2009
World	*0.07*	*0.07*
Developing economies	0.13	0.12
Developing economies – Africa	0.35	0.40
Developing economies – Americas	0.11	0.11
Developing economies – Asia	0.13	0.11
Africa		
Nigeria	0.93	0.83
São Tomé and Príncipe	0.90	0.70
Angola	0.89	0.96
Botswana	0.81	0.45
Equatorial Guinea	0.81	0.73
Comoros	0.77	0.51
Chad	0.74	0.87
Gabon	0.74	0.72
Burundi	0.70	0.59
Congo, Rep. of	0.69	0.71
Somalia	0.67	0.47
Mali	0.65	0.75
Central African Republic	0.64	0.40
Seychelles	0.64	0.52
Guinea-Bissau	0.62	0.93
Sudan	0.61	0.77
Congo, Dem. Rep. of	0.61	0.35
Malawi	0.59	0.63
Mayotte	0.58	0.23
Benin	0.58	0.35
Liberia	0.57	0.60
Guinea	0.57	0.49
Burkina Faso	0.56	0.34
Ethiopia	0.54	0.34
Zambia	0.52	0.66
Cape Verde	0.51	0.44
Sierra Leone	0.51	0.27
Mauritania	0.50	0.49
Cameroon	0.48	0.48
Lesotho	0.48	0.50
Gambia	0.46	0.26
Rwanda	0.46	0.40
Namibia	0.40	0.31
Niger	0.40	0.51
Mauritius	0.34	0.26
Uganda	0.33	0.23
Côte d'Ivoire	0.32	0.36
Ghana	0.31	0.44
Eritrea	0.31	0.22
Mozambique	0.31	0.32
Kenya	0.30	0.22
Zimbabwe	0.27	0.19
Tanzania	0.26	0.29
Madagascar	0.26	0.22
Swaziland	0.23	0.24
South Africa	0.14	0.15
Djibouti	0.13	0.33

Source: UNCTAD 2010b.
Notes: * The Herfindahl index ranges from 0 to 1, with higher values indicating higher levels of concentration.

index may not necessarily imply that exports are more diversified. One would need to know the cause of the decrease in the index and other details to make an informed determination.

In the late 1980s, many African countries started implementing programmes that were outward oriented and, more generally, market oriented, reducing some of the bottlenecks to diversification. There has also been a growing awareness in Africa of the need for an integrated approach in coordinating and implementing various diversification programmes. A programme to diversify agricultural exports, for example, which concentrates solely on obtaining aid and giving investment incentives to increase production, would not be successful without reliable infrastructure, property rights, and macroeconomic stability.

Consider the case of cut flowers in Tanzania. There was always suitable land for the production of cut flowers in Tanzania and a profitable foreign market for them in Europe. Nonetheless, actual production and exports did not take place until the early 1990s, after the following conditions were in place: producers had access to Nairobi International Airport in Kenya, an ordinance prohibiting the uprooting of coffee trees (in areas where cut flowers could be grown) was removed, export taxes were reduced, the foreign currency market was liberalized, and investment rules began to encourage direct foreign investment. These were changes that involved various government ministries, local governments, and a neighbouring country – changes that enabled Tanzania to take advantage of its difference with European countries in terms of climate, land, and labour costs. An important feature of the cut-flower industry is that 90 per cent of the employees are women. This is significant because women in general, for a variety of reasons, have fewer job opportunities. Tanzania's export revenue generated from cut flowers increased from US\$500,000 in 1990 to over \$33 million in 2007 (Golub and McManus 2009).

While diversification of products has been slow, diversification of markets has been growing relatively quickly. African countries in general continue to rely heavily on markets in developed countries. In addition, about 50 per cent of African countries' imports still come from developed countries. However, there has been a clear increase in African countries' exports to and imports from developing countries since the early 1990s, especially to and from Eastern, Southern, and Southeastern Asia, as shown in Table 28.3. This reflects economic reforms in Asia (China since 1978 and India since 1991) and also in African countries themselves. Those reforms have also been strengthened by trade agreements under the WTO.

Africa and the WTO

African countries' navigation in the global economy can be considered from various viewpoints. However, it is becoming increasingly important to examine Africa in the context of the WTO for several reasons. First, the WTO plays a pivotal role in setting trade rules and will continue to do so. Second, trade is and will continue to be a key source of economic growth in Africa. Third, African countries, especially in sub-Saharan Africa, have unique challenges which often call for special consideration by the WTO, separate from the consideration given to other developing countries. Fourth, African countries are continually gaining experience and confidence in negotiating in the WTO.

The WTO was born out of the General Agreement on Tariffs and Trade (GATT), which was established in 1947 when 23 countries signed the original treaty. In addition, participation in GATT was extended to colonies of GATT members, under Article XXVI: 5. GATT contracting countries applied this provision to all their colonies in Africa with the sole exception of Morocco, which was not sponsored by France to participate in GATT (Tomz *et al.* 2005). Thus, nearly all African countries were, by extension, part of GATT from its very inception.[3] To the extent that colonialism was, by design, fundamentally an exploitative political and economic system, the extension of GATT's rights and obligations to the colonies was also seen as a means for exploitation. When independence came, a colony to which GATT benefits and obligations were applied had three options: join GATT immediately as a full contracting party; establish *de facto* participation status while deciding about its future domestic trade policy; or simply end its participation in GATT.

While GATT was technically only a provisional treaty throughout its 48 years of existence, over time it actually amounted to an increasing number of complex agreements, administered and enforced by its operating body. These agreements were designed to reduce barriers to trade. There were eight rounds of multilateral trade negotiations under GATT, including the Uruguay Round (1986–93), from which the WTO was born. As of January 2011 the WTO had 153 members, including 42 African countries. In addition, 31 countries are observers, including nine African countries. Only two African countries – Eritrea and Somalia – had neither membership nor observer status.

The WTO (like its predecessor) strives to provide a more predictable trade environment and plays an important role in facilitating negotiations among many diverse countries. It is no secret or surprise that a country's economic strength is important in determining its leverage in negotiating agreements. Of course, this phenomenon is not unique to the WTO. Individual African countries do not have much economic leverage, given the small size of their economies, so African countries in the WTO have formed a coalition called the African Group, which affords them greater influence in negotiations. Many of them also belong to several other coalitions, including the African, Caribbean, and Pacific countries (ACP) Group, the Least-Developed Countries (LDC) Group, the G77, and the G33. The African Group, the ACP Group, and the LDC Group also coordinate under an umbrella group called the G90 (see Table 28.5).

Simply considering membership numbers, African countries enjoy significant representation in the WTO through various coalitions, as suggested by Table 28.6. All sub-Saharan African countries are members of the ACP Group. The G77 is a coalition of developing countries founded in 1964 to promote their interests in multilateral negotiations at various forums. The membership of the G77 grew from 77 countries when it was founded, to 130 countries in 2007. All 53 African countries are members of the G77. The G33 is a coalition of a subset of developing countries in the WTO that has focused on negotiations on agriculture, particularly on so-called 'special products', and a special safeguard mechanism.

The practice of belonging to these and other coalitions is explained by history, geography, common broad economic interests, and the efficiency of sharing information and scarce resources. More importantly, it is necessitated by the desire to have some leverage in the WTO negotiations, as leverage for African countries usually comes from their sheer number and the merits of their arguments rather than their economic strength.

The amendment of the Agreement on Trade-Related Aspects of Intellectual Property Rights (TRIPS) to address concerns of African countries is a good example of what can be achieved through coalitions. TRIPS was among the agreements that became effective at the establishment of the WTO in 1995. The Agreement sets a minimum uniform standard to protect intellectual property rights. The signing of the TRIPS Agreement was an achievement celebrated by developed countries, the main producers of technological knowledge. African and other developing countries, on the other hand, had all along been opposed to and wary of an agreement that might adversely affect their access to generic and cheaper medicines and hamper their adoption of new technology.

Certain provisions were included in the agreement to give governments, especially those in developing countries, some discretion to refuse to grant patents for public health reasons. Parallel importing, which is permitted by Article 6 of the TRIPS Agreement, refers to the practice of a

Table 28.5 African countries' membership of the WTO, ACP group, LDC group, and G33, December 2007

Country	WTO member (x) WTO observer (o)	ACP	LDC	G33
Algeria	o			
Angola	x	x	x	
Benin	x	x	x	x
Botswana	x	x		x
Burkina Faso	x	x	x	
Burundi	x	x	x	
Cameroon	x	x		
Cape Verde	x	x	x	
Central African Republic	x	x	x	
Chad	x	x	x	
Comoros	o	x	x	
Congo, Dem. Rep. of	x	x	x	x
Congo, Rep. of	x	x		
Côte d'Ivoire	x	x		x
Djibouti	x	x	x	
Egypt	x			
Equatorial Guinea	o	x	x	
Eritrea		x	x	
Ethiopia	o	x	x	
Gabon	x	x		
Gambia	x	x	x	
Ghana	x	x		
Guinea	x	x	x	
Guinea-Bissau	x	x	x	
Kenya	x	x		x
Lesotho	x	x	x	
Liberia	o	x	x	
Libya	o			
Madagascar	x	x	x	x
Malawi	x	x	x	
Mali	x	x	x	
Mauritania	x	x	x	
Mauritius	x	x		x
Morocco	x			
Mozambique	x	x	x	x
Namibia	x	x		
Niger	x	x	x	
Nigeria	x	x		x
Rwanda	x	x	x	
São Tomé and Príncipe	o	x	x	
Senegal	x	x	x	x
Seychelles	o	x		
Sierra Leone	x	x	x	
Somalia		x	x	
South Africa	x	x		
Sudan	o	x	x	
Swaziland	x	x		
Tanzania	x	x	x	x
Togo	x	x	x	
Tunisia	x			
Uganda	x	x	x	x
Zambia	x	x	x	x
Zimbabwe	x	x		x

Source: Table 1.1 (updated) from Mshomba 2009.

Table 28.6 African countries' relative membership in various groups, December 2007

Group	Total membership			Group members that are also WTO members		
	Total	African countries	Percentage African	Total	African countries	Percentage African
WTO	153	42	27	153	42	27
ACP	79	48	61	57	39	68
LDC	50	34	68	33	26	79
G77	133	53	40	102	42	41
G33	42	14	33	42	14	33

Source: Table 1.2 (updated) from Mshomba 2009.

third party reselling products without the approval of the patent holder. For example, suppose *Profitmax* pharmaceutical company sells a patented drug in Uganda and Zimbabwe, but sells it at a lower price in Uganda. If another company buys it in Uganda and sells it in Zimbabwe at a price lower than the price charged by *Profitmax*, such action would constitute parallel importing. Another example is compulsory licensing, permitted by Article 31 of TRIPS, which 'allows for other use of the subject matter of a patent without the authorization of the right holder'. Compulsory licensing takes place when a government allows a third party to produce a patented product without the consent of the patent holder.

Nonetheless, parallel importing and compulsory licensing are of little direct importance to most African countries. While drug prices in these countries are still high relative to purchasing ability, these prices tend to be lower, in absolute terms, than prices in other countries. Any parallel importing is likely to be from, rather than to, these countries. In fact, to help ensure the flow of relatively cheap drugs to African countries, these countries should be assuring pharmaceutical companies that they will not be party to parallel *exporting* and that they will work diligently to prevent the smuggling of drugs *from* Africa.

Compulsory licensing is a viable option if a country has the capacity to produce and market generic drugs, but most African countries do not have that capacity. For many African countries, this provision is thus useful only if they can import from other countries, such as India and Brazil, which can themselves take advantage of compulsory licensing to produce generic drugs. However, Article 31(f) of the TRIPS Agreement stipulates that any use of compulsory licensing 'shall be authorized predominantly for the supply of the market of the Member authorizing such use'. That is, compulsory licensing was to be authorized primarily for the domestic market. This has posed a significant problem for countries that lack production capacity.

At the same time, the TRIPS Agreement gave developing countries until 1 January 2006 to comply with its provisions. In 2002 the WTO extended the deadline, to 1 January 2016 for least-developed countries to begin to provide patent protection for pharmaceuticals. Other developing countries, however, were still bound by the original deadline. That meant that although India, for example, could still utilize the compulsory licensing provision to produce generic drugs, as of 1 January 2006 it could not export them. Although a country like Tanzania (still under the extended transitional period) would theoretically have been allowed to import generic drugs from India, India would have been bound by the TRIPS Agreement not to export the drugs. Tanzania would either have had to produce the drugs itself or find another least-developed country that produced the drugs.

Aware of what this predicament meant for Africa, the African Group in the WTO pushed for changes that produced what is referred to as the *August 2003 Decision* – a waiver of Article 31(f) of the TRIPS Agreement. This meant that countries that utilized compulsory licensing'to produce generic drugs were no longer constrained to their domestic markets; they could now export them to eligible importing countries or regional trading blocs. However, the waiver was agreed to only on a temporary basis. The African Group pushed to make the waiver permanent.

On 6 December 2005 WTO members gave their approval to make the August 2003 decision a permanent amendment to the TRIPS Agreement. To become a permanent amendment, two-thirds of the WTO members must ratify the changes. Initially the WTO gave itself a deadline of 1 December 2007 for ratification. By December 2007, with only 13 out of 152 countries having ratified the amendment, the WTO extended the deadline to the end of 2009. On 6 December 2005, WTO members gave their approval to make the August 2003 decision a permanent amendment to the TRIPS Agreement. To become a permanent amendment, two-thirds of the WTO members must ratify the changes. Initially the WTO gave itself a deadline of 1 December 2007 for ratification. By December 2007, with only 13 out of 152 countries having ratified the amendment, the WTO extended the deadline to the end of 2009. The deadline was pushed back again to December 2011 and later to December 2013. As of September 2012, only 44 countries had ratified the amendment so it is likely that the December 2013 deadline will be pushed back as well. Despite the delays in ratifying the waiver, the fact that the process has gotten this far must be considered a victory for the African Group, which clearly demonstrated its tenacity and ingenuity in the WTO TRIPS Council. If the waiver does become a permanent amendment, it will be the first time a core WTO Agreement has been amended.

In 2007 Rwanda became the first country to notify the WTO that it was going to apply the compulsory licensing provision to import HIV/AIDS generic drugs from Canada (ICTSD 2007). However, given the administrative and legal procedures involved, it took more than a year before the export of generic drugs from Canada to Rwanda actually began. In addition, the fact that Rwanda was already receiving some assistance for HIV/AIDS drugs through other initiatives reduced the urgency of the Canada-Rwanda deal.

It is unfortunate that African countries have had to expend so many of their meagre diplomatic resources fighting for access to cheap medicines. Nonetheless, the approval to amend the TRIPS Agreement is a victory, albeit modest, for the African Group. While the outcome shows how slow the WTO can be in making genuine changes, it also shows how important it is for African countries to be persistent with justifiable demands.

WTO agreements cannot be amended on a whim if they are to guide long-term trade policies and be applied to the filing and settlement of trade disputes. However, the WTO's rigidity in making corrections even in a case as clear as the one involving compulsory licensing, discussed above, makes African countries instinctively and, perhaps, justifiably hesitant about any proposed new agreements.

Most African countries are in an awkward situation because the constraints imposed by various agreements are often not aimed directly at them. The constraints usually target large developing countries, such as Argentina, Brazil, China, India, and South Africa, which are typically capable of taking advantage of any available loopholes. Of course, South Africa is in the African Group, and for various strategic, historical, and institutional reasons, the African Group tends to be in coalitions with other developing countries, even if their interests are not completely in harmony.

The TRIPS Agreement gave the African Group a unique opportunity to show its maturity and shrewdness in negotiations at the WTO. The experience the African Group acquired and the coalitions it forged in the process are assets transferable to other endeavours. Nonetheless, the capacity of African countries to negotiate will continue to be compromised so long as they are dependent on aid and special or preferential treatment.

Aid for Trade

Dependency on aid – in a direct form or in the form of preferential treatment – often undermines whatever leverage African countries might have in negotiating in the WTO. African countries, the leverage of which is typically small to begin with due to their small economies (notwithstanding the various coalitions to which they belong), negotiate from an even weaker position with donors and preference-giving countries. Only a naïve diplomat would approach WTO negotiations single-mindedly, without considering his or her country's aid dependency. In 2010 sub-Saharan Africa received 35 per cent of the world's total net official development assistance (ODA). Net ODA as a percentage of gross national income was highest in sub-Saharan Africa, at 4.3 per cent, followed by the Middle East and North Africa region at a distant second, with 0.9 per cent.

Given the declaration that the Doha Round was to be a *development* round, it was only a matter of time before aid became a central issue in the WTO negotiations. An Aid for Trade initiative was formally launched in December 2005 at the WTO Ministerial Conference in Hong Kong. The merit in the Aid for Trade initiative comes from the fact it can help to reduce supply-side constraints, thus improving production capacity and helping countries to diversify and add value to their exports.

In addition, African countries also want to be given aid for diminished preference margins. A basic principle of the WTO and its predecessor, GATT, is non-differentiated treatment, commonly called the most favoured nation (MFN) principle. The MFN principle means a member country must treat all other members equally in respect to trade policy. If a member country lowers the tariff rate on a commodity entering from one member country, for example, it must likewise lower the tariff rate on that commodity from all other member countries. Exceptions to the MFN rule are made for preferential tariff treatment for developing and least-developed countries, and for free trade areas and other levels of economic integration. Developing countries, and even more so least-developed countries, are accorded special and preferential treatment. However, their margin of preference erodes whenever MFN tariffs are lowered for goods covered by preferential programmes.

While the erosion of the preference margins seems to be a legitimate concern, it is interesting that a handful of countries that have been able to utilize preferential treatment, as well as those that have failed to take advantage of it, are asking for additional aid to help them adjust to reduced preferential margins.[4] Financial assistance for adjustment costs is to come from the same countries that have offered preferential treatment to African countries in the first place. In a way, countries that offer preferential treatment are held hostage by their preferential openness. Preferential treatment, which by its very design is meant to be temporary, is portrayed in the aid for trade initiative as if it were a perpetual entitlement for developing countries. What is even more ironic is that African countries that, for one reason or another, are not able to take advantage of preferential treatment stand a chance to benefit by receiving financial aid when the preferential treatment that they were not able to utilize erodes or expires. Whatever the reasons for requesting aid might be, however, dependence on aid and lobbying for preferential treatment reduces African countries' leverage in negotiations in the WTO (on aid and dependency see Williams, this volume).

Developed countries' agricultural policies

In general, developed countries have been generous to African countries and maintain lower trade barriers than African countries. However, their promises cannot always be taken at face value. Developed countries often make aid pledges that they do not always honour. Moreover, they still have some trade barriers and market distortions, especially in the agricultural sector, which hurt African countries.

It should be noted that the agricultural sector is a very important economic sector in most African countries. In 2010 it contributed 13 per cent of GDP in sub-Saharan Africa and 30 per cent in non-oil-exporting countries (World Bank 2012). Agricultural exports are the most important export sector for many African countries, contributing more than 60 per cent of export revenue in Benin, Burkina Faso, Burundi, Cape Verde, Djibouti, Ethiopia, Ghana, Guinea-Bissau, Kenya, Malawi, Seychelles, and Uganda in 2009 (UNCTAD 2010b). The importance of agriculture in Africa is even more pronounced when one considers that the sector employs 65 per cent of the labour force, most of whom are women.

The agricultural sector was brought under the WTO in 1995 when the Agreement on Agriculture took effect. The agreement's objectives are ostensibly to increase market access and to reduce domestic support and export subsidies in developed countries. Given how much leeway countries were given, it was clear early on that no significant liberalization could be expected. Further negotiations were needed to set the agricultural sector en route to more meaningful liberalization.

The Doha Round of negotiations was launched at the WTO Ministerial Conference in 2001 with this in mind. It was launched with the hope of bringing the agricultural sector into greater harmony with the development objectives of developing countries. The Doha Round was declared to be a development round and was acceptable to African countries because of its uniquely explicit development agenda and its attention to agriculture. However, the Doha Round has reached an impasse, partly due to the resistance of developed countries to making meaningful cuts in agricultural subsidies. These subsidies cause increases in production and decreases in world prices, hurting developing countries that depend on agricultural exports.

US cotton subsidies have come to symbolize the inconsistency of developed countries' policies (see the case study, 'Cotton producers in Benin squeezed by domestic policies and OECD subsidies', in Mshomba 2009). While the United States and other developed countries have found it politically difficult to remove cotton subsidies, they agreed to support the development and production of cotton in West African countries that have suffered the most due to those subsidies through its West Africa Cotton Improvement Program launched in 2006 (USAID 2006). This assistance provided by developed countries and multilateral agencies can have a positive impact on West African countries. However, elimination of subsidies will have a far greater positive impact on producer prices for African farmers, unlike financial aid, which may not even get to the capital city, let alone to the rural areas. Studies have shown that the removal of cotton subsidies worldwide would increase cotton export earnings in West Africa by 15 per cent to 36 per cent (Badiane et al. 2002; Gillson et al. 2004).

Conclusion

Globalization is an ongoing process whereby countries increasingly interact with each other, either by choice or circumstance. It is a dynamic process that will continue to change in magnitude and form. Because African countries are highly integrated into the global economy, external factors can affect them significantly, and all the more so since African economies are very specialized.

It is encouraging that the WTO has become more sensitive to the salient features and needs of developing countries, especially LDCs. If aid for trade is given and spent effectively and provisions for special and preferential treatment are used strategically, they can contribute to development in African countries. To make sure that aid is well targeted, aid should be determined by what needs to be done, rather than aid determining what should be done. It is important, for example, to evaluate the impact of liberalization on its own merit. Short of that, hasty adjustments and unexamined projects could be carried out only because aid was made available for that purpose. Likewise, trade- and growth-enhancing adjustments could be put off just because aid was not available. Aid should facilitate trade reforms; it should not be the reason for reforms.

As developing countries, African countries have ample policy space. This is especially true for the least-developed countries. The African Group in the WTO will continue to protect their policy space, which is meant to allow them to liberalize at a pace that they determine to be in harmony with their overall development strategies. Of course, external factors still matter. The elimination of developed country agricultural subsidies, especially for cotton, and increased market access for LDCs' products into developed countries, will boost sub-Saharan African exports and enhance their potential to develop.

Notes

1 Some of the discussion in this chapter is drawn from Mshomba (2000, 2009).
2 These data fluctuate from year to year, but major differences between countries are a common phenomenon.
3 South Africa and Southern Rhodesia (Zimbabwe) were among the original contracting countries of GATT. However, at the time each of these countries was under a white minority rule that was notoriously repressive of the majority black Africans.
4 See Brenton and Ikezuki (2005) and Hoekman *et al.* (2006) for utilization of preferential market access by African countries.

Bibliography

Badiane, O., Dhaneshwar, G., Goreux, L. and Masson, P. (2002) 'Cotton Sector Strategies in West and Central Africa', World Bank Policy Research Working Paper 2867, Washington, DC: World Bank.

Brenton, P. and Ikezuki, T. (2005) 'The Impact of Agricultural Trade Preferences, with Particular Attention to the Least-Developed Countries', in A. Aksoy and J. Benghin (eds) *Global Agriculture Trade and Developing Countries*, Washington, DC: World Bank.

Gillson, I., Poulton, C., Balcombe, K. and Page, S. (2004) 'Understanding the Impact of Cotton Subsidies on Developing Countries', Overseas Development Institute Working Paper AG0107, London: Overseas Development Institute.

Golub, S. and McManus, J. (2009) 'Horticulture Exports and African Development', Geneva: UNCTAD.

Hoekman, B., Martin, W. and Braga, C.P. (2006) 'Preference Erosion: The Terms of the Debate', in R. Newfarmer (ed.) *Trade, Doha, and Development: A Window into the Issues*, Washington, DC: World Bank.

ICTSD (International Centre for Trade and Sustainable Development) (2007) 'Rwanda Becomes First Country to Try to Use WTO Procedure to Import Patented HIV/AIDS Drugs', *BRIDGES Weekly Trade News Digest* 11(27), Geneva: ICSTD.

Mshomba, R. (2000) *Africa in the Global Economy*, Boulder, CO: Lynne Rienner Publishers.

——(2009) *Africa and the World Trade Organization*, New York, NY: Cambridge University Press.

Seyoum, B. (2007) 'Export Performance of Developing Countries under the African Growth and Opportunity Act: Experience from US Trade with sub-Saharan Africa', *Journal of Economic Studies* 34(6): 515–33.

Tomz, M., Goldstein, J. and Rivers, D. (2005) 'Membership has its Privileges: The Impact of GATT on International Trade', Working Paper, Stanford, CA: Stanford University.

UNCTAD (United Nations Conference on Trade and Development) (2009) 'Economic Development in Africa Report 2009: Strengthening Regional Economic Integration for Africa's Development', Geneva: UNCTAD.

——(2010a) 'Building Productive Capacities in LDCs for Inclusive and Sustainable Development', Geneva: UNCTAD.

——(2010b) 'Handbook of Statistics 2010', Geneva: UNCTAD.

USAID (United States Agency for International Development) (2006) 'West Africa Cotton Improvement Program: Program Description', Washington, DC: USAID, http://pdf.usaid.gov/pdf_docs/PDACK365.pdf (accessed 26 May 2012).

USITC (United States International Trade Commission) (2009) 'Textiles and Apparel: US Imports from Sub-Saharan Africa under the Generalized System of Preferences and the African Growth and Opportunity Act, year-to-date from Jan-Mar', http://reportweb.usitc.gov/africa/by_sectors_all.jsp?sectorcode=TX (accessed 14 December 2010).

World Bank (2007) *World Development Indicators*, Washington, DC: World Bank.

——(2008) *World Development Indicators*, Washington, DC: World Bank.

——(2009) *World Development Indicators*, Washington, DC: World Bank.

——(2010) *World Development Indicators*, Washington, DC: World Bank.

——(2012) *World Development Indicators*, Washington, DC: World Bank.

29

PAN-AFRICANISM AND
REGIONAL INTEGRATION

Gilbert M. Khadiagala

Regional integration has been a dominant process in African efforts to build multilateral institutions for development and economic coordination. Since the 1960s, African countries have invoked the importance of forging close economic cooperation to promote growth and development, overcome the impediments of political fragmentation, and increase Africa's competitiveness with the rest of the world. Meeting these objectives has entailed the construction of sub-regional and continental mechanisms for integration.

Throughout the four decades of regional integration schemes, African countries have sought to reconcile national and regional priorities against the backdrop of competing demands and expectations. Despite the broad consensus on the benefits of integration, there has been a mixed record of national commitment to regional institutions. Myriad developmental challenges accompanying state- and nation-building processes have stymied regional initiatives, saddling most of Africa with weak integration arrangements. Just as significantly, attempts to build regional integration schemes in Africa have oscillated between sub-regional and continental domains, raising profound questions about the geographical reach of regionalism. At the core of this problem is the issue of how to construct regional institutions, including defining memberships, and delineating responsibilities. Often regarded as the differences between minimalist and maximalist approaches to integration, these contrasting visions have framed the tenor and debates about the construction of integration schemes. Over the years, although there has emerged a tenuous compromise to simultaneously deepen integration at both levels, tensions still persist between sub-regionalism and continentalism.

This chapter provides a conceptual overview of key ideas, debates, and themes surrounding African regional integration schemes since the 1960s. It identifies two dominant phases in the construction of regional institutions (the first phase, 1960s–1990s, and the second phase, 1990s to recent times) to highlight various actors and processes that have animated the construction of continental and sub-regional institutions for economic integration and security collaboration. In addition, the chapter discusses the diverse roles of external actors and institutions in the articulation and support for the objectives of regional integration. In the concluding sections, the chapter will reflect on some of the key trends that may have an effect on future regional integration trends.

The first phase of regional integration schemes

Dominant scholarship in regionalism makes a distinction between regional cooperation and integration to differentiate between process and outcomes. Regional cooperation is a more flexible form of regionalism, denoting the coordination and coalescence of policies around common objectives. Regional integration, on the other hand, is perceived as a more weighty process of ceding sovereignty to new structures that acquire substantive roles that transcend cooperation. From this perspective, cooperation may be a process of attaining the ends of integration, a terminal stage where states lose some of the factual attributes of sovereignty.[1] Economic analyses of the progressive stages of integration also mirror the dynamic evolution from limited cooperation arrangements in the trade arena to broad-based forms of economic integration. The classical economic characterization of integration identifies five stages: preferential trade area; a free trade area; a customs union; a common market; and an economic union. Throughout these stages, increased trade and market cooperation builds the foundations for substantive integration. In the penultimate stage of economic union, states lose autonomy and sovereignty over economic policy.[2]

African attempts at integration have operated within the overarching framework of incrementally accelerating the capacity for shared sovereignties and problem solving in the economic and political realms. However, attaining these objectives has been difficult, primarily because of the problems of translating lofty ideals into realities and the array of challenges associated with managing Africa's economic, political, and geographical diversities. Mshomba has succinctly noted that 'part of what makes economic integration in Africa an interesting subject for research ... is the wide gap between the rhetorical support of politicians and the real state of economic integration' (Mshomba 2000: 175; see also this volume).

Since colonial times, authors of integration schemes in Africa have sought to overcome the deficiencies of fragile and fragmented economies and polities, redoing the territorial and political tapestry established in the partition of Africa. Questions of economies of scale and political viability have always framed integration arrangements, reflecting a yearning for political and economic communities that transcend existing structures. Thus colonial governments crafted the formative regional economic integration schemes by seeking to create large unions among the geographically diverse entities. Some of these efforts involved the economic rationalization of colonial territories to foster trade, industrial development, infrastructural cooperation, and shared services. One of the largest colonial initiatives was the French bid to group 13 territories into two federations: the French West Africa (*Afrique Occidental Française* – AOF – made up of Côte d'Ivoire, Dahomey, French Guinea, French Sudan, Mauritania, Niger, Senegal, and Upper Volta); and French Equatorial African Federation (*Afrique Equitorial Française* – AEF – made up of Chad, Central African Republic, Congo, Gabon, and Cameroon). Although each federation had its own currency and possessed the potential for political and economic development, France abandoned these schemes in 1958. Similarly, the East African Common Market Organization (EACMO, comprising Kenya, Tanganyika, and Uganda), the Central African Federation (CAF, comprising Nyasaland, Northern and Southern Rhodesia), and the Southern African Customs Union (SACU, comprising the Republic of South Africa, Bechuanaland, Basotholand, and Swaziland) were colonial bids to exploit geographical proximities to lay the foundations of trade, and monetary, industrial, and infrastructural cooperation.[3]

On the eve of decolonization in the late 1950s, the process of integration unleashed in Europe through the Treaty of Rome in 1957 had decisive influence on the trajectory of Africa's regionalism. While spearheading the formation of the European Economic Community (EEC), France also induced its European partners to provide aid, technical assistance, and trade preferences to its former colonies. The Treaty of Rome allowed for the association of former colonies and created the first European Overseas Development Fund (FEDOM) to meet thei economic needs. Association membership was subsequently formalized in the Yaoundé Agreements of 1963 and 1969. Alongside these agreements, France galvanized its former colonies to form new regional blocs such as the *Union Douaniere de L'Afrique de l'Ouest* (UDEAO, the West African Customs Union), and the *Union Africaine et Malgache de Coopération Économique* (UAMCE, the Economic Cooperation of Africa and Malagasy). The expansion of EEC membership in the early 1970s enabled the transformation of Yaoundé Agreements into the Lomé Conventions that benefitted more African countries. One of the objectives of these Conventions was to help deepen integration in Africa through strengthening trade and aid relationships.[4]

French-led regionalism in the post-independence period gave rise to a countervailing movement led primarily by Ghana's Kwame Nkrumah for indigenous approaches to African integration. Invoking Pan-Africanist ideals, Nkrumah opposed the Association of African countries with the EEC on the grounds of balkanizing Africa to the detriment of continental integration. Instead, Nkrumah suggested a grand continental union government, which would reduce colonial fragmentation, promote political unity by diminishing sovereignty, and foster economic development. Ranged against this vision was the gradualist approach articulated notably by Francophone countries, Tanzania, and Nigeria, which proposed basing Africa's integration schemes on sub-regional organizations. The gradualists saw economic integration beginning at the sub-regional level and proceeding in progressive stages until the attainment of a common market (Green and Seidman 1968).

The contest between continentalism and sub-regionalism was resolved in the formation of the Organization of African Unity (OAU) when African states opted for both continental institutions for security and political integration based on respect for sovereignty and territorial integrity coexisting alongside sub-regional economic institutions and arrangements. Assisting the OAU in the articulation of broad-based, all-inclusive Pan-African integration was the United Nations (UN) Economic Commission for Africa (ECA), created in 1958. From its formation, the ECA assumed a strategic position in the debates about the parameters of African integration and development. At the OAU heads of state conference in 1963, the ECA prescribed a pragmatic and gradualist approach to integration in Africa, arguing that the economic background is 'not yet ripe for a full economic union, quite apart from the political obstacles' (UNECA 1963: 397–98).

In proposing 'large-scale import substitution based on larger, sub-regional markets', the ECA nonetheless pointed to the major obstacles to integration in Africa: poor communications capacity and the lack of 'true national markets' within individual states (UNECA 1963: 397–98). The gradualist vision articulated by the ECA was to shape the course of African integration for decades to come. With the OAU providing the larger umbrella for the advancement of continental ideals of unity, self-determination, and security, African sub-regions became the critical locus for experiments with regional cooperation. Starting from the mid-1960s, sub-regional organizations such as the East African Community (EAC), the Economic Community of West African States (ECOWAS), the Inter-Governmental Authority on Development (IGAD), the Southern African Development Community (SADC), plus multiple others in West and Central Africa, evolved to articulate the economic component of regionalism that drew on geographical proximities and common objectives (Legum 1975; Meyers 1974).

Building on the inherited colonial trade and services institutions, Kenya, Uganda, and Tanzania led the process of East African integration. However, although hailed as a regional organization that mirrored the European experience, strains of nationalism appeared in the mid-1960s that were to impair integration. Beginning with the decision in 1966 to end the common monetary unit and the establishment of separate currencies, the three countries strayed away from the institutions and services erected by British authorities. In 1967 a Treaty of Cooperation created the EAC, whose objectives narrowly reflected the upsurge of nationalism and divergent ideological and political positions. Moreover, by vesting the decision-making power of the EAC in the hands of heads of state, the EAC became hostage to elite political consensus. When fissures surfaced over personalities, the gains from integration, and economic policies, the EAC collapsed in 1977 (Mead 1969; Mugomba 1978).

The disintegrative trends in East Africa belied the renewed momentum for integration in West Africa. Since the 1950s, West Africa had been a theatre of competing regional institutions. For a long time UDEAO, formed in 1959 and composed of most of the Francophone countries, dominated attempts to expand trade in the region. In 1972, however, Dahomey, Côte d'Ivoire, Mali, and Mauritania replaced UDEAO with the *Communauté Économique de l'Afrique de l'Ouest* (CEAO, Economic Community of West Africa), whose objectives were improvement of infrastructure, acceleration of joint industrialization, and expansion of trade. Parallel initiatives culminated in the formation of the most comprehensive economic cooperative network to emerge in Africa, ECOWAS, in May 1975. Since the mid-1960s, the ECA and Nigeria had spearheaded bids for a West African Economic Community through relentless meetings and studies. With the formation of ECOWAS, regional states started to confront ways of diminishing the debilitating Francophone-Anglophone divide that had long dominated the region (Yansane 1977; Ojo 1980). In conception and modalities, ECOWAS echoed the gradualist and functionalist intentions of most of Africa's regional integration schemes, putting emphasis on cooperation and harmonization in agriculture, trade, industry, transportation, finance, and labour mobility. Like the EAC, ECOWAS also accorded decision-making authority to the regional heads of state.

Beyond ECOWAS, Africa witnessed a spate of integration schemes in the 1980s, most of which built on sub-regional proximities and sought limited functional objectives. In Central and Equatorial Africa, the *Union Douanière et Économique de l'Afrique Centrale* (UDEAC, the Customs and Economic Union of Central Africa) with a common currency and central bank, had dominated regionalism since 1964. However, UDEAC faced competition from the *Communuaté Économique des Pays des Grand Lacs* (CEPGL, the Economic Community of the Great Lakes Countries), which was created in 1976 and comprised Burundi, Rwanda, and Zaire. Nonetheless, the search for a new regional institution in 1983 produced the *Communuaté Économique des États de l'Afrique Central* (CEEAC, the Economic Community of Central African States (ECCAS)), incorporating UDEAC and CEPGL plus Equatorial Guinea and São Tomé and Príncipe (Robson 1985).

In East and Southern Africa, a new organization – the Preferential Trading Area (PTA) for Eastern and Southern Africa, the precursor to the Common Market for Eastern and Southern African Countries (COMESA) – was formed in 1981 to promote trade among 18 diverse states ranging from Egypt to Zambia. In Southern Africa, the efforts by the Frontline States neighbouring minority regimes led to the formation of the Southern African Development Coordination Conference (SADCC) to reduce dependence on South Africa and foster sectoral collaboration in mainly transport and communications.

By the mid-1980s, Africa had made remarkable progress in realizing the ECA's vision of sub-regional entities as the bedrock of African integration, but amidst disappointing economic performance, the ECA alongside the OAU came up with a blueprint for Africa's self-reliance and industrialization geared toward the domestic market. The Lagos Plan of Action passed by the OAU in 1980 made the creation of regional organizations as the centrepiece for self-reliant development. Thus, as the Plan noted, given the small size of African domestic markets, regional organizations would enlarge market size through the protection of infant industries and the attraction of foreign direct investment. Consistent with the idea expressed since the early 1960s, the ECA continued to be an advocate of economic collaboration among states that also remained beholden to their sovereignties. Such integration would entail a common external tariff, free movement of peoples and goods, and coordination of macroeconomic policies to ensure mutual consistency of fiscal, monetary, and external payments, and exchange rate policies of member states. As part of the Lagos Plan of Action, the ECA envisioned broadening the existing regional institutions – ECOWAS, ECCAS, and PTA – and creating new ones as the foundational blocs for Africa-wide economic community.[5]

Weaknesses in the first phase of integration schemes

Despite the proliferation of regional integration schemes along functional and geographical lines, these arrangements faced profound questions of effectiveness in the 1980s. Although African countries pursued integration for the purposes of market enlargement, industrialization, sustained development and growth, and increased international competitiveness, for the most part it was difficult for these arrangements to translate these commitments into substantive goals. The growing scepticism about the contribution of regional integration to African development led some critics to contend that these institutions were unlikely to overcome the multiple obstacles confronting them in the short to medium term. Johnson (1991: 2) summarized the prevailing view, noting that '[t]he precise structure and details of the actual schemes being promoted have been unrealistic in the light of the costs and sacrifices that African governments and their citizens are willing to bear'.

A large part of the explanation for the lack of effectiveness was the unwillingness of governments to subordinate national political interests to long-term regional economic goals, a problem that was also compounded by the absence of a clear direction about the purposes of integration. In a review of ECOWAS in 1985, for instance, Robson argued that 'the right problems are not being addressed in the right order ... too much emphasis is being given to policy areas which are of little immediate relevance' (Robson 1985: 614). Furthermore, he suggested that the main weaknesses of ECOWAS – that decisions adopted by the heads of state or by ministers almost invariably fail to be implemented by action at the national levels – could be explained by two main factors: 'namely 1) the emphasis on trade liberalization; and 2) the lack of simultaneity in the obligations and benefits implied by the Community's programme' (ibid.: 616).

The uncertainty over the trade liberalization approach to integration that Robson raised with respect to ECOWAS signalled more widespread rethinking of the objectives of African integration in the late 1980s. Trade liberalization, the critics argued, was not feasible in the context of economic disparities among African countries and their dependence on foreign trade. This rethinking coincided with the debates that sought to diminish the applicability of European-style integration to African conditions because the European model was based on high levels of political and economic convergence.

While proponents of scaled-down regional integrative schemes cast doubt on the original ECA belief that African unity could be achieved through a slow process of functional integration, the ECA and OAU moved quickly from the mid-1980s toward reinvigoration of the idea of an African Common Market. Drawing from the Lagos Plan of Action, the ECA and OAU convened a series of exploratory meetings toward the formation of a continental economic community. These initiatives culminated in the Abuja Treaty of 1991 that proposed the gradual establishment of an African Economic Community (AEC) as an integral part of the OAU. According to its framers, the AEC was to be established over a 34-year period through coordination, harmonization, and progressive integration of the activities of the existing regional economic communities. Article 8(3) of the Treaty conferred on the Assembly of Heads of State and Government – the supreme organ of the AEC – the power to 'give directives, coordinate, and harmonize the economic, scientific, technical, cultural, and social policies of member states' (OAU 1991). Through the Abuja Treaty, African countries tried once more to reconcile the three decade-long contest between continentalism and sub-regionalism.

The second phase of regional integration schemes

The renewed drive for integration captured in the Abuja Treaty came against the backdrop of continuous economic crises that had beset Africa in the 1980s. Weakening of national economies had invariably affected regional integration by denuding the ability of states to be effective participants in these arrangements. Besides, as most of Africa confronted severe debt crisis and embarked on externally directed Structural Adjustment Programmes (SAPs) to reverse the precipitous economic decline, there was little attention paid to the coordination and harmonization of policies (see Williams, this volume). Yet, in the face of the implementation of SAPs and other donor-driven programmes, the political and economic circumstances for building the second phase of regional integration schemes began to take shape in the mid-1990s. Propelling the new impetus were reforms ushered by the collapse of state-run economies and protectionist economic policies that had been the foundations of the ECA's inward-looking project on integration; some of these reforms saw increasing convergence of African economies. As a result, there was a marked shift in integration toward outward-looking market enlargement via liberalization and a more frontal approach to cooperation and coordination in functional areas such as large-scale infrastructure. Writing in the mid-1980s, Robson pointed to the potential role of enforced economic adjustment in underwriting new trends in African regionalism, which he suggested meant that 'the lack of a will to give real priority to intra-regional adjustments and compromises, and to the development of practical integration strategies, could thereby conceivably prove to be less of an obstacle in the future than it has been during the past decade' (Robson 1985: 621–22).

As economic reforms induced more convergence in policies, particularly the shift from states to markets, African countries seemed more prepared to harmonize policies in regional arrangements. Equally significant, the momentum toward political renewal unleashed by the end of the Cold War and the rise of the democracy movements across Africa bolstered the new era of regionalism.

Analytical efforts to understand the new phase spoke of 'second-generation integration' attempts that have gained strength since 1992. In contrast to the first generation that was propelled primarily by political leaders and senior technocrats, the new phase promised to engage multifaceted actors, particularly the private sector, non-governmental organizations (NGOs), and parliaments in the integration agenda. As Mistry noted:

> In principle, the new approach has abandoned the ossified, static, protected-fortress approach to integration among closed, state-run economies. It lays more emphasis on development of thematic integration (i.e. cooperating to save on large-scale infrastructure costs and achieving economies of scale) and open, rather than protected, market enlargement as a means of consolidating national economic policy shifts towards greater liberalization, market orientation, competitiveness, and efficiency.
>
> (Mistry 2000: 559–60)

SADCC's sectoral focus toward integration in the 1980s in part influenced the shift in the approach to regionalism that was captured in the second generation. Although transport and infrastructural coordination became SADCC's major strength, when it was eventually transformed into the Southern African Development Community (SADC) in 1992, regional states worked to deepen sectoral coordination as they also embarked on the goal of regional integration for production. South Africa's accession to SADC membership in 1994 enhanced the viability of the organization because of its large economy and contribution to the region's gross domestic product (GDP). There was a realization that for market integration to succeed, it was important to focus on efficient cross-border infrastructure and services to allow for the free movement of persons, goods, and services. In 1996 SADC signed a trade protocol that phased out barriers among members as a preliminary step in the establishment of a Free Trade Area in 2008. The expansion of institutions around SADC, such as the SADC Parliamentary Forum, and the involvement of business groups in questions of integration made SADC the symbol of a new approach to regionalism (Jeffries 2007).

Similarly, after nearly a quarter century, Kenya, Tanzania, and Uganda re-established the East African Community (EAC) in 1999. Under the new arrangement, the EAC created a Common Market in 2010, plans to move into a Monetary Union by 2012, and eventually form a Political Federation. Although the timeframe for the Political Federation has not been fixed, the EAC has embarked on national consultations among the member states to gauge the readiness toward this goal. The three countries have also inaugurated a joint legislative assembly to handle regional policy matters and a regional court to settle cross-border disputes. In December 2006, Rwanda and Burundi were admitted as members of the EAC at the same time as the institution launched a 2006–10 regional development strategy.[6]

The 1990s also witnessed the revitalization and expansion of PTA through the formation of COMESA in 1994, the objective of which is to deepen regional integration through trade and investment. Since its formation, COMESA has expanded northwards to include Egypt, even as it shrunk southwards with the withdrawal of Lesotho, Mozambique, and Tanzania. To promote trade within the 19-member regional bloc, COMESA established three key instruments: COMESA Clearing House, COMESA Bank, and COMESA Travellers' Cheques. In June 2009, COMESA reached a milestone when it launched a customs union. Coming about a year behind schedule, it aims at removing tariff barriers among member states and harmonizing barriers with third parties through the Common External Tariff (CET), which was adopted in May 2007.

In 1996, some members of COMESA – Kenya, Uganda, Eritrea, Ethiopia, Sudan, and Djibouti – decided to transform the moribund Intergovernmental Authority on Drought and Desertification (IGADD) into the Intergovernmental Authority on Development (IGAD). Although the IGAD mandate has moved beyond alleviating drought and desertification in the Horn of Africa to address economic cooperation, it remains one of the weakest regional integration groups in Eastern Africa. In West Africa, CEAO – to which all Francophone countries except Togo belong – was replaced in 1994 by the more ambitious *Union Économique et Monétaire Ouest-Africaine* (UEMOA, the West African Monetary and Economic Union), which has increasingly competed with ECOWAS.

Central Africa has been slow in building functional regional integration schemes. Both the Abuja Treaty and the Constitutive Act of the African Union recognize ECCAS as one of the building blocks of the contemplated AEC. ECCAS has a membership of 11 countries: Angola, Burundi, Cameroon, Central African Republic, Chad, the Democratic Republic of Congo (DRC), the Republic of Congo, Equatorial Guinea, Gabon, Rwanda, and São Tomé and Príncipe. However, the grandiose goals of ECCAS – which includes gradual elimination of trade barriers; free movement of persons, capital, goods, and services; and the development of capacities to maintain peace, security, and stability – have not been accomplished. ECCAS is weak because the Central African region is riddled with civil conflicts, authoritarian regimes, and a lack of internal dynamism for integration. Moreover, ECCAS competes with the Central African Economic and Monetary Union (CEMAC), a much smaller community (with a membership of only six states, all of which are also members of ECCAS), which has made better efforts at integration.

Regional integration for security

The promise of new regionalism underpinned by markets and similar political ideals and practices faced the countervailing trends of state failure and civil conflicts that were to preoccupy regional institutions in Africa in the 1990s. The disintegrative trends of civil conflicts have weakened many African sub-regions and markedly slowed down the pace of functional cooperation. Although optimistic thinkers believed that regional integration would strengthen national autonomy, few African regional institutions were prepared for the convulsion that engulfed Africa from the early 1990s. Since the 1960s, most of Africa's regional schemes had given little attention to the dangers of state disintegration primarily because the norms of territorial integrity and sovereignty shielded these institutions from interference in domestic affairs.

The transformation of regional integration schemes into regional security mechanisms to stem the tide of civil wars began with an ECOWAS decision to send a Monitoring Group, ECOMOG, into Liberia in 1991. Throughout the almost decade-long engagement in the Liberian civil war, ECOWAS assumed security and peacekeeping functions under Nigerian leadership. During the same time, ECOWAS also intervened with mixed results in the civil war in Sierra Leone and Guinea-Bissau. These interventions sapped the resources of member countries and, in turn, produced regional strains that affected the agenda of integration (Arthur 2010; Adebajo 2002). In Southern Africa, SADC's intervention in Lesotho by South Africa and Botswana in 1998, and the engagement of Angola, Namibia, and Zimbabwe in the DRC between 1998 and 2000, were instances of the transformation of economic regionalism into security regionalism. Similarly, in the Horn of Africa, since its inception, IGAD was preoccupied with the mediation of conflicts in Sudan and Somalia.

The experience of ECOWAS, SADC, and IGAD in regional security coincided with a global push to build the capacity of African sub-regional organizations as vehicles of peacekeeping and conflict resolution. These donor-driven initiatives began in the early 1990s with the Clinton administration's programme on the African Crisis Response Initiative (ACRI), and have continued with various programmes by the European Union (EU) to boost the institutional capacity of African regional organizations in early warnings, preventive diplomacy, peace-keeping, and post-conflict reconstruction. In more recent years, the multiplication of mandates has been witnessed in external pressures on these institutions to engage in counter-terrorism efforts and anchor the African Standby Force (see Sarjoh Bah and Aning 2008; Youngs 2006; Mulugeta 2008).

Insecurity in Africa's sub-regions inevitably foisted conflict resolution roles on regional institutions, but the unanswered question has been whether these responsibilities dovetail with the long-term objectives of trade integration and investment mandates that these institutions were originally crafted to pursue. African sub-regional institutions such as ECOWAS, ECCAS, EAC, and SADC have understandably taken on security and conflict resolution roles which, while seeking to promote stability, may also in the short to medium term distract from the agenda of economic integration. As most of the civil conflicts started to wane in the mid-2000s, the salient issue that emerged on the sub-regional horizon was how to minimize the proliferation of security roles for regional economic communities (RECs) while they refocus on the priorities that initially animated integration. Some critics of the proliferation of security mandates have contended that framing the future trajectories of African regionalism will have to confront the question of separation of economic from security objectives, particularly since Africa is in the process of creating a new continental security architecture through the formation of the African Union (AU) in 2002 (Khadiagala 2006).

The creation of the AU marked another critical phase in Africa's regionalism at the turn of the new millennium. As part of the efforts to reignite the spirit of African problem-solving, the AU was restructured to meet the many challenges that Africa has confronted since the early 1990s. Breaking with the tradition established in the OAU Charter, the AU Constitutive Act envisages a common defence policy and regional intervention in response to war crimes, genocide, and crimes against humanity (Touray 2005). Building on the Abuja Treaty, the AU has designated the following RECs as the fulcrum for continental economic integration: COMESA, SADC, ECOWAS, IGAD, ECCAS, the Arab Maghreb Union (AMU), and the Senegalese Community for Aid and Self-Development (SENCAD). The AU has also established a new timeframe of 2034 by which the AEC would be operational. Perhaps as one of the initial steps toward the AEC, SADC, COMESA, and the ECA agreed in November 2008 to work toward creating Africa's largest trading bloc. At a meeting in Kampala, the three organizations agreed on a roadmap that provides for harmonization of trade and investment regulations among the three RECs with a combined population of over 527 million people and a combined GDP of US$624 billion. It also provides for consultation and the exchange of information and expertise, mobilization of financial resources to implement activities of common interest, work plans, and capacity building.

As part of Africa's determination for development and integration, the New Partnership for Africa's Development (NEPAD) sees RECs as the fundamental building blocks to achieve its multifaceted objectives. As it seeks to reduce poverty, promote sustainable socioeconomic development and growth, and foster regional and continental integration, NEPAD has made national, regional, and continental organizations the key implementers of its goals (Ikome 2007). At the January 2008 AU summit in Ethiopia, African leaders resolved to integrate NEPAD into AU structures as a way of promoting the continental ownership of NEPAD and making the AU the implementer of NEPAD programmes. The NEPAD framework is consistent with the principles of new regionalism to increase both the participation of the private sector through investments in a wide range of sectors and the direct involvement of civil society and non-state actors in regional and continental affairs. Within the context of the evolving reciprocal relations between NEPAD and RECs, there have been steps to apply NEPAD criteria in the identification and prioritization of programmes in RECs; deepening ownership of NEPAD within RECs; and reaching out to REC constituencies in the design and implementation of projects. In essence the RECs are the building blocks of NEPAD and are in a strategic position to guide the implementation of programmes and projects under NEPAD (see NEPAD 2001, 2008).

The resurgence of fast-track continental integration

The new structures and institutions embodied in the AU, NEPAD, and RECs have attempted to rebuild the division of labour between security and economic roles in integration that existed in the first three decades of African independence, when the OAU dealt primarily with political and security matters while sub-regional organizations focused on economic concerns. However, it would be difficult to obliterate the burgeoning security functions of RECs given their centrality in Africa's security initiatives. Although there have been more efforts to evolve better coordination mechanisms between the AU and the RECs in a wide range of areas, the problem of defining roles and mandates remains an impediment in the harmonization of policies among these institutions.

Since its formation, the AU has faced the most formidable challenge from a Libyan-led agenda for a Union government. Gaddafi forced debates on transcending AU structures to create a continental government in what has been billed as the grand debate on the Union government. Hardly had the AU institutions been given time to mature and prove themselves than discussions on the Union government began to overshadow its operations. The idea of a Union government came about when the AU Assembly of Heads of State in Abuja decided, in January 2005, to create a number of ministerial portfolios for the AU. Subsequently, the AU Assembly set up a committee of seven heads of state under President Yoweri Museveni of Uganda to examine the proposal. The committee hurriedly came up with a report that was submitted to the Assembly at the session held in Sirte, Libya, in July 2005. The report expressed the view that instead of creating ministerial portfolios in certain areas of the AU, Africa should work towards the formation of a United States of Africa.

Subsequently, Libya and its allies continued to press for the formation of additional AU committees and studies to examine the timeline for a Union government. However, the AU Executive Council report, submitted to the heads of state meeting in Addis Ababa, Ethiopia, in January 2007, revealed the wide rifts among members: 'all Member States accept the United States of Africa as a common and desirable goal [but] differences exist over the modalities and time frame for achieving this goal and the appropriate pace of integration' (Anon. 2007). These differences played out at the Accra summit of heads of state in July 2007. Although the summit reiterated the need to accelerate 'the economic and political integration of the African continent, including the formation of a Union Government for Africa with the ultimate objective of creating the United States of Africa', differences persisted as a majority of the AU conceded to accelerate the process set in motion by the Abuja Treaty of 1991 (see AU 2007). The Accra summit nonetheless established a ministerial committee to examine the functions of the Union government, identify its domains of competence, and define the relationship between it and the RECs.

When Gaddafi became the Chairman of the AU in 2009, he used the opportunity to harangue and cajole African leaders to agree to a central AU authority with powers over foreign affairs, economy, and defence. At the July 2009 summit in Sirte, this pressure yielded an announcement on the transformation of the AU Commission into an AU Authority. Facing objections from South Africa and Nigeria, Gaddafi pulled back from the immediate implementation of the transformation and, instead, requested the AU Commission to study the modalities of implementation. After the Sirte summit, Botswana's Vice-President Mompati Merafhe lashed out at Gaddafi's chairmanship of the AU, noting that:

> The chair has no respect for established procedures and processes of the African Union and this may be motivated by his burning desire to coerce everyone into the premature establishment of an African Union government ... Whilst the summit was forced to adopt a document most countries did not agree with, the test will be in its implementation.
>
> (Sudan Tribune *2009*)

In addition to resurrecting the old debates between continentalism and sub-regionalism, the debates on the Union government have overshadowed plans to revamp the professional competence and institutional integrity of the AU – problems identified in the AU audit report of 2008. While a bulk of the criticisms in the Audit Report were levelled at the dysfunctional nature of the AU Commission, the AU summit in Egypt accepted 19 recommendations, rejected 22, and referred 52 to the AU Commission for further study. To mollify the critics, President of the AU Commission Jean Ping outlined major reforms he sought to undertake to improve the AU, underscoring the importance of the recommendations in the AU audit report that gave priority to the values of competence, experience, efficiency, and justice (see AU 2008).

Regional integration and external actors

In the first and second phases of African regionalism, external actors, in particular donors, have featured prominently as providers of resources, investments, and markets. With the accession of African countries to the Lomé Convention in 1975, the debates against promoting Western ties that Nkrumah had assiduously propounded lost their policy significance. Over the years, funding through the Lomé process helped strengthen African regional institutions through investment in infrastructure and other projects with cross-regional impact. In most of the 1960s and 1970s multilateral and bilateral institutions devoted a portion of their development assistance to regional integration. As Africa faced severe economic crises in the 1980s, however, donor engagement in regional integration became less salient, particularly since adjustment policies were targeted to stabilize individual countries. The exceptions were SADCC (geared toward dependency reduction on minority regimes in southern Africa) and IGADD (with its focus on alleviating the problems of drought and desertification in the Horn of Africa).

Donor re-engagement with regional integration has occurred as part of boosting the ability of African institutions to strengthen economic reforms and participate effectively in the new global economy. As Goldstein notes:

> the term regionalism itself is acquiring a new meaning. Integration agreements are now about much more than reducing tariffs and quotas and explicitly include the goal of removing other barriers that segment markets and impede the free flow of goods, services, and factors of production; they are outward-looking, instead of attempting to apply to more than one country the import-substitution model of the past …
>
> *(Goldstein 2002: 11)*

A dominant issue in contemporary African regionalism is the impact of the Economic Partnership Agreements (EPAs) mandated as part of the Cotonou Partnership Agreement, the successor to the Lomé Agreements between Europe and African countries. Signed in 2000, the Cotonou Agreement reflected the changes in economic relationships between Europe and Africa, with the expansion of the EU and pressure from the World Trade Organization (WTO) to eliminate the long-standing generous trade preferences for African countries in EU markets. The Agreement envisaged the phasing out of the trade arrangements by January 2008 and their replacement by EPAs that would fulfil the requirements of the WTO.

Since the accession of the Cotonou Agreement, negotiations for EPAs have constituted a source of strife between the EU and African regional blocs. In conception, EPAs seek the establishment of new trading blocs among African states to negotiate free trade areas (FTAs) with Europe and better coordination of EU aid programmes with the EPAs (Draper 2007). Europe has frequently criticized African regionalism for overlapping memberships, incompatible goals, and unwieldy mandates. It has thus tried to project the EPAs as a means to rationalize African regionalism, contending that EPAs can only flourish in sub-regional contexts with distinct memberships and dense economic interactions. This has placed countries such as Tanzania in a quandary, forced to choose negotiating an EPA in SADC, the East African Customs Union (EACU), or the East and Southern Africa (ESA) grouping. Although in 2003 SADC proposed that Tanzania should continue negotiating EPAs under SADC, the EU demanded negotiations under the EACU. Similarly, Europe has pressured Kenya and Uganda to quit COMESA, despite the reluctance of these countries to negotiate under the EA Customs because of the infancy of the bloc and the weak economies of the member states (Edwin 2007).

Although EPAs are supposed to expand intra-regional trade and trade links with Europe, Stevens has observed that they may erect new trade barriers among African countries, defeating the objective of integration:

> By increasing the stakes, EPAs may make regional liberalization less likely. Some countries willing to remove barriers to imports from their neighbours with similar economies may be unwilling to offer the same terms to highly competitive (and possibly dumped) EU imports. Regional groups may splinter between those willing to liberalize towards the EU and the others.
>
> *(Stevens 2006: 447)*

Questions about the shape of EPAs and their impact on RECs and African regionalism in general will take time to unfold, but already the negotiations have exposed some profound tensions facing the construction of regional institutions. As part of the initiative to galvanize African efforts to understand the long-term implications of EPAs on African regionalism, the ECA has been organizing expert workshops across Africa to evaluate the effects of EPAs by focusing on issues of coordination and harmonization, as well as reviewing questions of trade facilitation, infrastructure development, and product quality. At the time of writing, individual states or groups of states had signed interim EPAs but permanent agreements had been delayed due to wrangles over the effects of trade liberalization on African economies.

Less certain on the trajectories of regionalism is also the involvement of new actors such as China. Although China has stepped up engagement with African countries on trade, invest-ment, and development assistance (see Alden, this volume), it is only beginning to address regional institutions. Since it hosted the annual meeting of the African Development Bank (AfDB) in Shanghai in 2007, China has signalled its interest to strengthen its ties to African regional and sub-regional organizations such as ECOWAS, COMESA, EAC, and SADC. For instance, in May 2008 a delegation of ministers responsible for EAC visited China to learn from the Chinese experience in infrastructure development and to garner support and partnership in developing the region's infrastructures as part of the overall EAC Infrastructure Development Plan. Under this Plan, the EAC seeks to develop roads, railways, civil aviation, and telecommunications to achieve higher standards of living and make the region competitive and attractive for sustainable investment, trade, and development. Similarly, China and the ECOWAS Bank for Investment and Development (EBID) signed a memorandum of understanding (MOU) in June 2007 to establish markets in China and the ECOWAS region that will enable their citizens to exploit trade and investment opportunities. As part of this initiative, China held an Economic and Trade Forum with ECOWAS in September 2008. At the continental level, China has associated itself closely with the ideas behind NEPAD.

Traditional multilateral actors such as the World Bank have recently recommitted to strengthening regional institutions in Africa. In September 2008 the World Bank signed an MOU with the AU aimed at deepening collaboration in the areas of regional integration, governance, post-conflict countries, relations with the diaspora, and HIV/AIDS and other communicable diseases. Collaboration is intended to be result focused, with the World Bank's technical expertise complementing the AU's political leadership. The MOU provides that spe-cific arrangements for individual activities in each substantive area will be set out in jointly formulated work plans, and the two institutions will periodically assess the effectiveness of the collaboration. The MOU also provides an overall framework for collaboration over an initial five-year period in each of these areas, which are priorities for both the World Bank and the AU.

Conclusion

African experiments with collective regional institutions for prosperity and security have been marked by both integrative and disintegrative trends. Geographical and cultural proximities constitute the impetus for integration in addition to the necessity of managing problems occasioned by small economies and political fragility. Disintegrative dynamics on the other hand have inhered in Africa's political diversity, fixation with national sovereignty, and inability to transform the ideals of regionalism into meaningful programmes. Over the years, regionalism for development and continental unity has entailed reconciling the opportunities of geographical and cultural contiguity with the divisive questions of sovereignty and political compatibility. These trends have been mediated by leadership, vision, and compromises around institutions and programmes that seek to build collective synergies, promote cooperation, and foster regional identities.

The current and future dimensions of regional integration in Africa are shaped largely by past practices established since the 1960s. The structural problems of underdevelopment, external orientation of primarily agricultural economies, and inadequate infrastructure for trade and investment have remained a constant in evaluating the obstacles of RECs to achieve the objectives of development. While some RECs have made efforts to deepen integration by creating institutions such as customs unions and free trade and incorporating more voices in integration debates, the first- and second-generation constraints loom large on the landscape of regionalism. These constraints are compounded by the ambivalence surrounding the construction of an AEC. Although most proponents of the AEC posit RECs as transitional vehicles for its realization, there are profound questions about whether RECs require sufficient time to evolve effective supra-national institutions before they are merged into the AEC. Timetables that anticipate the realization of the AEC do not necessarily take into the account the hurdles in constructing viable RECs. The 2008 MOU among the EAC, SADC, and COMESA for an incremental merger may point in the direction of rethinking the timetable for the AEC, but these institutions still have a lot of work to do in realizing this objective and, more importantly, in getting member states to buy into the merger project.

The future of regional integration hinges on the resolution of the tension between continentalism and sub-regionalism, a discourse that perennially resurfaces in African inter-state relations. As the debates on the Union government since the 1960s reveal, strong leaders with only tenuous links to their domestic constituencies have been the major proponents of continentalist visions. Nkrumah attempted to force the grand idea of African unity before the military overthrew him in 1966 (see Khadiagala 2010), and Gaddafi ultimately suffered the same fate, as domestic opponents contested his rule and challenged his fixation with the Union government in Africa. Of Gaddafi's autocratic allies in the AU, Senegal's Wade has already lost power, and Burkina Faso's Blaise Compaoré is unlikely to have the mettle to pursue the extravagant agenda of the Union government on his own. The defeat of continentalists may thus allow the sub-regionalists to forge ahead with the slow but steady process of building regional institutions that balance inter-governmentalism and supranationalism.

Notes

1 For some of the seminal debates on the subjects see Ernest Haas (1970), Asante (1997), and Gruhn (1979).
2 See, for instance, Balassa (1961), Viner (1950), and Robson (1998).

3 For wide-ranging discussions on colonial schemes see Green and Krishna (1967), Robson (1967), and Roland (1967).
4 For the evolution of European relations with Africa during this period see Zartman (1971).
5 For wide-ranging analyses of the ECA's position and the Lagos Plan see UNECA (1984) and Onwuka and Sesay (1985).
6 On recent trends in East Africa see Odhiambo (2011).

Bibliography

Adebajo, A. (2002) *Building Peace in West Africa: Liberia, Sierra Leone, and Guinea Bissau*, Boulder, CO: Lynne Rienner Publishers.
Anon. (2007) 'Grand Debate on Union Government for Africa Starts', *The Statesman* (Accra), 26 June.
Arthur, P. (2010) 'ECOWAS and Regional Peacekeeping Integration in West Africa: Lessons for the Future', *Africa Today* 57(2): 2–24.
Asante, S.K.B. (1997) '*Regionalism and Africa's Development: Expectations, Reality, and Challenges*', London: MacMillan.
AU (African Union) (2007) *Assembly of the African Union: Decisions and Declarations at the July 1–3, 2007*, Accra, Ghana.
——(2008) *Assembly of the African Union: Decisions and Declarations at the June 30–July 3, 2008*, Sharm el-Sheikh, Egypt.
Balassa, B. (1961) *The Theory of Economic Integration*, Baltimore, MD: Johns Hopkins University Press.
Draper, P. (2007) *EU–Africa Trade Relations: The Political Economy of Economic Partnership Agreements*, Brussels: Jan Tumlir Policy Essay No. 02.
Edwin, W. (2007) 'EU wants Dar to Decide Under Which Regional Bloc it Will Negotiate EPAs', *The East African*, Nairobi, 3 April.
Goldstein, A. (2002) 'The New Regionalism in Sub-Saharan Africa: More than Meets the Eye?' Policy Brief No. 20, Paris: OECD Development Centre.
Green, R.H. and Krishna, K.G. (1967) *Economic Cooperation in Africa: Retrospect and Prospects*, London: Oxford University Press.
Green, R.H. and Seidman, A. (1968) *Unity of Poverty? The Economics of Pan-Africanism*, London: Penguin.
Gruhn, I.V. (1979) *Regionalism Reconsidered: The Economic Commission for Africa*, Boulder, CO: Westview.
Haas, E. (1970) 'The Study of Regional Integration: Reflections on the Joy and Anguish of Pretheorizing', *International Organization* 24(4): 606–46.
Ikome, F. (2007) *From the Lagos Plan of Action to the New Partnership for Africa's Development: The Political Economy of African Regional Initiatives*, Midrand: Institute for Global Dialogue.
Jeffries, K. (2007) 'The Process of Monetary Integration in the SADC Region', *Journal of Southern African Studies* 33(1): 83–107.
Johnson, O.E.G. (1991) 'Economic Integration in Africa: Enhancing Prospects for Success', *Journal of Modern African Studies* 29(1): 1–26.
Khadiagala, G.M. (2006) 'Western Views of African Responses to Economic, Social, and Environmental Dimensions of the Global Agenda', in M. Mwagiru and O. Oculi (eds) *Rethinking Global Security: An African Perspective*, Nairobi: Heinrich Boll Foundation.
——(2010) 'Two Moments in African Political Thought: Ideas in African International Relations', *South African Journal of International Affairs* 23(3): 375–86.
Legum, C. (1975) 'The Organization of African Unity-Success or Failure?' *International Affairs* 51(2): 208–19.
Mead, D.C. (1969) 'Economic Cooperation in East Africa', *Journal of Modern African Studies* 7(2): 277–87.
Meyers, D.B. (1974) 'Intra-Regional Conflict Management by the Organization of African Unity', *International Organization* 28(3): 345–73.
Mistry, P. (2000) 'Africa's Record of Regional Cooperation and Integration', *African Affairs* 99(397): 553–73.
Mshomba, R.E. (2000) *Africa in the Global Economy*, Boulder, CO: Lynne Rienner Publishers.
Mugomba, A.T. (1978) 'Regional Organizations and African Underdevelopment: The Collapse of the East African Community', *Journal of Modern African Studies* 16(2): 261–72.
Mulugeta, A. (2008) 'Promises and Challenges of a Sub-Regional Force for the Horn of Africa', *International Peacekeeping* 15(2): 171–84.
NEPAD (The New Partnership for Africa's Development) (2001) 'The New Partnership for Africa's Development', Midrand: NEPAD Secretariat, October 2001.

——(2008) 'The AU/NEPAD African Action Plan', 10th Africa Partnership Forum, www.oecd.org/ dataoecd/28/10/41084201.pdf (accessed 4 January 2012).

OAU (Organization of African Unity) (1991) *The Abuja Treaty Toward the Establishment of the African Economic Community*, Addis Ababa: OAU.

Odhiambo, W. (2011) 'The Distribution of Costs and Benefits in Trade in the Context of the East African Integration Process', in Society for International Development, *East African Integration: Dynamics of Equity in Trade, Education, and Media*, Nairobi: SID.

Ojo, O.J.B. (1980) 'Nigeria and the Formation of ECOWAS', *International Organization* 34(4): 571–604.

Onwuka, R.I. and Sesay, A. (1985) *The Future of Regionalism in Africa*, London: MacMillan.

Robson, P. (1967) 'Economic Integration in Southern Africa', *Journal of Modern African Studies* 5(4): 469–90.

——(1985) 'Regional Integration and the Crisis in Sub-Saharan Africa', *Journal of Modern African Studies* 23(4): 603–22.

——(1998) *The Economics of International Integration*, London: Routledge.

Roland, J. (1967) 'The Experience of Integration in French-Speaking Africa', in A. Hazelwood (ed.) *African Integration and Disintegration*, New York, NY: Oxford University Press.

Sarjo Bah, A. and Aning, K. (2008) 'US Peace Operations Policy in Africa: From ACRI to AFRICOM', *International Peacekeeping* 15(1): 118–32.

Stevens, C. (2006) 'The EU, Africa, and Economic Partnership Agreements: Unintended Consequences of Policy Leverage', *Journal of Modern African Studies* 44(3): 441–58.

Sudan Tribune (2009) 'Botswana's VP Slams Libya, Claim Summit Failed Africa', 6 July, www.sudantribune. com/Botswana-s-VP-slams-Libya-says-AU,31740 (accessed 21 May 2012).

Touray, O.A. (2005) 'The Common African Defence and Security Policy', *African Affairs* 104(417): 635–56.

UNECA (United Nations Economic Commission for Africa) (1963) 'Approaches to African Economic Integration', *Journal of Modern African Studies* 1(3): 395–402.

——(1984) *Proposals for Strengthening Economic Integration in West Africa*, Addis Ababa: UNECA.

Viner, J. (1950) *The Customs Union Issue*, New York, NY: Carnegie Endowment for International Peace.

Yansane, A.Y. (1977) 'West African Economic Integration: Is ECOWAS the Answer?' *Africa Today* 24(3): 43–59.

Youngs, R. (2006) 'The EU and Conflict in West Africa', *European Foreign Affairs Review* 11: 333–52.

Zartman, I.W. (1971) *The Politics of Trade Negotiations between Africa and the Economic Community: The Weak Confronts the Strong*, Princeton, NJ: Princeton University Press.

30

TERRORISM, SECURITY, AND THE STATE

Ken Menkhaus

The actual threat posed by terrorism in Africa can be overstated, but it is difficult to exaggerate the impact that post-9/11 security concerns have had on the way analysts and practitioners understand and engage with Africa. While the new preoccupation with security threats in Africa manifests itself most explicitly as the counter-terrorism agenda, it encompasses a much wider range of international security concerns, some pre-dating the global 'war on terror'. Analytically, this has meant that a growing portion of research and analysis on Africa interprets the continent through a security lens. In the policy world, the trend has been toward the 'securitization' of humanitarian relief, development aid, state-building and democratization programmes, and peace-building and post-conflict initiatives (Curtis, this volume), as security priorities have subordinated and redefined those agendas. The reshuffling of priorities has produced stormy debates and power struggles inside donor governments and the United Nations (UN) system. At the same time, it has also brought external security actors – especially the US Department of Defense – into a much more robust role on the continent than was the case in the 1990s, when Africa was generally seen to have marginal importance to US and global security.

The securitization of external relations with Africa has also reshaped the behaviour and calculations of African political actors. In a reprise of political manoeuvring during the Cold War, some African governments and armed groups have sought to harness Western counter-terrorism concerns to advance more parochial interests – to demonize or eliminate local rivals, secure military aid, or deflect criticism of authoritarianism or human rights abuses. In other cases, African actors have energetically resisted external and local attempts to reframe Africa as a global security threat. In short, almost every topic examined in this *Handbook* has been affected, and in some cases transformed, by the rise of global security agendas since 2001. Getting both security analysis and security policies right in Africa is thus a matter of high importance. Unfortunately, that has not always been the case.

Contested concepts

All three of the concepts under consideration here – terrorism, security, and the state – are deeply contested. This has tended to result in analysts and observers talking past, rather than with, one another. Defining terrorism in the abstract is **not** especially contentious, but applying the label to specific groups certainly is. A number of African parties and governments – including, most notably, the African National Congress (ANC) of South Africa – were once armed resistance movements labelled as 'terrorists' by the West. More recently, the designation has tended to be applied to armed groups that attack Western targets, while other armed groups that have engaged in terrorist tactics against local populations or governments have not been so designated. Not surprisingly, many African observers are sceptical about what they see as the selective application of the terrorist label. Some of the worst instances of terrorism in Africa in recent decades have been conducted or sponsored by African governments themselves, sometimes with external support. The extensive governmental use of unaccountable paramilitaries – the most infamous of which was the Sudanese government's reliance on and support to the 'janjaweed' in the ethnic-cleansing campaign in Darfur – has produced horrific acts of terrorism against targeted civilians. For most African communities, the threat posed by state-sponsored terrorism is a more immediate danger than the remote machinations of al-Qaeda. By contrast, for most Western governments, terrorism in Africa is assumed to be about al-Qaeda, its affiliates, and other extremist Islamic movements on the continent.

Security is also a disputed concept. The debates surrounding this term boil down to two questions: 'whose security?' and 'security from what?' Conventional security studies focuses exclusively on security of the state against a physical attack. This national security perspective emphasizes either the security of African governments, or the states outside the continent – in this case Western states. However, the notion of human security – the physical protection of local communities from the threat of violence – has widened the definition of security in recent years. Security studies has broadened its focus to encompass a much wider range of threats, including disease, criminal violence, malnutrition, environmental degradation, and displacement. In Africa, where much of the continent has endured and emerged from horrific civil wars in the past 20 years, there is a particular emphasis on post-conflict security problems. Shockingly high levels of post-conflict violence in places like the Democratic Republic of Congo (DRC) have highlighted the chronic levels of insecurity in conditions of 'not war not peace' and underscore the ubiquity of criminal and political violence in areas beset by unresolved local disputes, small arms proliferation, and weak governance (Muggah 2009).

Finally, the concept of the state in Africa has been contested since independence. In some instances, what passes for a sovereign state is in fact a shell of a government controlled by a narrow band of political elites and/or ethnic interests with little legitimacy in the eyes of its citizens. In such a context, the very notion of state security becomes problematic and easily conflated with regime survival. In cases where African regimes are predatory and constitute a major threat to the security of portions of their own population, attempts to improve the state's security sector by outside actors can actually heighten the insecurity of the citizenry (Le Sage 2010: 74; Call 2008). In addition, most African states suffer from serious capacity deficits; in the worst cases, African states are unable to exercise even the most minimal powers expected of a sovereign authority. No fewer than 14 of the 20 states ranked at the top of the 2011 'Failed States Index' are located in sub-Saharan Africa (Foreign Policy 2011), hence most of the literature on the causes and problems of state failure are, with a few notable exceptions, virtually synonymous with assessment of the problem of weak governance in Africa. The failure and fragility of most African states – manifested in corruption, an ineffective rule of law, and poorly paid and controlled security-sector forces – is widely understood to be a major security threat to both the international community and to local citizens.

'Ungoverned space' and security threats

The most consequential theory linking terrorism, security, and the state in Africa involves making a threat assessment around the concept of 'ungoverned space'. In the months following the terrorist attacks of 11 September 2001 and America's subsequent military operation to oust al-Qaeda and the Taliban from Afghanistan, US counter-terrorism strategy anticipated that al-Qaeda would disperse and decentralize in new locations. The areas of greatest concern were what came to be called ungoverned space – territory beyond the effective control of state law enforcement, where al-Qaeda could presumably operate with impunity. This theory, and the national security strategy that emerged from it, was based on a plausible assumption that al-Qaeda needed two things: a physical base from which to operate; and one with as little government capacity as possible. The seminal 2002 US National Security Strategy encoded this reasoning, famously observing that the United States was 'now threatened less by conquering states than we are by failing ones' (White House 2002: 1). The precise link between failed states and terrorist safe havens subsequently became the focus of intense US government analysis, with more refined assessments eventually emerging from the Department of Defense's 'Ungoverned Areas Project' (Lamb 2007). Even so, the basic premise of the 2002 National Security Strategy has endured, as evidenced by the 2009 remarks of Ambassador Daniel Benjamin, the State Department Coordinator for Counter-Terrorism: 'Weakly-governed or entirely ungoverned areas are a major safe haven for al Qaida and its allies ... The problem of un- and under-governed spaces is one of the toughest ones this and future administrations will face' (Benjamin 2009).

The post-9/11 focus on denying al-Qaeda access to safe haven in weak states had several immediate consequences for Africa. First, portions of sub-Saharan Africa came under close scrutiny as likely sanctuaries for al-Qaeda cells. States that were institutionally weak, featured large, poor, and/or aggrieved Muslim populations, and possessed a pre-existing Salafist or Islamic jihadist movement made the top of the shortlist. Somalia met all those criteria, as did a number of other areas now seen as hotspots, including coastal Kenya and Tanzania, eastern Ethiopia, northern Nigeria, and the Sahel states. More generally, Islamic Africa – long treated as marginal in both academic and diplomatic circles – suddenly gained much greater attention from the West, and the United States in particular.

This new attention to Islamic Africa and to the 'hotspot' areas noted above prompted a major shift of Western government defence and intelligence assets to these countries of concern. This stood in stark contrast to the 1990s, when Western government analysis of and intelligence on Africa was slashed. The new attention to Islamic Africa also triggered a flood of commissioned studies of existing Islamist movements, al-Qaeda's presence in Africa, radicalization of African Muslims, African security sectors, and other related fields. Long a neglected field, African security studies mushroomed in importance, with new journals, workshops, and projects devoted to it. Academic area specialists with expertise in an African 'country of concern' suddenly found themselves awash with requests for studies for think tanks, contractors, and governments. They were joined by a flood of newcomers who quickly retooled to meet demand (Toolis 2004). In a sense, the academic enterprise in Africa became partially 'securitized', as research funding and consultancies became increasingly driven by counter-terrorism agendas. Africa's hotspots also became the target of much more frequent – though sometimes superficial – coverage by a host of defence monitoring and analysis publications.

In addition, the US military devoted much greater resources to the continent: the creation of a new Combatant Command devoted exclusively to Africa (AFRICOM), based in Stuttgart Germany; the establishment of a military base at Camp Lemonier in Djibouti, which hosts several thousand US force personnel comprising the Combined Joint Task Force – Horn of Africa (CJTF-HOA); the Trans-Saharan Counter-Terrorism Partnership (successor to the Pan-Sahel Initiative of 2004); and a robust increase in both Department of Defense (DOD) military attachés in US embassies, and training and support programmes to African militaries (Le Sage 2007). This major expansion of the presence and role of the US military sparked sharply negative reactions from many African observers and leaders, who feared it represented the militarization of US diplomacy. The creation of AFRICOM – seemingly an innocuous improvement of the Combatant Command structure, at least in the eyes of DOD officials – proved especially contentious, provoking a storm of criticism and debate in Africa. Most of the US military engagement on the continent has been in the form of military training and support, and some civil affairs work, but in a number of cases the US military and Central Intelligence Agency (CIA) have engaged in 'kinetic' operations against terrorist targets, especially in Somalia. The CIA also operates an interrogation facility in the Mogadishu airport in Somalia that has recently come under media scrutiny (Scahill 2011). In addition, parts of Africa have seen an increase in the number of private security firms operating on contract with foreign governments, international companies, or the host government. This trend has been especially pronounced in Somalia.

At the same time, some African governments have redirected their energies toward counter-terrorism, sometimes with substantial support from Western governments. One of the most dramatic instances of this has been the deployment of an African Union peacekeeping force to Somalia (AMISOM). The peacekeeping force's mandate includes protecting the Transitional Federal Government (TFG) and supporting its stabilization efforts. In reality, the 17,000-strong force, composed mainly of Ugandan, Burundian, and Kenyan troops, has (with support from private security firms) mainly been engaged in a prolonged war against the jihadist group al-Shabaab, which is committed to driving both the TFG and AMISOM out of Mogadishu. Some observers accuse Uganda and Burundi of serving as surrogates for Western militaries in Somalia and of being motivated by parochial economic interests. AMISOM's supporters dispute this, arguing that they are acting to promote stability in the troubled Horn of Africa.

Some African counter-terrorism operations have been unilateral. Prior to AMISOM's deployment to Somalia, the government of Ethiopia launched a major military offensive in stateless Somalia in December 2006 to oust what it believed to be a dangerous Islamist move-ment known as the Islamic Courts Union (ICU). The ensuing two-year Ethiopian military occupation and counter-insurgency against al-Shabaab plunged Somalia into a horrific crisis from which it has yet to recover, and ultimately fuelled the ascent of al-Shabaab from a small militia into the most radical and dangerous al-Qaeda affiliate on the continent. The ill-fated Ethiopian occupation of Somalia serves as a reminder that counter-terrorism operations are susceptible to the law of unintended consequences. Despite the problems encountered by Ethiopia in 2007 and 2008, both Kenya and Ethiopia sent their armed forces into southern Somalia in 2011 and 2012 in pursuit of al-Shabaab, relying heavily on local proxies. These more recent, unilateral counter-terrorism operations have encountered difficulties but did not trigger broad public mobilization by Somalis in support of al-Shabaab.

Securitization of state-building

Western counter-terrorism policies to deny al-Qaeda a base in Africa have sparked a security-driven focus on state-building, with the aim of strengthening local capacity to monitor, disrupt, and prevent terrorist activities. In the past, weak and failed African states had been seen as primarily a humanitarian problem or a constraint on development; after a brief and highly unsuccessful foray into state-building in Somalia in 1993–94, the United States and the West had shown little appetite for 'fixing failed states' in Africa. In the aftermath of 9/11, that changed. The Bush Administration's disdain for nation-building was replaced by urgent prioritization of state-building programmes in weak states. Selected African governments became major beneficiaries of this policy reversal. A significant portion of Western development budgets in Africa was devoted to state capacity building. Most of the work of AFRICOM consisted of military-to-military assistance in the form of training and equipment. Donor states and UN specialized agencies took on projects in security-sector reform that had them involved in equipping and training police and engaging with security forces to a degree that would have been unthinkable a decade earlier. The entire enterprise to strengthen the capacity of African states' police, military, and judiciary in order to build up local partners in the global war on terror represented the securitization of state-building in Africa.

The approach has enjoyed successes, but has also brewed controversies and seen its share of setbacks. First, it quickly encountered criticism when some of the security-sector capacity it had developed was misused by partner governments against their own populations. The heavy-handed Ethiopian crackdown in 2005 against protesters following a disputed election was the most dramatic of these incidents, but hardly the only one. This raised concerns that capacity-building projects had failed to consider the question 'capacity to do what?' In some cases the answer was to use the capacity against domestic rivals, not terrorists. Observers worried that securitized state-building would set back hard-earned democratic gains on the continent, as regimes exploited their new role as partners in the global war on terror to consolidate power, eliminate rivals, and curtail civil liberties. Others pointed out that state-building in the name of counter-terrorism presumed that the recipient government shared a common agenda with Western donors, when in fact they were often much more concerned with their own political survival and local threats, not with al-Qaeda. Put another way, the United States and some of its African allies were actually fighting somewhat different wars, so that counter-terrorism assistance was likely to be put to different uses than what the donor intended. Disputes between the government of Ethiopia and the United States over American contact with the Ogaden National Liberation Front – a movement the United States sees as a potential bulwark against al-Shabaab in the eastern Horn, but which Ethiopia views as a domestic terrorist group and a more immediate threat to its own security – is but one example.

Questions were also raised about the political will of some recipient governments to commit to state-building (Le Sage 2010: 73). The securitized state-building agenda assumed that the problem of Africa's weak states was a matter of capacity, not will. For many policymakers and analysts in the West, the idea that a government would not seek to maximize its power seemed counter-intuitive. Yet developments in a number of state-building settings, both in and beyond Africa, demonstrated that African government leaders often had powerful reasons not to extend the reach of their government. In some cases, leaders presided over lucrative criminal economies and so had little interest in promoting the rule of law; in others, leaders correctly surmised that efforts to extend state authority to remote, thinly populated, 'ungoverned' hinterlands was simply not economical; in still others, leaders were keen to embrace state-building in the name of counter-terrorism, but only as an ongoing income-generating project, not as an outcome (Reno 2000; Herbst 2000). In such cases – of which the Somali TFG is probably the best example – securitized state-building led to a perplexing case of moral hazard, in which local actors shared with the United States a powerful interest in addressing terrorism, but little interest at all in defeating it, as that would have the unwanted effect of reducing their strategic importance to the United States and would dry up military and state-building assistance (Menkhaus 2010c). Finally, some African heads of state resisted military aid aimed at strengthening their security sector out of concern that elite counter-terrorism units could create a rule of law unto themselves, accountable more to the external donor than to their own government. Recent research suggests that African heads of state tend to make decisions about the composition and capacity of their security sectors based on calculations on regime survival, even if that produces a greater likelihood of ethnic grievances, insurgencies, and civil war (Roessler 2011).

Time and again, Western donor agencies and militaries were perplexed and frustrated with the failure of some African governments to respond as they expected as partners in counter-terrorism and in state-building. These Western expectations reflected an inadequate understanding of the political economy of the state across much of the continent and a lack of appreciation for the ways in which local leaders sometimes view the state, the rule of law, and terrorist threats through a very different lens than do Western donors.

The privileging of state-building as a security issue also had major and unwanted implications for development agencies as they came under donor pressure to channel their aid through state agencies. This raised a difficult policy question: when should external actors work *with* African states in pursuit of their objectives, and when is it appropriate or necessary to work *around* the state? Many observers trace almost all of Africa's most pressing crises – food insecurity, humanitarian emergencies, underdevelopment, civil war, criminality, and terrorist threats – to the weakness of African states. For this school of thought the answer is clear: all external assistance and interventions must be designed to strengthen the capacity and legitimacy of the state. However, working with weak and sometimes venal state authorities comes at a cost: reduced effectiveness, reduced efficiency, and loss of neutrality, especially in cases where the state is party to an ongoing armed conflict. Not surprisingly, development and humanitarian agencies have been among the most vocal critics of efforts by donor governments to harness their aid in pursuit of state-building objectives. Claiming that the push to strengthen African states has been mainly driven by counter-terrorism concerns, these actors argue that pressure to channel humanitarian aid through states essentially 'securitizes' development and humanitarian aid as well, a policy that jeopardizes their neutrality in conflict situations (Muggah *et al.* 2010).

Importantly, though, schools of thought on the question of working with or around Africa's weak states do not fall neatly into counter-terrorism, development, democratization, or humanitarian camps. Counter-terrorism initiatives simultaneously work with and around the state, sometimes working at cross-purposes, and while some development agencies resist linkage of their operations to state-centric stabilization agendas, other development actors have eagerly embraced the securitization of their work as a means of attracting more funding.

Re-thinking ungoverned space

Meanwhile, the flurry of state capacity building that ensued following the 9/11 attacks rushed past the fundamental question of whether the threat assessment on which policy was based was in fact empirically correct. Were zones of ungoverned space in Africa in fact attractive safe havens for a dispersed al-Qaeda?

Counter-intuitively, the eventual answer was no, or at least not exactly. As evidence of al-Qaeda's operations and presence on the African continent was collected and assessed, it became increasingly clear that zones of complete state collapse proved to be just as 'non-permissive' an environment for terrorists as they were for international aid agencies. Close examination of al-Qaeda's experience in north-east Africa in 1991–96, a period when the organization was based in Sudan, revealed that the group's attempts to penetrate Somalia – which by 1991 was the scene of complete state collapse, massive displacement, civil war, and famine – met only setbacks, acrimony, and frustration (Watts *et al.* 2007). Al-Qaeda operatives were stymied by clannism, local distrust, corruption, logistical headaches, and disease, eventually prompting one operative to ask his superiors if efforts to build a training camp could be relocated back to Sudan, which was both safer and cheaper. Somalia's 'ungoverned space' was anything but conducive for al-Qaeda's nascent East Africa cell, which by 1995 withdrew from Somalia to Kenya (Menkhaus and Shapiro 2010). Instead, it was in neighbouring Kenya where the East Africa al-Qaeda (EAAQ) cell thrived. There it established residencies, set up businesses and charity fronts, rented light aircraft, intermarried, and planned and executed several major terrorist attacks – including the bombings of the US Embassies in Nairobi and Dar es Salaam in August 1998. Kenya in the 1990s had a weak state and a highly corrupt police force. It teemed with foreign missionaries, aid workers, businesspeople, and tourists, so foreign terrorists could easily go unnoticed; and Kenya was replete with soft Western targets. By contrast, Somalia featured almost no Western targets and had almost no foreign visitors, making it much harder for non-Somali operatives to go unnoticed. It seems al-Qaeda prefers a weak, penetrable government to no government at all. 'Not all weak and failing states are afflicted by terrorism', notes Stewart Patrick, 'nor are all weak and failing states equally attractive to transnational terrorists. In fact, terrorists are likely to find *weak but functioning* states like Kenya or Pakistan more congenial long term bases of operation' (Patrick 2011: 10). Instead, political commitment on the part of a weak government appears to be a more decisive factor in determining its vulnerability to terrorist infiltration (ibid.: 11).

In addition, the concept of ungoverned space came under scrutiny from those who challenged the premise that zones of state failure were 'ungoverned'. The dominant image of Africa's zones of state failure were as regions of lawless, violent anarchy. In reality, researchers and relief agencies pointed out that local African communities are not passive victims of state collapse, but quickly construct informal systems of 'governance without government' in an effort to provide some level of security and order (Menkhaus 2006–07, 2010b). Areas beyond the effective reach of the state in Africa usually feature a patchwork of hybrid governance arrangements. Some of these are impressive grassroots efforts enjoying strong legitimacy in the community; others are little more than warlord fiefdoms (Andersen *et al.* 2007). In either case, they are not Hobbesian anarchy.

The ubiquity of what Crawford and Miscik (2010) call 'mezzanine rulers' in weak states poses a range of interesting policy challenges. For African governments, the choice is whether to view these often powerful non-state actors as impediments to the expansion of the state's authority or as potential partners in negotiated governance arrangements. For Western governments pursuing counter-terrorism agendas, the choice is whether to partner with government security forces with limited capacity, or to circumvent the state and work directly with armed non-state partners in pursuit of terrorist groups. In the long term, all agree that an effective state security sector is key to preventing and monitoring terrorism and international criminal activities, but the building up of state capacity is a lengthy process. In the interim, more expedient logic often applies, enticing Western governments to work around rather than with weak African governments. As was learned in Afghanistan, this can inadvertently work against state-building, by strengthening forces opposing the expansion of state authority and incentivizing them to remain autonomous from the state. This has been particularly notable in the case of Somalia, where US and AMISOM counter-terrorism efforts have often relied on non-state armed groups as a more effective partner than the TFG.

Thus, despite mounting evidence from the field, conventional thinking on state-building, state failure, and security still presumes a compatibility between state-building and counter-terrorism objectives, and still clings to the questionable assumption that ungoverned space is a more attractive lair for transnational criminal and terrorist groups than are weak states. Deeply embedded Western belief systems about the nature of states, interests, and armed conflict fare poorly when they collide with the messy realities of 'post-modern' political violence in Africa and elsewhere (Keen 2012).

'Hearts and minds' – the securitization of development and humanitarian aid

Another piece of conventional wisdom in security studies – especially in counter-terrorism doctrine – is the importance of winning the 'hearts and minds' of local communities. This 'civ-mil' (civilian-military) work typically involves harnessing development and humanitarian projects with the specific intent of addressing local needs (especially youth unemployment), reducing local grievances, and combating perceptions of marginalization that insurgents can exploit. By demonstrating to recipient communities that their loyalty, support, and cooperation pay dividends, and by generating jobs that reduce the number of easy recruits into armed groups, the aim of 'hearts and minds' campaigns is to inoculate local communities for radicalization and render them non-permissive environments for terrorists or insurgents. This latter objective is based on the very important observation that the single most effective deterrent to terrorism is community policing.

The 'hearts and minds' strategy explicitly melds counter-terrorism operations with development and humanitarian projects, whether executed by civil affairs teams in the military or in partnership with development firms. In the US government this is referred to as the 'whole of government' approach, an effort to ensure that the '3 Ds' – defence, diplomacy, and development – are all working toward a common goal within a common strategy. Not surprisingly, this securitization of development assistance in Africa has met with resistance and alarm from many development and humanitarian actors. They insist that this approach in fact subordinates development aid to defence objectives. They argue further that the direct linkage between development projects and security operations creates enormous security risks for aid workers. They also question the effectiveness and appropriateness of aid projects driven by short-term, military objectives.

Beyond the debate over the securitization of development and humanitarian aid for counter-terrorism purposes, an equally pressing question has received less attention: winning 'hearts and minds' *for whom*? Is the aim of these projects to combat anti-American or anti-Western sentiment? Or to win local communities over to their own governments, against which they may have profound grievances? The tendency among US civil affairs programmes has been to privilege the former goal. Yet evidence suggests that programmes aimed at making aggrieved populations feel that they are stakeholders in their own country is a far more effective approach to countering radicalization.

In Africa, the effort to harness development and humanitarian aid to win over potentially hostile communities has been almost exclusively focused on Muslim populations. Numerous inquiries into the 'roots of radicalization' of African Islamic communities have been commissioned, which have in turn informed new programming designed to address – and presumably prevent – the radicalization of African Muslims. While the quality of the programming varies from project to project, the premises underpinning this 'hearts and minds' approach in African Islamic communities are questionable and have come under attack. First, the very notion of what constitutes 'radicalized' viewpoints among African Muslims is a matter of debate – to return to the question above, is it measured in levels of anti-Americanism or anti-Westernism? Affiliation with a Salafi movement? Support for al-Qaeda or its affiliates? Desire for an Islamic state rather than democracy? Is there any discernible link between extremist views and actual security threats? On the one hand, available evidence suggests that radical views do seem prevalent among at least some African Muslim communities. For instance, the Pew Global Attitudes Project found that Nigerian Muslims registered opinions on some questions that were more radical than Muslim counterparts from other continents. In polls conducted only with Muslim populations, Pew found that Nigeria was the only country surveyed which showed an increase in the percentage of respondents who expressed confidence in Osama bin Laden between 2003 and 2008 (from 44 per cent to 58 per cent), and revealed that support for bin Laden was by far higher in Nigeria than in any other Muslim country in the survey (Pew Research Center 2008). A higher percentage of Nigerian Muslims also agreed with the statement that suicide bombing is justified, though that number declined from 47 per cent to 32 per cent from 2003 to 2008. Nigerian Muslims also registered the highest level of favourable attitudes towards al-Qaeda – 49 per cent – of any of the countries surveyed in a follow-up 2010 poll (Pew Research Center 2011). Qualitative studies in other African countries with large Muslim population, such as Kenya, Somalia, and Ethiopia, document the dramatic increase in Salafi mosques and schools, and growing manifestations of Islamic radicalization manifested in verbal support of al-Qaeda and acceptance of al-Qaeda's master narrative (Carson 2005; Abbink 2011; ICG 2005; Møller 2006).

These reports raise concern, but also constitute a puzzle. If African Muslim populations are increasingly susceptible to radicalization, why has so little of that translated into action in the form of direct involvement in jihadi and terrorist organization? On paper, many African Muslim communities should be ripe for recruitment by al-Qaeda and its affiliates. In reality, sub-Saharan Africa has proven to be infertile ground for recruitment, with only a very small percentage of al-Qaeda's fighters coming from there. There are a variety of potential explanations, but the simplest appears to be that African Muslim grievances and agendas have been mainly local, not global, in nature; hence, their political mobilization has been directed at national-level concerns (Menkhaus 2009). These affiliations can shift quickly, of course, as the case of Somalia's jihadist group al-Shabaab demonstrates. Al-Shabaab's rapid ascent was fuelled mainly by Somali anger over a local calamity: the Ethiopian military invasion and occupation of southern Somalia. However, al-Shabaab leaders subsequently pushed the movement into affiliation with al-Qaeda for their own more parochial reasons.

That radicalization of parts of the African Muslim population has not (yet) translated into high levels of recruitment into al-Qaeda or its affiliates is reassuring, but is only one element of counter-terrorism policy. Of perhaps greater concern is the passive rather than active support that a large, partially radicalized, disaffected Muslim community in Africa could provide to a terrorist group (Le Sage 2010). That is, terrorists will be in a strong position to exploit operating environments in which aggrieved local communities do not have a sense of being stakeholders in the welfare of the state. This analysis is important because it points to a different type of development intervention – one which prioritizes reforms and service delivery by the local government to win over its own citizens, as opposed to trying to win over local communities to the United States or the West. If local populations have a sense of being stakeholders in their country, they are much more likely to engage in the kind of community policing that is central to prevention of terrorist and other armed insurgency attacks.

The harnessing of development work in pursuit of 'hearts and minds' campaigns also raises questions about the actual roots of radicalization. Why are some of Africa's Muslim populations apparently more prone to radicalism than others? The answer of course depends in part on the context of each state, but studies tend to focus on a general syndrome of radicalization 'drivers', including political marginalization, economic frustration, clashes over land, the more general politicization of identity politics across Africa's multi-ethnic and multi-sectarian states, the impact of the influx of Salafi mosques and clerics funded by groups in the Gulf, and greater exposure to global media and websites carrying radical messages and narratives. While this assessment is plausible, the prescription that has typically followed is not. Development projects put to use as tools of de-radicalization have shown no signs of effectiveness. Local communities that voice support for an al-Qaeda affiliate such as al-Qaeda in the Islamic Maghreb (AQIM) or al-Shabaab are not going to change their views simply because Western aid agencies or military civil affairs teams build them a new schoolhouse. A recent assessment of US civil affairs outreach in Kenya reached the sobering conclusion that the assumption that small-scale aid projects like repairing toilets, can win the 'hearts and minds' of people, help to stabilize a region, prevent the radicalization of populations and work to counter terrorism, suggests at best a simplistic – if not patronizing – view of the assisted communities (Bradbury and Kleinman 2010).

Most donor agencies and AFRICOM civil affairs teams are aware that their limited aid interventions are very unlikely to change public attitudes toward the state, the foreign donor, or the al-Qaeda master narrative. They nonetheless find such 'hearts and minds' work useful as a means of gauging local attitudes and gathering information. This, however, has sparked powerful disagreements with development and humanitarian agencies, which fear that such overt use of development work for what amounts to intelligence gathering will render all aid organizations vulnerable to charges that they are spies for the US military, an accusation that puts aid workers in grave danger. This is a major concern in parts of Islamic Africa, where humanitarian access has dramatically shrunk due to insecurity.

Finally, counter-terrorism operations in one African state, Somalia, have collided with the humanitarian imperative of access. One of the more effective counter-terrorism policies against al-Qaeda and its affiliates has been tight restrictions on financial transactions. The Patriot Act of 2001, which gave the US government greater freedom to investigate individuals suspected of terrorist activities, also prohibits material support to groups designated as terrorist. The law has subsequently been strictly interpreted by the US Supreme Court, in the Holder vs. Humanitarian Law Project Case of 2010; other Western states have passed similar laws. In effect, strict legal interpretation of these laws has virtually criminalized all humanitarian aid into zones controlled by terrorist groups, as these groups will almost certainly derive some material benefit from the aid. In response to this legal concern, in late 2009 the US Agency for International Development (USAID) announced the suspension of all food aid into southern Somalia, prompting an acrimonious debate with some relief agencies over the move, especially at a time of worsening humanitarian crisis in southern Somalia (Menkhaus 2010a: 337). The collision of counter-terrorism legislation with the humanitarian imperative of full access to those in need remained unresolved right through the Somali famine of 2011, and constituted one of a number of critical bottlenecks to effective delivery of emergency relief (Menkhaus 2012).

Evolving terrorist threats

What, in the end, is the actual terrorist threat in Africa, and who is most threatened? Two categories of threat are of particular concern.

The rise of al-Qaeda 'affiliates'

Al-Qaeda's affiliates are now considered to be a greater global and regional security threat than al-Qaeda itself. Many of these affiliates – al-Shabaab, AQIM, Boko Haram, Ansar al-Dine – are based in Africa. Nearly all of these groups have emerged relatively recently; this has placed the counter-terrorist spotlight squarely on Africa since 2008.

The actual threat posed by African jihadi movements has varied over time and by group. One of the oldest African jihadi groups, AQIM, has in recent years split and one wing has degenerated into a criminal syndicate, engaged in drug smuggling and kidnapping for ransom (Le Sage 2010: 60). Neither wing commands many fighters, and by 2011 experts perceived AQIM to be in 'survival mode'. Turmoil in parts of the Sahel since 2011 may, however, be providing the group with new opportunities, leading to warnings about AQIM from the US African Command (Marshall 2012). A second jihadi group, Boko Haram, has grown considerably as a threat to both Nigerians and the international community. It launched a major terrorist attack against the UN compound in Abuja in August 2011 that killed 23 people. Most of its political violence is directed at Nigerian Christians living in northern Nigeria: churches are one of the group's preferred targets. It is responsible for over 1,000 deaths since

2010, and is now a major security threat inside Nigeria. Boko Haram claims links to al-Qaeda but is not considered an affiliate. Its agenda and grievances have to date been local not global; it claims to want to bring strict *sharia* (Islamic) law to the country and rid it of all Western influences. A third West African jihadi group, Ansar al-Dine, emerged suddenly from the spill-over of armed groups from Libya and the ensuing disorder in northern Mali in 2012. It has links to AQIM, draws on the Tuareg people for support, and seeks to impose *sharia* law and an Islamic state over all of Mali. To date, most of its armed attacks have targeted sufi shrines and tombs, which, as a strict Salafi group, it views as a corrupted practice of Islam.

The African jihadi group that has generated by far the most concern as a security threat to its own people, neighbouring states, and global interests is Somalia's al-Shabaab. Al-Shabaab's influence and power actually peaked in 2008; since then, it has been beset by internal disputes, has lost legitimacy among most Somalis, and has lost territory in the face of military pressure from AMISOM forces and the militaries of neighbouring Ethiopia and Kenya (ICG 2010). Nonetheless, the group remains a real danger at home and abroad (Marchal 2009). Inside Somalia, it retains the capacity to launch daily attacks on AMISOM troops and the Somali transitional government. Under pressure in southern Somalia it has expanded operations in the north of the country, against the once stable regions of Puntland and Somaliland. It poses the greatest threat in Kenya and East Africa, where a large cell of non-Somali East Africans operate under the al-Shabaab franchise and have launched a series of terrorist attacks, most notably the World Cup bombings in 2010 in Kampala that killed 74 people.

Radicalization of African diasporas

One of the quiet – but seismic – transformations of parts of Africa is the rise of a large diaspora in the West and the Middle East. For many African states, remittances from the diaspora constitute the top source of hard currency and are critical to the economy. African diasporas are also a major source of leadership in African political, commercial, and civic life. The diasporization of some African countries has implications for violent extremism. When African Muslims migrate abroad to the Gulf states, Europe, or North America, they are often exposed to more strident forms of Salafi Islam and other forms of socialization which lead a small percentage to embrace radical interpretations of Islam (Menkhaus 2009). This concern is most pronounced in the case of the very large and poorly assimilated Somali refugee and immigrant communities abroad, many of which expressed sympathy and provided support to al-Shabaab during its battle with Ethiopian occupying troops in 2007–08. Indeed, much of the top leadership of al-Shabaab consists of Somali returnees from the diaspora.

Though the allure of both al-Shabaab in particular and al-Qaeda in general has faded in recent years, there remains a genuine concern over the possibilities of self-radicalization by Somali or other African Muslim youth in the West and ensuing 'home-grown' terrorist plots. This has securitized Western government policies towards African Muslim diaspora populations. Their remittances have come under much closer regulation out of fear they are financing terrorist groups, and their movements abroad, internet chat rooms, mosques, and political activism have all come under closer law enforcement scrutiny.

Conclusion

The threat of terrorism in Africa has reshaped international perceptions of and policies toward Africa. The result has been the partial 'securitization' of state-building, development aid, and humanitarian assistance as security agendas have come to dominate the new international relations with the continent. The impact of this shift has been felt unevenly across Africa, with Nigeria, Sahel countries, East Africa, and the Horn most affected. African governments that have succeeded in positioning themselves as allies in counter-terrorism, and programmes designed to combat violent extremism have fared well, securing such governments significant aid in the name of capacity building and earning them a greater degree of immunity from criticism over human rights abuses or democratic deficits.

Close examination of the theories and strategies underpinning counter-terrorism initiatives in Africa since 9/11 clearly suggests that some elements of Western – and African – counter-terrorism policies have been based on partially inaccurate assumptions. Zones of state failure are not in fact 'ungoverned space' but are populated by a complex array of informal security and governance arrangements. Zones of complete state collapse and civil war are not ideal operating environments for international terrorist or criminal networks; al-Qaeda's experience in East Africa suggests instead that it prefers to exploit weak, corrupt states. Al-Qaeda's exploitation of Africa's weak states does not require a strong network of true believers as much as it requires corrupt police and pragmatic businesspeople. African governments in some instances view counter-terrorism as an opportunity to be exploited, not a problem to be solved, and use this Western agenda to accrue aid and capacity that helps them solidify their position of power and suppress local rivals. State-building assistance provided in the name of counter-terrorism and stabilization cannot always presume that the recipient government shares an interest in improving the capacity of the state. In some cases, regimes have a stronger interest in perpetuating institutional weakness to facilitate patronage politics and allow criminal activities to go undetected (see also Brown, this volume). Civil affairs projects and 'securitized' development aid from the West are not in fact an effective means of winning 'hearts and minds' among aggrieved or marginalized African Muslims, whose demands are usually for political rights and reform in their own country rather than a new well or pit latrine. African jihadist groups have sought and secured affiliations with al-Qaeda and embraced their globalist rhetoric, but their agendas, like those of most African Muslims expressing 'radical' views, are primarily local, not global. Some of the most worrisome terrorist threats are increasingly coming not from radicalized African Muslims on the continent, but from a small number of African Muslims in the diaspora who have been radicalized while living in Europe or North America. Similarly, the main religious battle in Islamic Africa today does not in fact pit Muslims against Christians, but is instead a struggle between sufi and Salafi interpretations of Islam.

Finally, direct external military interventions to defeat a rising terrorist movement can inadvertently inflame local sentiment, earning the radical group more support from the population and allowing it to conflate its extremist ideology with ethnic or nationalist solidarity (Lyman 2009). Fortunately, many organizations involved in counter-terrorism and security matters have learned from these reconsiderations, giving reason for cautious optimism that 'second-generation' counter-terrorism policies in Africa will be better informed and less likely to produce unintended consequences. 'Without such an understanding', concludes Andre Le Sage, 'U.S. and other security assistance providers will not only be frustrated in achieving their goals, but their investments in Africa may actually reward those who allow violence, predation, and plundering to continue' (Le Sage 2010: 74).

Bibliography

Abbink, J. (2011) 'Religion in Public Spaces: Emerging Muslim–Christian Polemics in Ethiopia', *African Affairs* 110(439): 253–74.

Andersen, L., Møller, B. and Stepputat, F. (eds) (2007) *Fragile States and Insecure People? Violence, Security, and Statehood in the Twenty-First Century*, New York, NY: Palgrave.

Benjamin, D. (2009) 'International Counterterrorism Policy in the Obama Administration', Speech at the Jamestown Foundation, Washington, DC, 9 December, www.state.gov/j/ct/rls/rm/2009/133337.htm (accessed 18 April 2012).

Bradbury, M. and Kleinman, M. (2010) *Winning Hearts and Minds? Examining the Relationship between Aid and Security in Kenya*, Boston, MA: Feinstein International Center.

Call, C.T. (ed.) (2008) *Building States to Build Peace*, Boulder, CO: Lynne Rienner Publishers.

Carson, J. (2005) 'Kenya; The Struggle Against Terrorism', in R. Rotberg (ed.) *Battling Terror in the Horn of Africa and Yemen*, Washington, DC: Brookings Press.

Crawford, M. and Miscik, J. (2010) 'The Rise of the Mezzanine Rulers', *Foreign Affairs* 89(6): 123–32.

Foreign Policy (2011) 'The Failed States Index 2011', July, www.foreignpolicy.com/articles/2011/06/17/2011_failed_states_index_interactive_map_and_rankings (accessed 8 July 2012).

Herbst, J. (2000) *States and Power in Africa*, Princeton, NJ: Princeton University Press.

ICG (International Crisis Group) (2005) 'Counter-Terrorism in Somalia: Losing Hearts and Minds?', Africa Report No. 95, 11 July, Brussels/Nairobi: International Crisis Group.

——(2010) 'Somalia's Divided Islamists', Africa Briefing No. 74, 18 May, Brussels/Nairobi: International Crisis Group.

Keen, D. (2012) *Useful Enemies: When Waging Wars is More Important Than Winning Them*, New Haven, CT: Yale University Press.

Lamb, R.D. (2007) 'Ungoverned Areas and Threats from Safe Havens', Washington, DC: Office of the Under Secretary of Defense for Policy, www.cissm.umd.edu/papers/files/ugash_report_final.pdf (accessed 22 April 2012).

Le Sage, A. (2007) *African Counter-Terrorism Cooperation: Assessing Regional and Sub-Regional Initiatives*, Washington, DC: Potomac.

——(2010) 'Non-State Security Threats in Africa: Challenges for US Engagement', *PRISM* 2(1): 57–78.

Lyman, P. (2009) 'The War on Terrorism in Africa', in J. Harbeson and D. Rothchild (eds) *Africa in World Politics*, fourth edn, Boulder, CO: Westview Press.

Marchal, R. (2009) 'A Tentative Assessment of the Somali *Harakat al-Shabaab*', *Journal of Eastern African Studies* 3(3): 381–404.

Marshall, T. (2012) 'Africa: US Africom Commander Details Current, Emerging Threats', *United States Africa Command*, 26 June, http://allafrica.com/stories/201206260988.html (accessed 22 April 2012).

Menkhaus, K. (2006–07) 'Governance without Government in Somalia: Spoilers, State Building, and the Politics of Coping', *International Security* 31(3): 74–106.

——(2009) 'African Diasporas, Diasporas in Africa, and the Terrorist Threat', in D. Zimmerman and W. Rosenau (eds) *The Radicalization of Diasporas and Terrorism*, Zurich: ETH Center for Security Studies.

——(2010a) 'Stabilisation and Humanitarian Access in a Collapsed State: The Somali Case', *Disasters* 34(3): 320–41.

——(2010b) 'State Failure and Ungoverned Space', in M. Berdal and A. Wennmann (eds) *Ending Wars, Consolidating Peace: Economic Perspectives*, Abingdon: Routledge for the International Institute for Strategic Studies.

——(2010c) 'State Fragility as Wicked Problem', *PRISM* 1(2): 85–100.

——(2012) 'Critical Bottlenecks in the 2011 Somali Famine', *Global Food Security* 1(1): 29–35.

Menkhaus, K. and Shapiro, J. (2010) 'Non-State Actors and Failed States: Lessons from al-Qa'ida's Experiences in the Horn of Africa', in A.L. Clunan and H. Trinkunas (eds) *Ungoverned Spaces? Alternatives to State Authority in an Era of Softened Sovereignty*, Stanford, CA: Stanford University Press.

Møller, B. (2006) 'Political Islam in Kenya', DIIS Working Paper No. 2006/22, Copenhagen: Danish Institute for International Studies, www.diis.dk/graphics/Publications/WP2006/WP2006-22_web.pdf (accessed 8 April 2012).

Muggah, R. (2009) 'Securing the Peace: Post Conflict Security Promotion', in *Small Arms Survey 2009: Shadows of War*, Geneva: Small Arms Survey, www.smallarmssurvey.org/publications/by-type/yearbook/small-arms-survey-2009.html (accessed 8 April 2012).

Muggah, R., Collinson, S. and Elhawary, S. (eds) (2010) 'States of Fragility: Stabilisation and its Implications for Humanitarian Action', *Disasters* 34(s3): s275–96.

Patrick, S. (2011) *Weak Links: Fragile States, Global Threats, and International Security*, New York, NY: Oxford University Press.

Pew Research Center (2008) 'Global Public Opinion in the Bush Years (2001–8)', Pew Global Attitudes Project, 18 December, http://pewglobal.org/2008/12/18/global-public-opinion-in-the-bush-years-2001-2008/ (accessed 8 April 2012).

——(2011) 'Osama bin Laden Largely Discredited Among Muslim Publics in Recent Years', Pew Global Attitudes Project, 2 May, http://pewglobal.org/2011/05/02/osama-bin-laden-largely-discredited-among-muslim-publics-in-recent-years/ (accessed 8 July 2012).

Reno, W. (2000) *Warlord Politics and African States*, Boulder, CO: Lynne Rienner Publishers.

Roessler, P. (2011) 'The Enemy Within: Personal Rule, Coups and Civil War in Africa', *World Politics* 63(2): 300–46.

Scahill, C. (2011) 'The CIA's Secret Sites in Somalia', *The Nation*, 12 July, www.thenation.com/article/161936/cias-secret-sites-somalia (accessed 8 April 2012).

Toolis, K. (2004) 'Rise of the Terrorist Professors', *New Statesmen*, 14 June 2004.

Watts, C., Shapiro, J. and Brown, V. (2007) *Al Qa'ida's (Mis)Adventures in the Horn of Africa*, West Point, NY: Combating Terrorism Center, www.ctc.usma.edu/wp-content/uploads/2010/06/Al-Qaidas-Mis-Adventures-in-the-Horn-of-Africa.pdf (accessed 8 April 2012).

White House (2002) 'The National Security Strategy of the United States of America', Washington, DC: The White House, http://georgewbush-whitehouse.archives.gov/nsc/nss/2002/index.html (accessed 15 April 2012).

31

DEMOCRACY PROMOTION

Stephen Brown

Most African countries were democracies at the time of their independence, but by the late 1980s very few democracies remained. In the early 1990s, Western governments announced that democracy promotion would be a cornerstone of their aid to countries in Africa and elsewhere. However, 20 years later, remarkably few African countries can truly be described as democracies. Why did Western aid donors suddenly emphasize democracy in the early 1990s? Why is the track record of democracy promotion so poor? How serious are donors about promoting democracy when faced with competing foreign policy objectives? What enables African countries to resist pressure to democratize? Why has democracy promotion declined in the past decade?

This chapter attempts to answer these questions. First, it examines the rise of democracy promotion and the various forms it can take. Next, it analyses the lack of success and the factors that have contributed to it, including inherent limitations, donors' overall failure prioritizing it, and African governments' means of resisting the pressure. Then, it explains the decline of democracy promotion, before concluding with a discussion of the main factors that make advancing democracy abroad so difficult, the sincerity of the efforts of foreign actors, and the potential future impact of international assistance.

The rise of democracy promotion in Africa

In the late 1950s and early 1960s, as most African countries moved toward independence, the departing British and French colonial officials left in place democratic constitutions and institutions, albeit ones that were hastily assembled with minimal input from domestic populations.[1] In most countries, democracy did not last long, generally due to weak state institutions, a lack of experience with and commitment to democratic procedures, especially among elites, as well as intense political rivalries, often along ethnic lines. Single-party regimes or military dictatorships soon replaced democratic governments. For the most part, during the Cold War Western countries cared little about domestic governance issues in Africa; their main concern was African countries' foreign policy. Western countries, especially the United States, the UK, and France, were preoccupied with maintaining the stability of their client states and seeking to prevent those states from allying with the Soviet Union.

In the context of intense superpower rivalry, the excesses, corruption, and widespread human rights abuses in client states mattered little to the major Western countries. A democratic façade – and sometimes not even that – was all that was required to escape pressure to democratize. The superpowers continued to support dictators such as Mobutu Sese Seko of Zaire (today's Democratic Republic of Congo), providing vast amounts of foreign aid and, in some cases, military assistance. Despite some pro-democratic rhetoric and relatively weak condemnations of human rights abuses, the American government's attitude towards authoritarian rulers in Africa could be summed up by US President Franklin D. Roosevelt's comments about a Nicaraguan dictator: 'He may be a son-of-a-bitch, but he is our son-of-a-bitch'.

During this period, France and the UK also maintained close economic and commercial ties with their former colonies, with little concern for the regime type. Other Western European countries, including the Netherlands and the Nordic countries, had fewer economic, political, and security interests in Africa than did the United States, UK, and France, and adopted a more humanitarian approach. They focused more on local social and economic needs, sometimes emphasizing the importance of human rights rather than democracy per se.[2] From the mid-1970s to the early 1990s, they provided special economic support and development assistance to the largely undemocratic 'Frontline States', which in turn were supporting the struggle against the apartheid regime in South Africa.

In 1989, military, autocratic, or single-party regimes governed 38 out of 45 sub-Saharan African countries (Ake 1996: 135). At that time, only three African countries had remained democratic uninterrupted since independence: Botswana, the Gambia, and Mauritius (and the Gambia succumbed to a military coup a few years later). With low rates of literacy, high levels of poverty, and entrenched authoritarian rulers, African countries seemed unlikely to democratize, which made any normative suggestions of democracy promotion appear rather futile, and potentially counterproductive strategically if it meant losing useful authoritarian allies.

Contrary to expectations, following the end of the Cold War in 1989 a continent-wide wave of democratization began in Africa with the end of single-party rule and the completion of democratic elections in Benin, and proceeded to spread across the continent. According to Radelet's calculations, the number of democracies in sub-Saharan Africa 'jumped' from three to 23 between 1989 and 1998 (Radelet 2010: 93). This trend closely followed the end of single-party and authoritarian rule in Eastern Europe and the collapse of the USSR – events that many Africans followed closely, especially regime opponents.

Western governments had engaged in some democracy promotion activities prior to the early 1990s. However, they recognized an historic opportunity in the fall of communism as an alternative model to political and economic liberalism. With the collapse of the Soviet Bloc and the disappearance of the Cold War rivalry, along with the triumphalism that accompanied that 'unipolar moment', democracy promotion rose to the top of Western countries' agendas, especially with regard to Africa. The next section of this chapter examines why.

Why promote democracy?

Interpretations differ on why many Western countries (though not France or Japan) suddenly began to promote democracy proactively abroad. Some saw it as part of a package in which 'all good things go together': political and economic liberalization, free votes, and free markets. Especially to many Americans, the end of the Cold War heralded the definitive victory of Western liberalism and the defeat of alternatives. Henceforth, by this reasoning, economic and political development would go hand in hand. Though scholars have disputed the premise that democracy brought about a higher rate of economic growth, politicians and policy advisers continued to present the combination of economic and political liberalization as the joint path to global peace and prosperity.

Critical voices considered Western democracy promotion a component of capitalist imperialism, epitomized by the United States. They saw the West's newfound concern for domestic governance as an extension of attempts to impose neoliberal economic models upon the political realm. Some interpreted it as a means of replacing entrenched rulers in Africa with leaders more friendly to the West and, perhaps more importantly, more favourable to Western economic interests, including opening up profitable opportunities for private-sector actors. Others worried that the emphasis on democratization would justify the reduction of aid to Africa.

The truth lies somewhere in between these two caricatures. Many donor governments and aid officials value political and civil rights, including democratic competition for political power, in and of themselves. Such rights are beneficial to citizens, even if not accompanied by social and economic rights.[3] Those concerns, the argument goes, were always present, but it was the New World Order that was born in 1989–90 that virtually eliminated some competing threats and allowed democracy promotion to move up on Western countries' list of priorities. Their domestic media and development non-governmental organizations (NGOs) often supported the belief that countries that respected human rights and democratic principles should receive more aid than those that do not. Some civil society organizations in African countries have supported donors' decisions to freeze aid to their country until the domestic democracy movement succeeds in dislodging their dictator. In a few cases, they actually lobbied for aid sanctions. Accusations of self-interested donor behaviour are sometimes overstated. Donors have taken their strongest and most concerted efforts to promote democracy in some countries, such as Malawi, wherein democratization would provide very little benefit, if any, to Western countries. Despite fears to the contrary, aid levels to Africa have in fact increased; some donor countries have recently doubled their assistance to Africa or plan to do so within the next few years.

Some scepticism about the sincerity of democracy promotion, however, is also warranted. Clearly, pressure is not applied evenly to all countries. Western countries still support many non-democratic regimes that have pro-Western foreign policies or provide the West with important natural resources. The hypocrisy in the application of pressure to democratize is undeniable. Moreover, democracy promotion is often applied together with pressure for economic liberalization. Donors, especially the United States, are often content with only cosmetic political reform, and sometimes economic reform is all that is required to regain the status of aid-worthiness. Often, they openly express their desire to see African countries integrated fully with the global capitalist economy and open their markets to Western businesses. African countries are usually more accountable to aid donors than they are accountable to their own citizens, which is highly problematic for the application of the democratic label. For governing elites of developing countries, democracy promotion is a reminder of the international asymmetry of power. It is an infringement on their sovereignty and a display of Western claims to moral and intellectual superiority. In sum, Western countries undertake democracy promotion in Africa for a mix of normative and self-interested reasons that vary over time and by context. The following section examines the different forms that democracy promotion can take.

Forms of democracy promotion

Most Western aid donors issued statements in 1989–90 that future aid allocation levels would depend on the extent to which recipient countries had democratized. They used a combination of the carrot (increased development assistance) and the stick (aid sanctions) to promote democratization in African countries (for more on economic conditionality see Williams, this volume). This connection of aid flows to domestic modes of governance is generally referred to as political conditionality.

Donors applied negative political conditionality (the stick) to a number of authoritarian regimes – that is to say, they reduced or suspended development assistance, pending the authoritarian regimes' political (and often economic) liberalization. For example, Western countries adopted wide-ranging sanctions against apartheid South Africa in the 1980s and, two decades later, suspended aid to the Zimbabwean government and instituted 'smart sanctions' against its ruling elites – for instance, freezing their bank accounts abroad and denying them and their families visas to travel to Europe or North America.

Alternatively, positive political conditionality (the carrot) refers to the provision of aid to countries selected for their higher levels of democracy and good governance. The best example of this preferential treatment is the US Millennium Challenge Account (MCA), which provides extra assistance to countries that meet a certain number of criteria. Political indicators include civil liberties and political rights, as well as voice and accountability. MCA funds provide incentives for developing countries to reach the eligibility threshold on these and other indicators.

Most democracy assistance is focused on technical goals. It seeks to strengthen institutions that are essential for democracies to function. In the 1990s the United States channelled significant amounts of funding through a number of American democracy promotion organizations founded in the 1980s, namely the National Endowment for Democracy, the National Democratic Institute for International Affairs, and the International Republican Institute. To provide specialized assistance, some other donors also established government-funded, arm's length organizations, including Canada's International Centre for Human Rights and Democratic Development (1988), the UK's Westminster Foundation for Democracy (1992), and the Netherlands Institute for Multiparty Democracy (2000). During this period, other specialized institutions were also created, notably the Washington-based International Foundation for Electoral Systems (1987) and the Stockholm-based International Institute for Democracy and Electoral Assistance (1995). Together, these organizations – along with UN bodies, German political party foundations, private foundations, and numerous international NGOs – provided support to parliamentarians, political parties, independent electoral commissions, the judiciary, the media, and local civil society organizations in African countries.

As Thomas Carothers (2009) has noted, that type of technical approach, which he calls 'political assistance', is predicated on the assumption that democracy can emerge almost any-where with the right knowledge and institutions. This type of aid tends to be provided over a relatively short period of time, after which the country is expected to have acquired the necessary tools to make democracy work. That is the dominant perspective of US government policies. It relies on an optimistic conception of democracy highly based on human agency: the right people with some specific knowledge and abilities can not only overcome authoritarian rule but also replace it with a durable democracy. It also assumes that citizens favour democracy and, more problematically, that political, economic, and military elites will act democratically, rather than undermine democratic institutions when it might suit their interests.

Another form of assistance, which Carothers calls 'developmental', adopts a more structural approach. From this perspective, democracy depends more on its socioeconomic foundations for its longevity than on the people who would usher it in and sustain it. In other words, it sees democracy as the result of greater literacy and education, the rise of the middle class, and other benefits of successful development that have been found to be associated with the survival of democratic regimes (see Przeworski *et al.* 1996). Democracy promotion would thus best be served by more holistic support to social and economic development – that is to say, indirectly and over a long period of time. It is a more pessimistic outlook for democratization in Africa, and one generally adopted by the European Union (EU) and its member states.

The effectiveness of democracy promotion

Understanding the rationale for democracy promotion is merely the preface to analysing its real effects. This section explores whether democracy promotion has been able to achieve its objectives and what difficulties it continues to encounter.

The impact of democracy promotion

It is difficult to determine the exact impact of democracy promotion efforts because of the mix of complicated factors contributing to political change. Still, carefully researched qualitative case studies can assess the relative importance of Western donors in the democratization process. One such study identified 18 cases of aid suspension in sub-Saharan Africa between 1990 and 1995 and none north of the Sahara. It found that only in two of them did political conditionality clearly make a 'modest' or 'significant' contribution to democratization: Kenya and Malawi, discussed below. Elsewhere, the contribution was either unclear or absent (Crawford 1997). Bratton and van de Walle state that of the 25 cases of politically conditional aid in Africa, eight resulted in transition to democracy, constituting a modest success rate. However, their analysis also suggests that domestic factors are far more important that international ones (Bratton and van de Walle 1997: 219–20). Further complicating the efforts to quantify the impact of political conditionality is the fact that a 'large number' of authoritarian regimes pre-emptively enacted democratic reforms specifically to avoid a suspension of aid (ibid.: 182), though many of those reforms were merely cosmetic.

According to Freedom House (2012: 14–18), only nine out of 49 sub-Saharan African countries, and none in North Africa, could be classified as 'free electoral democracies' in 2012.[4] From this, one can conclude that 20 years of democracy promotion has had little visible impact in Africa, especially since two of those nine had been democratic since independence and donors played little or no role in the democratic transitions of most of the others. All too often, emerging 'success stories' were ruined by authoritarian backsliding, a military coup, or the resumption of civil war.

The first successful use of negative political conditionality occurred in Kenya. Donors coordinated a joint suspension of new development assistance in 1991, to last until the government had carried out important economic and political liberalization. Within a few weeks' time, authoritarian ruler Daniel arap Moi announced that the constitution would be amended to return Kenya to a multi-party system. Donor pressure was nonetheless insufficient to ensure that the 1992 and 1997 elections were reasonably free and fair, allowing Moi to remain in power, aided by a divided opposition. Donors undermined their own democracy promotion efforts when they settled for economic and minor political reforms and a promise of more to take place at a later date. On more than one occasion, Moi made sufficient changes for aid to be renewed, and then reneged on his commitments to further liberalization, eventually triggering renewed donor sanctions. It was only in 2002, after Moi retired, that the opposition – buoyed by massive defections from the ruling party and rallying around one main presidential candidate – was able to win. In that stage of the protracted democratization process, donors played a relatively minor part, though they may have influenced Moi's decision to retire (Brown 2007).

Malawi stands out as a case where Western countries unequivocally play a very important role in the democratization process, though domestic actors played crucial parts as well. First, donors acted in concert and suspended new, non-humanitarian assistance in 1992, demanding political liberalization. This quickly prompted a severe economic crisis and weakened the regime of 'Life President' Hastings Kamuzu Banda, who announced that a referendum would be held to determine whether Malawi should adopt a multi-party system. Donors supported the referendum process and ensured its fairness, leading to a two-to-one victory for the advocates of multi-partyism. The following year, with key support from donors, free and fair general elections led to Banda's defeat. For the first time, power was passed peacefully to a newly legalized opposition party. Though this was a great and rapid achievement, two decades after the ground-breaking referendum, Malawi's transition to democracy is still incomplete and the process seems to have stalled, leaving in place a hybrid regime (Brown 2004).

Perhaps more time is needed for African countries to continue in a slow process of democratization. Indeed, democracy promotion activities might have made positive contributions, especially by strengthening the structural underpinnings of democracy. That kind of impact, however, is even more difficult to measure than the more immediate effects of political conditionality.

The inherent difficulties of democracy promotion

Democratization follows a very uncertain and highly contingent path. Moreover, scholars almost unanimously agree that it is primarily a domestic process, nearly impossible to impose and depending above all on domestic actors, institutions, and conditions. As a result, effective democracy promotion efforts are inherently very difficult to design and implement. Only a relatively rare combination of circumstances is conducive to international pressure tilting the balance of forces in favour of a transition to democracy. Levitsky and Way describe these as strong 'Western *leverage* (governments' vulnerability to external pressure) and *linkage* to the West (the density of a country's ties to the United States, the European Union, and Western-led multi-lateral institutions)' (Levitsky and Way 2005: 21, italics in original). Thus, Western countries are most likely to promote democracy successfully in countries that are highly dependent on foreign aid, even if they do not have particularly close ties with the West. This level of leverage is found more often in Africa than other regions and certainly applies to Malawi and Kenya in the early 1990s.

There are nonetheless several important impediments to the use of political conditionality in Africa. Among other challenges, political conditionality is a very blunt instrument. Aid flows are not easily turned on and off – and doing so can be extremely disruptive to development efforts, potentially harming the poor more than authoritarian elites. Even if donors agree to suspend aid jointly (which is required for maximum impact), it is hard for them to agree on the minimum terms needed for aid to be resumed – especially if both economic and political liberalization are required – and even more difficult to reach a consensus on how much backsliding would warrant another suspension. In addition, recalcitrant authoritarian rulers in Africa have often rapidly discerned how to enact enough cosmetic reforms to please donors but not threaten their own hold on power (Brown 2005: 184–85).

Competing objectives and other donor deficiencies

Arguably, the most important donor characteristic that undermines their democracy promotion is the multitude of competing objectives that each donor government has. A study by Schraeder *et al.* (1998) examined the allocation of American, French, and Japanese aid to 36 African countries in the 1980s and found that the donors' own strategic interests were more important than the recipients' needs and that economic interests – especially commercial ones – were very important determinants of how donors distributed their aid budgets. It would be unrealistic to expect those Western interests to disappear with the rise of democracy promotion activities in the early 1990s.

Not all Western foreign policy objectives can become top priorities, and trade-offs become necessary. Not all donor governments will agree which ones to rank highest; so, barring exceptional coordination efforts, some donors may well undermine others' efforts. Moreover, Western governments can be internally divided over the relative importance of democracy. For instance, a Western ministry of defence will generally care less about the level of democracy in a strategically important recipient country than the ministry of foreign affairs or the official aid agency. The ministry of commerce might focus instead on economic reform, especially commercial policies such as tariffs and other barriers to trade.

Since the 1980s, economic liberalization has been the most important policy change required by Western donors in Africa, especially the international financial institutions, and constitutes the core of structural adjustment programmes (SAPs) and their latest reincarnation, poverty reduction strategy papers (PRSPs). Donors thus identify compliant economic reformers, including Ghana, Uganda, and most recently Rwanda, as 'success stories'. Since they are so few in number, many donors are reluctant to tarnish their star pupils' positive image with loud, governance-related complaints.

Security has also been a major consideration in Western relations with African countries, especially for the United States and since the terrorist attacks on 11 September 2001. The importance of security alliances often overshadows any efforts to promote democratization. In countries emerging from conflict, more emphasis is often placed on reconstruction and reconciliation, sometimes involving interim power-sharing arrangements, instead of rapid democratization.

There are other ways that donors often hamper their own democracy promotion efforts. For instance, they tend to have a shallow commitment to democratization beyond the holding of periodical elections and a semblance of basic civil rights. In many cases, Western countries endorse elections that are blatantly 'un-free' and unfair (for illustrations from Kenya, see Brown 2001). Moreover, after a formerly authoritarian country holds its first democratic elections, donors are less likely to invoke conditionality in response to subsequent backsliding.[5] Moreover, the United States and other donors tend to focus too much on the provision of technical assistance that treats the lack of democracy as if it were a technical problem, the result solely of a lack of institutional capacity, rather than a very deliberate lack of will at the political level (Brown 2005: 185–87).

Recipient countries' counter-leverage

Recipient countries can often play donor interests off each other and evade pressure for reform in a specific area. As mentioned above, during the Cold War, African 'client states' could satisfy their patrons through their actions on the international stage and thus avoid the scrutiny of their domestic political behaviour. African countries also held a variety of bargaining chips after the end of the Cold War. For example, the government of Kenya – both the authoritarian regime of the 1990s and early 2000s, and the more democratic governments since 2003 – has often benefited from donors' tolerance of corruption, important human rights abuses, and undemocratic behaviour because of 'counter-leverage' it has had over the West. Among other things, Kenya is an important player in regional politics and a base for numerous humanitarian and development efforts of Western countries, UN agencies, and NGOs in East Africa and the Horn. Kenya also provides access to air and naval bases for the United States, the UK, and other Western countries, especially important for surveillance of and operations in neighbouring Somalia. Kenya tries pirates who are arrested in the Indian Ocean by Western countries, which do not want to put them on trial at home, in part for fear of refugee claims. Western powers consider good relations with the Kenyan government key to their foreign policy objectives in that region.

Authoritarian African countries that are important to Western – and especially American – global security interests are highly unlikely to be subjected to strong pressure to democratize. Mauritania, for instance, rehabilitated itself almost overnight as an ally in George W. Bush's 'war on terror'. For decades, Western countries applied only feeble pressure on Egypt for support of its 'moderating' influence on Middle East politics as well as for fear of Islamists winning free and fair elections (as they had in the 1992 elections in Algeria, which were annulled as a result). Donors are also wary of criticizing the Ethiopian government's undemocratic behaviour, in part because of its role in fighting terrorism and Islamism, notably in Somalia. Actions against the Sudanese government for its major human rights abuses in the Darfur region are restrained because of its contributions to fighting al-Qaeda (for the impact of the 'war on terror' in Africa see Menkhaus, this volume).

Thus, a relatively high degree of linkage to Western countries does not necessarily increase the latter's capacity to influence African countries' internal politics, as Levitsky and Way (2005) suggest. Instead, various bargaining chips can create counter-leverage and serve as a means of reducing the West's influence on domestic political matters. For instance, if the Kenyan government is displeased by European criticisms of its undemocratic behaviour, it can credibly threaten to disband (and in fact has done so) the EU-funded special tribunals in Kenya that deal with the Somali pirates, whose kidnappings and extortion constitute a threat to donor countries' commercial and strategic interests.

Given the numerous inherent difficulties of political conditionality, the limitations of purely technical assistance, instances of feeble donor commitment, and authoritarian regimes' means of resistance, it is not surprising that democracy promotion slipped down donors' agendas.

The decline of democracy promotion

Democracy promotion proved to be a much harder task than many democracy promoters had expected. The euphoria that followed the fall of the Berlin Wall and numerous authoritarian regimes in Eastern Europe and Africa soon gave way to a more sober and realistic set of expectations, if not outright pessimism. In the second half of the 1990s, the wave of democratic transitions in Africa slowed and many African countries adapted to – and often circumvented – political conditionality, producing a large number of hybrid regimes – that is, countries with multi-party systems and periodic elections, but ones that were generally not free enough to remove the incumbent via the ballot box.

The New World Order that was to follow the crumbling of the Soviet empire would be described more accurately as a New World Disorder, with civil conflagrations erupting across Africa and elsewhere, most horrifically in the African Great Lakes region. Faced with such pressing issues, only smaller and less influential donors retained a focus on democracy promotion; the major ones reverted to outright economic and, especially, strategic self-interest.

The al-Qaeda attacks in the United States in September 2001 accelerated this trend. The United States and other Western countries increasingly viewed foreign policy through a security lens, including democracy promotion, even if sometimes merely instrumentally. For instance, to justify the subsequent US-led invasions of Afghanistan (2001) and Iraq (2003), donors invoked democracy and human rights, but the regimes that Western countries helped to set up after 'regime change' sorely lacked credibility in those areas. That in turn contributed to a further de-legitimization of democracy promotion – even when not carried out through coercion. Instead, donor countries focused more on state-building.

Other factors also contributed to the decline of Western democracy promotion. Western countries relied on natural resources from authoritarian African states, notably oil from Angola and increasingly Equatorial Guinea, thereby reducing their leverage or, rather, increasing African countries' counter-leverage. Several African countries could rely more on private investment and less on foreign aid. The rapid rise of China as an alternative source of aid, trade, and investment further reduced the strength of many African countries' linkages with the West, facilitating their circumvention of political and economic conditionality (Alden, this volume). What then to conclude on the West's experiences of democracy promotion on the African continent?

Conclusion

Democracy promotion in Africa reached its apogee during the brief period of time in the early 1990s when the Soviet threat had disappeared and Western liberalism appeared to have triumphed. Western countries used the window of opportunity to try to accelerate change elsewhere. Even at its height, however, democracy promoters could point to very few cases where they had made an important contribution, especially in Africa. Democracy promotion proved to be a more complicated task and African authoritarian leaders more resilient than most Western governments had realized. Faced with disappointing results (for reasons both endogenous and exogenous to their efforts, described above), and the resurgence of other priorities (especially security), donor countries soon returned democratization to its prior rhetorical role, raised in speeches and grand statements, but usually superseded by other priorities on the ground, especially for the more important players on the international stage, such as the United States.

Given the serious flaws in donors' democracy promotion strategies even in the first half of the 1990s, including lack of consistency and half-hearted efforts, one may wonder how committed Western countries ever were. Though some might be tempted to dismiss democracy promotion as a purely cosmetic and hypocritical endeavour, many Western actors involved were sincere, if perhaps somewhat naïve, in their desire to support the pro-democracy movements that appeared across the African continent. However, donor governments are fractured and different branches have different goals and priorities. As Crawford (1997: 103) notes, 'human rights and democracy principles appear to be always at the bottom of the pile'. Only in countries where donors have precious few interests at all, of which Malawi is the best example, will they apply political conditionality strongly and long enough to obtain results.

It is nonetheless too soon to dismiss democracy promotion efforts as ineffective. The fruits of the more technocratic or 'political' democracy assistance to date have indeed been meagre. However, in some cases over the longer term, those efforts may yet encourage and facilitate local actors' efforts to democratize their countries. In this they may be aided by slower structural changes, including those promoted through developmental assistance, which cannot only facilitate transitions to democracy in Africa, but also improve its odds of survival.

Notes

1 By way of contrast, armed insurrection in the 1970s forced the Portuguese to withdraw much more quickly from their African colonies, leaving in place newly independent, single-party, Marxist regimes, some plagued by civil war – notably, Angola and Mozambique.
2 Though at times they advocated greater freedom of expression and association and other civil rights that are essential for democracy, these donors applied little or no pressure for the short-term dismantling of one-party states.

3 Democracies, however, do not necessarily provide more social and economic rights than non-democracies – and those rights may have a greater impact on citizens' wellbeing.

4 They are: Benin, Botswana, Cape Verde, Ghana, Mali, Mauritius, Namibia, São Tomé and Príncipe, and South Africa.

5 The widely reported abuses in Zimbabwe and their extreme nature help explain why it constitutes an exception.

Bibliography

Ake, C. (1996) *Democracy and Development in Africa*, Washington, DC: Brookings Institution.

Bratton, M. and van de Walle, N. (1997) *Democratic Experiments in Africa: Regime Transition in Comparative Perspective*, New York, NY: Cambridge University Press.

Brown, S. (2001) 'Authoritarian Leaders and Multiparty Elections in Africa: How Foreign Donors Help to Keep Kenya's Daniel arap Moi in Power', *Third World Quarterly* 22(5): 725–39.

——(2004) '"Born-Again Politicians Hijacked Our Revolution!": Reassessing Malawi's Transition to Democracy', *Canadian Journal of African Studies* 38(3): 705–22.

——(2005) 'Foreign Aid and Democracy Promotion: Lessons from Africa', *European Journal of Development Research* 17(2): 179–98.

——(2007) 'From Demiurge to Midwife: Changing Donor Roles in Kenya's Democratisation Process', in G.R. Murunga and S.W. Nasong'o (eds) *Kenya: The Struggle for Democracy*, London: Zed Books.

Carothers, T. (2009) 'Democracy Assistance: Political vs. Developmental?' *Journal of Democracy* 20(1): 5–19.

Crawford, G. (1997) 'Foreign Aid and Political Conditionality: Issues of Effectiveness and Consistency', *Democratization* 4(3): 69–108.

Freedom House (2012) 'Freedom in the World 2012', www.freedomhouse.org/report/freedom-world/freedom-world-2012 (accessed 1 May 2012).

Levitsky, S. and Way, L.A. (2005) 'International Linkage and Democratization', *Journal of Democracy* 16(3): 20–34.

Przeworski, A., Alvarez, M., Cheibub, J.A. and Limongi, F. (1996) 'What Makes Democracies Endure?' *Journal of Democracy* 7(1): 39–55.

Radelet, S. (2010) 'Success Stories from "Emerging Africa"', *Journal of Democracy* 21(4): 87–101.

Schraeder, P.J., Hook, S.W. and Taylor, B. (1998) 'Clarifying the Foreign Aid Puzzle: A Comparison of American, Japanese, French and Swedish Aid Flows', *World Politics* 50(2): 294–323.

32

CHINA AND AFRICA

Chris Alden

The rise of China, from a stalwart of revolution in the 1950s to its emergence as a major global economic and political actor in the last decade, is one of the defining features of the twenty-first century. For the leading industrialized economies of the North, initial praise of China's gradualist shift to a market economy has evolved into a chorus bemoaning China's impact on trade competitiveness and growing concern as they are upstaged internationally by Beijing. These developments are most clearly visible in Africa, a continent that was languishing on the margins of international interest after the end of the Cold War.

China's forthright engagement with the African continent, built upon China's historic support for the independence struggle and the growing economic power wielded by Beijing, has helped re-ignite continental economies through new investment and trade opportunities. Perhaps more importantly, it has restored African political agency by increasing the choice available to African leaders with regard to with whom they do business and how they wish to do it – although this has inevitably been accompanied by a growing reliance on China itself. Indeed, one of the most striking developments over the past two decades has been the growing convergence between African development needs and Chinese economic interests. The structures and practices of an emerging mutually dependent relationship based on these realities are beginning to take fuller form, led by Beijing's promotion of Forum on China-Africa Cooperation (FOCAC) and the broadening of strategic dialogue with key African countries at the sub-state level, through national business councils and party-to-party links.

This chapter examines China's engagement with Africa by looking first at the sources of Chinese engagement with Africa; second, the proliferation of Chinese actors on the African continent; third, FOCAC (the diplomatic cornerstone of the relationship); and, finally, new trends in the relationship.

Sources of Chinese engagement with Africa

Since the onset of economic reform in 1978, China has had an unmatched record of sustained economic growth that has transformed key sectors of its economy into the global leader in manufacturing and production. To maintain these high levels of domestic output, crucial not only for the Chinese economy but for overall social and political stability in authoritarian China, the economy requires critical energy, mineral, and other resources from abroad (e.g. Downs

2004; Soares de Oliveira 2008). The promulgation of the government's 'going out' strategy – whereby over 100 restructured state-owned enterprises were given the legal and administrative means, preferential access to finance, and diplomatic support necessary to break into markets outside of China – has been the main policy response to this need. Given China's expansive financial resources, including the world's largest foreign capital reserves (US$2.4 trillion), carving out a position in the capital-starved energy and minerals markets in Africa was fairly straight-forward. Concurrently, the willingness of the Chinese government to provide a whole package of elite inducements – ranging from presidential palaces to large-scale infrastructure projects, alongside leasing and supply agreements for resources – has proved to be crucial to securing deals in Africa (Alden 2007: 11–36).

Underlying this approach is a highly publicized provision whereby the Chinese government forswears any interest in the domestic affairs of African governments, in direct contrast to the European Union (EU) or the United States, both of which have selectively applied conditions to their development assistance programmes and even some investments. In parallel with this state-led drive for resources abroad is a search for new markets aimed at expanding the invest-ment and trade opportunities for Chinese firms. The relatively small size of the African market, however, places some constraints on these ambitions. Finally, there is a diplomatic imperative tied to the decades of competition between Beijing and Taipei over official recognition, with countries in Africa being particularly targeted.

Resource security

China's position within Africa's resource sector has surged in the last decade and a half from that of a marginal player to a significant holder of interests in oil leases from Angola to Sudan, and mining concessions from the Democratic Republic of the Congo (DRC) to South Africa. Its two-way trade with Africa, exceeding $106 billion in 2008, is overwhelmingly based on the extraction of oil, strategic minerals, and raw materials in exchange for manufactured goods (Goldstein et al. 2006). Reflecting these trends, China went from being the leading Asian oil exporter in 1993, to the second-largest world consumer in 2003 and third-largest global importer in 2004. These statistics justify moving energy security to the core of Beijing's foreign policy formulation. Not only does China's continued economic growth depend on a secure resource supply but so, too, does its social stability and ultimately the survival of the Communist Party of China (CPC).[1]

Despite being a major oil producer (4.8 per cent of global production)[2] and second only to the United States in refinery capacity and output (8.5 per cent and 8.7 per cent, respectively),[3] China is only able to provide for less than half of its domestic oil needs. China's oil consumption has doubled in the last decade and, according to the Organization of the Petroleum Exporting Countries (OPEC), China's oil demand will show the world's fastest growth rate in the coming decades, doubling again by 2030 (BPC 2008: 47). Although China became a net oil importer in 1993, it was not until the new century that energy security became central to the political debate. Recent events – including the 2005 creation of the Energy Leading Group (the coordination body headed by premier Wen Jiabao), the publication of a White Paper on Energy ('China's Energy Conditions and Policies', Chinese State Council Information Office 2007) in December 2007, and the White Paper on Diplomacy (Hsiao 2008) – mark increasing uneasiness over this topic among the political elite.

China has become externally dependent on other resources in addition to oil, which has intensified its economic interaction with the African continent in the new century. Over the past decade, China surpassed the United States to become the world's leading consumer of most base metals. Chinese demand has been growing at a rate over 10 per cent a year since 1990, having only intensified further in recent years (Brett and Ericsson 2006: 22). China has been the major driver behind the soaring prices of metals in the international market. China is the world's largest consumer and producer of aluminium, iron ore, lead, and zinc, and holds significant shares in all other mineral supply and demand markets.

Finally, food security itself is becoming an area of great concern for China. The years of rapid economic development have, for the first time in decades, exposed China to the vagaries of supply-side and market constraints in agricultural commodities. In terms of overall agricultural imports, China leads the region with its import share of 44 per cent of the world's soybeans, 35 per cent of the world's cotton, 20 per cent of the world's palm oil, and 2.5 per cent of the world's rice, with Japanese, Indian, and South Korean demand trailing in its wake. Consumption patterns in China have changed dramatically since the gradualist introduction of market capitalism, and Chinese total caloric intake has risen to levels equivalent to the United States. While rising domestic demand would have been expected to open up opportunities for expanding local agriculture by Chinese farmers, China's physical constraints (despite its geographic size, it has only 7 per cent of the world's arable land) and the fact that rapid industrialization and accompanying urbanization over the last few decades has removed tens of thousands of hectares of fertile land from production. The result has been a steady rise in food imports, which in combination with Chinese (and Indian) energy needs, has increased food prices worldwide. For China in particular, the fear that inflation and dwindling supplies could contribute to periodic waves of domestic unrest that had begun to gather force was underscored in a report issued by the State Council on food security in 2005, the first year that China became a major importer of food since the CPC took over. In 2008 the National Development Reform Committee produced the preliminary findings of a 20-year Food Security Strategy, setting out the parameters of food security for the country as being met first and foremost through the maintenance of 125 million hectares of arable land and 95 per cent self-sufficiency in grains (Kelley 2009: 94).

The African resource bounty

Against this backdrop, Africa has assumed a critical role in China's search for resource security. The African continent possesses a generous endowment of natural resources – particularly hydrocarbons, minerals, and timber – which remain mostly untapped due to decades of political instability, poor infrastructure, and scarce investment. However, the Chinese foray into this sector had to take into account the prevailing dominance of established interests, primarily from the United States, France, and Great Britain, all of which produced a pattern of investment that replicated colonial-era divisions refracted through the politics of the Cold War. With the end of the bipolar conflict, economic interests rapidly pushed to the forefront and the geographic spheres of influence that had shaped energy investment gave way to direct competition between, for instance, French and American interests in West Africa (Schraeder 2000). Among the most prominent newcomers are Asian states – China, India, Malaysia, and Singapore – and Middle Eastern countries – Israel, Saudi Arabia, and Kuwait. This scenario sets the ground for growing competition for economic and political influence over the continent in the coming decades, something that is particularly astounding considering that less than a decade ago the African continent was suffering from a sharp decline in interest by its traditional Western partners.

In regional terms, Africa possesses the third-largest oil reserves, an estimated 9.5 per cent of global known deposits in 2007, behind the Middle East (61 per cent) and North America (11.6 per cent), and ahead of South and Central America (8.5 per cent). Africa boasts the fastest growth rate in oil reserves, having doubled in the past two decades (BPC 2008: 6). In sub-regional terms, North Africa and sub-Saharan Africa each account for half of the continent's known reserves. Libya (35 per cent), Nigeria (31 per cent), Algeria (10 per cent), and Angola (8 per cent) possess the largest reserves. In production, Africa comes fourth with a share of 12.5 per cent of the world total, but the rankings change a bit from those of oil reserves, with Nigeria as the main African oil producer (25 per cent), followed by Algeria (21 per cent), Libya (20 per cent), and Angola (18 per cent) (ibid.: 8). In recent years northern African countries' production has been showing signs of stabilization, while other countries have been expanding their share. For instance, Angola has registered the fastest growth rate in production during the past decade, having even overtaken Nigeria as sub-Saharan African's major oil producer in mid-2008.[4]

Africa's endowment of non-fuel minerals further complements the attractiveness of this picture, with South Africa possessing one of the world's richest mineral beds. Among other minerals, South Africa is the leading producer of platinum (80 per cent of total production and 90 per cent of world reserves), manganese (the country holds over 75 per cent of the world's reserve base), and the world's second gold mine producer (overtaken by Australia in 2007). Moreover, South Africa is a major coal producer and has developed the world's leading technology in converting coal to synthetic fuels (synfuels), introducing new possibilities for the coal-rich Chinese state. Recognition of this has factored into the joint venture between two Chinese firms and the South African parastatal, Sasol. By way of contrast, despite decades of neglect and internecine conflict, the DRC's mineral wealth is notoriously underutilized. Even so, the DRC has the world's most plentiful cobalt mines, providing 36 per cent of the world's cobalt and possessing half of the world's known reserves. DRC is also the world's leading diamond producer, with 33 per cent of the world total. Together with South Africa and Botswana, they account for over half of global diamond mining output and 60 per cent of known deposits (figures from 2007; USGS 2008). The African countries with significant mineral reserves that have attracted the most Chinese interest are Gabon (manganese), Zambia (copper and iron ore), Zimbabwe (platinum), and Angola (diamonds, copper, and iron ore).

Finally, African agriculture and forestry resources remain underdeveloped. According to the Food and Agriculture Organization (FAO), only 14 per cent of Africa's total 184 million hectares of available land is currently cultivated. Over 90 per cent of cultivated land is dependent upon rainfall, and few farms make effective use of modern fertilizers (Diouf 2008). African agriculture, which continues to serve as a mainstay of employment, suffers from low productivity, chronic under-investment and limited access to foreign export markets. Moreover, the environmental constraints that African agriculturalists face are familiar to Chinese farmers. Private Chinese farmers have already set up farms in Uganda, South Africa, and Zambia (23 in the latter case) (Spieldoch and Murphy 2009: 42), while larger agricultural firms are in negotiations with African governments to lease larger tracts of land for production. In forestry, hundreds of thousands of square kilometres of virgin timber abound in parts of tropical Africa and have inspired China's small and medium-sized companies to set up logging operations – both legal and illegal – across the continent.

These economic complementarities have spurred a dramatic increase in trade. Between 1995 and 2000 commercial exchanges more than doubled from $4 billion to $10 billion, and then quadrupled in the following five years ($42 billion in 2005), before the figure surpassed $106 billion – a full year before the 2010 target established by Hu Jintao during the FOCAC III summit in Beijing in 2006 (Chinese Ministry of Commerce 2008; WTO 2006). Even if in relative terms Africa represents only a meagre 3 per cent of China's overall foreign trade, it shows the highest growth rate among all regions. While Africa's share in Chinese exports grew from 1.7 per cent in 1996, to 2.7 per cent in 2006, the share in imports expanded from 1 per cent to 3.6 per cent in the same decade, revealing the nature of exchanges (World Trade Data 2007).

At the same time, the onset of the world's worst economic crisis since the Great Depression has challenged the newfound certainties of Chinese engagement in Africa. Some are already declaring that the withdrawal of dozens of Chinese firms from the mining sector and Beijing's push to re-open negotiations on the purported $9 billion investment package in the DRC signify that the high watermark of China–Africa economic ties has been reached. Western donors even criticized this investment package and pressured Kinshasa and Beijing to reduce it from $9 billion to $6 billion in February 2009 (Lokongo 2009). This pessimistic interpretation is misplaced, however. China's involvement in Africa remains a priority, albeit one that is subject to changing international and domestic economic circumstances, as well as the emergence of a reconsideration of risk in selective African environments.

New markets and diplomacy

Though resource security impulses are at the forefront of the contemporary push into Africa with China's energy state-owned enterprises (SOEs) taking the lead, there is also a desire to exploit commercial opportunities with increased trade. Using Chinese finance to support Chinese construction firms building infrastructure in Africa mitigates risk for these firms and, concurrently, provides incentives for them to seek new business opportunities abroad. Indeed, survey data suggest that once established in the African market, Chinese firms 'anticipated that they will secure further contracts' (Davies and Corkin 2007: 246). The over-supply of infrastructure firms and labour within China itself provides an additional rationale for this expansion into new markets. The appeal of this approach for African governments, despite some concerns around the use of Chinese labour, was that these were 'turnkey' operations; they placed few demands on the African recipients and produced a relatively inexpensive and functioning road, railroad, bridge, or dam quickly (Fletcher 2010: 7).

The need for Chinese manufacturing firms to find new outlets for their products, especially those at the low end of the consumer market (which were losing favour domestically and held little appeal in the more sophisticated Western markets), has also contributed to a surge in two-way trade (Broadman 2007). With manufacturing accounting for 32 per cent of China's gross domestic product (GDP) and 89 per cent of its merchandise exports by 2005, the importance of opening up new opportunities abroad was paramount (Biacuana *et al.* 2009: 10). At a different level, a new wave of Chinese migrants to Africa have opened up wholesale and retail shops across the continent, bringing low-cost goods to the African consumer and contributing to a boom in the purchase of items such as bicycles, radios, and watches which were once out of reach of ordinary Africans (see Dittigen 2010; Park 2009; Dobler 2008).

Diplomatic concerns, including the longstanding competition for recognition between the People's Republic of China and the Republic of China (Taiwan), have also led China to become more involved in African affairs, since Taiwan had been able to win recognition from a number of African states over the years (Rawnsley 2000). Beijing's drive to isolate the rebel province internationally meant that it actively sought to provide inducements for African governments to reconsider their links with Taipei.

As international pressure increased on China to play a more activist role on the global stage, building international alliances with like-minded states became imperative. Africa's position as a friendly environment for Beijing was underscored by its unwillingness to join in the Western sanctions campaign against China in the wake of Tiananmen Square. African states supported China in international fora as varied as the International Olympic Committee (where African votes helped secure Beijing's hosting of the 2008 Olympic Games) and the United Nations' (UN) Human Rights Commission. Sharing a common view on sovereignty and human rights – though one that was arguably in the process of changing through the African Union (AU) and the emergence of the UN's Responsibility to Protect (R2P) initiative in 2005 – enabled China to work in tandem on many issues with African states, the largest regional voting bloc in the UN (Alden 2007: 16). To address these complex diplomatic ends, the Chinese Ministry of Foreign Affairs established the multilateral FOCAC in 2000.

The Chinese in Africa: from state-owned enterprises to retail shopkeepers

Capturing the diversity of China's engagement in Africa is necessary to achieve any understanding of the complex and sometimes contradictory reactions that its presence inspires across Africa. Ranging from global parastatals like the China National Offshore Oil Corporation (CNOOC) to thousands of retail shops, the Chinese have made inroads in the economic life of ordinary Africans in an extraordinarily short period of time. Moreover, the rapidity with which these Chinese actors adapt to changing circumstances in Africa – in some part a product of the fast pace of change in China itself – challenges assumptions about what China's presence really means for the continent.

Where China's engagement in Africa might stoke additional conflict is with Chinese SOEs that have begun to gain access to resources and markets formerly dominated by Western and South African firms. Using a package of high-profile diplomatic and substantive financial incentives, these SOEs have been able to secure leases for oil in Angola, Sudan, and Nigeria, as well as deals gaining access to strategic minerals in countries such as Gabon, the DRC, and Zimbabwe. The proximity of top management of these SOEs to leading party officials, according to one study, 'affords certain strategic SOEs vital political connections and a measure of input into foreign policy decisions pertaining to their particular business interests' (Jakobson and Know 2010: 26). For developmentally minded African leaders, the attractiveness of Chinese support for infrastructure development, an area neglected by traditional Western donors in recent decades, is rooted in the visible and immediate impact that provisions for transportation and communication have on enhancing the economic potential in their respective countries, as well as improving livelihoods within beneficiary communities. These 'resources for infrastructure' deals, often involving billions of dollars-worth of low concessional loans by China ExIm Bank, have been carried out for the most part by Chinese construction firms, the use of contracted labourers and even basic supplies of which has been criticized in some African circles.

Moreover, the overall competitiveness of Chinese firms has meant that once exposed to the African environment, they have been able to capture a growing portion of the open tenders for infrastructure projects. According to one study, Chinese construction firms have succeeded in recent years in winning 30 per cent of the combined value of infrastructure contracts tendered by the African Development Bank (AfDB) and World Bank (Foster *et al.* 2007: 5–6). This trend is evident in the conduct of Chinese infrastructure and engineering firms operating in Africa as early as 1988, where in countries like Liberia, for example, the China State Construction Engineering Corporation was able to stay on and win contracts from the Liberian government to renovate the local hospital (Bräutigam 1998: 214). There are numerous contemporary examples of Chinese construction firms entering African markets via a Chinese-financed project and winning public tenders. As these contracts finish, an undetermined number of Chinese labourers brought in to work on these construction projects have stayed on in Africa to seek employment opportunities or open up small businesses.

While Chinese SOEs captivate the attention of the international media, there is an equivalent drive by Chinese small and medium-sized enterprises (SMEs) into the continent that has made as much or more impact on local African economies and the China–Africa relationship than aspiring multinationals. Many of the medium-sized companies are drawn from the ranks of the rehabilitated SOE sector, which has been undergoing a painful restructuring process that has cut it back from 300,000 to 150,000 firms over the last decade (CSIS/IIE 2006: 23–24).[5] In some cases these businesses were motivated by a desire on the part of a relatively large Chinese company to establish foreign subsidiaries so as to guarantee access to Western markets should protectionism take root (Hong and Sun 2006: 624). For many smaller businesses, the motivation, as noted above, is to make use of China's competitive advantage relative to the African companies where they possess the relatively advanced technologies and cost-effective production needed to give them a price advantage over other local and foreign firms (ibid.: 625). Surveys of 80 Chinese SMEs working in Africa confirm that gaining access to the continent's markets is the top business motivation (Gu 2009).

At the same time, the poor conduct of some Chinese firms operating in Africa has threatened to tarnish the overall reputation of China. China has been willing to ignore basic health and safety regulations, local labour laws, and even environmental standards within the industry by a number of Chinese mining companies based in Katanga province, DRC, which has inspired substantial criticism (Clark *et al.* 2008). That a collapse in commodity prices in late 2008 caused many of these companies to pull out of the DRC highlights these companies' opportunistic and exploitative character. While Zambia has been an exemplary partner in many ways, the poor practices of a leading Chinese mining firm resulted in a flurry of accidental deaths in 2006 and, in 2010, the shooting of African labourers by Chinese managers during a labour dispute, causing the opposition political party to use anti-Chinese feelings as a mobilization strategy in their election campaigns.

Finally, the growing trend of Chinese migration in parts of Africa has not passed unnoticed in communities unaccustomed to hosting foreigners from beyond the continent. Much of the Chinese immigration has been undocumented, leading to wild speculation as to the numbers of Chinese settling in the continent, a situation further compounded by the African tendency to identify all non-Indian Asians as being 'Chinese'. Within the continent's leading migration destination, South Africa, the Chinese community has surged from 80,000 in the 1980s to an estimated 350,000 in 2006, though overall migration to Africa is declared by Beijing to be only 750,000 (with other estimates higher) (Park 2009: 3). Concurrently, the lack of financial means and weak skill base of many of the migrants has raised concerns amongst educated Africans and small business owners alike. The proliferation of Chinese retail shops in urban and rural communities, bringing low-cost consumer goods to African markets for the first time, is driving African-owned businesses out of the retail trade and stoking resentment in local communities.

In short, during the last decade and a half, the Chinese presence in Africa has been marked by diversity in composition and depth, defying the easy stereotypes that have accompanied many portrayals in the Western and even African media. This spectrum of Chinese actors has been further matched by changing approaches to Africa at the highest levels by authorities in Beijing and, more prosaically, by individual migration strategies. Africa's resources may be the instigator of Chinese interests but it is clear that China's ties with the continent are increasingly set to be anchored by an expanding cast of characters and changing relationships. The opportunities are there for enhanced African influence aimed at addressing problems or managing conflicts through direct engagement with this array of Chinese actors, if applied with a strong sense of strategic purpose. So far, this sort of approach has been best mobilized by political parties in pursuit of their narrower and more parochial interests (Corkin 2012).

The diplomatic cornerstone of the relationship: the FOCAC process

A special dimension of China's engagement with the African continent has been the founding of a regionally tailored multilateral platform, the Forum for China-Africa Cooperation (FOCAC). This regularized structure provides a public setting for celebrating the achievements of the relationship, an opportunity to formulate a raft of economic targets aimed at fostering mutual development interests, and a stage on which to endorse common perspectives on global issues. While some might call this multilateralism, most of the substance of economic ties (notably aid and investment agreements) continues to be rooted in bilateral relations between China and individual African states.

The FOCAC process originated with the convergence of various economic and political factors. As noted above, the economic context of China's 'going out' strategy was significant, bringing with it a need for key resources which Africa could readily supply. Politically, there was a renewed push to counter Taiwan's so-called 'dollar diplomacy' on the continent, which had succeeded in winning back official recognition from a number of African states by the early 1990s. This corresponded with the broader aims of revitalizing diplomatic ties with the developing world in the wake of Tiananmen and the accompanying Western opprobrium and sanctions. However, the shape of Chinese engagement as it manifested in FOCAC mirrored Japan's Tokyo International Conference on African Development (TICAD) process, which, as interpreted by the CPC's Central Committee, had found a successful way of responding to African requests for changes to aid policy (Ling 2010: 13). This initiative came against the backdrop of the longstanding Franco-African Summit process and a new US-led approach that culminated in a ministerial conference on Africa in 1999 and a widely touted continental tour by US President Bill Clinton.

The first FOCAC ministerial meeting, held in Beijing in 2000, organized African ambassadors as an ad hoc unit within the Chinese Ministry of Foreign Affairs. The agenda ranged from strengthening development cooperation through expansion of Chinese credit facilities, to monitoring and reducing the flow of Chinese small arms. The second FOCAC ministerial meeting took place in December 2003 in Addis Ababa and produced a firm commitment to raise two-way trade to $30 billion by the next FOCAC meeting, to forgive the debt owed by 31 African countries, and to combat 'hegemony' in international affairs. It was, however, FOCAC III – designated a 'summit' by Chinese and Africans due to the invitation and participation of top political leadership – held in Beijing in November 2006, that attracted the world's attention by bringing together the largest-ever number of African leaders in a summit outside the continent. Indeed, in that same year, both top Chinese leaders visited the continent and the Chinese government released its first-ever 'White Paper on China's Africa Policy' (January 2006).

The declaration made at FOCAC III called for an increase in trade to $100 billion by the next ministerial meeting, as well as commitments to reduce tariffs on 440 items produced by Africa's least developed countries, the creation of a $5 billion investment fund, and numerous small grant and training programmes. More recently, FOCAC IV, held in Egypt in 2009, included commitments to: a $10 billion package of concessional loans; raise African agricultural productivity; reduce or eliminate tariff barriers for Africa's poorest countries; build hospitals and schools; establish new or expanded training programmes to address human development; provide for 100 clean energy projects; and increase support for peace and security.

What is striking about the contents of the FOCAC IV declaration is the degree to which, building upon the first three FOCAC meetings, this process reflects a growing and deliberately constructed convergence between African development needs and Chinese economic interests. It is a convergence that reflects the obvious economic asymmetries between China's activist form of state-led capitalism and Africa's exploitation of its under-developed resource base to attract Chinese investment and, concurrently, the paradoxical political symmetry implied in the mutual commitment to sovereign equality. For instance, in agriculture – a sector long recognized to be an area where Africa's potential comparative advantages have remained under-invested and under-utilized (and one in which the Chinese have provided technical assistance since the 1960s) – the Chinese propose to introduce new techniques, seed varieties, and training programmes, derived from their own experience of raising productivity amongst Chinese farmers.[6] To facilitate this process, the Chinese government is rolling out an additional 10 agricultural training centres across the continent in countries like Mozambique, Zimbabwe, and Senegal. Coupled with this are additional financial means aimed at providing financial support for commercial enterprises. Raising Africa's agricultural productivity will not only dramatically enhance the livelihoods of rural communities in Africa through improvements in income generation and employment, but it can address the growing food security problem in China itself.

Another example is the targeting of Africa's SMEs for development and growth through a special $1 billion fund. Moreover, signalling that they understand that a focus on the supply side is not enough to make real development gains, Beijing has agreed to end tariffs on 95 per cent of all products from Africa's less developed countries. Opening up China's market to African commerce has the potential to set off a virtuous cycle of development when linked with the support for African business. At the same time, it could end up like the US African Growth and Opportunity Act (AGOA), which gave preferential access to the American market in sectors like clothing which contributed to a surge not so much in African but rather Asian-based investment. Africans will nevertheless have to be nimble investors to make the most out of what seems to be genuinely liberal terms on offer. Indeed, they may even find that they are competing with the growing Chinese communities within their midst who have proven entrepreneurial acumen and understanding of how the Chinese domestic market has fuelled China's own economic transformation.

Moreover, the diversity of Chinese actors in Africa – contrary to the presumptions of the notion of 'China–Africa' as two unitary entities – poses a dilemma in structuring and managing the relationship. Once shaped and led by Beijing's political elites at the top in conjunction with their African counterparts, the steady diffusion of economic power to semi-autonomous SOEs, provincial authorities and a sometimes rapacious profit-seeking private sector has introduced a diversity of interests and practice that are as often at odds with Chinese unitary foreign policy aims. The actions of murky investment houses like the China International Fund and the state-owned Angolan national oil company, Sonangol, raise troubling questions about the long-term impact of China's role on the continent. Sonangol has leveraged Chinese (Hong Kong) finance to advance Angolan political interests and secure a huge stake in the illegal military regime in Guinea. Operating on the margins of respectability, these organizations can damage the positive intentions on display at FOCAC IV in their unwavering pursuit of profit and wilful distain for African sensibilities.

This situation also highlights one of the most notable gaps in the FOCAC process: the role of non-state actors. While much media attention was focused on what happened within the halls of the FOCAC ministerial and the press conferences, the FOCAC Business Forum met on the fringes of the event. Missing, however, was the once-mooted inclusion of a parallel Chinese-African civil society process. In the Western context, vibrant civil societies guard the underlying values that inform national foreign policies. Unabashedly critical of the state and private capital – and undoubtedly the bane of authoritarian and, at times, democratic governments alike – these sometimes self-appointed 'voices of the people' nonetheless serve a tremendously important function in reasserting the moral purpose of foreign policy actions. In Africa, China has seemingly exported many features of its domestic setting (such as opaque business and financial practices), including a weak civil society, the boundaries of action of which are circumscribed to varying degrees by the state. Whether the current situation, which places the burden of responsibility solely on the party leadership and bureaucracy to anticipate, manage, and ameliorate the conduct of a plethora of Chinese actors in Africa, is sufficient remains to be seen.

Conclusion

China's emergence as a leading trade and investment partner with Africa has had a number of impacts upon the continent that suggest interesting lessons for other regions, such as Latin America. China's economic engagement has revived the flagging fortunes of Africa's resource-based economies, providing new investment and new markets that have contributed to the global commodity boom. China's demand for resources has helped drive up commodity prices, while its focus on infrastructure has brought about a renewal of donor interest in financing vital improvements in that neglected sector. At the same time, the Chinese approach to financing its expanding role in the resource sector through provision for hard infrastructure, it could be argued, is crucially dependent upon the very dearth of that in the target country. As the South African case demonstrates, middle-income countries with reasonably well-developed infrastructure, existing local company expertise, strong labour unions, and an established regulatory environment can be less attractive investment destinations. However, other Chinese actors – notably those in the financial sector – are drawn to these settings as they provide a stronger institutional framework that supports their pursuit of profits.

In political terms, the African example suggests that China can provide a welcome alternative to the established sources of trade and investment, not least because they are less concerned with using the development process as an instrument for the imposition of normative transformation on target states, and more concerned with using mutual economic interests (*cf.* Williams, this volume). The revival of African economic fortunes has had a direct impact on the international stature of African leaders, allowing them to challenge the certitudes that informed the approach adopted by the Organisation for Economic Co-operation and Development (OECD) 'donor cartel'. The result is not, as some critics have feared, a shift away from the North, but rather a diversification of development partnerships which – at least in those African countries with sound and committed political leadership – offer an unprecedented opportunity to use all means available for achieving development.

Change and adaptability remain the hallmarks of China–Africa relations and – to the credit of the Chinese government's willingness to revisit and revise specific initiatives in light of experience on the ground – give the relationship a dynamism lacking in many other trans-regional initiatives (see Khadiagala; Mshomba, both this volume). China's experience in Africa in many ways has provided a short, sharp lesson in the ease of breaking into the relatively neglected African terrain (by China) and, at the same time, the increasing difficulties for African countries in securing their interests over the long term. Africa should welcome China's willingness to maintain its focus on building long-term economic relationships on the continent, despite obstacles encountered on the ground and, more recently, the adverse global economic climate. Africa has long complained about its investors' limited interests, but now it has met a different kind of partner. While there are many potential benefits for African states from their relationships with China, Chinese actors' narrower, and often self-serving, interests are a challenge to ensuring that this carefully constructed relationship with the continent stays on course.

Notes

1 For a detailed account on energy security emergence as China's foreign policy major driver see Zweig and Jianhai (2005).
2 China occupies the fifth position as producer after Saudi Arabia and the Russian Federation (both with 12.6 per cent), the United States (8 per cent) and Iran (5.4 per cent) (BPC 2008: 9).
3 US refinery capacity and output share are 20 per cent of total, over twice China's share (BPC 2008: 18).
4 Although Angola's production has been increasing exponentially, this situation is partly due to increasing unrest in Nigerian southern oil fields.
5 At a cost of 25 million unemployed, this sector having formerly employed 80 per cent of all Chinese workers.
6 For an overview of Chinese technical assistance in agricultural sector in Africa, see Bräutigam (1998).

Bibliography

Alden, C. (2007) *China in Africa*, London: Zed.
Biacuana, G., Disenyana, T., Draper, P. and Khumalo, N. (2009) *China's Manufacturing Exports and Africa's Deindustrialisation*, Braamfontein: South African Institute of International Affairs.
BPC (British Petroleum Company) (2008) 'BP Statistical Review of World Energy', June 2008, London: BP plc.
Bräutigam, D. (1998) *Chinese Aid and African Development: Exporting Green Revolution*, Basingstoke: Macmillan.
Brett, D. and Ericsson, M. (2006) 'Chinese Expansion to Create New Global Mining Companies', *Commodities Now*, October 2006: 22–28, www.rmg.se/RMG2005/pages/attachments/COMMODITIES_NOW_2006_Oct,_Chinese_Expansion_to_Create_New_Global_Mining_Companies.pdf (accessed 28 October 2011).
Broadman, H. (2007) *Africa's Silk Road*, Washington, DC: World Bank.
Chinese Ministry of Commerce (2008) *Total Import & Export Value by Country (Region) (2007/01–12)*, Beijing: Department of General Economic Affairs, http://english.mofcom.gov.cn/article/statistic/ie/200802/20080205371690.html (accessed 9 December 2011).
Chinese State Council Information Office (2007) *China's Energy Conditions and Policies*, Beijing: China Internet Information Center, www.china.org.cn/english/environment/236955.htm (accessed 7 July 2012).
Clark, S., Smith, M. and Wild, F. (2008) 'China Lets Child Workers Die Digging in Congo Mines for Copper', www.bloomberg.com/apps/news?pid=newsarchive&sid=aW8xVLQ4Xhr8 (accessed 23 July 2008).
Corkin, L. (2012) 'African Agency: Angolan Political Elites Management of Chinese Credit Lines', in M. Power and A.C. Alves (eds) *China and Angola: A Marriage of Convenience?* London: Fahamu.
CSIS/IIE (2006) *China: The Balance Sheet*, Washington, DC: Center for Strategic and International Studies/Institute for International Economics.
Davies, M. and Corkin, L. (2007) 'China's Entry into Africa's Construction Sector: The Case of Angola', in G. le Pere (ed.) *China in Africa: Mercantilist Predator or Partner in Development?* Midrand: SAIIA/IGD.
Diouf, J. (2008) Director General of Food and Agriculture Organisation, Regional Conference for Africa, 19 June, www.fao.org/newsroom/en/news/2008/1000868/index.html (accessed 25 March 2012).
Dittigen, R. (2010) 'From Isolation to Integration? A Study of Chinese Retailers in Dakar', South African Institute of International Affairs Occasional Paper No. 57, China in Africa Project.
Dobler, G. (2008) 'Solidarity, Xenophobia and the Regulation of Chinese Businesses in Namibia', in C. Alden, D. Large and R. Soares de Oliveira (eds) *China Returns to Africa: An Emerging Power and a Continent Embrace*, London: Hurst.
Downs, E. (2004) 'The Energy Security Debate', *China Quarterly* 177: 21–41.
Fletcher, H. (2010) 'Development Aid for Infrastructure Investment in Africa: Malian Relations with China, the European Commission and the World Bank', South African Institute of International Affairs Occasional Paper No. 58, China in Africa Project.
Foster, V., Butterfield, W., Chen, C. and Pushka, N. (2007) *Building Bridges: China's Growing Role as Infrastructure Financier in Africa*, Washington, DC: The World Bank.
Goldstein, A., Pinaud, N. and Reisen, H. (2006) 'The Rise of China and India: What's in it for Africa?', Organisation for Economic Co-operation and Development Policy Insights No. 19, www.oecd.org/dataoecd/52/4/36761102.pdf (accessed 7 January 2012).

Gu, J. (2009) 'China's Private Enterprises in Africa and the Implications for African Development', *European Journal of Development Research* 21(4): 570–85.

Hong, E. and Sun, L. (2006) 'Dynamics of Internationalisation and Outward Investment: Chinese Corporations' Strategies', *The China Quarterly* 187: 610–34.

Hsiao, R. (2008) 'Energy Security the Centrepiece of China's Foreign Policy', *China Brief* 8(16).

Jakobson, L. and Know, D. (2010) 'New Foreign Policy Actors in China', Stockholm International Peace Research Institute Policy Paper No. 26.

Kelley, J. (2009) In testimony before the European Union Committee, House of Lords, 30 April 2009, 7th Report of Session 2009–10, Vol. 2: Evidence.

Ling, J. (2010) 'Aid and Africa: What Can the EU, China and Africa Learn from Each Other?', South African Institute of International Affairs Occasional Paper No. 56.

Lokongo, A.R. (2009) 'Sino-DRC Contracts to Thwart the Return of Western Patronage', http://pambazuka.org/en/category/africa_china/54567 (accessed 24 March 2012).

Park, Y. (2009) 'Chinese Migration in Africa', South African Institute of International Affairs Occasional Paper No. 24, China in Africa Project.

Rawnsley, G. (2000) *Taiwan's Informal Diplomacy and Propaganda*, Basingstoke: Macmillan.

Schraeder, P.J. (2000) 'Cold War to Cold Peace: Explaining US-French Competition in Francophone Africa', *Political Science Quarterly* 115(3): 395–419.

Soares de Oliveira, R. (2008) 'Making Sense of Chinese Oil Investment in Africa', in C. Alden, D. Large and R. Soares de Oliveira (eds) *China Returns to Africa: An Emerging Power and a Continent Embrace*, London: Hurst.

Spieldoch, A. and Murphy, S. (2009) 'Agricultural Land Acquisitions: Implications for Food Security and Poverty Alleviation', in Michael Kugelman and Susan Levenstein (eds) *Land Grab? The Race for the World's Farmland*, Washington, DC: Woodrow Wilson Centre.

USGS (US Geological Survey) (2008) 'Mineral Commodity Summaries 2008', US Geological Survey, US Department of the Interior.

World Trade Data (2007) 'China Africa's Top 20'.

WTO (World Trade Organization) (2006) 'Merchandise Trade by Region and Economy, 1995–05 – China', Geneva: World Trade Organization, www.wto.org/english/res_e/statis_e/its2006_e/appendix_e/a14.xls (accessed 8 March 2012).

Zweig, D. and Jianhai, B. (2005) 'China's Global Hunt for Energy', *Foreign Affairs* 84(5): 25–38.

INDEX

426